Whitman Encyclopedia of Colonial and Early American Coins

"David Bowers's encyclopedic knowledge and devotion to American colonial and Confederation coinage are now transferred into a *published* encyclopedia for everyone to enjoy—so he can continue to write on even more topics."

—*Eric P. Newman,*
numismatic researcher and author

⁓⋙⋘⁓

"The extensive assortment of America's colonial and pre-federal coins and tokens is now presented in one convenient source by Q. David Bowers, who has spent a lifetime researching this absorbing topic. Each coin type has been carefully documented, as are all of the notable variations. The story of money in early America—of the winning of financial freedom for our emerging nation—is reflected and amplified in each of the coins described in this book."

—*Kenneth Bressett,*
numismatic researcher and author

⁓⋙⋘⁓

"The *Whitman Encyclopedia of Colonial and Early American Coins* is a wonderful, and much needed, platform for encouraging the historical research of our colonial time period."

—*Ray Williams,*
president, Colonial Coin Collectors Club

⁓⋙⋘⁓

"I am very impressed with the chapter on Virginia halfpence."

—*Alan Anthony,*
numismatist

⁓⋙⋘⁓

"A book like this is a great tool for any collector, beginning or advanced, especially one just starting in the early copper field."

—*Tony Carlotto,*
Vermont copper specialist

⁓⋙⋘⁓

"I think we finally have something that will replace S.S. Crosby's *Early American Coins*—in spades!"

—*George Fuld,*
numismatic researcher and author

"The *Whitman Encyclopedia of Colonial and Early American Coins* is very easy to read, while presenting a great deal of useful information. I especially like the finding guides included for the major series. Bowers's discussion of the Massachusetts coppers is one of the best I have read."

—Louis E. Jordan III,
Head of Special Collections and Medieval Institute Library,
University of Notre Dame

"A reference such as this has been needed for a long time. None of the standard references of the past are satisfactory. The *Whitman Encyclopedia of Colonial and Early American Coins* is a welcome addition to the libraries of colonial specialists as well as the more general collector of American coins—and I can't think of anyone better qualified than Q. David Bowers to accomplish this effort."

—Sydney Martin,
Connecticut copper specialist,
editor, Colonial Coin Collectors Club Newsletter

"David Bowers has written the book that collectors of colonial and early American coinage have waited 150 years to read—covering expert information with authority, yet written with such marvelous clarity that even novice collectors will find it indispensable."

—Joel J. Orosz,
numismatic researcher and author

"This book confirms that Q. David Bowers is, without question, one of the best numismatic authors and researchers of this century and the last."

—Jim Rosen,
Nova Constellatio specialist

"What an incredible, immensely useful, and important book Dave Bowers has put together!"

—Roger Siboni,
president, American Numismatic Society

Whitman Encyclopedia of Colonial and Early American Coins

Q. David Bowers

Foreword by
Kenneth Bressett

Valuations editor
Lawrence R. Stack

Whitman Publishing, LLC

WHITMAN ENCYCLOPEDIA
OF COLONIAL AND
EARLY AMERICAN COINS

Whitman Publishing, LLC

© 2009 Whitman Publishing, LLC
3101 Clairmont Road, Suite C, Atlanta, GA 30329

All rights reserved, including duplication of any kind or storage in electronic or visual retrieval systems. Permission is granted for writers to use a limited number of brief excerpts and quotations in printed reviews, magazine articles, and numismatic catalogs, provided credit is given to the title of the work and the author. The Whitman numbering system may be used without permission, although citation of this book will be appreciated. Written permission from Whitman Publishing, LLC, is required for other uses, including in books, any use of illustrations, and any use of any information or illustrations in electronic or other media.

Correspondence concerning this book may be directed to the publisher, Attn: Whitman Encyclopedia of Colonial and Early American Coins, at the address above.

ISBN: 0794825419
Printed in China

Disclaimer: No warranty or representation of any kind is made concerning the accuracy or completeness of the information presented, or its usefulness in numismatic purchases or sales. The opinions of others may vary. The author, a professional numismatist, regularly buys, sells, and sometimes holds certain of the items discussed in this book.

Caveat: The price estimates given are subject to variation and differences of opinion. Before making decisions to buy or sell, consult the latest information. For scarce and rare pieces, auction realizations can be very useful. For certain issues that are normally found with areas of light striking, well struck coins may command significantly higher prices. There are no universally agreed upon grading standards for colonial and early American coins, and opinions can vary widely, including among experts. Past performance of the rare coin market or any coin or series within that market is not necessarily an indication of future performance, as the future is unknown. Such factors as changing demand, popularity, variations (sometimes wide) in grading interpretations, strength of the overall coin market, and economic conditions will continue to be influences.

Valuations: Estimated market prices are given in various grades by valuations editor Lawrence R. Stack, with information from multiple sources. These are given simply as an opinion and guide at the time of compilation in 2008. Certain actual transactions may take place at higher or lower figures, especially in the case of particularly rare or high-grade coins.

Advertisements within this book: Whitman Publishing, LLC, does not endorse, warrant, or guarantee any of the products or services of its advertisers. All warranties and guarantees are the sole responsibility of the advertiser.

> *About the cover:* Massachusetts's Pine Tree coinage, struck from 1667 to 1682, was the third in a series, after its Willow Tree (1653–1660) and Oak Tree (1660–1667) coins. The piece pictured on the front cover is a silver Pine Tree shilling. This is America's iconic colonial coin, made in New England by the first mint set up in our country. Over the years it has gained great fame. Nathaniel Hawthorne wrote a romantic story featuring this coin. *On the back cover:* The famous Bar copper is undated and of uncertain origin, but its design was likely copied from a Continental button. The 13 bars represent the original states, separate but united into a single entity. This theme is strengthened by the interlocking letters of USA. The token is thought to have circulated in New York in late 1785.

If you enjoy the *Whitman Encyclopedia of Colonial and Early American Coins*, you'll also enjoy these books: *United States Pattern Coins*, 10th edition; *100 Greatest American Medals and Tokens*; *A Guide Book of United States Tokens and Medals*; *History of the United States Mint and Its Coinage*; and *The Expert's Guide to Collecting and Investing in Rare Coins*. The *Guide Book of United States Coins* (popularly known as the "Red Book") provides an annually updated overview of colonial and early American coins and tokens. *Obsolete Paper Money Issued by Banks in the United States 1782–1866* explores the colorful, ornate paper money that first circulated in the 13 colonies, and served American commerce up through the Civil War. *America's Money, America's Story* has much to offer the student of early American coinage, as does *Numismatic Art in America*, second edition.

For a complete catalog of numismatic reference books, supplies, and storage products,
visit Whitman Publishing online at www.whitman**books**.com.

Contents

Foreword *by Kenneth Bressett* vii

Credits and Acknowledgments ix

Introduction xi

1. Money in Early America 1

2. Minting and Distribution 6

3. Collecting Colonial Coins 15

4. How to Use This Book 29

5. Silver Coinage of Massachusetts, 1652–1682 32

6. British Coins and Tokens for America, Early Issues 50

7. American Coins and Tokens, 1783–1788 71

8. Other Early American Pieces 230

9. European Coins and Tokens for America, Later Issues 243

10. Early Washington Coins and Tokens 255

11. Unrelated Foreign Coins and Tokens 275

12. 19th-Century Colonial Copies and Fantasies 292

Selected Bibliography 317

About the Author 326

Index 327

FOREWORD

by Kenneth Bressett

The story of money, its everyday use in commerce, and how it is created for payment of taxes and use in trade, presents a chronicle of the people, the tribulations, and the progress of every nation. Knowledge of the various kinds of coins and other money used during the formation of the United States is essential to understanding the character of its early settlers, the problems they faced, and steps that were taken to overcome the many hardships associated with achieving some degree of economic freedom and stability.

Money that was used in early America was nothing at all like the coins, paper bills, and credit cards used today. It would have been as difficult for the original settlers to envision electronic transfers as it is for us to think about having to do without a standard monetary system, or the checks, coins, and currency we use to facilitate trade. For colonizers of a new land it was far more essential to journey with the essentials of life that must have included clothing, household goods, farm equipment, tools, and barter items. With no place to spend money, the early settlers in America were not overly concerned about bringing cash with them to their new home.

Most of the early American settlers were farmers or small merchants looking for a better life. They had heard stories about rivers teeming with gold and precious gems, and while both they and the English government longed for immediate riches, their goal was mainly to ensure economic growth. The men hunted, built homes, and farmed, while the women cooked, made preserves, spun, and made clothing. Theirs was a self-sufficient society that relied on barter and needed little outside assistance or money. But that was not what the king of England hoped to achieve in the plantations that were intended more as a source of exports to the mother country.

Early commerce in New England consisted of exchanging goods with the natives, by which valuable furs were obtained for export. In England they were used to acquire needed supplies and items that could not be produced locally. Beaver skins, wampum, imported trinkets, grain—and, in Virginia, tobacco—soon became the commonly accepted media of exchange for all other available commodities. The settlers had little use for coined money at first, but when traders came from foreign lands, coins were usually demanded in payment for goods. Coins that did occasionally come from England were immediately returned in payment for essential items from the homeland.

Gold and silver coins of all nations were accepted in normal dealings by the colonists who in turn used them to purchase imported goods. English copper and silver coins were familiar and desirable, but of equal value were the German thalers, Dutch silver lyon (lion) dollars and gold ducats, French louis, and of course, the ever-present gold doubloons and silver pieces-of-eight and their fractions from Spain as well as mints from Mexico to South America. English copper coins served the need for small change, but even these were scarce and rarely adequate for commercial needs.

In time, barter out of necessity became the prime medium of exchange within the colonies. Europeans were anxious to purchase fish and pelts from America, and the colonists were eager to accommodate them by bartering for those items with the Indians. Beads, knives, hatchets, and blankets were the favorite items. Trade with Europe was necessary and brought in powder, shot, guns, nails, and other provisions, thus adding to the shortage of coined money in the colonies. By and large, the colonization of British North America began and grew under the principles of mercantilism, a system whereby the colonies were expected to buy English finished goods and pay for them by sending locally abundant raw materials to England to supply her factories and stores. Colonial trade policy and England's mercantile system in general were governed by the English Board of Trade, which regulated commerce, raw materials, manufacturing, and shipping. Trade with any other country was discouraged in an effort to keep the colonies dependent on England.

The British mercantile system required gold and silver to be used in England, and largely prevented the colonies from using anything but barter. As inhibiting as this was, the barter system at least served communities well for domestic needs, and the Americans even continued to exchange goods, services, and products well beyond the period of British control.

Foreword

From 1637 to 1661, Indian wampum became a standard medium of exchange for trade with the Native Americans. Wampum, basically strings of colored shell beads, was highly coveted and could be exchanged for furs. Six white beads or three blue beads equaled one English penny. All financial records were kept in the traditional English pounds, shillings, and pence, but debts and taxes were often paid in corn, beaver, or whatever foreign coins were available. The terms "country pay" and "corn" referred to a number of different kinds of grain or even peas, and all were accepted by some colonial treasuries for payment of taxes.

To a great extent, the saga of the American colonization effort is a story of the settlers' struggle to achieve a degree of economic sufficiency in defiance of unsympathetic British policies. Self-sufficiency, which could be better called "liberty," meant the opportunity to market surplus produce at reasonable prices, and to use the income for necessities, or even an occasional luxury. This, however, was not the royal intent, and every possible obstacle was used to force a kind of restricted trade with England that would favor the Crown and leave the colonists with only the barest of necessities—and a continuing need to trade with the homeland.

Coining money was considered a royal prerogative and was forbidden to the colonists. Some trade did go on with other foreign merchants, and small quantities of Spanish-American coins did circulate here, as well as other gold and silver pieces, but most local transactions had to rely on barter or trade without the use of coins. In time, just about anything that even looked like a coin was considered spendable. It was not until 1652, during the reign of Oliver Cromwell, three years after King Charles was removed from the throne, that coinage became an issue, and the Massachusetts Bay Colony faced the issue squarely. A mint was established in Boston to provide a coinage that could be used to satisfy local needs and to counteract debased Spanish-American silver coins. The coins made at that historic facility were produced over the next 30 years in defiance of British law. The date 1652 was continued in use on them by convention, representing the date of authorization by the colony. It is a matter of debate as to whether the maintaining of this date was intended to hide from British authorities the fact that the coins were made far beyond Cromwell's time.

Mark Newby, a Quaker merchant, came to New Jersey in 1681 with a group of immigrants and a quantity of Irish coins known as St. Patrick's halfpence. The legislature of the colony made them legal tender for that amount. In 1688, Richard Holt, a British entrepreneur, arranged for a quantity of tin tokens to be made for the American plantations, but these never crossed the Atlantic.

Over the years British financial policies created many hardships and ill feelings towards the Crown. They prompted acts of defiance such as the Massachusetts coinage that was seen by some as the "first Declaration of Independence." Later there were other revolts against taxation and fiscal controls that seemed to be against the best interest of the colonists. The Stamp Act of 1765 was particularly offensive because it was seen as taxation without representation and a restriction on the freedom of the press. In Boston, reaction to the British tax on tea was swift and harsh.

Some relief from the always-prevalent coin shortage in America was promised to the colonies in 1722 when William Wood, an English businessman, obtained a patent from King George I to make tokens for Ireland and America. These were to be lightweight brass pieces that would facilitate trade in the colonies, and not likely to be returned to England because they were not made to the same standards as regal coins. Some were sent to America along with the "Rosa Americana" pieces that had been made expressly for the colonies. Both circulated for a short time, but despite the desperate need for small change, these coins were widely rejected because of their weight, and the experiment died the following year.

Among the many kinds of coins and tokens used to facilitate trade in the early colonies were those from France that were made either for homeland or colonial use, English merchants' coins and tokens, and nearly anything imported from Europe that could be called a "coin."

When the British government agreed to make an issue of copper coins exclusively for Virginia in 1773, they again were lightweight and included an image of George III, who by then was not very popular with Americans now on the verge of revolution. The coins were considered too little and too late to help with the economic future of a new country; it was time to begin thinking about becoming self-sufficient in every way. In 1776 the Continental Congress proposed an issue of coins with a design inspired by Benjamin Franklin. For some reason, that coinage never progressed far beyond a limited distribution of pewter pieces. Specimens are now considered to be rare and valuable collector items. New Hampshire proposed a coinage in 1776, but the idea did not progress past the pattern stage. Another early attempt to provide the states with a uniform coinage was tried when copper coins dated 1783 with the legend NOVA CONSTELLATIO were made under contract with a private mint in Birmingham, England, and imported for use in America.

Various other patterns and state-authorized coinages were proposed and started in the period from 1785 through 1788. Each is a chapter in the history of early America and tells of the measures taken by Vermont, Connecticut, New Jersey, New York, and Massachusetts to provide coinage for the beginning nation. Mixed with these states' efforts were a number of tokens and coins sent here in commerce, while others were imported by merchants from overseas for local use.

The extensive assortment of coins and tokens pressed into use prior to the establishment of the American monetary system is formidable. Detailed accounts of various segments of these have been published in many forms and are now presented in one convenient source by author Q. David Bowers, who has spent a lifetime researching this absorbing topic. Each coin type has been carefully documented, as are all of the notable variations that hold such high interest for collectors. The story of money in early America reflects the hardships, heartbreaks, opportunities, conquests, and political horse-trading that went into winning financial freedom for the emerging nation. It is a story reflected and amplified in each of the coins described in this book.

CREDITS AND ACKNOWLEDGMENTS

The **American Antiquarian Society,** Worcester, Massachusetts, provided information. The **American Numismatic Association,** Colorado Springs, Colorado, assisted in several ways. The **American Numismatic Society,** New York City, made its facilities available for research. The **Massachusetts Historical Society,** Boston, provided images and information. The **Smithsonian Institution** helped with research.

Alan Anthony reviewed the manuscript and made suggestions, especially regarding Bermuda and Virginia coinage. **William T. Anton Jr.** helped in several ways, including reviewing all of the listings in the New Jersey coppers section. **Richard August** made suggestions, provided coins for photography, advised concerning rarity ratings, and consulted on several matters.

Anne Bentley, curator, Massachusetts Historical Society, provided coins for photography and made suggestions for the manuscript. **Jerry Bobbe** provided photographs of certain Conder tokens. **Roy Bonjour** reviewed the Vermont listings, made suggestions, and supplied key photographs. **Wynn Bowers** reviewed the manuscript, made suggestions, and assisted on a research trip. **Kenneth Bressett** contributed the foreword, copyedited the text, and helped in other ways.

Randy Clark was essential for the Connecticut section and provided citations, comments, and corrections, and helped in other ways. **Judy Clevenger** provided an illustration. **Colonial Williamsburg Foundation** provided images of coins gifted by **Joseph R. and Ruth P. Lasser.**

Charles Davis reviewed the text and made suggestions. **Thomas Delorey** reviewed the manuscript and made suggestions.

George J. Fuld consulted on various series, made his studies of Washington pieces available, helped with rarity ratings, and assisted in other ways.

Larry Gaye provided photographs of Conder tokens. **David Gladfelter** reviewed the manuscript and made suggestions, with particular regard to monetary policies and circulation. He also suggested avenues of research. **Erik Goldstein,** curator, **Colonial Williamsburg,** made suggestions and furnished photographs of coins, including certain items donated by **Joseph Lasser.**

Heritage Auction Galleries, James Halperin co-chairman, provided images and prices from their past sales. **Michael J. Hodder** made suggestions regarding numismatic research past and present, provided rarity data on Massachusetts silver, reviewed the manuscript, and helped in many other ways. **Robert Hoge,** American Numismatic Society, helped secure images. **Jack Howes** reviewed the manuscript and made suggestions.

Katherine M. Jaeger provided information on 1818 New Spain jolas. **Louis E. Jordan** reviewed and contributed to the text, with special emphasis on Massachusetts and Maryland.

John Kleeberg reviewed the manuscript and made many additions and suggestions. **John Kraljevich** made contributions. **Robert Krajewski, Stack's,** provided photographs.

Robert Leonard reviewed the manuscript and provided suggestions, especially regarding monetary history. **Stuart Levine** provided photographs of two coins. **Dana Linett, Early American Numismatics and Early American History Auctions,** furnished auction data. **John N. Lupia III** made a valuable suggestion.

Robert M. Martin reviewed the manuscript and helped in other ways, including with rarity and grade information relating to Connecticut coppers (including photographs by Neil Rothschild). **Sydney F. Martin** reviewed the text, added several listings, provided photographs of coins in his collection (by Neil Rothschild; including many Connecticut coppers), provided rarity ratings and price suggestions for Connecticut coppers, assisted with Wood's Rosa Americana and Hibernia coinages, and helped in other ways. **Jack McNamara, Stack's,** assisted with valuations. **Priscilla Moore** reviewed the manuscript and made suggestions. **Roger Moore, MD,** provided extensive information on Virginia coinage, provided illustrations, and helped in other ways. **Philip L. Mossman, MD,** reviewed the manuscript and made suggestions concerning many historical aspects, especially with regard to early American monetary systems and policies. **Tom Mulvaney** provided a selection of photographs including many made to order.

Eric P. Newman reviewed the manuscript, suggested certain formats, and helped in many other ways. He was a valuable counsel. **Susan Novak** helped with correspondence, contacts, and coordination of research.

Joel J. Orosz reviewed the manuscript and made suggestions.

Mike Packard made die details, rarity data, and historical information available from his studies of Massachusetts copper coins of 1787 and 1788. **Donald Partrick** helped in several ways. **Douglas Plasencia** provided many photographs, including from Stack's and other auction catalogs, and assisted on a research trip. **Andrew W. Pollock III** made suggestions.

Robert Rhue reviewed the manuscript and made suggestions. **Tom Rinaldo** made suggestions. **Neil Rothschild** provided many illustrations, including specimens from the Robert M. Martin (Connecticut coppers), Sydney F. Martin (Connecticut coppers), and Roger S. Siboni (various series) collections.

Edwin Sarrafian reviewed the text and made suggestions, especially regarding state copper coinage and was important in the listings for Machin's Mills issues. **George Seifrit** provided images of a Machin's Mills halfpenny. **Leo Shane**, librarian of C4, provided reference works. **Roger S. Siboni** provided images of coins (by Neil Rothschild) from his collection (including extensive New Jersey coppers), reviewed the manuscript, made suggestions, and was a key figure in other ways. **James C. Spilman** reviewed the manuscript, made suggestions, provided photographs from his files, and granted permission to use material from the *Colonial Newsletter*. **Lawrence R. Stack** as valuations editor coordinated market information from many sources, and also helped with suggestions; he also provided archival photographs, including from the John J. Ford Jr. Collection and his own reference collection. **Elena Stolyarik** photographed coins in the American Numismatic Society's collection. **Geoffrey P. Stevens** helped with information. **David M. Sundman** reviewed the manuscript and made suggestions.

Anthony J. Terranova reviewed the manuscript, provided extensive photographic files from Pine Tree Auctions as well as coins for photography, Al Hoch plates, Richard Picker estate items, and helped in other ways. **Two Bits Photography** provided certain images of the Sydney Martin collection coins.

Robert A. Vlack helped with several specialties and shared information on die varieties.

Alan V. Weinberg read the manuscript, made suggestions, and provided coins for photography. **Robin Wells** reviewed the manuscript and made suggestions. **Ray Williams** reviewed the manuscript, made suggestions concerning avenues of research, shared notes concerning the history and characteristics of New Jersey coppers, and helped in other ways.

*This book is dedicated to
Eric P. Newman
and his lifetime devotion to
early American numismatics.*

INTRODUCTION

Welcome to the *Whitman Encyclopedia of Colonial and Early American Coins*. This project has been a dream of mine for many years. I'll share some recollections that may be of interest.

When I first began to collect coins in 1952, soon learning how to spell and pronounce *numismatist*, my first interest was Lincoln cents. That's how most people started back then, when there was a possibility of finding a 1909-S V.D.B. or 1914-D cent in circulation. I was never that lucky, but the coin bug bit me, and I soon went on to collect other things.

Within a year I discovered colonials. My first order of business was trying to track down a copy of Sylvester S. Crosby's *Early Coins of America*, 1875, which I was able to do after some difficulty—in an era in which there were no specialized numismatic booksellers, and the title was long out of print (save for a 1945 reprint of which I was not aware). I also found a copy of *The State Coinages of New England*, published by the American Numismatic Society in 1920, describing the copper issues of Vermont, Connecticut, and Massachusetts. Copies of Sydney P. Noe's studies of Massachusetts silver and Edward Maris's book on New Jersey coppers were also acquired, the latter being hard to find.

In the next several years my fascination grew, and I came to know others who were interested in colonial coins and their history. There weren't many of us. Eric Newman, author of texts on Virginia, Fugio, and Continental Currency coinage, among other accomplishments, stood at the top of the pyramid. Ken Bressett had a longtime interest and liked Vermont coppers in particular. Before long, Ken Rendell, also a teenager, became a fine friend and colonial collector. George Fuld had wide-ranging interests but particularly enjoyed Washington coins, tokens, and medals. Walter Breen was the most active researcher of the time and became a friend as well. Walter, a polymath, was simultaneously working on books on New Jersey coinage, Massachusetts silver, U.S. half cents, and other series. His New Jersey manuscript was the most advanced, not far from publication, he often said. (It never was published, although the manuscript survives.) Damon G. Douglas was an avid researcher, especially in the 1940s, and studied New Jersey and Fugio coppers. I never met him.

About the year 1957, Bressett, Rendell, Breen, Fuld, and I decided to form the Rittenhouse Society, a group of young people interested in research, with emphasis on colonial coins. Our original proposal was that members had to be under 30 years of age, but Eric Newman (born in 1911) would then be excluded, so all age requirements were dropped. Joining us in the Rittenhouse Society were several others who liked research but weren't colonial specialists, including D. Wayne Johnson (who in 1960 became founding editor of *Coin World*) and Grover Criswell, whose forte was Confederate bills and bonds. In 1960 in Boston, at the annual convention of the American Numismatic Association, we "formalized" the Rittenhouse Society and decided to have breakfast meetings each year at the same show.

By that time, I could probably recite by heart much, if not most, information in Crosby, except for the text of old legislative documents. I could identify by sight many Connecticut coppers, all the Vermonts, and most of the Massachusetts half cents and cents, and dearly loved the mystique surrounding Machin's Mills, having been drawn to the information about this establishment in Crosby. I had spent a fair amount of time on the last, tracking down information wherever I could, usually by lengthy correspondence in an era before the Internet and the availability of databases. I never did find anything significant beyond what Crosby knew in the olden days, combined with the findings of Newman and a few others.

Along the way I discovered some new die combinations in the Massachusetts and Connecticut series. My business partner, Jim Ruddy, with whom I formed the Empire Coin Company in April 1958, found a new obverse die of the famous 1786 "Date Under Plow Beam" New Jersey copper—a coup, as this style is perhaps the most famous of the types from that state. Although Jim was not deeply interested in research, he was an avid collector, and among other things bought the New Jersey coppers from the collection of King Farouk of Egypt when it was auctioned in Cairo in 1954.

John J. Ford Jr. was another early influence in the series. He and his employee, Walter Breen, seemed to have a love-hate relationship with each other, while at the same time they cooperated in business. In any event Walter did not want John to be a part of the Rittenhouse Society, and thus he was not invited. Otherwise he surely would have been among the founders. I spent many happy hours with John, going over his collection, which he was always willing to share with me—even, at a later time, allowing a staff photographer to join me on a visit to his underground vault in Rockville Centre, New York, to photograph his Vermont coppers. I enjoyed poking through his boxes of colonials, most still in the envelopes of earlier owners such as Wayte Raymond and F.C.C. Boyd. At the time I was planning to write a book on this fascinating Vermont series (but never did).

By that time, John Ford had isolated himself from many fine people in the hobby, becoming involved in controversies, and did not have the time or inclination to share his holdings except with a few close friends. John, now deceased, had one of the most complex personalities of anyone I ever met. One could either be a friend or be despised. John was particularly intolerant of dealers who achieved success in the marketplace with little knowledge of history, minting procedures, and other studies that make a true professional. He was fond of saying that *A Guide Book of United States Coins* (the "Red Book") was the one-book reference library of many if not most dealers, and that beyond its pages they were clueless. He was also a bit of a curmudgeon. Probably, if he had been introduced to Miss America, he would remark afterward that she had a pimple on her left ear.

In the 1950s the larger dealers rarely attributed colonial coins by die varieties. Connecticut coppers in particular were apt to be relegated to a back drawer, as most were well worn. To the uninitiated, Henry C. Miller's descriptive guidelines might as well have been written in Greek. The Hollinbeck Coin Company (Art and Paul Kagin, in Des Moines) shipped me boxes of Connecticuts they'd had for years. I marked my offer on each envelope, shipped them back, and back they came to me with an invoice. Offers ranged from about $2 to $10. Stack's had scads of Connecticuts, some marked with Miller numbers, others not. I was invited to look through the stock and make offers on any I could use.

Rendell, Breen, Ford, and others interested in state coinage of the 1780s found many rarities in dealers' stocks this way, often by looking through boxes at conventions. Groups of Uncirculated 1773 Virginia halfpence were common in dealers' stocks, particularly those of an old-timer in Syracuse, from whom I bought at least a couple hundred. He never would reveal how many he actually had—all remnants from the famous Cohen hoard. Eric Newman wrote a dandy book on these Virginia coins in 1956, but few readers were inspired to collect them by die varieties, for the differences were minute in many instances.

Richard ("Dick") Picker, trained as an accountant, became a coin dealer in the mid-1950s. His specialties were colonial and early U.S. coins. There were no generally accepted grading standards for colonial coins then (nor are there now). Tired of hearing "You call it Very Fine, but I think it is only Fine" from buyers, Dick opted not to grade his coins at all. And throughout the rest of his career he never did. He would say, "That Ryder-9 Vermont is one hundred dollars." It was not a Very Good coin, nor a Very Fine coin, but instead was whatever the buyer wanted to call it. Simply, it was a $100 coin. Take it or leave it. The system worked, and Dick came to be admired by collectors and dealers alike. In 1971 his inventory was stolen while in the care of the security service hired by the American Numismatic Association for its annual convention, held that year in Washington, D.C. The security service was sued (and never hired again), but the coins were never found. I remember that I was considering buying a Theatre at New York token on display for sale in his case, and had examined it, but was not sure if a tiny planchet crack on the lower part of the obverse would deter a future buyer from purchasing it from me. To this day, whenever I see one of these tokens, I check for the planchet crack. A unique white-metal 1792 Roman Head cent obverse die trial was swiped as well and has not been seen since.

I traveled to Europe frequently in the 1960s, visiting the leading London dealers. The largest and most important was Spink & Son, an old-line firm in the charge of Douglas Liddell, who in turn visited me in the United States a couple of times. B.A. Seaby, Ltd, had large stocks of popularly priced coins and was more willing to trade and make deals than Spink. Hibernia and Rosa Americana coins were common and inexpensive. Except for certain pieces with American connections, there was little interest in Conder tokens. Robert Bashlow was ahead of me on a visit to Seaby's when, for sixpence each, he bought their entire stock of Conder tokens—thousands of pieces. A.H. Baldwin & Sons was rumored to have a vast stock, but I never had access to it. "Mrs. Norweb gets first choice when we find something, and after that John Ford buys what we have available," I was told. I had the distinct feeling that I was regarded as a nuisance, so I visited their office only occasionally.

Talbot, Allum & Lee cents of 1795 could often be found in twos and threes in dealers' stocks in London, usually somewhat prooflike, while mulings with odd Conder token dies could be bought for the equivalent of a dollar or two, but were scarce. The 1783 Proof restrikes of the Washington Draped Bust cent were plentiful in copper, plus the occasional silver striking. Large Eagle and the scarcer Small Eagle Washington cents of 1791 were always easy to find.

Once, I spent a delightful afternoon in London with C. Wilson Peck, author of *English Copper, Tin and Bronze Coins in the British Museum, 1558–1978*, a monumental book that remains the standard today. He took a liking to me and invited me to view his collection, arranged in wooden cabinets in his home. I was allowed to pick out any items I found of interest to buy, after which he planned to offer the main collection to the London dealers. On another occasion, I visited with a Mr. Hammond in Torquay, on the coast in Devon, and bought his collection of British coins. Included were a large number of counterfeit halfpence dated in the 18th century. Upon returning home I shipped them to Eric P. Newman, the only person I knew who might be interested in such things. (Today, many people would be.)

The *Colonial Newsletter*, founded by Al Hoch, had its genesis at the ANA Convention in Boston in the summer of 1960, the same event during which the Rittenhouse Society was "formalized." Hoch gathered pictures of state-copper die varieties, and all of us helped with contributions. After a few issues, publication was taken over by James C. Spilman, who edited it for years afterward, during which time it became the journal of record for the colonial specialty. Following publication of issue number 103 in February 1996, the *Colonial Newsletter* was donated to the American Numismatic Society, which continues its publication today. Philip L. Mossman became editor as of number 104, in time followed by Gary Trudgen. With the contributions of many others, the *CNL* continued to new heights of excellence with an increased amount of information published each year. Today, a file of *CNL* remains fascinating to read. I did just that, poring through back issues, in the course of preparing this book.

The *CNL*, as it was nicknamed, was immediately appreciated by the current and growing field of colonial researchers, including Bob Vlack, a relative newcomer but already prominent in the field. A consummate student and observer, he learned quickly. It had been only a couple years earlier when he telephoned me at Empire Coin Company to buy a "starter collection" of Connecticut coppers, as he thought the description sounded interesting, and, somehow, he might like to see what such coins looked like! The rest is research and publication history. Today, his work on Machin's Mills and French colonial coinage is especially important.

Phil Greco was a bright star in colonials, and had an "internship" one summer at Empire Coin Company, where he helped assemble existing pictures of colonial and state coins to help us make out the different die varieties. Phil's interest must have turned elsewhere, for I do not recall having heard from him much after that time, although he was a contributor to the *CNL* in the early days. The *CNL* soon went from founder Hoch to James C. Spilman. Jim Spilman was a wonderful editor—caretaker and shepherd, actually—of the *CNL*. He had the rare talent of considering the opinions of others, printing them, and then gently suggesting modifications. All letters, articles, and comments were welcome.

Interest expanded, and colonial coins, while not in the top-10 series in the American numismatic hit parade, attracted many new faces. Other collectors, earlier not publicizing their holdings, came forward to share ideas and opinions. Edward "Ned" Barnsley loved Connecticut coppers and contributed extensive research notes to the *CNL*, while editor Spilman parried with his own erudite observations, plus studies of Fugio coppers and other specialties. Norman Bryant, Bob Hinkley, Howard Kurth, Ted Craige, Alan V. Weinberg, and others who enjoyed colonials were frequent correspondents.

In the years since then, colonials have come of age. *Walter Breen's Complete Encyclopedia of U.S. and Colonial Coins*, 1988, a most impressive work, became widely circulated and introduced the field to many. The venerable (since 1946) Red Book, now under the editorship of Ken Bressett, expanded its coverage. The Colonial Coin Collectors Club (C4) was founded by Mike Hodder in 1993 and is dynamic today, with the *C4 Newsletter* being a particularly active forum for the exchange of ideas and discoveries. An annual convention is held in Boston.

Many participants among modern researchers engage in "zero-based" thinking: carefully examining coins themselves as well as *original* documents, disregarding later theories and adding them if they can be supported by historical or other evidence. Many conclusions are far different from the web of theories presented by Walter Breen in his *Complete Encyclopedia of U.S. and Colonial Coins*.

Encapsulating U.S. coins in plastic and labeling them with a grade became popular in 1986 when the Professional Coin Grading Service (PCGS) was launched. This and other services went on to grade colonial coins, further increasing their popularity, especially to buyers who might be distrustful of a grade applied by a collector or dealer. Today, it is not at all unusual for a dealer to have, for example, a 1788 Massachusetts cent in a holder, labeled with a grade and assigned a price. The same dealer would not recognize such names as Hillyer C. Ryder, Joseph Callender, or Jacob Perkins—key people for anyone even casually studying this particular specialty. "Slabbing" coins has led to the democratization of collecting, with many new enthusiasts depending on the holder label for all of the information they need, without consulting traditional sources, never mind that a 1652 Pine Tree shilling might be clipped and significantly underweight but not so noted on the holder. Of course, clipped pieces on their own, if properly described, can be historical and desirable.

That said, the official weight for any Massachusetts shilling was 72 grains and proportionally less for the smaller denominations. This was the ideal weight and not one that could be maintained consistently because of the crudeness of the minting machinery and the planchet production. The actual weight of pieces unclipped after striking could range as high as 76 grains or more, and as low as 61 grains or so. That particular 61-grain piece was lot 43 in the Hain Family Collection Sale, conducted by Stack's in 2002, wherein the cataloger made the statement that this piece was, in his opinion, not clipped after striking, adding that "the Boston Mint did not always get its coins' weight right."

Moreover, the thickness of the planchet determines its weight as much as does its diameter. The thickness of the planchets on which Massachusetts silver coins were struck could vary significantly. Lots 34 and 35 of the above-referenced Hain sale are classic examples. These are two Oak Tree Shillings of the same Noe-9 variety. Lot 34 weighed 71.4 grains and was struck on an extremely thick and constricted planchet. That piece is smaller in diameter than lot 35, which weighed but 47.7 grains and was struck on an exceptionally thin planchet. Further, the "official" weight of an Oak Tree twopence is 12 grains, one-sixth that of a shilling. Yet numerous Oak Tree twopence, unclipped after striking, weigh 8 to 10 grains, a significant variance from the standard.

It seems to me that, to date, many certified colonial coins have been evaluated by commercial graders who do not necessarily have expertise in the colonial field. Such nuances as original weight differences vis-à-vis coins clipped after striking are in some instances not easily distinguished, as I have just indicated. In time, I expect that the staffs of the grading services will gain more knowledge.

Today, the field of colonial coins has attracted many devotees. Some stay but a short while. Others remain for the rest of their lives. While buying, selling, and swapping are always popular—everyone wants to add to his or her collection—it is perhaps the old-fashioned friendship that is the biggest draw. To immerse yourself with a group of colonial specialists is to join a warm, friendly circle. And then there is always the excitement of sharing a new find.

The present book is intended to be a general guide to the vast field of colonial coins. I and many fine consultants have created what I hope you will find to be a very useful text—giving the basics for each specialty, outlining the individual die varieties or an overview of them (depending upon the series), and assigning estimated market values. Beyond this book, I recommend the specialized texts on the different series. Remarkably, one of the best "reads" of all remains the 1875 work by Crosby, *The Early Coins of America*.

Welcome to a fascinating field of numismatic study and collecting.

1

MONEY IN EARLY AMERICA

COMMODITIES IN EXCHANGE

During most of the 17th century, the first century of permanent North American colonization by northern Europeans, coins were scarce in circulation. To fill the demand for media of exchange, many commodities and commercial products were used. In Maryland and Virginia, tobacco, powder, and shot traded at set rates. On March 4, 1635, the Massachusetts General Court adopted legislation that provided the following:

> It is likewise ordered that musket bullets of a full bore shall pass currently for a farthing apiece, provided that no man be compelled to take above XII [one shilling] at a time in them.

In the early days in some colonies, grain (a general term for corn, peas, and wheat), oat meal, cattle, furs, and fish were also used in payment of debt. Each of these had a utility value. Tobacco could be smoked, or if the recipient didn't indulge, a neighbor would. Fish could be eaten, and fur could be made into caps and clothing.

In New Hampshire dried and salted fish, lumber, and agricultural products saw service as currency. Citizens of the Carolinas often used tobacco, corn, peas, rice, and even pine tar for the same purpose. In New York beaver skins were sometimes specified as payment in contracts. Each of these things required effort to find or produce. Accordingly, the market could not be disturbed by an unexpected flood of animal skins or musket balls. This is the labor theory of value, originally developed by Adam Smith (and later extensively expanded by Karl Marx). Counterfeiting was not a problem. Unfortunately, tobacco depreciated so badly from overproduction in Virginia that, in 1640 (twenty-one years after tobacco was made the official currency), all the "bad" and half the "good" was ordered burned. This was not successful in decreasing the flood of tobacco on the market, so in 1666 both Virginia and Maryland banned the planting of tobacco entirely for a year. Prices in 1683 were so low from overproduction that there were riots when Virginia refused to order another one-year ban. The value of beaver skins fluctuated also.

Indian wampum, or shell money, was used, particularly in the northeastern areas. On November 15, 1637, the Massachusetts General Court ordered that wampum should pass at six per penny for any sum under 12 pence. Harvard College was founded in 1636. Tuition of £1 6s 8d could be paid several ways, including by about 1,900 beads of white whelk and blue (purple) quahog wampum.

On October 7, 1640, the General Court directed that white wampum should pass at four per penny and blue at two per penny, with no more than 12 pence worth to be used at one time unless the receiver desired more. Wampum had its problems, for similar glass beads later could be made cheaply in factories, and wampum also counterfeited from seashells. What had become an accepted medium of exchange among Indians became devalued when interfered with by white settlers.

Commodities used in exchange were often referred to as "country pay," a term still seen today in some historical accounts.

Coins Used in the Colonies

Prior to establishment of the United States Mint in Philadelphia in 1792 and its subsequent production of coinage for circulation in 1793, metallic money in the American colonies came in many forms. Foreign coins comprised a wide variety of copper, silver, and gold issues from Spanish America, England, Portugal, Holland, France, Germany, and elsewhere. Many of these were made legal tender by federal law.

As a general rule, in the 18th century copper coins used for small change were apt to be British. Silver and gold issues, used in larger transactions, were typically pieces struck at the Spanish-American mints in Mexico (in particular), Chile, Peru, and elsewhere. These were denominated in reales (sometimes given as *reals*), with 8 reales equaling a Spanish dollar. Gold coins were reckoned in escudos, with eight escudos equaling a gold doubloon, worth about 16 Spanish dollars. Deeds, contracts, and other documents involving money were usually drawn in English or Spanish money. Brazilian gold coins were important as well. In correspondence, numismatic historian John Kleeberg gave this summary:

> I like to apply a simple rule of thumb: the gold coins came from Brazil (the 6,400 reis, often called joes), the silver coins from Mexico (the 8 reales), and the copper from Britain and Ireland (the halfpence). Those were the workhorse coins. Then there were some additional "workhorse" coins—the pistareen from mainland Spain, for example, and the Spanish American 2 reales, reales, and 1/2 reales. As for the source of Spanish American silver, there's another simple rule of thumb—México in the 18th century, Potosí in the 17th century.

Holland isn't that important in North American circulation, except for a peculiar period during the War of the Spanish Succession (1701–1714), when lion daalders were pressed into service instead of 8-real coins because the latter were not obtainable. All our evidence (the Castine deposit, the early New York paper money issues, the *Feversham* shipwreck) for the use of lion daalders comes from that short period. German coins don't seem to be important at all. Thus a fairly complete list of countries from which came the early coins used in the American colonies would include Brazil, Mexico, Bolivia, Peru, Spain, Britain, and Ireland.

The popular Spanish milled dollar, or 8-real piece, was divided into eighths or bits, the one-real worth 12-1/2¢. From this, the term "two bits" for a twenty-five-cent coin passed into the modern idiom.

Indeed, long after the Philadelphia Mint and its several branches were in operation, most silver coins in circulation in the United States were Spanish-American types. In New York City, Boston, or Philadelphia in the 1850s, silver two-real coins were much more common than federal Liberty Seated coins. From 1821 until August 1834 there were no U.S. gold coins in circulation, as the value of that metal had risen to the point that it cost more than face value to mint a $5 gold coin. These continued to be struck to the order of those who deposited sufficient gold to make them. After they were delivered, the coins were used in international trade, where the face value made no difference. A five-dollar gold coin containing, for example, $5.05 worth of precious metal would be valued at $5.05 at a destination such as London or Vienna. In the meantime, Spanish-American doubloons and other gold coins were widely used.

Selected foreign silver and gold coins remained legal tender until after the Act of February 21, 1857, mandated their retirement. An extension was granted for two years, then another for six months, making them useful in commerce well into the year 1859.

It was difficult, if not impossible, for the average merchant or banker to know the exchange value of an eight-escudo gold doubloon from Mexico, as compared to one from Peru or Chile, or to figure the trade worth of a French silver five-franc coin. Exchange-rate tables published in newspapers and almanacs were a help. Most city newspapers had a "prices current" column listing values of popular gold and silver coins, as well as market values for commodities. A wide class of publications known as counterfeit detectors and bank-note reporters developed. These told the value of paper money in particular (in addition to endeavoring to identify counterfeits), but often gave exchange values for foreign coins.

Reckoning Monetary Accounts

In the early days, none of England's monetary colonies had any coins of their own. The only money available to purchase imported necessities was whatever the settlers may have brought with them. Then, as trade developed with the Spanish in the West Indies and the Dutch in New Netherland, new money was earned which expanded this meager supply.

Individual colonies had significant commercial interaction with companies in the mother country, in keeping with the principles of mercantilism previously discussed. Through this contact they dealt with England as if each colony were an independent nation. Surprising as it may seem today, as the new colonies struggled for their own existence, certain of them had little contact with each other. Thus the exchange value of the coins circulating in any particular colony was determined by its own economic factors. Frequently these exchange rates, set by local legislation, were very different from one colony to the next. The bookkeeping system by which colonies everywhere reckoned the money circulating within their jurisdictions was called "money of account." Quite consistently the "money of account" in every English colony was denominated in the same monetary units used in England, namely pounds, shillings, and pence (written as £, s, and d, respectively). Thus in 1750 a Spanish-American piece of eight or 8-real coin was quoted as worth 54d sterling in England. In the "monies of account" of the separate colonies it was worth 72d in New England and Virginia monies; 90d in Pennsylvania, Maryland, Delaware, and New Jersey; and 96d in New York. In Georgia it was worth 54d, the same rate as in England, as that colony was under direct English support.

The piece of eight was called "real [i.e., literal] money" because it actually existed as a Spanish-American coin. All of these money-of-account notations were called "imaginary money" because this was just a bookkeeping contrivance with nothing to do with the actual coins spent, just how the money was tracked. For example, a 90d Pennsylvania coin never existed. It was only a bookkeeping device by which to calculate relative values in Pennsylvania for any piece of eight that circulated there. The same coin would be worth 96d in "New York money," should a traveler take it there.

David Gladfelter commented:

> In New Jersey, after 1707 and until the Revolution, "money of account" was "proclamation money" (or "proc"), which was inflated a maximum of 33% over sterling in accordance with the proclamation of Queen Anne in 1704 and the act of Parliament in 1707 limiting this inflation to 33%. The inflation was an attempt by the colonists to keep silver coin in circulation. Thus, a six-shilling New Jersey bill of credit was authorized to pass for 17 dwt [pennyweight] and 12 grains of bullion, the amount of sterling silver in 4 shillings 6d of English money, and was equal to a Spanish pillar dollar. (Correspondence)

English coins in circulation were denominated in terms of a shilling composed of 12 pence, with divisions including the sixpence, fourpence (or groat), and threepence. There were no one-pound silver coins in America, and the largest value typically seen was the crown (5 shillings). Most often encountered was the silver shilling. In the British system, fractional parts of the penny were the halfpenny and farthing, the latter being a quarter-penny. During the 18th century, copper English halfpence and counterfeits of them were the most plentiful copper coins in circulation. Even after federal dollars became a reality during the Confederation, many commercial and civic accounts continued to be reckoned in British money. In some areas, any quarter-size silver coin, including U.S. coins and Spanish-American two-real pieces, were nicknamed "shillings." After the Philadelphia Mint went into operation federal cents were referred to as "pennies," and they still are.

From time to time, paper currency issues were produced by the various colonies, the earliest being the issue of Massachusetts dated December 10, 1690, on the old calendar in which the year began on March 25. Because of this, other Massachusetts bills dated "February 3, 1690," were printed before March 25, 1691, as authorized by the "order of February 3, 1690/91," the double date used by historians to explain this transitional period. Although dated earlier, the February 3, 1690, bills were actually printed later than the December 10, 1690, currency. Confusing? Under the old Julian calendar in use in Protestant England before 1752, New Year's Day came on March 25. The day before March 25, 1691, was thus March 24, 1690, in the old calendar. In 1752, England and her American colonies changed to the Gregorian calendar and to adjust for doing so dropped 11 days from the month of September. To make the conversion beginning in 1752, the year 1751 was a "short" year, beginning March 25, 1751, and ending December 31. Thus today we celebrate Benjamin Franklin's birthday on January 17 (1706), but the old-style date was January 6 (1705). Looking back from today, we use the double date to correct the Julian year to Gregorian but usually ignore the 11 days. The double date was not used in the 18th century.

Paper issues printed for colonial monies of account usually were reckoned either in English pounds, shillings, and pence, or in Spanish dollars. For example, an early note of Pennsylvania bore the following inscription:

> This bill shall pass current for five shillings within the Province of Pennsylvania according to an Act of Assembly made in the 31st year of the reign of King George II. Dated May 20, 1758.

A note of Delaware was inscribed thus:

> This indented bill shall pass current for Fifteen Shillings within the Government of the Counties of New Castle, Kent, Sussex on Delaware, according to an Act of Assembly of the said Government made in the 32nd Year of the Reign of our Sovereign Lord King George II. Dated the 1st Day of June, 1759.

When the first issues of the Continental Congress appeared in 1775 they specified payment in Spanish coins. For example, a typical note reads as follows:

> This Bill entitles the Bearer to receive EIGHT Spanish milled DOLLARS, or the Value thereof in Gold or Silver, according to the Resolutions of the CONGRESS, held at Philadelphia the 10th of May, 1775.

Paper Money of Limited Use

Paper money of various kinds, issued in large amounts during the 18th century, was often viewed with distrust. Counterfeiting was rife, notes or bills that were good in one area were valueless in another, and many other problems surfaced. Bills were often altered by removing one denomination and inking in a higher value. Counterfeits were made by various processes, including carefully drawing notes by hand as well as the more prolific making of a false printing plate. Because of counterfeits, official designs were often changed at short intervals, at which time earlier currency was called in, inspected for genuineness, and exchanged for the new. Very few people could tell genuine notes from counterfeits, some of which were so clever that numismatists today need to look for secret privy marks and other signs. Despite the warning "To Counterfeit Is Death" printed on many notes, the game continued. In practice, very few makers of false notes were ever executed, as juries were reluctant to apply the ultimate penalty.

Moreover, much paper money became devalued. It took ever-increasing amounts of paper to buy a given item. Such currency generally stayed within the colony of issue, or if taken across borders, was apt to sell at a deep discount. Older paper money of higher value was often referred to as "old tenor," as were earlier coins of higher weight. The quality and acceptance of paper varied from colony to colony—with some keeping tighter rein than others.

The saying, "never keep a paper dollar in your pocket till tomorrow," popularized by Aaron White around 1857, was just as applicable in colonial days. A citizen holding Spanish coins worth five pounds and an equivalent amount of paper money with the same value would nearly always spend the paper money first.

Continental currency was authorized by the Continental Congress and was issued in five series, in denominations from fractions of a dollar up to, eventually, $80. Although these notes were payable in Spanish milled dollars, as related previously, the federal treasury was empty. Accordingly, the bills depreciated rapidly from their first issue in 1775 to the last in 1779. In January 1777 it took $105 in Continental paper money to buy $100 in Spanish silver dollars at an exchange office. By February 1781 it took $7,500! After this time, the bills became virtually worthless. Some smart speculators made a market in them and were rewarded when, on August 4, 1790, Congress passed an act providing that Continental currency would be received at the Treasury until September 1, 1791, at the rate of $100 in bills to $1 in silver or gold coins. The Act of May 8, 1792, extended the redemption period of March 7, 1792, after which time the bills were repudiated, the status they retain today. Later paper money issues of the various states, similar in design to certain Continental notes, were guaranteed by the government. It is an arguable point as to the legal-tender status today of signed, unredeemed bills.

In April 1782 the Commonwealth of Pennsylvania affirmed the charter of the Bank of North America, the first such institution authorized by a state, although banks and money-exchange offices were hardly new. Soon the bank issued paper money with its imprint, redeemable in specie (gold and silver coins) at its office. This set the pace for more than 2,000 banks and other issuers of paper money from that time until the 1860s. It was not until 1861 that the federal government again issued currency in quantity for public use. The failure of Continental notes had warned the public, and it was thought that federal paper money would be questioned. As it developed, bills of banks ranged from worthless to fully redeemable in gold or silver, depending on the reputation and capital of the institution involved. The Bank of New York, founded in 1784, issued paper that was of solid value; while, for example, the Farmers Exchange Bank of Gloucester, Rhode Island, was simply a "paper mill" that paid out currency with no backing.

After 1861, the new federal Demand Notes, Legal Tender Notes, and other forms of paper money became common, although their exchange value in terms of gold and silver coins was apt to vary. This was true from 1862 until the late 1870s, when such coins were hoarded and not seen in circulation. At one point in 1865 it took more than $250 in Legal Tender bills to buy $100 in face value of U.S. gold coins. Paper money and silver coins achieved parity in April 1876, paper and gold in December 1878, after which currency and coins could be exchanged at par.

During the entire colonial era and extending well into the mid-19th century, gold and silver coins were always preferable to paper money. Anyone with a five-dollar gold coin and a $5 bill would spend the bill first.

EARLY COINAGE IN AND FOR AMERICA

In the 18th century, as part of the flood of European coins brought to America, such low-denomination coins as Mark Newby's St. Patrick and William Wood's Hibernia coppers were used here, although they were not made specifically for this side of the Atlantic, nor did they bear any inscriptions relating to the colonies. Mark Newby coppers were legal tender for a time in West Jersey (largely today's New Jersey), but no such mantle was ever placed on Hibernia coinage. Irish coins of the Voce Populi type have no known connection with America. These European coppers have been adopted into the American series by numismatists, although there is no logic for doing so. Mention is made of the brass pieces produced in England circa 1616 for the Sommer Islands (Bermuda). At the time, these were under the Virginia Company, but that division was separate from the colony on the American mainland. The authorization provided that these little coins, each depicting a wild hog, be used only on those islands. The main "currency" of the Sommer Islands during that time continued to be tobacco.

Curiously, the many other issues that were legal tender—various foreign gold and silver issues—are not collected as part of the American colonial series. Many are of significant related interest, however. Extensive collections could be made of Spanish-American dollars and their fractional parts, as these were the main coins in American circulation in the 18th and early 19th centuries, and were given legal-tender status.

In 1652 the first coins to be struck in what is now the United States were produced by the Massachusetts Bay Colony. This coinage continued for three decades, until 1682. Best known is the Pine Tree shilling, a coin of legend and lore.

Various coins were produced in England for specific distribution in America. For Maryland, Cecil Calvert, the second Lord Baltimore, caused a series of silver coins ranging from the groat (fourpence) to the shilling to be struck. Few American Plantation tokens struck in England in 1688 and intended for this side of the Atlantic ever reached what is now the United States. Copper halfpence for Virginia were struck at the Tower Mint in London in 1773 and shipped to that colony. William Wood, under a royal patent, produced the distinctive Rosa Americana issues, these in addition to his earlier-mentioned Hibernia coppers. To the coins in circulation were added coins and tokens of private issuers.

In Simsbury, Connecticut, in 1737, Dr. Samuel Higley struck copper threepence pieces made from metal taken from local mines; this coinage was continued after his death the same year. In 1783, John Chalmers, an Annapolis, Maryland, silversmith, issued his own coinage in that metal—pieces of good quality that were readily accepted in regional commerce. In the 1780s, following the Revolutionary War, copper coins were produced in large quantities under contracts awarded by Vermont, Connecticut, and New Jersey. Massachusetts operated its own mint to strike coppers. Fugio coppers, struck under the authority of Congress, made their appearance in 1787. Taken together, these diverse coinages and others featured in the present book are often referred to as "colonials" by numismatists today.

When the colonial era ended, exactly, can be debated. The Declaration of Independence, dated July 4, 1776, proclaimed that the colonies were henceforth independent. Therefore, they were no longer colonies. The Battle of Yorktown, 1781, marked the end of the war. The Treaty of Paris, signed in 1783, resulted in the recognition of the independence of the United States of America by all countries, including Britain.

Actual statehood commenced when the various former colonies ratified the United States Constitution. Delaware was the first in 1787. Complicating the discussion is the Continental Congress's issuance, in the late 1770s, of paper money specifically marked "United States." Coins and tokens of George Washington, struck from 1783 through the mid-1790s, are often collected with colonial issues and are included here. The nomenclature of "colonial and early American coins," as in the title of this book, will probably satisfy nearly everyone.

2

Minting and Distribution

Preparing Ingots, Strip, and Planchets

Buildings and Equipment

Although no single description fits all, a typical minting house or facility for colonial coins was apt to have certain essential equipment and space for several different operations. A wooden structure, referred to as a mint house, copper house, or some similar name, was likely to be framed in wood, covered on the outside with shingles or clapboard, and have a peaked roof. Windows were necessary to admit light but were probably equipped with bolts on the inside so they could be locked at night or when the facility was not in operation.

If metal was to be processed into ingots, then into strips for making planchets, external power was necessary. Accordingly, a constantly flowing large stream or river suitable for driving a water wheel was desired, as was the setting for Machin's Mills on the outlet of Orange Pond near Newburgh, New York, the Rahway mint for New Jersey coppers; and the Vermont facility on Millbrook in Pawlet (near Rupert). Horsepower in the literal sense was another possibility, with the animals harnessed to arms attached to a vertical pole, which would be rotated as the horses traveled in a small circle. In the early days the Philadelphia Mint used horses for this purpose. Although steam power was in use at the Soho Mint (Birmingham, England) and elsewhere in Europe, this mode of force is not known to have been employed at any facilities that struck colonial coins in America.

Copper and Silver Into Strip

A fully equipped mint required facilities for processing copper or silver into ingots. Both metals were often acquired in the form of scrap or worn foreign coins. Less often, ingots or sheet could be purchased from suppliers. Metal was heated in a crucible in a furnace fueled by charcoal (usually), after which it was poured into cast-iron molds to create ingots or billets. The finished ingots, while still hot, were made thinner with a triphammer to pound them flat, or with a rolling mill. The latter consisted of an upper and lower cast-iron roller, driven at the side, and adjustable for spacing. On the first pass a copper ingot would be reduced slightly in thickness, on the second pass even more, and on subsequent passes down to the thickness of the coin itself. In the meantime, the strip would expand laterally, requiring wide rollers from side to side, or cutting the strip so it could be passed through rollers with a smaller jaw.

Both the triphammer process and the more usual rolling mill caused the strip to harden as it was thinned. At intervals the strip would be reheated and cooled slowly, an annealing process that made it more malleable.

The melting of the ingots was a necessarily hot and messy process, and likely was conducted outside of the main mint building. Massachusetts copper half cents and cents dated 1787 and 1788 were struck at a mint in Boston, where ingots were also made from scrap and other copper. Ingots were processed into strip at a separate facility in Dedham. Machin's Mills, a private operation, seems to have had facilities for all operations, from casting and rolling ingots to striking coins. In the absence of details it may be logical to assume that minters in city locations, such as Ephraim Brasher and John Bailey in New York, obtained copper strip or even planchets from an outside supplier. One mint for making New Jersey coppers was set up in a room behind the kitchen in a private home. This operation probably obtained planchets from a vendor.

It is unlikely that assaying or evaluating the purity of copper took place. What came in, went out. The metal often came in many forms, including sheeting taken from roofs, bands from kegs and barrels, old brass cannon, and more. The melting of copper or silver scrap, coins, and other forms would cause impurities to rise to the surface where they could be drawn off, leaving the metal itself with whatever other elements it might contain. Silver, such as used for the 1652-dated Massachusetts coinage, John Chalmers's coins of 1783, and other issues, was refined to achieve a desired purity and was assayed at intervals. Similarly, Brasher's gold coinage of 1786 and 1787 underwent similar procedures.

The appearance of early American coins reflects that copper was of varying purity. Some metal produced coins that were light in color, this being generally true of Machin's Mills halfpence and the half cents and cents of Massachusetts. In contrast, coins struck at the mint in Rupert, Vermont, more often than not had a black surface, at least after some evidence of circulation, suggesting that the composition may have been different. The same can be said for many of the earlier Connecticut coins, especially the issues of 1785. The situation was not much different a few years later at the Philadelphia Mint. Numismatists are aware that cents of 1794 and 1795 are often light in color, while half cents of 1797 and 1808 are usually dark, as are cents of 1814.

As for silver, most was obtained from old tableware, jewelry scrap, and foreign coins. Most silversmiths routinely gave credit when old teapots, spoons, and the like were turned in. Silversmiths who struck coins, including John Chalmers of Annapolis and Standish Barry of Baltimore, probably used recycled metal. Much Massachusetts silver was obtained from foreign coins.

Planchet Preparation

The making of round planchets for coins was a time-consuming process. Copper strip of the required thickness was fed by hand into either a cutting or punch press, advancing the strip as each planchet was cut, trying to place the next punch hole as close as possible to the preceding. A top or hammer punch (essentially a round die with a sharp rim in the form of a knife) descended and pressed the strip against a bottom die made in the form of a tapered punch, also with a sharp rim, with a hole the size of the required planchet at the center. The sides sloped upward to the punch rim, which was sharp enough to cut the strip.

The upper and lower punches had to be in precise alignment, the top punch fitting slightly inside the bottom punch with a little leeway. If the alignment was not exact, the punches would be damaged. In the meantime, the used planchet strip (called scissel) was melted and recycled, as were planchets that were clipped or bent.

The resulting planchet would be punched out of the strip and fall through the hollow bottom die to a bin or container below. It would have a rough top edge or burr, from the hammer die being slightly smaller. Planchets were placed into a cylinder or barrel together with sawdust and sand, and rotated for a long period of time by water power or other means. It is said that at Machin's Mills this was done overnight while the other operations were closed. If bright planchets were desired, the pieces could be brightened by rinsing them in acid to remove surface oxidation, and tumbling them in sawdust or with small scraps of leather.

The type of planchet cutter commonly employed in America during the 1785–1789 era of extensive copper coinage has been described in detail by James C. Spilman in *CNL* 63, July 1982, in his "Overview of Early American Coining Technology," as two "telescoping cookie cutters." Evidence of this technique can be seen from the occurrence of planchet cutter marks occasionally seen on coppers of this era. The actual device consisted of

> a pair of cooking cutters with sharpened edges, with one of the pair being slightly larger than the other, allowing them to slip into each other. The copper strip was placed between these two opposing sharp edges. When the uppermost cutter was lowered by the movement of a screw press, the two cutters telescoped together, thus cutting the planchet stock from both sides simultaneously. The combined cutting action from the two cutters left the finished planchets with a very smooth, rounded edge.

Spilman further noted that this cookie-cutter was actually French, as described by Denis Diderot in *l'Encyclopedie*, originating at the Paris Mint in the 1750s. Planchets made this way have a *cut* edge. In contrast the English method consisted of using an hammer die with a flat face to punch strip placed on an anvil die with a steel area surrounding a circular hole (this being the type of punch press later used at the Philadelphia Mint). Planchets made this way have a *sheared* edge.

It was standard practice to "anneal" or soften the planchets by heating and slow cooling. This eliminated "work hardening" that took place during planchet preparation. Die patterns would be impressed more deeply on softened planchets. The striking process hardened the finished coins, making them more durable for circulation.

In addition, we know that counterfeit foreign coins, Nova Constellatio coppers, and other pieces were sometimes used as planchets for state copper and related coins. As such issues were apt to vary in value from state to state, the reasoning was that if depreciated coppers trading at 20 to 30 or even more per shilling could be overstamped with dies of more valuable coppers, an automatic profit would be made. At one time a New Jersey shilling would buy 45 old coppers. It thus became worthwhile to accumulate Connecticut coppers, counterfeit British and Irish halfpence, and other coins and stamp them with New Jersey dies, as the last had a higher value in commerce.

Dies and Coinage

Designs and Motifs

Dies for striking colonial coins were typically made of steel. Two dies were usually required, one for the obverse (or face design) and the other for the back (reverse). The side with a portrait or scene was usually designated as the obverse, and the side with an eagle or seated figure the reverse. Dates were usually on the reverse. There were many exceptions. While die faces were circular, the shanks could be any shape, but most seem to have been round cylinders.

Each die was made of distinctive character, so the finished coins would indicate the authority of the issuer and be familiar as to value. By the time state coinage commenced (in 1785 by Connecticut and Vermont) the most familiar coins in circulation were British halfpence. These depicted the king on the obverse and the seated figure of the goddess Britannia on the reverse. It was logical that Connecticut and Vermont (beginning in 1786, after the "landscape" coinage) placed a portrait on one side of their coins and a seated figure on the other. Such motifs gave instant credibility to new issues and implied that they were worth as much as a British halfpenny.

Regulations of the colonies and states specified the appearance of the coins, sometimes suggesting the lettering and designs. Latinizing place names and other words was very popular. NOVA CÆSAREA meant New Jersey and NOVA EBORAC (or NEO EBORACENSIS or NEO EBORACUS) New York, and another issuer's coins were variously imprinted VERMON, VERMONTS, VERMONTIS, and VERMONTENSIUM. On its early silver coins Massachusetts had MASATHVSETS, on its later coppers MASSACHUSETTS.

Other coppers of the 1780s had IMMUNIS COLUMBIA, NON VI VIRTUTE VICI, E PLURIBUS UNUM, LIBER NATUS LIBERTATEM DEFENDO, and other Latinized inscriptions, the meanings of which were probably unknown to many recipients. INDE ET LIB on the reverse of Connecticut and Vermont coppers meant "independence and liberty." The seated Britannia figure so familiar on British coppers was used on the coins of these two states as well as on the 1787 coppers of New York.

Values were stated on some coins, but not on others. Early Massachusetts silver coins were denominated in pence, as II, III, VI, and XII, the last equaling a shilling. Maryland coins were issued in values of IV (fourpence or groat), VI, and XII. Among state coppers, those of Massachusetts are marked HALF CENT and CENT, but others state no value.

Most colonial coins bore a date. The exceptions are the New England or "NE" coinage, Maryland, certain Higley coppers, and a few others.

Engraving the Dies

Die preparation is variously called engraving or cutting. Makers of dies were referred to as engravers or die cutters, these being synonymous. The process usually involved a combination of engraving or carefully cutting features into a die by hand, and punching in certain other elements. Die sinking is an appropriate term when punches were used.

To receive the impression in the face of the die, the blank steel cylinder was softened by heating to a cherry red for a sustained period of time, then cooled very slowly, the annealing process. That done, the die was cleaned to remove scale and oxidation, presenting a bright top face. If needed, it was ground perfectly flat. Sometimes a small depression was punched at the die's center to accommodate one arm of a compass, while the other end scribed circular lines around the border, spaced so as to indicate an area in which lettering could be added. Most often this nicety was probably skipped.

For the center, a design could be engraved by hand, or a hub punch could be used. Hand engraving was a meticulous process, in which the artist, using magnification, worked carefully to develop the contours of a portrait, details of the clothing and the hair, a laurel wreath, and other features as appropriate. For the reverse a similar operation was followed. Necessarily a tedious process, hand engraving was used on early colonial dies, such as Massachusetts silver, and some later dies as well, including some early issues in the Connecticut series in 1785. Later the hub punch came into general use and saved a lot of work.

A hub was prepared by cutting in relief a soft steel punch to represent a portrait, a seated figure, an eagle and shield, or some other motif. The punch was then hardened by heating to a high temperature, then quenching suddenly in a bath of water or oil, which crystallized the metal and made it very durable. The same quenching process was used when dies were completed.

A punch—say, of a portrait—was then impressed into the center of the soft steel blank intended to be the die. This was likely done by using a screw press and delivering intense pressure. The process was probably slow, forcing the punch into the die by exerting pressure on the long arms of a screw press. Alternatively, the punch could have received multiple blows. The last is less likely, as this would have produced the slight doubling of features on some dies, and such evidence is not seen today.

The die, complete with portrait or other central device, was then removed from the press and placed on a work bench, at which time individual letter and number punches were employed to add appropriate inscriptions. Although some hub punches also included lettering, it was generally the case that such delicate features as letters, the branch held by a seated figure, and other delicate parts of the design did not transfer well, and thus they were added by hand. Accordingly, a punch for a Liberty Seated figure could be used on the reverse of a Connecticut copper, but the branch and the Liberty Cap would be added by hand, as would be the line or lines under the figure.

For Fugio coppers of 1787, the obverse hub included the sundial, sun, rays, and base of the sundial. The reverse had the label inscribed UNITED STATES and the linked rings. Other features were added by hand, including the lettering and date.

Edge features such as dots, beads or pellets, and dentils (toothlike projections) could be added individually by hand. In some instances, punches were used to form an arc containing a number of adjacent ornaments, resulting in a higher speed operation. The spacing and alignment of such features is often irregular and crude.

Finishing the Dies

The finished die for a Connecticut copper, Fugio copper, or some other coin was again heated to a high temperature, then quenched. After hardening the die was cleaned to remove scale and rust, then was ready for use in coining.

Hardened dies were placed in the coining press and put into service. Specific figures for the life of a given die for a colonial or state coin are not known, but likely the typical number of impressions ranged widely from a few thousand to several tens of thousands. We believe that about three million New Jersey coppers were minted from 75 or more obverse dies (not counting imitation or counterfeit dies), yielding about 40,000 impressions per die. On the other hand, Mike Packard, in *The Colonial Newsletter*, August 1989, gave estimates for the production of Massachusetts coppers that indicated a much shorter die life: 1787 half cents, 65,000; 1788 half cents, 41,500; 1787 cents, 90,500; and 1788 cents, 205,500, for an overall estimate of 402,500. About 30 different obverse dies (not including suspected counterfeits) have been identified, which yields a production of 13,000 or so per die.

Some dies seem to have cracked early in their life, evidenced by all known coins from the die showing cracks or breaks (the last occurring when pieces fell from the die). Other dies probably served to make 50,000 or more coins. Factors affecting die life include the hardness of the steel and its overall quality, the hardness of the planchets, and the spacing between obverse and reverse dies. If the dies were spaced closely together, they would wear more quickly than if they were further apart.

While some mints probably made their own dies, it seems likely that in many instances certain jewelers and other artisans in major cities turned out dies on request as a manufactured product. Lines of communication were well established in colonial eras, and it would be a simple matter for a coiner of Connecticut, New Jersey, or other coins to send dies to an engraver in New York City or Philadelphia. This saved the cost of having a skilled artisan on the mint staff. Per figures cited by Crosby, we know the extensive coinage of Massachusetts coppers, involving perhaps 60 or so obverse and reverse dies was accomplished by dies obtained from Joseph Callender at the rate of £1 4s each and from Jacob Perkins at the rate of 1 percent of the value of the coins struck therefrom. The total payment to Callender was £48 12s for his work; for a smaller number of dies, Perkins received £3 18s, or about £52 total, less than £1 per die. In the same period other expenses included about £677 for erecting and equipping the mint and £477 for operating expenses (not including cost of metal). It is seen that die making was but a tiny expense, suggesting that for other mints, having an on-premises die cutter may have been highly unlikely.

Minting Procedures

In the striking of coins from dies, using prepared planchets, no single rule fits all minting procedures. Coins of the American colonial era were produced in many different ways, ranging from crude hammering of an upper die to strike a planchet placed on a lower die, to high-speed steam-powered presses (used by the Soho Mint in Birmingham, England, for certain Conder tokens shipped to the United States).

The earliest procedure for which we have knowledge is the method of striking the NE coinage for Massachusetts Bay Colony beginning in 1652. Small, simple, steel punches with NE and with denominations expressed as III, VI, or XII were used to impress opposite sides and ends of a blank silver planchet placed upon an anvil or hard surface. Such pieces were made by hand, with two punching operations. Afterward in Massachusetts other methods were used, including, it is believed, a rocker press, consisting of a fixed anvil die in a lower position, and above a small curved steel face upon which a design was engraved or punched. A planchet was fed into the space between the lower die and the upper rocker die, and as a lever was pulled, the rocker die exerted force across the planchet from one end to the other. The resulting coins had a slight undulating shape when viewed edge on. Otherwise simple obverse and reverse dies were employed, such as perhaps on the Willow Tree coinage. In such a scenario a fixed lower die was struck by a movable upper die, the top often enclosed in a tube but not fixed in position, allowing it to slip or rotate. Coins thus struck were usually blurred in terms of lettering and devices, as the planchets were loose and dies not fixed. Which processes were used has been a matter of discussion in the pages of the *Colonial Newsletter*, *C4 Newsletter*, and elsewhere.

The most standard coinage method used in the early days was the screw press, in which the hammer or top die was attached to a screw turned by two long lever arms, heavily weighted at the ends. The upper descended, struck the planchet, then went back to the starting position. Screw presses were widely used, including at the first Philadelphia Mint beginning in 1792. A screw press used to strike New Jersey copper coins was sold to the Mint in 1794.

An early screw-type coining press of the general type used to strike many colonial coins. One or two men tugged on the straps attached to the weighted arm, causing the screw to turn and the top or hammer die to descend to strike a planchet resting on the bottom or anvil die.

Although anecdotal accounts suggest such presses could strike more than 100 coins per minute, in actuality the operation was probably slow. In the absence of automatic mechanisms, each planchet had to be fed by hand into the press, stamped, ejected, then another planchet fed. The most common scenario seems to have been a worker seated on the floor opposite the base of the screw press, his head low enough for the arms to swing above and his legs in a hole or recess in the floor. Struck coins were brushed off the back of the die, falling into a container likewise in a hole or recess in the floor.

The same attendant would keep an eye on the dies, replacing them as they chipped, broke, or showed extensive wear. In some cases, such as the coinage of Virginia halfpence at the Royal Mint in London, some dies seem to have been replaced in pairs, perhaps after one showed damage. It may have been easier to replace both dies at the same time rather than wait for the second die to have problems. This was not consistent, as the Royal Mint also combined certain Virginia obverses and reverses with others. Similarly, among domestically produced coins, there are any number of Connecticut, Massachusetts, and other copper issues known only in single die pairs, not combined with other obverses or reverses.

Characteristics of Dies

To numismatists, the more hand work used in the creation of a die, the more interesting the coin produced from it. Rusticity is equivalent to desirability. Among early Massachusetts silver, all letters were hand engraved, with the result that a given letter in a die, such as the repeated N, would appear to be different in each instance or even backward. Similarly, pine trees, engraved by hand, could be thin, thick, large, or small.

Among later dies the size and shape of letter and number punches often varied. An A could be small, short, and wide, or tall, thin, and narrow. One distinctive A punch used on many dies is broken at the upper left. Apparently, a G punch was not on hand when certain Fugio dies were made, and a C punch was used, with a crossbar added in the die to make a G, to create FUGIO. This did not always happen, as dies lettered FUCIO demonstrate. An even wider variation is shown in date digits; those on New Jersey coppers are especially diverse.

The edge decorations mentioned earlier can be fascinating to contemplate. In the Connecticut series, short lines, sometimes thick, sometimes thin, were engraved or punched around the border, erratically spaced, giving an interesting appearance when viewed today. The use of triangular dentils, representing saw teeth, was often employed and is seen on a number of coinages, most notably those of Connecticut and New Jersey.

As the edge ornaments were on the rim of the dies—and in many series, such as Connecticuts, coins were not struck fully across obverse and reverse dies—only parts of the dentils are visible. Accordingly, what may be a series of large, closely spaced triangles on one striking can appear on another coin as tiny triangles widely spaced with only the tips of the dentils showing. To determine the true nature of dentils, multiple coins or images often need to be studied. Other dies had no dentils or edge ornaments at all.

Various ornaments were used for punctuation. The Connecticut series is particularly rich in variety, with pheons (tiny arrowheads), five-pointed and six-pointed stars, fleurons (tulip-shaped decorations placed sideways), crosses, cinquefoils (with five lobes), quatrefoils (with four lobes or petals), groups of dots, and more. Some New Jersey coppers feature what may be a little running fox as an ornament.

The bust on a Connecticut, Vermont, New York, or other copper, often laureated (with a wreath of leaves), can be tall and narrow or nearly round, can have drapery or armor, and can vary in many other ways. Horses on the obverse of New Jersey coppers can face right (usually) or left, can be bug-eyed or have small eyes, can display a neatly braided mane or a wild unruly one, and can have large ears or small.

Eagles on the reverse can have different numbers of arrows or olive leaves and can face left or right. Seated goddesses can hold a plain pole or one topped with a liberty cap, along with a branch that can be large or small, with many or few leaves.

Such characteristics are what the spirit of die variety collecting is all about. And, if the engraver made a mistake—such as placing the C in AUCTORI backward, or spelling AUCTOBI instead of AUCTORI, or placing ET LIB INDE on the die instead of INDE ET LIB—so much the better!

In the meantime in Europe, coining procedures were sophisticated by comparison. The Virginia halfpence of 1773, made at the Tower Mint in London, are masterpieces of quality, most so similar that magnification is needed to tell them apart. Even then, differentiating certain obverses can be difficult, with the only earmarks being tiny differences in the placement of letters in GEORGIVS III REX, or the presence or absence of a dot. The portrait punch was standard, and all the letters were from the same font of punches. Because of this, the discovery of a new obverse of a Virginia halfpenny would involve closer inspection, while the finding of a new 1785 Connecticut copper obverse, cut by hand, would be more obvious.

American Mints and Locations of Selected Colonial Mints

The descriptions of state and related copper coinages presented in chapter 7 give information about the mints used to make them. Separate buildings were used by Machin's Mills, Reuben Harmon in Rupert (Vermont), and certain coiners of New Jersey coppers. The Massachusetts Bay Colony mint that struck silver coins in the 17th century was in its own building in Boston. The later 1787–1788 copper half cents and cents struck by that state were in another structure in the same city.

Other mints were modest, perhaps not even deserving of that name. Ephraim Brasher, a New York City silversmith and goldsmith, plied his trade in the city, in one or several rooms, and probably had limited (but effective) facilities for melting metal into ingots and producing strip for planchets.

Minting and Distribution

THE BRITISH HALFPENNY AS MODEL

To gain ready acceptance of their coins in circulation, coiners of Vermont, Connecticut, and Machin's Mills copper coins copied the basic designs of genuine regal British halfpence made in London, never mind that the Revolutionary War with England had ended just a few years earlier. Examples are shown here.

Authentic British halfpenny of 1731 depicting King George II (on the throne from 1727 to 1760).

Authentic British halfpenny of 1772 depicting King George III (ruled 1760–1820), used on coppers from 1770 to 1775.

Vermont copper of 1786 with features of King George II adapted from the British halfpenny. (Variety RR-10, always lightly struck at the centers)

Vermont copper of 1788 with features of King George III adapted from the British halfpenny. (Variety RR-20)

Connecticut copper of 1786 with features of King George II adapted from the British halfpenny. (Variety Miller 5.8-H.2)

Connecticut copper of 1788 with features of King George III adapted from the British halfpenny. (Variety Miller 4.1-K)

Machin's Mills counterfeit halfpenny of 1747 of King George II. (Variety Vlack 1-47A)

Counterfeit British halfpenny with the fictitious date of 1778 made at Machin's Mills in Newburgh, New York. (Variety Vlack 11-78A)

One New Jersey minting facility was set up in a room behind a kitchen in a private house.

Accounts of Machin's Mills

From about 1786 to 1789, Machin's Mills operated as a private mint near Newburgh, New York. In chapter 7 an account is given of many coins attributed to that facility, including certain coppers of Vermont, Connecticut, and counterfeit British halfpence, among others. Two recollections of this mint survive, both from the 1850s, when Machin's Mills was probably hazy in the memory of anyone involved. Accordingly, they must be viewed with a grain of salt. The comments are valuable in a general way, however, in that they give a view of coinage operations that must have been similar to certain other facilities.

Charles I. Bushnell, who did research in the 1850s, including correspondence with Benjamin Hall of Troy, New York, provided this account to Sylvester S. Crosby:

> The mint house at Newburgh, Ulster County, New York, was situated on the east side of Machin's Lake or Pond, about one-eighth of a mile distant from the pond. The building was erected in 1784 by Thomas Machin, and was still standing in 1792, at which time the rollers, press, and cutting machine [cutting out press for planchet discs] were taken out. The coins were struck by means of a large bar loaded at each end with a 500-pound ball with ropes attached.

Two men were required on each side, making four in all to strike the pieces, plus a man to set the planchets. The metal

Die Features of Selected Colonial Coins

Variations in tree styles on Massachusetts shillings dated 1652: *(a)* Willow Tree, Noe-1-A; *(b)* Oak Tree, Noe-3; *(c)* Pine Tree, Noe-14; *(d)* Pine Tree, Noe-2.

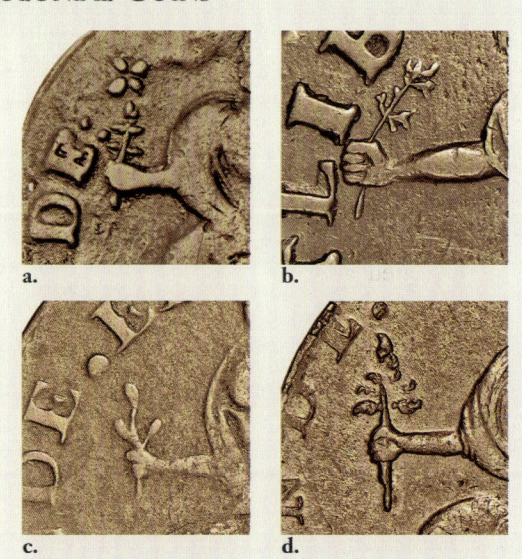

Variations in branches and their positions on the reverse of Connecticut coppers: *(a)* 1785 Miller 3.2-L; *(b)* 1787 Miller 1.1-A; *(c)* 1787 Miller 1.2-C; *(d)* 1788 Miller 6-H.

Mystery coins: *(a)* The 1787 Nova Eborac copper with Small Head (W-5765; attributed by Walter Breen to coiner Gilbert Rindell of Elizabethtown, New Jersey), and *(b)* the Connecticut "Muttonhead" copper, Miller 1.2-C (W-2720; from "undisclosed private mint, New York City?" per Breen). It seems these are both actually from dies by the same hand. In actuality, no facts are known about either coin. Such are the interesting mysteries of colonial coins.

More mystery coins: *(a)* The seated figure on the 1788 Vermont RR-27 (W-2205) and *(b)* the figure on the 1787 Nova Eborac copper (W-5755) were likely cut by the same engraver. The intricacy of the garment top is similar on both and is quite unlike anything else in the entire Vermont series.

Variations in date sizes and styles on New Jersey coppers: *(a)* 1786 Maris 18-J; *(b)* 1786 Maris 55-l; *(c)* 1787 Maris 6-C; *(d)* 1788 Maris 49-f.

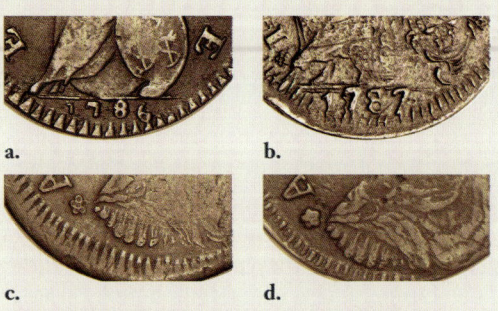

Variations in dentils on Connecticut coppers: *(a)* 1786 Miller 1-A; *(b)* 1787 Miller 12-Q; *(c)* 1787 Miller 50-F; *(d)* 1788 Miller 14.1-L.2.

of which the coins were struck was composed of old brass cannons and mortars, the zinc from the copper being extracted by smelting in a furnace. About 60 coins were struck a minute. For a number of years the sloop *Newburgh* (Capt. Isaac Belknap) carried the coining press as part of its ballast. The coins were made by James F. Atlee. Many bore on the obverse GEORGIUS III, and on the reverse INDE ET LIB. Others bore the figure of a plough on one side. The mint ceased operations in 1791.

A closely related account, penned generations later by Thomas N. Machin, son of the entrepreneur, to Franklin B. Hough, gave this information (cited by James C. Spilman in the *Colonial Newsletter*, March 1983) on the operation of the enterprise:

> The coinage mill was 40 to 50 rods below the pond, on a canal dug for the purpose. The building was of wood, 30 by 40 feet, and two stories high. The metal used was copper, obtained by melting up cannon and leaving out the zinc in the alloy. The copper was then run into moulds and rolled into flat sheets of the thickness of the coin, and from one to two feet wide. It was then punched with a screw, moved by a lever, so adjusted that half a revolution would punch out a disk the size of the coin.
>
> The blanks were then put into a cylinder and revolved with sand, sawdust, and water. They were generally left revolving through the night; and the coiners circulated the story that the devil came by night to work for them. They also sometimes worked in masks to create a terror in the neighborhood. One night in the cylinder would wear the edges of the blanks smooth.
>
> The coining press was a screw, with an iron bar about 10 feet long through the top. On each end of this bar was a leaden weight of perhaps 500 pounds. The threads of the screw were large and square and worked through an iron frame. Ropes were attached to each end of the bar, and it was swung about half way around by two men pulling upon the ropes; two other men pulled the lever back, and a fifth laid on the blank and took off the coin with his fingers. The last operative named sat in a pit so that the lever would not touch his head.
>
> The coinage was about 60 per minute. A little silver was coined, but mostly copper, and the work continued four or five years. Atlee the engraver wore a horrid mask, and frightened some boys who came to fish so that they never ventured near the mill again. The machinery was removed to New York, and the building was afterwards used as a grist mill. Machin abandoned the enterprise probably about 1790, on the adoption of the federal Constitution.

It is highly unlikely that 60 coins per minute, or one *per second*, could have been struck on a screw press with weighted arms with 500 pounds of lead at each end. With such a mass, it would have been a challenge to have made one coin each several seconds.

Information about James F. Atlee, mentioned in the above accounts, will be found under the Machin's Mills listings in chapter 7.

DISTRIBUTION AND ECONOMIC CONSIDERATIONS

Official, Unofficial, and Mysterious Coinage

Sylvester S. Crosby's *Early Coins of America*, 1875, and Philip L. Mossman's *Money of the American Colonies and Confederation: A Numismatic, Economic & Historical Correlation* are both excellent sources of information about the distribution of coins and surrounding economic circumstances. The emphasis of the present text is on the coins themselves. Necessarily, only a brief commentary on the other factors can be given.

Most coins we collect as part of the colonial and early American series were made pursuant to specific laws. The Massachusetts Bay Colony authorized the coinage of 1652 and later years and gave contracts respecting it; the later state of Massachusetts authorized another mint that struck copper coins in the 1780s.

Connecticut, Vermont, and New Jersey tapped private individuals to set up and manage minting facilities. Oversight was casual at best, and those holding coinage contracts sometimes failed to report on the quantities minted, or did not pay under terms of their agreements. The federal government placed the contract for the 1787 Fugio copper coinage, and this arrangement suffered from accounting problems as well. The entire business of contract coinage seems to have been one with high expectations followed by little in the way of real profit. An exception may have been John Hull, who held the contract for early Massachusetts silver. He became a wealthy man in the process.

The much-studied Machin's Mills enterprise was unofficial, except in a small part of its operations in which it had a legitimate contract to make coppers for Vermont (for which, it seems, the mint did not bother to report production). Other mints sprang up here and there, most in the form of counterfeiting operations that copied the designs of legitimate state or foreign coinage. Some were openly operated and filled a need for local or regional coins, such as the Higley copper production of 1737 to 1739 and silversmith John Chalmers's coinage of 1783, among others.

Little or no accounting was kept of coins made in England or other countries and shipped to America. If such an accounting were done, it is not known today. From the number of die varieties now known we can surmise, for example, that the 1722 to 1724 Rosa Americana coinage struck in England for America was very extensive, while the single die–pair production of 1796 Castorland medals, made in France, was modest.

Distribution

Colonial coins were distributed in various ways. Most minters simply spent their products to secure goods and profits, or to exchange for other coins. In some instances a percentage was paid into a state or colony treasury, which in turn paid them out.

We know from specific information surviving from the Hard Times token era of the 1830s that it was common practice for coiners to make tokens and sell them at, say, a 60 percent discount from face value, in exchange for other funds. Likely, Machin's Mills and certain coiners of the undocumented tokens of the 1790s (Immunis Columbia, George Washington, and the like) distributed similarly, wholesaling the tokens in bags or kegs at a discount in exchange for Spanish-American dollars or paper money of value.

It is well known that silver and gold coins were reckoned at specific exchange values, using charts printed in newspapers and elsewhere. For many transactions this was mostly done by sight, not by carefully weighing each incoming Spanish dollar, English shilling, or Mexican doubloon on a balance scale. So long as buyers and sellers had faith in the money they were using, it was simply passed along from one person to another. Widely circulated charts gave weights of silver and gold coins.

As for coppers, these were simply accepted at agreed upon values, such as 14 to a shilling, or 20 to a shilling, or whatever the prevailing local rate. It made no difference if they were British, Vermont, Connecticut, or other coppers, so long as they were round and about the size of a halfpenny. In the early 1780s there was a copper coin shortage, as no regal (official British) halfpence had been struck since 1775, and in the meantime the Revolutionary War had disrupted the monetary scene. Many different coppers were good in trade at the time. Values varied, and in time, as more issues were circulated, it seems that Nova Constellatio coppers, counterfeit halfpence, and some others were not as valuable as certain Connecticut, New Jersey, and Vermont coins.

Devaluation of Coppers

By the late 1780s, coppers became plentiful in circulation. In addition to those made officially and unofficially in America, vast numbers were imported from Birmingham and other foreign sources. This caused a glut and, by 1789, a deep devaluation known as the "coppers panic." Some banks and merchants refused to take coppers at all, and instead traded only in foreign coins of known value, or in paper money with good backing. *The Copper Coinage of New Jersey*, a manuscript by Damon G. Douglas, edited by Gary Trudgen, gives much information, including the following (lightly edited).

On July 25, 1789, the Common Council of New York City recommended that citizens receive and pay coppers only at the depreciated rate of 48 per shilling. On August 1, 1789, this was the situation in New York City:

> There has been a mighty convulsion here lately on account of the coppers. We abound with them in this place, and they are generally light and bad. The merchants refuse to take them at more than half [their past value] and some at no more than a third. At Philadelphia I hear they have fared much in the same manner.

On September 17, 1789, a traveler in New York City reported, "Coppers pass at 24 the shilling. Only the Jersey coins are current in the market." The same diarist noted on September 21 at New Haven, Connecticut, "Coppers are 72 the shilling at the ferry."

A summary report was filed by a Mr. Rutherford of the New Jersey General Assembly on June 7, 1790:

> That the depreciation of the copper coin appears to be entirely owing to the fraudulent practices of persons who have stamped Birmingham and Connecticut coppers with the same impression as those of this state, and have afterwards passed them to others; that the New Jersey coppers coined by law are superior in weight to the British, are of pure metal, and weigh six penny weight six grains each, and that most of the counterfeits are on base metal and weigh less than five pennyweight each. The New Jersey coppers lately passed at 15 for a shilling, the rate directed by law, and the Birmingham and Connecticut coppers could at the same time be procured for 45 for a shilling, and that some persons availed themselves of the difference and have changed the impression of a considerable quantity of light and base coppers, converting one shilling's worth of those coppers into three shillings worth of New Jersey coppers, which practice has occasioned so great a depreciation of the coppers in this state that in some places they do not circulate, and in other places they pass at an unequal and uncertain value from 48 to 36 for a shilling, though they lately circulated at their full value, even in the neighboring states where no other coppers could pass.

The preceding and similar reports reflect that by 1789 coppers traded at deep discounts, making their coining impractical. The Connecticut, Massachusetts, Vermont, New Jersey, and Machin's Mills coppers were last produced with the date of 1788. This also explains the reason why so many state and Machin's Mills coppers are overstruck. Those of lesser value could be purchased in quantity and overstamped with dies of New Jersey or some other entity whose coppers were more valuable, and a profit could be made.

In Later Years

Copper coins continued to circulate after 1789. As production ceased and it was no longer advantageous to import lightweight counterfeit coins from Birmingham, the panic abated. Coppers remained in circulation for years afterward, eventually trading at the value of one cent, on par with the first Philadelphia Mint cents released in early 1793. Wear on extant coins, plus scattered later accounts, reveal that some of the state coins remained familiar sights in commerce through the Hard Times era of the 1830s, and some were seen into the 1850s. Large cents and surviving tokens and state coins disappeared from U.S. circulation by the early 1860s, but remained in common use in Canada.

Coins and tokens depicting George Washington probably made their first appearance in circulation in the 1780s with the Georgius Triumpho coppers of 1783, supplemented by a relatively small number of copper tokens issued in the 1790s. Most Washington pieces of this era were made in England and either circulated there or were sold to British numismatists. Few were seen stateside.

Thus ended the production of colonial and early American coins treated in the present text.

3
Collecting Colonial Coins

Numismatic Traditions and Chronology

Numismatics Before 1850

Activity in Europe

The hobby of numismatics developed in a serious way in the 1850s in the United States. Before then, there were scattered collectors, historians, and museums interested in coins, but no groups or organizations, no publications, and no auctions of significance. The only way to learn the rarity, value, or history of a coin was through correspondence, or by the chance reading of an article or account.

In contrast, the art or science of numismatics—it was called both things—flourished in Europe. In England, many reference books were in print, coin auctions dispersed significant cabinets of numismatic treasures, and collectors eagerly sought specimens from the days of ancient Greece down to the latest patterns and Proof sets. American coins were of interest to the typical collector in the British Isles, including Pine Tree shillings, Rosa Americana pennies, and other pieces relating to the former British colonies. In the late 1780s and the 1790s there was a mad passion for collecting copper halfpenny tokens—hundreds of varieties of which were made with unusual edge lettering, interesting motifs, and even combinations of unrelated dies—to entice buyers. Some of these, today called Conder tokens (from Rev. James Conder, who wrote a reference book about them), alluded to George Washington or other American motifs.

In Paris, Vienna, Leipzig, and other centers of refinement and culture, national and city museums often had important coin collections, usually emphasizing ancient Greek and Roman issues and later issues of a particular country, but often including stray American pieces as well.

Activity in America

The earliest person of numismatic importance in America seems to have been Pierre Eugène Du Simitière (1737–1784), a Swiss immigrant who by 1774 had settled in Philadelphia. In the 1760s, certainly by 1766, he had a cabinet of coins, including examples acquired from John Smith of Burlington, New Jersey, whose collection was said to be extensive. Major James, of Philadelphia, also had an impressive holding.

On April 26, 1779, Du Simitière wrote about numismatics to Gov. George Clinton of New York, noting in part, "Coins and medals ancient and modern I have collection of, but nowadays these are become scarce, notwithstanding I meet with some now and then," quoted in the *American Antiquarian*, September 1871. By this time his cabinet included seven rare Higley coppers of the years 1737 to 1739 and nine Massachusetts silver pieces as part of an inventory of 135 specimens. Later Du Simitière prepared an outline titled "Sketch of a Plan of a Work intended to illustrate the Revolution in North America by Medals, Seals, Coins, Devices, Statues, Monuments,

Badges &c," which could have been America's first numismatic reference book, had it been published, but it wasn't. Du Simitière also maintained the American Museum, which included displays of coins and medals, in his home on Arch Street in Philadelphia.

There were others who possessed a few coins and medals of historical or curiosity interest. Among these was Rev. Andrew Eliot (1718–1778), pastor of the famous Old North Church in Boston, who by 1767 had an extensive cabinet that included many New England silver coins. By 1772, John Andrews, a Boston hardware merchant, had begun following numismatics. Long afterward, in the 1860s, his collection came to light in the estate of his son Henry, and was found to include several NE shillings and the exceedingly rare NE threepence. The coins were purchased by the Massachusetts Historical Society, which today maintains a magnificent collection.

In 1787, William Bentley of Salem, Massachusetts, entered in his diary some interesting observations of coins then in circulation, including this on September 2, 1787:

> About this time there was a great difficulty respecting the circulation of small copper coin. Those of George III, being well executed, were of uncommon thinness, and those stamped from the face of other coppers in sand, commonly called "Birmingham," were very badly executed. Beside these were the coppers bearing the authority of the states of Vermont, Connecticut and New York, etc., but no accounts how issued, regularly transmitted.
>
> The Connecticut copper has a face of general form resembling the Georges. . . . A mint is said preparing for the Commonwealth of Massachusetts. It may be noted that the New York and Connecticut coin face opposite ways.

Bentley's September 16, 1787, entry included what we know today as a Nova Constellatio (not Vermont) copper:

> A coin circulated with the apparent authority of Vermont. A star with an eye in the centre and between the rays other stars in number thirteen. On the reverse a wreath in which is enclosed the cyphers U.S. Inscription Libertas et Justitia, 1785.

The Philadelphia Museum (a.k.a. Peale's Museum and the American Museum), established by artist and naturalist Charles Willson Peale in 1784, had a cabinet of coins and medals that was sold to P.T. Barnum in the mid-1840s. Augustus B. Sage later recalled this in a letter published in the *American Journal of Numismatics* in May 1867:

> About seven years ago the old Museum (Barnum's) contained a very fair cabinet, a miscellaneous collection, it is true, scattered here and there in the cases were some very rare specimens of our earlier coinage. At the time of the "clock excitement" [actually in 1856, when Barnum, who had backed a loan, suffered financial duress when the Jerome Clock Co. failed] I believe the rarer specimens were purchased at *one dollar each* by a prominent collector of New Jersey. There can be no question, I take it, that the exhibition of the cases of coins in Barnum's, at the time I have referred to, was an incentive for a great number of present collectors to turn their attention to the subject; and the public exhibition of such frames in all museums tends greatly to stimulate the study.

The American Museum was gutted by fire on July 13, 1865, at which time a small replacement display of coins and medals was lost.

The Early 19th Century

An entry in *Norton's Literary Letter*, 1859, told of three collectors active in the 1830s:

> At a time when 'coin collectors' in the United States were popularly considered little better than monomaniacs, two or three gentlemen—Dr. J.B. Felt, of Salem, Mass., Mr. J. Francis Fisher, of Baltimore [actually from Philadelphia], and Dr. Jas. Mease, of Philadelphia— were deeply interested in the subject, and communicated the results of their investigations to societies of which they were members, or published them in a separate form.

In 1839, the first important numismatic reference work was published in America. Joseph Barlow Felt's book, *An Historical Account of Massachusetts Currency*, an impressive 248 pages in length (first edition), treated coins and paper money, including extensive details of the NE and later silver coinage. It was so well done that nearly all of it remains useful today. John H. Hickcox (1858) and Sylvester S. Crosby (1875) drew heavily from this work.

In June 1838, the Mint Cabinet was formed at the Philadelphia Mint. William F. Dubois and Jacob Reese Eckfeldt were the curators for years afterward. Adam Eckfeldt, a mechanic who had worked at the Mint since its founding in 1792, first as a contractor and then as an employee, collected coins and contributed pieces to the new display. In time, the curators bought and traded coins to expand the holdings. A memorable exchange was made in 1843, when the Mint traded an 1804 silver dollar to Matthew A. Stickney for a 1785 Immune Columbia coin struck in gold instead of the usual copper (probably of recent manufacture, along with silver impressions, from dies brought over from England). Stickney, born in 1805, became interested in numismatics as a youth, when he inherited a quantity of Continental paper bills his grandfather had received for services during the Revolutionary War. This inspired him to collect coins, with American colonials among his interests.

In 1843, Dubois at the Mint furnished Stickney with a list of active collectors, including Lewis Roper, Jacob G. Morris, Richard W. Davids (described as a "nephew of Mr. Morris"), W.G. Mason, C.C. Ashmead, John Reeve, Mr. Cooper (of Camden, New Jersey), Henry A. Muhlenberg (of Reading, Pennsylvania), Rev. Dr. Robbins (of Hartford, Connecticut, and an uncle of Stickney), and Edmund B. Wynn (of Hamilton, New York). To this roster could be added Joseph Mickley, the most prominent collector in Philadelphia, and John Allan of New York, who had dealt in rare coins since the 1820s. Robert Gilmor Jr., scion of a wealthy merchant family, was very active, and among his holdings was a gold 1787 Brasher doubloon. William G. Stearns, a Boston lawyer who pursued the hobby, in 1840 sent a contribution to the *Numismatic Chronicle* in London, mentioning Gilmor's doubloon.

Although dispersals of Pierre Du Simitière, the American Museum, and other properties had brought coins to the auction block, the June 12 and 13, 1828, offering of the Benjamin H. Watkins collection deserves a nod. Held in Salem, Massachusetts, it comprised 350 lots of coins, books, engravings, and other items, including two NE shillings, a Massachusetts silver threepence, and two silver twopence pieces.

Growth of the Hobby

Museums were popular with the public during the 19th century, and nearly every city of importance had at least one, a few of which had displays of numismatic interest. Coins and medals could be viewed at Economy Village (the Harmonist settlement near Pittsburgh), Peale displays in Philadelphia, New York, and Baltimore, the East India Marine Society in Salem, the Library Company of Philadelphia, Harrington's Museum and the Massachusetts Historical Society in Boston, and in New York City at the Tammany Museum, the New York Historical Society, the relic-laden Fifth Ward Museum Hotel, and Barnum's American Museum.

The New York State Library had eight medals in its collection by 1846. After this time, the holdings grew, and by 1853, when Richard W. Davids of Philadelphia described its holdings, 58 pages were required in the catalog. Davids, a nephew of numismatist Jacob G. Morris, had been interested in coins since at least the early 1840s.

In 1848 Philadelphia publishers Carey & Hart issued Thomas Wyatt's 315-page, extensively illustrated book, *Memoirs of the Generals, Commodores, and Other Commanders, Who Distinguished Themselves in the American Army and Navy During the War of the Revolution*. Wyatt achieved justified acclaim for his work and was considered an authority. The idol had clay feet, for later it was learned that he knowingly sold fake coins to Boston collector Winslow Lewis and others. Further, he struck (or had someone else strike) copies of certain early Massachusetts silver coins and passed them off as new discoveries from a long-buried hoard supposedly unearthed in Chelsea, near Boston (see chapter 12).

Numismatics Between 1850 and 1900

The Dynamic 1850's

American numismatics developed in a serious way in the 1850s. *The Documentary History of the State of New York*, by E.B. O'Callaghan, published in four volumes in 1850 by Weed, Parsons & Co., Albany, New York, included some numismatic information. Chapter 22, "Medals and Coins," featured three plates of coins engraved and separately printed by J.E. Gavit, probably the first high-quality collection of coin illustrations published in America. Depictions included Rosa Americana pieces of various denominations, copper coins identified with New York state, a 1794 Talbot, Allum & Lee cent, and a 1783 Washington Unity States cent.

1786 Non Vi Virtute Vici copper with reverse inscription of Neo Eboracensis (New York). Little is known about the history of this coin. (Engraving by John Gavit for O'Callaghan, *The Documentary History of the State of New-York*, 1850)

On February 20, 1851, under the title of *Executors' Sale. Valuable Collection of Gold and Silver Coins and Medals, Etc., Catalogue of the Entire Collection of Rare and Valuable Coins, Medals, Autographs, Mahogany Coins Case, Etc., Late of Doctor Lewis Roper, deceased*, a catalog described what is believe to be the first numismatic auction in America to realize over $1,000 (the exact figure was $1,172.47). Among the buyers was Ammi Brown, a Boston numismatist who collected Massachusetts silver coins among other things, and who owned the famous "1650" shillings (see chapter 12). On June 6, 1855, he was also a buyer, probably through an agent, in the Pierre (Peter) Flandin Collection sale held in New York City by Bangs, Brother & Co.

In January 1857 the Mint discontinued making large copper cents, soon changing production to the small copper-nickel Flying Eagle cents. This evoked a wave of nostalgia, and in 1858 and 1859 hundreds of enthusiasts combed through pocket change in the quest to build collections of as many different dates of large cents as possible. Examples could be found all the way back to the first year of issue, 1793, but earlier pieces were apt to be worn nearly smooth. The 1799 was viewed as very rare, the 1793 and 1804 as scarce, and the 1815 impossible to find. Jeremiah Colburn and others wrote about cents, and the collecting of them, in newspapers and magazines, advising readers that in 1815 the Mint did not make cents.

In 1856, Daniel Groux, a numismatist and exhibitor, issued a handsome, 17-page *Prospectus of an Important Work in Three Volumes, to be called, Numismatical History of the United States, Comprising a Full Description of its Medals & Coins, From the Earliest Period to Our Times*.

It seems that Groux, along with the nefarious Thomas Wyatt, sold Winslow Lewis some fake coins and deceived the good doctor in other ways. The books never materialized.

Historical Magazine, launched in January 1857, included many letters and notes about colonial coins. Jeremiah Colburn was a frequent contributor. The July 1857 issue revealed that the "Chelsea hoard" of Massachusetts silver coins was comprised of forgeries by a "smart Gothamite" (Thomas Wyatt). In August the first installment of Colburn's "The First Coinage of America" told of Massachusetts and other early silver issues. The July 1859 issue of *Historical Magazine* included "The First North American Coins," by "S.H.," of New York. Adapted from information in the *Massachusetts Historical Collections*, the feature discussed various colonial coins. As it contained the minutes of early numismatic societies, some consider it to be the first *numismatic* periodical in America. Another magazine, *Norton's Literary Letter*, was published in the late 1850s and contained limited information on early American coins.

In 1858 John Howard Hickcox published *An Historical Account of American Coinage*, though with a print run of just 205 copies, it did not have a memorable impact on the hobby. Hickcox's book contained many documents relevant to colonial coins and was a masterwork of research, considering that such information was widely scattered at the time. Five pages of plates engraved by John Gavit included illustrations from the 1850 *Documentary History of the State of New York*, some tinted brown. Hickcox's story does not end well. In March 1882, then working in the Copyright Division of the Library of Congress, he was implicated in stealing money from mail envelopes, to which he confessed.

In 1859, Montroville W. Dickeson's impressive *American Numismatical Manual* was published, with embossed metallic-toned plates of coins, including colonials. Detailed information was given on various issues. The book was widely circulated and followed by later editions in 1860 and 1864. Although some numismatists sneered at its errors, overall the volume provided tremendous impetus to the hobby. Today it remains a classic and is worthy of rediscovery by collectors. Similarly, the popular book by W.C. Prime, *Coins, Medals and Seals*, published in 1861, created wide interest.

In 1859, Augustus B. Sage prepared catalogs for three different coin auctions, launching what became a steady stream of sales that continues to the present day. The peak in the second half of the 19th century came in the 1880s, when the rate was about one sale per week. Catalogs prepared by W. Elliot Woodward, Edward D. Cogan, John W. Haseltine, W.H. Strobridge, Édouard Frossard, S.H. and Henry Chapman, and others offered many fine colonial and early American coins.

Societies and Publications

The Philadelphia Numismatic Society, organized on January 1, 1858, became the first coin club in America. Two more groups formed in March: the Boston Numismatic Society, on March 3, and the American Numismatic Society, founded by Augustus B. Sage and friends. Sage's group flourished for two years, then expired, or at least became comatose. In 1864 it was revived and renamed the American Numismatic and Archaeological Society. The "and Archaeological" addition was intended to widen its circle of members. In 1907 the original name was re-adopted. Today based in New York City, the society is a focal point for research, publication, and exhibition of colonial coins and information.

The society launched the *American Journal of Numismatics* in May 1866. It was the first magazine primarily devoted to coin collecting. In the same year, E.B. Mason Jr. published *Mason's Coin and Stamp Collectors' Magazine*, the first periodical issued by a dealer.

In 1870 the first single-subject study of importance on a colonial specialty, "The Vermont Coinage," by Rev. E.F. Slafter, was published in volume 1 of *The Collections of the Vermont Historical Society*. In 1875, Sylvester S. Crosby, a Boston watchmaker and jeweler who studied numismatics, published *The Early Coins of America*, sections of which had been distributed since 1873. This volume compiled everything worthwhile that had been published on colonial coins to that point, and much new information as well. Die variety descriptions were given for most of the larger series from Massachusetts onward. Today this book is still the foundation for any numismatic library on the subject. A few years later in 1881, Edward Maris produced the slim but elephant-folio-size study, *A Historic Sketch of the Coins of New Jersey With a Plate*, which became the standard on that subject. In all, many articles, several monographs, and a few books were published at this time dealing with early American and colonial issues.

Auction catalogs during this era, prepared by W. Elliot Woodward, John W. Haseltine, and others, offered many colonial coins, though descriptions were sparse in the 1860s and most of the 1870s. After Crosby's book became known, catalogs often referenced his numbers and many of his comments about rarity, history, and other aspects. State coppers of the 1780s, having relatively low market values, typically got short shrift in listings, so that modern scholars cannot attribute the specific varieties of most. There were exceptions, including John W. Haseltine's sales of the T.B. Gregory Collection in 1882 and the Crosby Collection in 1883, the Chapman brothers' sale of the Charles I. Bushnell Collection in 1882 (which brought the youthful Chapmans great fame), the Lorin G. Parmelee Collection by the New York Coin & Stamp Company in 1890, and a handful of others.

The Numismatist magazine made its debut in 1888 under the editorship of Dr. George F. Heath, a physician of Monroe, Michigan. In time this became the official publication of the American Numismatic Association (formed in November 1891).

By the end of the 19th century, colonial coins were an essential part of American numismatic activity. All American dealers handled them, and many important collections had been formed, the greatest being those of T. Harrison Garrett and Lorin G. Parmelee. Virgil M. Brand, James W. Ellsworth, Thomas Hall, Hillyer C. Ryder, Carl Würtzbach, and several others formed collections, mostly privately with little comment about their activities in the *American Journal of Numismatics* or *The Numismatist*.

The 20th Century Onward
The Numismatic Scene

At the turn of the 20th century, colonial coins were as popular as ever, joining tokens and medals in the numismatic limelight. In recent times New York City dealer Lyman H. Low, Ed Frossard, and others had showcased these specialties in auctions. *The Numismatist* and the *American Journal of Numismatics* printed occasional articles on colonial issues, although more ink was devoted to tokens and medals. State copper issues of the 1780s continued to be collected by types, with just a handful of specialists interested in die varieties. Crosby's *Early Coins of America* was the standard text. Maris's book on New Jersey coppers was hard to find, and beyond that hardly any information was available. Thomas

Collecting Colonial Coins

PLATE, IX.

Plate IX from Montroville W. Dickeson's *American Numismatical Manual*, 1859. This was the first comprehensive book published on colonial and United States coinage.

Hall compiled a manuscript on Connecticut coppers of 1787, but it was never published. His collection went *en bloc* to Virgil M. Brand.

Brand, who bid aggressively in nearly every important auction, had Theophile E. Leon and other scouts hunting material, and in time added the Dewitt S. Smith and Carl Würtzbach cabinets to his holdings. He was well on his way to becoming the greatest coin collector ever—in terms of both quality and quantity. Brand died in 1926, leaving an estate of about 350,000 coins from ancient to modern times, including duplicates of many rarities. His colonial coins were impressive and were parceled out into the marketplace over a long span of years by his heirs, brothers Horace and Armin.

Hillyer C. Ryder was a consummate student of the copper issues of the 1780s. He collected quietly but enthusiastically. His interest was well known to the dealers in Philadelphia, New York, and elsewhere, who furnished a steady stream of coppers as they came into stock. Ryder had been a buyer in the Bushnell sale in 1882 and the Parmelee auction of 1890.

In Baltimore, bank president Waldo C. Newcomer assembled one of the greatest American cabinets. His collection was consigned to Texas dealer B. Max Mehl in 1931, who sold about $250,000 worth of items from it, including rare colonials. Other pieces were auctioned. He died in Hawaii of a heart attack in 1934, leaving an estate valued at over $1 million. While colonial specialists were few, many collectors routinely added such pieces to general collections that emphasized federal coins. Accordingly, many important auctions held in the early 20th century included rare colonial and early American issues.

An Important Exhibition

In February 1907 in *The Numismatist*, America's most valuable coins formed the topic for an article. At the top of the list was the 1787 Brasher doubloon, estimated to be worth $3,000, followed by the 1822 half eagle (one of which had sold earlier for $2,165), the 1815 half eagle (valued at the odd price of $1,052, perhaps a typographical error), and the 1804 silver dollar at $1,000. Then came the 1783 Nova Constellatio pattern coins from the 1,000 mill to the 100 mill denominations, followed by the Washington New Jersey copper recently sold for $640, the 1776 Continental Currency dollar in silver, and, concluding the roster, the 1861 original Confederate States of America half dollar at $870.

In June 1907 the Matthew A. Stickney Collection was offered by Henry Chapman. A Brasher doubloon sold for $6,200, setting the record for any coin at auction. The unique 1776 Massachusetts Janus Head copper commanded $1,050 at the same event.

From January 17 to February 18, 1914, the American Numismatic Society sponsored the Exhibition of United States and Colonial Coins. A special catalog described rarities loaned by exhibitors including F.C.C. Boyd, Henry Chapman, S. Hudson Chapman, James W. Ellsworth, George French, H.O. Granberg, Waldo C. Newcomer, Wayte Raymond, Hillyer C. Ryder, Howland Wood, William H. Woodin, and Carl Würtzbach. Dazzling colonial and early American coins were on view, highlighted by the 1783 set of Nova Constellatio silver patterns.

In 1919 the *American Journal of Numismatics* published Hillyer C. Ryder's monographs on die varieties of Massachusetts and Vermont coins, and Henry C. Miller's "State Coinage of Connecticut." The three studies were issued in book form in 1920 as *The State Coinage of New England*. Ryder's and Miller's numbers quickly became standard, replacing the Crosby designations. Miller numbers in particular were difficult to figure out, at least quickly, leading some collectors (such as Frederick A. Canfield) to *paint* the attributions on the coins themselves—helpful if a coin became separated from its envelope or tag.

On the auction scene, B. Max Mehl's 1922 sale of the James Ten Eyck Collection included two varieties of 1787 Brasher doubloons.

Ellsworth and Garrett

On March 10, 1923, this appeared in the *New York Times*:

> Wayte Raymond, dealer in coins, of 489 Park Avenue, has bought from M. Knoedler & Co. the collection of early American and United States coins recently sold to the Knoedler Syndicate by James W. Ellsworth. Mr. Raymond paid about $100,000 for the coins, said to be the largest amount ever given for a numismatic collection in this country. The collection has been known for years as the finest in the United States, and Mr. Ellsworth, who has disposed of all his art works and other rare collections, with the exception of his Innes paintings and a Rembrandt, counted it as one of the most interesting and valuable of his possessions.
>
> Among the valuable coins is the unique set of Nova Constellatio patterns for a decimal system struck in 1783, in denominations of 100, 500 and 1,000 mills. This set was from the celebrated Parmelee Collection sold in New York in 1890.
>
> There was also the doubloon struck in New York in 1787 by Ephraim Brasher, of which there are only four specimens known. There are also pieces of the colonial period and early trial pieces used before the regular adopted coinage at the United States Mint in 1793, and a remarkable series of the gold, silver, and copper coins of the United States from the beginning of the coinage in 1793 up to the present time, including two 1804 dollars and the finest known specimens of many other rare dates.
>
> An interesting part of the collection is a series of the early private gold coins struck in California, Colorado, Utah, Oregon, North Carolina, and Georgia. There are about 2,000 coins in the collection, making it the most important coin set ever sold here.
>
> Mr. Ellsworth is said to have acquired one of his 1804 dollars and the Brasher doubloon at the Stickney sale, several years ago, paying $3,600 for the former and $6,200 for the latter.

Omitted from the account was the fact that John Work Garrett of Baltimore financed the transaction and was given first choice of the rarities in the purchase. These were added to the collection formed in the 1870s and 1880s by his father, T. Harrison Garrett.

In the same year the Mint Collection was moved from the Philadelphia Mint to the Smithsonian Institution in Washington, D.C. Today this is known as the National Numismatic Collection. Among its many treasures are colonial coins from Massachusetts silver onward.

The Frederick A. Canfield Collection of Connecticut coppers went from the New Jersey Historical Society to the American Numismatic Society in 1931, establishing the foundation of what remains today the best reference holding of this specialty.

The Changing Scene

Hillyer C. Ryder died in 1928. His estate, with its vast array of state coins as well as other early issues and U.S. coins, was appraised by Wayte Raymond. In 1945, Raymond received a call from those involved with the estate, asking if his 1928 appraisal and offer was still valid, perhaps thinking the Depression had diminished values in the meantime. Raymond affirmed that the offer was still good!

By this time, Frederick C.C. Boyd, known to his friends as "Fred," had been in numismatics for several decades. In the 1920s he was an active mail-order dealer, but by the 1940s he was busy with his position as an executive with the Union News Company. The firm maintained newsstands and kiosks in railroad stations and other locations. In the meantime he built extensive collections of U.S. coins, tokens, medals, and paper money. Tiring of the federal issues, he sold his magnificent collection of patterns to the Numismatic Gallery (Abe Kosoff and Abner Kreisberg), who placed it with King Farouk, the playboy king of Egypt. The silver and gold coins were auctioned under the title of "the World's Greatest Collection," which it hardly was, but the name created a lot of attention. Absent from the "greatest" collection were such rarities as the 1804 dollar and 1822 half eagle, and most mintmarks (even common ones).

Boyd bought the Ryder Collection from Raymond and focused his attention on colonials, as well as tokens, medals, and paper money. Raymond died in 1956. His widow, Olga, allowed John J. Ford Jr. to buy whatever he wanted for himself, after which the substantial remainder was auctioned by the New Netherlands Coin Company (in which Ford was a partner with Charles M. Wormser). Boyd passed away in 1958. Following a 1962 appraisal, Ford bought his choice of coins from that estate, with the important remainder items again going to New Netherlands. These coups netted Ford the Ryder, Raymond, and Boyd colonials.

After selling his cabinet to Virgil Brand, Carl Würtzbach remained active in the hobby. John Kleeberg (a contributor to this book) relates:

> Another important colonial collector was large-cent specialist George Hubbard Clapp's brother Charles Edwin Clapp Sr. He had a lot of trouble with his son, who was an alcoholic and a stockbroker. Being an alcoholic didn't cause any trouble, but being a stockbroker did, because he was trading at the time of the 1929 crash and lost $600,000 in a matter of months. A pity he went to the office each day—if he had stayed home and gotten blotto on a bottle of Scotch each morning, none of these problems would have happened. The father had to sell his colonial collection to bail out the son. The Massachusetts silver coins were sold to Carl Würtzbach. Then Würtzbach had to sell the Massachusetts silver when there was an embezzlement at the bank in Lee, Massachusetts, where he sat on the board of directors, and he had to bail out the bank. He sold the collection to T. James Clarke.
>
> Clarke died, and his large cent collection was plundered by William H. Sheldon. New Netherlands bought the Massachusetts silver in its turn, and sold it to Frederick C. C. Boyd. Then Boyd died a few years later, and John Ford scoffed up the Massachusetts silver, thereby contributing to the ruining of his friendships with Mrs. Norweb and Eric Newman. This is beginning to read like the Curse of Tutankhamun.

Along the way, auctions conducted by B. Max Mehl, Stack's, Numismatic Gallery, New Netherlands, and others offered colonial coins on a regular basis, sometimes as part of U.S. collections. Of particular note were rarities sold by the Numismatic Gallery at the 1947 American Numismatic Association convention in Buffalo, New York. *The Numismatist* gave this report:

> The Robert R. Prann Collection of colonials offered as fine a variety of rarities as has been sold at auction in many years. The Sommer Islands shillings sold for $170 and $190, the sixpence at $150 and $140, the threepence at $310, and the twopence at $190. The New England shilling sold for $270, the rare sixpence at $630, and the Willow Tree sixpence at $210. Many good buys were made by collectors of this series with a superb Chalmers sixpence selling at only $75, a New Hampshire cent at $105, a New York NON VI VIRTUTE VICI cent at $80, and two George Clinton cents at $250 and $225 respectively. Other bargains included a Confederatio cent at $230 and a Washington Roman Head cent at $150. Spirited bidding for the Perkins dollar started at $50 and was ended at $350.

More could be said about the Prann Collection. Another Roman Head cent, shipped in the early 1940s by New York dealer Abe Kosoff to Prann, who lived in Puerto Rico, remains on the ocean bottom in a torpedoed ship. Alas, the $230 Confederatio cent proved to be a Bolen copy.

In the 1940s and 1950s the American Numismatic Society remained a focal point for collectors and scholars interested in colonial coins. Society staffer Sydney P. Noe created studies of the die varieties of Massachusetts silver coins, updating the Crosby text and adding extensive illustrations. Wayte Raymond's *Standard Catalogue of United States Coins*, launched in 1934 and issued every year or so afterward, introduced many people to colonial coins, which the book covered extensively. In 1946 the new Whitman *Guide Book of United States Coins* (the Red Book) made its debut, also with valuable information. Interest in the field grew. Howard Kurth, John Richardson, W.P. Keller, and others found coppers of the 1780s especially interesting and studied them carefully, discovering important new varieties. Joseph R. Lasser, who as a young numismatist attended the 1937 American Numismatic Association convention in Washington, D.C., went on to form a magnificent cabinet of colonials.

Richard Kenney, an American Numismatic Society curator, produced a helpful monograph, *Struck Copies of Early American Coins*, published by Wayte Raymond in 1952. In the same year Raymond published Eric P. Newman's *The 1776 Continental Currency Coinage & Varieties of the Fugio Cent*, which became the standard reference on those series. In the 1950s, the New Netherlands Coin Company took the lead in featuring colonials in its auction sales, further increasing interest in the field. Walter Breen wrote most of the descriptions for New Netherlands, often adding historical and numismatic information and theories that made for fascinating reading. Not well remembered today is Oliver Eaton Futter, a Brooklyn, New York, numismatist who was a familiar figure at East Coast conventions and a frequent buyer at coin stores in New York City. In late 1953 his collection of colonial coins, said to be impressive, was purchased outright by B. Max Mehl of Fort Worth, Texas. A few years later Richard Picker began his rare coin dealership specializing in colonial and other early coins. In June 1956 in *The Numismatist*, Elston G. Bradfield reviewed the latest edition of the Red Book, noting, "Generally, colonials are up 5 percent to 10 percent, but some Pine Trees, Chalmers, Vermonts, New Yorks and Washington pieces have pushed into the plus-10 percent to 20 percent areas." In 1959, Kenneth Bressett joined the staff of Whitman Publishing Company, then located in Racine, Wisconsin. A news release of the time noted that he had discovered 12 varieties of colonial coins previously unrecorded.

The Rittenhouse Society, organized in 1957 and formally launched on an annual-meeting basis in 1960, drew a handful of specialists in the field. Apart from dedicated collectors of die varieties, the majority of numismatic activity was in the basic types listed in the Red Book (the *Standard Catalogue* having expired with its 1957 edition).

Colonial Coins to the Fore

Coin World, the first weekly numismatic publication, debuted in 1960. This and other factors (including the nationwide excitement for the 1960 Small Date Lincoln cent) propelled coin collecting into the mainstream. Before long, *Coin World*, *The Numismatist*, *The Numismatic Scrapbook Magazine*, and *Numismatic News* collectively claimed several hundred thousand subscribers. This catalyzed the publishing of more books, catalogs, and other information than the hobby had ever seen. Important to the present narrative, special interest groups were soon formed, including the Token and Medal Society (TAMS), the Early American Coppers Club (EAC), and the Society of Paper Money Collectors (SPMC), among others. Members enjoyed flocking together with others of the same feather to share new finds, ask questions, and further their enjoyment. EAC, in particular, attracted devotees of colonial coins, notably the state and related issues of the 1780s.

The *Colonial Newsletter*, launched in 1960 by Al Hoch and soon transferred to James C. Spilman, continued as the focal point for discoveries and new information in that specialty. In ensuing years, many discoveries were announced, old theories disproved, and other changes to conventional numismatic wisdom made, creating an archive that, fully indexed, serves as an important information source today (the index is online at the ANS Web site).

Hoch, through Quarterman Publications, reprinted Crosby's *Early Coins of America*, Sydney Noe's studies on Massachusetts silver, and other texts. Durst Publications, based in New York, issued further reprints. Books and monographs that had been difficult to obtain for many years were now available for low cost.

In the meantime, New Netherlands and Stack's led the way in colonial auction offerings, with continuing selections from the Boyd, Ryder, Raymond, and other estates, drawing many bidders. Cabinets such as those of the Massachusetts Historical Society, John Roper, Laird U. Park, Herbert M. Oechsner, and Ellis Robison scored successes for Stack's. In fact, there were many notable sales. In 1971 *Scott's Comprehensive Catalog and Encyclopedia of U.S. Coins*, by Don Taxay, was published. This contained much information on colonial coins, mostly furnished by Walter Breen. In 1988, *Walter Breen's Complete Encyclopedia of U.S. and Colonial Coins* featured extensive coverage of early issues from Bermuda coinage through coins of George Washington.

The Garrett Collection, bequeathed to the Johns Hopkins University in 1942, sold at auction in a series of four sales from 1979 to 1981. The colonials were mainly cataloged by this author, with excellent help from staff. Many records were set, including $725,000 for the finest known 1787 Brasher doubloon. The Norweb Collection and the Frederick Taylor Collection, both cataloged by Michael J. Hodder and me in the 1980s, were similarly laden with rarities in the colonial series and will be forever remembered.

Hodder went on to further accomplishments, such as founding the Colonial Coin Collectors Club and the *C4 Newsletter* in 1993. As if this were not enough, beginning in 2003 he was the lead cataloger for Stack's of the John J. Ford Jr. Collection, the greatest cabinet of colonials ever auctioned. Included were treasures from the long-hidden Boyd, Ryder, and Raymond collections, bringing these pieces to a new generation of enthusiasts. By autumn 2007 the Ford estate items, including tokens, medals, and paper money of various eras, had grossed over $55 million, the largest numismatic collection ever auctioned. Remarkably, there were no federal U.S. coins in it!

Into the 21st Century

Today, in the early 21st century, the field of colonial coin collecting is more enjoyable than ever. Available at one's fingertips is information that 50 years ago could not have been imagined. It's likely that at least several thousand people collect colonials casually, and the hundreds who belong to the Colonial Coin Collectors Club and/or subscribe to the *Colonial Newsletter* through the American Numismatic Society are very serious about the pursuit.

A grateful nod goes to the dealers who specialize in colonial coins, most of whom have taken a deep interest in the historical, technical, and numismatic aspects of the field, in addition to simply buying and selling. We all have benefited from their expertise and attention.

The unknown is always exciting to contemplate. In this field there are *many* varieties waiting to be discovered, perhaps by *you*, the reader. The Internet offers an instant link with buyers, sellers, and many sources of information. Camaraderie is better than ever. As a group, collectors in this field are willing to share information, often becoming good friends in the process. While there is certainly competition, there is also fellowship and good will. A visit to a gathering or seminar is always inspiring.

The key to success in collecting and enjoying colonials is *knowledge*. Because of this, as you meet other enthusiasts, you will find them both interested in and informed about the subject, but always eager to learn more. All of this adds up to a lot of excitement for the future.

Grading Colonial Coins

Introduction

In all instances the value of a colonial or early American coin is dependent upon its grade or preservation. The assigned grade refers to the amount of handling or wear it has received. Traditionally, adjectives have been used, ranging on the low end from Poor to Fair, then Good, the last representing what is often the minimal acceptable grade for a colonial coin, save for a rare variety. Upward from Good, we have Very Good, Fine, Very Fine, Extremely Fine, About Uncirculated, and Uncirculated, the last usually referred to as Mint State. Separately, Proof coins with mirrorlike surfaces represent a different method of manufacture and range from impaired Proofs to perfect.

For use in classifying early large copper cents dated from 1793 to 1814, William H. Sheldon, in his 1949 book, *Early American Cents* (followed by the 1958 updating, *Penny Whimsy*), delineated these levels (modern comments added in brackets):

A Quantitative Scale for Condition

Basal State 1-*Identifiable and unmutilated*, but so badly worn that only a portion of the legend or inscription is legible. Enough must remain for positive identification of the variety, although for some varieties this need not necessarily include a readable date. [Today, Poor-1 is used instead of Basal State 1.]

Fair 2-*The date and more than half of the inscription and detail can be made out, although perhaps faintly.*

Very Fair 3-*The date will be clear* and *practically all of the detail of the coin can be made out*, although faint areas are to be expected, and the coin as a whole may be well worn down. [Today, About Good–3, abbreviated as AG-3, is used.]

Good 4, 5, 6-*The date* together with *all of the detail* must be *very clear*. The general relief of the coin may be well worn down.

Very Good 7, 8, 10-*Everything is boldly clear*, but the sharpness of the coin may be largely gone. Signs of wear are seen uniformly over the whole coin, not merely on the high surfaces.

Fine 12, 15-*All of the design* and *all of the inscriptions* are sharp. Wear is appreciable only on the high surfaces. If the coin is examined with a glass, the *microscopic* detail is gone.

Very Fine 20, 30-*All of the detail is in sharp relief*, and *only the highest surfaces show wear*, even when the glass is applied. The microscopic detail is largely intact except on the high points. These high surfaces will show a little rubbing, or flattening, even to the unaided eye.

Extremely Fine 40-*Only the slightest trace of wear*, or of rubbing, is to be seen on the *high points.*

About Uncirculated 50-Close attention or the use of a glass should be necessary to make out that the coin is not in perfect Mint State. Typically, the AU-50 coin retains its full sharpness, but is darkened or is a little off-color.

Mint State 60, 65, 70-*Free from any wear*, and the color should be that of a copper coin which has been kept with great care. The color will vary from mint red to light brown or light olive. . . . For condition 70 the coin must be exactly as it left the dies, except for a slight mellowing of the color. Condition 60 means Mint State. Condition 70 means *perfect* Mint State.

These numerical classifications became popular, as it was easier for a beginning collector—or, for that matter, just about anyone—to understand that a coin described as VF-20 was better than one listed as G-4, but not as nice as an AU-50 or an MS-65. Importantly, Sheldon stated this:

> Many cents have injuries, scratches, or bruises which of course detract from numismatic value and modify condition. Since there is no way of standardizing how much a particular mutilation damages a coin, it is probably best to grade the coin *as if without* the injury, and then to list or describe the injury separately.

In the English language, adjectives such as *good, extremely fine, very good,* and so on are not arranged in any particular order when referring to objects in everyday life—say, a vacation experience or one's opinion of an antique chair. Therefore it takes some getting used to for new coin collectors to realize that Good is not as nice as Fine, and Extremely Fine is better than Very Fine. In fact a coin graded "Good" might not be *good* at all, in terms of desirability. Neither you nor I would probably want to buy a 1795 Talbot, Allum & Lee cent worn down to the point at which it is numismatically in Good grade.

Numbers help with the understanding. The Sheldon numbers were soon unofficially extended to use for half cents, later-date large cents, and colonial coins, but with no particular rules as to how a grade for colonial coins should be determined. Today, there are still no hard and fast rules, although *Walter Breen's Complete Encyclopedia of*

U.S. and Colonial Coins gives that author's guidelines for some issues.

The sharpness of the original strike can vary from completely detailed to flat, with the result of the latter being that a freshly minted coin can appear very worn. This is much more true of colonial coins than of the large copper cents treated by Sheldon. An example is found readily enough with the plentiful 1788 Vermont copper variety known as Richardson-Ryder number 16 (Whitman-2120 in this book), for which all specimens are flatly struck at the centers. If a non-specialist quickly looks at such a piece and it has no mint luster, he or she might designate it as VG-8 or F-12, whereas in actuality it might be a nice EF-40.

In contrast, the 1773 Virginia halfpenny is typically found sharply struck, and an About Uncirculated or Mint State example usually shows needle-sharp details. A quick glance at a Virginia halfpenny that is weak at the centers, with no details, earmarks it as being truly well worn, indeed perhaps G-4 or VG-8.

In reviewing auction catalogs, price lists, and other illustrations, it's apparent that, even among well-informed colonial collectors, one person's Very Fine can be another's Fine or Extremely Fine. As mentioned in this book's introduction, because of this uncertainty in grading, the late Richard Picker, prominent as a dealer in colonials from the late 1950s through the 1970s, did not assign grades to coins. He simply listed a given Massachusetts Pine Tree shilling, Vermont copper, or Fugio copper at, for example, $50, $200, or whatever. The buyer would examine the coin and, if he or she felt it was a "$50 coin" or a "$200 coin," would buy it. Otherwise the coin was passed by. For many years this worked very effectively for Dick Picker, as virtually all of his clients were knowledgeable.

In recent times, "gradeflation" has been the rule in the colonial field, including with certified coins. Many pieces graded Fine, Very Fine, and Extremely Fine in auctions of the 1950s and 1960s now are listed respectively as Very Fine, Extremely Fine, and About Uncirculated. Moreover, Sheldon's suggestion that defects be enumerated separately is *completely* ignored by certification services, a practice of which more will be said later.

Necessity for Grading Colonials

Many contemporary buyers enter the market for colonial and early American coins with well-endowed checkbooks but not a great deal of experience. Some are smart and learn the basics of grading. Many others naively trust the grading to certification services or coin sellers.

The best advice is to learn about grading by viewing coins in the marketplace—easy enough to do, for starters, simply by checking Internet postings. A lazy afternoon spent Web surfing for present and past auction listings of, for example, Massachusetts Pine Tree shillings of 1652 and Connecticut coppers from 1785 to 1788 will be more instructive than a dozen pages of written commentary.

Without realizing it, you will gain experience. In fact, a few dozen hours spent doing this will make you more knowledgeable than most of your peers. While you can obtain colonial coins by bidding in auction sales or ordering from price lists, it will not be very satisfying to receive them and wonder if the grades are correct. Is that Washington North Wales halfpenny really Very Fine, as labeled? It looks barely VG-8, if that. With knowledge, you can answer these questions.

No grading system can fit all colonial coins; it's important to know the characteristics of each series. Washington North Wales halfpence were miserably struck, and intentionally so. These were unofficial coins meant to be passed into circulation already with the appearance that they were well worn and had been accepted in trade for many years. Some understanding of this is necessary to be a smart buyer. On the other hand, 1796 Myddelton tokens were carefully struck with needle-sharp details and Proof finish, for sale to collectors. Today, nearly all are in choice or gem preservation. Likely, the label on a certified holder will do fine—no other knowledge necessary, other than to determine the coin has not been cleaned and that it has good eye appeal.

More Grading by the Numbers

In 1975 the American Numismatic Association board of governors appointed Abe Kosoff as chairman of the ANA Grading Service Study Committee, established to investigate its eponymous subject. This group expanded to become the American Numismatic Association Certification Service (ANACS), a facility that, for a fee, evaluates the authenticity of coins. In time, the ANA compiled findings and consulted experts with the thought of publishing a book that listed its grading standards. This evolved into the *Official American Numismatic Association Grading Standards for U.S. Coins*, published by the association in 1977 and in subsequent editions by Whitman Publishing, LLC. The original Sheldon system was eventually expanded to include many intermediate numbers, now including 11 classifications in Mint State alone, continuously from MS-60 to MS-70. In the About Uncirculated category Sheldon had only AU-50. Now there are also 53, 55, and 58.

While collectors of Morgan silver dollars and Saint-Gaudens double eagles can debate whether a given coin is just right if graded MS-64 or if it should be 63 or 65, collectors of colonial coins often differ widely in their interpretations. It is not unusual for a certified colonial to be labeled MS-60 or 63, while a long-time specialist may consider it no better than AU-50 or 55.

Certified Colonial Coins

In 1986 David Hall and a group of dealers banded together to create the Professional Coin Grading Service (PCGS), which charged a fee to examine a coin, have it reviewed by several dealers who consider themselves expert in grading, then encapsulate it in plastic and affix identification and a grade number. At first, colonial coins were not handled by PCGS. A typical coin sent to PCGS would be a federal issue such as a silver dollar that would be returned marked "1893-S MS-63."

In 1987 the Numismatic Guaranty Corporation of America (NGC) was founded, becoming the second dynamic force in the business. At present, PCGS, NGC, and ANACS are the only American grading services that regularly publish population reports, which list all known, certified coins. These are useful as they enable potential buyers to determine how scarce a coin from that particular service may be in a given grade.

Typically, only higher-value coins are submitted to population reports. For example, within a given colonial specialty, high-grade valuable coins are likely to be sent in, while well-worn examples might not be. Hence, such reports are only a guide, not a scientific posting. Adding further uncertainty is the fact that expensive coins are often submitted multiple times in an effort to secure upgrades. A coin submitted four times appears as four coins in a population report, whereas in reality only one coin is involved.

Other grading services are in business but do not publish reports. The quality of any given service can vary, and some collectors and dealers have preferences. Certain services (not mentioned by name here) simply are thought by some to be exploitative. These companies attach impressive-sounding labels to coins to be marketed on television, in newspaper advertisements, or in other media distributed to numismatically naive buyers. My advice is to stay with the leaders, and to consult with trustworthy dealers and collector friends to determine their favorites.

As a general observation, colonial coins certified by leading services tend to be more liberally graded than would be done by the usual old-line auction house or experienced dealer. Many coins that were Extremely Fine or About Uncirculated a few years ago now are in certified holders as Mint State, sometimes even up to MS-62 or MS-63. Many coins sold in the Ford Collection sales and carefully cataloged in circulated grades were sent to NGC and PCGS and—presto!—they are now Mint State. The coins themselves have not changed. Abraham Lincoln said, "How many legs does a dog have if you call the tail a leg? Four. Calling a tail a leg doesn't make it a leg." Similarly, if someone takes an Extremely Fine colonial coin and puts it in a certified holder and labels it as MS-63, it is still really Extremely Fine. As basic as this may seem, the reality in the marketplace, including in auction galleries, is that a genuine "dog" of a coin certified as MS-63 by a leading service will create a lot more attention than will an uncertified or "raw" coin with superb eye appeal.

Many collectors and dealers love holders as an aid to marketing coins. If a true AU-55 Oak Tree shilling lands in a holder marked MS-63, its value increases sharply. If a 1794 Talbot, Allum & Lee cent is as ugly as sin but is certified as EF-40, it will sell readily, especially if offered at a "bargain" price slightly below other EF-40 listings. Certified coins that are overgraded tend to stay in their holders. I have never heard of a single instance in which someone has sought to have a coin reholdered because it is overgraded!

In contrast, thousands of collectors and dealers resubmit coins to the services in hopes that they will be upgraded. If you were to use the original catalogs to research the details of the selected auction prices beginning in chapter 7, you would see multiple instances of coins once graded as circulated, such as Extremely Fine or About Uncirculated, and now certified as Mint State or higher, perhaps up to MS-65. This, within a short time, has doubled or tripled the price of many coins. Probably, a decade from now, the *majority* of expensive colonials that cross the auction block will be in certified holders—a simple matter of dollars and cents to the coins' owners. As a corollary, it is impossible to equate market prices of a generation ago to today's inflated values driven by liberal grading interpretations. Perhaps, if old Extremely Fine listings were moved up to About Uncirculated and old About Uncirculated listings to Mint State, one might come close, but there would still be instances of old Extremely Fine pieces now certified as Mint State.

Another problem with holders is that relatively few give information about die variety. A 1788 Vermont copper of the Mailed Bust Right type certified as F-12—if it is a Ryder-Richardson-16 variety—might be worth a few hundred dollars. A similar coin of the RR-33 variety would be worth more than $10,000! Another problem for most holders is that they include no information on the coin's weight or diameter, nor do they allow one to view the coin's edge. Often, metrology (diameter and weight) is useful in research. Finally, if a coin is damaged, such as a 1652 Pine Tree shilling by light clipping, this would rarely be mentioned on the holder.

Planchet flaws, porosity, and staining are likewise ignored. As one of many examples, experienced specialists know that such flaws are the norm and to be expected on Connecticut copper coins of 1785. Some have striations and rifts obliterating part of the design; others have minor flaws. A listing of a 1785 Connecticut certified as VF-20 doesn't mean much without a detailed description of the planchet to go with it. In addition, information about porosity, sharpness of strike, and eye appeal is needed to intelligently make a purchase. A certified VF-20 coin of a certain variety might be worth $400 if riddled with flaws, or it could be worth $3,000 if well struck and on a high quality planchet. Some sophistication is needed to examine certain coins; for example, some may show "roller marks" from the planchet strip process that were not flattened later by coining. Numismatically, these are not considered detrimental.

For *you* as a buyer of colonial coins, the information marked on a holder should be simply the beginning of a further investigation. If you fail to do this, you are apt to acquire some damaged or overgraded coins. Indeed, when it comes to grading, the best advice is *buyer beware*. The process is not the least bit scientific. If you're in doubt, just ask around the next time you meet with a few colonial specialists.

A Wonderful but Ironic Benefit of Unattributed Coins

In a way, the lack of information on certified coin holders—or, for that matter, on any coin holder—can be very beneficial. How? With some experience and knowledge, you can separate the wheat from the chaff, and buy nicer coins within any grade category than an uninformed collector could do. With some information, such as that found in the pages of this book, *you* might find a Vermont RR-33 copper offered simply as a 1788 "Mailed Bust Right" because the professional grader or rare coin dealer was unaware of die varieties of this state's coinage.

Or you may find a new variety of 1787 Fugio coppers, as Scott Mitchell did in autumn 2007 while reviewing a consignment of miscellaneous colonials sent to Stack's. This discovery is now known as Newman 13-JJ, and it sold for over $100,000 at auction in January 2008 (had Mitchell not made his discovery, the coin might have fetched a few hundred dollars).

Dealer Tony Terranova has found two new die varieties of Fugios; you could be next! Or you might find an unlisted die combination of a 1788 Connecticut copper. Or of a Machin's Mills copper. The possibility of fortune awaits you! Of course, you might just want to keep such a coin, as Richard August has done with several die varieties he discovered over the years.

Such "eureka moments" have happened many times—to *informed* buyers. Never has such a find happened to a buyer whose knowledge of an acquisition was limited to what was marked on the holder. Another advantage of certified coins is more obvious: most of the leading services guarantee the authenticity (genuineness) of the coins they certify.

Summary of Grading

Accurate grading of colonial and early American coins requires the experience that only comes through viewing many coins and becoming somewhat immersed in the marketplace. This is not particularly different from the discipline needed in collecting early American documents, antiques, or silverware. Each of these fields is dynamic, embraces many collectors, and has no uniformly agreed-upon grading standards. Generally, a collector or museum curator looks at a Paul Revere teapot, Duncan Phyfe chair, or Tanner map, then consults others in the particular field involved, and finally makes a purchase accordingly. Knowledge is an absolute requirement for success. Similarly, knowledge is needed to collect colonial coins.

On the other hand, clueless buyers are certainly an asset to the hobby, as they buy ugly and overgraded coins that specialists do not want! To these buyers, if a coin is certified, that is all that matters. The "funny" thing is they think they are acquiring bargains. We can all be grateful for these people. This comment may seem sarcastic and probably is. The fact is, many coins that specialists would not buy are eagerly snapped up by those who focus only on "getting good deals."

For colonial issues that trade regularly and exist in the market in quantity, an approximate order of grading will soon become apparent, and with some experience you will be able to grade, for example, a 1785 Vermont copper as VG-8, knowing it is not VF-20. Experienced dealers and collectors can be a great help, and I reiterate that the Internet can be educational, although not nearly as much as examining auction lots and dealer stocks in person.

When you become experienced in grading, you can evaluate the many differences of opinion. Take a 1652 Pine Tree shilling to a meeting of the Colonial Coin Collectors Club, or to a gathering sponsored by the American Numismatic Society, or some other area where collectors of a like mind congregate, pass it around, and ask the experts for their opinions. Grading is not now, never has been, and never will be precise. However, most will agree within a limited range of grading numbers. Use grading as an accessory, a tool, and not an object of worship or as something that affects your pleasure in collecting. Grading is an art, not a science.

The "Irresistible Charm" of Worn Coins

In many areas of numismatics, high grade is the lodestar of collecting. Not necessarily so with colonial coins. While an MS-60 or 63 or 65 coin is certainly worth owning, most early American coins are not found this way. A collector aspiring to own a set of the 39 different die varieties of Vermont coppers (with an unlimited bank account) might start as a teenager and die as an octogenarian before finding more than one, two, or three different coins in true MS-60 preservation. A specialist in Higley coppers minted in the 1730s would have the same experience if he set strictly graded VF-20 as a goal. Accordingly, when it comes to colonials, grading numbers are not the be-all and end-all they might be for Franklin half dollars of 1948 to 1963, or other modern series.

Most readers will agree that in the federal coin series, while silver and gold coins with scuffs, abrasions and the like are collected, if they are extensively *worn*, they would not be considered to be *charming*. However, most collectors of colonial copper coins have the opinion that well circulated examples can be great to own (not that there is a choice) and, further, they can be very appealing to contemplate. Perhaps that New England shilling was in someone's pocket during the Salem witch hunt, or that 1766 Pitt "halfpenny" might have been in a soldier's kit during the winter encampment at Valley Forge. This is difficult to explain in print, but the appeal is there and has lasted a long time. It is hard to improve on what William H. Sheldon had to say about this in 1949 in *Early American Cents*. His subject is early cents, but the sentiment is applicable to colonial coppers, as well:

> Old copper, like beauty, appears to possess a certain intrinsic quality or charm which for many people is irresistible. Gold, silver, and even bronze appear to be very much the same wherever you see them. Coins made of these metals become "old money" and "interesting," like the stuff seen in museums, but copper seems to possess an almost living warmth and a personality not encountered in any other metal. The big cent is something more than old money. Look at a handful of the cents dated before 1815, when they contained relatively pure copper. You see rich shades of green, red, brown, yellow, and even deep ebony; together with blending of these not elsewhere matched in nature save perhaps in autumn leaves. If the light is good (direct sunlight is preferable) you will possibly observe that no two of the coins are of quite the same color.

COLLECTING AND MARKET COMMENTS

Factors Affecting Prices

Apart from its grade, other factors can come into play to determine a colonial coin's value. The pedigree of a coin to a "name" sale can enhance its price. Two pieces in the same grade and of the same quality can have different values if one is pedigreed to, say, the Garrett Collection or the Ford Collection—which would enhance the value. If a colonial can be identified as a plate coin illustrated in a standard text such as Crosby, Maris, Miller, Newman, or Ryder, that also will increase its value.

An authoritative description in an auction catalog can draw a higher price if the writer correctly reviews other coins of the same variety and points out that the offered piece is exceptional in strike, eye appeal, or some other aspect.

While spans of a decade usually show an increase in prices for a given variety, individual results can vary. Sometimes additional pieces are discovered. If a colonial coin, of which just two or three are believed to exist, is auctioned today, it might sell for a record price. Some years from now, if 5 to 10 are known, it might bring less.

The coin market moves in cycles. While colonials have been largely immune to "hot" markets followed by "cold" markets, they do have their ups and downs. The long-term trend for just about every issue has been upward, as discussed below under a study of Red Book prices.

Competition is a main factor in setting prices. In a recent letter, William T. Anton Jr. reminisced about the first New Jersey Copper Coin Symposium in 1991. A show of hands revealed that six attendees collected these by die varieties; today that number is easily several dozen. It is not surprising for a "nice" New Jersey copper of medium scarcity to sell at a strong price with lots of bidding action. On a recent visit with Richard August, we both recalled that, when he began collecting colonials in the late 1950s, if a Connecticut copper of which 10 were known had come on the market, it would likely have sold for a basic "type" price—not as a rare variety, for there simply were not that many people specializing in the series. Today, a Connecticut with a population of 10 would likely sell for many multiples of a basic "type" valuation.

For certain expensive rarities in various colonial series, competition can be thin at high price levels. Three well-financed buyers may compete for a rarity in Sale A. But by the time Sale B occurs a few years later, one of the buyers may have sold his collection and another might have obtained a specimen of the coin by private treaty, meaning competition would be reduced and the price may be less. A case in point is a Very Fine example of the rare 1785 Inimica Tyrannis Americana copper (W-5635), an attraction at Stack's 1976 sale of the Laird U. Park Collection. Bidding opened at $25,000 with 140 people in the room and moved rapidly to $47,000, when it was sold to John L. Roper II. When Roper's collection was sold in December 1983, the same coin slept at $17,600. Demand had slackened. In 2004 the Ford Collection coin in the same grade went for $29,200. Most Park Collection coins, if sold today, would bring multiples of their 1976 prices, but there are exceptions, and it is wise to beware of such cases. The offering of the Ford coins electrified and catalyzed the market, and many of these pieces set records in later auctions.

Auction Prices: A Case Study

One of the most famous and popular colonial coins is the 1652 Massachusetts Pine Tree shilling variety known as Noe-1 (W-690). The following is a selection of auction prices realized from 2001 to date, grouped by grades (all Extremely Fine coins in one category, all About Uncirculated in another, etc.) and date offered. Coins described as clipped, bent, or with other significant problems are not included.

First, coins in Very Fine (VF) condition:

    Wayne S. Rich Sale (B&M 3/2002)—VF-30, $3,450

    Central States Sale (Heritage 4/2002)—VF-25 (PCGS), $3,105

    Lincoln Sale (Kingswood 1/2003)—VF-35 (PCGS), $2,415

    Long Beach Sale (Heritage 9/2003)—VF-35 (PCGS), $3,220

    Classics Sale (Stack's [ANR] 1/2004)—VF-35, $3,910

    Requa Sale (Stack's [ANR] 9/2006)—VF-30, $5,290

    Public Auction (Stack's 9/2006)—VF/EF, $4,888

    Long Beach Sale (Heritage 2/2007)—VF-25 (NGC), $4,025

Coins in Extremely Fine (EF) condition:

    Hain Family Sale (Stack's 1/2002)—EF, $8,625

    Pre–Long Beach Sale (Superior 2/2002)—EF-45, $2,933

    Monumental Sale (Scotsman 7/2003)—EF-45, $4,025

    Mid-Winter ANA Sale (Heritage 3/2004)—EF-45 (PCGS), $5,175

    Classics Sale (Stack's [ANR] 6/2004)—EF, $3,450

    John J. Ford Jr. XII Sale (Stack's 10/2005)—EF, $23,000; another EF, $23,000; Choice EF, $33,350

    FUN Sale (Heritage 1/2006)—EF-40 (PCGS), $5,980

    Denver ANA Sale (Heritage 8/2006)—EF-40 (PCGS), $6,325

    FUN Sale (Heritage 1/2007)—EF-40 (PCGS), $12,075

    Americana Sale (Stack's 1/2007)—EF-40 (PCGS), $12,075

Coins in About Uncirculated (AU) condition:

    Long Beach Sale (Heritage 2/2002)—AU-50 (PCGS), $6,325

    Central States Sale (Heritage 4/2002)—AU-50 (PCGS), $6,325; AU-55 (PCGS), $6,900

    Pre–Long Beach Sale (I. & L. Goldberg 9/2002)—AU-55 (PCGS), $6,612

    ANA Sale (Heritage 8/2004)—AU-55 (NGC), $11,500

    FUN Sale (Heritage 1/2005)—AU-53 (PCGS), $6,900

    New York Connoisseur's Collection (ANR 3/2006)—AU-50 (PCGS), $7,475

    Requa Sale (Stack's [ANR] 9/2006)—AU-55 (PCGS), $13,800

    FUN Sale (Heritage 1/2007)—AU-50 (NGC), $7,475; AU-50 (PCGS), $6,900

    Long Beach Auction (2/2007)—AU-58 (NGC), $8,625

Americana Sale (Stack's 1/2007)—AU-50 (PCGS), $6,900; AU-50 (NGC), $7,475

Long Beach Sale (Heritage 2/2007)—AU-58 (NGC), $8,625

Long Beach Sale (Heritage 5/2007)—AU-50 (PCGS), $7,475

FUN Sale (Heritage 1/2008)—AU-53 (PCGS), $9,775; AU-58 (PCGS), $16,900

Coins in Mint State (MS) condition:

66th Anniversary Sale / Strong Museum (Stack's 10/2001)—MS, $8,625

Hain Family Sale (Stack's 1/2002)—MS, $20,700

Central States Sale (Heritage 4/2002)—MS-60, $9,488

U.S. Coin Sale (Stack's 6/2002)—MS, $46,000

Public Auction (Stack's 5/2004)—MS-63 (PCGS), $33,350

John J. Ford Jr. XII Sale (Stack's 10/2005)—Gem MS Noe plate coin $43,125; another gem $48,875

What conclusions should be drawn? Here are some: generally, prices have risen in recent years. An auction price of 2001 or 2002 is likely a bargain today. Within any time period, prices can vary significantly for the same grade. The actual appearance of the coin, such as its striking and eye appeal, may be factors. When contemplating the purchase of a Noe-1, historical auction prices are interesting but should be cross-referenced with examination of the original catalogs and listings. Across the entire field of colonial coins, by matching pictures, grades of some coins may change in later offerings. In any event, past auction prices are only an approximate guide to bidding on a coin currently offered.

Also very important to remember is the fact that two different coins of the same date, type, and given grade may differ significantly in striking quality, planchet quality, damage, color, originality, and overall eye appeal. This can be true even for two coins certified in the same grade by the same services. Sometimes those differences can translate into one coin bringing a significantly higher price that its twin-graded coin—sometimes twice as much or more.

So, with colonials, perhaps more than most other slabbed coins, you should educate yourself about all of these nuances. Then you will be able to buy a coin based on its true merits, not on a single grade number.

Historical Price Trends

As a quick verification of the upward pricing trend of colonial coins, review these representative listings in *A Guide Book of United States Coins* (popularly known as the "Red Book") over a span of decades, from the first edition (cover date 1947) to recent times. Prices are from various editions, spaced 10 years apart, for coins listed in "Fine" grade (but see 1739 Higley for an exception, as grade reporting changed). In addition, the latest (2009 cover date) Red Book prices are listed in table 3.1.

The Whole Picture

There are many aspects to a colonial coin. Two of them, grade and price, are subject to opinion and change. These factors are important to evaluate, of course, when buying coins. Acquiring new pieces for your collection is one of the greatest pleasures and satisfactions of numismatics.

Beyond that the picture is larger. Every coin contains a generous measure of history. When was it made? By whom? What do the designs and inscriptions signify? What is the story and relative rarity of other specimens of a given variety? Simply looking at a coin for several minutes—noting the shape and position of the letters and digits, the features of the design, the dentils around the border, and other aspects—can be fascinating. Comparing two coins that differ only slightly can be even more interesting.

Study colonial coins carefully. Do this, and they will reward you immensely. This book contains much useful information beyond prices. Take advantage of the opportunity to learn as much as possible about any coin you own or contemplate acquiring. Your enjoyment will be enhanced.

Table 3.1 Red Book values for colonial coins since 1947 (in Fine except where noted otherwise)

	1947	1957	1967	1977	1987	1997	2007	2009
(1652) Massachusetts NE shilling	$250.00	$300.00	$1,350	$6,500	$8,500	$16,000	$90,000	$150,000
1652 Massachusetts Pine Tree shilling, large planchet	30.00	65.00	235	500	800	1,500	1,800	2,300
(1659) Maryland fourpence (groat)	175.00	225.00	575	4,000	4,000	4,750	6,750	7,000
1723 Rosa Americana twopence	4.00	12.00	65	160	200	200	300	300
1739 Higley threepence, "Broad Axe"	200.00	350.00	600[a]	16,000[b]	12,000	13,500	40,000	47,500
1766 Pitt "halfpenny" token	5.00	8.00	70	225	275	500	700	800
1773 Virginia halfpenny	1.25	4.50	40	45	60	75	110	110
1776 Continental dollar, "CURENCY" spelling	45.00	70.00	375	2,500	1,700[c]	3,200	11,000	11,000
1783 Chalmers threepence	50.00	80.00	325	1,400	1,700	1,800	3,000	3,500
1786 New York "Non Vi Virtute Vici" copper	200.00	225.00	575	4,500	3,000[c]	6,000	13,500	15,000
1786 Vermont "Baby Head" copper	10.00	20.00	125	550	550	825	1,200	1,750
1787 Connecticut copper "Muttonhead" variety	10.00	17.50	50	150	200	350	450	475
1787 New Jersey copper "PLURIBS" variety	6.00	7.50	40	100	150	275	475	500
1788 Massachusetts half cent	4.50	7.50	30	65	110	250	300	300
1785 Immune Columbia copper	350.00	350.00	350	—	6,000	8,250[d]	23,000	27,000[e]
(1785) Bar copper	10.00	20.00	175	600	350	900	2,750	3,250
1791 Washington Large Eagle cent	5.00	12.50	55	115	175	275	500	500
Washington "Success" token, small size	3.50	7.50	40	125	125	220	325	325
1787 Fugio "States United" copper	2.00	7.50	30	150	150	250	550	550

[a] Grade: Good (the only grade given). [b] Grade: Very Good (the highest grade listed). [c] *Sic;* a decrease. [d] Grade: None given (an error). [e] Grade: Very Fine (the only grade given).

4

HOW TO USE THIS BOOK

OVERVIEW

In the following chapters are listings for many different types and varieties of colonial coins. Each is accompanied by a history, then listings of important varieties. For many series, *all* known varieties are listed. Each is assigned an estimate of rarity per the Universal Rarity Scale (see below). These are estimates and, for many issues, are subject to change. The actual rarity of many varieties, including most of those listed in chapter 12, has not been widely studied. As time goes on, certain varieties that are rare today may become less so if two, three, or a half-dozen additional examples are discovered. As an example of this, today there are several varieties of 1787 Fugio coppers that were unknown to Eric P. Newman in his study of these in 1952. Sometimes several new varieties are discovered in the same collection.

As the majority of certified coins have not been attributed by die varieties, and as many coins exist outside the world of colonial specialists, it is likely that rarity estimates of many varieties will become more liberal in the future. By way of analogy, if on a nature walk in a park you see four deer, you know for sure that four exist. However, there may be eight others you don't see.

In many instances, attributions are cross referenced to studies by Walter H. Breen, Sylvester S. Crosby, George J. Fuld, Michael J. Hodder, Edward Maris, Sydney Martin, Henry Miller, Eric P. Newman, Hillyer C. Ryder, Robert A. Vlack, and other authors. See the Selected Bibliography for full titles. We all owe a great debt to those who have gone before us.

Most of the useful references are either available in original or reprint form, or can be acquired from dealers in out-of-print books. The Internet beckons with multiple sources, including professional numismatists. My recommendation is that you spend several hundred dollars to acquire a basic numismatic library. Crosby's *Early Coins of America* and *Walter Breen's Complete Encyclopedia of U.S. and Colonial Coins* are absolutely essential. Other titles are worthwhile and can be selected by topic. As each book yields general as well as specific information, the more you acquire, the better. There is no such thing as too much knowledge!

Membership in the Colonial Coin Collectors Club (C4) will bring you the *C4 Newsletter*, a key guide to market information, new varieties, and the overall collecting scene. The American Numismatic Society sponsors the *Colonial Newsletter*, an incomparable resource. Back issues are available on an inexpensive CD.

For many regularly traded varieties and types, this book provides estimated values, based upon auction records, information from contributors, and other sources. These have been compiled by a pricing panel chaired by Lawrence Stack. Prices can vary, sometimes widely. As discussed earlier, grading opinions and interpretations can vary widely as well. No claim, expressed or implied, is made that the present information is necessarily accurate or complete. The market continually changes, new things are learned, and opinions can be modified. That said, the text will be found as a useful and comprehensive guide to one of America's most fascinating areas of numismatics.

Whitman Numbers and Attributions

For quick reference, Whitman numbers have been assigned to each listing. As applicable, the most important or popular specialized text is cross referenced. As an example, a certain variety of 1787 Fugio copper is assigned Whitman number 6700, listed as W-6700, and a cross reference to Newman 10-G. The Whitman numbering system is open, with intervals between numbers, to permit listing of additional varieties as they are discovered.

Easy Finding Guides and Attribution

For certain series with many different die varieties, this book provides an Easy Finding Guide, listing the characteristics and, often, a photograph showing the distinguishing features. To attribute a variety, check both the obverse and reverse. Then look up the die combination, such as Obverse 4 and Reverse D, and study the entry for 4-D. If a variety seems to be very scarce or rare, double-check it. In instances of great rarity, have the coin checked by an expert. If there is a specialized text, such as Ryder-Richardson on Vermont coppers or Newman on Fugio coppers, then verify your rare find with that source. Although effort has been made with the listings and illustrations, there is always the possibility of error or the addition of new information.

Selected Auction Prices and Estimated Values

Cited under *"Selected auction price(s)"* are selected sales of important coins 2001 to date by Stack's, Heritage Auctions, McCawley & Grellman, Ira and Larry Goldberg, Bowers and Merena Galleries, Superior, and other firms. Selected earlier offerings are given for landmark rarities.

Beginning in 2003 and concluding in 2007, the John J. Ford Jr. Collection was auctioned by Stack's. The presentation far eclipsed any offering of colonial coins ever to cross the block, probably even more than any other two or three collections combined. The Ford holding comprised the essence of the Ryder, Raymond, and Boyd collections, as well as items separately gathered by Ford, including pieces from the Virgil Brand estate and the Garrett Collection. Certain of these coins are sufficiently rare that no counterparts will be available in the next two or three decades. In time, the usefulness of the Ford numbers will fade, but for the next several years they will certainly be a key to some values, although many pieces resold by Ford Collection bidders have brought higher prices. The Ford sales catalyzed the market and served as a springboard.

Citations are given only when auction offerings were described in their variety. A coin simply described as "1788 Vermont, Bust Right" and without a variety notation is not cited. Due to the knowledge needed to attribute them, many 1773 Virginia halfpence and 1785 to 1788 Connecticut coppers have been listed in catalogs only by type. Prices for such coins are not included here.

With regard to great rarities, the prices are simply guideposts. If a coin of which fewer than a half-dozen exist was sold for, say, $5,000, this does not mean that the same amount will secure another if it appears on the marketplace. The next time around, two competing bidders, each realizing that another such coin might not be offered for years, might bid it up to $10,000, $15,000, or even far more. In contrast, and to repeat an earlier comment, if at the time of a memorable offering only one or two coins were known of a die variety, but in the future a half dozen more are found, and in better average grade, a future auction price may be lower.

In recent years many colonial coin varieties often found in Mint State—such as certain Bank of New York hoard and "New Haven restrike" 1787 Fugio coppers; 1795 Talbot, Allum & Lee cents; 1773 Virginia halfpence; and certain Washington pieces—have sold for high prices if certified MS-63 or above. This reflects the entry of newcomers into the market in addition to demand from old-timers. Likely, a newcomer would not be attracted to or even be comfortable owning a Machin's Mills counterfeit halfpenny in Very Good grade. To desire and appreciate such pieces requires knowledge and understanding.

For all cited prices, refer to the catalogs themselves for complete information about the surface of the coins and other characteristics. These descriptions partly explain why some auction offerings of similarly graded coins can differ widely in price. An essential part of collecting colonial coins is the building of a useful reference library, including important auction catalogs.

Suggested valuations are provided for types and some varieties encountered with frequency, and the grids cover a wide range of grades. In such instances, selected auction prices are minimized or not given at all.

Rarity Scales

The Sheldon Rarity Scale is used in certain other texts and catalogs but not here. In that scale, an "R" or "Rarity" number is given, such as "R-5" or "Rarity-5." These numbers are estimates or guesses as to how many pieces are known. This can be translated per the following scale:

Rarity-1: More than 1,250 estimated known today.

Rarity-2: 501 to 1,250

Rarity-3: 201 to 500

Rarity-4: 76 to 200

Rarity-5: 31 to 75

Rarity-6: 13 to 30

Rarity-7: 4 to 12

Rarity-8: 2 or 3

Unique: 1 (sometimes called Rarity-9)

This text references the Universal Rarity Scale (URS). Mathematically sound in its progression and relationship among its divisions, the Universal Rarity Scale is applicable to any series. Stated simply, it is a geometric progression of numbers, rounded off for convenience in use, with each category containing about twice as many members as the preceding category. The Universal Rarity Scale uses a simple geometric progression of numbers, as 1, 2, 4, 8, 16, 32, and so on (see the rightmost of each number pair, rounded for the higher numbers).

Universal Rarity Scale

You may wish to bookmark this page for frequent reference.

URS-1	1 known, unique
URS-2	2 known
URS-3	3 or 4
URS-4	5 to 8
URS-5	9 to 16
URS-6	17 to 32
URS-7	33 to 64
URS-8	65 to 124
URS-9	125 to 249
URS-10	250 to 499
URS-11	500 to 999
URS-12	1,000 to 1,999
URS-13	2,000 to 3,999
URS-14	4,000 to 7,999
URS-15	8,000 to 15,999
URS-16	16,000 to 31,999

5
SILVER COINAGE OF MASSACHUSETTS
1652–1682

HISTORY OF THE COINAGE

Early Massachusetts Commerce

The Massachusetts Bay Colony traces its formation to the Puritan settlements of Salem (1628) and Boston (1629), a few years after the Pilgrims established the Plymouth Plantation in 1620. Under the new charter of 1691, these two colonies, together with Maine and Nova Scotia, were combined into a single political entity. In the early days, commerce was conducted by the barter system, as well as by assigning values to certain commodities. Grain, fish, cattle, and furs all were used as currency at one time or another. Indian wampum or shell money, earlier used as adornments by the natives, served in trade at set values established by the General Court. In 1635 the legislature enacted a provision ordering that musket bullets of a full bore should pass for a farthing (one-fourth of an English penny) apiece, provided that no man be compelled to take more than a shilling's worth (12 pence) of bullets at a time. Under the same law, British farthing coins in circulation were rendered invalid as currency. Crosby in *The Early Coins of America* notes:

> The purpose of this order may have been to compel a more thorough distribution of the munitions of war, which at that time were liable to be called into requisition at a moment's warning, rather than the desire to drive from circulation the small brass or copper coins of English origin which must have formed a much more agreeable medium of exchange than the bulky and inconvenient substitute here authorized.

These were the lightweight patent farthings, minted for England and Ireland under James I and Charles I, that were demonetized in 1635 because the Boston Puritans felt they were a cheat. Further, they disapproved of such monopolies. They were demonetized by the English Parliament nine years later in 1644. Many of these have been found in Virginia by metal detector–wielding coin hunters and others.

From time to time legislation was enacted to regulate the value of wampum, agricultural products, and other goods in commerce. For example, on September 27, 1642, it was ordered that wheat and barley should pass at the rate of four shillings per bushel; rye and peas at three shillings, four pence per bushel; and Indian corn at two shillings, six pence per bushel in payment of certain levies.

1652 Massachusetts Pine Tree shilling, large planchet type. (*Early Coins of America*, 1875)

Silver Coinage of Massachusetts, 1652–1682

Although English, Spanish, and other coins were occasionally seen in circulation in early Massachusetts, a large part of commerce (possibly the majority) apparently continued to be done on a barter basis. In October 1640, the shortage of circulating coins as money caused financial hardship. John Winthrop, first governor of the colony, noted in his journal:

> The scarcity of money made a great change in all commerce. Merchants could sell no wares but for ready money. Men could not pay their debts though they had enough, prices of lands and cattle fell soon to the one half and less, yea to a third, and after one fourth part.

The Massachusetts General Court on September 8, 1642, took its initial action to establish the value of foreign coins (original text):

> This Court considering the oft occasions wee have of trading with the Hollanders at the Dutch Plantation and otherwise, therefore order, that the Holland ducatoon being worth three gilders shalbee current at 6s in all payments within this jurisdicon. The rix-dollars being two and half gilders shalbee likewise current at 5s, and the ryall-of-eight shalbee also current at 5s.

Regal coins were common enough for the British colonies to sometimes reckon their accounts in pounds, shillings, and pence, but these were diluted with counterfeits. Silver shillings were met with on occasion; crown-size pieces were rare. As a result, Spanish-American 8-real coins ("Spanish dollars") and fractional parts were dominant. As described previously, "money of account" referred to bookkeeping notations used to compute the value of local circulating Massachusetts money against English monetary units, even though Spanish-American coins were more often involved than English.

As time went on, the quantity of foreign coins in circulation increased sharply, particularly issues from Spain mainly acquired through extensive trade with Europe and the West Indies. The value of such pieces was often subject to doubt, for counterfeits were abundant and coins often showed excessive wear or evidence of clipping (removing pieces of metal from the edge). In Massachusetts, it was proposed that a colonial official weigh and test individual coins and approve an official stamp to be impressed upon them, thus certifying their authenticity and weight. This proposal seems to have run into difficulties, and it is not known if coins were stamped accordingly.

It was common practice to make "change" by physically cutting coins apart. Thus, a silver shilling, if cut in half, was worth sixpence to the half. Spanish dollars or 8 reales could literally become "pieces of eight" if cut apart into pie-shaped segments, which they occasionally were. As might be expected, it was a common caper to cut an 8-real piece into nine sections and attempt to pass them off as eighths.

Establishing a Mint

On May 27, 1652, an act was passed in Massachusetts providing for the establishment of a mint, largely a reaction to the debased silver coins interfering with commerce. John Hull, who was appointed mint master, noted in his diary:

> Also upon occasion of much counterfeit coin brought into the country, and much loss accruing in that respect (and that did occasion a stoppage of trade), the General Court ordered "a mint to be set up, and to coin it, bringing it to the sterling standard for fineness, and for weight every shilling to be 3 pennyweight; that is, 9 pence at 5 shillings per ounce. And they made choice of me for that employment; and I chose my friend, Robert Sanderson, to be my partner to which the Court consented."

The act noted in part:

> After the first of September the money hereafter appointed and expressed shall be the current money of this commonwealth and no other, unless English, and except it be at the receiver's consent thereunto. In pursuance of the intent of this Court, herein be it further enacted, ordered, and enacted by the authority of this Court, that all persons whatsoever have liberty to bring into the mint house at Boston all bullion plate or Spanish coin there to be melted and brought to the alloy of sterling silver by John Hull, master of said mint, and sworn officers, and by him to be coined into 12 pence, 6 pence, and 3 pence pieces which shall be for form and flat and square on the sides and stamped on the one side with NE and on the other side with the figure XII, VI, and III—according to the value which shall be each piece, together with a privy mark—which shall be appointed every three months by the governor and known only to him and the sworn officers of the mint.
>
> And further the said master of the mint aforesaid is hereby required to coin all the said money of good silver of the just alloy of new sterling English money and for value to stamp two pence in a shilling of lesser value than the present English coin and the lesser pieces proportionately; and all such coin as aforesaid shall be acknowledged to be the current coin of this Commonwealth and passed from man to man and all payments accordingly within this jurisdiction only.
>
> And the mint master for himself and officers for their pains and labor in melting, refining, and coining is allowed by this Court to take one shilling three pence out of every twenty shillings which he shall stamp as aforesaid. And it shall be in the liberty of any person who brings into the mint house any bullion plate or Spanish coin as aforesaid to be present and see the same melted, refined, and alloyed, and then to take a receipt of the master of the mint for the weight of that which is good silver alloyed as aforesaid, for which the mint master shall deliver him the like weight in current money; that is, every shilling weighing three penny troy weight and lesser pieces proportionately, deducting allowance for coinage as before expressed. And that this order being of so great concernment may not in any particular thereof fall to the ground it is further ordered that Mr. Richard Bellingham, Mr. William Hibbens, the present Secretary Capt. John Leueret, and Mr. Thomas Clarke be a

committee appointed by this Court to appoint the mint house in some convenient place in Boston, to give John Hull, master of the mint, the oath suitable to his place, and to approve of all other officers and determine what else shall appear to them as necessary to be done for the caring and end of the whole order.

On June 22, 1652, the committee met and determined that a mint house would be built and the necessary tools and implements would be procured. The site was determined:

> The said mint house shall be set upon the land of the said John Hull; and if it is agreed between the said committee and said John Hull that when either by his death or otherwise the said John Hull shall cease to be mint master, then the country shall have the ground ye house stands upon at such price as two indifferent men, equally chosen by the country and ye said John Hull or his assigns shall determine, or else the said John Hull on the like term shall have the said house as two indifferent men shall judge it to be worth at the choice of the country.
>
> It is provided that the mint house be "16 feet square, 10 feet high, and substantially wrought."

In *The History of Massachusetts*, third edition, Hutchinson gives an account of this early mint:

> The trade of the province increasing, especially with the West Indies, where the buccaneers or pirates at this time were numerous, and part of the wealth which they took from the Spanish as well as what was produced by the trade being brought to New England in bullion, it was thought necessary, for preventing fraud in money, to erect a mint for coining shillings, sixpence, and threepence with no further impression at first than NE on one side and XII, VI, or III on the other; but in October, 1651 [*sic*, should be 1652] the Court ordered that all pieces of money should have a double ring with this inscription, MASSACHUSETTS, and a tree in the center on one side, and NEW-ENGLAND in the year of our Lord on the other side.
>
> The first money being struck in 1652, the same date was continued upon all that struck for 30 years after; and although there are a great variety of dies, it cannot be determined in what years the pieces were coined. No other colony ever presumed to coin any metal into money. It must be considered that at this time there was no king in Israel. No notice was taken of it by the Parliament or by Cromwell; in having been thus indulged, there was a tacit allowance of it afterwards even by King Charles II, for more than 20 years; and although it was made one of the charges against the colony when the charter was called in question, no great stress was laid upon it. It appeared to have been so beneficial that during Sir Edmund Andros' administration endeavors were used to obtain leave for continuing it, and the objections against it seemed not to have proceeded from its being an encroachment upon the prerogative, for the motion was referred to the master of the mint, and the report against it was upon mere prudential considerations.

> It is certain that great care was taken to preserve the purity of the coin. I do not find, notwithstanding, that it obtained a currency anywhere, otherwise than as bullion, except in the New England colonies. A very large sum was coined. The mint master, John Hull, raised a large fortune from it. He was to coin the money of the just alloy of the then new sterling English money; and for all charges which should attend melting, refining, and coining, he was to be allowed to take fifteen pence out of every twenty shillings. The Court were afterwards sensible that this was too advantageous a contract, and Mr. Hull was offered a sum of money by the Court to release them from it, but he refused to do it. [The accuracy of this statement was questioned by Crosby and others who could find no records to substantiate it.] He left a large personal estate, and one of the best real estates in the country.

Four Basic Designs Develop

Of the Pine Tree issues of the various denominations, Sydney P. Noe identified 37 different die varieties, some of these contemporary counterfeits.

In summary, the Massachusetts silver coinage comprised four different designs or formats, known by collectors as the NE (New England), Willow Tree, Oak Tree, and Pine Tree styles, extending from 1652 until 1682. The exact order of striking is not known. Other than the date 1662 for the inception of the Oak Tree twopence coinage, we know little about when types were changed—this despite many theories on the subject. Coinage was accomplished, in large quantities, and from all accounts the venture was a success. Royal opposition to the issues persisted, but no direct action was ever taken to force cessation of minting.

Today, examples of the NE coinage are rare and come on the market only occasionally. Willow Tree coins are exceedingly rare and not often encountered, even in larger collections. Oak Tree pieces are occasionally seen. Pine Tree issues, while scarce, are considerably more plentiful than the other styles, with the small-planchet Pine Tree shillings being the most common. Massachusetts silver coins, representing the first native coinage in North America, are particularly important historically.

Edge clipping of the tree coinages is a problem checked easily enough by weighing the coins. It cannot, in fact, be ascertained visually since the mint did its own clipping of planchets to reduce them to authorized weights. The standard weight for a shilling (12 pence) was 72 grains. Weights of unclipped specimens in the cabinet of the American Numismatic Society are generally from 70 to 72 grains. Fractional denominations are proportional. Regarding published weights in the Noe text, auction catalogs, and elsewhere, modern scholarship has shown that many earlier listed weights for individual specimens are incorrect when weighed today on precision scales. Most are, however, close to their stated weight.

Die descriptions in the following text are intended for easy attribution. For instances in which one die is diagnostic for the variety, the other die may not be described. More details, often fascinating and complex, can be found in Noe, the absolutely essential Ford catalog (by Michael J. Hodder, who has also helped with the present work), and other references. Rarity ratings are mostly adapted from the Ford catalog. Hodder's "A Plea for Reason" in the *Colonial Newsletter*, November 1994, commented that the Noe numbering system was clumsy in comparison to Crosby's designations of obverse and reverse dies. The Noe system outlined in *The Silver Coinage of Massachusetts* is the first cited here, despite its illogic, with cross-references to Crosby.

THE NE (NEW ENGLAND) COINAGE
1652

The initial Massachusetts silver coins consisted of three denominations: threepence, sixpence, and shilling. Although no precise record has survived, it is presumed that each piece was made by striking it twice, once on each side. First, at the top near the border of the planchet (today considered the obverse by numismatists), the letters NE were stamped by a prepared punch. Then on the reverse side of the piece, and at the other end of the planchet (so that the NE impression would not be flattened), the denomination III, VI, or XII was stamped with another prepared punch.

The coins' simplicity caused problems, so an official order was issued on October 19, 1652, providing that:

> For the prevention of washing [dissolving the silver metal by nitric acid] or clipping [trimming slivers of silver from the edge] of all such pieces of money as shall be coined within this jurisdiction:
>
> It is ordered by this Court and the authorities thereof that henceforth all pieces of money coined as aforesaid shall have a double ring on either side, with the inscription MASSACHUSETTS and a tree in the center on one side, and NEW ENGLAND in the year of our Lord on the other side, according to this drawing here in the margin. [Here was shown a crude sketch.]

While some historians have suggested that clipping and "washing" were problems at the time, surviving specimens of the NE coinage rarely show evidence of such damage. This is paradoxical, for later issues with tree designs often are found with extensive edge clipping.

It is believed that coinage of the NE series began sometime after the act became valid on September 1, 1652; Hull's assistant Sanderson had taken his oath of office on August 19. On October 19, new legislation provided for a design with double rings and other features, requiring more sophisticated technology than the device punches then in use. However, according to Louis E. Jordan's *John Hull, the Mint and the Economics of Massachusetts Coinage*, procurement and installation of a suitable coining press took time, and it was not until 1654 that the new coinage commenced.

Numismatists today have identified six different punch varieties of the NE shilling, which was the piece coined in the greatest quantities. If the privy marks specified were used on these or other coins, they have not been detected. Three different obverse NE punches and four different reverse XII punches were used in various combinations. Of the sixpence, two different punch variations are known, although one is a counterfeit of unknown age. Just one punch combination is known for the threepence, the obverse NE die being from the same punch as used on the larger sixpence.

Numismatic Aspects

(1652 Undated) NE Threepence

Whitman-1 · Noe 1-A

Obverse: NE in punched impression. Letters heavy. The same punches were used for certain VI pence. *Reverse:* III in punched impression. *Notes:* Only one authentic example is now securely located, in the Massachusetts Historical Society, ex William Sumner Appleton, 17.3 grains, holed. Another was stolen from Yale University but hopefully still exists. Fakes include examples on a bracelet with a false Timothy Dwight hallmark. *Rarity:* URS-2.

(1652 Undated) NE Sixpence

W-10 · Noe 1-A

Obverse: NE punch with heavy letters as used on the III pence. *Reverse:* VI in punch. Tall, narrow letters. *Notes:* Illustrated in Crosby as Plate I, No. 4. Not in the Hain or Ford collections. This is the genuine variety of the denomination. Examples include the Garrett, Roper, and ANS coins, plus one or two others. *Rarity:* URS-5.

G-4	VG-8	F-12	VF-20
$45,000	$90,000	$175,000	$325,000

W-20 · Noe 2-B

Obverse: NE punch with delicate letters. *Reverse:* VI in punch. Wide V, distant from bottom border of punch. *Notes:* Noe illustrates the T. James Clarke coin, ex Newcomer Collection; later in the Ford Collection; 38.3 grains and thus overweight. Michael J. Hodder in the Ford sale traces five, including one struck over a one-real coin. A counterfeit of unknown age, possibly contemporary, possibly not, this division of opinion accounting for the recent auction price. *Rarity:* URS-4.

Selected auction price(s): Garrett III Sale (B&R 10/1980), VF, $75,000. Americana Sale (Stack's 1/2008), VF-20, $13,800.

(1652 Undated) NE Shillings

W-40 · Noe I-A

Obverse: NE within border, N with diagonal extending as a tail below E. Same basic motif used on all NE shilling dies. Diagonal of N thick and becomes very thick past where the right stand of N intersects it. Serif on crossbar of E symmetrical, but with a thorn or spike extending upward from it, slightly to the right. *Reverse:* XII high in punch, X highest, second I lowest. Diagnostic. *Rarity:* URS-4.

Selected auction price(s): Ford XII Sale (Stack's 10/2005), Choice VF, Noe plate coin, $253,000.

W-50 · "Noe I-D"

Obverse: Same as preceding. *Reverse:* XII all on same level and close to bottom border. XI touch at bottom. Upper and lower left serifs of X touch edge of punch. Second I heavier than first. *Notes:* Unknown to Noe, although plated in the 1918 catalog of the Allison Jackman Collection. James Spilman and Michael J. Hodder, *CNL* May 1986, reported that three were known, and none have been located since. Finest is the Garrett coin. *Rarity:* URS-3.

Selected auction price(s): Garrett III Sale (B&R 10/1980), EF, $47,500. Hain Family Collection (Stack's 1/2002), EF, $161,000 and $172,500. Henry Leon Sale (Stack's 5/2007), EF-40, $414,000.

W-60 · Noe II-A

Obverse: Upper left serif of N gently curved. Diagonal of N thin, but becomes thick at tail. Right side of N thin. *Reverse:* Same as W-40. Usually with a die crack at the upper left of the X. *Rarity:* URS-5.

Selected auction price(s): Hain Family Sale (Stack's 1/2002), EF, $161,000 and $172,500.

W-70 · Noe III-A

Obverse: Upper left serif of N bent, with a straight section, then a tail to the left. Diagonal of N thin, but becomes thick at tail. Left upright of N wide, but becomes thin where it joins the top of the diagonal. Right side of N thin. *Reverse:* Same as W-40. With die crack at the upper left of the X. *Rarity:* URS-4.

W-80 · Noe III-B

Obverse: Same as preceding. Now with die crack diagonally down to the right from bottom of E. Serif right upright of N strengthened where it joins the diagonal. *Reverse:* X slightly lower than II; XI touch at bottom. Inside lower right serif of X is a small lump. Die crack from left bottom of second I down to border. *Rarity:* URS-4.

Selected auction price(s): Ford Collection Part XII (Stack's 10/2005), Choice VF, $345,000.

W-90 · Noe III-C

Obverse: Die crack diagonally down to the right from bottom of E. Serif on crossbar of E heavier on top. *Reverse:* X lower than II; XI do not touch at bottom. No lower left serif of X. Second I thickest. *Notes:* This is the variety most often seen. *Rarity:* URS-6.

G-4	VG-8	F-12	VF-20
$55,000	$100,000	$225,000	$325,000

THE WILLOW TREE COINAGE
1653–1660

Following the order of October 19, 1652, the design of Massachusetts coinage was changed accordingly, if a little slowly, as noted above. Obverse dies were prepared for three denominations: threepence, sixpence, and shilling. Surrounding the center tree was the legend in abbreviated form MASA THVSETS IN, and on the reverse, NEW ENGLAND AN DOM, with 1652 in the center and the denomination expressed as III, VI, or XII. These are the first dated coins struck in what would become the United States.

The tree is amorphous and consists of curls and squiggles, rather than a depiction of any particular botanical species. Collectors refer to this general type as the Willow Tree coinage, although Sydney P. Noe, in *The Silver Coinage of Massachusetts*, notes that early writers such as Joseph Felt and M.W. Dickeson did not use any particular term. W.E. Woodward, in his Sixth Sale, 1865, suggested a "palmetto tree." The earliest "willow" use found by Noe was in Woodward's 1867 sale of the Joseph Mickley Collection. The Willow Tree pieces, as they are universally designated today, were apparently produced by crude means, for all known specimens show evidence of multiple strikings.

It is probable that the blank silver planchet discs were placed into a rocker press, although details are not known. This efficient device forced a curved top die against a curved or flat bottom die. The pressure point moved as the roller moved, and greater force could be exerted than could be done with one flat die striking another. Louis E. Jordan attributes the multiple striking of details, seen especially on the earlier die varieties, to mint workers' inexperience with the press. As Willow Tree coins are slightly elongated and gently bent, the rocker press seems more likely.

Coinage of the Willow Tree series continued for an unknown time. Some scholars have suggested they were made until about 1660, which seems unlikely to this writer, unless the coinage was sporadic. All Willow Tree coins are rarities today.

The date of authorization remained constant as 1652 on this and on later coinages (excepting the 1662 Oak Tree twopence, authorized that year), although it should be mentioned that dates were not impressed on the coins until 1654. Some historians have proposed that this was to mislead the English authorities into thinking the silver coinage was temporary, for it had no authorization from the crown. However this theory raises several doubts. Massachusetts, under jurisdiction of a royal governor, openly operated a mint for many years after 1652. This fact, not to mention the continued circulation of freshly minted silver coins, belies any suggestion that coinage was kept a secret.

Sir Thomas Temple lived several years in New England during the Cromwell government. After the Restoration, he returned to England, where Charles II queried him about affairs in the Massachusetts colony. His Majesty complained that the colonists had invaded the royal prerogative by coining their own money. Temple, whose heart lay with the inhabitants of Massachusetts, informed the king that the colonists were not acquainted with detailed matters of law and that there was no criminal or subversive intent in coining their own money.

Another theory is quoted by Sylvester S. Crosby. It mentions the recollections of Edward Randolph, a commercial and political agent of the British crown who came to Boston in June 1676. A collection of Randolph's papers, issued in Boston in 1769, described the history of the Massachusetts Bay Colony and contained this account:

> As a mark of sovereignty they coin money, stamped with the inscription MATTACHUSETS, with a tree in the center, on the one side, and NEW ENGLAND, with the year 1652, and the value of the piece on the reverse. All the money is stamped with these figures, 1652, that year being the era of the common-wealth, wherein they erected themselves into a free state, enlarged their dominions, subjected the adjacent colonies under their obedience, and summoned the deputies to sit in the general court; which year is still commemorated on their coin.

The coinage apparently proceeded unhampered until 1665, when on May 8 the General Court recorded the letter sent by the king's commissioners:

> Gentlemen: We in His Majesty's name desire a book of your laws may be sent us, that we may have a perusal of your laws, such as are against this act, and such as are contrary and derogatory to the King's authority in government, mentioned in his gracious letter of June 28, 1662, may be annulled and repealed.

On May 24, 1665, the commissioners, having studied the book of laws, submitted a list of 26 items they required to be repealed or changed. The 22nd article noted:

> That page 61, title money, the law about a mint house, etc., be repealed, for coining is a royal prerogative, for the usurping of which ye act of indemnity is only a salvo.

Notwithstanding the threat, the General Court did not repeal the questioned law. Indeed, the mint's production increased over the years, apparently without royal reprisal. Regarding the 1652 date, the most likely explanation seems to be it was used simply because this was the year the coinage was authorized. Through generous mintages, Massachusetts coins were plentiful in circulation, and various laws were enacted to prevent the coins' export.

Numismatic Aspects

1652 Willow Tree Threepence

W-110 · Noe 1-A · unknown to Crosby

Obverse: Legend MASATHVSETS.IN starts at 12 o'clock. At center, within a circle of dots, a tree or bush with curved lines, designated a "willow," though bearing little relation to the appearance of that tree type in nature. Bold center dot. *Reverse:* Legend NEWENGLAND. A.D: starts at 3 o'clock. At center within a circle of dots, 1652 / III. Bold center dot. *Notes:* Only one die pair for this denomination. Three known: American Numismatic Society, Yale University (stolen and still missing), and Ford. *Rarity:* URS-3.

Selected auction price(s): Ford XII Sale (Stack's 10/2005), VF, Noe plate coin, "Only specimen ever available to collectors," $632,500.

1652 Willow Tree Sixpence

W-130 · Noe 1-A · Crosby 7

Obverse: The legend is MASATHVSETS.IN, and starts at 1 o'clock. At center, within a circle of dots, a tree or bush with curved lines. Bold center dot. *Reverse:* Legend, starting at 1 o'clock, is NEWENGLAND A. DOM:. At center, within a circle of dots, 1652 / VI. Bold center dot. *Notes:* Only one die pair for this denomination. *Rarity:* URS-6.

G-4	VG-8	F-12	VF-20	EF-40
$21,000	$37,500	$75,000	$170,000	$300,000

1652 Willow Tree Shillings

W-150 · Noe 1-A · Crosby 1-A

Obverse: Standard for type is MASATHVSETS IN around border (punctuation varies). At center, within a circle of dots, a "willow" tree. Colon after S, period after N. Per Noe, the uppermost branch touches the border and points slightly to the left of the fourth stroke of the M. A comparison of the forms and placement of the letter S, which occurs three times, is usually conclusive. The root forms have already been mentioned. *Reverse:* Standard for type is NEW ENGLAND AN DOM around border (punctuation varies). At center, within a circle of dots, 1652 / XII. Colon after D and N. Per Noe, the date and XII are high on the field. The E of NEW is small as compared with the N. A comparison of forms and placements of the four N's is frequently helpful, as the N of AN DOM has the third stroke short and heavy. *Punctuation:* NEWENGLAND : ANDOM : *Rarity:* URS-5.

Selected auction price(s): Garrett III Sale (B&R 10/1980), Superb AU, $35,000. Hain Family Sale (Stack's 1/2002), EF, Noe plate coin, $138,000. John J. Ford Jr. XII Sale (Stack's 10/2005), EF, Noe plate coin, $276,000.

W-160 · Noe 2-A · unknown to Crosby

Obverse: Per Noe, the shape of the tree is distinctive—so too is the shape of the roots. The horizontal hatchings of the trunk are peculiar to this die. The M is to be noted for its pronounced serifs. The line connecting the dots on the inner border is plainly visible. *Reverse:* Same as preceding. *Notes:* Discovered by Eric P. Newman (*ANS Notes and Monographs* 142). Two known: ANS and Norweb Collection (later in the Hain Family Collection). *Rarity:* URS-2.

Selected auction price(s): Norweb I Sale (B&M 10/1987), VF, $52,800. Hain Family Sale (Stack's 1/2002), now graded EF, $207,000.

W-170 · Noe 2-B · Crosby 2-B

Obverse: Same as preceding. *Reverse:* Per Noe, the letters are thin and elegant, with pronounced serifs—this is also true of the obverse. The border is distinctive for its fine dots. It follows the obverse in this regard. Punctuation as in Die A, but AN DOM shows differences in its spacing. *Rarity:* URS-4.

G-4	VG-8	F-12	VF-20	EF-40
$22,000	$40,000	$95,000	$200,000	$300,000

W-180 · Noe 3-C

Obverse: Per Noe, above the tree and just below the fourth stroke of the letter M is a tiny cross or other artifact, significance unknown. *Reverse:* Per Noe, die-flaw below the 5 of the date, while a crack extending downward to the right, starts from the first digit of the date, touches the 6, crosses the first I of the XII and terminates in the second I, giving the effect of a letter N following the X. *Punctuation:* NEWENGLAND : ANDOM. *Rarity:* URS-6.

Selected auction price(s): Roper Sale (Stack's 12/1983), EF, $28,600. Hain Family Sale (Stack's 1/2002), VF, mostly blank at centers, $16,100. 68th Anniversary Sale (Stack's 10/2003), VG, $14,950.

W-190 · Noe 3-D

Obverse: Same as preceding. *Reverse:* Per Noe, XII is large in scale and low on the field. The central dot is large and pronounced. *Punctuation:* NEWENGLAND ANDOM :. *Rarity:* URS-4.

Selected auction price(s): Norweb I Sale (B&M 10/1987), VF, $22,000; EF, $44,000. Hain Family Sale (Stack's 1/2002), VF, ex Norweb, $69,000; EF $172,500. John J. Ford Jr. XII Sale (Stack's 10/2005), Choice EF, Noe plate coin, $184,000.

W-200 · Noe 3-E

Obverse: Same as preceding. *Reverse:* Per Noe, lettering of border inscription is bolder and heavier than on any of preceding dies. The central dot small and light. A faint flaw connects the upper portions of the I's of XII. *Punctuation:* NEWENGLANDAN DOM. *Rarity:* URS-5.

Selected auction price(s): Hain Family Sale (Stack's 1/2002), VF, blank at centers, $19,550. John J. Ford Jr. XII Sale (Stack's 10/2005), EF, Noe plate coin, $184,000.

THE OAK TREE COINAGE
1660–1667

Following the Willow Tree coinage, the design was changed to the new so-called Oak Tree style. Certain of these were likely made by a rocker-type press, as used on the Willow Tree issues.

The term "Oak Tree" was used by numismatists at an early time. Crosby relates that Sir Thomas Temple, discussing the affairs of Massachusetts Bay in 1662, showed King Charles II pieces that must have been the Oak Tree coinage. When the king inquired as to the origin of the design, Temple said that it was the Royal Oak in which the king had secreted himself after his troops were defeated at the Battle of Worcester.

However, Louis E. Jordan pointed out that the original report, dated October 30, 1684, includes the following passage about the mint: "For in 1662, when our first agents were in England, some of our money was shown by Sir Thomas Temple at the Council-Table, and no dislike thereof manifested by any of those right honourable persons; much less a forbidding of it." The insertion of "Royal Oak" and mention of the Battle of Worcester are embellishments from later retellings.

Oak Tree coinage was made in several different denominations, including the customary threepence, sixpence, and shilling, all dated 1652. The series also introduced a new denomination, the twopence, which bore the date 1662 and was the only coin so dated among all Massachusetts silver coins. Did the date 1662 represent an error, or was 1662 used to observe the year in which this new denomination was authorized? Today, opinion among numismatists is divided on this point, with the present author inclined toward the latter explanation, for on May 16, 1662, the General Court ordered the mint master "to coin twopence pieces of silver, in proportion according to the just value and alloy of the monies, allowed here, to answer the occasions of the country for exchange." If anything, the 1662 date indicates that, by this time, Oak Tree coinage was taking place.

The arrangements with mint master Hull and his associate, Sanderson, were renegotiated on October 4, 1667. On May 12, 1675, another contract was arranged, extending the coining privilege to Hull and Sanderson for a further seven years. Crosby reports that, during the Massachusetts silver coinage period, numerous tributes—including ship masts, 3,000 codfish, and other material items—were sent to the king to incur his majesty's pleasure and to postpone any action on the Massachusetts coinage question.

Numismatic Aspects

1662 Oak Tree Twopence

W-240 · Noe-29 to 34 · Crosby 1-A.1, 1-A.2, 1-A.3

Notes: Unique denomination in the Massachusetts silver series. The variant date of 1662 refers to the year this denomination was first authorized. The span of Noe and Crosby references refers to the same die pair, but in different states. Noe-29 to 31 are Small Date; Noe-32 to 34 are Large Date, from recutting of the last two date digits. See Noe for details. Noe-31 illustrated. *Rarity:* URS-8.

G-4	VG-8	F-12	VF-20	EF-40	AU-50	MS-60
$600	$1,100	$2,300	$4,400	$7,500	$11,000	$18,000

1652 Oak Tree Threepence

W-260 · Noe-23 · Crosby 1-A.1

Obverse: S's are backward. MASATHVSETS begins near top of die. The only die with IN on the obverse. *Reverse:* In NEW the upper right of E and upper left of W nearly touch; W in right border. *Notes:* Usually slightly off center. *Rarity:* URS-6.

G-4	VG-8	F-12	VF-20	EF-40	AU-50
$675	$1,350	$3,250	$7,000	$13,000	$21,000

W-270 · Noe-24 · Crosby 2-A.1

Obverse: S's are normal. MASATHVSETS begins near top of die. Upper tip of lower left serif in E is close to and below left serif of T. *Notes:* Usually slightly off center. *Rarity:* URS-5.

Selected auction price(s): Norweb I Sale (B&M 10/1987), VF, $11,500. Hain Family Sale (Stack's 1/2002), Choice VF, $18,400; EF, $21,850. John J. Ford Jr. XII Sale (Stack's 10/2005), EF, Noe plate coin, $16,100.

W-280 · Noe-25 · Crosby 3-A.2

Obverse: S's are normal. MASATHVSETS begins near top of die. Long line to left, short line to right from base of tree.

Notes: Usually slightly off center, with extra metal beyond the outer circle of beads. *Rarity:* URS-5.

Selected auction price(s): Hain Family Sale (Stack's 1/2002), VF, irregular strike, $2,760; Choice VF, irregular strike, $4,600. John J. Ford Jr. XII Sale (Stack's 10/2005), Choice VF, Noe plate coin, $9,200; EF, $27,600.

W-290 · Noe-26 · Crosby 4-A.2

Obverse: S's are normal. MASATHVSETS begins near top of die. Curved line below tree intersects dot at its left end. *Notes:* Often with rough surfaces. Usually well centered on planchet. Michael J. Hodder comment: "Very rare, I know of 5 only. Henry Dittmer says there are 6, the last having shown up on eBay. This issue has many of the characteristics of the small planchet Pine Tree threepence and may have been struck on a screw press, too. Note it is always found perfectly centered, unlike all the other Oak Tree threepence." *Rarity:* URS-4.

Selected auction price(s): Hain Family Sale (Stack's 1/2002), Choice VF, $6,037.50. John J. Ford Jr. XII Sale (Stack's 10/2005), EF, Noe plate coin, $21,850.

W-300 · Noe-27 · Crosby 5-B

Obverse: S's are normal. MASATHVSETS begins near top of die. Five roots protrude downward from line below tree and point slightly to the left. *Notes:* Usually slightly off center. *Rarity:* URS-6.

G-4	VG-8	F-12	VF-20	EF-40
$675	$1,250	$3,100	$6,700	$11,000

W-310 · Noe-28 · Crosby 6-C

Obverse: MASATHVSETS begins at 7 o'clock; pellets in border below tree. *Reverse:* NEW begins at 7 o'clock; pellets in border below first I of date. *Notes:* Unique orientation of obverse and reverse legends on this die. Some strikes are centered, others are off center. *Rarity:* URS-6.

Selected auction price(s): Hain Family Sale (Stack's 1/2002), VF–EF, $6,325; MS, $19,550. John J. Ford Jr. XII Sale (Stack's 10/2005), F–VF, $6,325; VF, Noe plate coin, $9,200. FUN Sale (Heritage 1/2007), VF-35 (PCGS), $4,887.50.

W-320 · Noe-35 · unknown to Crosby
Obverse: MASATHVSETS begins at 8 o'clock; IN below tree. *Reverse:* Same as preceding, but later state. Three known, one holed. Walter Breen suggested that both sides are a reworking of Noe-28. *Rarity:* URS-3.

1652 Oak Tree Sixpence

W-350 · Noe-15 · Crosby 5-A
Obverse: Highest branch below space between T and H. *Reverse:* The 1 of date, if extended, points to O. *Notes:* The Bushnell coin, later owned by Stickney and Garrett, overstruck on a cut-down Massachusetts shilling with XII visible. A contemporary counterfeit in the view of some (*CNL* July 1969). "The dies of Noe-15 are excellent workmanship and the undertype is a genuine Hull shilling. It's my opinion that all Oak Tree sixpence struck over Oak Tree shillings are errors, sixpence-thick strip incorrectly run between shilling dies then run again between correct sixpence dies and the coins cut out leaving 'cut down' shilling undertypes visible. Note how the shilling undertype is always Oak Tree Noe-14, suggesting a single error event, but the sixpence overstrikes are Noe-15 or 20 or 21, suggesting several fix events." *Rarity:* URS-1.

W-360 · Noe-16 · Crosby 6-F
Obverse: Highest branch below right foot of A. *Reverse:* The 1 of date, if extended, points to bottom of left part of W. *Notes:* Usually well struck and well centered, but outer border of beads missing or incomplete. *Rarity:* URS-7.

G-4	VG-8	F-12	VF-20	EF-40	AU-50
$750	$1,300	$3,300	$7,750	$18,000	$22,000

W-370 · Noe-17 · Crosby 4-C
Obverse: Highest branch below space between T and H and points to leftmost serif of H. Tree trunk and base very distinctive; called the "Hydra Tree" by Michael J. Hodder. *Reverse:* The 1 of date, if extended, points to right foot of A. Tops of VI nearly touch. *Notes:* Likely a contemporary counterfeit. Usually with die defects on both sides. Eric P. Newman (1959) designates the perfect die as Noe-17.1. *Rarity:* URS-5.

Selected auction price(s): Norweb I Sale (B&M 10/1987), EF, $14,300. John J. Ford Jr. XII Sale (Stack's 10/2005), Choice AU, Noe plate coin, $40,250.

W-380 · Noe-18 · Crosby 2-B · Backward 2 variety
Obverse: Highest branch below space between T and H. *Reverse:* The 1 of date, if extended, points to right foot of A. Tops of VI not close. *Notes:* Obverse usually well off center. Possibly only three known. *Rarity:* URS-3.

Selected auction price(s): John J. Ford Jr. XII Sale (Stack's 10/2005), VF, Noe plate coin, $115,000.

W-390 · Noe-19 · Crosby 3-E
Obverse: Highest branch below center of H. *Reverse:* The 1 of date, if extended, points to right part of E. *Notes:* Illustrated in Crosby. Discussed by Eric P. Newman in *The Secret of the Good Samaritan Shilling* (pp. 45 ff). Considered by some (Richard August, Robert Vlack) as possibly a later (19th century) production. American Numismatic Society. Two others known, per Newman. *Rarity:* URS-3.

W-400 · Noe-20 to 22 · Crosby 1a-D, 1c-D, 1b-D
Obverse: Highest branch below left upright of H. Different obverse die states are described by Noe. *Reverse:* 1 of date if extended points to E. This reverse also used for Pine Tree sixpence Noe-32. *Notes:* At least one Noe-20 and four Noe-21 sixpence are known overstruck on cut-down Noe-14 Oak Tree shillings. Obverse typically off center, with blank planchet area at lower left. Exists in several die states, well delineated in the Ford catalog. The most available die combination of this type and denomination; among the varieties from Noe-20 to 22, Noe-22 is most often seen. Noe-21 illustrated. In general, Oak Tree sixpence are often seen with problems related to centering, weakly struck areas, and irregular planchets. Those pieces without such problems are worth a premium. *Rarity:* URS-9.

G-4	VG-8	F-12	VF-20	EF-40	AU-50	MS-60
$750	$1,300	$3,000	$7,200	$16,000	$20,000	$37,000

1652 Oak Tree Shillings

W-430 · Noe-1 · Crosby 9-H

Obverse: M at 11 o'clock. Diagnostic. *Reverse:* The 2 in date opposite first N in ENGLAND. *Notes:* Obverse border typically incomplete, reverse well centered. Usually sharply struck and very attractive. Popular and readily available variety. *Rarity:* URS-10.

G-4	VG-8	F-12	VF-20	EF-40	AU-50	MS-60
$750	$1,250	$3,400	$6,700	$11,000	$15,000	$30,000

W-440 · Noe-2 · Crosby 9-I

Obverse: Same as preceding. *Reverse:* Rosette after ANDO. The 2 in date opposite E in ENGLAND. *Notes:* Usually with several letters lightly struck on each side. Ford's Mint State may be finest. *Rarity:* URS-4.

Selected auction price(s): Norweb I Sale (B&M 10/1987), EF, light in some areas, $5,060. John J. Ford Jr. XII Sale (Stack's 10/2005), MS, Noe plate coin, $60,375.

W-450 · Noe-3 · Crosby 9-O

Obverse: Same as preceding. *Reverse:* The 2 in date opposite EW (NEW). *Notes:* Typically slightly off center. One of several Ford examples was on a very broad planchet, but of correct weight. *Rarity:* URS-6.

G-4	VG-8	F-12	VF-20	EF-40	AU-50
$1,000	$1,500	$3,750	$8,000	$12,500	$15,000

W-460 · Noe-4, Crosby 3-D

Obverse: M at 7 o'clock. Beads under left of M and under HV blended together. *Reverse:* The 6 is large; X is large. *Notes:* Obverse usually slightly off center, reverse better aligned. *Rarity:* URS-6.

G-4	VG-8	F-12	VF-20	EF-40	AU-50	MS-60
$750	$1,250	$3,300	$6,500	$10,000	$13,500	$27,000

W-470 · Noe-5 · Crosby 2-D

Obverse: M at 7 o'clock. Bottom limbs to left and right gently curved downward, then up. Highest branch points to right upright of H. Roots under line below tree (roots often resemble spikes on various Massachusetts coins). *Reverse:* Same as preceding. *Notes:* Obverse off center and slightly off planchet at the bottom. Some with tree lighter but border lettering stronger. Popular variety, readily available. *Rarity:* URS-11.

G-4	VG-8	F-12	VF-20	EF-40	AU-50	MS-60
$750	$1,250	$3,300	$6,500	$10,000	$13,500	$27,000

W-480 · Noe-6 and 7 · Crosby 1a-D and 1b-D

Obverse: M at 7 o'clock. Trunk wide and composed of vertical elements. Eleven or more roots point downward from line below tree, appearing like a rake. *Reverse:* Same as preceding. Noe-6 is very rare. Noe-7, constituting most of the population of this die combination, has tree re-engraved and D in ENGLAND nearly filled in. *Notes:* Obverse border beads missing on most. Noe-6 illustrated. *Rarity:* URS-7.

G-4	VG-8	F-12	VF-20	EF-40	AU-50
$750	$1,250	$3,300	$6,500	$10,000	$13,500

W-490 · Noe-8 · Crosby 5-A

Obverse: M at 7 o'clock. Trunk with heavy left and right outline, slight filling in between. Horizontal zig-zag serpentine line below base line of tree. Highest branch points to left upright of H. *Reverse:* 6 distant from border. Inside circle of beads mostly fused together from about 11 o'clock to 2 o'clock. *Notes:* Usually with lightness of striking in areas. *Rarity:* URS-5.

Selected auction price(s): Hain Family Sale (Stack's 1/2002), VF, $4,600; VF, sharper than preceding, $6,900. John J. Ford Jr. XII Sale (Stack's 10/2005), Choice VF, Noe plate coin, $20,700. Long Beach Sale (Heritage 6/2006), VG-10 (PCGS), $2,300. Requa Collection (Stack's [ANR] 9/2006), AU-55, $19,550. Norweb Collection (Stack's 11/2006), VF-30, $4,600.

W-500 · Noe-9 · Crosby 4-C

Obverse: M at 7 o'clock. Trunk wide and composed of multiple vertical and nearly vertical elements. Cross-hatching beneath line below tree. Beads mostly fused below MA. *Reverse:* Circles made up of elongated pellets rather than beads. Two center dots. *Notes:* Usually quite well centered. Sometimes with planchet clipped at edge, at mint, to reduce to authorized weight. *Rarity:* URS-7.

G-4	VG-8	F-12	VF-20	EF-40	AU-50
$750	$1,250	$3,300	$6,500	$10,000	$13,500

W-510 · Noe-10 to 12 · Crosby 6a-E.1 and 6b-E.2

Obverse: M at 7 o'clock. Backward N (IN). Trunk outlined to left and right, center filled with diagonal lines sloping up to right. *Notes:* In Noe-10 the tree is very light, Hodder's "Ghost Tree." This state is URS-5. Later considerably strengthened in the die. Noe-11 illustrated. *Rarity:* URS-7.

G-4	VG-8	F-12	VF-20	EF-40	AU-50
$750	$1,250	$3,300	$6,500	$10,000	$13,500

W-520 · Noe-13 · Crosby 8-F

Obverse: M at 7 o'clock. Trunk single and thin, no outline to sides. From line below tree, 4 roots slant down and to the left about 45 degrees. Backward N (IN). *Notes:* Early state of the obverse die used to coin Noe-14, listed here separately, as the alteration to Noe-14 was so extensive. Noe appears to have listed this and W-530 last among the Oak Trees because the tree shape resembles that on the large Pine Tree shillings, which he thought were struck after the Oak Trees. In actuality, the coinages may have overlapped. *Rarity:* URS-6.

G-4	VG-8	F-12	VF-20	EF-40	AU-50
$1,000	$1,500	$4,000	$8,000	$12,500	$15,000

W-530 · Noe-14 · Crosby 7-B · Spiny Tree

Obverse: As preceding, but now with extensive reworking, including a thicker trunk and thorns or spines added to the branches, now the "Spiny Tree." *Rarity:* URS-9.

G-4	VG-8	F-12	VF-20	EF-40	AU-50
$750	$1,250	$3,500	$7,000	$12,000	$17,000

THE PINE TREE COINAGE
1667–1682

Oak Tree coinage continued in production until the type was replaced by a new design displaying on the obverse a clear representation of a pine tree. This motif was not a whimsical choice but depicts the tree shown on Massachusetts Bay Colony flag. The flag's design featured a red field with a white canton in the upper left, in which was a red cross with a pine tree in its upper left quadrant.

Denominations in the Pine Tree coinage were threepence, sixpence, and shilling. Shillings were made in two formats, with earlier styles (until about 1675) made with a rocker press on thin, broad planchets, and later issues (1675–1682) struck with a screw press on smaller, thicker planchets. Both styles were made in large numbers, and the number of specimens existing today suggests that the small-planchet Pine Tree shillings may have been made in the largest quantities of all. Michael J. Hodder, student of the series and cataloger of colonials in the Ford Collection, suggests that certain coinages may have overlapped, such as Oak Tree and Pine Tree motifs.

Pine Tree coinage continued until at least 1682. Crosby cites documents from 1684 that mention the mint in the past tense, suggesting it closed prior to that date. The agreement with mint master Hull expired in May 1682, so this probably marked the latest date pieces were struck. Hull died on October 1, 1683.

It has been suggested by Crosby and seconded by Sydney P. Noe that the small-planchet Pine Tree issues were made to prolong the life of coinage dies.

Numismatic Aspects

1652 Pine Tree Threepence

W-630 · Noe-34 · Crosby 1-A.1

Obverse: Pellet to each side of tree (privy mark?). Four branches on left. V nearly touches bead. *Reverse:* First I (III) touches bead. Bottom of 2 points to interior right of N. *Rarity:* URS-8.

G-4	VG-8	F-12	VF-20	EF-40	AU-50
$550	$800	$1,800	$3,500	$6,250	$10,000

W-635 · Noe-35 · Crosby 1-A.2

Obverse: Same as preceding. *Reverse:* Die as preceding, reworked and now with ANO added. H recut, now smaller; a die break obscures the second A. *Rarity:* URS-4.

Selected auction price(s): Hain Family Sale (Stack's 1/2002), EF, $8,625. Pre–Long Beach (I. & L. Goldberg 9/2002), VF-20, $2,300. Long Beach (Heritage 9/2003), AU-50 (PCGS), $4,945. Baltimore (B&M 7/2004), AU-50 (PCGS), $5,520. John J. Ford Jr. XII Sale (Stack's 10/2005), EF, Noe plate coin, $9,775.

W-640 · Noe-36 and 37 · Crosby 2a-B and 2b-B

Obverse: No pellets to each side of trunk. Three branches on left. V distant from bead. *Reverse:* First I (III) distant from bead. Bottom of 2 points to left upright of N. *Notes:* Noe-36 is the more available of the two die states. Noe-36 illustrated. *Rarity:* URS-9.

G-4	VG-8	F-12	VF-20	EF-40	AU-50
$550	$800	$1,800	$3,500	$6,250	$10,000

1652 Pine Tree Sixpence

W-660 · Noe-32 · Crosby 2-D [Oak Tree reverse] · Spiny Tree

Obverse: "Spiny Tree." Cross-hatching below tree touches beads. No pellets. *Reverse:* 1 (1652) opposite W, right outside curve of 2 opposite left upright of N. *Notes:* Reverse used in the Oak Tree series, Noe-20 to 22. The only case of die linkage between two tree types. *Rarity:* URS-6.

G-4	VG-8	F-12	VF-20	EF-40	AU-50	MS-60
$600	$950	$2,000	$4,200	$7,500	$12,000	$22,000

W-670 · Noe-33 and 33a · Crosby 1-A

Obverse: Bottom of tree distant from beads. No cross-hatching. Pellet to each side of tree (privy mark?). *Reverse:* The 1 (1652) is opposite E; right outside curve of 2 opposite A. *Notes:* Noe-33 is usually slightly off center. The usually seen variety of this denomination. Noe-33 illustrated. *Rarity:* URS-10.

G-4	VG-8	F-12	VF-20	EF-40	AU-50	MS-60
$600	$925	$1,900	$3,900	$6,800	$11,000	$21,000

1652 Pine Tree Shillings, Large Planchet

W-690 · Noe-1 · Crosby 12-I

Obverse: Top of tree points to S. Diagnostic. Tree small. Pellet to each side of tree (privy mark?). Four roots extend from below tree down to right. *Notes:* This is considered by many to be the "poster example" of the classic Pine Tree shilling, or even the quintessential colonial coin. The Eliasberg Collection specimen was widely exhibited in this context. Fortunately for those seeking to acquire an example, Noe-1 is readily available in the marketplace. The assertion that this was the first Pine Tree shilling die variety struck has no substantiation. Massachusetts silver is one of the perennial favorites in the colonial series because it is the first coinage struck for the colonies in America; and also because it is one of few colonial series struck in silver. As with most Massachusetts silver pieces, Pine Tree shillings can come with a myriad of issues from irregular planchets to weakly struck areas to issues of centering. The more free of these issues any given piece is, the more premium it will carry in the marketplace. Richard Picker published a sub variety of Noe-1 in his dissertation in *Studies on Money in Early America*, ANS 1976; dies of Noe-1, but obverse and reverse reworked, with the date completely different. Probably unique. Quite remarkable. *Rarity:* URS-11.

G-4	VG-8	F-12	VF-20	EF-40	AU-50	MS-60
$700	$1,100	$2,300	$5,000	$8,500	$13,000	$24,000

W-700 · Noe-2 · Crosby 4-F · Straight Tree

Obverse: Top of tree points to slightly left of bottom point of V; seen only on Noe-2 and 3. No. pellets. Branches are straight and extend upward diagonally. *Notes:* Often called the Straight Tree, from the branches. Often with planchet clipped at the mint to reduce to authorized weight. *Rarity:* URS-7.

G-4	VG-8	F-12	VF-20	EF-40	AU-50
$700	$1,000	$2,300	$4,750	$8,250	$12,500

W-710 · Noe-3 · Crosby 3-F

Obverse: Top of tree points to slightly left of bottom point of V. Branches are gently curved. This die was made by completely re-engraving the center of Noe-2, creating a different tree. Some other changes were made as well, but the alignment of letters remains essentially the same. *Notes:* Usually well struck. Incomplete borders. *Rarity:* URS-6.

Selected auction price(s): Garrett III Sale (B&R 10/1980), AU, $11,000. Hain Family Sale (Stack's 1/2002), VF, $4,600; EF, ex Norweb, $9,200. John J. Ford Jr. XII Sale (Stack's 10/2005), Choice EF, $63,250.

W-720 · Noe-4 to 6 · Crosby 5-B.1, 5-B.2, 5a-B.2

Obverse: Top of tree points to right upright of H. First and second branches on left are close on trunk, third is distant; second left branch not split at end. Diagnostic. *Notes:* Noe-4 is the usually seen die state. Striking varies. Noe-4 illustrated. *Rarity:* URS-7.

G-4	VG-8	F-12	VF-20	EF-40	AU-50	MS-60
$700	$1,000	$2,300	$4,750	$8,250	$12,500	$25,000

W-730 · Noe-7 · Crosby 7-B.3

Obverse: Top of tree points to slightly left of S. Diagnostic. Center of M directly below tree trunk. *Notes:* Obverse typically slightly off center. *Rarity:* URS-5.

G-4	VG-8	F-12	VF-20	EF-40	AU-50	MS-60
$700	$1,000	$2,300	$4,750	$8,250	$12,500	$30,000

W-740 · Noe-8 · Crosby 1b-D
Obverse: Top of tree points to right upright of H. Beads below S at 1 o'clock can be normal, or on another state, missing. Early state of the same die used for Noe-8. *Reverse:* Bottom of 5 over first I. *Notes:* Obverse typically slightly off center. One of the more available large planchet varieties. Rarity: URS-9.

G-4	VG-8	F-12	VF-20	EF-40	AU-50	MS-60
$700	$1,100	$2,300	$5,000	$8,500	$13,000	$23,000

W-750 · Noe-9 and 10 · Crosby 1b-C, 1a-C
Obverse: Top of tree points to right upright of H. Late state with three tiny pellets below S at 1 o'clock. Diagnostic. *Reverse:* Bottom of 5 over upper right of X. *Notes:* Noe-10 (illustrated) has tree re-engraved and is considerably the more available of the two die states. Rarity: URS-10.

G-4	VG-8	F-12	VF-20	EF-40	AU-50
$700	$1,000	$2,300	$4,750	$8,250	$12,500

W-760 · Noe-11 · Crosby 2a-A.1
Obverse: Spelled MASATUSETS (without H). Diagnostic. Top of tree points to S between center and left serif. M at 7 o'clock. A at 3 o'clock. *Notes:* Usually with lightly struck reverse. Popular variety. Rediscovery of later state, Crosby 2b-A.2 reported by Walter Breen in *CNL* 4. Tree recut, branches no longer disconnected. Roots re-engraved. Colons added after D, N, and M. Serif added to top of G. Rarity: URS-7.

G-4	VG-8	F-12	VF-20	EF-40	AU-50
$900	$1,700	$3,500	$9,000	$17,000	$25,500

W-770 · Noe-12 · Crosby 6-K
Obverse: Top of tree points to space left of H. Diagnostic. Four pellets in border below trunk. N backward. *Notes:* Unique. Newman Collection, ex Castine hoard. Rarity: URS-1.

W-780 · Noe-13 · Crosby 9-G
Obverse: Top of tree points to center of S. Diagnostic. Six pairs of branches gently curved upward. *Notes:* Contemporary counterfeit. Usually in low grades with incomplete legends. Finest is Noe plate coin, Very Fine. Ford's (illustrated) was clipped and well worn with most legends gone. Rarity: URS-4.

Selected auction price(s): Hain Family Sale (Stack's 1/2002), VG, parts illegible, $2,415. John J. Ford Jr. XII Sale (Stack's 10/2005), F, with problems, $5,750.

W-790 · Noe-14 · unknown to Crosby
Obverse: Top of tree points to S(?). Trunk heavy at bottom, thinner toward top. Six pairs of branches curve gently upward. Space between A and T at the 3 o'clock position. *Reverse:* Right of base of 2 is thick with a point protruding to the left; I is close under it. *Notes:* A contemporary counterfeit. Two known to Noe, both worn and clipped, and held by Yale University; Richard August has owned three. Michael Hodder (Hain catalog) estimated "as few as 20." Rarity: URS-6.

Selected auction price(s): Hain Family Sale (Stack's 1/2002), VG, with problems, $1,725.

1652 Pine Tree Shillings, Small Planchet

W-830 · Noe-15 · Crosby 24-N
Obverse: Top of tree points to S. Diagnostic. *Notes:* Usually well struck. Later states are weak at lower right reverse. Small planchet Pine Trees, struck on a screw press, are generally sharper and better centered than the large planchet styles (made on a rocker press). *Rarity:* URS-7.

G-4	VG-8	F-12	VF-20	EF-40	AU-50
$600	$925	$1,900	$4,200	$7,500	$12,500

W-835 · Noe-16 · Crosby 21-L
Obverse: Top of tree points to outer left side of S. Diagnostic. *Reverse:* Inner circle is slightly misshapen and comes to a shallow "point" opposite 1 (1652). Lower left serif of 1 and upper left serif of X opposite each other. 5 and 2 on same level; tops of 5 and 2 not close. Long-lived die used on next several varieties. *Notes:* Usually well struck and very attractive. Readily available variety. *Rarity:* URS-11.

G-4	VG-8	F-12	VF-20	EF-40	AU-50	MS-60
$600	$925	$1,900	$4,200	$7,500	$12,500	

W-840 · Noe-17 · Crosby 22-L
Obverse: Top of tree points to just right of center point of V. TH nearly touch; lower right of H re-engraved. *Reverse:* Die of Noe-16. *Notes:* Usually well struck and attractive. Popular variety. *Rarity:* URS-9.

G-4	VG-8	F-12	VF-20	EF-40
$600	$925	$1,900	$4,200	$7,500

W-845 · Noe-18 · Crosby 23-L
Obverse: Top of tree points to left edge of side of V. Early state of die also used for Noe-24. *Reverse:* Die of Noe-16. *Notes:* Usually slightly off center on the obverse side. *Rarity:* URS-5.

Selected auction price(s): Hain Family Sale (Stack's 1/2002), EF, ex Parmelee Collection, $16,100. Kennywood Collection (Stack's [ANR] 1/2005), VF-20, $3,220. John J. Ford Jr. XII Sale (Stack's 10/2005), EF, $29,900.

W-850 · Noe-19 · Crosby 20-L
Obverse: Top of tree points to just right of center point of V. TH widely spaced; letters small. Bottom branch on each side normal thinness. *Reverse:* Die of Noe-16. A new die crack extends from the outer border to the top of the E in NEW. *Notes:* Often with areas of light striking. *Rarity:* URS-7.

G-4	VG-8	F-12	VF-20	EF-40
$600	$925	$1,900	$4,200	$7,500

W-860 · Noe-20 · Crosby 18-L
Obverse: Top of tree points to between H and V. Diagnostic. *Reverse:* Die of Noe-16. The 2 is opposite A. *Notes:* Obverse usually slightly off center. Rare variety. Ford had two. *Rarity:* URS-4.

Selected auction price(s): Hain Family Sale (Stack's 1/2002), VF, clipped, $3,737.50. FUN Sale (Heritage 1/2002), VF-30 (PCGS), $2,645. John J. Ford Jr. XII Sale (Stack's 10/2005), VF, $6,325; AU, Noe plate coin, $34,500. FUN Sale (Heritage 1/2007), VF-30 (PCGS), $4,025.

W-865 · Noe-21 · Crosby 17-L
Obverse: Top of tree points to just right of center point of V. TH widely spaced; letters small. Bottom branch on each side very thick. *Reverse:* Die of Noe-16. *Notes:* Not in the Ford Collection. Noe knew of just two, one in ANS and the other the Crosby plate coin. *Rarity:* URS-2.

W-870 · Noe-22 · Crosby 16-L
Obverse: Top of tree points to just right of center point of V. TH widely spaced; letters small. Curved ground below tree very wide with 10 pellets from left edge to right edge. *Reverse:* Die of Noe-16. *Notes:* Obverse usually slightly off center. Some lightness on reverse. *Rarity:* URS-4.

Selected auction price(s): Hain Family Sale (Stack's 1/2002), VF, $4,140; Noe plate coin, $4,891.50; EF, $5,462.50. John J. Ford Jr. XII Sale (Stack's 10/2005), Choice VF, $13,800.

W-875 · Noe-23 · Crosby 16-M
Obverse: Same as preceding. *Reverse:* W (NEW) as two V's. The 1 is heavy and leans right; positioned farther right than on Reverse L. Base of 5 lower than other digits. Tops of 5 and 2 closer than on Reverse L. G far too high and distant from inner circle. Some die deterioration below A (AN). *Notes:* Usually well centered. Obverse usually slightly lightly struck. *Rarity:* URS-5.

Selected auction price(s): C4 Convention (M&G 11/2002), VF-30, $4,550. Hain Family Sale (Stack's 1/2002), VF, $3,910; $5,462.50. Kennywood Collection (Stack's [ANR] 1/2005), F-15, $1,610. John J. Ford Jr. XII Sale (Stack's 10/2005), VF, $5,175; Noe plate coin, $9,200.

W-880 · Noe-24 · Crosby 23-M
Obverse: Later state of die used with Noe-18. *Reverse:* Same as preceding. Now with a cud under A (AN). *Notes:* Usually well centered. A rarity. Ford's was Very Fine. *Rarity:* URS-4.

Selected auction price(s): Norweb I Sale (B&M 10/1987), VF, $24,200; to Hain Family Sale (Stack's 1/2002), Choice VF, $21,850. John J. Ford Jr. XII Sale (Stack's 10/2005), VF, Noe plate coin, $23,000.

W-890 · Noe-25 · Crosby 16-O
Obverse: Same as used for Noe-22 and 23, but with signs of additional use. *Reverse:* W (NEW) as two V's. In date, 1 heavy and leans right; 16 slightly low; 2 heavy except for base. II's low and lean left, second I heavy. *Notes:* Usually slightly off center. Top of second A (MASATHVSETS) missing. *Rarity:* URS-7.

G-4	VG-8	F-12	VF-20	EF-40	AU-50	MS-60
$600	$925	$1,900	$4,200	$7,500	$12,500	$25,000

W-900 · Noe-26 · Crosby 15-O
Obverse: Top of tree points to right edge of side of V. *Reverse:* Same as preceding, now with slightly enlarged die cracks. *Notes:* Typically well centered and very attractive. *Rarity:* URS-7.

G-4	VG-8	F-12	VF-20	EF-40
$600	$925	$1,900	$4,200	$7,500

W-905 · Noe-unlisted · assigned "Crosby 15-Q"
Obverse: Same as preceding. *Reverse:* 65 and XI widely spaced. Per Noe, the X has a pigeon-toed appearance. *Notes:* Combination of the obverse of Noe-26 and the reverse of Noe-27. Reported by Walter Breen in *CNL* July 1961. Then in the Norweb Collection. *Rarity:* URS-1.

W-910 · Noe-27 · Crosby 18-Q
Obverse: Same die as used for Noe-20, but with further development of break at top of tree. *Reverse:* Same as preceding. *Notes:* Usually poorly struck, "dreadful" per Michael J. Hodder's comment in the Ford catalog. *Rarity:* URS-5.

Selected auction price(s): Hain Family Sale (Stack's 1/2002), F, $2,415; F to VF, $5,750. John J. Ford Jr. XII Sale (Stack's 10/2005), Choice F, Noe plate coin, $14,950.

W-920 · Noe-28 · Crosby 19-Q

Obverse: Top of tree points to upper right serif of V. *Reverse:* Same as preceding. *Notes:* Reverse usually lightly struck. Rare variety usually seen in lower grades. Ford's was Very Fine. *Rarity:* URS-5.

Selected auction price(s): Hain Family Sale (Stack's 1/2002), VF, $4,887.50. Mail Bid Sale (Coin Galleries 7/2005), Choice F, $2,300. John J. Ford Jr. XII Sale (Stack's 10/2005), VF, Noe plate coin, $7,475.

W-930 · Noe-29 · Crosby 14-R

Obverse: Top of tree points to tip of lower right serif of H. Diagnostic. Four pellets in border below and slightly left of trunk. *Reverse:* Colon after each word. *Notes:* Usually well struck. Popular variety. *Rarity:* URS-10.

G-4	VG-8	F-12	VF-20	EF-40	AU-50
$600	$925	$1,900	$4,200	$7,500	$12,500

W-935 · Noe-30 · Crosby 13-S

Obverse: Top of tree points to left edge of side of V. Four pellets in border below trunk. *Reverse:* Three dots after AN. In date, 5 shaped like a cedilla, with point opposite upper right serif of first I. The 2 is too far right and into beads. *Notes:* Usually well struck. Tops of some letters off planchet. *Rarity:* URS-10.

G-4	VG-8	F-12	VF-20	EF-40
$600	$925	$1,900	$4,200	$7,500

W-940 · Noe-31 · Crosby 8-E

Obverse: Per Noe, heavy-branched tree is set high in the field. Lower element of E is exceptionally long. The inner border has widely spaced dots. *Reverse:* Per Noe, only the last two digits of the date visible (on the only example known to Noe). The beads of the inner border are carelessly spaced. *Notes:* A contemporary counterfeit. Two or three known. *Rarity:* URS-2.

W-960 · Noe-18 · Crosby 22-M

Notes: Muling of two known dies. *Rarity:* URS-1.

6

British Coins and Tokens for America, Early Issues

Maryland (Lord Baltimore) Coinage
c. 1658

History

On June 20, 1632, Cecil Calvert, the second Lord Baltimore, received from King Charles I of England a grant for a new province to be named for the queen, Mary; it was designated "Terra Maria," or Maryland. The king's royalty was to consist of one fifth of any gold and silver found there, plus a yearly tribute of two Indian arrows. On November 22, 1633, the *Ark* and the *Dove* left the Isle of Wight, near the coast of England, and set sail for the new territory. On February 24, 1634, the adventurers arrived in the colony of Virginia. After spending nearly three months there, they left on May 8 for their new land. Much of what Sylvester S. Crosby presented in 1875 concerning early Maryland coinage was drawn from S.S. Streeter's "Sketch of the Early Currency in Maryland and Virginia," a paper read before the Historical Society of Maryland and published in *The Historical Magazine*, Volume II, 1858. Since then, other studies have been published, perhaps the most comprehensive being Louis E. Jordan's "Lord Baltimore Coinage and Daily Exchange in Early Maryland," in the *Colonial Newsletter*, August–December 2004.

Maryland's principal commodity in the early days was tobacco, as it was also in Virginia. For a time the crop saw service as a circulating medium; rents for certain land were payable in tobacco at a stated value. From time to time, corn, furs, wampum (called "roanoke"), powder and shot (one pound of powder equaling three pounds of shot), and other articles of trade and commerce also served as currency. Circulating metallic coinage was rare.

When Lord Baltimore regained control of Maryland in November 1657 (having lost it during the early part of the Commonwealth period), he appointed Josias Fendall as governor and Philip Calvert (Lord Baltimore's brother) as provincial secretary. Lord Baltimore initiated a coinage, and his brother was the "point man" for having it prepared in England for use in Maryland. Dies were prepared and specimens struck, probably at the Royal Mint (Richard Pight, mentioned below, was keeper of the dies there). On October 16, 1659, Cecil Calvert sent letters to the governor and the council and also to his brother. To the council went the following communication:

Maryland silver shilling. (Engraving by John Gavit for O'Callaghan, *The Documentary History of the State of New-York*, 1850)

50

After my hardy commendations, having of great pains and charges procured necessaries for a particular coin to be current in Maryland, a sample whereof, a piece of a shilling, a sixpence, and a groat [a silver coin of the value of four pence], I herewith send you, I recommend it to you to promote, all you can, to dispersing it, and by proclamation to make current within Maryland, for all payments upon contracts or causes happening or arising after a day to be by you limited in the said proclamation; and to procure an act of Assembly for the punishing of such as shall counterfeit the said coin or otherwise offend in that behalf, according to the form of an act recommended by me last year to my governor and secretary; or as near it as you can procure from the assembly, and to give me your advice next year touching upon what you think best to be further done in that matter touching coin; for its encouragement be given by the good success of it this year, there will be abundance of adventurers in it the next year.

At the same time the following letter went to Lord Baltimore's brother, Philip, then serving as secretary of state:

To my most affectionate, loving brother, Philip Calvert, Esq., at St. Mary's, in Maryland.

I sent a sample of the Maryland money, with directions for the procuring it to pass, because I understood by letters this year from the governor and you and others that there was no doubt but the people there would accept of it, which if we find they do, there will be means found to supply you all there with money enough; but though it would be a very great advantage of the Colony that it should pass current there, and an utter discouragement for the future supply of any more, if there be not a certain establishment this year, and assurance of its being vended and current there, yet it must not be imposed upon the people but by a law there made by their consent in a General Assembly, which I pray fail not to signify to the governor and Council there together from me, by showing them this letter from your most affectionate brother, C. Baltimore.

Lord Baltimore actively tried to get the Maryland Assembly to consent to accepting his coinage in 1659 and 1660, but the legislation was put on hold. There was serious Protestant opposition to Baltimore's stand on several issues that nearly resulted in the government's overthrow in 1660. Following this attempted coup, Baltimore put Governor Fendall on trial for treason and afterwards promoted his brother, Philip, to the governorship.

During Philip Calvert's first legislative session as governor, following the convening of the Assembly on April 17, 1661, the mint act was passed. Thus two years passed before Baltimore was able to issue the coins he had minted in 1659. In the meantime, England witnessed a significant event in 1660 with end of the Commonwealth (which had consented to Baltimore's coinage in 1659) and the restoration of the monarchy. Given this new political situation in England, several Marylanders were cautious about passing Baltimore's coinage legislation, even after the Protestant rebellion was suppressed. In fact, even in the governor's council, the final vote was 4-1, with one of Philip Calvert's hand-picked councilors opposed to it; this person was a Calvert supporter and three years later married Lord Baltimore's niece, so his opposition most likely was not a political statement against the Calvert rule. The 1661 act provided that a mint be established to coin pieces "as good silver as the current coin of English sterling money." Suitable punishment was specified for counterfeiters.

On April 12, 1662, the Assembly passed an act to promulgate the circulation of Maryland coinage. This legislation specified that every householder and freeman in the province must accept 10 shillings for every taxable individual in their charge or custody, and the silver was to be exchanged for casks of tobacco, valued at two pence per pound.

This caused a mandated exchange by every taxable person of 60 pounds of tobacco for 10 shillings of the new coinage. Although Streeter estimated there were at least 5,500 taxable persons in Maryland at the time, Louis E. Jordan found that in 1663 there were 2,873 taxables (records for 1662 do not exist). At full participation, this would calculate to an emission of £1,436 10s in Baltimore silver.

In 1662 the price of tobacco dropped to 1.6d per pound. Baltimore had anticipated a return of 2d per pound, which would have given him about a 20 percent profit (after factoring in minting and transportation costs). Based on the lower tobacco price, Baltimore actually lost money on the exchange of tobacco for coinage.

In 1671, Ogilby, referring to Maryland in his *Description of the New World*, noted that

the general way of traffic in commerce there is chiefly by barter, or exchange of one commodity for another; yet there wants not, besides English and other foreign coins, some of his lordship's own coin, as groats, sixpences, and shillings, which his Lordship at his own charge caused to be coined and dispersed throughout that province; 'tis equal in fineness of silver to English sterling, being of the same standard, but of somewhat less weight, and hath on one side his Lordship's coat of arms stamped, with this motto circumscribed Crescite & Multiplicamini, and on the other side his Lordship's effigies, circumscribed thus, Caecilius Dominus Terrae-Mariae, &c.

The fact that certain coinage was actually done in England is attested to by the orders of the Council of State in England (reference: *State Papers*, London, Volume 157) which noted:

Tuesday, 4 October, 1659. Lord Baltimore to be apprehended. Upon information given by Richard Pight, Clerk of the Irons in the Mint, Cecil Lord Baltimore and diverse others with him, and for him, have made and transported great sums of money and due still go on to make more,

Ordered, that a warrant be issued forth to the said Richard Pight for the apprehending of the Lord Baltimore and such others as are suspected to be engaged with him in the said offence, and for the ceasing of all such monies, stamps, tools, instruments for coining the same as can be met with, and to bring them in safe custody to the Council.

On the following day a somewhat similar action was taken by the same group:

> Wednesday, 5 October, 1659. Lord Baltimore to attend. The Council being informed that great quantities of silver is coined into pieces of diverse rates and values and sent to Maryland by the Lord Baltimore or his order,
>
> Ordered, that the said Lord Baltimore be summoned to attend the Committee of the Council for Plantations, who are to inquire into the whole business and to report the state thereof to the Council.

The fate of the Council inquiry is unknown. Importantly, the alleged offense was the *exporting* of specie, not the actual making of the coins. The success of the Maryland pieces in circulation has led historians to believe that some type of arrangement was made that did not prohibit the coins' further issue. Although the legislation of May 1, 1661, provided for the establishment of a native mint, no record of such an operation has been found.

Numismatic Aspects

Specimens exist today of the various silver denominations, the groat, sixpence, and shilling. In addition, at least eight specimens are known of the copper alloy denarium or penny. The last may have been a pattern, or there may have been limited circulation (as evidenced by wear on some specimens and one being found with a metal detector).

Michael J. Hodder has furnished this commentary:

> Calvert's charter granted him palatine rights in Maryland. Notice the crown on the reverse of his silver coinage. It is an earl's (British equivalent to a German count palatine) coronet, but has an arch above it surmounted by an orb crucifer, symbols of sovereignty.
>
> The terms of the charter were written to be as broad, and the rights granted Calvert as sweeping, as those ever enjoyed by any bishop of Durham. Durham had full sovereign rights over his lands. Only the king's personal presence trumped his control. In medieval times even the king's writ didn't run there! Thus, Calvert could appoint a governor and council for Maryland, fix its prices and wages, and control its commerce and diplomacy. He also had the coinage right, as Durham always had.
>
> There is a facsimile in the Maryland Historical Society of Cecil Calvert's 1632 grant of arms. It shows a ducal crown with two staves flying pennons. This is exactly the type seen on the back of the denarium. I suspect the type difference is to be explained by the fact that copper was never considered (until 1772) a medium suitable for a royal coinage (as opposed to tokens), and in the absence of laws against coining in that metal Calvert felt no pressing need to justify his denarii by iconographically pleading his charter.

There never was a question raised about Calvert's charter granting him the right to coin. Nor his right to put his own head on his coins. He was brought up on charges of illegally exporting silver out of the Commonwealth. Attacks against him took the form of challenges to his right to hold his charter at all. Calvert's coinage was the first struck in England specifically for any American colony. Like the Massachusetts Bay colony, Calvert kept his coinage's fineness sterling but held his coins' weights to nine pence in the shilling. Both Maryland and Massachusetts did this in the hopes of restricting circulation to within their borders. Massachusetts failed because initial quantities (Oaks and large Pines) were high enough that its consistent weight and fineness made it popular. Seeing a chance at profit Hull just increased output. In contrast, Maryland succeeded because its initial output was small, its external trade negligible, its local economy moribund, and its politics violent.

The legend on the reverse of the silver coinage is from Genesis I, 28: "Benedixitque illis Deus, et ait: Crescite et multiplicamini, et replete terram." translating to "and God blessed them (i.e., Adam & Eve) and said Increase and be multiplied and fill the earth." The Dns after Caecilivs on the obverse is the standard medieval abbreviation for Dominus, meaning Lord.

On the coins' obverse is the bust (head and shoulders) of Cecil Calvert facing left. CÆCILIUS Dns TERRÆ-MARIÆ &C. (or &CT. on the shillings) is around the border, with punctuation and cross. The reverse of the denarium features a crown. The silver issues have the Calvert arms crowned, orb and cross above, with the denomination divided by the shield, as I V, V I, and X II. Around the border is CRESCITE ET MVLTIPLICAMINI. Diameters are about 20.5 mm for the denarium, 16.3 mm for the fourpence, 21 mm for the sixpence, and 27 mm for the shilling.

The silver issues enjoyed an extensive circulation, and most examples seen today show considerable wear. Very Good, Fine, and Very Fine are typical grades, often with surface marks or damage. Any coin conservatively graded About Uncirculated or higher is a major rarity. Attributions are to Michael J. Hodder's delineation in the Norweb catalog.

Maryland Denarium (Penny)

W-1000 · Hodder 1-A

Obverse: Head of Cecil Calvert facing left, inscription around. *Reverse:* Baronial crown with two flags. DENARIVM TERRÆ MARIÆ around the border, with punctuation and cross. Edge plain. *Notes:* Breen-76. 20.7 mm. Hodder has traced seven examples. Finest is the Ford coin. *Portsmouth* [N.H.] *Journal*, October 1, 1859: "Great Prices for Old Coins—A great sale of old coins [Joseph Martin

Collection], by auction, has recently taken place in London, and enormous prices were obtained. . . . Among the coins struck for America may be mentioned the Lord Baltimore penny, said to be unique, $362." *Rarity:* URS-4.

Selected auction price(s): Roper Sale (Stack's 12/1983), VF, $13,200. John J. Ford Jr. II Sale (5/2004), AU, $241,500. J.A. Sherman Collection (Stack's 8/2007), VG-7, $41,400.

Maryland Fourpence (Groats)

W-1010 · Hodder 1-A · Large Bust, hyphen in TERRÆ-MARIÆ
Obverse: Head of Cecil Calvert facing left, inscription around. Hyphen in TERRÆ-MARIÆ. *Reverse:* Calvert arms and inscription. I and V divided by shield. *Notes:* Breen-74. *Rarity:* URS-6.

G-4	VG-8	F-12	VF-20	EF-40	AU-50
$5,000	$7,500	$12,000	$24,000	$40,000	$70,000

W-1020 · Hodder 2-B · Small Bust, no hyphen in TERRÆ MARIÆ
Obverse: Head of Cecil Calvert facing left, inscription around. No hyphen in TERRÆ MARIÆ. *Reverse:* Calvert arms and inscription. I and V divided by shield. Unique. Stolen from the Massachusetts Historical Society. Acquired unknowingly by Richard Picker and sold into the Norweb Collection. Auctioned in the Norweb sale by agreement, with proceeds to the MHS. Now in a New York collection. *Notes:* Breen-75. *Rarity:* URS-1.

Selected auction price(s): Norweb III Sale (11/1988), EF, $26,400.

Maryland Sixpence

W-1030 · Hodder 1-A · Large Bust, copper
Obverse: Head of Cecil Calvert facing left, inscription around. *Reverse:* Calvert arms and inscription. Dot after MVLTIPLICAMINI, shield point between VL. Denomination V and I divided by shield. *Notes:* Breen-unlisted. Unique in copper. British Museum. *Rarity:* URS-1.

W-1040 · Hodder 1-B · Large Bust
Obverse: Head of Cecil Calvert facing left, inscription around. *Reverse:* Calvert arms and inscription. Dot after MVLTIPLICAMINI, shield point between MV. Denomination V and I divided by shield. *Notes:* Breen-unlisted. Unique. Discovery coin in the Norweb Collection. *Rarity:* URS-1.

W-1050 · Hodder 2-B · Small Bust
Obverse: Head of Cecil Calvert facing left, inscription around. *Reverse:* Same as preceding. *Notes:* Breen-70. *Rarity:* URS-3.

Selected auction price(s): Ford II Sale (5/2004), VF, $13,800. Public Auction Sale (Stack's 9/2005), VF, $7,475; Choice VF, $7,475.

W-1052 · Hodder 2-B · copper
As preceding, but struck in copper. *Notes:* Breen-71. Unique. British Museum. *Rarity:* URS-1.

W-1060 · Hodder 2-C · Small Bust
Obverse: Head of Cecil Calvert facing left, inscription around. *Reverse:* Calvert arms and inscription. No dot after MVLTIPLICAMINI. Denomination V and I divided by shield. This is the variety usually encountered today. Some were among 19 sixpence found in a silver tube at Fulbeck Hall in Lincolnshire and auctioned on November 13, 2002, by Morton & Eden. These typically are found with localized striking weakness. *Notes:* Breen-68. *Rarity:* URS-7.

G-4	VG-8	F-12	VF-20	EF-40	AU-50
$2,000	$4,500	$8,000	$15,000	$20,000	$40,000

W-1062 · Hodder 2-C · copper
As preceding, but struck in copper. *Notes:* Breen-71. Unique. British Museum. *Rarity:* URS-1.

W-1070 · Hodder 2-D · Small Bust
Obverse: Head of Cecil Calvert facing left, inscription around. *Reverse:* Calvert arms and inscription. MVLTILICAMINI error. Denomination V and I divided by shield. *Notes:* Breen-72. Three known: Garrett, Norweb, and one sold by Morton & Eden in November 2002, found in a silver tube (see W-1060). The Garrett and Norweb coins show bulging from a sunken area on the reverse die. *Rarity:* URS-3.

Selected auction price(s): Garrett III Sale (B&R 10/1980), VF, $13,500. Later in the Ford II Sale (5/2004), EF, $31,625. Norweb III Sale (11/1988), AU or finer, $27,500.

Maryland Shillings

W-1080 · Hodder 1-A · Large Bust, MARIAE

Obverse: Head of Cecil Calvert facing left, inscription around, ending with &CT. *Reverse:* Calvert arms and inscription. Shield point above side of M toward V (MVLTIPLICAMINI). Denomination X and II divided by shield. *Notes:* Breen-64. Most have striking weakness in one area or another. Around the turn of the 21st century, a hoard of about 20 pieces was found in England. *Rarity:* URS-6.

G-4	VG-8	F-12	VF-20	EF-40	AU-50
$4,000	$6,500	$12,000	$23,000	$35,000	$55,000

W-1090 · Hodder 2-B · Small Bust, MARIÆ

Obverse: Head of Cecil Calvert facing left, inscription around. *Reverse:* Calvert arms and inscription. Shield point touches V (MVLTIPLICAMINI). Denomination X and II divided by shield. *Notes:* Breen-68. Two known, the AU-55 to MS-60 (with scratches) Norweb Collection coin and one in the American Numismatic Society. *Rarity:* URS-2.

W-1092 · Hodder 2-B · copper

As preceding, but struck in copper. *Notes:* Breen-66. Breen traces five, one in the British Museum and another in the Glasgow University Museum Collection. *Rarity:* URS-5.

Selected auction price(s): Garrett III Sale (B&R 10/1980), F, countermarked, $7,500. Norweb III Sale (11/1988), EF–AU, $12,100.

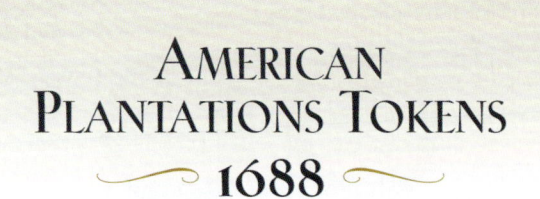

AMERICAN PLANTATIONS TOKENS 1688

Coins for the English Colonies

Tin tokens bearing the obverse design of King James II on horseback are identified with the American series. These were struck under a patent granted in August 1688 to Richard Holt, an agent for the owners of several tin mines. Holt proposed that new issues for the plantations in the New World be made of tin and of Spanish monetary designation to facilitate their acceptance in the channels of American commerce. Interestingly, in the colonies, 1/24th of a real would have equaled one and one-half farthings. In English documents discussing the production of this piece, it is generally referred to as a "farthing."

The dies were cut by John Roettier, one of England's most accomplished engravers. Eric P. Newman ("The James II 1/24th Real for the American Plantations," *Museum Notes 11*. American Numismatic Society, 1964) has identified seven obverse and seven reverse die varieties, indicating coinage must have been extensive. The coins were composed of 97.5 percent tin, with an overall weight of about 135 grains, although individual specimens can vary, sometimes widely.

Newman found no records that their distribution was ever authorized by the Crown. Still, some seem to have reached circulation in Britain and the Western Hemisphere. One was found in an excavation in Jamestown, Virginia, and some were recovered from excavations at Billingsgate Dock in London.

William of Orange arrived in England on November 5, 1688, claiming his right to the throne. James II fled to France on December 11. The next month, on January 28, William III became king and Mary was seated as queen, the only instance in English history of a monarch sharing his or her image on coinage with the portrait of a spouse. The regal coinage of William and Mary had two portraits.

Numismatic Aspects

The obverses of American Plantations tokens bear the equestrian statue of James II, surrounded by a Latin legend in abbreviated form: JACOBUS II D.G. MAG. BRI. FRAN. ET HIB. REX. An error die has HB instead of HIB. The reverse is lettered HISPAN VAL 24 PART REAL. At the center are four heraldic shields connected by chains. In the 12 o'clock position is the English shield with three couchant lions, then clockwise: Scottish shield with rampant lion, French shield with three fleurs-de-lys, and the Irish shield with a harp. On one die the Irish and Scottish shields are transposed. The edge is beaded. These are denominated in the Spanish system, not English pence. The Irish shield can vary in the number of harp strings, a key feature in identification.

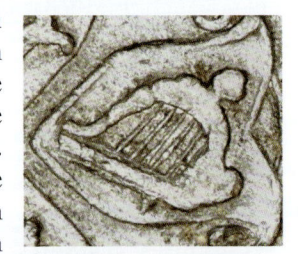

Illustrating 5 (transposed) strings in harp.

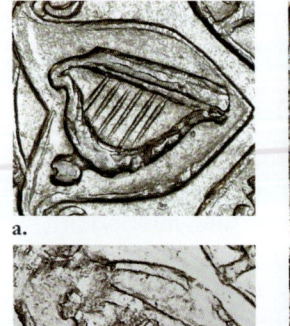

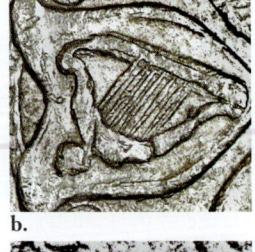

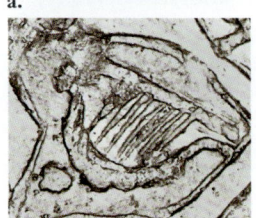

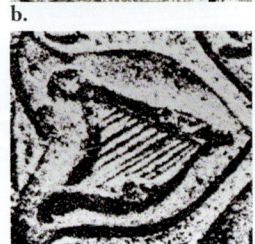

Illustrating (a) 6, (b) 7, (c) 8, and (d) 11 strings in harp (regular orientation).

Around 1828, the dies were acquired by Matthew Young, a London coin dealer. Most were sold to the British Museum, but two pairs were retained. Restrikes made from these were disseminated by W.S. Lincoln & Son, another London coin dealership. In the 1950s and 1960s these were seen with some frequency in the stocks of dealers in that city, but since that time most have been widely dispersed.

Today, examples of the American Plantations tokens are occasionally encountered, often restrikes of Newman die combination 4-E and the most plentiful, 5-D. These were made in a pewter-like metal.

Originals usually have black oxidation called "tinpest," which can result when tin is subjected to low temperatures. Restrikes sometimes have oxidation but can be found with original bright white surfaces. The rims are sometimes irregular. Easy Finding Guides are given on pages 56 and 57. It is often easier to attribute the coins by the reverse first. Rarity estimates are based upon Roger S. Siboni's studies plus extrapolation. No doubt other coins await attribution.

American Plantations Tokens

W-1130 · Newman 1-A
Six strings in harp; HB REX error. *Notes:* Seemingly rarer than generally known. *Rarity:* URS-4.

VF-20	EF-40	AU-50	MS-60
$1,400	$3,200	$8,500	$12,000

W-1135 · Newman 2-B
Seven strings in harp. *Notes:* Finest is Mint State. *Rarity:* URS-6.

VF-20	EF-40	AU-50	MS-60
$800	$1,400	$2,000	$5,000

W-1140 · Newman 2-G
Five strings in harp. Transposed Scottish lion and Irish harp. *Notes:* This is a classic scarcity, eagerly sought. In his 1988 *Encyclopedia*, Walter Breen knew of six. More have since been identified. *Rarity:* URS-4.

VF-20	EF-40	AU-50
$4,250	$8,000	$11,000

W-1145 · Newman 3-C
Eight strings in harp; sideways 4 (in 24). *Notes:* Finest is Mint State. *Rarity:* URS-4.

VF-20	EF-40	AU-50	MS-60
$3,500	$6,500	$10,000	$20,000

W-1150 · Newman 4-D
Eleven strings in harp. *Notes:* Existence not confirmed.

W-1155 · Newman 4-E
Seven strings in harp. Originals (possibly) and restrikes. *Notes:* Originals are in tin, restrikes are in pewter. Most if not all examples in the marketplace are restrikes. Although originals are believed to have been made, Roger S. Siboni has not being able to determine any variety other than the restrikes. While many restrikes are Mint State, others are in lower grades. Values are for restrikes. *Rarity:* URS-7 (restrikes).

EF-40	AU-50	MS-60
$800	$1,100	$2,000

W-1160 · Newman 5-D
Eleven strings in harp. Originals (possibly) and restrikes. *Notes:* All have a die crack on the obverse from A (FRAN) downward, below ET, to base of HI. On restrikes the break is continued through B (HIB). The positive existence of an original has not been confirmed. While many restrikes are Mint State, others are in lower grades. Prices are for restrikes. *Rarity:* URS-6 (restrikes).

EF-40	AU-50	MS-60
$800	$1,100	$2,000

W-1165 · Newman 6-F
Six strings in harp. *Notes:* Finest is Mint State, next several About Uncirculated. Two different obverse die states; see listing for die 6 below. *Rarity:* URS-6.

Selected auction price(s): Wayne S. Rich Collection (B&M 3/2002), AU, $3,910.

W-1170 · Newman 7-F
Six strings in harp. *Notes:* Existence not confirmed today. May be a high grade 6-F (possibility raised by Roger S. Siboni). *Rarity:* URS-1(?)

W-1175 · Newman 8-C
Eight strings in harp; sideways 4 (in 24) *Notes:* Finest is Mint State. First example noted by David Sonderman, who cataloged the Roper Collection sale for Stack's. *Rarity:* URS-4.

Easy Finding Guide
American Plantations Obverse Dies

HEAD DIRECTLY UNDER G

Newman 1. HB instead of HIB. Dot after X. Diagnostic. *Used for:* W-1080, Newman 1-A.

Newman 2. Correct HIB spelling. No dot after X. Diagnostic. *Used for:* W-1090, Newman 2-B, W-1100, Newman 2-G.

HEAD UNDER SPACE BETWEEN G AND B

Newman 3. Forehead below left serif of B. Tip of hoof opposite right foot of X. Diagnostic. *Used for:* W-1110, Newman 3-C.

Newman 4. Forehead below center of B. Tip of hoof barely past X. Distinctive long curve to the horse's tail. Diagnostic. *Used for:* W-1130, Newman 4-E.

Newman 5. Forehead below center of B. Tip of hoof opposite right foot of X and close to edge of X. Diagnostic. *Used for:* W-1140, Newman 5-D.

Newman 6. Spike on forehead connects to B. Tip of hoof opposite left tip of X. DG spaced closer than on any other die. Two obverse die states. First with horse's tail thin and with A (MAG) small (first identified in the Roger Siboni Collection, 2008; illustrated); second with broader tail, larger A, and other differences, from the die having been slightly reworked. The latter is the die state usually seen. Diagnostic. *Used for:* W-1150, Newman 6-F.

Newman 7. Forehead below upright of B; top of head heavily connected to B. G (MAG) low. Tip of hoof opposite center of X. First I in II higher. Diagnostic. *Used for:* W-1160, Newman 7-F.

Newman 8. Forehead below upright of B. G (MAG) slightly high. Tip of hoof opposite center of X. No dot after X. The G is close to the head. The letters MA are both the same height. Diagnostic. *Used for:* W-1170, Newman 8-C.

Easy Finding Guide
American Plantations Reverse Dies

HARP IN 9 O'CLOCK POSITION EXCEPT FOR REVERSE G

5 STRINGS IN HARP

Newman G. Transposed Scottish lion and Irish harp. Harp in 3 o'clock position. Features cut deeply in die. Diagnostic. *Used for:* W-1140, Newman 2-G.

6 STRINGS IN HARP

Newman A. In shield, head of lowest lion is slightly to the right. N (HISPAN) and 4 (24) each distant from crown. Rearmost legs of top two lions are distant from shield border; leg of lowest lion runs into border. As observed with harp horizontal, the fourth and fifth harp strings from the right are more widely spaced than are the others. IS (HISPAN) are on same level. Diagnostic. *Used for:* W-1080, Newman 1-A.

Newman F. In shield, lion's heads are directly under each other. S (HISPAN) lower than I. Rearmost legs of top two lions are close to the shield border; leg of lowest lion runs into border. Five of the chain links have thin or defective outside (toward the rim). Diagnostic. *Used for:* W-1150, Newman 6-F, W-1160, Newman 7-F.

7 STRINGS IN HARP

Newman B. Fleurs in bottom shield are large and are close to or touch edge. Leftmost (as viewed) harp strings are long. The 24 is normally spaced; AR (PART) is normally spaced. Diagnostic. *Used for:* W-1090, Newman 2-B.

Newman E. Fleurs in bottom shield are small and do not touch edge. Leftmost harp strings are short. The 24 is widely spaced; AR (PART) is wide, A slightly low, P very low. Diagnostic. *Used for:* W-1130, Newman 4-E.

8 STRINGS IN HARP

Newman C. Sideways 4 in 24. Diagnostic. *Used for:* W-1110, Newman 3-C, W-1170, Newman 8-C.

11 STRINGS IN HARP

Newman D. Diagnostic. *Used for:* W-1140, Newman 5-D.

Wood's Rosa Americana Coinage 1717–1733

William Wood's 1722 Rosa Americana penny struck for circulation in the American colonies. (Engraving by John Gavit for O'Callaghan, *The Documentary History of the State of New-York*, 1850)

History

William Wood, a metallurgist of Wolverhampton, county of Stafford, England, became interested in coinage as early as 1717. That year he caused several pattern halfpenny, penny, and twopence coins to be prepared. On July 12, 1722, he obtained a patent or contract from King George I, who granted him the right to produce 100 tons of coins to be distributed in the "American plantations." Some have said the duchess of Kendal, a German baroness who endeared herself to the king, helped Wood secure the royal privilege in return for £10,000.

There was at the time a severe shortage of circulating coins in the American colonies. Wood's proposed issues were to be of a new alloy, called Bath metal, consisting of 75 percent copper, 24.7 percent zinc, and 0.3 percent silver, which Wood claimed as his invention. The royal patent specified that the privilege was to last 14 years, during which time 300 tons of tokens could be struck in halfpenny, penny, and twopence denominations. During the first four years of the term no more than 200 tons were to be struck, and for the last 10 years, no more than 10 tons were to be struck in any given year. Coinage was performed by drop press.

Circulation for the pieces designated for America was limited to the "islands, dominions, or territories belonging to His Majesty, His heirs, or His successors in America, or any of them." Elaborate provisions were made for assaying the coins at regular intervals to verify their metallic content. Legal precautions were taken against counterfeiting.

In his 1762 work, *A View of the Silver Coin and Coinage of England, From the Norman Conquest to the Present Time*, Thomas Snelling included this:

> We have also been informed that Kingsmill Eyres, Esq.; Mr. Marshland, a hardwareman in Cornhill, and several others were concerned in the scheme, the last mentioned person had great quantities of them in his cellar, was ruined by it, and died housekeeper at Gresham College; the dyes were engraved by Mr. Lammas, Mr. Standbroke, and Mr. Harold, some of which were in the possession of Mr. Winthorpe, who went to New-York, his father lies buried at Beckingham; they were struck at the French Change, in Hogg Lane, Seven Dials, by an engine that raised and let fall an heavy weight upon them when made hot, which is the most expeditious way of striking Bath metal, which was the sort of metal they were made of.

Numismatic Aspects

Although the pieces made for America, designated as the Rosa Americana coinage, were given the nominal values of halfpenny, penny, and twopence, in actuality they were only about half the weight of similar English denominations. For example, the Rosa Americana penny was of the same approximate size as an English halfpenny. Modern scholars have found that at least some coins do not contain silver, and thus depart from the Bath metal alloy described above.

Efforts were made to have the pieces circulate in America. On October 29, 1725, the duke of Newcastle wrote to the governor of Massachusetts Bay, enclosing a copy of the Wood patent and requesting that the governor give "all due encouragement and assistance" to have the pieces used in the channels of commerce. Despite these and other efforts, Rosa Americana coins were not popular on this side of the Atlantic. They circulated only to a very limited extent. Most specimens known today in American cabinets were acquired from English sources, indicating that the Rosa Americana pieces, rejected in America, did see circulation in England, probably at values reduced from the denominations originally assigned to them.

The 1717 pre-patent coins depict George I on the obverse and, on the reverse, the denomination 1/2, I, or II, with a crown above. No reference was made to America. Beginning in 1722 an extensive series of Rosa Americana issues made its appearance, most dated 1722 or 1723. Issues of 1724, 1727, and 1733, considered patterns, were also struck.

Typically the obverse of the Rosa Americana twopence coinage consists of a bold portrait of George I surrounded by the legend GEORGIUS D:G: MAG: BRI FRA: ET HIB:REX., which signifies that George was king of Britain and her possessions. The reverse depicts a rose surrounded by: ROSA AMERICANA and UTILE DULCI, translating to "the American rose" and "useful and sweet." The intention was to prepare a coinage that would be distinctly American, in contrast with the English coins in colonial circulation at the time.

In 1724 several interesting patterns were produced, all of which are exceedingly rare today. An interesting design used on two issues depicted a rose bush with the legend ROSA SINE SPINA ("rose without thorns"). One depicted the bust of Wilhelmina on the obverse. Wilhelmina Charlotte Caroline was the wife of the king's son, who in time became King George II.

In 1727 a presently unique pattern halfpenny appeared with the bust of George II on the obverse and the ROSA SINE SPINA legend on the reverse. In 1733 a large pattern twopence depicting George II facing left with a redesigned rose on the reverse was made. Varieties of these rare twopence exist, such as off metal and uniface trials.

The typical Rosa Americana coin shows file marks on the edge from planchet preparation. Many show bubbles, pinpoint "pockmarks," or cracks from the heating of the planchet prior to striking. Planchet color can vary. All but a few patterns have a plain edge. Average diameters are 21.5 mm (halfpenny), 27.5 mm (penny), and 32.5 mm (twopence), but coins can vary by a millimeter or slightly more. The Norweb II Collection catalog (1987) is a useful source for information. In that catalog Michael J. Hodder commented:

> Given the very complexity of the coinage it is probably impossible to ever present the issues in a simple, straightforward fashion. The Rosa Americana coinage, of all the coinages commonly called "colonial," is the most difficult to approach or master. Consequently, many opportunities arise for the sophisticated student of the series, as in numismatics knowledge is the true key to success, whether it be collecting or enterprise.

Sydney F. Martin provided much of the information used here, generally divided into types and major differences within styles. He also provided URS ratings, noting that research is still in progress. Many other die varieties exist, as do strikings in copper, silver, on wide planchets, and so on. In the future, should it be desired to create expanded listings of the Martin types, this could be done by adding decimal points to the group number, such as W-1220.1, W-1220.2, and so on.

1717 Pre-Patent Coinage

W-1200 · Martin 1-A · (1717) pre-patent halfpenny

Obverse: Draped bust of George facing right. Short curls tied with a ribbon at the back of the nape of the neck. GEORGIVS • REX • around border. *Reverse:* Crowned fraction 1/2. DAT PACEM • ET • AUGET • OPES • around border. *Notes:* Undated, but presumed 1717. Four known to Sydney Martin. *Rarity:* URS-3.

Selected auction price(s): Norweb II Sale (3/1988), EF, $4,070. John J. Ford Jr. IX Sale (Stack's 5/2005), EF–AU, $7,475; EF–AU, $10,925.

W-1202 · Martin 1-A · (1717) pre-patent penny

Obverse: Squat, draped bust of George facing right. Long curls tied with a ribbon. GEORGIUS • D: G: M: BRI: FRA: ET • HIB: REX • around border. *Reverse:* Crowned roman numeral I. DAT • PACEM • ET • NOUAS • PREBET • ET • AUGET • OPES • around border. *Notes:* Undated, but presumed 1717. Three known, the Norweb coin being pictured by Crosby. *Rarity:* URS-3.

Selected auction price(s): Norweb II Sale (3/1988), VF, $2,090. To John J. Ford Jr. IX Sale (Stack's 5/2005), VF, $3,737.50.

W-1204 · Martin 1-B · (1717) pre-patent penny

Obverse: Same as preceding. *Reverse:* Crowned roman numeral I. Leafed branch to each side, crossing at bottom. BRVN: ET • LVN: DVX: SA: ROM: MI: ARC + THE: ET • PR: ELEC • around border. *Notes:* Undated, but presumed 1717. In the Norweb catalog, Michael J. Hodder delineated 10 examples. *Rarity:* URS-5.

Selected auction price(s): Garrett III Sale (B&R 10/1980), MS, $5,750. Norweb II Sale (3/1988), EF, $2,970. John J. Ford Jr. IX Sale (Stack's 5/2005), MS, $16,100; EF, $10,925.

W-1206 · Martin 2-C · (1717) pre-patent penny

Obverse: Tall, well-proportioned, mailed bust of George facing right. Long curls tied with a ribbon at the back of the head. GEORGIVS:D:G M:B:F: ET • HIB around border. *Reverse:* Crowned roman numeral I surrounded by a ring, the legend, and a second ring. 1717 • MAG • BRIT • GRA • ET • HIBER • REX • around border with a dot after the date and each word. *Rarity:* URS-1.

Selected auction price(s): John J. Ford Jr. IX Sale (Stack's 5/2005), F, $4,600.

W-1210 · Martin 1-A · 1717 pre-patent twopence

Obverse: Large well-proportioned mailed bust of George facing right. Long curls tied with a ribbon. GEORGIVS • D: G M:B:FR: ET • H: REX • around border. *Reverse:* Crowned roman numeral II surrounded by a ring, the legend, and another ring. 1717 • MAG • BRIT • FRA • ET • HIBER • REX: • around border. *Notes:* Two known. *Rarity:* URS-2.

Selected auction price(s): Norweb II Sale (3/1988), MS, $6,820, to Ford. John J. Ford Jr. IX Sale (Stack's 5/2005), About Fine, $4,600; MS, $17,250.

Rosa Americana Halfpence

W-1214 · Martin 1-A · 1722 halfpenny · VTILE · DVLCI
Obverse: Laureated bust of George facing right, with flowing hair tied by a ribbon. GEORGIUS • DEI to left, • GRATIA • REX • to right. *Reverse:* Uncrowned rose. • ROSA • AMERI : VTILE • DVLCI • 1722 around border. *Notes:* Breen-132. *Rarity:* URS-5.

Selected auction price(s): John J. Ford Jr. IX Sale (Stack's 5/2005), VF, $4,312.50; AU, $6,325. Americana Sale (Stack's 1/2008), EF-40, $10,350.

W-1218 · Martin 2-B · 1722 halfpenny · UTILE · DULCI
Obverse: Laureated bust of George facing right, with flowing hair tied by a ribbon. GEORGIUS to left, • D : G : REX • to right at border. *Reverse:* Uncrowned rose. • ROSA • AMERI : UTILE • DULCI • 1722 around border. U's punched over earlier V's. *Notes:* Breen-133. *Rarity:* URS-8.

VG-8	F-12	VF-20	EF-40	AU-50	MS-60
$150	$275	$575	$1,200	$2,400	$4,500

W-1222 · Martin 3-C · 1722 halfpenny · UTILE · DULCI
Obverse: Laureated bust of George facing right, with flowing hair tied by a ribbon. GEORGIUS • DEI • GRATIA • REX • around border. *Reverse:* Uncrowned rose. ROSA • AMERICANA • UTILE • DULCI • 1722 around border; rosette after date. *Notes:* Breen-134. Repunched date. *Rarity:* URS-11.

VG-8	F-12	VF-20	EF-40	AU-50	MS-60
$150	$275	$575	$1,200	$2,100	$4,000

W-1226 · Martin 3-D · 1723/2 halfpenny · Uncrowned Rose
Obverse: Same as preceding. *Reverse:* Uncrowned rose. ROSA • AMERICANA UTILE • DULCI • 1723/2 around border; rosette before UTILE and after date. *Notes:* Breen-136. *Rarity:* URS-6.

Selected auction price(s): John J. Ford Jr. IX Sale (Stack's 5/2005), EF, $5,175; AU, $6,325.

W-1232 · Martin 3-E · 1723 halfpenny
Obverse: Same as preceding. *Reverse:* Uncrowned rose. ROSA • AMERICANA UTILE • DULCI • 1723 around border; rosette before UTILE and after date. *Notes:* Breen-138. *Rarity:* URS-5.

Selected auction price(s): John J. Ford Jr. IX Sale (Stack's 5/2005), AU, $5,175. Americana Sale (Stack's 1/2008), F-15, $1,093.

W-1236 · Martin 3-F · 1723 halfpenny · Crowned Rose · no dot after 1723
Obverse: Same as preceding. *Reverse:* Crowned rose. ROSA • AMERICANA • 1723 around border. UTILE • DULCI on label below rose. Varieties exist with large or small 3. *Notes:* Breen-140. *Rarity:* URS-7.

VG-8	F-12	VF-20	EF-40	AU-50	MS-60
$120	$175	$1,200	$2,600	$5,250	

W-1240 · Martin 3-F · 1723 halfpenny
As preceding, but in silver. *Notes:* Breen-139. *Rarity:* URS-1.

Selected auction price(s): John J. Ford Jr. IX Sale (Stack's 5/2005), Near VF, $12,650.

W-1244 · Martin 4-G · 1723 halfpenny · dot after 1723
Obverse: Laureated bust of George facing right, with flowing hair tied by a stubby ribbon. GEORGIUS • DEI • GRATIA : REX • around border. *Reverse:* Crowned rose, label below. ROSA • AMERICANA • 1723 • at border. UTILE • DULCI on label below rose. *Notes:* Breen-141. *Rarity:* URS-1.

W-1248 · Martin 4-H · 1723 halfpenny · colon after 1723 · silver
Obverse: Same as preceding. *Reverse:* Crowned rose, label below. ROSA • AMERICANA • 1723: at border. UTILE • DULCI on label. *Notes:* Breen-142. *Rarity:* URS-2.

Selected auction price(s): John J. Ford Jr. IX Sale (Stack's 5/2005), Choice AU, $27,600.

Rosa Americana Pence

W-1252 · Martin 1-A · 1722 penny · GEORGIVS
Obverse: Laureated head of George facing right. Tight curls. Head narrower than later obverses. GEORGIVS • DEI to left, • GRATIA • REX • to right. *Reverse:* Uncrowned rose. ROSA • AMERICANA VTILE • DVLCI • 1722 around border. Rosette before VTILE and after date. *Notes:* Breen-110 (brass), 111 (copper), 112 (copper variety). *Rarity:* URS-4 (for Breen-110), URS-2 (Breen-111), URS-3 or 4 (Breen-112).

VG-8	F-12	VF-20	EF-40	AU-50	MS-60
		$12,000	$17,500	$28,000	$40,000

W-1256 · Martin 2-A · 1722 penny · GEORGIUS
Obverse: Laureated head of George facing right. Tight curls. GEORGIUS • DEI to left, • over head, GRATIA • REX • to right. *Reverse:* Same as preceding. *Notes:* Breen-113. *Rarity:* URS-6.

VG-8	F-12	VF-20	EF-40	AU-50	MS-60
$170	$300	$800	$1,500	$3,100	$6,250

W-1258 · Martin 2-A · 1722 penny
As preceding, but struck in copper and showing much longer hair ribbons. *Rarity:* URS-1.

Selected auction price(s): John J. Ford Jr. IX Sale (Stack's 5/2005), VF, $8,050.

W-1260 · Martin 2-B · 1722 penny
Obverse: Same as preceding. *Reverse:* Uncrowned rose. ROSA • AMERICANA • UTILE • DULCI • 1722 around border. *Notes:* Breen-114. *Rarity:* URS-6.

VG-8	F-12	VF-20	EF-40	AU-50	MS-60
$150	$260	$500	$1,100	$1,900	$4,200

W-1264 · Martin 2-C · 1722 penny
Obverse: Same as preceding. *Reverse:* Uncrowned rose. ROSA • AMERICANA • UTILE • DULCI • 1722 around border. Rosette after date. *Notes:* Breen-115. *Rarity:* URS-9.

VG-8	F-12	VF-20	EF-40	AU-50	MS-60
$150	$260	$500	$1,100	$1,900	$4,200

W-1268 · Martin 2-D · 1722 penny
Obverse: Same as preceding. *Reverse:* Uncrowned rose. ROSA • AMERICANA UTILE • DULCI • 1722 around border. Rosette after AMERICANA and date. *Notes:* Breen-116, 117, and 118. *Rarity:* URS-8.

VG-8	F-12	VF-20	EF-40	AU-50	MS-60
$150	$260	$500	$1,100	$1,900	$4,200

W-1272 · Martin 3-D · 1722 penny
Obverse: Laureated head of George facing right. Tight curls. GEORGIUS • DEI to left, • over head, GRATIA • REX to right. *Reverse:* Same as preceding. *Notes:* Breen-119. *Rarity:* URS-4.

Selected auction price(s): New York Sale (Heritage 6/2005), AU-58 (PCGS), $3,220. Long Beach Auction (2/2007), AU-58 (PCGS), $4,312.50.

W-1278 · Martin 2-E · 1723 penny
Obverse: See Martin 2-A above. *Reverse:* Crowned rose with label below. ROSA • AMERICANA • 1723 at border. UTILE • DULCI on label. *Notes:* Breen-121 (larger 3) and 122 (smaller 3); date differences hardly discernible. *Rarity:* URS-11.

VG-8	F-12	VF-20	EF-40	AU-50	MS-60
$115	$170	$450	$1,000	$1,600	$3,600

W-1282 · Martin 2-F · 1723 penny
Obverse: Same as preceding. *Reverse:* Crowned rose with label below. ROSA • AMERICANA • 1723 • at border (dot after date). UTILE • DULCI on label. *Notes:* Breen-124. *Rarity:* URS-4.

Selected auction price(s): John J. Ford Jr. IX Sale (Stack's 5/2005), Choice VF, $1,093.

W-1286 · Martin 2-G · 1724/3 penny · REX •
Obverse: Same as preceding. *Reverse:* Crowned rose with label below. ROSA : AME RICANA • 1724/3 at border (AME and RICANA divided by cross at top of crown). UTILE • DULCI on label. *Notes:* Breen-128; only example seen is silvered. *Rarity:* URS-1.

Selected auction price(s): John J. Ford Jr. IX Sale (Stack's 5/2005), Choice Unc., $24,000; F–VF, $14,950.

W-1294 · Martin 3-G · 1724/3 penny · REX
Obverse: See W-1272 (Martin 3-D). *Reverse:* Same as preceding. *Notes:* Breen-130; only example seen is in copper. *Rarity:* URS-1.

Selected auction price(s): John J. Ford Jr. IX Sale (Stack's 5/2005), VF, $12,650.

W-1302 · Martin 4-G · 1724/3 pattern penny · GEORGIUS • D •

Obverse: Laureated head of George facing right. Long flowing curls. Goiter-like projection at throat. GEORGIUS • D • to left, GRATIA • REX • to right. *Reverse:* Same as preceding. *Notes:* Breen-126. *Rarity:* URS-3.

Selected auction price(s): John J. Ford Jr. IX Sale (Stack's 5/2005), Choice Unc., $27,600.

W-1306 · Martin 5-G · 1724/3 pattern penny · GEORGIUS • DEI •

Obverse: Laureated head of George facing right. Long flowing curls. Goiter-like projection at throat. GEORGIUS • DEI • GRATIA • REX • around border. *Reverse:* Same as preceding. *Notes:* Breen-unlisted; only observed example is in silver. *Rarity:* URS-1.

Selected auction price(s): John J. Ford Jr. IX Sale (Stack's 5/2005), VF, inscribed, $6,325.

W-1310 · Martin 6-H · (1724) pattern · ROSA : SINE : SPINA •

Obverse: Laureated head of George facing right. Long flowing curls. Goiter-like projection at throat. GEORGIUS • DEI • GRATIA • REX around border. *Reverse:* Rose bush with flowering rose at top, with two lower stems, each with a bud and a half-opened rose. ROSA : SINE : SPINA • at border. *Notes:* Undated, but presumed 1724. The reverse legend translates to "rose without thorns." Called a "pattern" by some, but seemingly unlikely as most show evidence of circulation. *Rarity:* URS-4.

Selected auction price(s): Garrett III Sale (B&R 10/1980), VF, appearance of copper, $5,000. John J. Ford Jr. IX Sale (Stack's 5/2005), VF, $21,850.

W-1312 · Martin 7-H · undated pattern penny · Wilhelmina

Obverse: Bust of Wilhelmina left. WILHELMINA : CHARLOTTA • PR • WALLIA (inscription LLIA very small and below bust). *Reverse:* Same as preceding. *Rarity:* URS-3.

Selected auction price(s): John J. Ford Jr. IX Sale (Stack's 5/2005), Choice VF, $7,475; Choice EF, $11,500.

Rosa Americana Twopence

W-1318 · Martin 1-A · undated twopence

Obverse: "Early Head." George faces right; curls only at the back of neck. Very tiny ribbons. Head appears "squat." Three upper leaves. GEORGIVS • D : G : MAG: BRI : FRA : ET • HIB : REX around border. *Reverse:* Uncrowned rose. At top border, • ROSA • AMERICANA •. At bottom border, • UTILE • DULCI •. *Notes:* Breen-87. *Rarity:* URS-4.

Selected auction price(s): John J. Ford Jr. IX Sale (Stack's 5/2005), $25,300.

W-1322 · Martin 2-B · undated twopence · Young Head

Obverse: Young-appearing head of George facing right. Flowing curls tied with a ribbon. Prominent laurel wreath with several berries. GEORGIVS • D : G : MAG : BRI : FRA : ET • HIB : REX • around border. *Reverse:* Uncrowned rose. At top border, • ROSA • AMERICANA •. At bottom border, within label, • UTILE • DULCI. *Notes:* Breen-88. *Rarity:* URS-6.

G-4	VG-8	F-12	VF-20	EF-40	AU-50	MS-60
$200	$425	$750	$1,500	$3,600		$6,500

W-1326 · Martin 3-C · 1722 twopence · Old Head

Obverse: Older head of George facing right. Flowing curls tied with a ribbon. Prominent laurel wreath with no berries. GEORGIUS • D : G : MAG : BRI : FRA : ET • HIB : REX • around border. *Reverse:* Uncrowned rose. At top border, • ROSA • AMERICANA • 1722 •. At bottom border, within label, UTILE • DULCI. *Notes:* Breen-89. *Rarity:* URS-6.

G-4	VG-8	F-12	VF-20	EF-40	AU-50	MS-60
$170	$275	$800	$1,600	$3,500		$6,000

W-1330 · Martin 4-C · 1722 twopence

Obverse: Head style as above. GEORGIUS • D : G MAG : BRI : FRA : ET • HIB : REX around border. *Reverse:* Same as preceding. *Notes:* Breen-90. *Rarity:* URS-5.

Selected auction price(s): ANA Sale (Heritage 8/2001), AU-53 (PCGS), $1,840. John J. Ford Jr. IX Sale (Stack's 5/2005), AU, $2,300.

W-1334 · Martin 3-D · 1723 twopence
Obverse: See Martin 3-C above. *Reverse:* Crowned rose. At top border, ROSA • AMERICANA • 1723. At bottom border, within label, UTILE • DULCI. *Notes:* Breen-92. *Rarity:* URS-11.

W-1338 · Martin 3-E · 1723 twopence
Obverse: Same as preceding. GEORGIUS • D : G : MAG : BRI : FRA : ET • HIB : REX •. *Reverse:* Crowned rose. At top border, • ROSA + AME RICANA : 1723 • (AME and RICANA divided by cross at top of crown). At bottom border, within label, UTILE • DULCI. *Notes:* Breen-91. *Rarity:* URS-2.

G-4	VG-8	F-12	VF-20	EF-40	AU-50	MS-60
	$175	$300	$575	$1,300	$2,000	$7,500

W-1342 · Martin 3-F · 1723 twopence
Obverse: Same as preceding. *Reverse:* Crowned rose. At top border, • ROSA • AMERICANA • 1723 •. At bottom border, within label, UTILE • DULCI. *Notes:* Breen-94. *Rarity:* URS-5.

Selected auction price(s): John J. Ford Jr. IX Sale (Stack's 5/2005), EF, $920; Choice EF, $1,495. Requa Collection (Stack's [ANR] 9/2006), AU-55 (PCGS), $1,668.

W-1346 · Martin 4-E · 1723 twopence
Obverse: GEORGIUS • D : G: MAG: BRI : FRA : ET • HIB : REX around border. *Reverse:* Crowned rose. At top border, • ROSA • AMERICANA • 1723. At bottom border, within label, • UTILE • DULCI •. *Notes:* Breen-96. *Rarity:* URS-10.

Selected auction price(s): Logan & Steinberg Collections (B&M 11/2002), AU-58 (PCGS), $1,380. John J. Ford Jr. IX Sale (Stack's 5/2005), EF, $1,955; AU, $1,955; MS, $2,185.

W-1348 · Martin 4-E · 1723 twopence
As preceding, nickel plated. Originally thought to be in German silver; now determined to have been made on a planchet plated prior to striking. *Notes:* Breen-98. *Rarity:* URS-1.

Selected auction price(s): John J. Ford Jr. IX Sale (Stack's 5/2005), Choice MS, $40,250.

W-1350 · Martin 4-F · 1723 twopence
Obverse: Same as preceding. *Reverse:* Crowned rose. At top border, • ROSA • AMERICANA • 1723 •. At bottom border, within label, UTILE • DULCI. *Notes:* Breen-95. *Rarity:* URS-6.

Selected auction price(s): John J. Ford Jr. IX Sale (Stack's 5/2005), EF, $1,035. Long Beach Sale (Heritage 9/2005), AU-58 (PCGS), $2,300. Henry Leon Sale (Stack's 5/2007), EF-45, $1,035.

W-1358 · Martin 5-H · 1724 twopence · Goiter Head
Obverse: Young head of George facing right. Long, flowing curls tied by a ribbon and with a laurel wreath. Bulge on throat. GEORGIUS • D : G • M A to left, • above head, B • FRA • ET • HIB • REX • to right. *Reverse:* Uncrowned rose. At top border, • ROSA • AMERICANA • 1724 •. At bottom border, within label, UTILE • DULCI •. *Notes:* Breen-99. Martin knows of eight examples. *Rarity:* URS-4.

Selected auction price(s): John J. Ford Jr. IX Sale (Stack's 5/2005), Choice AU, $25,300.

W-1360 · Martin 5-H · 1724 twopence
As preceding, but silvered. The cataloger of the Ford sale suggests this may have been Wood's personal pocket piece. *Rarity:* URS-1.

Selected auction price(s): John J. Ford Jr. IX Sale (Stack's 5/2005), VF, inscribed, $11,500.

W-1362 · Martin 6-I · 1724 twopence
Obverse: GEORGIUS • D : G • M • B to left, • above head, FRA • ET • HIB • REX • to right. *Reverse:* Uncrowned rose. At top border, • ROSA • AMERICANA • 1724 •. At bottom border, within label, UTILE • DULCI. *Notes:* Breen-102. *Rarity:* URS-3.

Selected auction price(s): John J. Ford Jr. IX Sale (Stack's 5/2005), EF, $12,650; Choice MS, $25,300.

Later Patterns

W-1366 · Martin Pattern 1-A · 1727 pattern coin
Obverse: Head of George II facing right. GEORGIUS to left, D : GRA • REX • to right. *Reverse:* Rose bush with flowering rose at top, with two lower stems, each with a bud and a half-opened rose. ROSA : SINE : SPINA • at border. Date 1727 in exergue. *Rarity:* URS-1.

Selected auction price(s): John J. Ford Jr. IX Sale (Stack's 5/2005), VF, problems, $2,760. Americana Sale (Stack's 1/2008), VF-30, problems, $3,220.

63

W-1370 · Martin Pattern 1-A · 1733 pattern twopence
Obverse: Head of George II facing left. GEORGIVS at left, II • D • G • REX • at right. *Reverse:* Crowned rose in full bloom, on stem with leaves, turned slightly to the viewer's right. ROSA • AMER to the left, ICANA • 1733 • to the right. Below on two labels, UTILE DULCI. *Notes:* Breen-107. One lost aboard the S.S. *Arctic* in the Atlantic Ocean en route from England to New York on September 27, 1854 (Dickeson, pp. 76–78). These examples traced: Norweb, Nelson-Boyd-Ford, Crosby-Garrett-Roper, British Museum. In *A View of the Silver Coin and Coinage of England, From the Norman Conquest to the Present Time,* 1762, Thomas Snelling included this: "George II. 1733. We never heard of any proposals made about the year 1733, for an American coinage; No. 28. has the appearance of a pattern piece for some such scheme; it has the king's head laureate, inscribed, GEORGIUS II. D. G. REX, and on the reverse a leafed rose crowned, inscribed, ROSA AMERICANA 1733—UTILE DULCI. The only piece we know of, is in the collection of Thomas Hollis, Esq; we have also seen a Proof of the head in steel, said to be struck on that metal to show how malleable they could make it by smelting it with pit coal, by a scheme then on foot." Steel uniface strikes and lead trials both exist. *Rarity:* URS-3.

Selected auction price(s): Garrett III Sale (B&R 10/1980), PF, $22,500. To the Roper Sale (Stack's 12/1983), Choice PF, $18,800. Norweb II Sale (3/1988), PF, $19,800. John J. Ford Jr. IX Sale (Stack's 5/2005), Choice PF, $57,500; Gem PF, ex Norweb, $63,250.

Virginia Coinage 1773–1774

1773 Virginia copper halfpenny. (*Early Coins of America,* 1875)

Introduction

The April 10, 1606, charter granted by King James to Virginia specifically provided for the coinage privilege:

> And that they shall or lawfully may establish and cause be made a coin, to pass current there between the people of the several colonies for the more ease of traffic and bargaining between and amongst them and the natives there, of such metal, and in such manner or form, as the several councils there shall limit and appoint.

No coinage was ever produced within the colony of Virginia. The coins that circulated and were used in commerce throughout the colony were a mixture of English, Spanish, Portuguese, and Dutch, with most silver and gold coins of Spanish-American origin. On November 20, 1645, the Virginia colony passed legislation permitting 10,000 pounds of copper coinage to be produced, in the values of two-, three-, six-, and ninepence, as a substitute for tobacco, which was then used for small change and circulation. No coining was ever performed under this authorization.

Due to increasing pressure from tradesmen to acquire copper coins for use in commerce, on December 20, 1769, the Virginia House of Burgesses passed an act allowing the use of up to £2,500 to pay for the mintage of copper coins in Britain. However, it was not until 1772 that the final designs for the coinage was formulated. On May 20, 1773, the English Crown authorized the coinage of halfpennies for Virginia, not to exceed a total of 25 tons weight. This was five times the quantity requested by the colony. A total of 40 obverse dies and 30 reverse dies were produced. Minting took place in the Royal Mint in the Tower of London. This was the first and only colonial coinage authorized and produced in Britain for use in an American colony, thereby giving the Virginia pieces the unique claim of being the only true American colonial coinage.

On February 14, 1774, the ship *Virginia,* under the command of Howard Esten, arrived in New York with five tons of halfpence, which Eric P. Newman, student of the series, has equated to about 672,000 individual pieces. The vessel then continued to Virginia to make the delivery. Robert Nicholas, treasurer of the colony, was reluctant to distribute the halfpennies in absence of specific instructions from Britain authorizing him to do so. On November 16, 1774, a royal proclamation provided that

> the said pieces of copper money so coined, stamped, and impressed, shall be current and lawful money of and in our said colony of Virginia and of and within the districts and precincts of the same; and shall pass and be received therein after the rate following, that is to say, twenty-four of the said pieces shall pass and be received for the sum of one shilling, according to the currency of our said province of Virginia.

The pieces were made current up to the value of 60 halfpence for a payment of 20 shillings or more, and up to 24 halfpence for smaller payments. This proclamation did not arrive in Virginia until several months later. The first notice of it appeared in the *Virginia Gazette* on February 23, 1775. By that time the seeds of the Revolutionary War had been sown. Fears of war and inflation were rampant, motivating many citizens to hoard coins. Nevertheless, Virginia halfpence circulated extensively, as evidenced by worn examples surviving today, though this may well have occurred after the war ended.

Classification of Varieties

Eric P. Newman's 1956 book, *Coinage for Colonial Virginia*, Newman's 1964 addendum in *American Numismatic Society Museum Notes* 10, and "Virginia Halfpence Variety Update with Revised Die Interlock Chart" (by Alan Anthony, Roger A. Moore, and Eric P. Newman in the *Colonial Newsletter*, April 2005), provide the collector a solid basis for attributing the varieties of Virginia halfpence provided in the listing below.

Newman's original work explores the civil and economic history of the Virginia colony as well as the background of the coinage effected in England, and describes the characteristics of various dies and combinations thought to have been produced by Richard Yeo and/or Thomas Pingo at the Tower mint.

Basically, halfpence obverses are grouped into categories—with period after GEORGIVS (10 dies) and without a period after GEORGIVS (14 dies)—and each obverse is assigned a number designation. Reverses are classified by the number of strings in the harp on the coat of arms, either six (2 dies), seven (14 dies), or eight (6 dies), each assigned a letter. With the knowledge that 40 obverse and 30 reverse dies were made, it is likely that additional varieties remain to be discovered, assuming most or all dies were used for coinage.

Accordingly, the designation of a particular coin is made by using a number to describe the specific obverse and a letter to describe a specific reverse, such that one coin might be called a Newman 3-P, while another is designated as Newman 21-N, and so on. The halfpence have a very consistent diameter of between 24.7 and 26.1 mm. A number of fakes and facsimiles have been described by Roger Moore, et al., which can vary widely in diameter and weight but usually are easily identified.

In 1774, a limited number of impressions were struck in silver from dies of the same diameter as the halfpenny but with the obverse portrait of George III much larger in size. Traditionally these have been known as Virginia "shillings" due to their metallic content, but the weight falls about 10 percent below the English standards for shillings of the time, and no official shilling coinage was contemplated for Virginia. Accordingly, these 1774 pieces are better described as pattern halfpence in silver. Another interesting rare issue is the so-called 1773 copper "penny," actually a halfpenny struck in Proof grade on a broad planchet with a milled border. These occur on an Irish halfpenny blank weighing about 135 grains.

Numismatic Aspects

General description of the 1773 Virginia halfpenny: On the obverse is a portrait of George III facing right. GEORGIVS III REX at top and side border, some with period after GEORGIVS, others without. On the reverse, the coat of arms of the House of Hanover is at the center. The Hanoverian kings of England gave Virginia the singular honor among the colonies of using their coat of arms as a reward for Virginia's staunch support of the monarchy during the English Civil War (Alan Anthony). Reading the legend from left to right, there is seemingly a transposition of logical order. To the far left is NIA; next comes the date in the center divided by a crown, appearing as 17 [crown] 73; and finally the legend is completed by VIRGI to the far right. The lower left quadrant of the state arms shows a harp, which can have six, seven, or eight strings. A die preserved in the Royal Mint Museum has nine harp strings but is not known to have been used for coinage.

Illustrating *(a)* 6, *(b)* 7, and *(c)* 8 strings in the harp.

Although worn halfpence are seen with frequency today (especially on eBay), many encountered in the marketplace are Uncirculated. Some of these have come from the hoard of over 5,000 Uncirculated Virginia halfpence once held by Col. Mendes I. Cohen, Baltimore, Maryland. The circumstance surrounding this finding is not known. Walter Breen, in *The Numismatist*, January 1952, suggested that the discovery occurred within a government building in Annapolis, Maryland, where the coins "might have been" in an original keg. By the time of his *Encyclopedia*, 1988, this description had changed to "a keg found in Richmond before the Civil War," this based on reading of Eric P. Newman's 1964 article in *ANS Museum Notes*. Michael J. Hodder (communication to the author) states that the hoard came to Cohen from his father, Israel I. Cohen, who died in 1801. The Cohen family was prominent in Baltimore banking, and their establishment is depicted on certain bank notes.

Cohen's cache was dispersed slowly and carefully from 1875 until 1929, as they passed from his estate to his nieces and nephews. In the latter year the remaining coins, approximately 2,200, the property of Bertha Cohen, were dispersed at auction in one lot in Baltimore. Later many of these went to Wayte Raymond. Scattered groups of Uncirculated halfpence were available on the market as late as the 1950s, when a Mr. Gottschalk of Syracuse, New York, had hundreds and was frequently tapped by dealers as a source. Likely, these are from the cache held by dealer Barney Bluestone of the same city (see *The Numismatist*, August 1931, in which Bluestone lists these in 14 different varieties). By now, nearly all have been dispersed.

Montroville W. Dickeson, in his 1859 work, *American Numismatical Manual*, commented on two hoards of 1773 Virginia halfpence:

> Some few years since, a quantity of these copper coins was dug up from the summit of the hill on which the college now stands at Knoxville, Tennessee; and quite a number were exhumed from a locality near Easton, Pennsylvania, showing that they must have been extensively circulated, and have amply rewarded the projectors.

Little if any other information is known about the Knoxville and Easton finds, the condition of the pieces, or where they went. Apparently, Dickeson did not know of the Cohen holding.

The typical Uncirculated Virginia halfpenny in the marketplace is bright red-orange with some flecks and spots, but well struck and attractive. Today, most buyers seek a single Virginia halfpenny for the type. Fewer collect them by harp string count, though obtaining such a set is quite possible. A classification by Newman varieties divided into harp string counts and the presence or absence of a period after GEORGIVS is given below. At present, there is not a price differential for most of these varieties, though generally the varieties with no period on the obverse are less common than those with a period.

Prices are presently generic, including scarce and rare Newman varieties. Ongoing research will shed better light on the true rarity of some Virginia halfpence varieties. An opportunity now exists to acquire scarce varieties at prices paid for the more common types, but this may not last long if collector interest expands.

The following die varieties are from "Virginia Halfpence Variety Update With Revised Die Interlock Chart," by Anthony, Moore, and Newman. Alan Anthony and Roger Moore provided special assistance for the present book, including the rarity ratings and market notes.

1773 Halfpenny Varieties

6 Harp Strings · No Dot After GEORGIVS · Large Diameter

W-1390 · Newman 1-A · 1773 Virginia halfpenny · large planchet

Six harp strings. No dot after GEORGIVS. *Notes:* Known as the "Virginia Penny." Struck on a planchet 1-1/8 inches in diameter, 135 grains. Eric P. Newman attributes this as a trial or test striking before regular coinage commenced. Struck with a mirror Proof finish. *Rarity:* URS-6.

VF-20	EF-40	AU-PF	PF
—	—	$12,000	$26,000

6 Harp Strings · No Dot After GEORGIVS

W-1410 · Newman 5-B
Rarity: URS-6.
Selected auction price(s): John J. Ford Jr. VII Sale (Stack's 1/2005), Choice VF, $2,300. Long Beach Sale (Heritage 9/2005), AU-58 (PCGS), $1,725.

W-1420 · Newman 9-B
Rarity: URS-9.
Selected auction price(s): John J. Ford Jr. VII Sale (Stack's 1/2005), F–VG, $115. Long Beach Sale (Heritage 9/2005), MS-63BB (NGC), $1,093. CSNS Sale (Heritage 5/2007), MS-64BN (PCGS), $1,265.

7 Harp Strings · No Dot After GEORGIVS

W-1450 · Newman 2-D
Rarity: URS-6.
Selected auction price(s): John J. Ford Jr. VII Sale (Stack's 1/2005), Choice MS, listed as 2-E, $1,840. CSNS Sale (Heritage 4/2006), MS-61BN (PCGS), listed as 2-E, $1,150.

W-1455 · Newman 3-F
Notes: Often found with prooflike surfaces; do not confuse with the Proof Newman 1-A. *Rarity:* URS-8.
Selected auction price(s): John J. Ford Jr. VII Sale (Stack's 1/2005), Choice MS, $4,600. Long Beach Sale (Heritage 9/2005), MS-64BB (PCGS), $1,610. New York Connoisseur's Collection (B&M 3/2006), MS-64BN (NGC), $1,840. CSNS Sale (Heritage 5/2007), MS-64BN (PCGS), $1,265. Milwaukee Sale (Heritage 8/2007), MS-65BN (NGC), $2,990.

W-1460 · Newman 4-G
Rarity: URS-10.
Selected auction price(s): John J. Ford Jr. VII Sale (Stack's 1/2005), Choice MS, $1,840. Denver Sale (Heritage 8/2006), MS-63BD (PCGS), $2,990.

W-1470 · Newman 4-O
Rarity: URS-8.
Selected auction price(s): John J. Ford Jr. VII Sale (Stack's 1/2005), Choice MS, $2,300. Long Beach Sale (Heritage 9/2005), MS-64BN (PCGS), $1,955. Signature Sale (Heritage 11/2007), MS-64BN (PCGS), $1,380.

W-1475 · Newman 4-P
Rarity: URS-7.

Selected auction price(s): CSNS Sale (Heritage 4/2002), MS-64BN (PCGS), $1,208. CSNS Sale (Heritage 5/2004), MS-63BB (PCGS), $2,013. John J. Ford Jr. VII Sale (Stack's 1/2005), Choice MS, Newman plate coin, $3,450. Long Beach Sale (Heritage 9/2005), MS-63BB (PCGS), $1,955.

W-1480 · Newman 7-D
Rarity: URS-11.
Selected auction price(s): Long Beach Sale (Heritage 9/2005), MS-64 BN (PCGS), $1,150. FUN Sale (Heritage 1/2006), AU-50 (PCGS), $4,025. Long Beach Auction (Heritage 6/2006), MS-65BN (PCGS), $4,200. Houston U.S. Coin Auction (11/2007), MS-67BB (NGC), $13,800.

W-1490 · Newman 8-H
Notes: Very rare in grades of Very Fine or better. This variety has not been seen in Mint State. *Rarity:* URS-9.
Selected auction price(s): John J. Ford Jr. VII Sale (Stack's 1/2005), F, $977.50.

W-1495 · Newman 13-T
Notes: Discovered by Paul Weinstein (*CNL* December 1961). *Rarity:* URS-6.
Selected auction price(s): Private sale, VG, $560.

W-1500 · Newman 15-D
Notes: Discovered by Richard Picker. *Rarity:* URS-5.
Selected auction price(s): Private sale, VG, $255.

7 Harp Strings · Dot After GEORGIVS

W-1540 · Newman 20-N
Notes: See comment under Newman 29-N (W-1595). *Rarity:* URS-9.
Selected auction price(s): John J. Ford Jr. VII Sale (Stack's 1/2005), Choice MS, $2,185. CSNS Sale (Heritage 4/2006), MS-63BD (PCGS), $1,725. Dallas Sale #428 (Heritage 10/2006), MS-64BB (PCGS), $1,265. Milwaukee Sale (Heritage 8/2007), MS-65BB (PCGS), $2,760.

W-1545 · Newman 21-N
Rarity: URS-8.
Selected auction price(s): John J. Ford Jr. VII Sale (Stack's 1/2005), Choice MS BB, $1,725.

W-1550 · Newman 22-S
Rarity: URS-7.
Selected auction price(s): John J. Ford Jr. VII Sale (Stack's 1/2005), Choice MS, $1,955. Americana Sale (Stack's 1/2007), MS-63BB, $1,093. Brooklyn Sale (Stack's 3/2007), MS-64BN (PCGS), $1,035.

W-1560 · Newman 23-Q
Rarity: URS-10.
Selected auction price(s): John J. Ford Jr. VII Sale (Stack's 1/2005), MS–Choice MS, $1,265. Long Beach Sale (Heritage 6/2006), MS-63BB (PCGS), $1,150.

W-1565 · Newman 23-R
Rarity: URS-9.
Selected auction price(s): John J. Ford Jr. VII Sale (Stack's 1/2005), Choice MS, $1,265. Palm Beach Auction #368 (Heritage 3/2005), MS-63BB (PCGS), $2,880. FUN Sale (Heritage 1/2007), MS-64BD (PCGS), $2,185.

W-1570 · Newman 24-K
Notes: This is the most plentiful of all Virginia halfpence and is nearly always found in higher grades. *Rarity:* URS-12.
Selected auction price(s): John J. Ford Jr. VII Sale (Stack's 1/2005), Choice MS, $1,725; $2,530. CSNS Sale (Heritage 5/2005), MS-64BN (PCGS), $2,530. Atlanta Sale (Stack's [ANR] 10/2005), MS-63BD, $1,495. Denver Sale (Heritage 8/2006), MS-65BB (PCGS), $3,450. Signature Sale (Heritage 11/2007), MS-64BB (PCGS), $1,265. FUN Sale (Heritage 1/2008), MS-65BB (PCGS), $3,220.

W-1580 · Newman 25-M
Notes: This is a plentiful variety, but scarcer than W-1565 (cf. Alan Anthony). *Rarity:* URS-11.
Selected auction price(s): FUN Sale (Heritage 1/2005), MS-65BB (NGC), $1,800. John J. Ford Jr. VII Sale (Stack's 1/2005), Choice MS BD, $1,610. Long Beach Sale (Heritage 2/2005), MS-63BD (PCGS), $1,725. Atlanta Sale (Stack's [ANR] 10/2005), MS-63BD, $1,725. FUN Sale (Heritage 1/2006), MS-65BB (NGC), $2,185. Long Beach Sale (Heritage 6/2006), MS-64BD (PCGS), $1,840. Denver Sale (Heritage 8/2006), MS-64BD (PCGS), $2,185. Americana Sale (Stack's 1/2007), MS-63BB, $1,035. Brooklyn Sale (Stack's 3/2007), MS-63BB, $1,150. Long Beach Sale (Heritage 9/2007), MS-64BB (PCGS), $1,265. Pre–Long Beach Elite (Superior 9/2007), MS-64BB (PCGS), $1,092. 72nd Anniversary Sale (Stack's 10/2007), MS-64BB (PCGS), $1,725. Signature Sale (Heritage 11/2007), MS-65BN (PCGS), $2,530.

W-1585 · Newman 27-J
Rarity: URS-11.
Selected auction price(s): John J. Ford Jr. VII Sale (Stack's 1/2005), Gem MS, $2,070. Sanctuary Sale (B&M 6/2003), MS-63BD, $1,035. Classics Sale (Stack's [ANR] 6/2004), MS-64BB (PCGS), $1,035. John J. Ford Jr. VII Sale (Stack's 1/2005), Gem MS BN, $2,070. Dallas Coin Auction (Heritage 11/2006), MS-64BB (NGC), $1,150. Norweb Collection (Stack's 11/2006), MS-64BB (PCGS), $1,150. Long Beach Sale (Heritage 9/2007), MS-63BB (NGC), $1,001.

W-1590 · Newman 28-N
Notes: Discovered by Robert A. Vlack. *Rarity:* URS-2.
Selected auction price(s): No public sale.

W-1595 · Newman 29-N
Notes: Discovered by Mike Ringo. Alan Anthony (contribution): "During my research I have made photo overlays that seem to show that this is a Newman 20-N with a striking anomaly. It is not listed in my unpublished manuscript." *Rarity:* URS-2.
Selected auction price(s): No public sale.

8 Harp Strings · No Dot After GEORGIVS

W-1600 · Newman 5-Z
Notes: Rare in higher grades. *Rarity:* URS-9.
Selected auction price(s): John J. Ford Jr. VII Sale (Stack's 1/2005), Choice MS, Newman plate coin, $2,760. Long Beach Sale (Heritage 9/2005), MS-63BB (PCGS), $1,093.

W-1610 · Newman 6-X
Rarity: URS-10.
Selected auction price(s): John J. Ford Jr. VII Sale (Stack's 1/2005), Choice MS, $2,070.

W-1620 · Newman 10-W
Notes: Discovered by Walter Breen; see New Netherlands Sale #51, June 19, 1958. *Rarity:* URS-6.
Selected auction price(s): Private sale, MS, $1,200.

W-1630 · Newman 12-W
Notes: Discovered by Richard Picker. *Rarity:* URS-4.

W-1640 · Newman 13-V
Notes: Discovered by Ted Craige (*CNL* April–June 1962). *Rarity:* URS-4.
Selected auction price(s): Mail & Internet Bid Sale (Coin Galleries 4/2006), Choice AU, $1,323.

W-1650 · Newman 15-W
Notes: Discovered by Alan Anthony (*CNL* December 2005). *Rarity:* URS-2.

W-1650 · Newman 16-U
Rarity: URS-3.
Selected auction price(s): Heritage sale (1/2004), MS, $4,000.

8 Harp Strings · Dot After GEORGIVS

W-1670 · Newman 20-X
Rarity: URS-10.
Selected auction price(s): John J. Ford Jr. VII Sale (Stack's 1/2005), Choice MS, $1,725. Atlanta Sale (Stack's [ANR] 10/2005), MS-63BD, $1,380.

W-1680 · Newman 26-Y
Rarity: URS-11.
Selected auction price(s): John J. Ford Jr. VII Sale (Stack's 1/2005), Choice MS, $1,610. Atlanta Sale (Stack's [ANR] 10/2005), MS-63BD, $1,438. Atlanta ANA Sale #402 (Heritage 4/2006), MS-63BB (PCGS), $1,955. Long Beach Sale (Heritage 6/2006), MS-64BD (PCGS), $1,840.

Generic Market Values

The following values are for a generic 1773 halfpenny as might be found on the market today. In the future, there likely will be differentials based upon Newman varieties identified as such and expertly cataloged. Wide ranges are anticipated for rare varieties.

Varieties With Period After GEORGIVS

VG-8	F-12	VF-20	EF-40	AU-50	MS-60	MS-63
$50	$110	$240	$450	$650	$1,200	$2,000

Varieties With No Period After GEORGIVS

VG-8	F-12	VF-20	EF-40	AU-50	MS-60	MS-63
$75	$140	$300	$550	$850	$1,500	$2,600

1774 Pattern Silver Halfpenny ("Shilling")

W-1695 · 1774/3 Virginia pattern halfpenny or "shilling"

Obverse: Portrait of King George III facing right, different than on the halfpence. GEORGIVS III DEI GRATIA ("George III, by the grace of God") around the border. *Reverse:* Similar to the halfpenny, but with date 17 74/3 (also divided). *Notes:* Breen-183, Newman pp. 37–38, and Plate I. Pattern halfpenny struck in silver. Edge plain. No denomination given. Traditionally called a shilling in numismatic circles. *Rarity:* URS-4.
Selected auction price(s): Garrett III Sale (B&R 10/1980), PF, $23,000. Roper Sale (Stack's 12/1983), PF, $14,300. John J. Ford Jr. VII Sale (Stack's 1/2005), Gem BrPF, $115,000 (now at Colonial Williamsburg).

New Yorke in America Token
c. 1670

History

This undated token has puzzled many scholars over the years. Perhaps the most definitive study is that by John Kleeberg, "New Yorke in America Token," *Money of Pre-Federal America*, American Numismatic Society, 1992. The obverse shows Cupid and Psyche, a rebus on the name Lovelace, under a palm tree. The reverse illustrates the arms of Francis Lovelace, governor of New York from 1667 to 1673. "The New Yorke in America token is a farthing issued under Governor Lovelace, with the crest of his own arms serving as the arms of New York," the same writer concludes.

Specimens are known in copper (or with slight alloy as brass) and white metal.

W-1705 · New Yorke in America token
Obverse: Allegorical figures of Cupid and Psyche under a palm tree. *Reverse:* Perched eagle, arms of the Lovelace family. NEW YORKE IN AMERICA around the border. *Notes:* Breen-245. Struck in copper alloy. Edge plain. 22 mm. Possibly issued as a farthing (one-fourth of a penny). John Kleeberg (correspondence, 2008): "There are at least 13 known, possibly upwards of 21." Notwithstanding this, examples are few and far between in the marketplace. *Rarity:* URS-6.

VG-8	F-12	VF-20	EF-40
$8,000	$20,000	$30,000	$70,000

W-1710 · New Yorke in America token
Notes: As preceding, but struck in white-metal alloy. Breen-unlisted. John Kleeberg knows of four. *Rarity:* URS-3.

VG-8	F-12	VF-20	EF-40
—	—	—	—

Rhode Island Ship Medals
c. 1780

History

Circumstances surrounding the issue of the Rhode Island ship medal, sometimes referred to as a token, are shrouded in mystery. The piece was virtually unknown to American collectors until a specimen appeared in W. Elliot Woodward's sale of the Seavey Collection on June 21 and 22, 1864, at which time it sold for $40, an extraordinarily high price at the time.

The piece bears on the obverse an outline of an island with stylized soldiers superimposed. Ships are to the left, and men in 13 whaleboats fleeing to the right, a scene set in August 1778. The reverse has a sailing ship with sails furled and an inscription relating to the flight of Admiral Howe's flagship from Narragansett Bay, Rhode Island, in October 1779.

The flight of the Continental Army on August 30, 1778, seems to be ridiculed on one side, and on the other side Admiral Howe's flagship, attesting to his inability to retain the fruits of victory, is satirized. One 19th-century numismatist, George T. Paine, believed the coin may have been struck in Holland by a sympathizer with the American cause who intended one side of the medal as a compliment to Americans on their successful retreat, and the other side as a scorning of the English fleet. Michael J. Hodder believes these were struck in England in 1780 as a propaganda piece, heralding a English victory, scarce at this point, with inscriptions meant to be read by the Dutch (*C4 Newsletter*, Summer 2002). John Kleeberg (correspondence, 2008) offers this:

> A Dutch source is actually likelier than an English source. I have also thought the idea that it refers to Admiral Howe's retreat is a bit far-fetched—it certainly isn't obvious on the medal. I regard it as a wholly pro-British medal, part of the series of Dutch political and satirical medals, issued in the Netherlands as part of the debate within that country as to whether they should enter the war against Britain (which they eventually did). We know that at least one piece did pass through Dutch hands, because the first publication took place in a Japanese book, the *Seiyo Sempu* of 1785, and at that period only the Dutch were permitted to trade with Japan (via Deshima). Interestingly the medal must have traveled east on the ships of the Dutch East India Company—the same company that was shipping zinc westwards to Europe.

Specimens were issued in brass and pewter, the pewter pieces being elusive today. The word *vlugtende* ("fleeing") appears on the earlier issues below Howe's flagship, an engraving error. After a limited number of pieces were struck with this word, it was erased on most coins. A wreath was added, eliminating *vlugtende*, after which the final coinage took place.

W-1725 · Betts-561 · Rhode Island Ship Medal · "vlugtende" Below Ship

Obverse: Outline of Aquidneck Island or Newport Island with stylized soldiers bearing guns and headed to the shore on the right; to the left, English sailing vessels; in water to the right, Americans fleeing in 13 whaleboats. Inscription around border: D'vlugtende AMERICAANEN van ROHDE YLAND Aug,t 1778. Crossed branches below. *Reverse:* Sailing ship with sails furled. Around border: DE ADMIRAALS FLAG van ADMIRAAL HOWE 1779. Below ship: vlugtende. *Notes:* Breen-1138. Edge plain. 32 mm. *Rarity:* URS-2.

Selected auction price(s): Garrett III Sale (B&R 10/1980), EF, $16,000. To JWA collection, Roper Sale (Stack's 12/1983), EF, $9,900.

W-1730 · Betts-562 · Rhode Island Ship Medal · "vlugtende" Removed · brass or related copper alloy

As preceding, but "vlugtende" below ship removed. Obvious traces of the removal remain. *Notes:* Breen-1139. *Rarity:* URS-10.

G-4	VG-8	F-12	VF-20	EF-40	AU-50	MS-60
			$1,200	$2,200	$5,000	$8,000

W-1735 · Betts-562 · Rhode Island Ship Medal · "vlugtende" Removed · pewter

As preceding, but struck in pewter. *Notes:* Breen-1140. *Rarity:* URS-3.

Selected auction price(s): Garrett III Sale (B&R 10/1980), F, $5,000. Long Beach Sale (Heritage 9/2005), EF-45 (PCGS), $9,775.

W-1740 · Betts-563 · Rhode Island Ship Medal · Branches Below Ship · brass

As preceding, but branches or a floral ornament has been added to the die where "vlugtende" once was. *Notes:* Breen-1141. Brass. *Rarity:* URS-9.

VG-8	F-12	VF-20	EF-40	AU-50	MS-60	MS-63
		$1,200	$2,200	$3,300	$7,500	$15,000

W-1745 · Betts-563 · Rhode Island Ship Medal · Branches Below Ship · pewter

As preceding, but struck in pewter. *Notes:* Breen-1142. *Rarity:* URS-5.

VG-8	F-12	VF-20	EF-40	AU-50	MS-60	MS-63
		$5,500	$9,000	$12,000	$15,000	$17,500

7

AMERICAN COINS AND TOKENS 1783–1788

CHALMERS SILVER COINAGE
1783

History

John Chalmers, an Annapolis, Maryland, goldsmith and silversmith, produced in 1783 a series of silver coins of his own design. Values were of threepence, sixpence, and shilling. Several varieties were made.

Dr. Johann David Schoepf, a German who visited America in 1783 and 1784, wrote of his visit to Annapolis (in *Travels in the Confederation, 1783–1784*, cited by Crosby pp. 329, 330). Schoepf noted that the Chalmers coinage was initiated to prevent some of the abuses then being practiced with fractional parts of the Spanish dollar. It was customary at the time to cut a Spanish silver dollar into halves, quarters, and eighths, with the eighths being known as "one bit" or 12-1/2¢. Unscrupulous persons would attempt to cut five "quarters" or nine or ten "eighths" out of one coin, thereby realizing a proportional profit. Schoepf reported that Chalmers redeemed various fractional parts and exchanged his own coins for them, charging a commission to do so.

The building in which these pieces were coined stood at Fleet and Cornhill streets. Although the coins had no official status and were privately issued, apparently the government took no exception to them. Some, perhaps all, dies were engraved by Thomas Sparrow, who also made plates for Maryland paper money. Some could have been engraved by Chalmers, who certainly had the talent. Coinage apparently was quite extensive, for several hundred examples are known today. Most show evidence of considerable use in commerce.

Numismatic Aspects

The shilling denomination apparently was produced in the largest quantities for these are most often seen today. Two birds tugging on the same worm furnished the motif for the reverse of this issue. Diameters vary but average for the threepence is 13 mm, sixpence 17.5 mm, and shilling 22 mm. Edges were reeded by hand.

All Chalmers issues are elusive today. Most show extensive wear, with grades such as Fine and Very Fine being typical in most collections. Die varieties exist and are described below. They have not been widely sought, as most numismatists desire just one of each denomination and major style. The threepence is exceedingly rare. Remarkably, this denomination was lacking in the Ford Collection. One variety of the 1783 shilling with rings and stars on the reverse is exceedingly rare, with fewer than a half dozen known to exist.

1783 Chalmers Threepence

W-1760 · 1783 Chalmers threepence
Obverse: I. CHALMERS ANNAP's around border. Within, two clasped hands. *Reverse:* THREE PENCE 1783 and punctuation around border. At the center, a branch surrounded by a wreath. *Notes:* Breen-1018. *Rarity:* URS-7.

VG-8	F-12	VF-20	EF-40	AU-50
$2,400	$5,000	$7,500	$20,000	$40,000

1783 Chalmers Sixpence

W-1765 · Large Date · date as 17.83
Obverse: I. CHALMERS ANNAPOLIS 1783 and punctuation around border. At the center, a five-pointed star enclosed by a wreath. *Reverse:* I.C. SIX PENCE 17.83 around border. Within, a cross with two arms having a star at the end and two having a crescent. At the center of the cross are two clasped hands with ornaments in the field nearby. The "period" dividing the date is actually an ornament found on other dies as well, but in this instance intruding slightly into the date. *Notes:* Breen-1013. *Rarity:* URS-2 or 3(?).

VG-8	F-12	VF-20	EF-40	AU-50
$3,000	$7,000	$15,000	$25,000	$50,000

W-1770 · Large Date · period after date
General style as preceding, except as noted in the title. The period after date is very small. Initials T and S (for Thomas Sparrow) within crescents at end of cross. *Notes:* Breen-1014. *Rarity:* URS-6.

VG-8	F-12	VF-20	EF-40	AU-50
$3,000	$7,000	$10,000	$25,000	$50,000

W-1775 · Small Date · 8-pointed star after SIX
General style as preceding, except as noted in the title. *Notes:* Breen-1015. *Rarity:* URS-5.

VG-8	F-12	VF-20	EF-40	AU-50
$3,500	$8,000	$17,500	$30,000	$60,000

W-1780 · Small Date · 6-pointed star after SIX
General style as preceding, except as noted in the title. *Notes:* Breen-1017. *Rarity:* URS-5.

VG-8	F-12	VF-20	EF-40	AU-50
$3,500	$8,000	$17,500	$30,000	$60,000

1783 Chalmers Shillings

W-1785 · Short Worm
Obverse: I. CHALMERS, ANNAPOLIS and rosette around the border. Within, two clasped hand encircled by a wreath. *Reverse:* ONE SHILLING 1783 divided by rosettes around the border. At the center a beaded circle and adjacent circular line encloses a scene with a bar or fence across, a serpent above, and below, two birds competing for the same worm (or a "branch," per Crosby). Right end of bar opposite N (SHILLING). *Notes:* Usually with areas of localized weakness from misaligned dies or uneven planchet thickness. Breen-1011. *Rarity:* URS-8.

VG-8	F-12	VF-20	EF-40	AU-50
$2,500	$3,500	$6,800	$15,000	$30,000

W-1790 · Long Worm
Obverse: Same die as preceding. *Reverse:* General style as preceding. Worm longer than on the preceding. Right end of bar opposite second I (SHILLING). *Notes:* Obverse usually with areas of weakness. Breen-1012. *Rarity:* URS-9.

VG-8	F-12	VF-20	EF-40	AU-50
$2,500	$3,800	$7,500	$17,500	$35,000

W-1795 · Rings on reverse
Obverse: I. CHALMERS ANNAPOLIS 1783 with ornaments around border. At the center in three lines of script: EQUAL / TO ONE SHI. Ornament above, clasped hands below. *Reverse:* Twelve linked rings around border, 11 of which enclose a five-pointed star. At center, a ring from which a liberty pole and cap extend upward; five-pointed star to each side of the cap. *Notes:* Five reported: Mickley-Ford (VF–EF, the only example known to Crosby), Garrett (F–VF), Norweb-Smithsonian, Eric P. Newman (holed), and Loye Lauder (Poor, holed and plugged). All range from weak to indistinct at the centers. Breen-1010. *Rarity:* URS-4.

VG-8	F-12	VF-20
—	—	$175,000

Nova Constellatio Patterns
1783

1783 Nova Constellatio silver pattern 1,000 units or mark. (Early Coins of America, 1875)

History

In 1783 a remarkable group of pattern coins made its appearance: the "bit" of 100 units, the "quint" of 500 units, and the "mark" of 1,000 units. Sylvester S. Crosby said: "These are undoubtedly the first patterns for coinage of the United States and command an interest exceeding that of any others of this class." To these can be added a 5-unit piece in copper, unknown to Crosby. These were intended to illustrate coinage to be produced in the proposed North American Mint, operated under government auspices.

Gouverneur Morris, who had been assistant financier of the Confederation, proposed these pieces. Jared Sparks, in *The Life of Gouverneur Morris* (1832), quotes Morris:

> The various coins which have circulated in America have undergone different changes in their value so that there is hardly any which can be considered of the general standard, unless it be Spanish dollars. These pass in Georgia at five shillings, in North Carolina and New York at eight shillings, in Virginia and the four eastern states at six shillings, and in all other states, excepting South Carolina, at seven shillings and sixpence, and in South Carolina at thirty-two shillings and sixpence. The money unit of a new coin to agree, without a fraction, with all these different values of a dollar, excepting the last, will be the fourteen hundred and fortieth part of a dollar, equal to the sixteenth hundredth part of a crown. Of these units, twenty-four will be a penny of Georgia, fifteen will be a penny of North Carolina or New York, twenty will be a penny of Virginia and the four eastern states, sixteen will be a penny of all the other states, excepting South Carolina, and forty-eight will be thirteen pence of South Carolina.
>
> It has already been observed that to have the money unit very small is advantageous to commerce; but there is no necessity that this money unit be exactly represented in coin; it is sufficient that its value be precisely known. On the present occasion, two copper coins will be proper, the one of eight units, and the other of five. These may be called an Eight and a Five. Two of the former will make a penny proclamation, or Pennsylvania money, and three a penny Georgia money. Of the latter, three will make a penny New York money and four a penny lawful, or Virginia money. The money unit will be equal to a quarter of a grain of fine silver in coined money. Proceeding thence in a decimal ratio, one hundred would be the lowest silver coin, and might be called a Cent. It would contain twenty-five grains of fine silver, to which may be added two grains of copper, and the whole would weigh one pennyweight and three grains. Five of these would make a Quint or five hundred units, weighing five pennyweight and fifteen grains; and ten would make a Mark, or one thousand units weighing eleven pennyweight and six grains.

The preceding is also a dramatic exposition of how moneys of account varied from one state to another at the time.

Some of the circumstances surrounding the issue of 1783 pattern coins were recorded by Robert R. Morris, the financier. His diary noted that on April 2, 1783, "I sent for Mr. [Benjamin] Dudley who delivered me a piece of silver coin, being the first that has been struck as an American coin."

On April 16 it was noted that he "sent for Mr. Dudley and urged him to produce the coin to lay before the Congress to establish a mint." On the following day, April 17, he "sent for Mr. Dudley to urge the preparing of coins, etc. for establishing a mint."

Morris reported on April 22nd that: "Mr. Dudley sent in several pieces of money as patterns of the intended American coins." On July 5th he noted that "Mr. Benjamin Dudley also informs of a minting press being in New York for sale, and urges me to purchase for the use of the American Mint."

On August 19 he reports as follows:

> I sent for Mr. Benjamin Dudley, informed him of my doubts about the establishment of a mint and desired him to think of some employment in private service, in which I am willing to assist him in all my power. I told him to make out an account for the services he had performed for the public and submit at the Treasury office for inspection and settlement.

On August 30 it was reported that "Mr. Dudley brought the dies for coining in the American Mint."

The dies for the bit and quint denominations were cut by hand. The largest value, the mark, was made by the use of prepared punches. The pedigree of two pieces, the mark and the quint, obtained by John W. Haseltine in 1872 and years later sold into the Garrett Collection, was attested to by the seller, Rathmell Wilson, who on May 28, 1872, stated,

> The history of the two coins which you obtained from me, viz. Nova Constellatio 1783, U.S. 1,000, Nova Constellatio, 1783 U.S. 500 is as follows.
>
> They were the property of Hon. Charles Thomson, secretary of the first Congress. At his death the property was left by will to his nephew, John Thomson, of Newark, state of Delaware. These two coins were found

in the desk of the said deceased Charles Thomson, and preserved by his nephew during his life; at his death they came into the possession of his son Samuel E. Thomson of Newark, Delaware, from whom I received them. So you will perceive that their genuineness cannot be questioned; as they were never out of the possession of the Thomson family, until I received them.

Among the accounts of the United States, under the category of "Expenditure for Contingencies," between January and July 1783, the following entries appear in relation to coinage:

February 8. Jacob Eckfeldt, for dies for the Mint of North America, $5 and 18/90ths.

March 21. Benjamin Dudley employed in preparing a mint. $75 and 24/90ths.

April 17. John Swanwick, for dies for the public mint $22 and 42/90ths.

May 5. A. Dubois, for sinking, casehardening, etc., for pairs of dies for the public mint $72.

June 30. Benjamin Dudley employed in preparing a mint $77 and 60/90ths.

These patterns were created with care and with the intention of initiating a federal coinage. Their time had not come, and had it not been for the fortuitous saving of the silver pieces by Thomson, we might not know of them today. The copper five-unit piece is a later discovery found in Europe in 1977. Most of the different 1783 Nova Constellatio issues were acquired at the Garrett Collection sale by John J. Ford Jr., and later went into another fine private cabinet, along with the five-unit coin.

The North American Mint did not come to pass. The primary 1783 pattern designs were later used in a private venture to coin and distribute Nova Constellatio copper coins mostly dated 1783 and 1785.

Numismatic Aspects

The group of Nova Constellatio silver patterns obtained from Thomson's heirs was sold to Lorin G. Parmelee. In the 1890 sale of that collection the buyer was James W. Ellsworth. In 1923 the Ellsworth Collection was purchased by Wayte Raymond and John Work Garrett, with the latter retaining the Nova Constellatio patterns. In 1942 the Garrett coins went to The Johns Hopkins University. The present writer described the coins when they were auctioned in 1979, with the buyer being John J. Ford Jr. Sitting in the front row, and with Herbert I. Melnick as one of his agents, Ford developed a complicated scenario in which he (Ford) would bid, then ostensibly drop out, after which Melnick, seemingly acting for someone else, would commence bidding. Signals became crossed, and Ford had to break his plan to shout across the row to Melnick with further instructions. In the early 21st century Stack's, acting on behalf of the Ford family, sold the coins to a private collector.

1783 Nova Constellatio Pattern Coinage

W-1810 · 5 units
Obverse: All-seeing eye with rays surrounding, 13 stars between longest rays. NOVA CONSTELLATIO around border. *Reverse:* U.S / . . . 5 [three dots and 5] at center, ring of double leaves surrounding. LIBERTAS JUSTITIA / 1783 around border. *Edge:* Plain. *Notes:* 24 mm. Breen-1105. *Rarity:* URS-1. European dealer, John J. Ford Jr. Collection, private collection.

W-1815 · 100 units or 1 bit · ornamented edge
Obverse: All-seeing eye with rays surrounding, 13 stars between longest rays. NOVA CONSTELLATIO around border. *Reverse:* U.S / 100 at center, ring of double leaves surrounding. LIBERTAS JUSTITIA / 1783 around border. *Edge:* Ornamented with leaves. *Notes:* 18 mm. Silver. Breen-1103. *Rarity:* URS-2.

Selected auction price(s): Garrett I Sale (B&R 11/1979), MS-65, prooflike, $97,500 to Ford. Pedigree: ex Thomson heirs to Haseltine, Parmelee, Ellsworth, Garrett, and Ford, now in a private collection via Stack's.

W-1820 · 100 units or 1 bit · plain edge
As preceding, but with plain edge. Breen-1104. *Rarity:* URS-1. Eric P. Newman collection.

W-1825 · 500 units or 1 quint
Obverse: All-seeing eye with rays surrounding, 13 stars between longest rays. NOVA CONSTELLATIO around border. *Reverse:* U.S / 500 at center, ring of double leaves surrounding. LIBERTAS JUSTITIA / 1783 around border. *Edge:* Ornamented with leaves. *Notes:* 24 mm. Silver. Breen-1101. *Rarity:* URS-1.

Selected auction price(s): Garrett I Sale (B&R 11/1979), MS-65, prooflike, $165,000 to Ford. Pedigree: ex Thomson heirs to Haseltine, Parmelee, Ellsworth, Garrett, and Ford, now in a private collection via Stack's.

W-1830 · 500 units or 1 quint

Obverse: All-seeing eye with 13 closely spaced rays surrounding, 13 stars between highest tips of rays. No inscription. *Reverse:* Same as preceding. *Edge:* Ornamented with leaves. *Notes:* Parmelee Collection 1890 to Col. J.W. Ellsworth to John Work Garrett. Possibly owned by S.S. Crosby earlier. 24 mm. Silver. Breen-1102. *Rarity:* URS-1.

Selected auction price(s): Garrett I Sale (B&R 11/1979), AU-55, prooflike, $55,000 to Walter Perschke.

W-1835 · 1,000 units or 1 mark

Obverse: All-seeing eye with rays surrounding, 13 stars between longest rays. NOVA CONSTELLATIO around border. *Reverse:* U.S / 1.000 at center, ring of double leaves surrounding. LIBERTAS JUSTITIA / 1783 around border. *Edge:* Ornamented with leaves. *Notes:* 33 mm. Silver. Breen-1099. *Rarity:* URS-1.

Selected auction price(s): Garrett I Sale (B&R 11/1979), MS-60, prooflike, $190,000 to Ford. Pedigree: ex Thomson heirs to Haseltine, Parmelee, Ellsworth, Garrett, and Ford, now in a private collection via Stack's.

Nova Constellatio Coppers
1783–1786

1783 Nova Constellatio copper, type with pointed rays. (*Early Coins of America*, 1875)

History

The most comprehensive coverage of this series is by Eric P. Newman, "New Thoughts on the Nova Constellatio Private Copper Coinage," 1996. His conclusions deeply influenced the present narrative, the history of the coinage being different from that given in earlier texts. This was followed by Louis E. Jordan's "An Examination of the 'New Constellation' Coppers in Relation to the Nova Constellatio—Constellatio Nova Debate" in the *Colonial Newsletter*, December 2000. (At one time, Walter Breen proposed to use the Constellatio Nova word order, but this has since been discredited.) Together, these constitute most of the present state of the art concerning the history of these pieces.

In the early 1780s Gouverneur Morris, assistant superintendent of finance with the Continental Congress from 1781 to 1785, and a proponent of the 1,000-unit decimal coins and their fractional parts (the quint and the bit), joined with Robert Morris and William Constable as principals in William Constable & Co., a commercial house in New York City. In June 1784, John Rucker, residing in London, was admitted to the firm, and the name was changed to Constable, Rucker & Co. As a private venture the company ordered a large number of copper coins bearing designs artistically related to the 1783 Nova Constellatio silver patterns and copied from them. By this time the idea of creating the North American Mint to be run by the federal government had been abandoned. It is believed that the Nova Constellatio copper issues were struck by a private mint in Birmingham, England. Years later, William Constable was involved in the laying out of Castorland, a French settlement upstate New York that issued tokens (see listing).

Newman suggests that the 1783-dated pieces may not have been struck until 1785, for no contemporary accounts concerning them have been located before that year. The design seems to have been copied from the 1783 five-unit decimal pattern piece.

The obverse of the 1783 coins depicts an all-seeing eye at the center surrounded with rays and stars and with the legend NOVA CONSTELLATIO. Styles were made with blunt as well as pointed rays (the blunt-rays coins were the inspiration for the 1785 Vermont coppers with a related central motif). The reverse of each piece bears the inscription LIBERTAS JUSTITIA, a wreath within, and the block letters U S. This is a reference to the "new constellation" or group of colonies which together formed the United States. The 1785 coins have a modified reverse with script letters US and the motto expanded by ET, now as LIBERTAS ET JUSTITIA. The assigning of the NOVA CONSTELLATIO side follows Crosby. Others have called this the reverse.

Specimens were made in large quantities with the 1783 and 1785 dates. Numerous die variations occur and were first described in detail by Crosby (as delineated below), a system still useful today. A few specimens dated 1786 are known, but these are contemporary counterfeits attributed by some to Machin's Mills. The edge is plain on all. Crosby, the Red Book, and most others designate the rays side as the obverse, but Breen calls this the reverse. Crosby's obverse dies 2 and 3 of the 1783-dated coinage and obverse 3 of 1785 were muled with IMMUNE COLUMBIA dies.

The Nova Constellatio coppers were well received and saw extensive use in commerce, as evidenced by the wear seen on typical specimens today. Later, they were devalued, and many were used as undertypes (planchets) for Connecticut and, to a lesser extent, New Jersey and Vermont coppers.

75

1783 Nova Constellatio Coppers

W-1860 · Crosby 1-A · Large U • S

Obverse: Pointed rays. Ray points at bottom of first O (CONSTELLATIO). *Reverse:* U • S in larger block letters (S noticeably larger than U), circle of 24 pairs of leaves surrounding. LIBERTAS JUSTITIA / 1783 around border. This variety is often called "Large US." *Notes:* Usually seen in low grades. This and other 1783-dated coins may have been struck in 1785; see above narrative. The date numerals on W-1860 are similar to those on the 1783-dated GEORGIVS TRIUMPHO token, W-9310. The die work indicates a hand not as experienced as that which made the rest of the coinage (genuine issues). The obverse die was damaged by another die falling on it, below center, leaving dentil impressions opposite STEL and ATIO. The lower right portion of the wreath is always lightly struck. As to whether W-1860 is a contemporary counterfeit, or an authorized issue by a different diesinker, is unknown. Unlike any other in this series it is punch-linked to the 1783 Georgivs Triumpho token (W-10100). Breen-1106. *Rarity:* URS-8 or 9.

VG-8	F-12	VF-20	EF-40	AU-50	MS-60	MS-63
$120	$275	$750	$1,650	$3,700	$5,500	$8,000

W-1865 · Crosby 2-B · Pointed Rays · Small U • S

Obverse: Pointed rays. Ray points between C and O (CONSTELLATIO). *Reverse:* U • S in small block letters (smaller than on W-1860), circle of 24 pairs of leaves surrounding. LIBERTAS JUSTITIA / 1783 around border. *Rarity:* URS-11.

VG-8	F-12	VF-20	EF-40	AU-50	MS-60	MS-63
$110	$250	$500	$1,100	$2,000	$4,000	$6,000

W-1875 · Crosby 3-C · CONSTELATIO · Blunt Rays

Obverse: Blunt rays. CONSTELATIO misspelling. Also used for W-1880. *Reverse:* U • S in small block letters, circle of 23 pairs of leaves surrounding. LIBERTAS JUSTITIA / 1783 around border. *Rarity:* URS-10.

VG-8	F-12	VF-20	EF-40	AU-50	MS-60	MS-63
$120	$275	$700	$1,600	$2,800	$5,000	$7,000

1785 Nova Constellatio Coppers

W-1880 · Crosby 1-B · script US

Obverse: Same as W-1875. *Reverse:* US in large overlapping script letters, circle of 30 pairs of leaves surrounding. LIBERTAS ET JUSTITIA / 1785 around border. The 5 (1785) with wide flag at top extending past lower curve of 5. Large piece out of die above date. *Rarity:* URS-9.

VG-8	F-12	VF-20	EF-40	AU-50	MS-60	MS-63
$120	$275	$700	$1,800	$4,000	$5,000	$8,000

W-1885 · Crosby 2-A · Small Date

Obverse: Pointed rays. One ray points to left foot of N and ray points to right foot of A (NOVA). Another ray points slightly right of bottom of first O (CONSTELLATIO), and another points to just past base of upright of T. *Reverse:* US in large overlapping script letters, circle of 30 pairs of leaves surrounding. LIBERTAS ET JUSTITIA / 1785 around border. The 17 (1785) very close, 5 rotated too far left. Date distant from letters at each side. *Rarity:* URS-9.

VG-8	F-12	VF-20	EF-40	AU-50	MS-60	MS-63
$375	$850	$4,000	$7,000	$9,000	$12,500	$15,000

W-1895 · Crosby 3-B · Pointed Rays · script US

Obverse: Pointed rays. One ray points to left foot of N; one points to right foot of A (NOVA); one points to slightly left of bottom of first O (CONSTELLATIO); and one points to base of I. *Reverse:* Same as W-1880, but earlier state with smaller piece out of die. *Notes:* Obverse die usually heavily rusted. Theoretically this variety may exist without the reverse break, but none has been seen. *Rarity:* URS-11.

VG-8	F-12	VF-20	EF-40	AU-50	MS-60	MS-63
$110	$250	$525	$1,100	$2,000	$3,000	$5,000

W-1915 · Crosby 5-E

Obverse: Pointed rays. One ray points to past left foot of N; one points to left foot of A (NOVA); one points between C and O; and one points to between T and I. *Reverse:* US in large overlapping script letters, circle of 26 pairs of leaves surrounding. LIBERTAS ET JUSTITIA / 1785 around border. The 17 (1785) close, top of 7 wide. *Notes:* Both dies for this variety are very distinctive. *Rarity:* URS-8.

VG-8	F-12	VF-20	EF-40	AU-50	MS-60	MS-63
$110	$250	$525	$1,100	$2,000	$3,000	$5,000

W-1900 · Crosby 4-C

Obverse: Pointed rays. One ray points to just past left foot of N; one points to near center of A (NOVA); one points slightly left of bottom of first O (CONSTELLATIO); and one points to just past base of upright of T. Die also used for W-1910. *Reverse:* US in large overlapping script letters, circle of 30 pairs of leaves surrounding. LIBERTAS ET JUSTITIA / 1785 around border. *Notes:* Usually seen in low grades. The finest may be a choice Mint State in the Roger S. Siboni Collection (ex Stack's, September 2006). *Rarity:* URS-7.

VG-8	F-12	VF-20	EF-40	AU-50	MS-60	MS-63
$110	$250	$525	$1,100	$2,000	$3,000	$5,000

W-1920 · Crosby unlisted · 12 Stars

Obverse: NOVA CONSTELLATIO. Only 12 stars. *Reverse:* US in large overlapping script letters, circle of 23 pairs of leaves surrounding. LIBERTAS ET JUSTITIA / 1785 around border. Letters irregularly formed and spaced. *Notes:* Early die-struck counterfeit. Very crude. Eric P. Newman, owner of this unique coin, suggests an American origin. *Rarity:* URS-1.

1786 Nova Constellatio Copper

W-1940 · Crosby 1-A

Obverse: Nova Constellatio with pointed rays. *Reverse:* U • S in small letters, circle of double leaves surrounding. LIBERTAS JUSTITIA / 1786 around border. *Notes:* This coin, of unique date, is believed to have been made at Machin's Mills. All examples show extensive wear. *Rarity:* URS-5 or barely 6.

G-4	VG-8	F-12	VF-20
—		$10,500	

W-1910 · Crosby 4-D

Obverse: Same as preceding. *Reverse:* US in large overlapping script letters, circle of 29 pairs of leaves surrounding. LIBERTAS ET JUSTITIA / 1785 around border. *Rarity:* URS-8.

VG-8	F-12	VF-20	EF-40	AU-50	MS-60	MS-63
$110	$250	$525	$1,100	$2,000	$3,000	$5,000

1785 Nova Constellatio / 1785 Confederatio Muling

W-1950 · Crosby Plate VII, No. 10 · Large Stars
Obverse: Nova Constellatio reverse die, Crosby C, with script US, 30 pairs of leaves surrounding. *Reverse:* Large circle at center enclosing 13 large stars, rays around circle. CONFEDERATIO around border, 1785 below. *Rarity:* URS-1.

Selected auction price(s): Ford II Sale (5/2004), AG–VG, $6,037.50.

Immune Columbia Coinage 1785

1785 Immune Columbia copper with Nova Constellatio reverse. (*Early Coins of America*, 1875)

Stylistically related to the Nova Constellatio coppers are certain other pieces with an obverse from the Immune Columbia die combined with several different reverses. It has been suggested that the legend refers to America (Columbia) being immune to the problems of distant Europe. Three of these reverses are of the Nova Constellatio design, two with pointed rays and one with blunt rays. Other coins are mulings of irrelevant dies and are thought to have been produced at Machin's Mills in Newburgh, New York. Certain strikings in silver and gold were probably made as numismatic curiosities, possibly after Machin's Mills closed. Once again, facts are scarce and theories plentiful.

Eric P. Newman, in "New Thoughts on the Nova Constellatio Private Copper Coinage," 1996, discusses the relationship between certain Nova Constellatio and Immune Columbia coppers. The Breen *Encyclopedia* arranges the coins in an entirely different order from that used here, and gives his views of who made them and why, much of which is unsupported by documentation.

1785 Immune Columbia Issues

W-1960 · Immune Columbia / Nova Constellatio · Star in Border · copper
Obverse: Seated Liberty on a box or crate, with pole and cap and scales of justice. IMMUNE / COLUMBIA • to left and right, 1785 and ornaments below. *Reverse:* NOVA CONSTELLATIO with pointed rays. Star and dot in border. *Notes:* 27.1 mm. Breen-1117. *Rarity:* URS-5.

VG-8	F-12	VF-20	EF-40	AU-50
		$30,000	$45,000	$75,000

W-1970 · Immune Columbia / Nova Constellatio · gold
As preceding but struck in gold, over an English guinea. Likely made at a later date. *Notes:* Unique. Traded to the Mint Cabinet by Matthew Stickney on May 9, 1843, in exchange for an 1804 Class I silver dollar. Breen-1118. In the Smithsonian Institution. *Rarity:* URS-1.

W-1980 · Immune Columbia / Nova Constellatio · No Star in Border · copper
Obverse: Same as preceding. *Reverse:* NOVA CONSTELLATIO with pointed rays (Crosby obverse 3). No ornaments in border. *Notes:* Likely the gold and silver impressions (see following) were made in the 19th century (see Eric P. Newman and Kenneth E. Bressett, *The Fantastic 1804 Dollar*, 1962). Breen-1119. *Rarity:* URS-4.

VG-8	F-12	VF-20	EF-40
		$30,000	$45,000

W-1982 · Immune Columbia / Nova Constellatio · silver · plain edge
As preceding but struck in silver. Plain edge. *Notes:* Likely made at a later date. Breen-1121. *Rarity:* URS-3.

W-1985 · Immune Columbia / Nova Constellatio · silver · reeded edge

As preceding, struck in silver, but with diagonally reeded edge. *Notes:* Likely made at a later date. Breen-1120. *Rarity:* URS-4(?).

VF-20	EF-40	AU-50
$50,000	$75,000	

W-1990 · Immune Columbia / Blunt Rays CONSTELATIO · copper

Obverse: Same as preceding. *Reverse:* NOVA CONSTELATIO (misspelled) with blunt rays. A die used for regular Nova Constellatio coinage. *Notes:* Breen-1122. *Rarity:* URS-2.

Selected auction price(s): Garrett III Sale (B&R 10/1980), VG–F, $17,900. To Roper Sale (Stack's 12/1983), VG, $11,000. Norweb II Sale (3/1988), VF, $22,000.

W-1995 · Vlack 15-85 NY · George III / Immune Columbia

Obverse: CEORCIVS spelling. CEO widely spaced, RCIVS close. VS letters touch head. S leans left. Bow opposite O. Roman numeral III tight and angles downward. R (REX) closer to the period. Die deeply cut, so that central detail on struck coins is virtually absent. *Reverse:* Immune Columbia. *Notes:* Most are found in low grade and/or have defective planchets. The reverse is found with the Ryder-Richardson-1 Vermont. Breen-1000. *Condition Census:* VF-20 to EF-40. *Rarity:* URS-5.

G-4	VG-8	F-12	VF-20	EF-40
$7,500	$11,500	$14,000	$21,000	$42,000

(W-2250) · Immune Columbia / VERMON AUCTORI

Muling with Machin's Mills obverse die for a Vermont copper. See W-2250 in the Vermont section.

REPUBLIC OF VERMONT COPPERS
1785–1788

Preparations

Of the several states that issued copper coins during the 1780s, the earliest was the Republic of Vermont. Although it considered itself a state, the Republic of Vermont was not formally a state until its admittance to the Union in 1791.

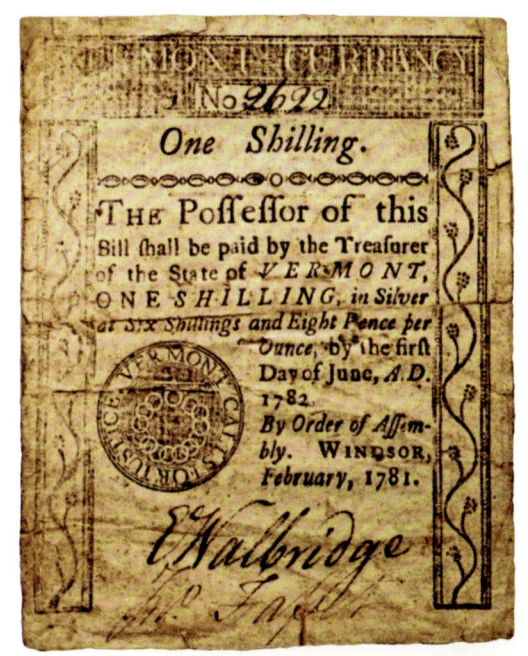

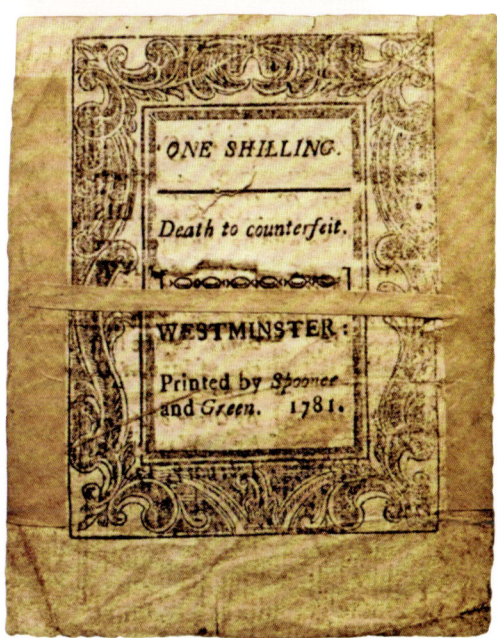

Vermont one-shilling note of 1781, issued by the *state* several years before the official coinage.

On June 10, 1785, Reuben Harmon Jr., a storekeeper and entrepreneur of Rupert, Bennington County, petitioned the House of Representatives for permission to produce coinage for Vermont. A committee consisting of Messrs. Tichenor, Strong, and Williams, with the addition of Ira Allen from the Legislative Council, was formed to consider the proposal. On June 15, 1785, a bill authorizing Harmon to coin copper pieces was sent to the governor and council for consideration and possible amendment:

> Whereas Reuben Harmon Jr., Esq., of Rupert in the county of Bennington, by his petition has represented that he has purchased a quantity of copper suitable for coining, and praying this legislature to grant him a right to coin copper, under such regulations as this assembly shall think meet; and this assembly being willing to encourage an undertaking that promises so much public utility, therefore:
>
> Be it enacted and it is hereby enacted . . . that there be and hereby is granted to the said Reuben Harmon Jr., Esq., the exclusive right of coining copper within this state for the term of two years from the first day of July, in the present year of our Lord one thousand seven hundred and eighty-five; and all coppers by him coined shall be in pieces of one third of an ounce troy each, with such devices and mottoes as shall be agreed on by the committee appointed for that purpose by this assembly.
>
> And be it further enacted . . . that the said Reuben Harmon before he enter on the business of coining, or take any benefit of this act, shall enter into a bond of five thousand pounds, to the treasurer of the state, with two or more good and sufficient sureties, freeholders of this state, conditioned that all the copper by him coined as aforesaid, shall be a full weight as specified in this act, and that the same shall be made of good and genuine metal.

The bill was passed on the same day. On June 16 the required financial bond was obtained. Harmon found that his coins, regulated to be the weight of one-third ounce each, would be too heavy and would weigh more than pieces of halfpenny size circulating at that time throughout the United States. Accordingly, an amendment was passed on October 27, 1785:

> Be it enacted and it is hereby enacted . . . that all coppers coined by said Reuben Harmon Jr., Esq., shall be of genuine copper in pieces weighing not less than four pennyweight fifteen grains each, and so much of the aforesaid act that regulates the weight of said coins is hereby repealed.

Reuben Harmon Jr. and the Rupert Mint

Sylvester S. Crosby quotes a letter from historian Benjamin H. Hall of Troy, New York, to Charles I. Bushnell, of New York City, dated March 3, 1855, which gives a brief biography of Harmon and tells of the mint:

> Reuben Harmon Jr. came from Suffield, Connecticut, in company with his father, Reuben Harmon, Sr., about the year 1768, and settled in the northeast part of Rupert, Vermont. He was a man of some note and influence while there. At a meeting of the inhabitants of the New Hampshire Grants held at Dorset, September 25, 1776, initiatory to their Declaration of Independence, Mr. Reuben Harmon [probably Jr.] was one of the representatives from Rupert. He was representative in the Vermont Legislature from Rupert in 1780, was justice of the peace from 1780 to 1790, and held several minor offices. In the year 1790 or thereabouts he left Rupert, for that part of the State of Ohio called New Connecticut, and there died long since.
>
> His Mint House was located near the northeast corner of Rupert, a little east of the main road leading from Dorset to Pawlet, on a small stream of water called Millbrook, which empties into Pawlet River. It was a small building, about 16 by 18 feet, made of rough materials; sided with unplaned and unpainted boards. It is still standing, but its location and uses are entirely different from what they were originally. Its situation at present is on the border of the adjoining town of Pawlet whither it was long since removed, and what was once a coin house is now a corn house.
>
> Col. William Cooley [Coley], who had worked at the goldsmith's trade in the city of New York, and who afterwards moved to Rupert, made the dies and assisted in striking the coin.

The Vermont Mint and Coinage

The same correspondent wrote to Charles I. Bushnell on July 18, 1855, with additional information:

> The sundial, or "Mind Your Business" copper coin, common in New England at the close of the last and at the commencement of the present century, was first manufactured by Abel Buel [*Buell* is the preferred spelling in numismatic circles today] at New Haven, Connecticut, the original dies having been designed and cut by himself. Not long after this, his son William Buel, removed from the manufactory to the town of Rupert, Bennington County, Vermont, and in connection with a Mr. Harmon, established the mint-house on what is now known as Millbrook.
>
> William had taken with him the original dies used by his father at New Haven, and continued at Rupert the coinage of the coppers above referred to, until the coin had depreciated so much in value as to be worthless or nearly so, for circulation. The remains of the dam which rendered the waters of Millbrook eligible are still to be seen, and pieces of copper and specimens of the old coin are still occasionally picked up on the site of the old mill and in the brook below.

It is doubted today that 1787-dated Fugio coppers, referred to as the "Mind Your Business copper coin" above, were actually struck in Vermont, for the act which authorized Reuben Harmon Jr. to strike coins specifically delineated the type of coins to be produced and provided strong penalties if there were deviations from those authorized. Eric P. Newman, writing "A Recently Discovered Coin Solves a

Vermont Numismatic Enigma" in *The Centennial Publication of the American Numismatic Society*, New York, 1958, gives the opinion that Buell brought with him punches and tools but not coining dies. These would have been Abel Buell's punches that were used to create the 1786 and 1787 Mailed Bust Left dies, similar in style to those used on Connecticut coppers. However, the workmanship of the lettering placement and style on the obverses and reverses is amateurish in comparison to the Connecticut dies believed to have been completely done (punches plus lettering) by Abel Buell.

It was related that William Buell had become involved in an altercation with Indians who accused Buell of killing one of their friends. It seems that Buell had obtained from a druggist a quantity of nitric acid, and upon returning to his residence with a jug of this substance he was approached by some Indians who wanted to drink what they thought was rum. Buell told them the jug contained acid and would poison them, but the Indians did not believe it. Taking the jug, one of them swallowed a substantial portion and died soon thereafter from the effects. Buell was then accused of killing the Indian, and in accordance with tradition, the dead man's companions sought revenge in kind. To escape the situation Buell is said to have fled to Rupert, Vermont, conveniently distant from Connecticut.

Abel Buell, as a young man, was convicted of counterfeiting Connecticut paper currency by altering four bills from 2s 6d to 30s (for which he had an ear cropped as punishment). He atoned for his youthful folly and, becoming a skilled silversmith, he engraved authorized dies for the Connecticut copper coinage.

Julian Harmon, the grandson of Reuben Harmon Jr., shed some further light on the early Vermont coiners in a letter dated June 4, 1855. He believed that Reuben Jr. came to Vermont about 1760, having moved from Sandisfield, Massachusetts. He verified that William Buell of New Haven cut the dies, and stated,

> The mint house stood on Pawlet River, three rods from [Reuben Harmon Jr.'s] house, a story and a half house, not painted, a furnace in one end for melting copper and rolling the bars, and in the other [west] end machinery for stamping, and in the center that for cutting. The stamping was done by means of an iron screw attached to heavy timbers above and moved by hand through the aid of ropes. Sixty per minute *could* be stamped, although 30 per minute was the usual number. William Buel assisted in striking the coins. Three persons were required for the purpose, one to place the copper, and two to swing the stamp. At first, the coins passed two for a penny, then four, then eight, when it ceased to pay expenses. The English imported so many of the "Bungtown coppers," which were of a much lighter color.

It was further stated that the coiner moved to Ohio about 1800 and engaged in the business of making salt at the Salt Spring Tract in Wethersfield Township, Trumbull County, in which business he continued until his death on October 29, 1806, in his 56th year.

B.H. Hall, in a letter to Charles I. Bushnell, dated June 14, 1856, gave another view of the mint:

> On the north side of Millbrook the "old copper house" was first erected.... From this location, in the town of Rupert, the "Mint House" was afterwards removed to and placed on the eastern bank of Pawlet River in the same town. Here it was also used for minting purposes. When the manufacture of coins was abolished, it was allowed to remain on Pawlet River for several years, but we could not learn to what uses it was put. Its third removal was to a spot north of the house of John Harwood, Esq., in the town of Rupert, on the east side of the main road. While here it was occupied as a residence by a family named Goff. It was again removed from its third location to a site nearly opposite, where it remained until its final journey which took place many years ago. This placed it on the farm of William Phelps about a mile north of John Harwood's residence in "the edge" of the town of Pawlet. Here it stood until last winter, when it was blown down.

Certain related information from Hall appears in *An Historical Account of American Coinage*, by John H. Hickcox, 1858, including portions of the above.

Z. Humphrey, in *The History of Dorset*, 1924 (cited by Everett T. Sipsey in *CNL* 13), states that William Coley, a New York City goldsmith (and silversmith), did not come to Rupert until after the Legislature extended the coinage franchise in 1786, nor did William Buell arrive with "dies" until after that time. We do know that Coley was in Rupert by 1787 (see Machin's Mills account below). The federal census taken on July 6, 1790, listed Coley as residing in Rupert and the head of a household there (including, in addition to Coley, three males under age 15 and two females with ages not specified).

Vermont "Landscape-Type" Coins

The first coins produced by Harmon, probably mostly if not entirely at the first mint location on Millbrook, have a scenic motif and portray on the obverse a typical Vermont rocky mountain ridge forested with pine trees. The dies were probably by Coley or by another craftsman at the partnership of Van Voorhis and Coley at 27 Hanover Square, New York City (Coley later moved to Rupert). Today, numismatists often refer to these as the "landscape type." To the right a sun peeping over the ridge is seen. Below is a plow. Around the border is the legend VERMONTIS RES PUBLICA and the date 1785.

VERMONTIS was the latinization of "Vermont." This translation of "Vermont" was not standardized, so in 1785 and continuing into 1786, such other variations as VERMONTS and the lengthy VERMONTENSIUM (creating "Republic of the Vermonters" in literal translation) were used.

The reverse depicts an all-seeing eye from which emanats 13 short rays, with a star above each, and 13 long rays. The orientation of the eye (with eyebrow on top) varies on certain dies. The legend STELLA QUARTA DECIMA ("the 14th star," a reference to Vermont's ambition to become the

14th state) surrounded. The orientation of the eye (with the eyebrow above the eyeball) varies with regard to the surrounding inscription. The central motif was copied from the reverse of a 1783-dated Nova Constellatio "Blunt Rays" copper, a coin then in general circulation (see earlier discussion of Nova Constellatio copper coinage). Later issues are of the "Pointed Rays" style. Vermont would have been one of the original states had it not been for a border dispute with New York, which prevented its entry into the Union until 1791.

Portrait Coinage

It is likely that in 1786 it was decided that the Vermont coppers, being of a unique obverse design not familiar to the citizens of Vermont or surrounding states, did not circulate as well as they would have if the design had been a more standard motif. Accordingly, new obverses and reverses were adopted, imitating the coinage of England, with a portrait on the obverse of George II and on the reverse a seated figure (Britannia on the English issues).

A different style, known today as the "Baby Head" variety, depicts a boyish bust facing right, with the legend AUCTORI VERMON: ("by the authority of Vermont") surrounding. The reverse shows the seated figure of a woman with INDE ET LIB (an abbreviation for "independence and liberty") at the border. The date 1786 is below. Later Vermont coins depict George III.

The initial coining franchise was granted to Harmon for a period of two years. Before the expiration, Harmon, on October 23, 1786, petitioned the General Assembly to extend the term on the grounds that it was too short to indemnify him for the great expense of erecting a factory, acquiring machinery, and otherwise beginning the coinage of copper. On October 24, 1786, the franchise was extended. The coinage design was officially modified to copy the English style, and following an initial period, Harmon was to pay a royalty for the coining privilege:

> Be it enacted by the General Assembly in the State of Vermont that there be and hereby is granted and confirmed to the said Reuben Harmon Jr., Esq., the exclusive right of coining copper within the state, for a further term of eight years from the first day of July, 1787; and that all copper by him coined shall be in pieces weighing not less than four pennyweight, fifteen grains each; and that the device for all coppers by him hereafter coined shall be, on the one side, a head with the motto "Auctoritate Vermontensium" abridged, and on the reverse a woman with the lettering INDE: ET LIB:, for "Independence and Liberty."
>
> And be it further enacted by the authority aforesaid that the said Reuben shall have and enjoy the aforesaid privilege of coining coppers within the state free from any duty to this state as a compensation therefore, for the full term of three years from the first day of July, 1787; and from and after the expiration of said three the said Reuben shall pay for the use of this state two and one-half percent of all the copper he shall coin for and during the remainder of aforesaid term of eight years.

It was further specified that appropriate bonds and guarantees were to be provided. Presumably, the "landscape" coins were discontinued about this time, and the "head" type with the George II portrait was instituted.

Coinage Removed to Machin's Mills

In 1787 Harmon entered into an arrangement with a number of other individuals involved in coinage. Ownership interest and connection was formed between the Vermont coining enterprises and Machin's Mills, a private mint, located on the shores of Orange County near Newburgh, New York. This was a partnership formed under an agreement dated April 18, 1787, that united the interests of Samuel Atlee, James F. Atlee, David Brooks, James Grier, and James Giles, all of New York City, with Thomas Machin of Ulster County, New York. Details are given under Machin's Mills coinage (of counterfeit English coppers) later in this chapter.

On June 7, 1787, another agreement was drawn up. Ten partners participated, including the original six involved in the Machin's Mills enterprise, plus four others: Reuben Harmon Jr., the Rupert, Vermont, coiner; William Coley, also of Rupert; Elias Jackson of Litchfield County, Connecticut; and Daniel Van Voorhis, a New York City goldsmith. The last had worked as a silversmith in Princeton, New Jersey, circa 1782 to 1784, then in New York City with Coley, Simeon Bayley, and Albion Cox in the same trade in the firm of Van Voorhis, Bayley, Coley & Cox, which dissolved in April 1785. (It was succeeded by Van Voorhis, Bayley & Coley, which ended in July of the same year, after which the business was continued as Van Voorhis & Coley at 27 Hanover Square. This arrangement continued until Coley moved to Rupert. Later, Albion Cox became involved in the coinage of coppers for the state of New Jersey.)

It was noted in the agreement that Reuben Harmon, after obtaining the coinage privilege from the legislature of Vermont, had taken in William Coley, Elias Jackson, and Daniel Van Voorhis as equal partners. Now it was intended to merge the interests of Machin's Mills with those of the Rupert, Vermont, minters. It was proposed that coinage be conducted in two locations: Machin's Mills, then in the process of readying for coinage; and at Rupert, Vermont, in the existing facilities there. Duties were divided among the various partners, with due provision being made for audits, settling accounts, and other business necessities. As to how long coinage actually continued at Rupert is an open question. Based upon an examination of planchet quality, it seems likely to me that just one 1787 variety was made there, RR-15 (W-2045). Others believe the Rupert mint may have coined coppers into 1789. If this is true, all of a sudden the Rupert mint was able to acquire planchets made from smooth copper stock and of much higher quality than those used on the "landscape," Baby Head, and George II portrait coinage.

In any event, production of Vermont coppers commenced at Machin's Mills in 1787, now with the portrait of King George III (instead of George II) with Vermont inscriptions. The coinage there was on better-quality planchets and of generally lighter weight. Dies were of mixed quality, often with crudely aligned lettering. As the Machin enterprise was involved in counterfeiting various other copper coins, including state issues as well as English halfpence, sometimes the dies were mixed. The result was curious "Vermont" coppers with reverse dies of the IMMUNE COLUMBIA and BRITANNIA coppers, a combination of a Vermont die with a Connecticut reverse, and a English-inscription obverse with a Vermont reverse.

The Machin enterprise is believed to have wound down in 1789, at which time the coppers panic made further production of coppers unprofitable.

The James F. Atlee Problem

While no one questions that at Machin's Mills certain of "the coins were made by James F. Atlee" (see 19th-century recollections in chapter 2), there is no contemporary evidence of any kind indicating he was an engraver. Some modern writers, Walter Breen in particular, have stated as fact that Atlee was an accomplished engraver across various state coinages. Others have taken the Breen information as correct, and have compounded his errors. It seems more likely that James F. Atlee was a mechanic and coiner, not a diecutting artist. He and Samuel Atlee (a brewer by trade) likely had equipment such as striking and coining presses.

In the *Colonial Newsletter*, January 1976, Edward R. Barnsley, in "The Problem of James F. Atlee," took issue with the popular idea that James F. Atlee cut dies for Machin's Mills, Connecticut, Vermont, New Jersey, and certain other coins. A misreading of Crosby may have led to this. Editor James C. Spilman concurred: "Nowhere in Crosby have we been able to connect James F. Atlee with any coinage dies." However, Crosby on pages 191 and 192 *does* state: "There is strong reason to believe that Atlee, who is said to have made the dies for all the coins struck at Newburgh, made dies for others of the Vermont coins." Crosby's "strong reason" is now out of favor with a number of scholars. In any event, "is said to have made" indicates Crosby was presenting conjecture, not fact.

As to Samuel Atlee, he was a brewmaster and entrepreneur. There is not a shred of evidence that he ever cut any dies, either. Michael J. Hodder's masterful "The 1787 'New York' Immunis Columbia; A Mystery Re-Ravelled," in the *Colonial Newsletter*, January 1991, debunks this myth. Related commentary will be found in John Lorenzo's "Atlee Broken 'A' Letter Punch," in the proceedings from the Coinage of the Americas Conference, 1995.

Lorenzo points out that punches and dies could be obtained from common sources, and that, for one, Abel Buell advertised that he had such for sale. It seems likely that certain entrepreneurs primarily occupied with stamping coins simply ordered dies from jewelers and engravers at a distance. Regarding the ubiquitous broken "A" punch, it is found on a wide variety of dies displaying workmanship that ranges from exceedingly amateurish (as on Vermont coppers RR-1 and 30) to sophisticated (the 1787 Immunis Columbia is an example). Either this punch was passed around among various engravers, or a common source of hardware and jewelers' supplies sold fonts in which the A's were broken.

In the *Colonial Newsletter* of October 1985, editor James C. Spilman synopsized the practice of creating "facts" from notions:

> A substantial amount of current "fact" regarding the origins of various early American coinages is based on speculation. We must be prepared to admit to ourselves that new findings may substantially change earlier concepts. Speculation is perhaps too harsh a word. In its place we might have said conjecture or assumption. But the fact is that there remains to be accomplished a great amount of research before many of these areas can be sorted out with a high degree of confidence in the accuracy of the conclusions. It is very good to develop theories so long as we do not translate them through long time acceptance into fact, and become trapped in this mindset.

a.   b.

Workmanship on Vermont dies varies widely, from incredibly amateurish to fairly sophisticated. (*a*) The most rustic of all Vermont dies is the obverse of RR-30, best known for its backward C in AUCTORI, but naive in other aspects as well. (*b*) The obverse of RR-1 was probably cut by the same hand.

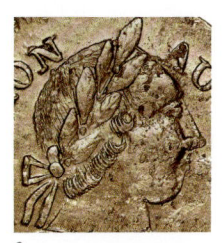

a.   b.

The head on RR-13 (*a*) surely was engraved by the same hand as the one that engraved RR-27 (*b*)—the hand of a skilled artist whose talent is seen only on these two Vermont dies.

Numismatic Aspects

Vermont coppers have always been popular with numismatists. Edmund F. Slafter, in "The Vermont Coinage" (an 1870 essay), described issues known to him, soon followed by Sylvester S. Crosby in his *Early Coins of America*, 1875. The latter was the standard reference for Vermont coins until 1919 or 1920.

Today, 39 different varieties represent more than a dozen distinctive types—a remarkable number for such an abbreviated coinage. Attributions are traditionally to the system by Hillyer C. Ryder in the *American Journal of Numismatics* in 1919, and published with information on Connecticut and Massachusetts coppers in *The State Coinage of New England*, 1920, by the American Numismatic Society. In *The Numismatist* in May 1947, John M. Richardson's "Colonial Coins of Vermont" added discoveries made since 1920. Both of these listings mixed varieties, interweaving early Rupert coins with later Machin's Mills issues, and, in fact, beginning the list with RR (Ryder-Richardson)-1, the odd muling of a crude Vermont obverse with an irrelevant IMMUNE COLUMBIA reverse. The system became ingrained with specialists, and today most of us can declaim on varieties of Vermont coppers, describing them by these numbers (to which cross-references are given in the present text).

The next major scholarship was Kenneth E. Bressett's "Vermont Copper Coinage," published as part of *Studies on Money in Early America*, 1976. For the first time a scientific/historical enumeration of the die characteristics was presented, assigning numbers from 1 onward to obverse dies, and letters from A onward to reverse dies. By this arrangement it was easy to identify the multiple uses of certain dies. Unfortunately, this study was not widely published and never became accepted in the mainstream, although it was a godsend to specialists. No doubt, if it had been published separately and widely distributed, we would be using Bressett numbers today.

In 1998 the Colonial Coin Collectors Club (C4) published *The Copper Coins of Vermont and Those Bearing the Vermont Name*, by Tony Carlotto, an enthusiastic student and devotee of the subject. The arrangement continued the Ryder-Richardson sequence, with cross references to the Bressett attributions. This book was a tour de force and today offers just about anything anyone might care to know on the title subject.

To the preceding comprehensive studies, many articles, mentions, and essays in the *C4 Newsletter* and the *Colonial Newsletter*, detailed listings in auction catalogs, and other publications have added to the information on the series. Roy E. Bonjour's *Survey of the Rarest Vermonts*, 2005, a supplement to the *C4 Newsletter*, is notable.

Availability and Characteristics of Vermont Coppers

The Vermont coppers struck in Rupert were made on rough copper planchets, often with streaks and fissures, and probably darkened or discolored from oxidation at the time they were used. Conditions must have been primitive. Dies were cut by several artisans, as noted previously. Basic types from the Rupert period include the "landscape" varieties with a sun peeping over a forested ridge, with spellings including VERMONTS, VERMONTIS, and VERMONTENSIUM (each having a slightly different meaning in Latin). All of these are readily enough found in the marketplace in usual grades from G-4 to F-15 or so, dark and with a rustic appearance. Then comes the Baby Head variety, scarce but collectible, and the Mailed Bust Left type of 1786 and 1787, the last date rare and always seen with a massive die break obscuring most of the date. Again, these are usually dark and with planchet problems. This rusticity contributes a great deal to the charm they offer.

After the move of operations to Machin's Mills in Newburgh, New York, coins were made lighter in weight, but usually on far better planchets. Today these later issues are found in varying shades of brown color. Nearly all have light striking at the centers, with few details. Likely, the dies were made this way, so that a freshly minted coin, if darkened, could be passed readily in circulation, giving the impression it had gone from hand to hand for a long time. Among the Machin's Mills coins are a half dozen or so major rarities. Most of these are not identifiable quickly by amateurs, giving Vermont specialists ample opportunity to cherrypick to find such pieces, as has been done many times.

Shield Styles

Using the Bressett system of reverse letters it is found that the seated figure as used on Machin's Mills dies specifically intended for Vermont can be neatly classified into two main groups of designs, which can be differentiated quickly by the high or low position of the interior oval on the shield:

1. *Low Shield*—Reverses J, K, L, M, O, S, and X. This includes reverses J and K, the only ones dated 1787. All others are dated 1788. It would seem likely that dies in this group were made first.
2. *High Shield with large support below it*—Reverses N, P, Q, R, T, U, and Y. All are dated 1788. Certain details including the branch and pole were added to each die by hand and were not in the design punch.
3. *Anomalous*—Reverse V (used on RR-13, Bressett 17-V) the BRITANNIA reverse made for a counterfeit English halfpenny.
4. *Anomalous*—Reverse W (used on RR-27, Bressett 18-W), a combination for which the obverse was finely engraved by an artist whose work has no counterpart on any other Vermont copper.

Low Shield and High Shield types, details:
(a) RR-20, Bressett 10-L with Low Shield;
(b) RR-22, Bressett 10-Q with High Shield.

Grading

As to grading Vermont coppers, the American Numismatic Association numbers, 1 to 70, such as G-4, F-12, EF-40, and so on, are often used. Neither the ANA nor anyone else has ever formalized rules. Almost every variety has its own characteristics, so no generalizations can be made. A weak or blank center in a Vermont landscape copper of 1785 or 1786 would be a negative and would deter many from buying it. On the other hand, all known Whitman-2225 (RR-30) coppers were flatly struck in the centers to begin with. In the 1960s I acquired a W-2120 (RR-16) copper I graded as About Uncirculated. It was lustrous brown with some tinges of mint red (not that Machin's Mills coppers were ever issued fully red to begin with). It was passed around among several professionals, none of whom was a colonial specialist. Expert opinions ranged from Fine to About Uncirculated.

Grading Vermont coppers is quite a challenge. The answer is to study each variety by looking at pictures in texts and catalogs, see what is being offered in the marketplace at different grades, and endeavor to develop a feeling for approximate grade. This should serve you well. If the presentation in this text evokes an interest in Vermont coppers, I recommend that you acquire a copy of Tony Carlotto's book as the next step.

Landscape Types (Rupert Mint)

W-2005 · RR-2 · Bressett 1-A · 1785 VERMONTS

Obverse: Ray of sun points to period after RES. *Reverse:* Period after STELLA. above left element of ray, tail of Q above double points of ray, star points to right leg of second A (QUARTA). The reverse of this and other issues of the landscape type are loosely copied after the 1783 Blunt Rays Nova Constellatio copper then in circulation. *Notes:* This is the first and most widely available of the 1785-dated landscape types. Planchet fissures of one degree or another are the rule, but exceptions occur. Often with areas of light striking. On late states there is a large die crack extending upward from 8 (1785). It is not known whether this or W-2010 was the first struck. No doubt both were from the mint building in its first location. *Rarity:* URS-11.

G-4	VG-8	F-12	VF-20	EF-40
$650	$1,000	$2,000	$5,500	$12,500

W-2010 · RR-3 · Bressett 2-B

Obverse: Ray of sun points to right of period after RES. *Reverse:* Blunt rays. Period after STELLA. above star, tail of Q between star and tip of ray, star points to period after QUARTA. *Notes:* Scarcest of the 1785 landscape varieties. Planchet flaws are common. Sometimes on a wide planchet with extensive dentils visible on both sides, but these are in the minority. Tony Carlotto wrote, "Probably the most intriguing coin in the landscape series. This is because of the striking peculiarities and planchet oddities." One struck over a 1785 Connecticut, Miller 4.1-F-4. *Rarity:* URS-7.

G-4	VG-8	F-12	VF-20	EF-40
$650	$1,000	$3,000	$7,000	$15,000

W-2015 · RR-4 · Bressett 3-C · 1785 VERMONTIS

Obverse: No lettering below date. *Reverse:* Blunt rays. Period after STELLA. above ray, tail of Q between star and tip of ray, star points to left leg of second A in QUARTA. The all-seeing eye at the center is inverted, a detail first noted by Tony Terranova. Die not used elsewhere. *Notes:* Planchet defects are common. In its late state the obverse die bulged considerably at the center. *Rarity:* URS-8.

VG-8	F-12	VF-20	EF-40
$850	$2,400	$6,000	$17,000

W-2020 · RR-6 · Bressett 4-D · 1786 VERMONTENSIUM

Obverse: Ray of sun points to upright of R in RES. *Reverse:* Pointed rays. Ray points at tail of Q. *Notes:* Usually with planchet flaws and rifts and lightly struck in areas. This is the most widely available 1786 landscape type and is more often seen than any of the 1785 issues. *Rarity:* URS-11.

VG-8	F-12	VF-20	EF-40
$600	$1,200	$3,400	$8,500

W-2025 · RR-7 · Bressett 5-E

Obverse: Ray of sun points to right foot of R. Tree touches lower left of N. *Reverse:* Pointed rays. Ray points at U. *Notes:* Often seen on nice planchets, though usually with some lightness of strike in areas. First of the Vermont varieties with normal die rotation (180° difference between obverse and reverse), although variations from rotated dies occur throughout the later series. Roy Bonjour considers this to be the most elusive of the VERMONTENSIUM varieties. *Rarity:* URS-8.

G-4	VG-8	F-12	VF-20	EF-40
$400	$600	$1,200	$3,200	$8,000

85

W-2030 · RR-8 · Bressett 6-E

Obverse: Ray of sun points to right foot of R. Tree distant from N. The 1 (1785) is sharply double-punched. *Reverse:* Same die as preceding. *Notes:* Scarcest of the three 1786 landscape varieties. Often seen well struck (except for the central part of the rocky ledge, which on this variety is not as well defined as on the other two VERMONTENSIUM dies), but planchet flaws are common. *Rarity:* URS-9.

G-4	VG-8	F-12	VF-20	EF-40
$350	$800	$1,200	$3,200	$8,000

Portrait Types (Rupert Mint)

1786 Head Right

W-2040 · RR-9 · Bressett 7-F · Baby Head · AUCTORI: / VERMON:

Obverse: Infantile portrait. Only variety with AUCTORI at left and VERMON to the right. *Reverse:* INDE: [group of dots] ET: LIB. Prominent cloth or sash from seated figure's shoulder near branch hand. Four wheat sheaves on the shield, reflective of Vermont agriculture. *Notes:* Nearly always seen on imperfect planchets with fissures and usually in lower grades. Usually dark brown or black. The wheat sheaves are usually mostly or completely missing. The inspiration for the youthful portrait has been a matter of conjecture. For many years this has been one of the most popular and sought-after Vermont varieties. *Rarity:* URS-10.

G-4	VG-8	F-12	VF-20	EF-40
$450	$750	$2,700	$10,500	$38,000

1786 Head [Mailed Bust] Left

W-2045 · RR-10 · Bressett 8-G · VERMON: / AUCTORI:

Obverse: Portrait of King George II copied from English coinage. VERMON: / AUCTORI: [colon after both words]. V distant from bust. *Reverse:* Branch hand is opposite space past E. Wheat sheaf on shield, a distinctive feature that is visible on only a few specimens. *Notes:* Planchet usually dark and with laminations or rifts. The date on the reverse of this is very close to that used on a 1786 Connecticut copper, Miller 5.9-B-1, but other topological features are different. Dies of this and the next two are attributed to Abel Buell, who was a principal in Connecticut of the Company for Coining Coppers. *Rarity:* URS-9.

G-4	VG-8	F-12	VF-20	EF-40
$250	$550	$1,200	$4,700	$9,500

W-2050 · RR-11 · Bressett 9-H · VERMON: / AUCTORI

Obverse: Portrait of King George II copied from English coinage. V closer to bust than on preceding, C too small and placed high. *Reverse:* Branch hand is opposite the upright of E. *Notes:* Usually with planchet defects and dark surfaces. The obverse die was used to strike some examples of RR-11, then RR-15, then more of RR-11. *Rarity:* URS-8.

VG-8	F-12	VF-20	EF-40
$550	$1,300	$5,500	$11,500

1787 Head [Mailed Bust] Left

W-2060 · RR-15 · Bressett 9-I

Obverse: Same as W-2045. *Reverse:* All seen have a massive die crack obscuring much of the date. The rarity of this issue suggests that the die had a very short life. *Notes:* Usually with planchet defects and dark surfaces. The obverse die was first used to strike W-2050, then some of W-2060 as here, then additional specimens of W-2050. While this is a rare variety, its market value goes beyond that consideration as it is actively collected as the only year in which this type was made, and is listed in the Red Book. Known struck over a W-2015 (RR-4) and a George III halfpence; the latter is most curious. *Rarity:* URS-6.

G-4	VG-8	F-12	VF-20	EF-40
$2,800	$6,500	$14,000	$26,000	$48,000

Portrait Issues (Machin's Mills)

1787 Mailed Bust Right

W-2100 · RR-34 · Bressett 10-J · VERMON / AUCTORI ·
Obverse: N very close to head. Fillet ends centered opposite V. This is the earliest combination in the long use of an obverse that was mated with nine reverses. *Reverse:* Low Shield style. First of only two 1787-dated dies used with Mailed Bust Right coinage. INDE ETLIB. The B (ETLIB) close to shield and directly opposite stripe in shield. Pole ends above top left of 1 (1787). Bottom of shield is a loop and rests on the higher of two lines. This is the only use of this reverse. *Notes:* One of the key issues in the series. Bonjour census: four Very Fine (including untraced Crosby plate coin); one G-4. To these can be added a Fine-to-Very-Fine and two Very Fine coins, for a total of eight. *Rarity:* URS-4.

G-4	VG-8	F-12	VF-20
—	—	—	$65,000

W-2105 · RR-14 · Bressett 10-K
Obverse: Same as W-2100. *Reverse:* Low Shield style. INDE ET LIB. The B is distant from shield. Pole ends far left of 1 (1787). Bottom of shield is solid and rests on the higher of two lines. Also used on RR-12 and RR-32. *Notes:* A few are overstruck on Nova Constellatio coppers. Usually on a smooth, pleasing planchet. *Rarity:* URS-10.

G-4	VG-8	F-12	VF-20	EF-40
$200	$350	$650	$2,400	$6,500

W-2110 · RR-12 · Bressett 11-K · VERMON / AUCTORI ·
Obverse: V close to top of the two fillets; I distant from bust. Unique use of this obverse. *Reverse:* Low Shield style. Same as W-2105. *Notes:* Small and large planchet varieties, the last usually over Nova Constellatio coppers (illustrated). *Rarity:* URS-10.

G-4	VG-8	F-12	VF-20	EF-40
$200	$350	$650	$2,400	$6,500

W-2115 · RR-32 · Bressett 12-K
Obverse: Base of I opposite point of bust. Unique use of this obverse. *Reverse:* Low Shield style. Same as W-2105. *Notes:* It may be that all are struck over Nova Constellatio coppers (see Carlotto), but not all show traces. Roy Bonjour now (2008) lists an EF-45, an EF-45 over Nova Constellatio, and an F-15/G-4, plus an example reported by Gregory Field. Another is in the Bennington Museum. Yet another recent find is Very Fine to Extremely Fine. *Rarity:* URS-4.

G-4	VG-8	F-12	VF-20
—	—	$58,500	—

1788 Mailed Bust Right

W-2120 · RR-16 · Bressett 15-S · VERMON / AUCTORI · no periods in legend
Obverse: N distant from head. Upper left of A broken. Raised dots on breastplate. Unique use of this die. *Reverse:* Low Shield style. INDE / ET LIB. *Notes:* Always weak at centers. Usually on a smooth planchet and quite attractive overall. Often seen in higher grades such as Extremely Fine or even About Uncirculated, but a puzzlement to grade for those who are not familiar with the idiosyncrasies of Vermont coppers. This is one of the most plentiful of all Vermont issues, sharing that distinction with W-2255. *Rarity:* URS-12.

G-4	VG-8	F-12	VF-20	EF-40	AU-50
$120	$170	$425	$1,000	$2,000	$3,750

W-2125 · RR-17 · Bressett 14-S
Obverse: N close to head. Upper left of A intact. Unique use of this die. *Reverse:* Same as preceding. *Notes:* Usually seen with smooth surfaces and excellent eye appeal. Lightly struck at the centers, typical for all but a few Machin's Mills coppers of this general style. *Rarity:* URS-7.

G-4	VG-8	F-12	VF-20	EF-40
$200	$300	$750	$2,400	$8,000

W-2130 · RR-35 · Bressett 20-X

Obverse: Upper of the two fillet ribbons extends part way to upright of E. Upper left of A broken. Known specimens are weakly struck at the right side of the obverse. Unique use of this die. *Reverse:* Low Shield style. *ET LIB* *INDE. Only die with ET LIB at the left and INDE to the right. In late states a piece fell from the die obliterating the top of E (INDE). Used on W-2135 in later state. *Notes:* One of the classic Machin's Mills rarities in the Vermont series. Carlotto states that all were struck over counterfeit Irish halfpence, as the weights match. Evidence of the undertype is not visible on all. Bonjour census: a dozen or so known, typically Very Good to Fine. *Rarity:* URS-5.

G-4	VG-8	F-12	VF-20	EF-40
—	—	$25,000	—	—

W-2135 · RR-18 · Bressett 19-X

Obverse: The letter A distant from head. Bottom fillet points to center of V. Raised dots on breastplate. A vertical die crack bisects the die, but there may have been early impressions without this feature. Unique use of this die. *Reverse:* Same as preceding. *Notes:* Known struck over English and Irish coppers (see Mossman, p. 269). *Rarity:* URS-7.

G-4	VG-8	F-12	VF-20	EF-40
$400	$750	$1,700	$5,000	$15,000

W-2150 · RR-20 · Bressett 10-L · VERMON · / AUCTORI · · periods after words

Obverse: Same as W-2100 of 1787. N very close to head. Long-lived die used with a total of 10 reverses. *Reverse:* Low Shield style. One line above date. Branch hand opposite right part of D. All digits significantly below date line. *Notes:* Usually on a smooth planchet and light or medium brown in color. Weakly struck at the centers as expected, but sometimes with full rims to the shield. *Rarity:* URS-9.

G-4	VG-8	F-12	VF-20	EF-40
$250	$300	$800	$4,000	$11,000

W-2155 · RR-21 · Bressett 10-R

Obverse: Same as preceding. *Reverse:* High Shield, line above date. Branch hand opposite upright of E. The 7 is low; 88 touches date line. *Notes:* Usually on a nice planchet, light to medium brown. Lightly struck at the centers, but often with most interior shield details present. *Rarity:* URS-7.

G-4	VG-8	F-12	VF-20
$400	$650	$2,100	$6,200

W-2160 · RR-38 · Bressett 10-N

Obverse: Same as preceding. *Reverse:* High Shield, Line above date. Branch hand opposite space between D and E. All digits significantly below date line; 1 very low; 7 low. *Notes:* Unknown to Ryder and Richardson, this was revealed by colonial dealer-specialist Richard Picker in the 1960s. This is the most recent new variety to be discovered in the Vermont series. *Rarity:* URS-4. Bonjour census plus updates: five Very Good or so; one Fine; and one Very Fine (some planchet flaws), for a total of seven.

W-2165 · RR-22 · Bressett 10-Q

Obverse: Same as preceding. *Reverse:* High Shield style. Two lines above date. Branch hand opposite right part of D. The 7 in date is very low. Typically seen with two die cracks at the left. Later die states show advanced cracks and bulging. Unique use of this die. *Notes:* Usually seen on a high quality planchet. Weak at the centers. *Rarity:* URS-7.

G-4	VG-8	F-12	VF-20
$200	$450	$850	$3,500

W-2170 · RR-37 · Bressett 10-M

Obverse: Same as preceding. *Reverse:* Low Shield style. Two lines above date. Branch hand opposite right part of D. *Notes:* This variety, unknown to Ryder and Richardson, was discovered by Al Hoch and published in the first issue of the *Colonial Newsletter* in 1960. Since that time four more have been identified. Bonjour census: VF-20, F-12, VG-8, G-4, to which can be added a Very Fine to Extremely Fine (but porous) example found by Edwin Sarrafian on eBay in 2005. *Rarity:* URS-4.

W-2175 · RR-23 · Bressett 10-O

Obverse: Same as preceding. *Reverse:* Low Shield style. Two lines above date. Branch hand opposite upright of E. Branch very close to E. The digits 88 touch date line. *Notes:* Usually attractive and on a nice-quality planchet. Lightly struck at centers, but some are above average in this regard. *Rarity:* URS-9.

G-4	VG-8	F-12	VF-20	EF-40
$200	$400	$850	$3,200	$8,500

W-2180 · RR-36 · Bressett 10-P

Obverse: Same as preceding. *Reverse:* High Shield style. Two lines above date. Branch hand opposite E. Branch distant from E. Only the second 8 touches the date line. *Notes:* Published in *The Numismatist*, February 1955. *Rarity:* URS-5.

Selected auction price(s): Norweb I Sale (B&M 10/1987), F-VF, $3,300; VF, planchet flaw, $2,090. Hinkley Collection (B&M 11/2001), VF-20, $9,775. C4 Convention (M&G 11/2001), G-6, $1,300. Logan & Steinberg Collections (B&M 11/2002), VG-10, $4,830.

W-2185 · RR-19 · Bressett 13-L · 1788

Obverse: Different obverse. N significantly above head. O and N widely spaced. Upper left of A broken. Usually (but not always) seen with a rim cud break from R (AUCTORI) clockwise to about halfway below the portrait. Unique use of this die. *Reverse:* Low Shield style. One line above date. Branch hand opposite right part of D. *Notes:* Always lightly struck at the centers. Planchet quality varies but is often quite good. *Rarity:* URS-7.

G-4	VG-8	F-12	VF-20	EF-40
$400	$800	$1,500	$3,500	$9,000

W-2190 · RR-26 · Bressett 16-T · VERMON + AUCTORI +

Obverse: Unique with this punctuation. Portrait larger than on typical Vermont coppers. *Reverse:* High Shield style. INDE+ ET • LIB+. Branch hand is opposite upright of E. Always seen in shallow relief. All seen have a prominent die crack extended from E (INDE) across the neck and arm to E (ET). Unique use of this reverse die. *Notes:* This is one of the well-known key rarities in the original Ryder listing. All are lightly struck on both sides, but especially on the reverse. *Rarity:* URS-5.

Selected auction price(s): Hinkley Collection (B&M 11/2001), VG-8, $3,220. C4 Convention (M&G 11/2001), F-12, $4,250. Logan & Steinberg Collections (B&M 11/2002), VF-35, $3,680; VF-35, $8,913. Smith & Youngman Collections (B&M 3/2003), F-12, $3,738. John J. Ford Jr. I Sale (Stack's 10/2003), Choice VF, $12,650. C4 Convention (M&G 11/2005), VG-8, $4,500.

W-2195 · RR-25 · Bressett 16-U

Obverse: Same as preceding. With break, actually a small rectangular piece out of the die, where the neck meets the mail. *Reverse:* High Shield style. INDE+ ET • LIB+. Branch hand shows distinct fingers and is opposite the upright of D; pole ends to left of 1; single line above date. Used on W-2195 (as here), 2210, 2220, 2260, and 2265 (also Miller 1788 Connecticut reverse I). *Notes:* Those overstruck on Irish halfpence are rarer; Carlotto gives details. *Rarity:* URS-10.

G-4	VG-8	F-12	VF-20	EF-40
$250	$300	$750	$2,500	$5,800

W-2200 · RR-24 · Bressett 16-S

Obverse: Same as preceding. Last use of the obverse die with break or crack extending slightly into the field. *Reverse:* Low Shield style. Branch hand is opposite upright of D. INDE / ET LIB (no punctuation). Used on W-2120, 2125, 2200 (as here), and 2225. *Notes:* Usually on a nice planchet. Lightness of strike at the centers, as usual. *Rarity:* URS-10.

G-4	VG-8	F-12	VF-20	EF-40
$250	$400	$1,000	$4,500	$10,500

1788 Mailed Bust Right · VERMON · AUCTORI +

W-2205 · RR-27 · Bressett 18-W

Obverse: Unique punctuation. Head particularly rounded with hair strands mostly emanating from below N. Unique use of this die. *Reverse:* INDE * ET LIB *. Unique punctuation. Branch hand opposite space between E and star; top of pole extends above hand; bottom of pole to left of feet; single line above date; second 8 closest to line. Unique use of this die. *Notes:* A very distinctive die combination in terms of punctuation and details of the obverse and reverse figures. The dies seem to be by the same hand as the 1787 Nova Eborac Medium Head, Reverse Figure Left dies (W-5755). Perhaps the most carefully cut die in the Vermont series. Reverse seated figure punch also used on Machin's Mills coppers Vlack 9-76B and 15-86NY. Usually much better struck at the centers (but still weak in many details) than a Vermont copper of this year. One of the more available issues in this series. Tony Carlotto suggests that more than 1,250 are known. *Rarity:* URS-11.

G-4	VG-8	F-12	VF-20	EF-40
$240	$350	$950	$2,800	$7,500

1788 Mailed Bust Right · VERMON* / *AUCTORI

W-2210 · RR-33 · Bressett 21-Y

Obverse: Unique punctuation. Stars each close to portrait. *Reverse:* High Shield style. *INDE ETLIB*. Unique punctuation arrangement. Single line above date; first 8 touches line; second 8 embedded in line. Die crack horizontally below center. Unique use of this die. *Notes:* Tony Carlotto reports only three known, each over a counterfeit Irish halfpenny. Bonjour census: VF-20 (over counterfeit 1782 Irish halfpenny); August Collection Very Fine to Extremely Fine (over a counterfeit 1782 Irish halfpenny, finest known); VG-8/G-4 (little detail, ex Bowers; also over counterfeit English halfpenny); Bennington Museum. *Rarity:* URS-3.

W-2215 · RR-28 · Bressett 21-U

Obverse: Same as W-2210. *Reverse:* High Shield style. Used on W-2195, 2215 (as here), 2220, 2260, and 2265 (also Miller 1788 Connecticut reverse I). Later use with die crack more prominent. *Notes:* Lightly struck at the centers and usually weaker on the reverse. Many are overstruck on counterfeit Irish and English halfpence, but the undertype is not always visible. Some auctions list such overstrikes when visible, others ignore this feature. *Rarity:* URS-6.

G-4	VG-8	F-12	VF-20	EF-40
$2,000	$3,500	$8,000	$17,000	$25,000

1788 Mailed Bust Right · *VERMON* *AUCTORI*

W-2220 · RR-29 · Bressett 22-U

Obverse: Unique punctuation arrangement. First two stars are close to portrait. Seen with distinctive die crack from above the head, extending along forehead and nose to R at the right. Unique use of this die. *Reverse:* High Shield style. Used on W-2195, 2215, 2220 (as here), 2260, and 2265 (also Miller 1788 Connecticut reverse I). *Notes:* There are two distinct die-state combinations for this variety. Both have the obverse crack. The first run produced coins of higher quality. After that, the reverse was used to coin other varieties. Then it was reunited with the obverse, and coins were struck with weaker definition of the features. Early strikes are from a perfect die, later coins with the die shattered. Known struck over Irish halfpence. *Rarity:* URS-7.

G-4	VG-8	F-12	VF-20	EF-40
$450	$700	$1,500	$4,000	$10,000

1788 Mailed Bust Right · VERMON* / AUCTORI

W-2225 · RR-30 · Bressett 23-S · inverted or backward C

Obverse: Inverted C. Lettering crudely aligned, MO overlap. Ropelike, ragged border to bottom of portrait. Unique use of this die. *Reverse:* Low Shield style. Used on W-2120, 2125, 2200, and 2225 (as here). *Notes:* One of the most distinctive Machin's Mills Vermonts, and one of the most sought after. This variety is especially desirable if at least a third or half of the backward C is clear, although on the majority some or even most of the letter is usually missing (off the planchet). Years ago this was considered to be a great rarity, but with expanded interest in die varieties and a greater collector base, many have been found since the 1950s. The finest may be the lustrous AU-50 coin owned by the late Robert Hinkley, who specialized in Vermont coppers for a long period of time. This shows microscopic die-finish lines. Other high-grade examples are owned by Roger S. Siboni and Anthony J. Terranova; the coin owned by the latter with the obverse C fully visible (illustrated). *Rarity:* URS-6.

G-4	VG-8	F-12	VF-20	EF-40	AU-50
$9,500	$12,500	$28,000	$60,000	—	

Illogical Mulings (Machin's Mills)

W-2250 · RR-1 · Bressett 26-Z · 1785 IMMUNE COLUMBIA

Obverse: From crudely cut die with VERMON AUCTORI and head of George III style. *Reverse:* Seated figure, IMMUNE COLUMBIA / 1785. Always seen on a small planchet that did not permit the border inscriptions to be completely struck. Usually of pleasing, light-brown appearance without porosity. Machin's Mills issue. *Notes:* The origin of the reverse die is not known, but is likely American. Breen attributed it to Wyon in England, stating that the IMMUNE (instead of IMMUNIS) misspelling caused it to be rejected and sent to America, but the workmanship does not match that of the Wyon shop. The IMMUNE die was combined with others, including Nova Constellatio dies (made in England). Due to its early date and unique style this was listed by Hillyer C. Ryder as number 1 in his text. Despite their peculiar nature, this and other Machin's Mills mulings are "official," as that mint was an authorized producer of Vermont issues. *Rarity:* URS-6.

G-4	VG-8	F-12	VF-20	EF-40
$7,500	$14,000	$20,000	$50,000	—

W-2255 · RR-13 · Bressett 17-V · 1787 BRITANNIA

Obverse: From die with VERMON AUCTORI and head of George III style. Perhaps the most finely drawn head in the Vermont series. *Reverse:* Seated figure, BRITANNIA / 1787, a die intended for a counterfeit English halfpenny. Machin's Mills issue. *Notes:* Most but not all have the lettering very weak on the reverse, seemingly from a die ground down to give the coins a worn appearance, thus suggesting that they are "good" and have been circulating for a long time. Alternatively, the reverse could have been used to strike W-2255, then extensively for counterfeit English halfpence, then in a worn state, more Vermonts. Hickcox (1858) and Dickeson (1859), copying Hickcox, presented the novel statement that these pieces were produced deliberately by Vermont coiners who were aware that Vermont legislators were negotiating with England to join the English (rather than becoming part of the United States). This is one of the most plentiful of all Vermont coppers, sharing that distinction with W-2120. Tony Carlotto suggests that more than 1,250 are known. Usually a pleasing, light brown in color. Also known as Vlack Machin's Mills halfpenny VT-87C. *Rarity:* URS-12.

G-4	VG-8	F-12	VF-20	EF-40	AU-50
$200	$250	$375	$950	$2,800	$5,500

W-2260 · RR-31 · Bressett 24-U · 1788 GEORGIVS III REX

Obverse: Counterfeit halfpenny die with English inscription and portrait. *Reverse:* Used on W-2195, 2215, 2220, 2260 (as here), and 2265 (also Miller 1788 Connecticut reverse I). Machin's Mills issue. *Notes:* Usually seen on a small planchet and with the obverse well struck (in the context of a Machin's Mill Vermont copper). Sometimes known as Vlack Machin's Mills halfpenny 22-88VT (W-8090). *Rarity:* URS-8.

G-4	VG-8	F-12	VF-20	EF-40
$800	$1,400	$3,400	$6,500	$18,000

W-2265 (same as W-4400) · RR-39 · Bressett 25-U · 1788

Obverse: Same as W-4400 of Connecticut; 1787 Miller 1.1-A, I, VV, and 1788 1-I (see W-4400 for illustration). *Reverse:* Used on W-2195, 2215, 2220, 2260, and 2265 (as here). *Notes:* Shared reverse with a later Connecticut copper. Not listed with Vermont coppers until recent generations. *Rarity:* URS-6.

G-4	VG-8	F-12	VF-20
$4,000	$7,000	$14,000	$22,000

Early Counterfeit · 1785 VERMONTIS

W-2270 · RR-5 · struck

Contemporary counterfeit, sometimes struck, other times cast (see next entry). Sun rises on left side of mountain. Lettering all around border, including below date. Not an official issue, but sometimes added to Vermont collections. Dismissed by Kenneth Bressett and Tony Carlotto. *Rarity:* URS-4.

Selected auction price(s): Norweb I Sale (B&M 10/1987), VG, $37,400.

W-2275 · RR-5 · cast

Contemporary counterfeit as described above, cast. *Rarity:* URS-5.

Selected auction price(s): Norweb I Sale (B&M 10/1987), VG, $7,040. C4 Convention (M&G 11/2001), Fair-2/AG-3, $2,000. Mid-Winter ANA Sale (B&M 4/2005), Fair-2, $3,450.

Connecticut Coppers 1785–1788

Connecticut copper of 1785. (Engraving by John Gavit for Hickcox, *An Historical Account of American Coinage*, 1858)

Authorization of the Coinage

On October 18, 1785, Samuel Bishop, James Hillhouse, Joseph Hopkins, and John Goodrich petitioned the General Assembly of Connecticut to authorize the production of copper coins. They stated that there was a great scarcity of small circulating coins in the state, and those seen were apt to be counterfeits. Two days later, on October 20, they were granted the right to establish a mint under the direction and superintendence of the General Assembly, with a royalty of 1/20th part of all copper coins to be paid into the treasury of the state.

The authorization was given to coin no more than £10,000 lawful money in value of the standard of English halfpence, to weigh six pennyweight (equal to 144 grains) each, and to bear a design of a man's head on one side with the letters AUCTORI: CONNEC: ("by the authority of Connecticut"). The reverse side was to depict the emblem of Liberty with an olive branch in her hand and with the inscription INDE: ET. LIB: 1785, the lettering being an abbreviation of the Latin words for "independence and liberty."

Yet another condition was specifically stated: "Nothing in this act shall be construed to make such coppers a legal tender in payment of any debt, except for the purpose of making even change, for any sum not exceeding three shillings." At the time, many regal, counterfeit, and other coppers were in circulation, including Nova Constellatio issues. The willingness of customers and tradesmen to accept them varied. Not wishing to disturb this situation, the General Assembly authorized their use as small change only. The next week, on October 24, another act was drawn up to prevent counterfeiting:

> No person whatever shall coin or manufacture any copper coin of any description or size without permission . . . from the General Assembly on pain of forfeiting for each offense the sum of one hundred pounds lawful money.

Counterfeiting of coins and paper money was a common crime in Connecticut and other states at the time. Gradually, the typical weight and percentage of authentic copper coins in circulation declined, leading to devaluation culminating in what historians refer to as the coppers panic of 1789. As such coins became worth a fraction of their former values, this effectively ended the era of state and related copper coinage in America.

The Company for Coining Coppers

Oversight by the state on the new coining operation was slight. In 1787 a committee was appointed to review the coinage. Likely, other reviews were held, but no information has been found concerning them. Later, in May 1789, the committee gave an overall review to the assembly. It was related that on April 7, 1789, a meeting of the parties involved at the inception of minting was held at a private home in New Haven. Attending were Samuel Bishop, James Hillhouse, Mark Leavenworth, and John Goodrich. The history of the coinage was revealed.

On November 12, 1785, Samuel Bishop, James Hillhouse, Joseph Hopkins, and John Goodrich, the original persons named in the coinage act, entered into an agreement with Pierpoint Edwards, Jonathan Ingersoll, Abel Buell, and Elias Shipman to form the Company for Coining Coppers. Buell was an experienced plate and die engraver, and brought his expertise to the enterprise. The others were citizens of high integrity and repute, men who were important in the state. While the partners hoped to make a profit, it is likely that they also sought to benefit Connecticut by providing coins for commerce.

This arrangement continued until February 1786, when Ingersoll and Edwards sold 1/16th part of the company each to Goodrich. In March 1786 Hopkins sold 1/16th part to Goodrich, and in April 1786 Edwards, Shipman, and Ingersoll each sold 1/16th part to James Jarvis. The latter continued production of Connecticut coppers until some time in the summer of 1786, when the supply of copper metal was depleted.

On September 10, 1786, the company leased its minting apparatus to Mark Leavenworth, Isaac Baldwin, and William Leavenworth for a period of six weeks. Likely, the latter individuals had access to copper. Additional transfers of interest took place, so that in June 1787 the ownership stood as follows: James Jarvis, 9/16th part; James Hillhouse, 1/8th part; Mark Leavenworth, 1/8th part; Abel Buell, 1/8th part; and John Goodrich, 1/16th part. In early summer 1787 the Company for Coining Coppers wound down, and the enterprise became known as James Jarvis & Co.

Inspectors from the legislature found out that 28,944 pounds' weight of coppers was produced by the Company for Coining Coppers, with 1/20th part, or 1,477 pounds and a few ounces, being transmitted to Connecticut as a royalty. At the time, the coppers passed in circulation at 18 pieces to a shilling.

No records have been located as to the extent of the Jarvis operation, or indicating whether its coinage was officially sanctioned by the state. Its main business was the production of 1787-dated Fugio coppers, and emphasis was on trying to make as much profit as possible.

The committee further learned that Major Eli Leavenworth, apparently a relative of the other two Leavenworths earlier associated with the venture, made blank coppers in autumn 1788 and had them stamped in New York with various impressions. Some of these apparently had inscriptions relating to Connecticut, but others were of different designs.

It was disclosed that Abel Buell had gone to Europe. Before leaving he gave Benjamin Buell, believed to be a son, the right to produce coppers. As of the committee report in 1789, Benjamin had just begun to issue pieces of undetermined design, which would have been dated 1788 or earlier.

On June 20, 1789, the right to coin coppers was suspended. Thus concluded the official Connecticut production, although it is likely that most coinage after the Company for Coining Coppers dissolved was not reported to the state. About this time, the "coppers panic" sharply devalued Connecticut and other coins, making further production unprofitable, even for counterfeiters. Machin's Mills was shuttered about this time. As a further end to such business, the Constitution became effective on March 9, 1789, after which the federal government reserved the exclusive right to produce coins.

Accounts of the Mints

Charles I. Bushnell, who in the late 1850s did extensive research in the field of early American coins, medals, and tokens, entered the following in his manuscript notes:

> Hon. Henry Meigs, late of this city (New York), deceased, informed me in September 1854 that Connecticut coins were made in a building situated under the Southern Bluff, near the center of the north shore of the harbor in New Haven, west of the Broome and Platt houses. Mr. Meigs lived at the time between the latter residences, at a short distance from the mint house. He visited it frequently and saw the press in operation.
>
> The building was a small frame house, and he thinks was painted red. Messrs. Broome and Platt, who had formerly been merchants in the city of New York, and who were men of fortune, he thinks must have had a subcontract for the manufacture of the state coinage, as Mr. Broome superintended the mint, and gave orders to the men, not more than three of whom were seen at work at one time. Both members of the firm would sometimes distribute some of the coins among the boys, among whom was my informant.
>
> Mr. Meigs said he saw the mint in operation in 1788, and that it had been in operation some considerable time before that. The coins were struck by means of a

Connecticut copper of 1785. W-2340, Miller 3.4-F.1, an example in extraordinary preservation. The typical copper of this year is apt to be Very Good to Very Fine and with planchet defects.

powerful iron screw. Mr. F. Kingsbury thinks that the house described by Mr. Meigs was probably at a place at Morris Cove, now so called, which is on the right hand side of the harbor going up, and about two miles above the lighthouse. The firm of Broome and Platt was composed of Samuel Broome and Jeremiah Platt.

I have understood from another source that a building at Westville, at the foot of West Rock, about two miles inland from New Haven, was likewise used for the coinage of Connecticut coppers. At the time the old building was last seen, it contained an old coining press, and the remnants of copper castings.

The dies for coins struck by the Company for Coining Coppers are thought to have been made by Abel Buell, a partner. Others are thought to have produced many other dies of different styles used by counterfeiters, notably Machin's Mills, to which coinage of many pieces dated from 1786 to 1788 are attributed.

As a general rule, the weight of these coppers declined steadily, with those of the first year, 1785, being much heavier than those of the last, 1788. During this interim more than 350 die combinations were made, by far the largest number of any state copper coinage. Connecticut coppers, which circulated widely, were considered to be fair game for other coiners. In addition to unofficial coinage at Machin's Mills, other pieces were struck outside of the state, and we know some were made in New York City. Walter Breen, in his *Encyclopedia* and also in his description of the present writer's Connecticut collection for Pine Tree Auctions in 1975, proposed a new arrangement of classifying these coppers to a half dozen different minting locations. Today, certain of these theories are taken with a grain of salt by specialists. As die-engraving punches, craftsmen, and dies were apt to move from one location to another, it is unlikely that definitive attributions will ever be made for all varieties. If a letter punch on a Connecticut copper is identical to one used on a New Jersey copper, it does not logically follow that a mint in New Jersey was busy making Connecticut coins. It could have been that various dies for Connecticut and New Jersey were made in the same shop, not necessarily in either state.

As Connecticut coppers circulated at a higher value than certain of their contemporaries, many Nova Constellatio and some other pieces were overstruck with Connecticut designs, probably at Machin's Mills near Newburgh, New York. As Connecticut coppers never had legal-tender status to begin with, it can be argued that no laws were broken when maverick mints made their own versions. Although no single rule applies to all, it seems that in prefederal times, those who counterfeited currency and silver and gold coins were punished, but the making of false copper coins was a misdemeanor, if indeed it was noticed at all.

Classifying and Studying Connecticut Coppers

The first extensive study of Connecticut coppers appeared in Montroville W. Dickeson's *American Numismatical Manual* in 1859. As he was starting without building on any other published numismatic information of significance, this work is remarkable for the useful information it contained. Connecticut types were arranged by numbers, and descriptions were given of the ornaments included in certain of the legends, a remarkable sophistication for the era. The book went through later editions in 1860 and 1865. Sylvester S. Crosby's *Early Coins of America*, 1875, contained much more information and remains useful today, while Dickeson is largely forgotten. Crosby presented legislative and contractual background to the coins and described many die combinations. These were classified by head style, inscriptions, punctuation, and ornaments, with a scheme of numbers for obverse dies and letters for reverses, starting anew with each year. The ornaments included pheons (tiny horizontal arrowheads), cinquefoils (five-lobed decorations), fleurons (horizontal elements somewhat resembling a tulip or the head of a rag mop), and so on. This was followed in 1892 by Dr. Thomas Hall's masterful 58-page study of the most extensive coinage year, *A Descriptive List of the Coppers Issued by Authority, for the State of Connecticut, for the Year 1787*.

In a 1919 study in the *American Journal of Numismatics*, published in book form in 1920 in *The State Coinages of New England*, Henry C. Miller used and expanded the system originated by Dickeson, amplified by Crosby and used by Hall, adding to nomenclature still in effect today. Obverses of a given year and basic style, based on the portrait, punctuation, and other obvious features, were given a number beginning with 1, similar to Crosby. If several different dies had the same style, but slightly different features, the 1 would be given a superscript, such as 1^1, 1^2, or 1^3, these being additions to the Crosby schedule. Reverses were given letters starting with capital A, continuing through capital Z, then lowercase a through z, then double capitals starting with AA, BB, and so on. Accordingly, a certain variety of 1787 might be described as 33^{33}-ff^1. As the use of superscript numbers is sometimes clumsy, today a period is used to separate the superscript, as 33.33-ff.1. The Miller numbers are cross-referenced in all listings below. As the 1787 dies are more extensive and complex than are those of the other three dates, additional information about them (letter positions, fillets, dentils, etc.) is given in many instances, to aid identification. Evaluating dentils can be challenging, as on many coins only the tips of long dentils are shown. Often, several different specimens need to be examined to determine the actual length and spacing. There are many coins for which this has not been done, suggesting that some designated as "short" or "medium" length might actually be longer.

In our own time there is no lack of reading material for the specialist. Issues of the *Colonial Newsletter* have many articles by James C. Spilman and Edward Barnsley, including diagrams of die combinations and linkages, and studies of weights, not to overlook many valuable contributions by Walter Breen and, later, by Philip L. Mossman. These remain a rich resource. A contributor to the present book is preparing a definitive work on Connecticut coppers, which will be essential to specialists in the series.

Notable Collectors of the Past

The pursuit of Connecticut coppers has attracted many numismatists over the years. Prominent specialists include pioneer Thomas Hall, who was an avid collector as early as the 1870s and advertised for these coins. His obituary in *The Numismatist*, June 1909, included this:

> The very sudden death, in May last, at his summer home in Chelmsford, Mass., of Dr. Thomas Hall, for many years a member of the Boston Numismatic Society, leaves a vacancy in the ranks of prominent collectors of Americana. Dr. Hall's cabinet was remarkable in many ways; his sets of early U.S. cents, especially those of 1793 and '94, had few if any equals. His Rosa Americanas comprised nearly if not quite all the known varieties, while his colonial and state issues, from the early N.E. silver to the New Jersey, Vermont, and especially the Connecticut Cents, was remarkable for its completeness; he had in preparation a monograph of some of these, and a portion of it he had privately printed; but we fear that physical infirmity prevented him from bringing it to a conclusion.

Dr. Hall was never happier than when opening his cabinet to some friend of congenial tastes, especially as his failing health kept him at home for much of the time in the latter years of life. He had carefully studied its wealth of choice and interesting pieces.

The Hall collection went en bloc to Virgil M. Brand in the same year.

Mention is made of William W. Hays, who must have furnished strong competition to all comers in the late 19th century, for his collection offered by Charles Steigerwalt in October 1903 included the remarkable count of 277 pieces. These went to Hillyer C. Ryder, whose holdings passed to F.C.C. Boyd to Wayte Raymond, then to John J. Ford Jr. The state coppers in both the Boyd and Raymond estates were acquired by Ford, who had the knack of being in the right place at the right time. Boyd, Raymond, and Ford were caretakers and appreciative owners, but added little to study and research. Henry C. Miller, of reference renown, must be mentioned among specialists and connoisseurs, along with Frederick A. Canfield (whose collection of 285 coins formed the core of the American Numismatic Society's holdings, which stands at over 310 today), Norman Bryant (whose coins went to Craige), Edward ("Ned") Barnsley, Ted Craige (to Bowers), Frederick Taylor, and Emery May Holden Norweb, among others.

Aspects of Collecting

The Miller system of die-variety attribution is daunting to many, especially with the Draped Bust Left coins of 1787. Well-worn coins are sometimes difficult or impossible to classify. Moreover, the prospect of gathering several hundred die combinations, many of which take careful study with a magnifying glass to differentiate, deters many. A convenient alternative is to collect by basic dates and types as outlined in the Red Book or in *Walter Breen's Complete Encyclopedia of U.S. and Colonial Coins*.

Although there are many exceptions, in general the first issues of 1785 are on heavy planchets, dark in hue or even black, and with small rifts and fissures. This is particularly true of the earlier die combinations of the Mailed Bust Right type, many of these being from hand-cut dies (not from punches for the portrait and seated figure). As a result, the early varieties are especially interesting to study. All dies were made with three grapevines on the shield, these being part of the arms of the state. Most coins are not struck up sufficiently to show these, although parts may be visible.

The Mailed Bust Left type was introduced this year and continued into 1788. The portrait is that of King George II, similar to that found on regal halfpence. The dies were cut by Abel Buell, whose techniques have been extensively studied in the *Colonial Newsletter*. He devised a system of hub dies containing the portrait, seated figure, and, sometimes, other information, but always with punctuation added by hand. These can be challenging to attribute.

Coppers of 1786 included Mailed Bust Left, Draped Bust Left, and Mailed Bust Right types. Many of the last are styled after the portrait of King George III found on regal halfpence and are probably counterfeits. Machin's Mills made many coppers of this and later dates, usually on lightweight planchets of high quality, but with the dies sometimes containing errors and often with irregular spacing or arrangement of the letters and date numerals.

Dies of 1787 and 1788 by Buell used Mailed Bust Left or Draped Bust Left obverses, and seated-figure reverse punches. Letters, numerals, punctuation, and ornaments were added individually by hand. It is thought that *all* legal Connecticut coppers after 1785 are from Buell's punches. It remains a puzzle why counterfeiters created the Mailed Bust Right coinage, rather than imitating Buell's head of King George II. The portrait coinages of Vermont and Connecticut are very similar in style and include dies by Buell and unknown others.

The largest number of varieties is found among the 1787 issues. Most are of the Draped Bust Left type, divided into Small Letters (attributed to James Jarvis) and Large Letters (Company for Coining Coppers) styles. These can be difficult to differentiate as to individual die varieties, such as many from the 33-style obverse and Z-reverse dies. Others are obvious, such as with arrowheads (pheons) at the date or the reverse lettered ETLIB INDE rather than INDE ET LIB. Most of this year are on decent planchets. The last date is 1788, made in several types, but with fewer varieties overall. Generally, these are on thin planchets of good quality.

Basic types of Connecticut coppers can be collected easily—a very pleasant pursuit—with typical grades ranging from Good to Fine. Those at the Very Fine level are scarcer, and Extremely Fine or finer coins are rare. There are many exceptions. The 1787 "Laughing Head," Miller 6.1-M, is often found in high grades, as is 4-L ("Horned Bust") of the same year. The Red Book describes basic types of Connecticuts and furnishes ideas for interesting varieties. Although the standard spelling in the reverse legend was INDE ET LIB, close spacing to produce ETLIB is a common feature, as is an R instead of a B in LIB, to create ET LIR or ETLIR.

In many instances an F punch was altered in the die to become an E. Although some have been called INDE over INDF (but not in the present text), no comprehensive study has ever been made of them.

Punctuation found on Connecticut coppers includes periods, sometimes called dots or (English style) stops. These can be centered after a word or can be low. Crosses can be vertical, as +, or diagonal, as x. Miller called larger ornaments of this type a *cross*, smaller versions a *crosslet*. Quatrefoils have four lobes or petals, while cinquefoils have five. Dots were arranged in various ways, such as groups of four in a diamond pattern, or a central dot with others surrounding. A pheon is a horizontal ornaments resembling an arrowhead. A fleuron is horizontal, with a head or bud, with a tail above and below the shaft, starting a small distance in from the head of the shaft. The reasons for using such a wide variety of ornaments and arrangements on Connecticut dies is unknown today. Suggestions include control of the use of the dies or evaluation the length of time they served, or the source or distribution of a particular batch of copper or the coppers struck from them. In any event, it seems logical that a given die was used until it cracked or otherwise became unserviceable.

The sharpness of details on the coins varies widely. Very few Connecticuts are boldly struck with all portrait and seated figure details complete, and with full lettering and borders. Machin's Mills coins usually have incomplete borders and always are weak at the centers, since the dies were made this way to simulate wear. If a freshly minted copper appeared to have been used for a long time, and thus accepted in commerce, it was easier for the Machin's Mills coiners to distribute. The extensive Mailed Bust Left and Draped Bust Left coinage from Abel Buell dies can be well struck, but is usually seen with lightness at the center of the obverse and, in particular, the center of the reverse. Planchet flaws are the rule, not the exception. Machin's Mills issues are often on good planchets, but are weakly struck at the centers.

Market prices for basic types in grades from Good to Fine or even Very Fine are quite reasonable. Familiarity with the different types will be useful when buying. In that way you will know, for example, that a 1787 "Laughing Head" in Fine grade is of so-so significance, but that a 1787 Miller 1.1-VV, a Machin's Mills counterfeit, in Fine is scarce and well worth buying in that grade.

More so than in any other state-coinage series, planchet flaws, lightness of strike, and other problems are very common and are to be expected. In the selected auction prices below, problems have been mentioned if they are important; most other coins have granularity, some roughness, or other aspects affecting value. For complete information check the auction catalogs. If you desire problem-free coins, try Massachusetts coppers instead! Of course, the variable quality of striking and planchets adds a generous measure of appeal to the series. One of the most desired of all varieties is the 1787 Miller 1.4-WW (check the listing). Be prepared to be aware, learn, and then enjoy!

Easy Finding Guide
1785 Mailed Bust Right Obverse Dies

For this and other Easy Finding Guides, descriptions are given to quickly identify dies in many instances. If the punctuation and ornaments are unique to a die, little if anything further is stated. For types that include multiple dies, read up to "Diagnostic" to attribute the die.

AUCTORI. / CONNEC.

Miller 1 · Legend AUCTORI. CONNEC. with periods. Diagnostic. *Used for:* W-2300, Miller 1-E.

AUCTORI: / CONNEC:

Miller 2 · Roman Head · Lower dot of colon after AUCTORI clear of head. Upper fillet is serpentine and points just right of foot of A, bottom fillet points at center of A. Diagnostic. *Used for:* W-2305, Miller 2-A.1. W-2310, Miller 2-A.4.

Miller 3.1 · Lower dot of colon touches head. Hair curl above forehead. Upper curved line of mail ends abruptly at lower left corner and does not connect with inner line. Five dots below upper curved line. Four dots on mail above breast. Upper fillet is looped at end and is below U. Lower fillet curves down and is distant from A. Diagnostic. *Used for:* W-2315, Miller 3.1-A.3. W-2320, Miller 3.1-F.3, W-2325, Miller 3.1-L.

Miller 3.2 · Lower dot of colon heavy and partly on head. A single sprig from near top of upper front leaf is joined by a second, both terminating in a prominent berry on forehead. T tilted right. I thick and low. Upper fillet ends below space between A and U. Lower fillet distant and follows neck. The curved lines of the mail at lower left corner form a rounded extremity. Top curved lines on shoulder double. Diagnostic. *Used for:* W-2330, Miller 3.2-L.

Miller 3.3 · Lower dot of colon touches head. Curl above forehead. Both colons heavy. Last colon close to C and low. Upper fillet ends below U. Lower fillet ends below center of A. Diagnostic. *Used for:* W-2335, Miller 3.3-F.3.

Miller 3.4 · Lower colon near hair, which is indented at that point. Small head; hair brushed to back as to form a dome. 5 large laurel leaves; prominent curl above forehead. Upper fillet below center of U. Lower fillet below right center of A (can appear split on some specimens). Diagnostic. *Used for:* W-2340, Miller 3.4-F.1. W-2345, Miller 3.4-F.2.

Miller 3.5 · Lower dot of colon very close to head. Four hair locks emerge from upper front leaf, uniting over forehead. T thick. A line joins T and O at top. I low. EC low. Diagnostic. *Used for:* W-2350, Miller 3.5-B.

Miller 4.1 · **African Head** · Head in high relief, large and close to bottom border. Hair thick and brushed upward, like tiny leaves. 6 large laurel leaves. Diagnostic. *Used for:* W-2355, Miller 4.1-F.4.

Miller 4.2 · **African Head** · Similar to 4.1 but hair brushed back. Lower dot of first colon heavy. Diagnostic. *Used for:* W-2360, Miller 4.2-F.6 (listed by Miller as 4.2-F.4).

Miller 4.3 · Lower dot of colon partly on head. Upper fillet ends below U. Lower fillet-end distant from A. AUCTORI closely spaced. Hair brushed back, forehead receding. Last colon midway between C and mail. Crack from lower left corner of mail. Diagnostic. *Used for:* W-2365, Miller 4.3-A.2. W-2370, Miller 4.3-D.

Miller 4.4 · Lower dot of colon partly on head. I low. Four hair locks from upper front leaf unite in a prominent berry over forehead. Mail at lower left corner has rounded extremity. Long pointed nose, lips thick. Upper fillet points between A and U. EC low. Diagnostic. *Used for:* W-2375, Miller 4.4-C. W-2380, Miller 4.4-D.

Miller 5 · Lower dot of colon half on head. Upper fillet ends below U. Lower fillet ends below center and left foot of A and is not close to it. Top left of T thick. R leans right. Lower dot of last colon slightly below line of C. C in CONNEC closed. Hair brushed back in nearly parallel lines to northwest. Neck large and badly shaped. Two oblong die-breaks between chin and bust. Diagnostic. *Used for:* W-2385, Miller 5-F.5.

Miller 6.1 · **Round Head** · Lower dot of colon entirely on head. I partly on head. Prominent berry on forehead. Tail of R close to I and touches head. Last colon distant from mail and much nearer C. Diagnostic. *Used for:* W-2390, Miller 6.1-A.1.

1785 OBVERSE DIES (continued)

Miller 6.2 · Lower dot of colon very heavy and entirely on head. I partly on head. A and U not close. Tail of R touches I but is clear of head. Last colon slightly low and close to C. Diagnostic. *Used for:* W-2395, Miller 6.2-F.1.

Miller 6.3 · Lower dot of colon entirely on head. I partly on head. Hair coarse and brushed back and down. Fillets are heavy and end between bust and A. A touches upper fillet. C distant from forehead. Diagnostic. *Used for:* W-2400, Miller 6.3-G.1. W-2410, Miller 6.3-G.2.

Miller 6.4 · Lower dot of colon entirely on head. I low and partly on head. Hair brushed to back. Upper fillet end below U. Lower fillet-end distant from A. Lower left corner of mail ends in sharp point. T in AUCTORI high. Last colon nearly equidistant from C and mail. Diagnostic. *Used for:* W-2415, Miller 6.4-F.5. W-2420, Miller 6.4-I. W-2425, Miller 6.4-K.

Miller 6.5 · Lower dot of colon entirely on head. I partly on head. Fillet-ends between bust and A. Letters light and tall. I low. Last colon more distant from the bust than in obverse 6.3. Diagnostic. *Used for:* W-2430, Miller 6.5-M.

Miller 6.6 · Lower dot of colon entirely on head. I touches head. Hair coarse and brushed in parallel strokes in northwest direction. Upper fillet opposite U; lower opposite space between AU. Nose on head points to center of second N, unlike any other 1785 obverse. Vertical crack bisects obverse 11:30 to 6:30. *Used for:* W-2435, Miller 6.6-A.3.

EASY FINDING GUIDE
1785 MAILED BUST LEFT OBVERSE DIES

Obverse 7 and 8 were called "Head of 1786" by Miller, but as the style was first used in 1785, the 1786 version should be called Head of 1785. Miller's obverse 7 is now known to represent three varieties; photographs should be studied for comparison. Miller listed just 7-D.

AUCTORI / CONNEC

The differences among the three obverse 7 dies are very subtle. Careful examination is recommended, best in conjunction with detailed photographs.

Miller 7.1 · Narrow gap between AUCTORI and the dentils. The letters are thicker than on 7.3, with which this die is easily confused. Diagnostic. *Used for:* W-2440, 7.1-D.

Miller 7.2 · Same die as Miller 1786 4.2, the only instance of a 1785 die carried over to a later year. Diagnostic break on neck extending right, through the fillets. Semicircle below the mail. Diagnostic. *Used for:* W-2445, 7.2-D.

Miller 7.3 · Wide space between AUCTORI and the dentils. Diagnostic. *Used for:* W-2450, 7.3-D.

AUCTORI: / CONNEC:

Miller 8 · Legend and punctuation diagnostic. *Used for:* W-2455, 8-D.

Easy Finding Guide
1785 Reverse Dies

Compare B, D, I, K, and L, which are similar; check other features if dots are weak.

INDE: / ETLIB:

Miller A.1 · Branch hand opposite curve of D. Top leaf close to and only slightly beyond colon. Diagnostic. *Used for:* W-2305, Miller 2-A.1. W-2390, Miller 6.1-A.1.

Miller A.2 · Branch hand opposite lower right of E. Diagnostic. *Used for:* W-2365, Miller 4.3-A.2.

Miller A.3 · Branch hand opposite colon. Diagnostic. *Used for:* W-2315, Miller 3.1-A.3. W-2435, Miller 6.6-A.3.

Miller A.4 · Branch hand opposite curve of D. Top leaf mostly above colon. Diagnostic. *Used for:* W-2310, Miller 2-A.4.

INDE: ❖ / ETLIB:

Miller B · Branch hand opposite center of E. Miller: Cross formed by four irregular heavy dots with light connecting line. Top of branch close to cross. Diagnostic. Earlier, this die was known as K.2 (*CNL*, May 1991). *Used for:* W-2350, Miller 3.5-B.

INDE: ❖❖ / ETLIB:

Miller C · Branch hand opposite upright of E (compare to the next several following). Diagnostic. *Used for:* W-2375, Miller 4.4-C.

INDE: ❖ / ETLIB:

Miller D · Branch hand opposite colon. Colon distant from E. Diagnostic. *Used for:* W-2370, Miller 4.3-D. W-2380, Miller 4.4-D. W-2440, Miller 7.1-D. W-2445, Miller 7.2-D. W-2450, Miller 7.3-D. W-2455, Miller 8-D.

INDE. ❖❖ / ETLIB. ❖

Miller E · Branch hand opposite center of E. Small letters. Two groups of four dots in a diamond pattern past INDE: (left and right dots heavier than dots between them, but all can be weakly defined). Diagnostic. *Used for:* W-2300, Miller 1-E.

INDE: ✤ / ET LIB:

Miller F.1 · Branch hand opposite center of D. Diagnostic. *Used for:* W-2340, Miller 3.4-F.1. W-2395, Miller 6.2-F.1.

1785
Reverse Dies
(continued)

INDE: ✜ / ET LIR: (F.2 ONLY)

Miller F.2 · ETLIR spelling. Diagnostic. Could be listed under a separate heading, but Miller order is preserved here. *Used for:* W-2345, Miller 3.4-F.2.

INDE: ✜ / ET LIB:

Miller F.3 · Branch hand opposite colon. Colon distant from E. 1 slightly farther below date line than is 7; 8 low. Diagnostic. *Used for:* W-2320, Miller 3.1-F.3. W-2335, Miller 3.3-F.3.

Miller F.4 · Branch hand opposite center of E. First colon close to E, dots large and equally sized, lower dot closer to E. Last colon wide and low. Diagnostic. Compare to F.6. *Used for:* W-2355, Miller 4.1-F.4.

Miller F.5 · Branch hand opposite colon. Colon distant from E. In date, 1 thick and defective at upper right. 8 leans right. Bottom date line wavy. Diagnostic. *Used for:* W-2385, Miller 5-F.5. W-2415, Miller 6.4-F.5.

Miller F.6 · Branch hand opposite center of E. First colon more distant from E than with F.4 and parallel to it. Last colon closer and higher than with F.4. Diagnostic. Compare to F-4. *Used for:* W-2360, Miller 4.2-F.6.

INDE: ✜ ✜ / ET LIB:

Miller G.1 · Branch tip opposite center of first quatrefoil. Edge of cap close to upright of E. Diagnostic. *Used for:* W-2400, Miller 6.3-G.1.

Miller G.2 · Branch tip below quatrefoil. Edge of cap distant from upright of E. Diagnostic. *Used for:* W-2410, Miller 6.3-G.2.

INDE: ⁙ / ET LIB:

Miller I · Legend and punctuation diagnostic. *Used for:* W-2420, Miller 6.4-I.

INDE: ⁙ / ET LIB:

Miller K · Legend and punctuation diagnostic. *Used for:* W-2425, Miller 6.4-K.

INDE: ✣ / ET LIB:

Miller L · Legend and punctuation diagnostic. *Used for:* W-2325, Miller 3.1-L. W-2330, Miller 3.2-L.

INDE: ✜ / ET LIB: ✜

Miller M · Legend and punctuation diagnostic. *Used for:* W-2430, Miller 6.5-M.

1785 Connecticut Coppers

1785 Mailed Bust Right

W-2300 · Miller 1-E
Rarity: URS-9.

G-4	VG-8	F-12	VF-20	EF-40	AU-50
$60	$100	$220	$700	$2,000	$4,200

W-2305 · Miller 2-A.1 · Roman Head
Notes: The obverse portrait is deep in the die, absorbing much of the planchet metal and characteristically creating a weak reverse. *Rarity:* URS-7.

G-4	VG-8	F-12	VF-20	EF-40	AU-50
$60	$200	$500	$1,200	$3,000	$6,000

W-2310 · Miller 2-A.4
Rarity: URS-6.

G-4	VG-8	F-12	VF-20	EF-40	AU-50
$60	$100	$220	$700	$2,000	$4,200

W-2315 · Miller 3.1-A.3
Rarity: URS-9.

G-4	VG-8	F-12	VF-20	EF-40	AU-50
$60	$100	$220	$700	$2,000	$4,200

W-2320 · Miller 3.1-F.3
Notes: First identified circa 1955 from the Canfield specimen (ANS) and reported by Richard Picker in *CNL* 1961. By 1991 more than a half dozen had been found. *Rarity:* URS-5.

G-4	VG-8	F-12	VF-20	EF-40	AU-50
$60	$100	$220	$700	$2,000	$4,200

W-2325 · Miller 3.1-L
Obverse: Same as preceding. *Rarity:* URS-8.

G-4	VG-8	F-12	VF-20	EF-40	AU-50
$60	$100	$220	$700	$2,000	$4,200

W-2330 · Miller 3.2-L
Reverse: As preceding. *Rarity:* URS-8.

G-4	VG-8	F-12	VF-20	EF-40	AU-50
$60	$100	$220	$700	$2,000	$4,200

W-2335 · Miller 3.3-F.3
Rarity: URS-9.

G-4	VG-8	F-12	VF-20	EF-40	AU-50
$60	$100	$220	$700	$2,000	$4,200

W-2340 · Miller 3.4-F.1
Rarity: URS-10.

G-4	VG-8	F-12	VF-20	EF-40	AU-50
$60	$100	$220	$700	$2,000	$4,200

W-2345 · Miller 3.4-F.2 · ETLIR
Notes: Only ETLIR reverse of 1785. Usually on a rough planchet. *Rarity:* URS-11.

G-4	VG-8	F-12	VF-20	EF-40	AU-50
$60	$100	$220	$700	$2,000	$4,200

W-2350 · Miller 3.5-B
Rarity: URS-7.

Selected auction price(s): John J. Ford Jr. IX Sale (Stack's 5/2005), VF, $546.25.

W-2355 · Miller 4.1-F.4 · African Head
Notes: Sometimes called Negro Head, a name used by M.W. Dickeson (1859) and perhaps earlier, although Dickeson's die cannot be attributed specifically today. Usually on dark, heavy planchets. Usually with weak obverse border and weak reverse. Scarce with a combination of high grade and good eye appeal. This has long been one of the most popular Connecticut coppers, due in part to its inclusion as a major type in the Red Book. *Rarity:* URS-12.

G-4	VG-8	F-12	VF-20	EF-40	AU-50
$90	$150	$575	$1,500	$3,900	$9,000

W-2360 · Miller 4.2-F.6
Notes: Listed in the original Miller text as 4.2-F.4. Discovered by Eric P. Newman (*CNL*, January 1972). *Rarity:* URS-2.

W-2365 · Miller 4.3-A.2
Rarity: URS-10.

G-4	VG-8	F-12	VF-20	EF-40	AU-50
$60	$100	$220	$700	$2,000	$4,200

W-2370 · Miller 4.3-D
Rarity: URS-6.

Selected auction price(s): John J. Ford Jr. IX Sale (Stack's 5/2005), F, rough, $460.

W-2375 · Miller 4.4-C
Rarity: URS-10.

G-4	VG-8	F-12	VF-20	EF-40	AU-50
$60	$100	$220	$700	$2,000	$4,200

W-2380 · Miller 4.4-D
Rarity: URS-5.

Selected auction price(s): Perkins Collection (1/2000), F–VF, $4,600.

W-2385 · Miller 5-F.5
Notes: Miller listed obverses 5.1 and 5.2, but 5.2 is simply a later state of 5.1, and there is just one die. *Rarity:* URS-9.

G-4	VG-8	F-12	VF-20	EF-40	AU-50
$60	$100	$220	$700	$2,000	$4,200

W-2390 · Miller 6.1-A.1
Rarity: URS-7.

G-4	VG-8	F-12	VF-20	EF-40	AU-50
$60	$100	$220	$700	$2,000	$4,200

W-2395 · Miller 6.2-F.1 · "Goatee" variety

Notes: With prominent die crack from front of face downward, actually much more than a goatee. *Rarity:* URS-10.

G-4	VG-8	F-12	VF-20	EF-40	AU-50
$60	$100	$220	$700	$2,000	$4,200

W-2400 · Miller 6.3-G.1

Rarity: URS-10.

G-4	VG-8	F-12	VF-20	EF-40	AU-50
$60	$100	$220	$700	$2,000	$4,200

W-2410 · Miller 6.3-G.2

Notes: Struck from heavily damaged dies. Usually seen in lower grades. *Rarity:* URS-6.

Selected auction price(s): Perkins Collection (1/2000), AU, but "peppered" with marks, $1,610. C4 Convention (M&G 11/2002), VF-30, $2,200.

W-2415 · Miller 6.4-F.5

Rarity: URS-5.

Selected auction price(s): Perkins Collection (1/2000), F/VG, $4,887.50. John J. Ford Jr. IX Sale (Stack's 5/2005), VF, rough reverse, $8,625; Choice VF, rough reverse, $8,625.

W-2420 · Miller 6.4-I

Rarity: URS-11.

G-4	VG-8	F-12	VF-20	EF-40	AU-50
$60	$100	$220	$700	$2,000	$4,200

W-2425 · Miller 6.4-K

Notes: Called 6.4-K.1 in the Miller text, when it was thought that there were two K reverses, a theory now discredited. *Rarity:* URS-6.

Selected auction price(s): Perkins Collection (1/2000), VG, $2,760. C4 Convention (M&G 11/2002), F-12, $650. Mail Bid Sale (Coin Galleries 4/2004), VG, $1,167. John J. Ford Jr. IX Sale (Stack's 5/2005), EF, $25,300.

W-2430 · Miller 6.5-M

Rarity: URS-6.

Selected auction price(s): Perkins Collection (1/2000), F, lightly pitted, $4,025. John J. Ford Jr. IX Sale (Stack's 5/2005), AU, reverse slightly off center with only part of date visible, $27,600.

W-2435 · Miller 6.6-A.3

Notes: This is the rarest die combination of 1785. Illustrated on CoinFacts (PCGS website, courtesy of Ron Guth). Discovery coin identified by Robert M. Martin and published and illustrated in *CNL*, April 2004. *Rarity:* URS-1.

G-4	VG-8	F-12	VF-20	EF-40	AU-50
$60	$100	$220	$700	$2,000	$4,200

1785 Mailed Bust Left

W-2440 · Miller 7.1-D

Notes: Typically from damaged dies, with obverse die deeply sunken, making the coins concave. *Rarity:* URS-8.

G-4	VG-8	F-12	VF-20	EF-40	AU-50
$225	$375	$700	$1,750	$4,000	$8,500

W-2445 · Miller 7.2-D

Notes: Discovered by Frederick Canfield in the early 1920s. *Rarity:* URS-6.

Selected auction price(s): Perkins Collection (1/2000), VG–G [or finer], $4,025. C4 Convention (M&G 11/2001), VG-8, $500. John J. Ford Jr. IX Sale (Stack's 5/2005), F, $3,737.50.

W-2450 · Miller 7.3-D

Notes: Discovered by Robert Lindesmith in 1973; one in the Taylor sale (1987) was miscataloged as 7.1-D. (*CNL*, May 1991). *Rarity:* URS-3.

W-2455 · Miller 8-D

Rarity: URS-7.

G-4	VG-8	F-12	VF-20	EF-40	AU-50
$225	$375	$700	$1,750	$4,000	$8,500

Easy Finding Guide
1786 Mailed Bust Right Obverse Dies

AUCTORI / CONNEC

Miller 1 · Double Chin · Legend and punctuation diagnostic. Used for: W-2460, Miller 1-A.

AUCTORI · / CONNEC ·

Miller 2.1 · Round Head · Legend and punctuation diagnostic. Dickeson (1859): "Bears the appellation of the round head, the features being quite small and delicately proportioned. The hair is brought out artistically, and the wreath around the head is well arranged." Used for: W-2465, Miller 2.1-A. W-2470, Miller 2.1-D.3.

AUCTORI. / CONNEC.

Miller 2.2 · Broad-Shouldered Head · Periods low after each word. Diagnostic. Used for: W-2475, Miller 2.2-D.2.

· AUCTORI · / · CONNEC ·

Miller 2.3 · Ornate Mailed Bust · Contemporary counterfeit. Ornate or frilly details on mail. Diagnostic. Used for: W-2485, Miller 2.3-T.

AUCTORI: / CONNEC:

Miller 3 · Scholar's Head · Legend and punctuation diagnostic. Nickname popular since the 1990s, originated by Michael J. Hodder. Earlier called Large Head. Used for: W-2510, Miller 3-D.1. W-2515, Miller 3-D.4.

Easy Finding Guide
1786 Mailed Bust Left Obverse Dies

AUCTORI / CONNEC

Miller 4.1 · Dentils large, spike-like, and triangular. Letters very close to or touching dentils; dentil pierces top of O (AUCTORI) and first C in CONNEC. Tip of highest leaf is close to or touches dentil. Diagnostic. Used for: W-2520, Miller 4.1-C. W-2525, Miller 4.1-G.

Miller 4.2 · Same die as Miller 1785 7.2. Most letters distant from dentils. Dentils tiny. Semicircle below the mail. Diagnostic. Used for: W-2530, Miller 4.2-R. W-2535, Miller 4.2-S.

Miller 4.3 · Unknown to Miller. Dentils large, spike-like, and triangular. Tip of highest leaf is opposite space between two dentils. Dentil does not pierce top of C. Diagnostic. Used for: W-2537, Miller 4.3-H.2.

AUCTORI: / CONNEC:

Details for obverse 5 are mainly from Miller. All obverses except 5.1 and 5.3 seem to be from a hub that included the lettering; NE (CONNEC) close on all. Small differences in spacing are due to either relapping or the depth of the impression of the hub into the working die. Punctuation was added by hand, and some portrait details were adjusted or strengthened. Close examination of the different possibilities is required.

1786 Mailed Bust Left Obverse Dies (continued)

Miller 5.1 · Dentils large, spike-like, and triangular. TOR very widely spaced. The upper border of mail beneath the throat consists of a double curved line and is not fluted. The tail of the R extends too far to the right. Upper fillet ends opposite left side of C or slightly above it. Obverses 5.1 (as here) and 5.3 are not from the standard hub. Diagnostic. *Used for:* W-2540, Miller 5.1-H.1.

Miller 5.2 · Upper dot of both colons low. NE close. Bottom colon after C two or three times farther from C than is top colon. Four leaves on back of wreath. Three stemmed berries within wreath. Lowest curl ends in a berry which it partly includes. Diagnostic. *Used for:* W-2545, Miller 5.2-H.1. W-2550, Miller 5.2-I. W-2555, Miller 5.2-L. W-2560, Miller 5.2-O.2.

Miller 5.3 · **Hercules Head** · Distinctive head in high relief due to sinking of die, obverses 5.1 and 5.3 (as here) are not from the standard hub. Diagnostic. Dickeson (1859) "The workmanship differs from any of the whole series, the die being deeper, and hence the muscular development of feature surpasses any other issue. To distinguish it, I have called it the type Hercules." *Used for:* W-2565, Miller 5.3-B.2. W-2570, Miller 5.3-G. W-2575, Miller 5.3-N.

Miller 5.4 · First colon leans left. NEC letters touch dentils. Semi-spherical protrusion below the front mail. Medium size triangular dentils. Diagnostic. *Used for:* W-2580, Miller 5.4-G. W-2585, Miller 5.4-N. W-2590, Miller 5.4-O.1.

Miller 5.5 · Dentils small. Over C: they are heavier, extend farther into the field, and are fused together. Four leaves on front, three on back of wreath. Semi-circle below mail. Edges of leaves rough and irregular. Lowest curl encircles a berry. First colon sloping, the lower dot nearer I. Upper dot of last colon nearly level with top of C. Diagnostic. *Used for:* W-2595, Miller 5.5-M.

Miller 5.6 · Four leaves on back of wreath. Dentils small. Semi-circular line below mail. Both colons low, dots large and heavy. Diagnostic. *Used for:* W-2600, Miller 5.6-M.

Miller 5.7 · Upper dots of both colons about on a level with the tops of the preceding letters and somewhat farther from I and C than the lower dots. Four leaves back of wreath with rough, irregular edges. The letters NEC repunched. Diagnostic. *Used for:* W-2605, Miller 5.7-G. W-2610, Miller 5.7-H.1. W-2615, Miller 5.7-O.2.

Miller 5.8 · Upper dots of both colons farthest from letters. Four leaves on back of wreath. Semi-circular line heavy, touching dentils. Partial double cutting of fluted border. Diagnostic. *Used for:* W-2620, Miller 5.8-F. W-2625, Miller 5.8-H.2. W-2630, Miller 5.8-O.2.

Miller 5.9 · Upper dots of both colons low. Upper dot of first colon the nearer to I. Four leaves on back of wreath with edges smooth and not outlined. Three berries with stems in wreath. The lowest curl ends in a berry, but does not encircle it. Diagnostic. *Used for:* W-2635, Miller 5.9-B.1. W-2640, Miller 5.9-L. W-2645, Miller 5.9-Q.

Miller 5.10 · Upper dot of both colons low. First colon has both dots near I. Four outlined leaves back of wreath. Lowest curl ends in a berry, but does not encircle it. First C in CONNEC shows double punching. Crack closing first C in CONNEC. Another closing and extending slightly below last C. Diagnostic. *Used for:* W-2650, Miller 5.10-L. W-2655, Miller 5.10-P.

Miller 5.11 · Upper dot of both colons low, the dots much smaller than those on other dies of obverse 5. Four leaves on back of wreath with smooth edges, not outlined. No berries. Lowest curl heavy, without berry. No semi-circular line. Diagnostic. *Used for:* W-2660, Miller 5.11-R.

Miller 5.13 · Both colons incline to right. Semicircular breastplate. Roman nose. Colons heavy and even. Upper dot of first colon low, and much larger than lower dot. Two dots between forelock and wreath. Serifs of E closed. Dentils fine and ragged. Diagnostic. *Used for:* W-2665, Miller 5.13-I.

Miller 5.14 · Lower dot of first colon a little below the bottom of I. Bottom dot of second colon even with bottom of C. Colons nearly parallel with letters. No semicircular breastplate. Three side curls enclose dots. The curved band on armor, under fluting, on throat, tapers into almost a crescent at the ends. Dentils fine. Diagnostic. *Used for:* W-2670, Miller 5.14-S.

Miller 5.15 · Second colon close to C and parallel to it; top dot opposite upper tip of C; bottom dot about centered with bottom part of C. No semicircular breastplate. Lower fillet follows neck, then turns right to point at bottom of C; top fillet points between colon and armor. A (AUCTORI) close to but distinctly separated from the armor; UC close. *Used for:* W-2675, Miller 5.15-S.

EASY FINDING GUIDE
1786 DRAPED BUST LEFT OBVERSE DIES

AUCTORI: / CONNEC:

Miller 6 · Legend and punctuation diagnostic. *Used for:* W-2690, Miller 6-K.

AUCTORI: ❋ / ❋ CONNEC: ❋

Miller 7 · Legend and punctuation diagnostic. *Used for:* W-2695, Miller 7-K.

EASY FINDING GUIDE
1786 REVERSE DIES

ET LIB / INDE

Miller A · Transposed legend and punctuation diagnostic. Tiny date as on certain NJ coppers. Sawtooth dentils. *Used for:* W-2460, Miller 1-A. W-2465, Miller 2.1-A.

INDE / ET LIB

Miller B.1 · Branch hand opposite upright of D. IN close. DE heavy and partially filled. E nearly touches branch hand. Diagnostic. *Used for:* W-2635, Miller 5.9-B.1.

1786
Reverse Dies
(continued)

Miller B.2 · Branch hand opposite upright and left of D. IN widely separated. E heavy. Diagnostic. Buckled at center. *Used for:* W-2565, Miller 5.3-B.2.

INDE. — — / ET LIB:

Miller C · Legend and punctuation diagnostic. *Used for:* W-2520, Miller 4.1-C.

INDE. / ET LIB.

Miller D.1 · Branch hand opposite D. Diagnostic. *Used for:* W-2510, Miller 3-D.1.

Miller D.2 · Branch hand opposite upright of D. Diagnostic. *Used for:* W-2475, Miller 2.2-D.2.

Miller D.3 · Branch hand opposite center and right upright of N. Diagnostic. *Used for:* W-2470, Miller 2.1-D.3.

Miller D.4 · Branch hand opposite space between N and D. Diagnostic. *Used for:* W-2515, Miller 3-D.4.

INDE. ✥ / ET LIB.

Miller F · Legend and punctuation diagnostic. *Used for:* W-2620, Miller 5.8-F.

INDE: -:- / ET LIB:

Miller G · Legend and punctuation diagnostic. *Used for:* W-2525, Miller 4.1-G. W-2570, Miller 5.3-G. W-2580, Miller 5.4-G. W-2605, Miller 5.7-G.

INDE: / ET · LIB:

Miller H.1 · No liberty cap. Diagnostic. *Used for:* W-2540, Miller 5.1-H.1. W-2545, Miller 5.2-H.1. W-2610, Miller 5.7-H.1.

Miller H.2 · With liberty cap. Diagnostic. *Used for:* W-2625, Miller 5.8-H.2.

INDE: ✤ / ET · LIB:

Miller I · Legend and punctuation diagnostic. *Used for:* W-2550, Miller 5.2-I. W-2665, Miller 5.13-I.

-:- INDE: -:- / -:- ET · LIB:

Miller K · Used with Draped Bust Left obverse. Diagnostic. Legend and punctuation also diagnostic. *Used for:* W-2690, Miller 6-K. W-2695, Miller 7-K.

INDE: ≋ / ET — LIB:

Miller L · Legend and punctuation diagnostic. *Used for:* W-2555, Miller 5.2-L. W-2640, Miller 5.9-L. W-2650, Miller 5.10-L.

INDE ⬟ / ET LIB

Miller M · Legend and punctuation diagnostic. *Used for:* W-2595, Miller 5.5-M. W-2600, Miller 5.6-M.

INDE: -:- / ET · LIB:

Miller N · Legend and punctuation diagnostic. *Used for:* W-2575, Miller 5.3-N. W-2585, Miller 5.4-N.

INDE: ·:· / ET LIB·

Miller O.1 · With liberty cap. Diagnostic. *Used for:* W-2590, Miller 5.4-O.1.

INDE: ·:· / ET LIB·

Miller O.2 · No liberty cap. Diagnostic. *Used for:* W-2560, Miller 5.2-O.2. W-2615, Miller 5.7-O.2. W-2630, Miller 5.8-O.2.

INDE: / ET — LIB:

Miller P · Legend and punctuation diagnostic. *Used for:* W-2655, Miller 5.10-P.

INDE: · ⬅ / ET — LIB:

Miller Q · Punctuation subject to interpretation (see Taylor-2376 discussion). *Used for:* W-2645, Miller 5.9-Q.

INDE: ✤ / ET — LIB:

Miller R · Punctuation diagnostic. *Used for:* W-2530, Miller 4.2-R. W-2660, Miller 5.11-R.

107

1786 Reverse Dies (continued)

INDE:/ET·LIB:

Miller S · Sword Hilt and Guard reverse. Legend and punctuation definitive, but best known for the addition of a sword hilt and guard at the goddess' waist, visible to the right. This feature is sometimes weakly defined. Unique in the Connecticut series. (*CNL*, May 1991). *Used for:* W-2535, Miller 4.2-S. W-2670, Miller 5.14-S. W-2675, Miller 5.15-S.

INDE. : / ?

Miller T · **Backward D in INDE** · Seated figure with puffy blouse leans to left. 1 low, 88 high. Knowledge of other details incomplete. Contemporary counterfeit. *Used for:* W-2485, Miller 2.3-T.

1786 Connecticut Coppers

1786 Mailed Bust Right

W-2460 · **Miller 1-A** · **Double Chin**
Notes: Nickname from Dickeson (1859), not often used later. *Rarity:* URS-8.
  Selected auction price(s): Perkins Collection (1/2000), F–VF, some roughness, $1,035. Pre–Long Beach Sale (Superior 6/2002), AU-55, $10,925. John J. Ford Jr. IX Sale (Stack's 5/2005), Choice VF, centers rough, $4,887.50; Choice VF, centers rough, $1,955.

W-2465 · **Miller 2.1-A** · **Round Head**
Notes: Another nickname from Dickeson (1859), not often used later. *Rarity:* URS-10.

G-4	VG-8	F-12	VF-20	EF-40	AU-50	MS-60
$250	$325	$1,000	$3,500	$8,000	$15,000	

W-2470 · **Miller 2.1-D.3**
Notes: See above. *Rarity:* URS-5.
  Selected auction price(s): Perkins Collection (1/2000), VF, granular; "possibly finest known," $13,800.

W-2475 · **Miller 2.2-D.2** · **Broad-Shouldered Head**
Notes: Struck on small-diameter planchets; date usually not visible. *Rarity:* URS-5.
  Selected auction price(s): John J. Ford Jr. IX Sale (Stack's 5/2005), VG–F, Miller plate coin, $13,800.

1786 "Miller" Connecticut Addenda

The dies for W-8145 through W-8160 are "evasion" or "bungtown" coppers. Each has English arms on the reverse shield, otherwise unknown in the Connecticut series. These are new listings to the Miller series. See "Corrigenda Millerensis Revisited," Jeff Rock, *CNL*, May 1991. Their proper place among copper listings of the 1780s has not been resolved by scholars, and some may opt to include them with Connecticuts.

W-2485 · **Miller 2.3-T** · **Backward D in INDE**
Notes: "First reported by C. Wyllys Betts in *Counterfeit Half-Pence Current in the American Colonies*, 1886, and illustrated there-in by a line engraving" (*CNL*, March 1964). Contemporary counterfeit of the "African Head" style. Two believed known: the Betts coin (later, Ford collection) and Newman-collection specimen. Breen-761. *Rarity:* URS-2.
  Selected auction price(s): John J. Ford Jr. IX Sale (Stack's 5/2005), F, irregularly struck, $92,000.

W-2490 · **Miller 2.4-U**
Notes: Discovered by Al Hoch around 1963. (*CNL*, May 1991). Breen-760. *Rarity:* URS-2.

W-2495 · **Miller 2.5-V**
Notes: "Since all four or five specimens of the above three varieties (2.3-T, 2.4-U, and 2.5-V) are weakly and unevenly struck, on wretched planchets, there is a strong possibility that the same reverse die was used on all three. The branch details visible on reverses T and V are identical, as are some other details." Discovered in 1975 by Edward R. Barnsley (*CNL*, May 1991). *Rarity:* URS-2.

W-2500 · **Miller 2.6-BRI** · **Vlack CT-86A**
Notes: Reverse with BRITA / NIA, a counterfeit English halfpenny die. Discovered in 1975 by Edward R. Barnsley. Vlack CT-86-A (1974 plate; *CNL*, May 1991). *Rarity:* URS-2.

1786 Mailed Bust Right (continued)

W-2510 · Miller 3-D.1 · Scholar's Head
Notes: Relatively new nickname for this obverse, but one that has caught on. In especially strong demand due to the distinctive appearance of the portrait. *Rarity:* URS-7.

G-4	VG-8	F-12	VF-20	EF-40	AU-50	MS-60
$1,000	$2,000	$5,000	$7,500	$10,000	$15,000	

W-2515 · Miller 3-D.4 · Scholar's Head
Notes: Three known; one in ANS, this, one in the Robert M. Martin Collection, and the other in Stack's sale of June 1995. *Rarity:* URS-3.
Selected auction price(s): Perkins Collection (1/2000), AG, $6,612.50.

1786 Mailed Bust Left

W-2520 · Miller 4.1-C
Notes: Listed by Crosby, but later untraced until the 1940s. Two believed known, one the Taylor coin, this being the inaugural auction appearance of the variety. Published by Edward R. Barnsley in *EAC*, March 1964. *Rarity:* URS-2.
Selected auction price(s): John J. Ford Jr. IX Sale (Stack's 5/2005), F–VF, "finer of two known," $40,250.

W-2525 · Miller 4.1-G
Rarity: URS-10.

G-4	VG-8	F-12	VF-20	EF-40	AU-50	MS-60
$60	$100	$190	$550	$1,400	$2,800	

W-2530 · Miller 4.2-R
Notes: Robert M. Martin recorded 22 specimens. *Rarity:* URS-6.
Selected auction price(s): John J. Ford Jr. IX Sale (Stack's 5/2005), F, planchet rifts, $402.

W-2535 · Miller 4.2-S · Sword Hilt and Guard reverse
Notes: Discovered by Norman Bryant in the early 1960s, after which more were identified. One of the most distinctive types in the series. *Rarity:* URS-5.
Selected auction price(s): Perkins Collection (1/2000), G, some problems, $4,600.

W-2540 · Miller 5.1-H.1
Rarity: URS-7.
Selected auction price(s): Perkins Collection (1/2000), VF, $1,035. John J. Ford Jr. IX Sale (Stack's 5/2005), VG–F, some roughness, $4,600; EF, planchet flaws, some serious, $1,092.50.

W-2545 · Miller 5.2-H.1
Rarity: URS-5.
Selected auction price(s): Perkins Collection (1/2000), net VF, $4,889.50. C4 Convention (M&G 11/2002), G-7, $4,250. John J. Ford Jr. IX Sale (Stack's 5/2005), EF, planchet flaws, $1,725. Palm Beach Auction (Heritage 3/2006), EF-45 (PCGS), $8,050. Henry Leon Sale (Stack's 5/2007), EF-45, $4,600.

W-2550 · Miller 5.2-I
Rarity: URS-9.
Selected auction price(s): Perkins Collection (1/2000), EF, $974.50.

W-2555 · Miller 5.2-L
Rarity: URS-7.

W-2560 · Miller 5.2-O.2
Rarity: URS-6.
Selected auction price(s): Perkins Collection (1/2000), net VF, $1,265.50. John J. Ford Jr. IX Sale (Stack's 5/2005), F–VF, rough, $1,265 (misattributed as 5.8-O.2).

W-2565 · Miller 5.3-B.2 · Hercules Head
Notes: Garrett sale; Miller sale; this coin. Always irregularly struck. *Rarity:* URS-3.
Selected auction price(s): Perkins Collection (1/2000), VF, $21,850. John J. Ford Jr. IX Sale (Stack's 5/2005), MS, Miller plate coin, heavy flaws, $80,500.

W-2570 · Miller 5.3-G · Hercules Head
Rarity: URS-3.

W-2575 · Miller 5.3-N · Hercules Head
Notes: Very popular due to its distinctive appearance, availability, and listing in the Red Book. Typically on a flawed planchet. Reverse weak due to a worn and buckled die. *Rarity:* URS-11.

G-4	VG-8	F-12	VF-20	EF-40	AU-50	MS-60
$120	$225	$650	$2,750	$6,000		

W-2580 · Miller 5.4-G
Rarity: URS-11.

G-4	VG-8	F-12	VF-20	EF-40	AU-50	MS-60
$60	$100	$190	$550	$1,400	$2,800	

W-2585 · Miller 5.4-N
Rarity: URS-6.
Selected auction price(s): Perkins Collection (1/2000), VF, $4,312.50. John J. Ford Jr. IX Sale (Stack's 5/2005), AU, top of reverse indistinct, some flaws, $27,600.

W-2590 · Miller 5.4-O.1
Rarity: URS-11.

G-4	VG-8	F-12	VF-20	EF-40	AU-50	MS-60
$60	$100	$190	$550	$1,400	$2,800	$20,000

W-2595 · Miller 5.5-M
Rarity: URS-10.

G-4	VG-8	F-12	VF-20	EF-40	AU-50	MS-60
$60	$100	$190	$550	$1,400	$2,800	

W-2600 · Miller 5.6-M
Rarity: URS-7.
Selected auction price(s): Perkins Collection (1/2000), VF, some flaws, $1,035. John J. Ford Jr. IX Sale (Stack's 5/2005), VF, some lightness of strike, $1,610.

W-2605 · Miller 5.7-G
Rarity: URS-1.

W-2610 · Miller 5.7-H.1
Rarity: URS-7.
  Selected auction price(s): Perkins Collection (1/2000), VF, some problems, $1,063.75. John J. Ford Jr. IX Sale (Stack's 5/2005), EF, granular, $5,462.50. Public Auction Sale (Stack's 9/2005), Choice AU, $8,050.

W-2615 · Miller 5.7-O.2
Rarity: URS-6.
  Selected auction price(s): John J. Ford Jr. IX Sale (Stack's 5/2005), VF, $6,325.

W-2620 · Miller 5.8-F
Notes: Once considered to be very rare (see notes in Perkins catalog under Lot 239), now relatively available. *Rarity:* URS-8.
  Selected auction price(s): John J. Ford Jr. IX Sale (Stack's 5/2005), EF, some roughness, $2,070.

W-2625 · Miller 5.8-H.2
Rarity: URS-7.
  Selected auction price(s): John J. Ford Jr. IX Sale (Stack's 5/2005), Choice AU, some problems, but the finest seen by the cataloger, $8,050. Americana Sale (Stack's 1/2007), AU-50, $1,495.

W-2630 · Miller 5.8-O.2
Rarity: URS-7.
  Selected auction price(s): Perkins Collection (1/2000), VF, $1,840. Americana Sale (Stack's 1/2007), EF-40, $1,265.

W-2635 · Miller 5.9-B.1
Rarity: URS-7.
  Selected auction price(s): John J. Ford Jr. IX Sale (Stack's 5/2005), EF, flaws, $1,840.

W-2640 · Miller 5.9-L
Notes: First identified in the 1950s, after which others were found. (*CNL*, March 1964). *Rarity:* URS-5.
  Selected auction price(s): Perkins Collection (1/2000), F/VF, $4,600.

W-2645 · Miller 5.9-Q
Rarity: URS-7.

W-2650 · Miller 5.10-L
Rarity: URS-6.
  Selected auction price(s): Perkins Collection (1/2000), F, $1,840. John J. Ford Jr. IX Sale (Stack's 5/2005), F, once cleaned, some roughness, $3,220.

W-2655 · Miller 5.10-P
Rarity: URS-7.
  Selected auction price(s): John J. Ford Jr. IX Sale (Stack's 5/2005), VF, rough, $1,265.

W-2660 · Miller 5.11-R
Rarity: URS-7 or 8.
  Selected auction price(s): Perkins Collection (1/2000), VF, $1,610. John J. Ford Jr. IX Sale (Stack's 5/2005), AU, a few problems, $9,200.

W-2665 · Miller 5.13-I
Notes: New addition to the Miller list. (*CNL*, March 1964) Two believed known, Canfield collection (ANS) and in a California collection. *Rarity:* URS-2.

W-2670 · Miller 5.14-S · Sword Hilt and Guard reverse
Notes: New addition to the Miller list. (*CNL*, May 1991). *Rarity:* URS-7.
  Selected auction price(s): Perkins Collection (1/2000), VF, flaws, "possibly finest known," $2,185.

W-2675 · Miller 5.15-S · Sword Hilt and Guard reverse
Notes: Earlier listed as a Miller variety, then delisted as none could be found. Richard August identified one in his collection in 2007 (illustrated; see the relevant Easy Finding Guides), confirming its existence. *Rarity:* URS-1.

1786 Draped Bust Left

W-2690 · Miller 6-K
Rarity: URS-7.

G-4	VG-8	F-12	VF-20	EF-40	AU-50	MS-60
$100	$200	$525	$2,000	$5,500		

W-2695 · Miller 7-K
Rarity: URS-4.
  Selected auction price(s): Perkins Collection (1/2000), VF, $6,900. John J. Ford Jr. IX Sale (Stack's 5/2005), VG–F, $9,200.

Easy Finding Guide
1787 Mailed Bust Right Obverse Dies

AUCTORI / CONNEC

Miller 1.1 · Small Head · Edge of shoulder concave. Diagnostic. *Used for:* W-2700, Miller 1.1-A. W-2710, Miller 1.1-VV.

Miller 1.2 · Muttonhead · Large head. 7 prominent vertical plates on shoulder. 3 rounded-top otherwise rectangular plates in front of neck. Diagnostic. *Details:* Largest head of the year. A close to mail, final C distant. On most specimens CONNEC weakly struck, the E not showing. Nicknames include "Muttonhead" (or Mutton Head), "Bull's Head," and "Bradford Head." *Used for:* W-2720, Miller 1.2-C. W-2730, Miller 1.2-mm.

Miller 1.3 · 6-pointed star in front of lower edge of mail. Diagnostic. *Used for:* W-2735, Miller 1.3-L.

Miller 1.4 · Head outlined and left of center of planchet. Diagnostic. *Used for:* W-2740, Miller 1.4-WW.

AUCTORI / CONNEC·

Miller 52 · Roman Head · Legend and punctuation diagnostic. *Used for:* W-2745, Miller 52-G.1. W-2750, Miller 52-G.2.

Easy Finding Guide
1787 Mailed Bust Left Obverse Dies

AUCTORI / CONNEC

Miller 2 · Legend and punctuation diagnostic. *Used for:* W-2755, Miller 2-B.

AUCTORI / CONNEC·

Miller 3 · Legend and punctuation diagnostic. *Used for:* W-2805, Miller 3-G.1.

AUCTORI· / CONNEC·

Miller 4 · Horned Bust (later die states) · Legend and punctuation diagnostic. *Details:* Most often seen with crescent shaped die crack in front of throat that starts as a small lune and develops into a major crack. Occasional examples with this die crack are found on unusually large planchets. On later issues, the die crack becomes more extended and forms a horn-like projection from the mail. *Used for:* W-2810, Miller 4-L.

1787 Mailed Bust Left Obverse Dies (continued)

·AUCTORI· / · CONNEC

Miller 5 · Legend and punctuation diagnostic. *Used for:* W-2815, Miller 5-P.

·AUCTORI· / · CONNEC·

Miller 6.1 · **Laughing Head** · Dot after AUCTORI above tip of highest leaf. Diagnostic. *Used for:* W-2820, Miller 6.1-M.

Miller 6.2 · **Laughing Head / Outlined Head** · Dot after AUCTORI to left of and distant from tip of highest leaf. Diagnostic. *Used for:* W-2825, Miller 6.2-M.

AUCTORI: / CONNEC:

Miller 7 · **Hercules Head** · Legend and punctuation diagnostic. Head distinctive. *Used for:* W-2830, Miller 7-I.

AUCTORI: ⋮ / ⋮ CONNEC: ⋮

Miller 8 · Punctuation definitive (but first group of dots sometimes not clear). Three fillet-ends, the bottom light and stringlike. A leans left, with right foot far above bottom of U. Diagnostic. *Notes:* This die is a later state of Miller Draped Bust Left obverse die Miller 16.5, only such instance in state coppers of such a dramatic conversion (Randy Clark, *C4 Newsletter*, Summer 2007). *Used for:* W-2835, Miller 8-N. W-2840, Miller 8-O. W-2845, Miller 8-a.1.

✠ AUCTORI ✠ / ✠ ✠ CONNEC ✠

Miller 9 · Legend and punctuation diagnostic. *Used for:* W-2850, Miller 9-D. W-2855, Miller 9-E. W-2860, Miller 9-R.

✠ AUCTORI ✠ ✠ / ✠ ✠ CONNEC ✠

Miller 10 · Legend and punctuation diagnostic. *Used for:* W-2865, Miller 10-E.

✤ AUCTORI ✤ / ✤ CONNEC ✤

Miller 11.1 · First star very close to mail, but not touching. Final star touches mail. Diagnostic. *Used for:* W-2870, Miller 11.1-E.

Miller 11.2 · Neither first nor last star touches mail. Diagnostic. *Used for:* W-2875, Miller 11.2-K.

Miller 11.3 • First star touches mail. Diagnostic. *Used for:* W-2880, Miller 11.3-K.

AUCTORI. ❋ / CONNEC ❋

Miller 12 • Legend and punctuation diagnostic. *Used for:* W-2885, Miller 12-Q.

AUCTORI ✱ / ✱ CONNEC ✱

Miller 13 • Legend and punctuation diagnostic. *Used for:* W-2890, Miller 13-D.

➤ AUCTORI ◀ / ➤➤ CONNEC • ◀

Miller 14 • Legend and punctuation diagnostic. *Used for:* W-2895, Miller 14-H.

❋ AUCTORI ❋❋ / ❋❋ CONNECT ❋❋

Miller 15 • **CONNECT** • Spelling diagnostic. *Used for:* W-2900, Miller 15-F. W-2910, Miller 15-R. W-2915, Miller 15-S.

EASY FINDING GUIDE
1787 DRAPED BUST LEFT OBVERSE DIES

AUCTORI: / CONNEC:

Miller 16.1 • First C in CONNEC embedded in hair. Lower curve of C not visible. Diagnostic. *Details:* Large letters. A near point of bust; UC wide; tail of R touches base of I. O close to head. Last C low and opposite bulky upper fillet. A curved fold of the toga projects from the bust near the lower left corner of A. Short triangular dentils. Diagnostic. *Used for:* W-3000, Miller 16.1-m.

Miller 16.2 • Large letters. AUCT wide; I low; lower colon heavy and opposite and slightly below lower right serif of I. C close to head. Upper fillet opposite upright of C; lower fillet opposite right side of C. Diagnostic. *Used for:* W-3005, Miller 16.2-NN.1. W-3010, Miller 16.2-NN.2.

Miller 16.3 • Small letters. A far from toga and partly filled; UC widely spaced; T leans left. Diagnostic. *Used for:* W-3015, Miller 16.3-l.2.

Miller 16.4 • Large letters. Tops of both colons low. A high; AUC wide; RI close. Upper fillet opposite right part of C; lower fillet opposite colon. Diagnostic. *Used for:* W-3020, Miller 16.4-n.

113

1787 Draped Bust Left Obverse Dies (continued)

Miller 16.5 · Large letters. A leans slightly left and has right foot above base of U; letters fairly evenly spaced; I low. Upper fillet opposite center of C; lower fillet opposite colon. Diagnostic. *Notes:* This die was later reground and altered to become Mailed Bust Left die Miller 8, the only such instance in state coppers of such a dramatic conversion (Randy Clark, *C4 Newsletter*, Summer 2007). *Used for:* W-3025, Miller 16.5-n. W-3030, Miller 16.5-p.

Miller 16.6 · Large letters. A leans slightly left; UC wide; colon low and with bottom dot close to head. First C (CONNEC) partly in hair. Diagnostic. *Used for:* W-3035, Miller 16.6-NN.2.

AUCTORI: / — ✠ — CONNEC:

Miller 17 · Legend and punctuation diagnostic. *Used for:* W-3040, Miller 17-g.3.

AUCTORI: ✠ / ✠ CONNEC

Miller 18 · Legend and punctuation diagnostic. *Used for:* W-3045, Miller 18-g.1.

AUCTORI: ✠ / ✠ CONNEC:

Miller 19 · Legend and punctuation diagnostic. *Used for:* W-3050, Miller 19-g.4.

AUCTORI: ✣ / ✣ CONNEC:

Miller 20 · Legend and punctuation diagnostic. *Used for:* W-3055, Miller 20-a.2.

AUCTORI: ✵ / — ✠ — CONNEC: ✵

Miller 21 · Legend and punctuation diagnostic. *Used for:* W-3060, Miller 21-DD.

AUCTORI: ✣ / ✠ CONNEC: ✠

Miller 22 · Legend and punctuation diagnostic. *Used for:* W-3065, Miller 22-g.2.

— ✠ — AUCTORI: / — ✠ — CONNEC:

Miller 24 · Legend and punctuation diagnostic. *Used for:* W-3070, Miller 24-g.3. W-3075, Miller 24-g.5. W-3080, Miller 24-FF.

✣ AUCTORI: ✵ / ✣ CONNEC:

Miller 25 · Legend and punctuation diagnostic. *Used for:* W-3100, Miller 25-b. W-3105, Miller 25-m.

✤ AUCTORI: / ✖ CONNEC: ✖

Miller 26 · Legend and punctuation diagnostic. *Used for:* W-3110, Miller 26-a.1. W-3120, Miller 26-AA. W-3115, Miller 26-kk.1.

✢ AUCTORI: ✖ / ✖ CONNEC: ✖

Miller 27 · Legend and punctuation diagnostic. *Used for:* W-3125, Miller 27-a.1.

AUCTORI: ✤ / ✤ CONNEC:

Miller 28 · Legend and punctuation diagnostic. *Used for:* W-3130, Miller 28-m. W-3135, Miller 28-n. W-3140, Miller 28-o.

AUCTORI: ✤ / ✤ CONNEC: ✤

Miller 29.1 · A almost touches bust. Diagnostic. *Used for:* W-3145, Miller 29.1-a.2. W-3150, Miller 29.1-n. W-3155, Miller 29.1-p.

Miller 29.2 · A distinctly separated from bust. Diagnostic. *Used for:* W-3160, Miller 29.2-N. W-3165, Miller 29.2-o.

AUCTORI: ❀ / ❀ CONNEC: ❀

Miller 30 · Legend and punctuation diagnostic. *Used for:* W-3170, Miller 30-X.1. W-3175, Miller 30-hh.1.

❀ AUCTORI: ❀ / ❀ CONNEC:

Miller 31.1 · AU farther apart than UC. Two lobes of second cinquefoil point to border; no lobe points to forehead. Bottom of C touches head. Top dot of final colon opposite top end of C. Diagnostic. *Used for:* W-3200, Miller 31.1-r.4. W-3205, Miller 31.1-gg.1.

Miller 31.2 · AU and UC about the same spacing. One lobe of second cinquefoil points to border; another lobe points to forehead. Bottom of C well within head. Top dot of final colon opposite space of C. Diagnostic. *Used for:* W-3210, Miller 31.2-r.3.

❀ AUCTORI. ❀ / ❀ CONNEC. ❀

Obverse 32 dies include many with only slight differences. Some may have been hubbed with lettering, but others differ in letter spacing and alignment. The dentils are often quite different, and merit checking.

Miller 32.1 · *Cinquefoils:* First, half under bust; second, distant from period and well to left of hair; third, above head, closer to C than to tip of wreath; fourth, close to period and toga. UC wide; OR wide; heavy dot about half below serif of I. C close to head; O distant from head; CON wide. *Fillet ends opposite:* C; space between C and dot. *Dentils:* Medium length, widely spaced, erratic alignment. Diagnostic. *Used for:* W-3215, Miller 32.1-X.3.

1787 Draped Bust Left Obverse Dies (continued)

Miller 32.2 · *Cinquefoils:* First, nearly half under bust; second, near period and distant from hair; third, above head, U leans right; fourth, about equidistant between dot and toga. CTO widely spaced; I heavy and with base on same level as R. *Fillet ends opposite:* Dot; space after dot. *Dentils:* Small to medium with variable spacing. Diagnostic. *Used for:* W-3220, Miller 32.2-X.1. W-3225, Miller 32.2-X.2. W-3230, Miller 32.2-X.4.

Miller 32.3 · Later state of die 43.2, with CONNFC corrected to CONNEC. *Cinquefoils:* First, about one-fourth under bust; second, distant from period and most of it above hair; third, at moderate distance from head; fourth, below lower fillet end. AU more widely spaced than UC; O low; I heavy; dot slightly more than half below serif of I. C on head; E low and with a line added to the bottom as an F punch was used; C lower yet. *Fillet ends opposite:* Right side of C; dot. *Dentils:* Short, some triangular, others as lines, the last widely spaced. Diagnostic. *Used for:* W-3235, Miller 32.3-X.4.

Miller 32.4 · *Cinquefoils:* First, entirely to left of bust; second, distant from period and much to left of hair; third, distant from head, and nearly midway between wreath and C; fourth, opposite lower fillet end. A low; CT close; I heavy; period mostly below serif of I. C grazes head; NN high. *Fillet ends opposite:* Dot; cinquefoil. *Dentils:* Medium to long lines, widely spaced, irregularly aligned. Diagnostic. *Used for:* W-3240, Miller 32.4-F. W-3245, Miller 32.4-X.5. W-3250, Miller 32.4-Z.3. W-3255, Miller 32.4-Z.20.

Miller 32.5 · *Cinquefoils:* First, half under bust and very high; second, low, not far from period and distant from hair; third, a little distant from head and midway between nearest wreath leaf tip and C; fourth, opposite upper fillet end and distant from toga. First period further from I than from cinquefoil. Last period equidistant from C and cinquefoil. U leans right; CT widely spaced; upper right arm of T too long; O small; I thick; dot mostly above serif of I. C touches head; CON wide; NN close; EC close; C low. *Fillet ends opposite:* Space between dot and cinquefoil, cinquefoil. *Dentils:* Spaced thick lines, some with pointed tips. Diagnostic. *Used for:* W-3260, Miller 32.5-aa.

Miller 32.6 · *Cinquefoils:* First, entirely to left of bust; second, low and near period; third, high and much nearer to tip of wreath than to C; fourth, opposite lower fillet-end and distant from toga. First period low and very close to base of I. Last period above fillet-end and rather close to C. A mostly filled and closer to U than U is to C; TOR wide; O low; lower right of I missing. C near head, leans right, and is distant from O; E low, C lower yet. *Fillet ends opposite:* Dot; cinquefoil. *Dentils:* Short and medium lengths, thick, widely spaced, erratic alignment. Diagnostic. *Used for:* W-3265, Miller 32.6-X.6.

Miller 32.7 · *Cinquefoils:* First, about one-fourth under bust and distant from A; second, near period and distant from hair; third, high, distant from head; fourth, twice as close to dot as to toga. First period close to I and cinquefoil, but not so low nor so close to I as in 32.6. Last period midway between C and cinquefoil. A mostly filled; top left of T heavy, top right light; R mostly filled; I heavy; dot about level with serif of I. *Fillet ends opposite:* Dot; cinquefoil. *Dentils:* Tiny triangles. Diagnostic. *Used for:* W-3270, Miller 32.7-X.1.

Miller 32.8 · *Cinquefoils:* First, close to bust; second, close to wreath; third, above head, closer to C than to tip of wreath; fourth, distant from C, close to toga. First period near cinquefoil and opposite hair. No berries in wreath. A large

and high; uprights of T and I thick. C close to head; NE very widely spaced. *Fillet ends opposite:* Last dot; left edge of cinquefoil. *Dentils:* Short, closely spaced. Diagnostic. *Used for:* W-3275, Miller 32.8-aa.

❋ AUCTORI: ❋ / ❋ CONNEC: ❋

Obverse 33, the most extensive of the Miller types, has been the nemesis of many specialists. Examples that are extensively worn may be difficult if not impossible to attribute by narrative descriptions, and require photographs. Examination of the dentils can be very helpful, as styles vary widely (and are not treated by Miller). The Miller groups have been retained, but in the study, what the fillet ends are opposite, rather than points to, has been used.

GROUP I

Upper fillet end points to lower dot of last colon. Dies 33.1 to 33.22. Miller categories (but see descriptions).

Miller 33.1 · *Cinquefoils:* First, entirely left of bust, about on a line with the middle of A; second, close to colon; third, nearly equidistant from wreath and C; fourth, close to colon, distant from toga. Colons small and close to I and C. AUCTORI becomes progressively distant from dentils so that ORI are about 3 to 4 times the distance that A is; OR low; dot mostly above lower serif of I. C low and on head; NNE slightly high. *Fillet ends opposite:* Colon; cinquefoil. *Dentils:* Small dots and horizontal pellets, irregularly shaped and spaced. Diagnostic. *Details:* Cracks from edge through top of A to U; from I through second cinquefoil and hair; from C through top of O to border; from border to end of toga. Diagnostic. *Used for:* W-3310, Miller 33.1-Z.13. W-3330, Miller 33.1-Z.19.

Miller 33.2 · *Cinquefoils:* First, almost wholly left of bust; second, close to forelock; third, close to head and much nearer to C than to wreath; fourth, rather close to colon and toga. First colon equidistant from I and cinquefoil. Last colon close to C. AU wide; lower dot about halfway below serif of I. C large and on head; O close; NN close. *Fillet ends opposite:* Colon; cinquefoil. *Dentils:* Long and thin, widely spaced. Diagnostic. *Details:* In some combinations of this obverse, die cracks occur along the top and bottom of most of the letters; also from the top of I to the wreath and through the last colon and cinquefoil to the toga. Diagnostic. *Used for:* W-3360, Miller 33.2-Z.12. W-3370, Miller 33.2-Z.17. W-3380, Miller 33.2-Z.21. W-3390, Miller 33.2-Z.22. W-3340, Miller 33.2-Z.5.

Miller 33.3 · *Cinquefoils:* First, almost wholly left of bust; second, midway between colon and wreath and mostly above hair; third, distant from head and a little nearer to C than to wreath; fourth, near toga and about twice as far from last colon. A distant from cinquefoil; AU wide; R and I lean right; I heavy; lower dot of colon closer to I than is top colon. C into head; O close to first N double punched; NN and EC close; E from altered F punch. *Fillet ends opposite:* Colon; cinquefoil. *Dentils:* Lines ranging in length from short to medium, of irregular thickness and spacing; short and very widely spaced over NE; heavy and one doubled over EC. Perfect die; also crack from dentils through E. In some cases this die-crack changes the E into F and makes the legend read CONNFC. (See obverse 43.2.) Diagnostic. *Used for:* W-3400, Miller 33.3-W.1.

Miller 33.4 · *Cinquefoils:* First, close to point of bust, nearly all to left of it; second, opposite forelock and nearer colon than wreath; third, nearer C than tip of wreath; fourth, a little closer to colon than to end of toga. First colon close to I, slanting to right, the lower dot nearer I than is top dot. Last colon low, the lower dot mostly below C. UC wide; C low; OR wide; R leans right; I heavy, with lower dot closer. C very close to head; CO and NN wide; E double punched. *Fillet ends opposite:* Colon; cinquefoil. *Dentils:* Short to medium lines, variable thickness and spacing. Usually only partially visible. Diagnostic. *Used for:* W-3410, Miller 33.4-Z.2. W-3415, Miller 33.4-q.

Miller 33.5 · *Cinquefoils:* First, close to bust, almost entirely to left of it; second, a little distant from forelock and midway between colon and wreath; third, clear of head and about equidistant from wreath and C; fourth, equally distant from upper dot of last colon and toga. First colon wide, nearer to I than to cinquefoil. Last colon low, the lower dot mostly below C. A distant from cinquefoil and slightly high; C large; T leans left; O low; I thick with lower dot closer. C on head; O close to head; NN close to each other. *Fillet ends opposite:* Colon; cinquefoil. *Dentils:* Mostly short and closely spaced. Diagnostic. *Used for:* W-3420, Miller 33.5-T.2.

1787 Draped Bust Left Obverse Dies (continued)

Miller 33.6 · *Cinquefoils:* First, considerably below point of bust and almost entirely to left of it; second, distant to left of hair and midway between colon and wreath; third, high, distant from head and a little nearer to C than to wreath; fourth, high and opposite the upper dot of the colon. First colon slanting, the lower dot nearer to I and distant from cinquefoil. Last colon wide, near to C and cinquefoil. A tall and thin; UC and TO wide; R leans right; I thick. C close to head. CON wide. Three fillet-ends. Toga double cut. *Three fillet ends opposite:* Center of C; colon; left side of cinquefoil. *Dentils:* Mostly short, thick, and widely and irregularly spaced. Diagnostic. *Used for:* W-3425, Miller 33.6-KK.

Miller 33.7 · *Cinquefoils:* First, about three-fourths left of bust and distant from A; second, opposite upper dot of colon and nearer to it than to wreath; third, high, nearer to C than to wreath; fourth, mostly beyond end of toga and equally distant from colon and toga. Dots of both colons heavy and close. AU wide; O low; I thick, lower dot about half below serif of I. C low and close to head; letters about evenly spaced. *Fillet ends opposite:* Space between C and colon; space between colon and cinquefoil; lower fillet very thick. *Dentils:* Mostly short, thick, and widely and irregularly spaced. Diagnostic. *Used for:* W-3430, Miller 33.7-Z.9. W-3435, Miller 33.7-Z.10. W-3440, Miller 33.7-r.2. W-3450, Miller 33.7-r.4.

Miller 33.8 · *Cinquefoils:* First, one-fourth under bust and high, distant from A; second, fairly distant from colon and hair; third, distant from head, nearer C than to wreath; fourth, midway between colon and toga. First colon close to I the lower dot touching the base of that letter. Last colon a little nearer C than to cinquefoil. R high, leaning to right. Irregularity in die at right of I making the I thick and blurred. C clear of head, but close to it. O distant from head. E high, the top leaning to right. *Fillet ends opposite:* Colon; cinquefoil; lower fillet thick. *Dentils:* Medium length, thick, tapered, irregularly but mostly closely spaced. Diagnostic. *Used for:* W-3470, Miller 33.8-Z.13. W-3480, Miller 33.8-Z.19.

Miller 33.9 · *Cinquefoils:* First, close to bust and about three-fourths to left of it; second, distant from colon and well to left of hair; third, distant from head and about equidistant from wreath and C; fourth, nearer to end of toga than to colon. Upper dot of both colons low. AUC wide; U leans right; O low; R leans right. C near head; CO and EC wide. *Fillet ends opposite:* Colon; left side of cinquefoil. *Dentils:* Medium length, closely spaced. Diagnostic. *Used for:* W-3490, Miller 33.9-s.2.

Miller 33.10 · *Cinquefoils:* First, high, partly under bust, but mostly to left of it; second, partly over and very close to hair; third, near wreath; fourth, distant from colon and very close to end of toga. First colon low, nearly midway between I and cinquefoil. Last colon in regular position, a little nearer to C than to cinquefoil. AU close; U leans right; UC wide. CO touch head; ONN wide. *Fillet ends opposite:* Colon; space between colon and cinquefoil. *Dentils:* Short and irregularly but mostly closely spaced. Diagnostic. *Used for:* W-3500, Miller 33.10-W.6. W-3505, Miller 33.10-Z.7. W-3510, Miller 33.10-Z.8.

Miller 33.11 · *Cinquefoils:* First, high, more than half to left of bust; second, near colon, partly over and near hair; third, close to head, and nearer to C than tip of wreath; fourth, low, midway between colon and end of toga. First colon low, a little nearer to I than to cinquefoil. Last colon not far from C. AUCTORI widely spaced. C touches head, O well clear of it. Top of E leans to right. *Fillet ends opposite:* Colon; left side of cinquefoil. *Dentils:* Medium length, thick, and closely spaced. Diagnostic. *Used for:* W-3515, Miller 33.11-Z.18. W-3520, Miller 33.11-gg.1.

Miller 33.12 · *Cinquefoils:* First, high, more than half to left of bust; second, distant from colon and hair; third, high, nearer C than tip of wreath; fourth, close to toga, the upper part in line with upper dot of colon. First colon low, the lower dot half below I and nearer to I than to cinquefoil. AUCTORI widely spaced; O low; R with weak right tail; I very thick. C touches head or is close; CO very close; ON wide; EC close. *Fillet ends opposite:* Colon; space between colon and cinquefoil. *Dentils:* Medium length, mostly closely spaced, more consistent than most dentils of 33 obverses. Diagnostic. *Used for:* W-3525, Miller 33.12-W.3. W-3530, Miller 33.12-Z.10. W-3535, Miller 33.12-Z.16. W-3540, Miller 33.12-Z.21. W-3545, Miller 33.12-Z.24.

Miller 33.13 · *Cinquefoils:* First, low, nearly half under and touching bust; second, very low and almost touching lower dot of colon; third, low, touching head; fourth, midway between final colon and end of toga. Colon dots close, the upper dot of both colons low and close to letters. A slightly high; CT wide; I heavy, with colon low and light in the die. C on head; NN close. *Fillet ends opposite:* Right side of colon; cinquefoil. *Dentils:* Medium length, medium spacing, well arranged. Diagnostic. *Used for:* W-3550, Miller 33.13-Z.1. W-3555, Miller 33.13-Z.6. W-3560, Miller 33.13-Z.7. W-3565, Miller 33.13-q. W-3570, Miller 33.13-ff.1. W-3575, Miller 33.13-hh.2.

Miller 33.14 · *Cinquefoils:* First, about half under bust; second, high, distant from colon and partly above forelock; third, distant from head, much closer to C than tip of wreath; fourth, high, mostly above end of toga and rather nearer to toga than to colon. Colons distant from letters and cinquefoils. A slightly high and distant from U; upper left of T short; I thick, with bottom dot nearly all above I. C near or touches head; O close to head, CONN wide; EC close. *Fillet ends opposite:* Colon; left side of cinquefoil. *Dentils:* Short and mostly closely spaced. Diagnostic. *Used for:* W-3580, Miller 33.14-Z.2. W-3600, Miller 33.14-Z.14.

Miller 33.15 · *Cinquefoils:* First, half under bust and very distant from A; second, high, opposite upper dot of colon, distant from colon and hair; third, high, midway between C and wreath; fourth, distant from colon, close to toga and mostly above it. O low; colon very heavy with bottom dot about half below base of I. C close to head; letters mostly evenly spaced; second N high and leans to right; colon very heavy. *Fillet ends opposite:* Colon; just past colon; upper fillet looped at end. *Dentils:* Short and mostly closely spaced. Diagnostic. *Used for:* W-3605, Miller 33.15-r.1.

Miller 33.16 · *Cinquefoils:* First, about half under bust; second, high, distant from colon and partly above forelock; third, above head, slightly closer to C than tip of wreath; fourth, high, mostly above end of toga very close to it. In AUCTORI, O low; I heavy; colon heavy with lower dot slightly more than half below base of I. *Fillet ends opposite:* Colon; space between colon and cinquefoil. *Dentils:* Short and closely spaced. Diagnostic. *Used for:* W-3610, Miller 33.16-T.2. W-3615, Miller 33.16-Z.15. W-3620, Miller 33.16-l.2.

Miller 33.17 · *Cinquefoils:* First, half under bust and a little more distant from it than in variety 33.15; second, high, a trifle over but not so far from hair as in variety 33.15; third, not very distant from head; fourth, nearly all above end of toga and well separated from it. Letters widely separated; left upright of U especially thick; O low; tail of R weak; I heavy, lower dot slightly more than half below base. *Fillet ends opposite:* Space between C and colon but closer to colon; past right side of colon. *Dentils:* Medium-length lines very widely spaced and not extending to rim. Diagnostic. *Used for:* W-3625, Miller 33.17-r.1. W-3630, Miller 33.17-r.5. W-3635, Miller 33.17-gg.2.

Miller 33.18 · *Cinquefoils:* First, about half under bust and close to drapery; second, distant from colon, hair, and wreath; third, high, distant from head and a little nearer to C than to wreath; fourth, about equidistant from colon and toga. First colon slanting to right, the lower dot nearly all below I and nearer than the upper dot to I. Last colon also low, the dots close, and midway between C and last cinquefoil. *Fillet ends opposite:* Colon; cinquefoil. *Dentils:* Long, of variable thickness and spacing. Very crude. Diagnostic. *Used for:* W-3640, Miller 33.18-Z.24.

1787 Draped Bust Left Obverse Dies (continued)

Miller 33.19 · *Cinquefoils:* First, close to bust and almost wholly under it; second, very close to colon and distant from hair; third, high; fourth, close to colon and toga. Both colons low and close to letters and cinquefoils. AU and CT wide; I thick and low; colon leans left. C touches head; EC very close. *Fillet ends opposite:* Colon; space between colon and cinquefoil. *Dentils:* Short and closely spaced. Diagnostic. *Used for:* W-3645, Miller 33.19-Z.1. W-3650, Miller 33.19-Z.2. W-3655, Miller 33.19-Z.4. W-3660, Miller 33.19-q.

Miller 33.20 · *Cinquefoils:* First, almost entirely below drapery and very distant from A; second, partly over and distant from hair, its center on a line with upper dot of colon and nearer to colon than to hair; third, midway between wreath and C; fourth, nearer to end of toga than to colon. First colon wide, nearly equidistant from I and cinquefoil, the lower dot partly below I. Last colon nearer to C than to cinquefoil. AU wide; U leans right; T leans right; O lower than R. CO touch head; second N leans right; EC very close. *Fillet ends opposite:* Colon; left part of cinquefoil; both fillets heavy. *Dentils:* Small with tapered ends, closely spaced. Diagnostic. CONNFC corrected to CONNEC by adding bottom line, but not obvious. *Used for:* W-3665, Miller 33.20-Z.9. W-3670, Miller 33.20-Z.11.

Miller 33.21 · *Cinquefoils:* First, nearly completely under bust; second, about equidistant between colon and forelock; third, closer to C than tip of wreath; fourth, near toga, which is defective at its end. AU and CTO closer than are other letters; I distant from R; bottom dot about halfway below base of I. C clear of head, CONN wide; NEC closer; second N low. *Fillet ends opposite:* Space between C and colon; colon. *Dentils:* Short to medium with tapered ends; mostly widely spaced. Diagnostic. *Used for:* W-3675, Miller 33.21-Z.13. W-3680, Miller 33.21-k.4. W-3700, Miller 33.21-EE.

Miller 33.22 · *Cinquefoils:* First, partly below bust and close to A than usual, AUCTORI widely spaced, UC closer than the other letters; second, low, its center on a line with lower dot of colon; third, distant from head and midway between tip of wreath and C; fourth, low, nearer colon than end of toga. Last colon low and close to C. I (AUCTORI) over erroneous O; C (CONNEC) close to head. Miller: "The fillet-ends are not clear enough to decide whether it should be placed in the first or second group." *Dentils:* Small and widely spaced. Diagnostic. *Used for:* W-3705, Miller 33.22-II.

Group II

Upper fillet end points to area between last colon and cinquefoil. Dies 33.23 to 33.28. Miller categories (but see descriptions).

- In dies 23 to 25 the first cinquefoil is entirely left of bust
- In die 26 the first cinquefoil is about one-half under bust
- In dies 27 and 28 the first cinquefoil is more than half under bust

Miller 33.23 · *Cinquefoils:* First, entirely to left of bust; second, distant from colon and near hair; third, high; fourth, nearly midway between colon and toga. First colon low, the dots close and not far from I. Last colon near C. AUCT widely spaced. U slopes to left, its top above that of C. C touches head, O very close. NE high. E leans to right. *Fillet ends opposite:* Between colon and cinquefoil; right side of cinquefoil. *Dentils:* Short and closely spaced. Diagnostic. *Used for:* W-3710, Miller 33.23-Z.4. W-3715, Miller 33.23-hh.2.

Miller 33.24 · *Cinquefoils:* First, entirely to left of bust; second, midway between colon and leaf; third, about midway between head and dentils; fourth, high, closer to toga than to colon. Miller: "Top of U on same curve as adjoining C. C on head. CO closely spaced. E low." *Fillet ends opposite:* Colon; cinquefoil. *Dentils:* Short, irregular, closely spaced. Diagnostic. *Used for:* W-3720, Miller 33.24-Z.10.

Miller 33.25 · *Cinquefoils:* First, entirely to left of bust; second, partly above forelock and nearer to it than to colon; third, high; fourth, distant both from colon and toga. Both colons a little low and distant from letters, the colon dots heavy. AU close; U leans right; tail of R weak; I heavy and high. C very close to head; all letters fairly close; NN closest. *Fillet ends opposite:* Space just beyond colon; cinquefoil. *Dentils:* Short and closely spaced. Diagnostic. *Used for:* W-3725, Miller 33.25-W.3. W-3730, Miller 33.25-Z.10. W-3735, Miller 33.25-Z.24.

Miller 33.26 · *Cinquefoils:* First, half under, nearly touching bust; second, very near, or touching hair, near wreath; third, near wreath; fourth, opposite and near lower fillet-end, distant from toga. AU close; U leans right; UCT wide; TO close; R leans right; heavy, bottom dot nearly completely below base of I. CO low and on head; EC close. *Fillet ends opposite:* Space between colon and cinquefoil; cinquefoil. *Dentils:* Medium length, closely spaced. Mostly missing on most specimens. Diagnostic. *Used for:* W-3740, Miller 33.26-W.3. W-3745, Miller 33.26-W.5.

Miller 33.27 · *Cinquefoils:* First, more than half under bust and very close to drapery; second, distant from colon and hair; third, low, close to head; fourth, a little nearer to end of toga than to colon. Colons in regular position, the first midway between I and cinquefoil, the last not far from C. AU wide; OR wide; R leans right and has weak tail; I thick; bottom dot mostly above base. C on head; O close or touches; NN and EC close. *Fillet ends opposite:* Just past colon; cinquefoil. *Dentils:* Short and medium lengths, irregularly aligned and spaced; amateurish in appearance. Diagnostic. *Used for:* W-3750, Miller 33.27-Z.16. W-3755, Miller 33.27-r.4.

Miller 33.28 · *Cinquefoils:* First, most all under bust, below the drapery; second, distant from colon and hair; third, touches dentils, closer to C than tip of wreath; fourth, between C and toga, slightly closer to toga, which ends in two heavy dots. Colons nearer to letters than to cinquefoils. U leans right; I heavy; bottom dot about half below base. C very close to head; CO low; base of E long; final C slightly low. *Fillet ends opposite:* Colon; cinquefoil. *Dentils:* Medium lines irregularly spaced. Diagnostic. *Used for:* W-3760, Miller 33.28-Z.7. W-3765, Miller 33.28-Z.11. W-3770, Miller 33.28-Z.16. W-3775, Miller 33.28-Z.20.

Group III

Lower fillet end points at the last colon. Dies 33.29 to 33.41 (but see descriptions).

- In dies 29 to 34 the first cinquefoil is entirely or almost entirely left of bust.
- In dies 35 to 39 the first cinquefoil is partly under the bust but mostly left of it.
- In die 40 the cinquefoil is half under the bust.
- In die 41 the cinquefoil is entirely under the bust.

Miller 33.29 · *Cinquefoils:* First, left of bust and nearer A than usual; second, opposite space between colon dots and not far from hair; third, clear of head, nearer to C than to wreath; fourth, touches end of toga. First colon sloping, the lower dot almost all below I. Last colon near C and a little further from cinquefoil, the upper dot low. Letters in AUCTORI well spaced; tail of R weak; I thick and slightly low; lower dot mostly below base. C on head; CO low; NN and EC close. *Fillet ends opposite:* Bottom and right part of C; colon. *Dentils:* Medium to long, thick, and mostly closely spaced. Diagnostic. *Used for:* W-3780, Miller 33.29-Z.7. W-3800, Miller 33.29-Z.25. W-3805, Miller 33.29- s.1. W-3810, Miller 33.29-gg.1.

Miller 33.30 · *Cinquefoils:* First, very high, entirely left of bust; second, above hair, its top on about the same curve as the tops of I and wreath; third, distant from head, slightly nearer to C than to wreath; fourth, high, near end of toga and distant from colon. First colon midway between I and cinquefoil. Upper dot of last colon weak, the lower dot below C. A slightly high and mostly filled; AU and RI closer than other letters; T leans left; I thick. CO near head. NN high. *Fillet ends opposite:* Center and right part of C; colon. *Dentils:* Medium to long, widely spaced. Diagnostic. *Used for:* W-3815, Miller 33.30-EE. W-3820, Miller 33.30-SS.

1787 Draped Bust Left Obverse Dies (continued)

Miller 33.31 · *Cinquefoils:* First, below point of bust and entirely left of it; second, distant from colon and not far to left of hair; third, close to head and nearer C than usual; fourth, nearly touches end of toga. Lower dot of first colon close to I. Last colon midway between C and cinquefoil, the upper dot low. AU and OR wide; I thick; lower dot about even with base of I. C low and touches head; NNE high. *Fillet ends opposite:* Right part of C; right part of colon. *Dentils:* Medium, widely but erratically spaced. Diagnostic. *Used for:* W-3825, Miller 33.31-gg.2.

Miller 33.32 · *Cinquefoils:* First, entirely left of bust, its top on a level with the top of A; second, near hair; third, close to head and near C; fourth, close to end of toga, about twice as far from colon. First colon slanting to right, the lower dot nearer I. Lower dot of last colon heavy, partly below C. A and top of R mostly filled; TO and RI close. C close to head; E double punched; final C low. *Fillet ends opposite:* Right side of C; colon. *Dentils:* Short to medium, mostly widely spaced. Diagnostic. *Used for:* W-3830, Miller 33.32-Z.13.

Miller 33.33 · *Cinquefoils:* First, beyond point of bust, between drapery and A; second, midway between colon and wreath, partly over hair; third, not far from head, a little nearer C than tip of wreath; fourth, between end of toga and dentils and very close to toga. First colon very low, the lower dot much below the base of I. Last colon widely spaced, the upper dot partly above the top of C. A low and closer to cinquefoil than to U; CT very wide; other letters fairly widely spaced; I leans left; lower dot far below base. C touches head; CO low; ONN very wide. *Fillet ends opposite:* C; colon. *Dentils:* Medium to long, toothlike, irregularly aligned. Diagnostic. *Used for:* W-3835, Miller 33.33-Z.3. W-3840, Miller 33.33-Z.11.

Miller 33.34 · *Cinquefoils:* First, close to point of bust and nearly all to left of it; second, above hair, midway between upper dot of colon and wreath; third, high; fourth, opposite space between colon dots and very close to end of toga. Colons with larger, heavy dots, the lower dot of first colon partly below I. Last colon wide, equidistant from C and cinquefoil. A mostly filled and closer to cinquefoil than to U; U leans right; UCT wide; O low; ORI very wide; I low. C touches head; ONNE wide; E leans sharply left; C very low. Die displays amateurish workmanship and is distinctive as such. *Fillet ends opposite:* C; colon. *Dentils:* Short and irregular. Diagnostic. *Used for:* W-3845, Miller 33.34-W.2. W-3850, Miller 33.34-Z.3. W-3860, Miller 33.34-Z.11.

Miller 33.35 · *Cinquefoils:* First, nearly touching bust and about three-quarters left of it; second, near colon; third, close to head; fourth, near colon. AUCTORI distant from border; UCT wide; ORI wide; colon small and above base of I. C close to head; NNE high; EC close; final C low. *Fillet ends opposite:* C; colon. *Dentils:* Short, erratically spaced. Diagnostic. *Used for:* W-3865, Miller 33.35-Z.1. W-3870, Miller 33.35-Z.9.

Miller 33.36 · *Cinquefoils:* First, about three-quarters beyond bust and well clear of it; second, close to colon and distant to left from hair; third, high, nearer to C than to wreath; fourth, opposite space between colon dots, and nearly equidistant from colon and end of toga. Colons wide, in regular position. AU wide; U leans right; TO wide; tail of R defective; I heavy; lower dot about even with base of I. C touches head; O leans left; NN high; base of E heavy; C slightly low; letters fairly evenly spaced. *Fillet ends opposite:* C; colon. *Dentils:* Short to medium, most are widely spaced. Diagnostic. *Used for:* W-3875, Miller 33.36-T.1. W-3900, Miller 33.36-T.2. W-3905, Miller 33.36-T.3. W-3910, Miller 33.36-SS.

Miller 33.37 · *Cinquefoils:* First, about three-quarters beyond bust; second, above hair, equidistant from colon and wreath; third, close to head, nearer C than tip of wreath; fourth, mostly above upper dot of colon and end of toga and quite

close to the toga. First colon distant from I and cinquefoil, the upper dot low. Last colon very low, the lower dot entirely below C. A low and slightly closer to cinquefoil than to U; all letters fairly widely spaced, CT and RI especially so. C low and on head; ONN high; E altered from an F punch, with base line too short; C low; colon low. Raised lump touches dentils just past colon. *Fillet ends opposite:* Right edge of C; right edge of colon. *Dentils:* Small, medium spacing, and one of the most regularly aligned among obverse 33 dies. Diagnostic. *Used for:* W-3915, Miller 33.37-Z.9. W-3920, Miller 33.37-Z.11.

Miller 33.38 · *Cinquefoils:* First, below bust and more than half to left of it; second, near and partly over hair, a little closer to upper dot of colon than to wreath; third, nearer C than tip of wreath; fourth, midway between colon and end of toga. Upper dot of colon low. AU wide; I thick and leans right. C close to head; NNE high; final C low. *Fillet ends opposite:* C; colon. *Dentils:* Thin lines, medium to long, widely spaced, irregularly aligned. Diagnostic. *Used for:* W-3925, Miller 33.38-Z.1. W-3930, Miller 33.38-Z.6. W-3935, Miller 33.38-Z.18. W-3940, Miller 33.38-Z.23. W-3945, Miller 33.38-gg.1.

Miller 33.39 · *Cinquefoils:* First, close to bust and more than half to left of it; second, distant from colon and hair; third, distant from head, much nearer to C than to wreath; fourth, very close to end of toga. Colons close, the upper dot of both low. A mostly filled and about equidistant from cinquefoil and U; CTO close; I heavy; lower dot about half below base. C low and clear of head; CO wide; final C low. *Fillet ends opposite:* Right part of C; colon. *Dentils:* Medium lines mostly widely spaced and of the same length. Diagnostic. *Used for:* W-3950, Miller 33.39-Z.13. W-3955, Miller 33.39-Z.20. W-3960, Miller 33.39-s.1.

Miller 33.40 · *Cinquefoils:* First, one-half or more under bust; second, high, opposite upper dot of colon, distant from colon, hair and wreath; third, very high, distant from head, wreath and C; fourth, not far from colon, opposite upper dot. First colon nearer I than cinquefoil, but distant from both. Last colon near C, the dots close, the upper one low. A mostly filled; UCTO widely spaced. C low and on head; NEC close; final C slightly low. *Fillet ends opposite:* C; colon. *Dentils:* Short and closely spaced. Diagnostic. *Used for:* W-3965, Miller 33.40-Z.1. W-3970, Miller 33.40-Z.2.

Miller 33.41 · *Cinquefoils:* First, very far under bust and very distant from A; second, distant from colon and hair; third, distant from head, wreath and C; fourth, opposite and close to end of toga. Dots of both colons small, the upper ones low. Letters in both words widely spaced. A mostly filled; U leans right; UC closer; tail of R weak; colon about equidistant from I and cinquefoil and not close to either. C low and barely touches head; ON especially wide. *Fillet ends opposite:* Right edge of C; colon. *Dentils:* Thick, medium length, irregularly spaced and sometimes fused. Diagnostic. *Used for:* W-3975, Miller 33.41-Z.11.

GROUP IV

Miller categories, but see descriptions.

- In die 42 the lower fillet end points at the last cinquefoil.
- In dies 43 to 45 both fillet ends point at the last cinquefoil.

Miller 33.42 · *Cinquefoils:* First, entirely left of bust; second, high, very near upper dot of first colon; third, distant from head; fourth, opposite lower fillet end. Both colons lean sharply left. Letters in both words fairly widely spaced. A mostly filled. C close to head; NEC closest. *Fillet ends opposite:* Right edge of C; colon. *Dentils:* Short to medium, thick, closely spaced. Diagnostic. *Used for:* W-4000, Miller 33.42-Z.2.

Miller 33.43 · *Cinquefoils:* First, close to point of bust and wholly to left of it; second, left of hair, distant both from colon and hair; third, nearer wreath than C; fourth, midway between colon and end of toga and distant from both. Upper dot of both colons low. O low; I heavy; letters about evenly spaced. C touches head; CO low; ONNE wide; EC close and low. *Fillet ends opposite:* Space between colon and cinquefoil; cinquefoil. *Dentils:* Short, thick, widely spaced. Diagnostic. *Used for:* W-4005, Miller 33.43-q. W-4010, Miller 33.43-hh.2.

1787 Draped Bust Left Obverse Dies (continued)

Miller 33.44 · *Cinquefoils:* First, very high, above top of A and about three-fourths left of bust; second, very close to forelock; third, touches head; fourth, distant from colon, fillet-ends and toga. First colon wide, midway between I and cinquefoil. Last colon low, the lower dot below C. Letters in both words fairly widely spaced. AU distant; U leans right; UC close; lower dot more than half below base. C touches head; CO low; colon low. *Fillet ends opposite:* Left of cinquefoil; right side of cinquefoil. *Dentils:* Short to medium, closely spaced. Diagnostic. *Used for:* W-4015, Miller 33.44-W.3.

Miller 33.45 · *Cinquefoils:* First, about half under bust, distant from A; second, distant from colon, near forelock and partly above it; third, touching head; fourth, distant from toga and fully twice as far from colon. First colon wide, the lower dot nearer I. Lower dot of last colon a little low. UC close; T leans right; RI wide; I heavy. C low and touches head. O close to head; NNE wide; final C slightly low. *Fillet ends opposite:* Left of cinquefoil; right side of cinquefoil. *Dentils:* Long, widely spaced, and of about the same length. Diagnostic. *Used for:* W-4020, Miller 33.45-W.2.

Varieties Not Listed in Miller

Miller 33.46 · Taylor catalog: First cinquefoil three quarters clear of bust; AUCTORI widely spaced, O low and I high; first colon leans slightly right, lower dot half below baseline of I; C and O barely touch head; second N high; EC close; final colon well centered; fourth cinquefoil close to but free of toga end. Final colon between upper and lower fillet ends. A mostly filled and distant from U; O low; RI wide; generous spacing between letters overall. C touches head; CO low; final C low. *Fillet ends opposite:* Left side of colon; past right side of colon. *Dentils:* Short, tightly spaced, some fused. Diagnostic die crack from rim to second leaf of wreath, wide and deep. Diagnostic. *Used for:* W-4025, Miller 33.46-Z.21. W-4030, Miller 33.46-Z.22.

Miller 33.47 · *Cinquefoils:* First, joined to bust, which is markedly rounded at lower edge of armor; second, far from colon and much farther (about 1/8") from hair; third, midway between C and wreath, close to hair; fourth, almost midway between colon and toga, not far from either. Colons normal and about opposite nearby letters. AUCTORI widely spaced; AU and TO closer. C touches head; letters very widely spaced. ON repunched. *Fillet ends opposite:* Left side of colon; past right side of colon. *Dentils:* Short to medium, irregularly but mostly widely spaced, misaligned, the work of an amateur. Diagnostic. *Used for:* W-4035, Miller 33.47-TT.

Miller 33.48 · *Cinquefoils:* First, about 1/3 under bust; second, slightly high and close to forelock; third, closer to C than peak of wreath, about twice as close to head as to dentils; fourth, twice as close to toga as to C. First colon light and leans slightly left; second heavier and leans slightly right. Letters in both words fairly widely spaced. AU wide; ORI especially wide. C low and close to head; CO low. *Fillet ends opposite:* Right side of colon and past it; cinquefoil. *Dentils:* Short, widely spaced. Diagnostic. *Used for:* W-4040, Miller 33.48-Z.25.

Miller 33.49 · *CNL,* November 1974: The position of the first cinquefoil and the A are different from any known variety. There is a little too much space between the A and U of AUCTORI and the U tilts slightly to the right. The R of AUCTORI is high and its tail is close to the base of the I. The colon after AUCTORI is quite low and leans markedly to the left. Second cinquefoil is nearly equidistant between the colon and the hair and one arm of the cinquefoil points to the top dot of the colon. Diagnostic. *Used for:* W-4045, Miller 33.49-Z.7.

Miller 33.50 · *CNL,* April 1997: CONNEC is shifted far to the right. A vertical line drawn from the inside bottom point of the first C would bypass the back of the head. The last C of CONNEC would be nearly bisected by a line drawn from the top of the ribbon end to it. Diagnostic. *Used for:* W-4050, Miller 33.50-Z.24.

AUCTORI: ← / → CONNEC: ←

Miller 34 · Legend and punctuation diagnostic. *Used for:* W-4055, Miller 34-k.3. W-4060, Miller 34-ff.1.

→ AUCTORI: ← / → CONNEC:

Miller 36 · Legend and punctuation diagnostic. *Used for:* W-4065, Miller 36-k.3. W-4070, Miller 36-l.1. W-4075, Miller 36-ff.2.

→ AUCTORI: ← / → CONNEC: ←

- First fleuron entirely left of bust: Dies 1 and 2.
- First fleuron mostly left of bust: Dies 3 to 7.
- First fleuron half under bust: Dies 8 to 10.
- First fleuron mostly under bust: Die 11.
- First fleuron entirely under bust: Dies 12 to 14.

Miller 37.1 · *Fleurons:* First, left of bust; second, distant from colon; third, clear of head, nearer C than tip of wreath; fourth, close to end of toga. First colon nearer to I than to fleuron. Last colon about equidistant from C and final fleuron. U leans right; UC wide; I low. C clear of head; EC close. *Fillet ends opposite:* Right side of C; right side of colon. *Dentils:* Thick, medium length, many with pointed ends, closely spaced. Diagnostic. *Used for:* W-4100, Miller 37.1-cc.1.

Miller 37.2 · *Fleurons:* First, almost entirely left of bust; second, distant from colon, hair, and wreath; third, close to head; fourth, midway between final colon and toga. First colon sloping, the lower dot nearer I and about one half below that letter. Last colon also sloping to right and opposite upper fillet end. U high and leans left; UCT wide; ORI wide. C on head; CO and NN wide; final C defective. *Fillet ends opposite:* Colon; fleuron. *Dentils:* Medium length, thick, medium spacing. Diagnostic. *Used for:* W-4105, Miller 37.2-k.5.

Miller 37.3 · *Fleurons:* First, close to bust, partly under, but mostly left; second, distant from colon, very close to hair; third, not far from head, and nearer C than tip of wreath; fourth, near colon and toga. Both colons slightly low and well separated from letters. A mostly filled; UC wide; other letters mostly wide; RI closer; R with thin tail. C on head; ON close. *Fillet ends opposite:* Space between C and colon; past colon. *Dentils:* Medium length, most pointed, irregular alignment and spacing. Diagnostic. *Used for:* W-4110, Miller 37.3-i.

Miller 37.4 · *Fleurons:* First, partly under, but more than half to left of bust; second, distant from colon and hair; third, very close to head; fourth, distant from colon and end of toga. First colon distant from I. Last colon rather distant from C. AUC and ORI wide; I very low. C on head; O close or touching; letters widely spaced; NE closer; final C low. *Fillet ends opposite:* Colon; fleuron. *Dentils:* Short, irregular, widely spaced. Diagnostic. *Used for:* W-4115, Miller 37.4-k.1. W-4120, Miller 37.4-RR.

Miller 37.5 · *Fleurons:* First, close to bust, and more than half to left of it; second, distant from colon and hair; third, near head; fourth, about midway between colon and end of toga. Upper dot of first colon low and distant from I. Last colon low, well separated from C and fleuron. TO and RI close; thick tail to R. C on head; O close; letters well spaced. *Fillet ends opposite:* Colon; fleuron. *Dentils:* Short to medium length, thick, medium spacing. Diagnostic. *Used for:* W-4125, Miller 37.5-e.

Miller 37.6 · *Fleurons:* First, near bust, more than half to left of it; second, near, but clear of hair; third, clear of head, and closer to C than to wreath; fourth, rather closer to end of toga than to upper dot of colon. First colon sloping, the upper dot more distant from I. Last colon very low, the lower dot mostly below C. Letters in both words fairly widely spaced. A mostly filled; long tail to R. C on head; final C low. *Fillet ends opposite:* Left side of colon; space between colon and fleuron. *Dentils:* Small, medium spacing. Diagnostic. *Used for:* W-4130, Miller 37.6-B. W-4135, Miller 37.6-k.4.

1787 DRAPED BUST LEFT OBVERSE DIES (continued)

Miller 37.7 · *Fleurons:* First, more than half left of bust and almost touching it; second, opposite center of colon and farther from it than colon is to I; third, closer to C than to nearest leaf in wreath; fourth, fleuron near toga. Dots of first colon equidistant from I. Three berries in wreath. Letters in both words fairly widely spaced. CT and RI closer. C touches head; final C low. *Fillet ends opposite:* Space between C and colon; right of colon. *Dentils:* Long, thick lines, widely spaced, not quite extending to rim. Diagnostic. *Used for:* W-4140, Miller 37.7-h.2.

Miller 37.8 · *Fleurons:* First, about half under and clear of bust; second, near colon, a little further from hair; third, close to head and much nearer to C than to wreath; fourth, close to colon and end of toga. Colons well apart from letters. Last colon points at low part of upper fillet-end. CTO close; other letters wide; R low; I lower. C on head; O close; ON wide. *Fillet ends opposite:* Space between C and colon; past colon. *Dentils:* Short, closely spaced. Diagnostic. *Used for:* W-4145, Miller 37.8-HH. W-4150, Miller 37.8-LL. W-4155, Miller 37.8-k.2.

Miller 37.9 · *Fleurons:* First, half under bust; second, very distant from colon and distant to left of hair; third, well above head and midway between wreath and C; fourth, distant from colon and toga. Both fillet ends point to last fleuron. Colons well spaced and nearer to the letters than to the fleurons. Last colon above the fillet end. Three berries in wreath. Letters in both words fairly widely spaced. T leans left. C close to head; final C low. *Fillet ends opposite:* Space between colon and fleuron; right part of fleuron. *Dentils:* Short, medium spacing. Diagnostic. *Used for:* W-4160, Miller 37.9-e.

Miller 37.10 · *Fleurons:* First, half under and close to bust; second, distant from upper dot of colon and considerably to left of hair; third, nearer to C than to top of wreath; fourth, distant slightly from colon and toga. Both colons sloping to right, the lower dots nearer the letters. Lower dot of last colon one half below C. Letters in both words fairly widely spaced. C (CONNEC) on head; last C low. *Fillet ends opposite:* Colon; space between colon and fleuron. *Dentils:* Short, medium spacing. Diagnostic. *Used for:* W-4165, Miller 37.10-RR.

Miller 37.11 · *Fleurons:* First, more than half under bust; second, distant from colon and hair; third, close to head; fourth, a little further from space between colon dots than from end of toga. First colon low. The dots of last colon nearer to C than to fleuron. Letters in both words fairly widely spaced. U leans sharply right. C on head, O close; final C low. *Fillet ends opposite:* Colon; left side of fleuron. *Dentils:* Short, mostly pointed ends, medium spacing. Diagnostic. *Used for:* W-4170, Miller 37.11-ff.2.

Miller 37.12 · *Fleurons:* First, entirely under bust, touching drapery; second, distant from colon and hair; third, close to head, about halfway between wreath and C; fourth, low, midway between lower dot of colon and toga. Both colons sloping, the lower dots nearer letters. Letters in both words fairly widely spaced. A mostly filled; I slightly low. C on head; O very close. *Fillet ends opposite:* Colon; fleuron. *Dentils:* Small, closely spaced. Diagnostic. *Used for:* W-4175, Miller 37.12-LL. W-4180, Miller 37.12-TT.

Miller 37.13 · *Fleurons:* First, wholly under bust, distant from A; second, close to upper dot of colon, distant from hair; third, well separated from head; fourth, close to space between colon dots and pointing to lower edge of upper dot. First colon slopes decidedly to right, with the lower dot much nearer to I. Last colon slightly low, the lower dot about halfway between C and fleuron. Letters in both words fairly widely spaced. U leans right; R leans sharply right. C on head; ON widest. *Fillet ends opposite:* Space between C and colon; space between colon and fleuron. *Dentils:* Short, closely spaced. Diagnostic. *Used for:* W-4185, Miller 37.13-HH.

Miller 37.14 · *Fleurons:* First, high, entirely under bust; curved fold of the toga extends from point of bust uniting with fleuron; second, slightly distant from colon, pointing between the dots; third, close to head; fourth, distant from colon and low, pointing at lower dot of colon; both colons low and sloping to right. Letters in both words fairly widely spaced. UC and ORI widest. C on head; O close. *Fillet ends opposite:* Left tip of fleuron; fleuron. *Dentils:* Short, closely spaced. Diagnostic. *Used for:* W-4190, Miller 37.14-cc.2.

Miller 37.15 · *Fleurons:* First, small and close to left of bust; second, near hair; third, close to head, near to C, and distant from wreath; fourth, opposite space between dots of last colon—near colon and toga. First colon leans to right—lower dot near I. Second colon parallel with C. Letters in both words fairly widely spaced. A mostly filled; I low; C on head. *Fillet ends opposite:* Colon; space between colon and fleuron. *Dentils:* Medium length, widely spaced, erratic alignment. Diagnostic. *Used for:* W-4195, Miller 37.15-h.3.

AUCIORI: / ✠ CONNEC: ✠

Miller 38 · **AUCIORI** · AUCIORI spelling diagnostic. *Used for:* W-4200, Miller 38-l.2. W-4205, Miller 38-GG.

➤ AUCTOBI: ⬅ / ➤ CONNEC: ⬅

Miller 39.1 · **AUCTOBI** · Colon after final C widely spaced, lower dot slightly below base of C. Diagnostic. *Used for:* W-4210, Miller 39.1-h.1. W-4215, Miller 39.1-ff.2.

Miller 39.2 · **AUCTOBI** · Colon after final C closely spaced, lower dot above base of C. Diagnostic. *Used for:* W-4220, Miller 39.2-ee.

AUCTOPI ✤ / ✤ CONNEC

Miller 40 · **AUCTOPI** · AUCTOPI with this punctuation diagnostic. *Used for:* W-4240, Miller 40-N. W-4230, Miller 40-kk.1.

✤ AUCTOPI: ✤ / ✤ CONNEC:

Miller 41 · **AUCTOPI** · AUCTOPI with this punctuation diagnostic. Crosby and Hall give the final punctuation of the legend as a period. Sharp specimens indicate that it is more likely a colon, the lower dot touching and blending with the end of the toga adjacent to C. *Used for:* W-4235, Miller 41-ii.

✤ AUCTOPI: / ✤ CONNEC: ✤

Miller 42 · **AUCTOPI** · AUCTOPI with this punctuation diagnostic. *Used for:* W-4240, Miller 42-o. W-4245, Miller 42-kk.2.

✿ AUCTORI. ✿ / ✿ CONNFC. ✿

Miller 43.1 · **CONNFC** · Cinquefoil much closer to I than to head. Diagnostic. *Used for:* W-4250, Miller 43.1-Y.

Miller 43.2 · **CONNFC** · Cinquefoil much closer to head than to I. Diagnostic. This is a "CONNFC" and was struck from the die before the F was changed to E and became obverse 32.3. A different view: "The obverse is actually a reground and slightly reworked state of obverse 32.3, causing the E in CONNEC to look like an F. Unlike some of the other regrinding, this one actually changed the obverse legend, and as such, is listed by a different obverse number in the Miller taxonomy" (*CNL*, January 1972). If such regrinding took place, it should have weakened other nearby features such as the other letters and the cinquefoil, which does not seem to be the case. *Used for:* W-4255, Miller 43.2-X.4.

1787 Draped Bust Left Obverse Dies
(continued)

✣ AUCTORI: / ✣ CONNEC: ✣

Miller 44 · Legend and punctuation diagnostic. *Used for:* W-4260, Miller 44-W.4. W-4290, Miller 44-W.5. W-4295, Miller 44-Z.10.

— ✠ — AUCTORI: — ✠ — / — ✠ — CONNEC: — ✠ —

Miller 45 · Legend and punctuation diagnostic. *Used for:* W-4300, Miller 45-CC.

✣ AUCTORI: ✖ — / — ✖ — CONNEC: — ✖ —

Miller 46 · Legend and punctuation diagnostic. *Used for:* W-4305, Miller 46-BB.

✣ AUCTORI: — ✖ — / — ✖ — CONNEC:

Miller 47 · Legend and punctuation diagnostic. *Used for:* W-4310, Miller 47-a.3.

→ AUCTORI: ← / → CONNEC: ←

Miller 48 · Legend and punctuation diagnostic. *Used for:* W-4315, Miller 48-g.5. W-4305, Miller 48-k.3.

✣ AUCTORI: ✣ / ✣✣ CONNEC: ✣

Miller 49.1 · A mostly filled; U leans right and is close to C; I heavy and slightly high. *Fillet ends opposite:* Left side of colon; space between colon and cinquefoil. *Dentils:* Medium, closely spaced. Die failure from border past C (AUCTORI) to chin caused bulge and lower level above die crack. *Used for:* W-4310, Miller 49.1-Z.1.

Miller 49.2 · A filled; AUC about evenly spaced; OR wide; O lower than R. CO low; EC very close; colon appears as a bar with dots connected. *Dentils:* Small, triangular. *Used for:* W-4315, Miller 49.2-Z.1. W-4320, Miller 49.2-Z.26. W-4325, Miller 49.2-Z.27.

✣ AUCTORI. ✣ / ✣ CONNLC. ✣

Miller 50 · **CONNLC** · Punctuation and spelling diagnostic. Same die as obverse 17 of 1788. *Used for:* W-4330, Miller 50-F.

→ AUCTORI: ← / · → CONNEC: ←

Miller 53 · Legend and punctuation diagnostic. *Used for:* W-4335, Miller 53-FF.

← AUCTORI: ← / ← CONNEC:

Miller 56 · First pheon points away from A. Diagnostic. *Used for:* W-4340, Miller 56-XX.

Easy Finding Guide
1787 Reverse Dies

On various dies ET LIB should be two words, sometimes it appears as ETLIB. In other cases it is difficult to determine whether it is one word or two. In instances in which ETLIB is given as one word, other features should also be checked to verify the attribution.

ETLIB / INDE

Miller A · ETLIB INDE · Transposition diagnostic. *Used for:* W-2700, Miller 1.1-A.

INDE ET / LIB

Miller B · Legend definitive with INDE ET left. *Used for:* W-2755, Miller 2-B. W-4130, Miller 37.6-B.

INDE · ET / LIB

Miller C · Legend definitive with INDE ET left and dot after INDE. *Used for:* W-2720, Miller 1.2-C.

✚ INDE ✚ ET ✚ ✚ / ✚ ✚ LIB ✚ ✚

Miller D · Legend and punctuation diagnostic. *Used for:* W-2850, Miller 9-D. W-2890, Miller 13-D.

✣ INDE ✣ ET ✣ / ✣ LIB ✣ ✣

Miller E · Legend and punctuation diagnostic. *Used for:* W-2855, Miller 9-E. W-2865, Miller 10-E. W-2870, Miller 11.1-E.

✣ INDE ✣ ET ✣✣ / ✣✣ LIB ✣✣

Miller F · Legend and punctuation diagnostic. *Used for:* W-2900, Miller 15-F. W-3240, Miller 32.4-F. W-4330, Miller 50-F.

INDE ✱ ET / LIB ✱

Miller G.1 · Branch hand opposite upright of E (INDE). Pole points to left of 7. Diagnostic. *Used for:* W-2745, Miller 52-G.1. W-2805, Miller 3-G.1.

Miller G.2 · Branch hand opposite lower right of E (INDE). Pole points to right of 7. Diagnostic. Die used on counterfeit Machin's Mills halfpenny Vlack 13-87CT. *Used for:* W-2750, Miller 52-G.2.

INDE · ET / ➤➤ LIB · ◀◀
[plus ➤ and ◀ at each side of date]

Miller H · Legend and punctuation diagnostic. With pheons at each side of date, "arrows at date" variety. *Used for:* W-2895, Miller 14-H.

1787
Reverse Dies
(continued)

INDE: ⁂ / ET LIB.

Miller I · Legend and punctuation diagnostic. *Used for:* W-2830, Miller 7-I.

✤ INDE ✤ / ✤ ET LIB ✤

Miller K · Legend and punctuation diagnostic. *Used for:* W-2875, Miller 11.2-K. W-2880, Miller 11.3-K.

INDE · / ET · LIB ·

Miller L · Legend and punctuation diagnostic. *Used for:* W-2735, Miller 1.3-L. W-2810, Miller 4-L.

INDE: ✤ ✤ / ✤ ET · LIB:

Miller M · Legend and punctuation diagnostic. *Used for:* W-2820, Miller 6.1-M. W-2825, Miller 6.2-M.

INDE ✤ ✤ / ✤ ETLIB ✤

Miller N · Legend and punctuation diagnostic. *Used for:* W-2835, Miller 8-N. W-3160, Miller 29.2-N. W-4240, Miller 40-N.

✤ INDE: ✤ ✤ / ✤ ETLIB: ✤

Miller O · Legend and punctuation diagnostic. *Used for:* W-2840, Miller 8-O.

· IN DE · / ET LIB ·

Miller P · IN and DE separated by hand and branch. This and punctuation diagnostic. *Used for:* W-2815, Miller 5-P.

✤ IN DE · / ET LIB · ✤

Miller Q · IN and DE separated by hand and branch. Date blundered as 1787 over 1877. This and punctuation diagnostic. *Used for:* W-2885, Miller 12-Q.

✚ IND ✖✖✖ ET✚ / ✖✖✖ LIB ✚✖✖

Miller R · Legend and punctuation diagnostic. Corrected overdate, 1787 over 1788. *Used for:* W-2860, Miller 9-R. W-2910, Miller 15-R.

✤ INDL ✤ ET ✤ / ✤ LIB ✤

Miller S · Legend and punctuation diagnostic. *Used for:* W-2915, Miller 15-S.

❋ INDE: ❋❋ / ❋ ETLIB: ❋

Miller T.1 · In date, 1 thick, leans left, and touches single date line. Diagnostic. *Used for:* W-3875, Miller 33.36-T.1.

Miller T.2 · All digits touch lower date line; 17 wide; 8 leans left. Date line double. Diagnostic. *Used for:* W-3420, Miller 33.5-T.2. W-3610, Miller 33.16-T.2. W-3900, Miller 33.36-T.2.

Miller T.3 · In date, 78 high; 8 doubled; second 7 very low and distant from date line and touches dentil. Date line double. Diagnostic. *Used for:* W-3905, Miller 33.36-T.3.

❋ INDE: ❋❋❋ / ❋ ETLIB:

Miller W.1 · Branch hand opposite right part of E. Second 7 low; 1 and 8 high. Bottom date line weak. Diagnostic. *Used for:* W-3400, Miller 33.3-W.1.

Miller W.2 · Branch hand opposite E; base of E slants downward. Digits all close to or touching bottom date line. Left part of date-line triple. Pole points to left of 1. Diagnostic. *Used for:* W-3845, Miller 33.34-W.2. W-4020, Miller 33.45-W.2.

Miller W.3 · Branch hand opposite upright of E. In date, 8 high and leans slightly left. Diagnostic. *Used for:* W-3525, Miller 33.12-W.3. W-3725, Miller 33.25-W.3. W-3740, Miller 33.26-W.3. W-4015, Miller 33.44-W.3.

Miller W.4 · Second 7 very high. Pole points to left of 1. Diagnostic. *Used for:* W-4260, Miller 44-W.4.

Miller W.5 · Branch hand opposite space between D and E. Diagnostic. *Used for:* W-3745, Miller 33.26-W.5. W-4290, Miller 44-W.5.

Miller W.6 · Pole points to between 1 and 7. Diagnostic. *Used for:* W-3500, Miller 33.10-W.6.

❋ INDE. ❋❋❋ / ❋ ETLIB. ❋

Miller X.1 · Branch hand opposite right part of E. Cinquefoil closer to pole than to hair. In date, 1 higher than other numbers and pierces bottom date line. Diagnostic. *Used for:* W-3170, Miller 30-X.1. W-3220, Miller 32.2-X.1. W-3270, Miller 32.7-X.1.

Miller X.2 · Branch hand opposite E. Cinquefoil equidistant between hair and pole. In date, 1 high, heavy, distant, and leans left; 8 high; second 7 very low. Diagnostic. *Used for:* W-3225, Miller 32.2-X.2.

1787
Reverse Dies
(continued)

Miller X.3 · Branch hand opposite right part of E. Cinquefoil equidistant between hair and pole. In date, 1 higher than other digits and leans left; 8 slightly high; 7's lower. Diagnostic. *Used for:* W-3215, Miller 32.1-X.3.

Miller X.4 · Branch hand opposite right part of E. Cinquefoil equidistant between hair and pole. In date, 1 higher than other digits; 8 lowest. Diagnostic. *Used for:* W-3230, Miller 32.2-X.4. W-3235, Miller 32.3-X.4. W-4255, Miller 43.2-X.4.

Miller X.5 · Branch hand opposite space between right tip of E and dot. Cinquefoil equidistant between hair and pole and very low. Diagnostic. *Used for:* W-3245, Miller 32.4-X.5.

Miller X.6 · Branch hand opposite upright of E. Cinquefoil twice as close to hair than to pole. Diagnostic. *Used for:* W-3265, Miller 32.6-X.6.

❀ INDE. ❀ — ❀ — ❀ / ❀ ETLIB. ❀

Miller Y · Legend and punctuation diagnostic. *Used for:* W-4250, Miller 43.1-Y.

❀ INDE: ❀❀❀ / ❀ ETLIB: ❀

Miller Z.1 · **INDE Over INDN** · Branch hand opposite E. E corrected from erroneous N. Diagnostic. *Used for:* W-3550, Miller 33.13-Z.1. W-3645, Miller 33.19-Z.1. W-3865, Miller 33.35-Z.1. W-3925, Miller 33.38-Z.1. W-3965, Miller 33.40-Z.1. W-4310, Miller 49.1-Z.1. W-4315, Miller 49.2-Z.1.

Miller Z.2 · Branch hand very thin and opposite right part of E. All digits below dateline and about the same height; 78 slightly wide. Pole points to left tip of 7. Diagnostic. *Used for:* W-3410, Miller 33.4-Z.2. W-3580, Miller 33.14-Z.2. W-3650, Miller 33.19-Z.2. W-3970, Miller 33.40-Z.2. W-4000, Miller 33.42-Z.2.

Miller Z.3 · Branch hand opposite upright of E. In date, 1 heavy; second 7 highest. Pole points to left of 1. Diagnostic. *Used for:* W-3250, Miller 32.4-Z.3. W-3835, Miller 33.33-Z.3. W-3850, Miller 33.34-Z.3.

Miller Z.4 · Branch hand opposite upright of E. In date, 1 low, 8 touches line, which is curved over both 7's. Pole points to between 1 and 7. Diagnostic. *Used for:* W-3655, Miller 33.19-Z.4. W-3710, Miller 33.23-Z.4.

Miller Z.5 · Branch hand opposite E. Digits touch bottom date line; 1 and 8 highest. Pole points to left top of 7. Diagnostic. *Used for:* W-3340, Miller 33.2-Z.5.

Miller Z.6 · Branch hand opposite upright and left edge of E. No digits touch date line; second 7 low. Pole points to top left of 7. Diagnostic. *Used for:* W-3555, Miller 33.13-Z.6. W-3930, Miller 33.38-Z.6.

Miller Z.7 · Branch hand opposite E. In date, 1 high and distant; 787 progressively lower. Pole points to left side of 1. Diagnostic. *Used for:* W-3505, Miller 33.10-Z.7. W-3560, Miller 33.13-Z.7. W-3760, Miller 33.28-Z.7. W-3780, Miller 33.29-Z.7. W-4045, Miller 33.49-Z.7.

Miller Z.8 · Branch hand opposite upright and left side of E. In date, 1 distant; 1 and second 7 slightly low; bottom date line very irregular. Pole points to left of 7. Diagnostic. *Used for:* W-3510, Miller 33.10-Z.8.

Miller Z.9 · Branch hand opposite upright of E. In date, 1 distant; date line curved over both 7's; 78 high. 1 touches the line. 8 encroaches on it. Pole points to between 1 and 7. Diagnostic. *Used for:* W-3430, Miller 33.7-Z.9. W-3665, Miller 33.20-Z.9. W-3870, Miller 33.35-Z.9. W-3915, Miller 33.37-Z.9.

Miller Z.10 · Branch hand opposite right part of E. In date, 1 thick and high; first 7 lowest; 8 slightly high; lower date line defective. Pole points to upper right top of 1. Diagnostic. *Used for:* W-3435, Miller 33.7-Z.10. W-3530, Miller 33.12-Z.10. W-3720, Miller 33.24-Z.10. W-3730, Miller 33.25-Z.10. W-4295, Miller 44-Z.10.

Miller Z.11 · Branch hand opposite upright of E. In date, 1 leans slightly left; first 7 high; second 7 very low. Pole points to left tip of 7. Diagnostic. *Used for:* W-3670, Miller 33.20-Z.11. W-3765, Miller 33.28-Z.11. W-3840, Miller 33.33-Z.11. W-3860, Miller 33.34-Z.11. W-3920, Miller 33.37-Z.11. W-3975, Miller 33.41-Z.11.

Miller Z.12 · Branch hand opposite space between DE, closer to E. All digits touch date line, 8 low. Pole points to left of 7. Diagnostic. *Used for:* W-3360, Miller 33.2-Z.12.

Miller Z.13 · Branch hand opposite E. In date, 1 highest; 7's low and below date line; 8 barely touches date line. Pole points to upper left of 7. Diagnostic. *Used for:* W-3310, Miller 33.1-Z.13. W-3470, Miller 33.8-Z.13. W-3675, Miller 33.21-Z.13. W-3830, Miller 33.32-Z.13. W-3950, Miller 33.39-Z.13.

Miller Z.14 · Branch hand opposite space to right of colon. In date, 1 high; 8 low. Pole points to left tip of 7. Cinquefoil touches skirt. Diagnostic. *Used for:* W-3600, Miller 33.14-Z.14.

Miller Z.15 · Branch hand opposite E. In date, 1 and 87 touch date line; first 7 slightly below. Pole points to upper right tip of 1. Diagnostic. *Used for:* W-3615, Miller 33.16-Z.15.

Miller Z.16 · Branch hand opposite upright of E and space to left. In date, 1 high; 7's slightly low; 8 lower. Pole points to just left of 7. Diagnostic. *Used for:* W-3535, Miller 33.12-Z.16. W-3750, Miller 33.27-Z.16. W-3770, Miller 33.28-Z.16.

1787 REVERSE DIES (continued)

Miller Z.17 · Branch hand opposite space between E and colon; unusual. Pole points just past left top of 7. Date about evenly spaced and digits about the same height; 1 straddles 2 triangular dentils. Diagnostic. *Used for:* W-3370, Miller 33.2-Z.17.

Miller Z.18 · Branch hand opposite E. In date, 1 and 8 slightly high; both 7's slightly below date line; 1 and 8 are above dentil spaces; tips of 7's run into dentils. Pole points to upper left of 7. Diagnostic. *Used for:* W-3515, Miller 33.11-Z.18. W-3935, Miller 33.38-Z.18.

Miller Z.19 · Branch hand opposite E. Date about evenly spaced; 8 high and well into date line. Pole points just past left of 7. Diagnostic. *Used for:* W-3330, Miller 33.1-Z.19. W-3480, Miller 33.8-Z.19.

Miller Z.20 · Branch hand opposite space between D and E. Second 7 very low. Pole points to upper left of 7. Diagnostic. *Used for:* W-3255, Miller 32.4-Z.20. W-3775, Miller 33.28-Z.20. W-3955, Miller 33.39-Z.20.

Miller Z.21 · **INDE Over IODE** · Branch hand opposite right part of E and space between E and colon. N over earlier erroneous O, as also with Z-22. In date, 1 thick; first 7 slightly low and is the only digit to touch a dentil. Pole points to just past left of 7. Diagnostic. *Used for:* W-3380, Miller 33.2-Z.21. W-3540, Miller 33.12-Z.21. W-4025, Miller 33.46-Z.21.

Miller Z.22 · **INDE Over IODE** · Branch hand opposite E. N over earlier erroneous O, as also with Z-21. Numerals large; 178 wide; 1 highest; all are in the heavy date line, actually two lines mostly merged. Pole points to slightly right of left edge of 7. Diagnostic. *Used for:* W-3390, Miller 33.2-Z.22. W-4030, Miller 33.46-Z.22.

Miller Z.23 · Branch hand thin near drapery and is opposite space between D and E. Digits high; 8 very high. Pole points to just left of 7. Diagnostic. *Used for:* W-3940, Miller 33.38-Z.23.

Miller Z.24 · Branch hand opposite right part of E. In date, 17 merges into date line; 8 very high and leans left; second 7 lowest digit (somewhat similar to Z.25). Pole points to right side of 1. Diagnostic. *Used for:* W-3545, Miller 33.12-Z.24. W-3640, Miller 33.18-Z.24. W-3735, Miller 33.25-Z.24. W-4050, Miller 33.50-Z.24.

Miller Z.25 · Branch hand opposite upright of E and space to left. In date, 17 merges into date line; 8 very high and leans left; second 7 lowest digit (somewhat similar to Z.24). Pole points to just left of 7. Diagnostic. *Used for:* W-3800, Miller 33.29-Z.25. W-4040, Miller 33.48-Z.25.

Miller Z.26 · Branch hand opposite E. Pole points to left side of 1. Horizontal crack from waistband through upright of L to rim at 3 o'clock. *Used for:* W-4320, Miller 49.2-Z.26.

Miller Z.27 · Branch hand opposite colon. Pole points to center of 7. *Dentils:* Fine and distant from legend. *Used for:* W-4325, Miller 49.2-Z.27.

✺ INDE: — ✢ — — ✢ — / — ✢ — ETLIB:

Miller a.1 · Branch hand opposite E. In date, 1 high, second 7 very high. Pole points to upper left of 7. Diagnostic. *Used for:* W-2845, Miller 8-a.1. W-3110, Miller 26-a.1. W-3125, Miller 27-a.1.

Miller a.2 · Branch hand opposite D. In date, 8 slightly high; date line cut away above second 7. Pole thick at end and points to center and left of 7. Diagnostic. *Used for:* W-3055, Miller 20-a.2. W-3145, Miller 29.1-a.2.

Miller a.3 · Branch hand opposite upright of E. In date, 1 and both 7's high and into date line; 8 lower and touches dateline; 87 closer than are other figures. Pole points to upper left of 7. Diagnostic. *Used for:* W-4310, Miller 47-a.3.

✺ INDE: — ✢ — — ✢ — / ✢ — ETLIB:

Miller b · Legend and punctuation diagnostic. *Used for:* W-3100, Miller 25-b.

✢ INDE: ☙ ☙ / ✢ ETLIB:

Miller e · Legend and punctuation diagnostic. *Used for:* W-4125, Miller 37.5-e. W-4160, Miller 37.9-e.

— ✢ — INDE: — ✢ — — ✢ — /
— ✢ — ET—LIB:

Miller g.1 · Branch hand opposite upright of E and space between D and E. In date, 1 slightly high; 8 weak at top; second 2 low. Pole touches top date line and points to between 1 and 7. Diagnostic. *Used for:* W-3045, Miller 18-g.1.

Miller g.2 · Branch hand opposite upright of E. Pole points to upper left of 7. Diagnostic. *Used for:* W-3065, Miller 22-g.2.

Miller g.3 · Branch hand opposite D. In date, 17 high; 87 lower. Pole points to right side of 1. Diagnostic. *Used for:* W-3040, Miller 17-g.3. W-3070, Miller 24-g.3.

Miller g.4 · Branch hand opposite right part of D. Date wide; 8 high and into date line. Pole points to upper left of 1. Diagnostic. *Used for:* W-3050, Miller 19-g.4.

Miller g.5 · Branch hand opposite space between D and E. In date, 17 wide; 8 high and thin at top and touches date line. Pole points to tip of 1. Diagnostic. *Used for:* W-3075, Miller 24-g.5. W-4315, Miller 48-g.5.

✢ INDE: ☙ ☙ / ✺ ET—LIB:

Miller h.1 · Branch hand opposite D. In date, 17 wide; all digits high and close to or touching date line. Pole points left of 7. Diagnostic. *Used for:* W-4210, 39.1-h.1.

1787
Reverse Dies (continued)

Miller h.2 · Branch hand opposite space between D and E, closer to D. In date, 78 slightly high. Pole points to between 1 and 7. Diagnostic. *Used for:* W-4140, Miller 37.7-h.2.

Miller h.3 · Branch hand opposite D. Lower date-line cuts top of figure 8. Pole points to between 1 and 7. Diagnostic. *Used for:* W-4195, Miller 37.15-h.3.

✠ INDE: ❦❦ / ∝ ET — LIB: ✖

Miller i · Legend and punctuation diagnostic. *Used for:* W-4110, Miller 37.3-i.

∝ INDE: ❦❦ / ∝ ET—LIB:

Miller k.1 · Branch hand opposite space between D and E. Top of branch distant from fleuron; no terminal leaf. Diagnostic. B altered from erroneous R. *Used for:* W-4115, Miller 37.4-k.1.

Miller k.2 · Branch hand opposite right part of D. Second 7 very low. Diagnostic. *Used for:* W-4155, Miller 37.8-k.2.

Miller k.3 · Branch hand opposite space between D and E. Terminal leaf of branch large and ends close to fleuron. Diagnostic. *Used for:* W-4055, Miller 34-k.3. W-4065, Miller 36-k.3. W-4305, Miller 48-k.3.

Miller k.4 · Branch hand opposite space between D and E. In date, 1 thick and very high, ends near foot; second 7 low. Diagnostic. "Skeleton Hand." *Used for:* W-3680, Miller 33.21-k.4. W-4135, Miller 37.6-k.4.

Miller k.5 · Branch hand opposite right side of D. In date, 8 higher than other digits. Second leaf on right large and prominent. Diagnostic. *Used for:* W-4105, Miller 37.2-k.5.

❦❦ INDE: ❦❦ / ❦❦ ET—LIB: ❦

Miller l.1 · Branch hand opposite D. Diagnostic. *Used for:* W-4070, Miller 36-l.1.

Miller l.2 · Branch hand opposite right edge of D and space beyond. Diagnostic. *Used for:* W-3015, Miller 16.3-l.2. W-3620, Miller 33.16-l.2. W-4200, Miller 38-l.2.

✣ INDE ✣ ✣ / ✣ ET—LIB ✣

Miller m · Legend and punctuation diagnostic. *Used for:* W-3000, Miller 16.1-m. W-3105, Miller 25-m. W-3130, Miller 28-m.

✤ INDE: ✤ ✤ / ✤ ET—LIB:

Miller n · Legend and punctuation diagnostic. *Used for:* W-3020, Miller 16.4-n. W-3025, Miller 16.5-n. W-3135, Miller 28-n. W-3150, Miller 29.1-n.

✤ INDE ✤ ✤ / ETLIB ✤

Miller o · Legend and punctuation diagnostic. *Used for:* W-3140, Miller 28-o. W-3165, Miller 29.2-o. W-4240, Miller 42-o.

✤ INDE ✤ ✤ / ✤ ETLIB ✤

Miller p · Legend and punctuation diagnostic. *Used for:* W-3030, Miller 16.5-p. W-3155, Miller 29.1-p.

INDE: ✤✤✤ / ✤ ETLIB: ✤

Miller q · Legend and punctuation diagnostic. *Used for:* W-3415, Miller 33.4-q. W-3565, Miller 33.13-q. W-3660, Miller 33.19-q. W-4005, Miller 33.43-q.

✤ INDE: ✤✤ / ✤ ETLIB:

Miller r.1 · **B (LIB) Over a Cinquefoil** · Branch hand opposite E. Lowest colon dot after B touches shield. In date, 1 and 8 high; second 7 lowest. Diagnostic. *Notes:* This error is unusual, for one would suppose that cinquefoils would have been added to the die after the lettering was in place. *Used for:* W-3605, Miller 33.15-r.1. W-3625, Miller 33.17-r.1.

Miller r.2 · Branch hand opposite upright of E. Lowest colon dot after B distant from shield. In date, 178 high, second 7 slightly low. Diagnostic. *Used for:* W-3440, Miller 33.7-r.2.

Miller r.3 · Branch hand opposite upright of E and space to its left. Terminal leaf below and slightly left of cinquefoil. Diagnostic. *Used for:* W-3210, Miller 31.2-r.3.

Miller r.4 · Branch hand opposite E. Second 7 highest digit in date. Diagnostic. *Used for:* W-3200, Miller 31.1-r.4. W-3450, Miller 33.7-r.4. W-3755, Miller 33.27-r.4.

Miller r.5 · Branch hand opposite space between D and E. Diagnostic. *Used for:* W-3630, Miller 33.17-r.5.

✤ INDE: ✤✤ / ✤ ET—LIB: ✤

Miller s.1 · Second left leaf on branch short. In date, 8 slightly lower than second 7. Diagnostic. *Used for:* W-3805, Miller 33.29-s.1 · W-3960, Miller 33.39-s.1

Miller s.2 · Second left leaf on branch large. In date, 8 slightly higher than second 7. Diagnostic. *Used for:* W-3490, Miller 33.9-s.2.

1787 REVERSE DIES (continued)

✤ INDE OVER FUDE. ✤✤✤ / ✤ ETLIB. ✤

Miller aa · INDE Over FUDE · Legend and punctuation diagnostic. The engraver thought he was working on a Fugio copper, realized his error, and corrected it. *Used for:* W-3260, Miller 32.5-aa. W-3275, Miller 32.8-aa.

⚜ INDE: ⚜⚜⚜ / ⚜ ET–LIR:

Miller cc.1 · Branch hand opposite space between right side of D and space between D and E. Diagnostic. *Used for:* W-4100, Miller 37.1-cc.1.

Miller cc.2 · Branch hand opposite D. Diagnostic. *Used for:* W-4190, Miller 37.14-cc.2.

❧ INDE: ❧❧❧ / ❧ ET–LIR:

Miller ee · Legend and punctuation diagnostic. *Used for:* W-4220, Miller 39.2-ee.

⮜⮜ INDE: ⮜⮜⮜ / ⮜⮜ ET–LIR: ⮜

Miller ff.1 · On top of head, plume of hair turns to the right and ends above fleuron. E (ET) touches hand (poorly formed). Diagnostic. *Used for:* W-3570, Miller 33.13-ff.1. W-4060, Miller 34-ff.1.

Miller ff.2 · On top of head, plume of hair or ribbon turns upward toward rim. E (ET) distant from branch hand and pole. Diagnostic. *Used for:* W-4075, Miller 36-ff.2. W-4170, Miller 37.11-ff.2. W-4215, Miller 39.1-ff.2.

✤ INDE: ✤✤ / ✤ ETLIR: ✤

Miller gg.1 · Branch hand thin and opposite center of E. First 7 into bottom date line. Diagnostic. *Used for:* W-3205, Miller 31.1-gg.1. W-3520, Miller 33.11-gg.1. W-3810, Miller 33.29-gg.1. W-3945, Miller 33.38-gg.1.

Miller gg.2 · Branch hand normal thickness and opposite upright of E. First 7 below bottom date line. Diagnostic. *Used for:* W-3635, Miller 33.17-gg.2. W-3825, Miller 33.31-gg.2.

✤ INDE: ✤✤✤ / ✤ ETLIR: ✤

Miller hh.1 · Terminal leaf opposite first cinquefoil after INDE. Diagnostic. *Used for:* W-3175, Miller 30-hh.1.

Miller hh.2 · Terminal leaf under and close to second cinquefoil after INDE. Diagnostic. *Used for:* W-3575, Miller 33.13-hh.2. W-3715, Miller 33.23-hh.2. W-4010, Miller 33.43-hh.2.

✱ INDE: ✱✱ / ✱ ETIIB:

Miller ii · ETIIB · Legend and punctuation diagnostic. *Used for:* W-4235, Miller 41-ii.

❈ INDE: ❈❈ / ❈ ETIIB: ❈

Miller kk.1 · Branch hand opposite upright of E and space to its left. I (INDE) low. Bottom of colon on shield. Diagnostic. *Used for:* W-3115, Miller 26-kk.1. W-4230, Miller 40-kk.1.

Miller kk.2 · Branch hand opposite upright of E. Bottom of colon clear of shield. AUCTOPI spelling on obverse. Diagnostic. *Used for:* W-4245, Miller 42-kk.2.

INDE / ET.LIB

Miller mm · Legend and punctuation diagnostic. *Notes:* Pellet between T and L. Bulge across the top, probably accounting for the seemingly short life of this die. *Used for:* W-2730, Miller 1.2-mm.

❈ INDE: ✛ — ✛ / ✛ ETLIB:

Miller AA · Legend and punctuation diagnostic. *Used for:* W-3120, Miller 26-AA.

✖ INDE: ✛ — ✛ — / ✛ ETLIB ·

Miller BB · Legend and punctuation diagnostic. *Used for:* W-4305, Miller 46-BB.

✛ INDE: — ✛ — ✛ — / — ✛ — ETLIB:

Miller CC · Legend and punctuation diagnostic. *Used for:* W-4300, Miller 45-CC.

— ✛ — INDE: ✛ — ✛ — / — ✛ — ET—LIB:

Miller DD · Legend and punctuation diagnostic. *Used for:* W-3060, Miller 21-DD.

❈ INDE: ❈ — ❈ — / — ❈ ET—LIB: ❈

Miller EE · Legend and punctuation diagnostic. On the reverse the second and third cinquefoils were altered from crosses. *Used for:* W-3700, Miller 33.21-EE. W-3815, Miller 33.30-EE.

— ✛ — INDE: ✛ ✛ / ✛ ET—LIB:

Miller FF · Legend and punctuation diagnostic. *Used for:* W-3080, Miller 24-FF. W-4335, Miller 53-FF.

— ✛ — INDE: — ✛ = ✛ — / — ✛ — ET—LIB:

Miller GG · Legend and punctuation diagnostic. "Skeleton Hand." Third + is low. *Used for:* W-4205, Miller 38-GG.

➤❈ INDE: ❦ ❦ — / ❦ ET—LIB: ❦

Miller HH · Legend and punctuation diagnostic. *Used for:* W-4145, Miller 37.8-HH. W-4185, Miller 37.13-HH.

❈ INDE ❈❈❈ / ❈ ETLIB ❈

Miller II · Legend and punctuation diagnostic. *Used for:* W-3705, Miller 33.22-II.

1787 REVERSE DIES (continued)

✤ INDE: ✤✤✤ / ETLIB: ✤

Miller KK · Legend and punctuation diagnostic. *Used for:* W-3425, Miller 33.6-KK.

✤ INDE: ✤ ✤ / ✤ ET · IIB: ✤

Miller LL · Legend and punctuation diagnostic. *Used for:* W-4150, Miller 37.8-LL. W-4175, Miller 37.12-LL.

✤ INDE: ✤ ✤ / ✤ ET · LIB:

Miller NN.1 · Two date lines, usually appears as one thick date line. In date, 17 closer than 78. Diagnostic. *Used for:* W-3005, Miller 16.2-NN.1.

Miller NN.2 · Three date lines with suggestion of a fourth. In date, 17 farther apart than 78. Diagnostic. *Used for:* W-3010, Miller 16.2-NN.2. W-3035, Miller 16.6-NN.2.

⇶ INDE: ⇶ ⇇ / ⇶ ET–LIB: ⇇

Miller RR · Legend and punctuation diagnostic. *Used for:* W-4120, Miller 37.4-RR. W-4165, Miller 37.10-RR.

✤ INDE: ✤ ·✤· — / — ✤ ET · LIB: ✤

Miller SS · Legend and punctuation diagnostic. *Used for:* W-3820, Miller 33.30-SS. W-3910, Miller 33.36-SS.

— ✤ — INDE: ✤✤ / — ✤ — ETLIB: ✤

Miller TT · Legend and punctuation diagnostic. From the 1975 Pine Tree sale: "Originally nearest die style CC but the crosses were altered to cinquefoils with another cinquefoil added after ETLIB making a die ostensibly of type T but with some dashes remaining." *Used for:* W-4035, Miller 33.47-TT. W-4180, Miller 37.12-TT.

INDE / ETLIB

Miller VV · Legend and punctuation diagnostic. *Notes:* In date, 8 originally punched too high, then corrected. *Used for:* W-2710, Miller 1.1-VV.

ETLIB / INDE

Miller WW · Seated figure reversed, holding staff with liberty cap in right hand, branch in left. ETLIB / INDE. Diagnostic. *Used for:* W-2740, Miller 1.4-WW.

⇇⇇ INDE ⇇⇇⇇ / ⇶⇇ ET–LIB: ⇇

Miller XX · Legend and punctuation diagnostic. *Used for:* W-4340, Miller 56-XX.

1787 Connecticut Coppers

1787 Mailed Bust Right

W-2700 · Miller 1.1-A · Small Head · ETLIB / INDE reverse

Notes: One of most distinctive die pairs of the year. Often with roughness at the center of the reverse, an unstruck area of the original planchet. *Rarity:* URS-10.

Selected auction price(s): Perkins Collection (1/2000), EF, $2,760. C4 Convention (M&G 11/2001), VF-30, $1,050. Public Auction (Stack's 1/2004), Choice VF, $1,208. John J. Ford Jr. IX Sale (Stack's 5/2005), EF–AU, $4,887.50; AU, "finest seen," $4,370. ANA Las Vegas Sale (B&M 10/2005), AU-58 (PCGS), $11,500. Baltimore Sale (B&M 11/2007), EF, $1,150. Amherst & Waccabuc Collections (Stack's 11/2007), VF-25 (PCGS), $2,070.

G-4	VG-8	F-12	VF-20	EF-40	AU-50	MS-60
$120	$200	$400	$1,800	$4,200	$8,500	

W-2710 · Miller 1.1-VV · Small Head

Notes: Nearly always with planchet problems. *Rarity:* URS-5.

Selected auction price(s): John J. Ford Jr. IX Sale (Stack's 5/2005), VF, light at the centers, $34,500.

W-2720 · Miller 1.2-C · Muttonhead · Topless Liberty

Notes: Obverse with letters weak or missing, save for several very rare examples with most letters sharp. Perhaps the die was later ground down to make the coins appear worn, to facilitate circulation. This is one of the most distinctive, famous, and also available issues in the Connecticut series. Believed to be a contemporary counterfeit, the workmanship of the dies is unlike any others in the series save for Miller 1.2-mm (also compare to Nova Eborac W-5765). Called the Bull's Head by Dickeson (1859), nomenclature no longer used. "The topless liberty engraved on this die is indeed unique among the known Connecticut reverses. This female figure, dressed in the haute couture of the Court of Louis XVI, wears a combed wig, and on ankle length gown with full skirt fitted with three-quarter length flared sleeves, and square neck bodice cut well below the bosom. A stole is draped over her right shoulder, under her left arm, and across her lap in such a way as not to screen her bare chest. There she sits on top of the world, a proud 'emblem of liberty with an olive branch in her hand' as called for by the Connecticut legislature which specified the redesign of their copper pieces. Reverse C remains, therefore, the only die of Topless Liberty design used on any early American coinage" (*CNL*, January 1973). *Rarity:* URS-10.

G-4	VG-8	F-12	VF-20	EF-40	AU-50	MS-60
$100	$175	$475	$2,250	$4,750	$10,000	

W-2730 · Miller 1.2-mm · Muttonhead / Topless Liberty

Notes: Discovered by Robert A. Vlack in 1960. All with fairly sharp obverse, suggesting this variety was struck before Miller 1.2-C. Reverse with different punctuation from the preceding, but both with liberty cap in the form of a brimmed hat. Very rare. *Rarity:* URS-3.

W-2735 · Miller 1.3-L

Rarity: URS-6.

Selected auction price(s): Perkins Collection (1/2000), F, $2,300. John J. Ford Jr. IX Sale (Stack's 5/2005), VF, some lightness and so on, "finest seen," $21,850.

W-2740 · Miller 1.4-WW · ETLIB / INDE · transposed figure on reverse

Notes: Probably the most famous, rare, and coveted Connecticut type; the only die in the entire series with the seated figure reversed left to right, with branch arm on right. Two known: Norweb (now in a New York collection) and Newman collections. *Rarity:* URS-2.

Selected auction price(s): Norweb II Sale (3/1988), VF, lightly struck at the centers, $30,800.

W-2745 · Miller 52-G.1 · Roman Head

Notes: Two in ANS. *Rarity:* URS-6.

Selected auction price(s): Perkins Collection (1/2000), VG–F, $5,175. John J. Ford Jr. IX Sale (Stack's 5/2005), G, rough, $10,350.

W-2750 · Miller 52-G.2 · Roman Head

Notes: Discovery coin in *CNL*, December 1968, identified by Ted Craige as a second G reverse, earlier overlooked; 1975 Pine Tree, Lot 77, Extremely Fine, to Richard August collection. The other is Very Good and is owned by a New York collector. *Rarity:* URS-2.

1787 Mailed Bust Left

W-2755 · Miller 2-B

Rarity: URS-10.

G-4	VG-8	F-12	VF-20	EF-40	AU-50	MS-60
$60	$90	$170	$525	$1,500	$3,200	

W-2805 · Miller 3-G.1

Rarity: URS-6.

Selected auction price(s): Perkins Collection (1/2000), F–VF, some granularity, $4,312.50. September Sale (Stack's 9/2003), F, $1,150. John J. Ford Jr. IX Sale (Stack's 5/2005), AU, Miller plate coin, "finest seen" $20,700.

W-2810 · Miller 4-L · Horned Bust (later die states)

Notes: The obverse die developed a break (piece missing) in the left obverse field, which expanded to become a "horn" protruding from the bust. The nickname was assigned by Crosby in 1875. One of the most common Connecticut varieties and also one of the most popular, due to its nickname and easy recognition. The early die state (beginning aspects of the horn) is rare. *Rarity:* URS-12.

G-4	VG-8	F-12	VF-20	EF-40	AU-50	MS-60
$50	$75	$175	$500	$1,500	$4,000	

W-2815 · Miller 5-P

Notes: Branch hand divides IN DE (as also with reverse Q). Known over Nova Constellatio coppers and a counterfeit 1781 Irish halfpenny. Usually lightly struck and/or off center, a particular challenge to grade. *Rarity:* URS-6.

Selected auction price(s): Perkins Collection (1/2000), technically AU but variable sharpness in areas, etc., $1,725. Notre Dame Collection (Stack's 3/2001), AU, $1,955. John J. Ford Jr. IX Sale (Stack's 5/2005), EF, nicks, flaws, $2,070.

W-2820 · Miller 6.1-M · Laughing Head

Notes: Dickeson (1859): "The head small and round, facing to the left, and the hair a series of continuous small lines. The fillet terminates in a bow, in the center of which there is a circular ring. This type is quite thin, the lightest, we believe, coined in this year. It is known as the laughing effigy piece." This common variety and the next (scarcer) display an especially high degree of diecutting excellence in the context of the Connecticut series. *Rarity:* URS-12.

G-4	VG-8	F-12	VF-20	EF-40	AU-50	MS-60
$60	$125	$250	$700	$2,000	$4,000	

W-2825 · Miller 6.2-M · Laughing Head

Notes: Sometimes also called the "Outlined Head," but this term is equally applicable to Miller 6.1. Also known as the "Simple Head," from Crosby's comment, "a very simple expression." *Rarity:* URS-7.

G-4	VG-8	F-12	VF-20	EF-40	AU-50	MS-60
$60	$125	$250	$700	$2,000	$3,500	

W-2830 · Miller 7-I · Hercules Head

Notes: Same as 1786 obverse die Miller 5.3. The 1787 dated version is elusive. Lot 83 in the 1975 Pine Tree sale was said to be the first auctioned in more than 50 years. Robert M. Martin has tracked 22 different coins. *Rarity:* URS-6.

G-4	VG-8	F-12	VF-20	EF-40	AU-50	MS-60
$400	$800	$1,700	$4,000	$6,500	—	

W-2835 · Miller 8-N

Notes: Called "Tallest Head" in the 1975 Pine Tree sale. This die is a later state of Miller Draped Bust Left obverse die Miller 16.5. The remarkable nature of this obverse is not widely known beyond specialists. *Rarity:* URS-7.

Selected auction price(s): C4 Convention (M&G 11/2002), VF-20, $500, $575; VF-35, $575.

W-2840 · Miller 8-O

Notes: "Tallest head." *Rarity:* URS-10.

G-4	VG-8	F-12	VF-20	EF-40	AU-50	MS-60
$60	$90	$170	$525	$1,500	$3,200	

W-2845 · Miller 8-a.1

Notes: Unique. Reported by Edward R. Barnsley (*CNL*, December 1963, May 1991). *Rarity:* URS-1.

W-2850 · Miller 9-D

Rarity: URS-7.

W-2855 · Miller 9-E

Rarity: URS-7.

Selected auction price(s): Perkins Collection (1/2000), EF, some roughness, $1,610. Notre Dame Collection (Stack's 3/2001), AU, $1,006.

W-2860 · Miller 9-R · IND · 1787 Over 1788

Notes: Same double-error reverse die was used on Miller 9-R and 15-R. IND ET LIB instead of INDE ET LIB. Date first cut as 1788 then corrected. *Rarity:* URS-8.

Selected auction price(s): Pre–Long Beach Sale (Superior 9/2003), VF-30 (NGC), $1,035. John J. Ford Jr. IX Sale (Stack's 5/2005), Choice VF, $3,450.

W-2865 · Miller 10-E

Rarity: URS-7.

Selected auction price(s): C4 Convention (M&G 11/2001), VF-20, $650. John J. Ford Jr. IX Sale (Stack's 5/2005), EF, Miller plate coin, rough and granular, $3,450.

W-2870 · Miller 11.1-E

Rarity: URS-11.

G-4	VG-8	F-12	VF-20	EF-40	AU-50	MS-60
$60	$90	$170	$525	$1,500	$3,200	

W-2875 · Miller 11.2-K

Rarity: URS-10.

G-4	VG-8	F-12	VF-20	EF-40	AU-50	MS-60
$60	$90	$170	$525	$1,500	$3,200	

W-2880 · Miller 11.3-K

Notes: In Miller's time (1919) this was thought to be unique. *Rarity:* URS-2.

W-2885 · Miller 12-Q · 1787 Over 1877

Notes: Date corrected by repunching of the central digits. Also with branch hand dividing IN DE (as also with reverse P). Very crude dentils on reverse. Defective planchets are the rule. *Rarity:* URS-10.

G-4	VG-8	F-12	VF-20	EF-40	AU-50	MS-60
$100	$200	$700	$1,800	$4,750		

W-2890 · Miller 13-D · Childish Face

Notes: Crosby noted this has "a childish face," but the nomenclature was not picked up by Miller. *Rarity:* URS-11.

G-4	VG-8	F-12	VF-20	EF-40	AU-50	MS-60
$60	$90	$170	$525	$1,500	$3,200	$5,000

W-2895 · Miller 14-H · Arrows (Pheons) at Date

Notes: Unique reverse die with a pheon (arrowhead) to each side of the date. Curious and distinctive style. *Rarity:* URS-10.

G-4	VG-8	F-12	VF-20	EF-40	AU-50	MS-60
$60	$90	$170	$525	$1,500	$3,200	$5,000

W-2900 · Miller 15-F · CONNECT

Rarity: URS-10.

G-4	VG-8	F-12	VF-20	EF-40	AU-50	MS-60
$60	$150	$280	$800	$2,000	$3,350	$15,000

W-2910 · Miller 15-R · CONNECT / IND · 1787 Over 1788

Notes: Error obverse combined with same double-error reverse die used on Miller 9-R. IND ET LIB instead of INDE ET LIB. Date first cut as 1788, then corrected. A highly desirable rarity with errors on both sides. *Rarity:* URS-4.

Selected auction price(s): John J. Ford Jr. IX Sale (Stack's 5/2005), VF, flaws, "chip out of edge," $34,500.

W-2915 · Miller 15-S · CONNECT · INDL reverse

Notes: An error on each side. Robert M. Martin knows of 30 different coins. *Rarity:* URS-7.

Selected auction price(s): Perkins Collection (1/2000), F, $2,300. John J. Ford Jr. IX Sale (Stack's 5/2005), VG, nearly black, light at centers, $1,150. Americana Sale (Stack's 1/2007), VG-10, $1,006.

1787 Draped Bust Left

W-3000 · Miller 16.1-m
Rarity: URS-8.

W-3005 · Miller 16.2-NN.1
Rarity: URS-7.

Selected auction price(s): John J. Ford Jr. IX Sale (Stack's 5/2005), VF, $1,035.

W-3010 · Miller 16.2-NN.2
Notes: Discovered in 1977 by Robert A. Vlack. (*CNL*, October 1978). Taylor-2436 was first auction appearance. *Rarity:* URS-3.

W-3015 · Miller 16.3-l.2
Rarity: URS-5.

Selected auction price(s): Perkins Collection (1/2000), F, $7,475. Logan & Steinberg Collections (B&M 11/2002), F-12, $4,830.

W-3020 · Miller 16.4-n
Rarity: URS-6.

Selected auction price(s): Perkins Collection (1/2000), F, cleaned, $1,285.

W-3025 · Miller 16.5-n
Notes: This obverse was later reworked to make Miller obverse 8, a different type! *Rarity:* URS-6.

Selected auction price(s): Perkins Collection (1/2000), sharpness of EF, $1,955. C4 Convention (M&G 11/2001), double struck, EF-40, $800. John J. Ford Jr. IX Sale (Stack's 5/2005), About VF, $1,150. Pre–Long Beach Sale (I. & L. Goldberg 9/2006), VF-30, $1,610.

W-3030 · Miller 16.5-p
Notes: See above. *Rarity:* URS-5.

Selected auction price(s): John J. Ford Jr. IX Sale (Stack's 5/2005), EF, flaws, $13,800.

W-3035 · Miller 16.6-NN.2
Rarity: URS-7.

W-3040 · Miller 17-g.3
Rarity: URS-9.

Selected auction price(s): John J. Ford Jr. IX Sale (Stack's 5/2005), AU, $2,070.

W-3045 · Miller 18-g.1
Rarity: URS-7.

Selected auction price(s): Pre–Long Beach Sale (Superior 5/2001), VF-25, $1,265. John J. Ford Jr. IX Sale (Stack's 5/2005), Choice VF, some roughness, $900.

W-3050 · Miller 19-g.4
Rarity: URS-10.

G-4	VG-8	F-12	VF-20	EF-40	AU-50	MS-60
$50	$85	$140	$400	$1,000	$2,000	$7,500

W-3055 · Miller 20-a.2
Rarity: URS-7.

Selected auction price(s): John J. Ford Jr. IX Sale (Stack's 5/2005), Choice VF, slightly off center, $3,737.50.

W-3060 · Miller 21-DD
Rarity: URS-7.

Selected auction price(s): John J. Ford Jr. IX Sale (Stack's 5/2005), VF, Miller plate coin, minor problems, $1,500.

W-3065 · Miller 22-g.2
Rarity: URS-7.

Selected auction price(s): Perkins Collection (1/2000), VF, $1,380. John J. Ford Jr. IX Sale (Stack's 5/2005), AU, $10,350. Long Beach Sale (Heritage 9/2005), VF-35 (PCGS), $1,840.

W-3070 · Miller 24-g.3
Rarity: URS-6.

Selected auction price(s): C4 Convention (M&G 11/2001), VF-20, $550. Smith & Youngman Collections (B&M 3/2003), F-15, 30 percent off center, $2,990.

W-3075 · Miller 24-g.5
Rarity: URS-7.

Selected auction price(s): John J. Ford Jr. IX Sale (Stack's 5/2005), AU, flaws and areas of light striking, $7,475.

W-3080 · Miller 24-FF
Rarity: URS-6.

Selected auction price(s): Perkins Collection (1/2000), VF, "probably finest known," $5,462.50. C4 Convention (M&G 11/2002), F-12, $650. Public Auction Sale (Stack's 5/2004), VF, $3,565.

W-3100 · Miller 25-b
Rarity: URS-10.

G-4	VG-8	F-12	VF-20	EF-40	AU-50	MS-60
$50	$85	$140	$400	$1,000	$2,000	$10,000

W-3105 · Miller 25-m
Rarity: URS-7.

Selected auction price(s): C4 Convention (M&G 11/2002), EF-45, $3,400.

W-3110 · Miller 26-a.1
Rarity: URS-6.

Selected auction price(s): Perkins Collection (1/2000), EF, $4,887.50. John J. Ford Jr. IX Sale (Stack's 5/2005), F, areas of light striking, $2,990.

W-3115 · Miller 26-kk.1
Rarity: URS-7.

Selected auction price(s): Perkins Collection (1/2000), VF, $2,520.

W-3120 · Miller 26-AA
Rarity: URS-7.

Selected auction price(s): C4 Convention (M&G 11/2001), VF-20, double struck, $3,200. John J. Ford Jr. IX Sale (Stack's 5/2005), VF, some roughness, $1,840.

W-3125 · Miller 27-a.1
Rarity: URS-7.

Selected auction price(s): Perkins Collection (1/2000), EF, $2,760. John J. Ford Jr. IX Sale (Stack's 5/2005), Choice EF, Miller plate coin, part of date not visible, $6,325.

W-3130 · Miller 28-m
Rarity: URS-7.

Selected auction price(s): Garrett III Sale (B&R 10/1980), Choice MS, $7,200. Perkins Collection (1/2000), AU, $3,162.50. John J. Ford Jr. IX Sale (Stack's 5/2005), EF, $1,265; AU, "the finest seen," $4,887.50.

W-3135 · Miller 28-n
Rarity: URS-6.

W-3140 · Miller 28-o
Rarity: URS-6.

Selected auction price(s): C4 Convention (M&G 11/2002), VF-20, $1,700.

W-3145 · Miller 29.1-a.2
Rarity: URS-6.

Selected auction price(s): Perkins Collection (1/2000), AG obverse, F reverse, $1,380. John J. Ford Jr. IX Sale (Stack's 5/2005), Choice F, rough, $2,990.

W-3150 · Miller 29.1-n
Rarity: URS-6.

W-3155 · Miller 29.1-p
Rarity: URS-7.

Selected auction price(s): John J. Ford Jr. IX Sale (Stack's 5/2005), VF, normal roughness, $2,530.

W-3160 · Miller 29.2-N
Rarity: URS-6.

Selected auction price(s): John J. Ford Jr. IX Sale (Stack's 5/2005), Choice VF, rough at centers, $6,325.

W-3165 · Miller 29.2-o
Rarity: URS-7.

Selected auction price(s): John J. Ford Jr. IX Sale (Stack's 5/2005), Choice EF, $4,312.50.

W-3170 · Miller 30-X.1
Rarity: URS-6.

W-3175 · Miller 30-hh.1 · ETLIR
Rarity: URS-11.

G-4	VG-8	F-12	VF-20	EF-40	AU-50	MS-60
$55	$90	$190	$550	$1,450	$6,000	$7,000

W-3200 · Miller 31.1-r.4
Rarity: URS-11.

G-4	VG-8	F-12	VF-20	EF-40	AU-50	MS-60
$50	$85	$140	$400	$1,000	$2,000	$3,000

W-3205 · Miller 31.1-gg.1 · ETLIR
Rarity: URS-10.

G-4	VG-8	F-12	VF-20	EF-40	AU-50	MS-60
$55	$90	$190	$550	$1,450	$2,650	

W-3210 · Miller 31.2-r.3
Rarity: URS-12.

G-4	VG-8	F-12	VF-20	EF-40	AU-50	MS-60
$50	$85	$140	$400	$1,000	$2,000	$3,000

W-3215 · Miller 32.1-X.3
Rarity: URS-9.

G-4	VG-8	F-12	VF-20	EF-40	AU-50	MS-60
$50	$85	$140	$400	$1,000	$2,000	$5,000

W-3220 · Miller 32.2-X.1
Rarity: URS-10.

G-4	VG-8	F-12	VF-20	EF-40	AU-50	MS-60
$50	$85	$140	$400	$1,000	$2,000	$3,500

W-3225 · Miller 32.2-X.2
Rarity: URS-7.

Selected auction price(s): C4 Convention (M&G 11/2002), AU-50, $1,300. John J. Ford Jr. IX Sale (Stack's 5/2005), Choice EF, $1,495.

W-3230 · Miller 32.2-X.4
Rarity: URS-7.

Selected auction price(s): Garrett III Sale (B&R 10/1980), Choice MS, $7,000.

W-3235 · Miller 32.3-X.4
Rarity: URS-11.

G-4	VG-8	F-12	VF-20	EF-40	AU-50	MS-60
$50	$85	$140	$400	$1,000	$2,000	$3,000

W-3240 · Miller 32.4-F
Notes: The Taylor catalog (2486) gives a detailed discussion of this variety. *Rarity*: URS-6.

Selected auction price(s): Perkins Collection (1/2000), VG–VF, $1,955.

W-3245 · Miller 32.4-X.5
Rarity: URS-7.

Selected auction price(s): C4 Convention (M&G 11/2002), F-12, $500.

W-3250 · Miller 32.4-Z.3
Rarity: URS-7.

W-3255 · Miller 32.4-Z.20
Notes: First described by Walter Breen in 1951. Two known, one in ANS, another the Norweb coin (*CNL*, March 1964, May 1991). *Rarity:* URS-2.

Selected auction price(s): Perkins Collection (1/2000), G–VG, ex Norweb, $8,855.

W-3260 · Miller 32.5-aa · INDE Over FUDE
Notes: The engraver thought he was working on a Fugio copper, then corrected his error. Usually seen in low grades. Examples in the Taylor and Ford collections. *Rarity:* URS-9.

G-4	VG-8	F-12	VF-20	EF-40	AU-50	MS-60
$75	$150	$650	$1,000	$3,000	$5,000	

W-3265 · Miller 32.6-X.6
Rarity: URS-6.

Selected auction price(s): Perkins Collection (1/2000), F, $1,385. C4 Convention (M&G 11/2002), F-15, $600. John J. Ford Jr. IX Sale (Stack's 5/2005), EF, some roughness, better than most seen, $3,737.50. CSNS Sale (Heritage 4/2006), AU-50 (PCGS), $1,955.

W-3270 · Miller 32.7-X.1
Rarity: URS-7.

Selected auction price(s): C4 Convention (M&G 11/2002), VF-25, $600. John J. Ford Jr. IX Sale (Stack's 5/2005), EF, $2,760.

W-3275 · Miller 32.8-aa · INDE Over FUDE
Notes: The engraver thought he was working on a Fugio copper, then corrected his error. *Rarity:* URS-6.

Selected auction price(s): Perkins Collection (1/2000), VF, $2,530. John J. Ford Jr. IX Sale (Stack's 5/2005), Choice F, rough with loss of detail, $2,185.

W-3310 · Miller 33.1-Z.13
Rarity: URS-7.

Selected auction price(s): FUN Sale (Heritage 1/2007), AU-50 (PCGS), $1,035. Pre–Long Beach Sale (Superior 5/2001), EF-40, $2,530.

W-3330 · Miller 33.1-Z.19
Rarity: URS-7.

W-3340 · Miller 33.2-Z.5
Notes: Struck from damaged dies. *Rarity:* URS-12.

G-4	VG-8	F-12	VF-20	EF-40	AU-50	MS-60
$50	$85	$140	$400	$1,000	$2,000	

W-3360 · Miller 33.2-Z.12
Rarity: URS-12.

G-4	VG-8	F-12	VF-20	EF-40	AU-50	MS-60
$50	$85	$140	$400	$1,000	$2,000	

W-3370 · Miller 33.2-Z.17
Rarity: URS-6.

Selected auction price(s): Perkins Collection (1/2000), VF, $3,450. John J. Ford Jr. IX Sale (Stack's 5/2005), AU, some roughness, traces of mint color, $17,250.

W-3380 · Miller 33.2-Z.21 · INDE Over IODE
Notes: Erroneous O changed to N. *Rarity:* URS-6.

W-3390 · Miller 33.2-Z.22
Notes: Erroneous O changed to N. *Rarity:* URS-6.

Selected auction price(s): Perkins Collection (1/2000), F, dark, $1,265. C4 Convention (M&G 11/2002), F-12, $800.

W-3400 · Miller 33.3-W.1
Rarity: URS-8.

G-4	VG-8	F-12	VF-20	EF-40	AU-50	MS-60
$50	$85	$140	$400	$1,000	$2,000	

W-3410 · Miller 33.4-Z.2
Rarity: URS-5.

Selected auction price(s): Perkins Collection (1/2000), VF, $4,887.50. Mail Bid Sale (Coin Galleries 4/2004), VF, $1,714. John J. Ford Jr. IX Sale (Stack's 5/2005), VF, $6,900.

W-3415 · Miller 33.4-q
Rarity: URS-7.

Selected auction price(s): C4 Convention (M&G 11/2002), VF-30, $525. Public Auction Sale (Stack's 5/2004), M.33.4-q, EF, $1,955. John J. Ford Jr. IX Sale (Stack's 5/2005), EF, $2,070. Lake Michigan & Springdale Collections (Stacks [ANR] 6/2006), AU-50 (NGC), $1,668.

W-3420 · Miller 33.5-T.2 · Skeleton Hand
Notes: Hall and Miller called this the "Skeleton Hand," but other reverses (such as k.4 and GG) have the same skeletal features (*CNL*, January 1973). *Rarity:* URS-7.

Selected auction price(s): Perkins Collection (1/2000), VF, $1,725. John J. Ford Jr. IX Sale (Stack's 5/2005), EF, $1,955.

W-3425 · Miller 33.6-KK
Rarity: URS-11.

G-4	VG-8	F-12	VF-20	EF-40	AU-50	MS-60
$50	$85	$140	$400	$1,000	$2,000	

W-3430 · Miller 33.7-Z.9
Notes: Die combination discovered by Walter Breen in 1951. One or two exist, one confirmed (*CNL*, May 1991). *Rarity:* URS-1 or 2.

W-3435 · Miller 33.7-Z.10
Rarity: URS-2.

W-3440 · Miller 33.7-r.2
Rarity: URS-12.

G-4	VG-8	F-12	VF-20	EF-40	AU-50	MS-60
$50	$85	$140	$400	$1,000	$2,000	

W-3450 · Miller 33.7-r.4
Rarity: URS-7.

Selected auction price(s): Pre–Long Beach Sale (I. & L. Goldberg 9/2006), EF-40, $1,150.

W-3470 · Miller 33.8-Z.13
Rarity: URS-7.
Selected auction price(s): C4 Convention (M&G 11/2002), EF-40, $900. John J. Ford Jr. IX Sale (Stack's 5/2005), F, $517.50.

W-3480 · Miller 33.8-Z.19
Rarity: URS-6.
Selected auction price(s): Perkins Collection (1/2000), VF, $3,737.50. John J. Ford Jr. IX Sale (Stack's 5/2005), VF, $4,025.

W-3490 · Miller 33.9-s.2
Notes: Typically with extensive die cracks. *Rarity:* URS-11.

G-4	VG-8	F-12	VF-20	EF-40	AU-50	MS-60
$50	$85	$140	$400	$1,000	$2,000	

W-3500 · Miller 33.10-W.6
Rarity: URS-5.
Selected auction price(s): Perkins Collection (1/2000), sharpness of G–VG, technically VF, $1,610. John J. Ford Jr. IX Sale (Stack's 5/2005), VG–F, area of light striking, $3,737.50.

W-3505 · Miller 33.10-Z.7
Rarity: URS-6.
Selected auction price(s): Perkins Collection (1/2000), AU, $8,912.50. John J. Ford Jr. IX Sale (Stack's 5/2005), VF, $1,265.

W-3510 · Miller 33.10-Z.8
Rarity: URS-7.
Selected auction price(s): John J. Ford Jr. IX Sale (Stack's 5/2005), Choice AU, $4,025.

W-3515 · Miller 33.11-Z.18
Rarity: URS-7.

W-3520 · Miller 33.11-gg.1 · ETLIR
Rarity: URS-6.
Selected auction price(s): Perkins Collection (1/2000), VF, $2,185. C4 Convention (M&G 11/2002), VG-10, $2,200. John J. Ford Jr. IX Sale (Stack's 5/2005), VF, some roughness, $2,760. Americana Sale (Stack's 1/2007), VF-25, $1,150.

W-3525 · Miller 33.12-W.3
Rarity: URS-5.
Selected auction price(s): Perkins Collection (1/2000), VF/VG, $1,725. Mail Bid Sale (Coin Galleries 4/2004), Choice, $5,146. John J. Ford Jr. IX Sale (Stack's 5/2005), Choice EF, rough, $25,300.

W-3530 · Miller 33.12-Z.10
Notes: Discovered by Jesse Patrick in 1982 (*CNL*, May 1991). *Rarity:* URS-2.
Selected auction price(s): C4 Convention (M&G 11/2002), VG-10, $22,000.

W-3535 · Miller 33.12-Z.16
Rarity: URS-7.
Selected auction price(s): C4 Convention (M&G 11/2001), VF-20, $600. C4 Convention (M&G 11/2002), VF-35, $1,400; AU-50, $850. John J. Ford Jr. IX Sale (Stack's 5/2005), EF, flaws, $1,006.25.

W-3540 · Miller 33.12-Z.21 · INDE Over IODE
Notes: Erroneous O changed to N. *Rarity:* URS-5.
Selected auction price(s): Perkins Collection (1/2000), F, $2,530.

W-3545 · Miller 33.12-Z.24
Rarity: URS-6.

W-3550 · Miller 33.13-Z.1 · INDE Over INDN
Notes: E corrected from erroneous N. *Rarity:* URS-6.

W-3555 · Miller 33.13-Z.6
Rarity: URS-7.
Selected auction price(s): John J. Ford Jr. IX Sale (Stack's 5/2005), EF, some roughness, $2,300.

W-3560 · Miller 33.13-Z.7
Rarity: URS-7.
Selected auction price(s): Hain Family Collection Part II (Stack's 1/2002), MS, $6,325. John J. Ford Jr. IX Sale (Stack's 5/2005), EF, rough, $2,070.

W-3565 · Miller 33.13-q
Rarity: URS-4.
Selected auction price(s): Pre–Long Beach Sale (Superior 2/2003), VG-8, $9,775. John J. Ford Jr. IX Sale (Stack's 5/2005), F–VF, "a little rough and battered, edge hammered around" [an example of a rarity selling for a strong price, never mind the condition], $10,350.

W-3570 · Miller 33.13-ff.1 · ETLIR
Rarity: URS-3.
Selected auction price(s): Perkins Collection (1/2000), F, $9,775.

W-3575 · Miller 33.13-hh.2
Rarity: URS-5.
Selected auction price(s): Perkins Collection (1/2000), F/VG, $2,530.

W-3580 · Miller 33.14-Z.2
Notes: Discovered by Robert A. Vlack in 1962. Another rumored but not located (*CNL*, May 1991). *Rarity:* URS-1 or 2.

W-3600 · Miller 33.14- Z.14
Rarity: URS-7.

W-3605 · Miller 33.15-r.1 · B (LIB) Over Cinquefoil
Rarity: URS-11.

G-4	VG-8	F-12	VF-20	EF-40	AU-50	MS-60
$50	$85	$140	$400	$100	$2,000	$7,500

W-3610 · Miller 33.16-T.2
Rarity: URS-4.
Selected auction price(s): Mail Bid Sale (Coin Galleries 4/2004), AG, $3,910.

W-3615 · Miller 33.16-Z.15
Rarity: URS-9.

G-4	VG-8	F-12	VF-20	EF-40	AU-50	MS-60
$50	$85	$140	$400	$1,000	$2,000	$5,000

W-3620 · Miller 33.16-I.2
Rarity: URS-7.

W-3625 · Miller 33.17-r.1 · B (LIB) Over Cinquefoil
Rarity: URS-12.

G-4	VG-8	F-12	VF-20	EF-40	AU-50	MS-60
			$1,000	$2,000	$5,000	

W-3630 · Miller 33.17-r.5
Notes: Discovered by Thomas Hall prior to 1910. Only use of this reverse die. *Rarity:* URS-6

Selected auction price(s): John J. Ford Jr. IX Sale (Stack's 5/2005), VF, flaws, $3,450.

W-3635 · Miller 33.17-gg.2 · ETLIR
Rarity: URS-7.

W-3640 · Miller 33.18-Z.24
Rarity: URS-4.

W-3645 · Miller 33.19-Z.1 · INDE Over INDN
Notes: E corrected from erroneous N. *Rarity:* URS-9.

G-4	VG-8	F-12	VF-20	EF-40	AU-50	MS-60
$50	$85	$140	$400	$1,000	$2,000	$5,000

W-3650 · Miller 33.19-Z.2
Rarity: URS-7.

Selected auction price(s): C4 Convention (M&G 11/2002), EF-45, $900. John J. Ford Jr. IX Sale (Stack's 5/2005), Choice AU, some problems, $4,312.

W-3655 · Miller 33.19-Z.4
Notes: Discovered by John M. Richardson in the 1940s and reported in Stack's *Numismatic Review*, 1946; sold as Taylor-2548, sharpness of VG-8 with some aspects of F-12. Robert M. Martin records 9 listings. *Rarity:* URS-4 or 5.

Selected auction price(s): Perkins Collection (1/2000), VG, "one of four known," $6,325.

W-3660 · Miller 33.19-q
Rarity: URS-5.

Selected auction price(s): Perkins Collection (1/2000), F–VF, $4,312.50. CSNS Sale (Heritage 4/2002), VG-10, corroded, $2,070. John J. Ford Jr. IX Sale (Stack's 5/2005), F, rough, $2,300.

W-3665 · Miller 33.20-Z.9
Rarity: URS-7.

Selected auction price(s): Perkins Collection (1/2000), EF, $1,380. C4 Convention (M&G 11/2001), AU-50, $2,100. Public Auction Sale (Stack's 5/2004), AU, $2,530. John J. Ford Jr. IX Sale (Stack's 5/2005), Choice EF, minor problems, $3,737.

W-3670 · Miller 33.20-Z.11
Rarity: URS-5.

Selected auction price(s): Perkins Collection (1/2000), F, $5,750.

W-3675 · Miller 33.21-Z.13
Rarity: URS-6.

Selected auction price(s): C4 Convention (M&G 11/2001), VF-30, $1,450. Public Auction Sale (Stack's 9/2005), AG, $1,150.

W-3680 · Miller 33.21-k.4 · Skeleton Hand
Notes: One of several "Skeleton Hand" varieties. Discovered by John M. Richardson in the 1940s and reported in Stack's *Numismatic Review*, 1946. Robert M. Martin lists nine coins. *Rarity:* URS-5.

Selected auction price(s): Perkins Collection (1/2000), F, flaws, "possibly finest known," $13,900.

W-3700 · Miller 33.21-EE
Notes: Reverse die discovered by C.F. Luther in 1928 (but misattributed as to obverse), die combination first correctly reported in Stack's *Numismatic Review*, 1946. On the reverse the second and third cinquefoils were altered from crosses. *Rarity:* URS-4.

Selected auction price(s): Perkins Collection (1/2000), F, "possibly finest known," $6,037.50.

W-3705 · Miller 33.22-ll
Notes: Ryder Collection, later Ford Collection (lot 394), Good to Very Good. *Rarity:* URS-1.

Selected auction price(s): John J. Ford Jr. IX Sale (Stack's 5/2005), G–VG, rough, "first auction appearance ever," $92,000.

W-3710 · Miller 33.23-Z.4
Rarity: URS-7.

Selected auction price(s): Perkins Collection (1/2000), VF–EF, $1,150. John J. Ford Jr. IX Sale (Stack's 5/2005), Choice VF, $1,610.

W-3715 · Miller 33.23-hh.2 · ETLIR
Rarity: URS-6.

Selected auction price(s): Perkins Collection (1/2000), EF, $4,025. John J. Ford Jr. IX Sale (Stack's 5/2005), VF, rough, $3,220. Long Beach Sale (Heritage 9/2005), EF-45 (NGC), $1,955.

W-3720 · Miller 33.24-Z.10
Rarity: URS-4.

Selected auction price(s): John J. Ford Jr. IX Sale (Stack's 5/2005), VG–F, some usual flaws, $29,900.

W-3725 · Miller 33.25-W.3
Rarity: URS-6.

Selected auction price(s): Perkins Collection (1/2000), EF, granular, $1,160. John J. Ford Jr. IX Sale (Stack's 5/2005), Choice AU, some typical roughness at centers, $12,650.

W-3730 · Miller 33.25-Z.10
Rarity: URS-6.

Selected auction price(s): Perkins Collection (1/2000), VF, $1,955. John J. Ford Jr. IX Sale (Stack's 5/2005), F–VF, rough, $1,150.

W-3735 · Miller 33.25-Z.24
Rarity: URS-6.

Selected auction price(s): Perkins Collection (1/2000), VF, $3,450. John J. Ford Jr. IX Sale (Stack's 5/2005), F, planchet flaws, $1,150.

W-3740 · Miller 33.26-W.3
Rarity: URS-6.
Selected auction price(s): Perkins Collection (1/2000), F, $3,450. John J. Ford Jr. IX Sale (Stack's 5/2005), EF, minor flaws, $23,000.

W-3745 · Miller 33.26-W.5
Notes: This variety was known to both Thomas Hall and Henry C. Miller, but was not publicized until later. *Rarity:* URS-3.
Selected auction price(s): Perkins Collection (1/2000), VG, porous, "only one available of the three known," $6,325.

W-3750 · Miller 33.27-Z.16
Rarity: URS-1.

W-3755 · Miller 33.27-r.4
Rarity: URS-6.
Selected auction price(s): John J. Ford Jr. IX Sale (Stack's 5/2005), Choice AU, heavy flaws on reverse, $5,175.

W-3760 · Miller 33.28-Z.7 · Snipe Nose
Notes: So called from a crack that begins at the right, then expands to extend from the nose, left to the border. This combination discovered by a California dealer in 1984. (*CNL*, May 1991). *Rarity:* URS-1.

W-3765 · Miller 33.28-Z.11 · Snipe Nose
Rarity: URS-6.
Selected auction price(s): Perkins Collection (1/2000), VF, $2,070. C4 Convention (M&G 11/2001), $775. John J. Ford Jr. IX Sale (Stack's 5/2005), AU, minor flaws, $2,760. New York City Winter Auction (R.M. Smythe 3/2006), AU, $2,530.

W-3770 · Miller 33.28-Z.16 · Snipe Nose
Rarity: URS-8.

G-4	VG-8	F-12	VF-20	EF-40	AU-50	MS-60
$1,000	$2,000	$6,000				

W-3775 · Miller 33.28-Z.20 · Snipe Nose
Notes: Early states do not show the eponymous crack. *Rarity:* URS-4.
Selected auction price(s): Perkins Collection (1/2000), F, $17,250. John J. Ford Jr. IX Sale (Stack's 5/2005), VG–F, $32,200.

W-3780 · Miller 33.29-Z.7
Rarity: URS-7.
Selected auction price(s): Perkins Collection (1/2000), EF, $1,380. John J. Ford Jr. IX Sale (Stack's 5/2005), AU, minor flaws, $11,500.

W-3800 · Miller 33.29-Z.25
Notes: Discovered by Cyril Hawley and reported in *CNL*, July 1961. *Rarity:* URS-3.

W-3805 · Miller 33.29-s.1
Notes: Discovered by Mike Ringo at the FUN Convention in January 1993. Others have been found since, including an example (making five known) discovered in January 2008 by Andrew W. Pollock III while cataloging a miscellaneous group of Connecticut coppers consigned to Stack's. *Rarity:* URS-4.
Selected auction price(s): Baltimore Sale (B&M 11/2006), F-15, $43,125.

W-3810 · Miller 33.29-gg.1 · ETLIR
Rarity: URS-7.
Selected auction price(s): ANA Sale (Heritage 7/2005), AU-55 (PCGS), $3,163. Pre–Long Beach Sale (I. & L. Goldberg 9/2006), VF-20, $2,300.

W-3815 · Miller 33.30-EE
Notes: On the reverse the second and third cinquefoils were altered from crosses. *Rarity:* URS-6.
Selected auction price(s): John J. Ford Jr. IX Sale (Stack's 5/2005), About F, rough, $2,300.

W-3820 · Miller 33.30-SS
Rarity: URS-5.
Selected auction price(s): Perkins Collection (1/2000), VF, "finest known," $14,950.

W-3825 · Miller 33.31-gg.2 · ETLIR
Rarity: URS-7.
Selected auction price(s): Perkins Collection (1/2000), VF, $1,150. C4 Convention (M&G 11/2002), AU-50, $9,500. John J. Ford Jr. IX Sale (Stack's 5/2005), Choice EF, lacquer on reverse, $1,725.

W-3830 · Miller 33.32-Z.13
Rarity: URS-12.

G-4	VG-8	F-12	VF-20	EF-40	AU-50	MS-60
$50	$85	$140	$400	$1,000	$2,000	$5,000

W-3835 · Miller 33.33-Z.3
Rarity: URS-7.
Selected auction price(s): John J. Ford Jr. IX Sale (Stack's 5/2005), EF, light flaws, $2,070.

W-3840 · Miller 33.33-Z.11
Rarity: URS-6.
Selected auction price(s): Perkins Collection (1/2000), VF, $4,025. John J. Ford Jr. IX Sale (Stack's 5/2005), AU, rough, $5,750.

W-3845 · Miller 33.34-W.2
Rarity: URS-7.
Selected auction price(s): Strong Museum Collection (Stack's 10/2001), Choice EF, $1,093.

W-3850 · Miller 33.34-Z.3
Rarity: URS-7.

W-3860 · Miller 33.34-Z.11
Rarity: URS-7.
Selected auction price(s): C4 Convention (M&G 11/2002), EF-40, $1,700; EF-45, $850.

W-3865 · Miller 33.35-Z.1 · INDE Over INDN
Notes: E corrected from erroneous N. Die combination discovered in the Yale University collection and reported by Theodore V. Buttrey in *CNL*, January–March 1962. A second example was found by Jeff Rock. *Rarity:* URS-2.

W-3870 · Miller 33.35-Z.9
Rarity: URS-4.
 Selected auction price(s): Perkins Collection (1/2000), G–VG, $4,025.

W-3875 · Miller 33.36-T.1
Rarity: URS-6.

W-3900 · Miller 33.36-T.2
Rarity: URS-12.

G-4	VG-8	F-12	VF-20	EF-40	AU-50	MS-60
$50	$85	$140	$400	$1,000	$4,000	$7,500

W-3905 · Miller 33.36-T.3
Notes: Discovered by Ted Craige in November 1965, and reported in *CNL*, March–June 1966, then to Bowers / Pine Tree sale in 1975. Another rumored. *Rarity:* URS-2.

W-3910 · Miller 33.36-SS
Rarity: URS-3.

W-3915 · Miller 33.37-Z.9
Rarity: URS-8.

G-4	VG-8	F-12	VF-20	EF-40
$50	$85	$140	$400	$1,000

W-3920 · Miller 33.37-Z.11
Notes: One in ANS. *Rarity:* URS-4.
 Selected auction price(s): Perkins Collection (1/2000), VG, rough, $5,175.

W-3925 · Miller 33.38-Z.1 · INDE Over INDN
Notes: E corrected from erroneous N. *Rarity:* URS-7.
 Selected auction price(s): John J. Ford Jr. IX Sale (Stack's 5/2005), EF, rough, $2,990; AU, rough, $5,175.

W-3930 · Miller 33.38-Z.6
Rarity: URS-7.
 Selected auction price(s): John J. Ford Jr. IX Sale (Stack's 5/2005), F, rough, $1,725.

W-3935 · Miller 33.38-Z.18
Rarity: URS-3.

W-3940 · Miller 33.38-Z.23
Rarity: URS-7.
 Selected auction price(s): C4 Convention (M&G 11/2002), EF-45, $2,700. John J. Ford Jr. IX Sale (Stack's 5/2005), VF, $1,006.25.

W-3945 · Miller 33.38-gg.1 · ETLIR
Rarity: URS-6.
 Selected auction price(s): Perkins Collection (1/2000), F, $1,380. William O'Donnell (Stack's 1/2001), VF, $1,035.

W-3950 · Miller 33.39-Z.13
Notes: Discovered by Norman Bryant and reported to J.M. Richardson, who published it in Stack's *Numismatic Review*, 1946. *Rarity:* URS-5.
 Selected auction price(s): Perkins Collection (1/2000), VF, $10,350. C4 Convention (M&G 11/2002), F-12, $6,750.

W-3955 · Miller 33.39-Z.20
Rarity: URS-5.
 Selected auction price(s): Perkins Collection (1/2000), VG, $3,220. Public Auction Sale (Stack's 9/2005), VG, $1,955.

W-3960 · Miller 33.39-s.1
Rarity: URS-9.

G-4	VG-8	F-12	VF-20	EF-40
$50	$85	$140	$400	$1,000

W-3965 · Miller 33.40-Z.1 · INDE Over INDN
Notes: E corrected from erroneous N. *Rarity:* URS-7.
 Selected auction price(s): John J. Ford Jr. IX Sale (Stack's 5/2005), Choice EF, obverse cleaned, $1,150.

W-3970 · Miller 33.40-Z.2
Rarity: URS-6.
 Selected auction price(s): C4 Convention (M&G 11/2002), VF-30, $850; $1,000. John J. Ford Jr. IX Sale (Stack's 5/2005), EF, some flaws, $1,265.

W-3975 · Miller 33.41-Z.11
Rarity: URS-5.
 Selected auction price(s): Perkins Collection (1/2000), VF, granular, $4,025. John J. Ford Jr. IX Sale (Stack's 5/2005), VF, $8,625.

W-4000 · Miller 33.42-Z.2
Rarity: URS-5.
 Selected auction price(s): Perkins Collection (1/2000), F, flaws, $4,312.

W-4005 · Miller 33.43-q
Rarity: URS-7.

W-4010 · Miller 33.43-hh.2 · ETLIR
Rarity: URS-7.
 Selected auction price(s): Perkins Collection (1/2000), VF, $1,035. John J. Ford Jr. IX Sale (Stack's 5/2005), EF, minor problems, $2,185.

W-4015 · Miller 33.44-W.3
Rarity: URS-6.
 Selected auction price(s): Mail Bid Sale (Coin Galleries 7/2002), Choice EF, $1,265. Long Beach Sale (Heritage 9/2005), AU-50 (PCGS), $2,990.

W-4020 · Miller 33.45- W.2
Rarity: URS-6.
 Selected auction price(s): John J. Ford Jr. IX Sale (Stack's 5/2005), EF, cleaned and recolored, $2,530.

W-4025 · Miller 33.46-Z.21 · INDE Over IODE
Notes: Erroneous O changed to N. Die combination reported by Edward R. Barnsley in *CNL*, July 1961. One in ANS, two in the Taylor Collection, a fourth in the W.P. Keller Collection (*CNL*, May 1991). *Rarity:* URS-4.

W-4030 · Miller 33.46-Z.22 · INDE Over IODE
Notes: Erroneous O changed to N. Die combination reported by George C. Perkins in *CNL*, December 1989. Three known. *Rarity:* URS-3.
 Selected auction price(s): Perkins Collection (1/2000), F, $14,590.

W-4035 · Miller 33.47-TT
Notes: Discovered by Ted Craige in 1969 (*CNL*, September 1969). On reverse, first three cinquefoils altered from crosses. *Rarity:* URS-2.

W-4040 · Miller 33.48-Z.25
Notes: Discovered by Richard Picker in 1970 when he was cataloging the Massachusetts Historical Society Collection for Stack's. *Rarity:* URS-3.

W-4045 · Miller 33.49-Z.7
Notes: Reported by Ken Mote and Jeff Rock in *CNL*, November 1994. *Rarity:* URS-1.

W-4050 · Miller 33.50-Z.24
Notes: Reported by Ken Mote and Jeff Rock in *CNL*, April 1997. *Rarity:* URS-1.
Selected auction price(s): C4 Convention (M&G 11/2002), G-4, $3,600.

W-4055 · Miller 34-k.3
Rarity: URS-4.

W-4060 · Miller 34-ff.1 · ETLIR
Rarity: URS-7.
Selected auction price(s): Perkins Collection (1/2000), EF, $1,955. John J. Ford Jr. IX Sale (Stack's 5/2005), MS, $9,775.

W-4065 · Miller 36-k.3
Rarity: URS-4.

W-4070 · Miller 36-l.1
Rarity: URS-7.

W-4075 · Miller 36-ff.2 · ETLIR
Rarity: URS-6.
Selected auction price(s): Perkins Collection (1/2000), F, $2,530. Mail Bid Sale (Coin Galleries 4/2004), VG, $3,163. John J. Ford Jr. IX Sale (Stack's 5/2005), AU, rough, $5,175.

W-4100 · Miller 37.1-cc.1 · ETLIR
Rarity: URS-8.

G-4	VG-8	F-12	VF-20	EF-40
$55	$90	$190	$550	$1,450

W-4105 · Miller 37.2-k.5
Rarity: URS-7.
Selected auction price(s): C4 Convention (M&G 11/2002), EF-40, $2,500.

W-4110 · Miller 37.3-i
Rarity: URS-9.

G-4	VG-8	F-12	VF-20	EF-40
$50	$85	$140	$400	$1,000

W-4115 · Miller 37.4-k.1
Rarity: URS-9.

G-4	VG-8	F-12	VF-20	EF-40
$50	$85	$140	$400	$1,000

W-4120 · Miller 37.4-RR
Rarity: URS-1.
Selected auction price(s): John J. Ford Jr. IX Sale (Stack's 5/2005), VF, minor problems, $97,750.

W-4125 · Miller 37.5-e
Rarity: URS-8.

G-4	VG-8	F-12	VF-20	EF-40
$50	$85	$140	$400	$1,000

W-4130 · Miller 37.6-B
Rarity: URS-4.
Selected auction price(s): Perkins Collection (1/2000), VG–F, $3,737.50.

W-4135 · Miller 37.6-k.4 · Skeleton Hand
Notes: One of several "Skeleton Hand" varieties. *Rarity:* URS-7.
Selected auction price(s): Perkins Collection (1/2000), VF, $1,150. John J. Ford Jr. IX Sale (Stack's 5/2005), AU, flaws, $6,325.

W-4140 · Miller 37.7-h.2
Rarity: URS-6.
Selected auction price(s): Perkins Collection (1/2000), VF, $1,265.

W-4145 · Miller 37.8-HH
Rarity: URS-7.
Selected auction price(s): Pre–Long Beach Sale (Superior 6/2002), F-15, $2,123.

W-4150 · Miller 37.8-LL · ET-IIB
Notes: Reverse misspelling. *Rarity:* URS-7.
Selected auction price(s): C4 Convention (M&G 11/2002), $500.

W-4155 · Miller 37.8-k.2
Rarity: URS-7.

W-4160 · Miller 37.9-e
Rarity: URS-7.
Selected auction price(s): John J. Ford Jr. IX Sale (Stack's 5/2005), AU, $6,900.

W-4165 · Miller 37.10-RR
Rarity: URS-6.
Selected auction price(s): John J. Ford Jr. IX Sale (Stack's 5/2005), F–VF, Miller plate coin, cleaned and recolored, rough, flawed, $1,380.

W-4170 · Miller 37.11-ff.2 · ETLIR
Rarity: URS-7.
Selected auction price(s): John J. Ford Jr. IX Sale (Stack's 5/2005), F–VF, rough, $2,070.

W-4175 · Miller 37.12-LL · ET-IIB
Notes: Reverse misspelling. *Rarity:* URS-6.
Selected auction price(s): John J. Ford Jr. IX Sale (Stack's 5/2005), F–VF, $1,495.

W-4180 · Miller 37.12-TT
Notes: On reverse, first three cinquefoils altered from crosses. *Rarity:* URS-6.

W-4185 · Miller 37.13-HH
Rarity: URS-7.
　Selected auction price(s): John J. Ford Jr. IX Sale (Stack's 5/2005), EF, flaws, $1,380.

W-4190 · Miller 37.14-cc.2
Rarity: URS-6.
　Selected auction price(s): Perkins Collection (1/2000), VF, $3,220. Mail Bid Sale (Coin Galleries 4/2004), F, $1,208.

W-4195 · Miller 37.15-h.3
Notes: Not known in Miller in 1919, but identified soon thereafter. *Rarity:* URS-4.
　Selected auction price(s): C4 Convention (M&G 11/2002), G-6, $7,500.

W-4200 · Miller 38-I.2 · AUCIORI
Notes: Popular misspelling. Also see next. *Rarity:* URS-8.

W-4205 · Miller 38-GG · AUCIORI / Skeleton Hand
Notes: Popular AUCIORI misspelling. One of several "Skeleton Hand" reverse varieties. *Rarity:* URS-9.

G-4	VG-8	F-12	VF-20	EF-40
$50	$85	$170	$500	$1,200

W-4210 · Miller 39.1-h.1 · AUCTOBI
Notes: Popular misspelling. Also see next. *Rarity:* URS-7.

G-4	VG-8	F-12	VF-20	EF-40
$60	$100	$220	$675	$1,700

W-4215 · Miller 39.1-ff.2 · AUCTOBI / · ETLIR
Notes: Popular misspelling. *Rarity:* URS-7.

G-4	VG-8	F-12	VF-20	EF-40
$60	$100	$220	$675	$1,700

W-4220 · Miller 39.2-ee · AUCTOBI / · ETLIR
Notes: Very rare AUCTOBI obverse die. *Rarity:* URS-8.

G-4	VG-8	F-12	VF-20	EF-40
$60	$100	$220	$675	$1,700

W-4240 · Miller 40-N · AUCTOPI
Notes: Popular misspelling used on several varieties. *Rarity:* URS-6.
　Selected auction price(s): Perkins Collection (1/2000), F, $1,150. John J. Ford Jr. IX Sale (Stack's 5/2005), EF, Miller plate coin, rough, $5,750.

W-4230 · Miller 40-kk.1 · AUCTOPI
Notes: Popular misspelling. *Rarity:* URS-6.
　Selected auction price(s): Perkins Collection (1/2000), VG-F, $1,150.

W-4235 · Miller 41-ii · AUCTOPI / ETIIB
Notes: Rarest of the three "AUCTOPI" dies, its desirability compounded by the only use of the ETIIB error reverse. *Rarity:* URS-9.

G-4	VG-8	F-12	VF-20	EF-40
$60	$90	$190	$550	$1,450

W-4240 · Miller 42-o · AUCTOPI
Notes: Scarce "AUCTOPI" die. Also used on next. *Rarity:* URS-4.
　Selected auction price(s): Perkins Collection (1/2000), VG-F, $7,762.50. John J. Ford Jr. IX Sale (Stack's 5/2005), Choice F, some problems, $13,800.

W-4245 · Miller 42-kk.2 · AUCTOPI
Rarity: URS-8.

G-4	VG-8	F-12	VF-20	EF-40
$60	$100	$220	$700	$1,750

W-4250 · Miller 43.1-Y · CONNFC
Notes: Popular misspelling. Readily available. *Rarity:* URS-11.

G-4	VG-8	F-12	VF-20	EF-40
$55	$85	$175	$550	$1,200

W-4255 · Miller 43.2-X.4 · CONNFC
Notes: Second and rarer "CONNFC" die; this was later corrected to become obverse 32.3. *Rarity:* URS-7.

W-4260 · Miller 44-W.4
Rarity: URS-8.

G-4	VG-8	F-12	VF-20	EF-40
$50	$85	$140	$400	$1,000

W-4290 · Miller 44-W.5
Rarity: URS-6.
　Selected auction price(s): Perkins Collection (1/2000), VG-F, $1,840. John J. Ford Jr. IX Sale (Stack's 5/2005), VG-F, cleaned, pitted, $1,495.

W-4295 · Miller 44-Z.10
Rarity: URS-6.
　Selected auction price(s): Perkins Collection (1/2000), VF, $1,265. John J. Ford Jr. IX Sale (Stack's 5/2005), VG-F, $1,150.

W-4300 · Miller 45-CC
Rarity: URS-7.
　Selected auction price(s): Perkins Collection (1/2000), VF, "Hapsburg Jaw variety," $2,185.

W-4305 · Miller 46-BB
Rarity: URS-7.
　Selected auction price(s): Perkins Collection (1/2000), VF, Miller plate coin, 1,380. Logan & Steinberg Collections (B&M 11/2002), EF-40, $2,530. John J. Ford Jr. IX Sale (Stack's 5/2005), VF, $1,265.

W-4310 · Miller 47-a.3
Rarity: URS-5.
　Selected auction price(s): John J. Ford Jr. IX Sale (Stack's 5/2005), F, some roughness, $1,725.

W-4315 · Miller 48-g.5
Rarity: URS-7.

W-4305 · Miller 48-k.3
Notes: Reported by Robert A. Vlack in *CNL*, April–June 1967. *Rarity:* URS-4.
  Selected auction price(s): Perkins Collection (1/2000), VF/VG, $4,600.

W-4310 · Miller 49.1-Z.1 · INDE Over INDN
Notes: E corrected from erroneous N. *Rarity:* URS-5.

W-4315 · Miller 49.2-Z.1 · INDE Over INDN
Notes: E corrected from erroneous N. Die combination discovered by Michael J. Hodder. Extremely Fine grade (*CNL*, February 1993). *Rarity:* URS-1.

W-4320 · Miller 49.2-Z.26
Notes: Discovered by Stephen Tanenbaum in 1986. (*CNL*, May 1991). *Rarity:* URS-1.

W-4325 · Miller 49.2-Z.27
Notes: Discovered by Chris Young (*C4 Newsletter*, Fall 2007). Fine, holed. *Rarity:* URS-1.

W-4330 · Miller 50-F · CONNLC
Notes: In the 1975 Pine Tree sale Walter Breen stated that lot 82 was the first of this variety auctioned in more than 50 years. *Rarity:* URS-6.
  Selected auction price(s): Mail Bid Sale (Coin Galleries 4/2004), VF, $2,128. John J. Ford Jr. IX Sale (Stack's 5/2005), VG–F, rough, $1,955.

W-4335 · Miller 53-FF
Rarity: URS-7.
  Selected auction price(s): C4 Convention (M&G 11/2001), VF-20, $800. Henry Leon Sale (Stack's 5/2007), MS-60BN, $2,530.

W-4340 · Miller 56-XX
Notes: Also known as Miller 56-RR (*CNL*, May 1991). Discovered and described by C.F. Luther in 1928, but not given a designation until years later. *Rarity:* URS-5.

Easy Finding Guide
1788 Mailed Bust Right Obverse Dies

AUCTORI / CONNEC

Miller 1 · Legend and punctuation diagnostic. *Used for:* W-4400, Miller 1-I.

❋ AUCTORI. / CONNEC ❋

Miller 2 · Legend and punctuation diagnostic. *Used for:* W-4405, Miller 2-D.

❋ AUCTORI ❋ / ❋ CONNEC ❋

Miller 3 · Legend and punctuation diagnostic. *Used for:* W-4410, Miller 3-B.1. W-4415, Miller 3-B.2.

AUCTORI ❋ / ❋ CONNEC ❋

Miller 4.1 · Both fillets are outlined. Tip of wreath about even with highest point of star to right. Diagnostic. *Used for:* W-4420, Miller 4.1-B.1. W-4425, Miller 4.1-B.2. W-4430, Miller 4.1-K.

Miller 4.2 · Both fillets are solid. Tip of wreath far above star to right. Diagnostic. *Used for:* W-4435, Miller 4.2-R.

✸ AUCTORI ✸ / ✸ CONNEC ✿

Miller 5 · Legend and punctuation diagnostic. *Used for:* W-4440, Miller 5-B.2.

AUCTORI ✸ / ✸ CONNEC ✸

Miller 6 · Legend and punctuation diagnostic. *Used for:* W-4445, Miller 6-H.

Easy Finding Guide
1788 Mailed Bust Left Obverse Dies

✣ AUCTORI ✸ / ✸ CONNEC ✸

Miller 7 · Legend and punctuation diagnostic. *Used for:* W-4480, Miller 7-E. W-4485, Miller 7-F.2. W-4490, Miller 7-K.

AUCTORI. ✿ / CONNEC ✿

Miller 8 · Legend and punctuation diagnostic. *Used for:* W-4495, Miller 8-K.

AUCTORI / CONNEC ✸

Miller 9 · Legend and punctuation diagnostic. *Used for:* W-4500, Miller 9-E.

AUCTORI ✸ / ✸ CONNEC ✸

Miller 10 · Legend and punctuation diagnostic. *Used for:* W-4505, Miller 10-C.

✸ AUCTORI / ✸ CONNEC ✸

Miller 11 · Legend and punctuation diagnostic. *Used for:* W-4510, Miller 11-G.

✸ AUCTORI ✸ / ✸ CONNEC ✸

Miller 12.1 · Upper fillet points downward and is distant from star. Diagnostic. *Used for:* W-4515, Miller 12.1-E. W-4520, Miller 12.1-F.1.

Miller 12.2 · Upper fillet points to star and is close to it. Diagnostic. *Used for:* W-4525, Miller 12.2-C. W-4530, Miller 12.2-E.

✿ AUCTORI ✿ / ✿ CONNLC ✿

Miller 13 · **CONNLC** · Misspelling diagnostic. *Used for:* W-4535, Miller 13-A.1.

153

Easy Finding Guide
1788 Draped Bust Obverse Dies

❁ AUCTORI ❁ / ❁ CONNEC ❁

Miller 14.1 · Two lobes of cinquefoil touch top of head. Diagnostic. *Used for:* W-4570, Miller 14.1-L.2. W-4575, Miller 14.1-S.

Miller 14.2 · Cinquefoil separated from head with one lobe pointing toward it. Diagnostic. *Used for:* W-4580, Miller 14.2-A.2.

❁ AUCTORI ❁ / ❁ CONNEC. ❁

Miller 15.1 · Last cinquefoil below edge of toga and opposite opening. Diagnostic. *Used for:* W-4585, Miller 15.1-L.1.

Miller 15.2 · Last cinquefoil above toga. Diagnostic. *Used for:* W-4590, Miller 15.2-P.

❁ AUCTORI. ❁ / ❁ CONNEC. ❁

Miller 16.1 · First cinquefoil about half under bust. AU on same level. Cinquefoil distant from first C (in CONNEC); C close to head or touching it; second C distant and low. Diagnostic. *Used for:* W-4595, Miller 16.1-D. W-4600, Miller 16.1-H.

Miller 16.2 · First cinquefoil to left of bust. CO above head, fillet opposite dot and below dot. Diagnostic. *Used for:* W-4605, Miller 16.2-O.

Miller 16.3 · First cinquefoil mostly under bust. Large dot after I is about equidistant from I and cinquefoil. Diagnostic. *Used for:* W-4610, Miller 16.3-N.

Miller 16.4 · First cinquefoil to left of bust. C above head, fillet ends opposite above and below dot. Diagnostic. *Used for:* W-4615, Miller 16.4-A.2. W-4620, Miller 16.4-L.2.

Miller 16.5 · First cinquefoil about half under bust. A higher than U. Cinquefoil, C and O about the same distance apart. Diagnostic. *Used for:* W-4625, Miller 16.5-H.

Miller 16.7 · First cinquefoil mostly under bust. Fillet ends opposite last cinquefoil. Diagnostic. *Used for:* W-4630, Miller 16.7-P.

❁ AUCTORI. ❁ / ❁ CONNLC. ❁

Miller 17 · **CONNLC** · Misspelling diagnostic. *Used for:* W-4635, Miller 17-O. W-4640, Miller 17-Q.

Easy Finding Guide
1788 Reverse Dies

❋ INDE ❋ ET ❋ / ❋❋ LIB ❋

Miller A.1 · Branch hand normal. 1 and second 8 slightly high. Diagnostic. *Used for:* W-4535, Miller 13-A.1.

Miller A.2 · Branch hand becomes very thin near branch. In date, 1 very high; 7 lower; 8's very low and lean right. Diagnostic. *Used for:* W-4580, Miller 14.2-A.2. W-4615, Miller 16.4-A.2.

INDE ❋ ET / LIB ❖

Miller B.1 · Branch hand opposite right part of E; star opposite base of E. In date, 1 leans right and is close to 7. Diagnostic. *Used for:* W-4410, Miller 3-B.1. W-4420, Miller 4.1-B.1.

Miller B.2 · Branch hand opposite E; star opposite center of E. In date, 1 upright and distant from 7. Diagnostic. *Used for:* W-4415, Miller 3-B.2. W-4425, Miller 4.1-B.2. W-4440, Miller 5-B.2.

INDE ❋ ET / LIB ❋

Miller C · Legend and punctuation diagnostic. *Used for:* W-4505, Miller 10-C. W-4525, Miller 12.2-C.

INDE ❋ ET ❋ / LIB ❋

Miller D · Legend and punctuation diagnostic. Die for counterfeit English halfpenny Vlack 13-88CT (W-8080). *Used for:* W-4405, Miller 2-D. W-4595, Miller 16.1-D.

INDE ❋ ET ❋ / ❋ LIB ❖

Miller E · Legend and punctuation diagnostic. *Used for:* W-4480, Miller 7-E. W-4500, Miller 9-E. W-4515, Miller 12.1-E. W-4530, Miller 12.2-E.

INDE ❋ ET ❋ / ❋ / LIB ❋

Miller F.1 · In date, 17 high and into date line. Diagnostic. *Used for:* W-4520, Miller 12.1-F.1.

Miller F.2 · In date, 17 below date line. Diagnostic. *Used for:* W-4485, Miller 7-F.2.

INDE ❋ ET ❋ / ❋ LIB ❋

Miller G · Legend and punctuation diagnostic. *Used for:* W-4510, Miller 11-G.

❂ INDE · ❂❂ / ❂ ETLIB · ❂

Miller H · Legend and punctuation diagnostic. *Used for:* W-4445, Miller 6-H. W-4600, Miller 16.1-H. W-4625, Miller 16.5-H.

INDE ✖ / ET · LIB ✖

Miller I · Legend and punctuation diagnostic. *Used for:* W-4400, Miller 1-I (a.k.a. Vermont RR-39).

✱ INDE ✱ / ET ✱ LIB ✱

Miller K · Legend and punctuation diagnostic. *Used for:* W-4430, Miller 4.1-K. W-4490, Miller 7-K. W-4495, Miller 8-K.

❂ INDE · ET ❂ / ❂ LIB. ❂

Miller L.1 · Base of ET on same level. In date, 1 higher than 7; 88 upright. Diagnostic. *Used for:* W-4585, Miller 15.1-L.1.

Miller L.2 · Base of E higher than T. In date, 1 higher than highest part of 7; 88 lean left. Diagnostic. *Used for:* W-4570, Miller 14.1-L.2. W-4620, Miller 16.4-L.2.

❂ IN DE · ❂❂ / ❂❂ ETLIB. ❂

Miller N · Legend and punctuation diagnostic. *Used for:* W-4610, Miller 16.3-N.

❂ INDL. ET ❂❂ / ❂ / ❂ LIB. ❂

Miller O · **INDL** · Legend and punctuation diagnostic. *Used for:* W-4605, Miller 16.2-O. W-4635, Miller 17-O.

❂ INDE · ET ❂❂ / ❂ / ❂ LIB. ❂

Miller P · Legend and punctuation diagnostic. *Used for:* W-4590, Miller 15.2-P. W-4630, Miller 16.7-P.

❂ INDE · ET ❂ / ❂ / ❂ LIB. ❂

Miller Q · Legend and punctuation diagnostic. *Used for:* W-4640, Miller 17-Q.

✱ INDE ✱ / ✱ ET ✱ LIB ✱

Miller R · Legend and punctuation diagnostic. *Used for:* W-4435, Miller 4.2-R.

❂ INDE ❂ ET ❂ / ❂ / ❂ LIB.

Miller S · Legend and punctuation diagnostic. *Used for:* W-4575, Miller 14.1-S.

1788 Connecticut Coppers

1788 Mailed Bust Right

W-4400 (same as W-2265) · Miller 1-I · Vermont reverse die

Notes: Reverse die also used for W-2265 (RR-39, Bressett 25-U) of Vermont. Also used on several other Vermont varieties. The obverse is also known as Miller 1787 1.1. Always weak at the center, from buckled dies. Usually in low grades. *Rarity:* URS-7.

Selected auction price(s): Perkins Collection (1/2000), G/Fair, $1,840. C4 Convention (M&G 11/2001), VG-8, $5,500. C4 Convention (M&G 11/2002), F-15, $11,500. John J. Ford Jr. IX Sale (Stack's 5/2005), F, rough, $14,950. Long Beach Sale (Heritage 9/2005), VG/Fair, $4,025.

G-4	VG-8	F-12	VF-20	EF-40
$1,000	$4,000	$10,000	$15,000	$20,000

W-4405 · Miller 2-D

Rarity: URS-12.

Selected auction price(s): John J. Ford Jr. IX Sale (Stack's 5/2005), MS, $5,175. Palm Beach Auction (Heritage 3/2006), AU-50 (PCGS), $4,025. Denver Auction (Heritage 8/2006), ex Ford, MS-62BN (PCGS), $19,550.

W-4410 · Miller 3-B.1

Rarity: URS-7.

Selected auction price(s): Perkins Collection (1/2000), F, $2,990. Jewell Collection (Stack's [ANR] 3/2005), VF-20, $1,725.

W-4415 · Miller 3-B.2

Notes: The 1975 Pine Tree sale coin (lot 289) was overstruck on a 1785 Nova Constellatio (possibly Crosby 4-C). *Rarity:* URS-6.

Selected auction price(s): Perkins Collection (1/2000), VF, $3,737.50. John J. Ford Jr. IX Sale (Stack's 5/2005), F, over a Nova Constellatio, $14,950. CSNS Sale (Heritage 4/2006), VF-20 (PCGS), $1,265.

W-4420 · Miller 4.1-B.1

Notes: Some are overstruck on Nova Constellatio coppers. *Rarity:* URS-7.

Selected auction price(s): Perkins Collection (1/2000), G–VF, $1,265. C4 Convention (M&G 11/2002), VF-35, $1,200. John J. Ford Jr. IX Sale (Stack's 5/2005), Choice AU, $9,775.

W-4425 · Miller 4.1-B.2

Notes: Unique. Collection of the American Numismatic Society. *Rarity:* URS-1.

W-4430 · Miller 4.1-K

Rarity: URS-7.

Selected auction price(s): Perkins Collection (1/2000), EF or finer, $2,300. John J. Ford Jr. IX Sale (Stack's 5/2005), Choice AU, $5,750.

W-4435 · Miller 4.2-R

Notes: All seen are over Nova Constellatio coppers. *Rarity:* URS-6.

Selected auction price(s): Perkins Collection (1/2000), VG/AG, $3,737.50. John J. Ford Jr. IX Sale (Stack's 5/2005), F, $4,600. Mail / Internet Bid Sale (Coin Galleries 12/2005), About Fair–AG, $1,323.

W-4440 · Miller 5-B.2

Notes: The 1975 Pine Tree sale coin (lot 290) was overstruck on a 1785 Nova Constellatio (Crosby 5-E). *Rarity:* URS-8.

G-4	VG-8	F-12	VF-20	EF-40
$50	$100	$220	$700	$1,750

W-4445 · Miller 6-H

Rarity: URS-7.

Selected auction price(s): Perkins Collection (1/2000), VF, $1,150. O'Donnell Collection (Stack's 1/2001), VF, $1,495. John J. Ford Jr. IX Sale (Stack's 5/2005), MS, Miller plate coin, $19,550.

1788 Mailed Bust Left

W-4480 · Miller 7-E

Rarity: URS-8.

G-4	VG-8	F-12	VF-20	EF-40
$50	$80	$175	$550	$1,200

W-4485 · Miller 7-F.2

Rarity: URS-6.

Selected auction price(s): John J. Ford Jr. IX Sale (Stack's 5/2005), VF, rough, $1,725.

W-4490 · Miller 7-K

Rarity: URS-5.

Selected auction price(s): Perkins Collection (1/2000), F, $6,325. John J. Ford Jr. IX Sale (Stack's 5/2005), G–VG, flaws, $6,900.

W-4495 · Miller 8-K

Rarity: URS-5.

Selected auction price(s): Perkins Collection (1/2000), F–G, $4,025. C4 Convention (M&G 11/2002), F-12, $11,000. John J. Ford Jr. IX Sale (Stack's 5/2005), Choice VF, $23,000.

W-4500 · Miller 9-E

Rarity: URS-8.

G-4	VG-8	F-12	VF-20	EF-40
$50	$80	$175	$550	$1,200

W-4505 · Miller 10-C

Notes: Typically overstruck on a Nova Constellatio copper. *Rarity:* URS-7.

Selected auction price(s): John J. Ford Jr. IX Sale (Stack's 5/2005), MS, over Nova Constellatio, $12,650.

W-4510 · Miller 11-G

Rarity: URS-11.

G-4	VG-8	F-12	VF-20	EF-40
$50	$80	$175	$550	$1,200

W-4515 · Miller 12.1-E
Rarity: URS-8.

G-4	VG-8	F-12	VF-20	EF-40
$50	$80	$175	$550	$1,200

W-4520 · Miller 12.1-F.1
Rarity: URS-8.

G-4	VG-8	F-12	VF-20	EF-40
$50	$80	$175	$550	$1,200

W-4525 · Miller 12.2-C
Rarity: URS-8.

G-4	VG-8	F-12	VF-20	EF-40
$50	$80	$175	$550	$1,200

W-4530 · Miller 12.2-E
Rarity: URS-6.

Selected auction price(s): C4 Convention (M&G 11/2001), AU-50, $4,600. C4 Convention (M&G 11/2002), F-12, $625. John J. Ford Jr. IX Sale (Stack's 5/2005), AU, $8,050.

W-4535 · Miller 13-A.1 · CONNLC
Notes: Popular error obverse die. *Rarity:* URS-8.

G-4	VG-8	F-12	VF-20	EF-40
$70	$145	$300	$800	$2,300

1788 Draped Bust

W-4570 · Miller 14.1-L.2
Notes: With large die break across coin below of center; substantial pieces out of the die. *Rarity:* URS-6.

Selected auction price(s): C4 Convention (M&G 11/2002), VF-30, $700. John J. Ford Jr. IX Sale (Stack's 5/2005), EF, rough, $1,725

W-4575 · Miller 14.1-S
Notes: Discovered by Theodore V. Buttrey, 1962. Not in Miller. *Rarity:* URS-4.

W-4580 · Miller 14.2-A.2
Rarity: URS-8.

G-4	VG-8	F-12	VF-20	EF-40
$55	$85	$220	$550	$1,350

W-4585 · Miller 15.1-L.1
Rarity: URS-9.

G-4	VG-8	F-12	VF-20	EF-40
$55	$85	$220	$550	$1,350

W-4590 · Miller 15.2-P
Rarity: URS-7.

Selected auction price(s): John J. Ford Jr. IX Sale (Stack's 5/2005), VF, some problems, $1,380.

W-4595 · Miller 16.1-D
Rarity: URS-10.

G-4	VG-8	F-12	VF-20	EF-40
$55	$85	$220	$550	$1,350

W-4600 · Miller 16.1-H
Rarity: URS-9.

G-4	VG-8	F-12	VF-20	EF-40
$55	$85	$220	$550	$1,350

W-4605 · Miller 16.2-O · INDL
Notes: Reverse misspelling. *Rarity:* URS-7.

Selected auction price(s): John J. Ford Jr. IX Sale (Stack's 5/2005), EF, some problems, $3,450.

W-4610 · Miller 16.3-N
Notes: Some are struck over 1787 Ryder 1-B Massachusetts contemporary counterfeit cents (Philip Mossman records nine examples; see W-6030). *Rarity:* URS-11.

G-4	VG-8	F-12	VF-20	EF-40
$55	$85	$220	$550	$1,350

W-4615 · Miller 16.4-A.2
Notes: Discovered by Theodore V. Buttrey, 1962. *Rarity:* URS-3.

W-4620 · Miller 16.4-L.2
Rarity: URS-7.

Selected auction price(s): John J. Ford Jr. IX Sale (Stack's 5/2005), Choice VF, Miller plate coin, $4,600.

W-4625 · Miller 16.5-H
Rarity: URS-7.

Selected auction price(s): John J. Ford Jr. IX Sale (Stack's 5/2005), AU, $4,025; MS, $4,312.50.

W-4630 · Miller 16.7-P
Notes: Erroneously listed by Miller as 15.3-P. Nearly all are well worn. *Rarity:* URS-5.

Selected auction price(s): Perkins Collection (1/2000), technically F, $3,737.50.

W-4635 · Miller 17-O · CONNLC / INDL
Notes: Misspelled obverse and reverse. Unique. ANS Collection. *Rarity:* URS-1.

W-4640 · Miller 17-Q · CONNLC
Notes: Misspelled obverse. *Rarity:* URS-7.

Selected auction price(s): John J. Ford Jr. IX Sale (Stack's 5/2005), Choice AU, $20,700.

New Jersey Coppers 1786–1788

Mints and Minting

On June 1, 1786, primarily through the efforts of Matthias Ogden, the Council and General Assembly of New Jersey granted a coining privilege to a group of entrepreneurs composed of Walter Mould, Thomas Goadsby, and Albion Cox. Goadsby was a businessman and investor, and Cox, later employed by the Philadelphia Mint, was a skilled silversmith and assayer. Ogden was involved later at his home in Elizabethtown. Ogden, who had served with distinction in the Revolution, was a stage-line owner who had a contract for delivering mail between New York City and Philadelphia. It was specified that 3,000,000 copper coins be produced, each weighing 150 grains of pure copper. Inscriptions were to be provided by the justices of the state supreme court. These were to be valued in commerce at the rate of 15 to a New Jersey shilling. The coiners were to pay to the state on a quarterly basis a royalty of 10 percent of the coins struck. The contract was to be in effect for two years. Although it probably would have made the best economic sense to pay the state in newly minted coppers, the percentage could have been in gold or silver as well.

Historian Damon G. Douglas related that the first coinage by Mould, Goadsby, and Cox took place in Rahway, in mills leased from Daniel Marsh for an annual rent of £130. The facility was on the south bank of the Rahway River and was supplied with water power. The mint included equipment for casting ingots and rolling strip. One coining press was used. Presumably, coinage commenced by the autumn of 1786.

On November 17, 1786, Goadsby and Cox petitioned the General Assembly to give them separately a two-thirds interest in the business, with Walter Mould to independently conduct the remaining third. This bill was passed on November 22. Goadsby and Cox obtained the right to coin £6,666 13s 4d worth of coppers. Mould was given the separate right to coin a third of the total amount, or £3,333 6s 8d value. Walter Mould's mint was located in Morristown, New Jersey, while Goadsby and Cox remained in Rahway. The first quarterly payment of royalties by Mould was receipted for on May 8, 1787.

New Jersey copper of 1787. (Engraving by John Gavit for Hickcox, *An Historical Account of American Coinage*, 1858)

The Morristown mint and a later mint in Elizabethtown, which apparently superseded that at Rahway, were described in a letter dated August 8, 1855, from W. C. Baker to Charles I. Bushnell:

> There were two mint-houses in this state. One located in Morristown, and the other in Elizabethtown. The mint house of the former place, which is still standing, was the residence of John Cleve Symmes, chief justice of the state of New Jersey, uncle to John Cleve Symmes, author of *The Hole at the North Pole* [popularizing the theory of concentric spheres] and father-in-law of Gen. William H. Harrison, president of the United States. The residence was called "Solitude." It was at one time occupied by Mr. Holloway, and is known by some as the "Holloway House." The mint here was carried on by Walter Mould, an Englishman, who previous to his coming to America, had been employed in a similar way in Birmingham. In the coinage of the New Jersey coppers, a screw with a long lever was employed. This information is vouched for by Mr. Lewis Condict, of Morristown, who saw the mint in operation.
>
> The building in Elizabethtown, used as a mint-house, is near to the house formerly occupied by Col. Francis Barber, of the Revolutionary Army, and is known as the "Old Armstrong House." It is still standing and is situated in Water Street, and the coins were made in a shed back of the main building. The coining here was carried on by a man named Gilbert Rindle, probably for the account of Messrs. Goadsby and Cox. I have this from Mrs. — of Elizabethtown, who remembers the circumstance.

Later, the Rahway minting equipment was moved to Matthias Ogden's residence in Elizabethtown, where coinage continued in a room behind the kitchen. It is theorized that, in the absence of water power to drive machinery for strip and planchet preparation, the coins made there were struck over other coppers of lesser commercial value, acquired at a discount.

Bushnell mentioned another New Jersey coiner:

> Mr. J.R. Halsted informed me some 20 years ago that an acquaintance of his knew a Mr. Hatfield, who claimed to have made dies and coined New Jersey coppers, in a barn (Mr. Halsted thought) below Elizabethtown, in striking which he was assisted by a Negro.

Ray Williams (correspondence) suggested that the preceding may refer to the Rahway mint, a facility unknown to Bushnell (it was Damon G. Douglas who discovered it and published the information in the *Proceedings of the New Jersey Historical Society*, vol. 69, no. 3, July 1951).

Bushnell possessed a copy of an affidavit of John Bailey, who, it appears, also was involved in the coinage of New Jersey coppers, likely a subcontractor for Walter Mould, pursuing ordinary business and complying with state regulations:

City of New York,

Personally appeared before me, Jeremiah Wool, one of the Aldermen of the said City. John Bailey, of the said City of New York, cutler, who being duly sworn, deposeth and saith That since the fifteenth day of April 1788 he hath not either by himself or others, made or struck any coppers bearing the impression of those circulated by the state of New Jersey, commonly called Jersey coppers; and that what he so made previous to the said fifteenth of April was in conformity to, and by authority derived from, an Act of the State of New Jersey entitled, An Act for the Establishment of a Coinage of Copper" in that state, passed June the first, 1786.

(signed) John Bailey.

Sworn this first day of August 1789 Before me, Jeremiah Wool, alderman.

John H. Hickcox, of Albany, New York, who in 1858 wrote *An Historical Account of American Coinage*, received a letter from F.B. Chetwood, of Elizabeth, New Jersey, dated March 19, 1858:

My mother, the daughter of Col. Francis Barber, is now seventy-six years old and says that all of her recollection of the subject of your inquiry is that when she was a child ten or twelve years old she used to go into the house on the adjoining premises to her father's residence in this place to see them make coppers. The business was carried on in a room behind the kitchen, by Gilbert Rindle and a person whose name she thinks is Cox.

The modus operandi was as follows: in the middle of the room was a wooden box or pit sunk in the floor several feet deep, in the middle of which pit was placed an iron die, the top of which was about level with the floor of the room. A workman sat on the floor, with his legs inside the pit. He placed the smooth coppers on the die, and when stamped, brushed them off the die into the pit. The impression on the copper was made by a screw-press, which was worked by two men, one on each end of an iron bar or horizontal lever, attached to the screw at the center of its length, which was about nine or ten feet long.

My mother thinks it was in operation only a year or two, but her recollection on this point is not very reliable. The copper was brought to that house, all finished, as she thinks, except the stamping. She has no recollection at all of any other branch of the business being carried on there. She recollects that the copper when coined was put into kegs and sent off somewhere, and that her mother used to purchase a bureau drawer nearly full at a time, and pay them out in daily use for household expenses.

In addition to the pieces produced at various locations in New Jersey and by Bailey in New York City, some numismatists have stated that Machin's Mills produced coppers bearing the New Jersey design, but no facts have been found to substantiate this. Various other counterfeiters and imitators produced still other varieties, mostly of very crude workmanship.

Although numismatists can now identify with reasonable certainty some of the varieties of coppers that were produced at the Morristown mint, studies are continuing on ascribing the coppers minted at Rahway, Elizabethtown, and other locations.

The coppers panic of 1789 reduced the value of nearly all small change in this metal. Those with the New Jersey imprint were valued higher than most of the others as they were accepted for tax payments in the state, making it profitable to overstrike such coins with New Jersey dies, an activity that may have continued into early 1790, per Damon G. Douglas. The *American Journal of Numismatics*, March 1870, included this under "Transactions of Societies":

March 3, 1870, Boston Numismatic Society. Dr. S.A. Green read the following paper: In Samuel Davis' "Journal of a Tour to Connecticut," in 1789, (*Proceedings Mass. Hist. Soc.* for April 1869) allusion is made to the copper coinage of the states. In speaking of New Haven. Davis says, "We find some difficulty in making change in this place. Coppers pass at six the penny. Even those graced with the legend 'Auctori Conn.' are included. Feel chagrined that old Massachusetts, with his bow and arrow, should be under-valued. New York regulates their trade. The crown passes there, and here now, at 6s. 9d." While speaking of the New York fruit-market, he says that "coppers pass at twenty-four the shilling, only the Jersey coinage are current in the market." Of Voluntown, Conn., he says that "coppers pass at forty-eight the shilling, to those going east, as they pass thus at Providence."

On June 3, 1794, the widow of Matthias Ogden sold a coining press to the Philadelphia Mint for $47.44, as noted on page 75 of Frank Stewart's *History of the First United States Mint*.

Description of the New Jersey Coppers

New Jersey coppers were produced with a single motif, but with variations, based on the state arms. The obverse depicts a truncated horse head, usually facing to the right (although on a few varieties it faces to the left), with a plow below, and the inscription NOVA CÆSAREA ("New Caesar," from the Isle of Caesar, or Isle of Jersey) surrounding, with Æ as a ligature. The name NOVA CÆSAREA was first used in the original 1664 indenture specifying the boundaries of New Jersey, written by Charles II. The agrarian design is adapted from the state seal designed by Pierre du Simitière. The date—1786, 1787, or 1788—appears near the bottom rim. A rare style of 1786 has the date under the plow beam rather than at the bottom border. Attached to the front of the plow beam is a singletree, also called a whiffletree (or, inaccurately, a swingletree), a pivoted swinging bar to which the traces of a horse can be attached. This is seen on all New Jersey copper varieties.

1787 New Jersey copper variety Maris 56-n struck over a 1787 New York George Clinton / Excelsior copper (W-5970), a variety much rarer than the New Jersey coin it produced.

The coulter, a vertical knife or blade mounted on the plow beam, broke the earth in advance of the plowshare, and is a feature of most New Jersey coppers. Exceptions are the 1786 Date Under Plow Beam varieties and the related issues known as Coulterless. These are thought to have been the first coppers coined.

The reverse displays a shield in the center with E PLURIBUS UNUM surrounding, the first coin to use America's national motto. A few have ornamentation, such as sprigs or a running fox.

Many New Jersey coins were produced by overstriking Connecticut coppers, Irish halfpence, counterfeit English halfpence, and other pieces, probably because these could be bought at a sharp discount in comparison to the going rate in commerce for New Jersey issues. Such coins were ready-made planchets not requiring melting, casting, rolling, and cutting. Particularly notable in this regard is the 1787 Maris 56-n variety.

Dr. Edward Maris

New Jersey coppers attracted the attention of early writers, including John Hickcox, Montroville W. Dickeson, and Sylvester S. Crosby, whose works are commented upon in the Connecticut section of this chapter.

In 1881, *A Historic Sketch of the Coins of New Jersey With a Plate*, by Dr. Edward Maris (March 15, 1832–June 13, 1900), was published. This was an elephant-folio-size production, large and unwieldy, but eminently useful. Matching coins to the plates is quite easy. Described were more than 110 die varieties of New Jersey coppers plus a brief description of the imported "Mark Newby" coins (generally referred to as St. Patrick's coinage today). Maris was the first serious student of New Jersey coppers. His personal collection of them was sold at auction and eventually went to Baltimore & Ohio Railroad scion T. Harrison Garrett. Today, die varieties of New Jersey coppers are still described by Maris's alphanumerical designations, with many new discoveries added in the subsequent generations.

Maris, a physician, was very knowledgeable in several branches of numismatics and was a respected authority in his time. His interest in coins began in the late 1850s, an era of growth in the hobby spurred by the discontinuation of the old copper "large" cents in January 1857. His interest piqued, his first endeavor was to obtain as many dates of cents as he could find. Within a few years he became well read on the subject and formed collections in other areas. On page 193 of the 1876 volume of the *Coin Collector's Journal*, we find that Edward Maris, Joseph J. Mickley, Montroville W. Dickeson, and others were allowed access to "thousands" of old coppers being turned in to the Mint in exchange for the new Flying Eagle cents. In 1866 Maris sold his main collection of federal coins and devoted his interest to ancient and foreign coins, early American and colonial coins and paper money, and historical medals.

In 1869 his *Varieties of the Copper Issues of the United States Mint in the Year 1794* was published. This charming work described the dies and, for the cents, assigned names (some of which derived from medicine and mythology): Double Chin, Sans Milling, Tilted 4, Young Head, The Coquette, Crooked 7, Pyramidal Head, Mint Marked Head, Scarred Head, Standless 4, Abrupt Hair, Severed Hairs, The Ornate, Venus Marina, Fallen 4, Short Bust, Egeria (an elusive nymph who inspired Numa Pompilius), Patagonian, Nondescript, Amatory Face, Large Planchet, Marred Field, Distant 1, Shielded Hair, The Plicae (for a group of varieties), Roman Plica, and '95 Head. Significantly, this was the first extensive text published on die varieties for any American coin series.

In the meantime, Maris was a busy figure in the numismatic scene in Philadelphia. In 1873 he unexpectedly came upon 11 hitherto unknown copper-nickel Confederate States of America cents made on contract in 1861 by engraver Robert Lovett Jr., as a proposal for a Southern coinage. These were publicized afterward, with most of the credit going to local dealer John W. Haseltine, who handled many of them. Maris assisted with coin attributions and auction cataloging for his own consignments and for other dealers.

In *The Numismatist*, January 1895, as part of "A Tour Among the Coin Dealers," Augustus G. Heaton described Maris as being "rather advanced in age" and occupying a large, plain dwelling in the lower part of Philadelphia. "The genial doctor is one of the kindest and most conscientious of men. He is rather tall and spare, has a prominent nose and a face of generally strong character, clean shaven, except short side whiskers." He was a member of the Society of Friends (Quakers), it was reported, and was respected for his great moral character. Earlier he was a coin dealer on a casual basis, having had occasional collections given to him on consignment.

Numismatic Aspects

In the years after Maris's 1881 book, numismatic interest continued in the New Jersey copper series. Most often, representative dates and types were collected. Interest in specialized die varieties was minimal, and often Crosby's 1875 book was the guide, as only about 115 or 120 copies of Maris's study had been distributed.

In 1925, Julius and Henry Guttag published a guide to New Jersey coppers illustrated with high-quality line drawings taken from a combination of the Dr. Jacob Spiro Collection and Maris's original text. Several new varieties were described. In the *Colonial Newsletter*, December 1997, Roger Moore gave this update:

> The last hundred years have witnessed reprints of Dr. Maris's original work, modified reprints with an updating of the varieties, and attempts to develop rapid attribution systems, but no work has yet come close to challenging Dr. Maris's monograph as the single undisputed authority on N.J. copper coins. Since its publication in 1881 only one variety has been invalidated—#82. [And Maris 78-dd has been recognized as a die state of 77-dd, not a different variety.] Additions to Maris's list include 11 new varieties with an undescribed obverse, three varieties with an undescribed reverse, four varieties with an undescribed obverse and reverse, and 11 new mulings of previously known obverses and reverses.

New varieties discovered since the Moore update include 59-mm and 77-cc.

Today, thanks to the *Colonial Newsletter*, the more recent *C4 Newsletter*, and a general awareness and appreciation of early American coins in general, plus reprinting of the Maris text, New Jersey copper coins of the years 1786 to 1788 are in unceasing demand at all grade levels, including basic types as well as varieties by Maris numbers. Attributions are fairly easy. A good method is to check the reverse first, to see where the top point of the shield is in relation to the letters, then check other positions. Then check the obverse die with relation to the horse's ears and letters, and the style and position of the date. Refine your search by checking other features. An Easy Finding Guide is given in this text.

Many of the following notes and rarity ratings are courtesy of Ray Williams. Roger S. Siboni and Jack Howes, who are preparing a new book on New Jersey coppers, provided much information. William T. Anton Jr. reviewed this section and contributed annotations for listings.

Easy Finding Guide
New Jersey Obverse Dies

First, check the date of the coin. Then go to the listing for that date and begin with the title of the first set of descriptions. If your coin does not fit that set, go to succeeding descriptions until a title is appropriate. Next, check the listings within that title to find the variety. Always begin with the first headings for each year.

1786 DATE BELOW PLOW BEAM

1786 · Maris 7 · The digits 17 level, 8 and 6 progressively lower. Diagnostic. Leftmost ear points to C; other ear points to left foot of A. No period after final A. N is closer to plow handle than to O. Singletree touches plow beam. *Used for:* W-4700, 1786 Maris 7-C. W-4710, 1786 Maris 7-E.

1786 · Maris 8 · Digit 1 low and leans left; 786 higher. Diagnostic. N is close to O and distant from plow handle. *Used for:* W-4720, 1786 Maris 8-F.

1786 COULTERLESS

The coulter is the knifelike blade on the beam in front of the plow.

1786 · Maris 8.5 · Dot after final A. Leftmost ear small and under C; other ear under right edge of C. Diagnostic. N closer to plow handle than to O. The 1 (1786) high. *Used for:* W-4730, 1786 Maris 8.5-C.

1786 · Maris 9 · No dot after final A. Leftmost ear left of C. Diagnostic. Other ear between C and A. Only Coulterless with lower plow handle next to rim. N distant from plow handle only on Maris 9 and 11.5. *Used for:* W-4735, 1786 Maris 9-G.

1786 · Maris 10 · Dot after final A. Leftmost ear slightly right of C; other ear under A. Diagnostic. Upper plow handle close to N and nearly as high. *Used for:* W-4740, 1786 Maris 10-G. W-4745, 1786 Maris 10-h. W-4750, 1786 Maris 10-gg. W-4760, 1786 Maris 10-oo.

1786 · Maris 10.5 · Dot after final A. Leftmost ear under C; other ear under right inside serif of A. Diagnostic. Mane tousled. Plow beam points to right foot of A. *Used for:* W-4765, 1786 Maris 10.5-C.

1786 · Maris 11 · No dot after final A. Leftmost ear under C; other ear under upright of E. Diagnostic. *Used for:* W-4770, 1786 Maris 11-G. W-4775, 1786 Maris 11-H. W-4780, 1786 Maris 11-hh.

1786 · Maris 11.5 · No dot after final A. Leftmost ear under C; other ear under left foot of A. Diagnostic. N distant from plow handle only on Maris 9 and 11.5. *Used for:* W-4785, 1786 Maris 11.5-G.

1786 · Maris 12 · No dot after final A. Leftmost ear under left foot of A; other ear slightly right of tip of E. Diagnostic. *Used for:* W-4790, 1786 Maris 12-G. W-4795, 1786 Maris 12-I.

1786 · Maris 22 · Dot after final A. Leftmost ear under C; other ear under center of A. Dot after final A. Diagnostic. Upper plow handle distant from N and A about even with the base of N. *Used for:* W-4935, 1786 Maris 22-P.

1786 WITH COULTER, LEFTMOST EAR TO LEFT OF C

1786 · Maris 14 · Straight plow beam. Coulter points to second ornament from front of horse. Diagnostic. Other ear under right part of C. Ridge on front of neck. Plow distant from N and A. Date figures low; 7 lowest. Tip of singletree touches border. *Used for:* W-4810, 1786 Maris 14-J.

1786 · Maris 15 · Straight plow beam. Coulter points to rightmost ornament under horse. Diagnostic. Other ear under center of C. Date figures low; bottom of 6 incomplete. Point of plow close to tip of triangular sawtooth dentil. *Used for:* W-4815, 1786 Maris 15-J. W-4820, 1786 Maris 15-L. W-4825, 1786 Maris 15-T. W-4830, 1786 Maris 15-U.

1786 · Maris 21 · Curved plow beam. Ridge on front of neck. Top handle end close to N and nearly as high. Diagnostic. Other ear under slightly right of center of C. Top of 7 closest to line; 6 farthest and with top pointing to the right. *Used for:* W-4910, 1786 Maris 21-N. W-4915, 1786 Maris 21-O. W-4920, 1786 Maris 21-P. W-4925, 1786 Maris 21-R.

1786 · Maris 23 · Curved plow beam. Lower right tip of singletree touches edge. Top handle end farther from N than on Maris-21 and slightly less than half as high as N. Diagnostic. Other ear small and under right part of C. Date digits high; 8 and 6 into line. *Used for:* W-4940, 1786 Maris 23-P. W-4945, 1786 Maris 23-R.

1786 · Maris 25 · Straight plow beam. Coulter points to fourth ornament from front of horse. Diagnostic. Top plow handle 3/4 height of and close to N. Other ear under upright of C. Date digits low. *Used for:* W-4980, 1786 Maris 25-S.

New Jersey Obverse Dies (continued)

1786 WITH COULTER, LEFTMOST EAR UNDER C

1786 · Maris 13 · N nearly touches plow handle. Diagnostic. Leftmost ear tip far below right side of C; other ear under A. Diagnostic. The 1 and 6 high; only 6 touches date line. *Used for:* W-4800, 1786 Maris 13-J.

1786 · Maris 18 · Horse head normal, 1 tilted to left. (Bridle Variety on late state.) Diagnostic date and head details (die crack varies). On late die state, crack vertically from nose to chest, the "Bridle Variety." Leftmost ear under C; other ear under leftmost serif of A. Plow beam curved and recurved; bottom of singletree close to and parallel to coulter. The 1 and 6 high and touching line; 7 low with top touching triangular dentil. Traces of a mispunched 6 can be seen in the plowshare. *Used for:* W-4875, 1786 Maris 18-J. W-4880, 1786 Maris 18-L. W-4890, 1786 Maris 18-M (with or without Bridle crack). W-4895, 1786 Maris 18-N.

1786 · Maris 19 · Horse head and 1 tilted to left. A distant from head. Diagnostic. Leftmost ear under upright of C; other ear under right edge of C. A close to plow beam. *Used for:* W-4900, 1786 Maris 19-M.

1786 · Maris 20 · Horse head and 1 tilted to left. A close to head. Diagnostic. Leftmost ear under upright of C; other ear under center of C; both ears very small. Island or die defect in field below head and near plow. A distant from end of plow beam. *Used for:* W-4905, 1786 Maris 20-N.

1786 · Maris 21.5 · Dot centered after final A. Diagnostic. Leftmost ear under C; other ear under left foot of A. Top of singletree very high and opposite ornament below head. *Used for:* W-4930, 1786 Maris 21.5-R.

1786 · Maris 23.5 · The 7 about centered under left edge of plow. Diagnostic. Leftmost ear under C; other ear under leftmost serif of A. The 7 and 6 high. Top of coulter high. Top of singletree opposite center of ornament below head. *Used for:* W-4950, 1786 Maris 23.5-R.

1786 · Maris 24 · The 8 about centered under left edge of plow. Diagnostic. Leftmost ear under left edge of C; other ear tiny and below right part of C. Mane braided in two vertical rows, outer row erratic. NO (NOVA) close to dentils. Tip of plow beam close to right foot of A. Coulter with raised ridge outline below beam. Date digits low; bottom of 7 light (sometimes appears missing). *Used for:* W-4955, 1786 Maris 24-I. W-4960, 1786 Maris 24-M. W-4965, 1786 Maris 24-P. W-4970, 1786 Maris 24-Q. W-4975, 1786 Maris 24-R.

1786 WITH COULTER, LEFTMOST EAR RIGHT OF C

1786 · Maris 16 · Leftmost ear under left tip of A. No knobs on plow handles. Diagnostic. Other ear under center of A. N close to plow handle. Rightmost serif of A near top of singletree. Date figures low; 86 lowest, but tip of 6 closest to date line. *Used for:* W-4835, 1786 Maris 16-J. W-4840, 1786 Maris 16-L. W-4845, 1786 Maris 16-S. W-4850, 1786 Maris 16-d.

1786 · Maris 17 · Leftmost ear under left tip of A. Knobs on plow handles. Diagnostic. Leftmost ear tip below leftmost serif of A; other ear under upright of E. Dot centered after final A. Date low. *Used for:* W-4860, 1786 Maris 17-J. W-4865, 1786 Maris 17-K. W-4870, 1786 Maris 17-b.

1787 WITH KNOBS ON PLOW HANDLES

1787 · Maris 27 · Leftmost ear under space left of C. The 17 left of plow. Diagnostic. *Notes:* Other ear under right part of C. Second A in CÆSAREA punched over an erroneous I. *Used for:* W-5055, 1787 Maris 27-S. W-5060, 1787 Maris 27-j.

1787 · Maris 28 · Leftmost ear points at left side of C. The 1 left of plow, 7 under plow. Diagnostic. Early state of this die. Later, the knobs fade away. Other ear under C slightly right of center. *Used for:* W-5065, 1787 Maris 28-L. W-5070, 1787 Maris 28-S.

1787 · Maris 29 · Leftmost ear under space between C and A. Diagnostic. Other ear under upright of E. The 8 low; 7 very low with bottom between tips of two dentils. *Used for:* W-5075, 1787 Maris 29-L.

1787 · Maris 30 · Knobs very close to dentils. The 1 left of plow. Diagnostic. Leftmost ear hollow, larger, and under right part of C; other ear small and under left foot of A. The 1 slightly high and leans slightly left; top second 7 slightly lower than top of 8. Defective dentil to right of end of singletree. *Used for:* W-5090, 1787 Maris 30-L.

1787 · Maris 32 · Leftmost ear close to A (NOVA) and distant from C. Diagnostic. Other ear under upright of C. Singletree ends to the left of and below the tip of a dentil. Second 7 ends left of triangular dentil tip. *Used for:* W-5100, 1787 Maris 32-T.

1787 · Maris 55 · Knobs close to dentils. The 1 close under plow and touches it. Diagnostic. Leftmost ear hollow and under right edge of C; other ear below center of A. The 1 and 8 high; second 7 low and runs into dentils. *Used for:* W-5300, 1787 Maris 55-l. W-5305, 1787 Maris 55-m.

1787 WITH THREE LEAVES BELOW HORSE

1787 · Maris 34 · Top plow handle close to N and about half its height. Diagnostic. Leftmost ear hollow and below left foot of A; other ear much smaller and under left serif of E. Left end of date line near dentil. Digits lean right; second 7 touches dentil. *Used for:* W-5115, 1787 Maris 34-J. W-5120, 1787 Maris 34-V.

1787 · Maris 35 · Date repunched, 8 over 7. Diagnostic. Beam end points far to right of A. Ears distant from Æ. Leftmost ear hollow with tip below right edge of C; other ear under A. The 1 high. *Used for:* W-5125, 1787 Maris 35-J. W-5130, 1787 Maris 35-W.

1787 · Maris 40 · Beam end points far to right of A. Ears close to Æ. Diagnostic. Leftmost ear hollow and under left leg of A; other ear under right leg of A. Bottom plow handle thin. Coulter tapers to point. Tops of digits about the same level; 1 and 8 large lean right. *Used for:* W-5200, 1787 Maris 40-b.

1787 · Maris 60 · Beam end points to top of A. Left end of date line distant from dentils. Diagnostic. Leftmost ear below right edge of C; other ear below A. Digits irregularly aligned; first 7 high. *Used for:* W-5340, 1787 Maris 60-p.

New Jersey Obverse Dies (continued)

1787 · Maris 61 · Beam ends under left foot of A. Diagnostic. Leftmost ear under slightly left of center of C; other ear under space after C. Mane flows to the left. Break at left of mane. Beam ends opposite right inside serif of A. Lower handle shorter; 1 slightly low; second 7 over dentil tip. *Used for:* W-5345, 1787 Maris 61-p.

1787 · Maris 62 · Dot centered after final A. Diagnostic. Leftmost ear under leftmost serif of A; other ear under upright of A. Dot after final A. The 1 low; 8 small and high. *Notes:* Under the left and right leaves on the sprig are the initials W and M, for Walter Mould. *Used for:* W-5350, 1787 Maris 62-q. W-5355, 1787 Maris 62-r.

1787 · Maris 62.5 · WM on obverse. Diagnostic. *Used for:* W-5360, 1787 Maris 62.5-r.

1787 · Maris 63 · Beam end points to just right of A. Left end of date line touches a dentil. Diagnostic. Leftmost ear hollow and below right part of C; other ear smaller, hollow, and below left inside serif of A. Plow and coulter outlined. The 1 thick; 8 small and low. *Used for:* W-5365, 1787 Maris 63-q. W-5370, 1787 Maris 63-r. W-5375, 1787 Maris 63-s.

1787 · Maris 70 · Quatrefoil before N. Diagnostic. Leftmost ear under space between C and A; other ear under left foot of A. *Used for:* W-5410, 1787 Maris 70-x.

1787 · Maris 71 · Quatrefoil after second A. Diagnostic. *Used for:* W-5415, 1787 Maris 71-y.

1787 · Maris 72 · Star after each A. Final star slightly closer to plow beam than to A. Diagnostic. Leftmost ear under slightly right of E; other ear under S. *Used for:* W-5420, 1787 Maris 72-z.

1787 · Maris 73 · Star after each A. Final star closer to A than to plow beam. Diagnostic. Leftmost ear under upright of E; other ear under lower right part of E. Second 7 low. *Used for:* W-5430, 1787 Maris 73-aa.

1787 Dies with Unusual Features

1787 · Maris 6 · Raised outlines on plow handles and front of neck. Period after second A. Diagnostic. Leftmost ear under leftmost tip of A; other ear under upright of E. Pair of ears shaped like an M. S (CÆSAREA) too large. Coulter very close to decoration under head. Upright of 1 curved slightly to right; 78 high; 7's near tips of sawtooth dentils. *Used for:* W-5040, 1787 Maris 6-C. W-5050, 1787 Maris 6-D.

1787 · Maris 37 · Goiter variety with lump under neck. Diagnostic. Leftmost ear under slightly right of center of C; other ear under leftmost serif of A. Plow curves upward and points to right foot of A. Second 7 very low and close to dentil. *Used for:* W-5140, 1787 Maris 37-J. W-5145, 1787 Maris 37-X. W-5150, 1787 Maris 37-Y. W-5155, 1787 Maris 37-f.

1787 · Maris 69 · CESEREA misspelling. Star after A (NOVA). Diagnostic. *Used for:* W-5405, 1787 Maris 69-w.

1787 WITH LEFTMOST EAR TO LEFT OF C

1787 · Maris 33 · Coulter straight. Right ear under C. Top handle distant from N. Diagnostic. Beam distant from A. Dateline touches dentil to right. Second 7 low and touches dentil tip. *Used for:* W-5110, 1787 Maris 33-U.

1787 · Maris 46 · Coulter straight. Right ear under C. Top handle near N. Diagnostic. Beam close to A; tip of singletree almost touches right serif of A. The 1 leans slightly left; first 7 high. *Used for:* W-5250, 1787 Maris 46-e.

1787 · Maris 57 · Coulter tip bent at bottom right. Leftmost ear close to A (NOVA). Diagnostic. Other ear tiny; ear left of C. Singletree close to right foot of A. The 1 small; 8 large and above two dentil points. *Used for:* W-5315, 1787 Maris 57-n.

1787 · Maris 58 · Coulter tip bent at bottom right. Leftmost ear very high (almost as high as the letters) and is between A and C. Diagnostic. Other ear tiny and left of C. Curious five-pointed star below plow handles. The 1 high; 8 large; second 7 directly over tip of dentil. *Used for:* W-5320, 1787 Maris 58-n.

1787 WITH STRAIGHT PLOW BEAM

1787 · Maris 28 · End of plow distant from A. Diagnostic. Late state of die with knobs on plow weak or missing. Also listed under dies with knobs, above. Leftmost ear under left edge of C; other ear under C slightly right of center. Plow handles slightly shorter than base of N. The 1 leans slightly left. *Used for:* W-5065, 1787 Maris 28-L. W-5070, 1787 Maris 28-S.

1787 · Maris 36 · Letters hand-engraved in die and thus irregular. Diagnostic. Leftmost ear under C; other ear under left foot of A. Plow handle short and ends lower than baseline of N. The 1 high and leans right; overly large dentil below 8; second 7 heavy. *Used for:* W-5135, 1787 Maris 36-J.

1787 · Maris 38 · Tip of singletree misaligned and close to end of beam. Diagnostic. Leftmost ear under leftmost serif of A; other ear under A. End of plow beam curved and points to right foot of A. The 1 high; 8 highest; 7's low. *Used for:* W-5160, 1787 Maris 38-L. W-5170, 1787 Maris 38-Y. W-5175, 1787 Maris 38-Z. W-5180, 1787 Maris 38-a. W-5185, 1787 Maris 38-b. W-5190, 1787 Maris 38-c.

1787 · Maris 52 · Tip of singletree distant from end of beam. Diagnostic. Leftmost ear under left edge of C; other ear under space between C and E. The 8 low; second 7 lowest. *Used for:* W-5280, 1787 Maris 52-i.

New Jersey Obverse Dies (continued)

1787 · Maris 59 · Large sawtooth dentils completely around border. Diagnostic. Leftmost ear under left edge of C; other ear under right edge of C. Beam straight and ends near right foot of A. Figures about equidistant below date line; 1 and 8 small; 78 wide. *Used for:* W-5335, 1787 Maris 59-m. W-5335, 1787 Maris 59-o.

1787 · Maris 64 · Six separate tufts under horse head. Coulter points to first tuft. Diagnostic. Leftmost ear hollow and close below C; other ear hollow and just left of A. Mane flows upward to left. Cheek and neck with raised outline. Beam ends opposite foot of A; bottom of singletree points slightly right of tip of dentil. *Used for:* W-5380, 1787 Maris 64-t. W-5390, 1787 Maris 64-u.

1787 · Maris 83 · Little or no mane on horse. Diagnostic. Leftmost ear under right of C; other ear under left foot of A. *Used for:* W-5445, 1787 Maris 83-ii.

1787 · Maris 84 · The 17 left of left edge of plow. Diagnostic. *Used for:* W-5455, 1787 Maris 84-kk.

1787 With Curved Plow Beam

1787 · Maris 31 · Beam straight to singletree, then curves upward. Leftmost ear under C; other ear slightly left of A. Letters very close to sawtooth dentils. Lower left tip of singletree close to coulter. Date widely spaced. *Used for:* W-5095, 1787 Maris 31-L.

1787 · Maris 39 · Second 7 far too low. Diagnostic. Leftmost ear slightly right of C; other ear below left leg of A. The 8 is high. *Used for:* W-5195, 1787 Maris 39-a.

1787 · Maris 41 · Handle end under lower left serif of N. Rightmost tuft completely below horse's chest. Diagnostic. Leftmost ear under leftmost serif of A; other ear under A. Space between plow handles narrow and points to lower left of N. Top of singletree very short. Digits widely spaced; top of first 7 narrower than on Maris 42; 8 large and leans right; second 7 small. *Used for:* W-5205, 1787 Maris 41-c.

1787 · Maris 42 · Handle end under lower left serif of N. Rightmost tuft protrudes to right below horse's chest. Diagnostic. Leftmost ear under left leg of A; other ear under right leg of A. Upper plow handle points to left upright of N. The 1 high; tops of 7's wide; 8 very heavy. *Used for:* W-5210, 1787 Maris 42-c.

1787 · Maris 42.5 · Plow handles short and distant from N. Leftmost ear under slightly left of A. Diagnostic. Other ear under A. Illustrated in *CNL*, May 1996. *Used for:* W-5215, 1787 Maris 42.5-c.

1787 · Maris 43 · The 1 is at far left of edge of plow. Leftmost ear hollow and under space to right of C. Tufts below horse's head. Diagnostic. Handles close. Other ear under left leg of A. Beam points to rightmost serif of A. Lower right of singletree double the length of lower left element. Digits widely spaced; 1 slightly high; second 7 level with first 7. *Used for:* W-5220, 1787 Maris 43-Y. W-5225, 1787 Maris 43-d.

1787 · Maris 44 · Leftmost ear leans right and is under left foot of A. Top part of coulter slightly misaligned to left. Diagnostic. Leftmost ear hollow and under leftmost serif of A; other ear hollow and under right leg of A. Upper tip of top plow handle near leftmost serif of N. Digits about the same distance below line; 78 wide. *Used for:* W-5230, 1787 Maris 44-c. W-5235, 1787 Maris 44-d.

1787 · Maris 45 · Leftmost ear very large and leans left. Diagnostic. Leftmost ear hollow and under left leg of A; other ear small and under upright of E. Upper tip of top plow handle near leftmost serif of N. Eight tufts below horse's head. Sawtooth dentils; dentil over upright of R has doubled tip. The 1 slightly high; digits widely spaced. Plow beam end distant from A and points to it. *Used for:* W-5240, 1787 Maris 45-d. W-5245, 1787 Maris 45-e.

1787 · Maris 47 · Leftmost ear under center of C; other ear slightly left of A. The 1 left of plow second 7 low. Definitive. *Used for:* W-5255, 1787 Maris 47-e.

1787 · Maris 47.5 · Leftmost ear under heavy part of C; other ear slightly left of A. The 8 heavy and mostly filled. Definitive. *Used for:* W-5260, 1787 Maris 47.5-e.

1787 · Maris 48 · The digits 17 are at left of edge of plow. Diagnostic. Leftmost ear hollow and barely right of C; other ear small and under left of A. Mane in thick vertical ridge. Digits widely spaced; 1 slightly high. *Used for:* W-5265, 1787 Maris 48-X. W-5270, 1787 Maris 48-f. W-5275, 1787 Maris 48-g.

1787 · Maris 53 · Dot centered after second A. Plow handles not outlined. Diagnostic. Leftmost ear under left part of C; other ear barely past C. Period after final A. The digits 17 wide; 1 and 8 small. *Used for:* W-5290, 1787 Maris 53-j.

1787 · Maris 54 · Beam curves downward and ends close to A. Diagnostic. Leftmost ear under right edge of C; other ear under leftmost serif of A. Outline of chest incomplete where it joins neck. Mane prominent and in two vertical rows. Plow elements mostly outlined. Digits widely spaced and bottom of second 7 directly above tip of dentil. *Used for:* W-5295, 1787 Maris 54-k.

1787 · Maris 56 · Leftmost ear under left edge of C; other ear touches C. Diagnostic. Lower handle measurably longer. The 1 small; 8 large. *Used for:* W-5310, 1787 Maris 56-n.

1787 · Maris 68 · Handle end under lower left serif of N. Tip of singletree close to and points to lower right serif of A. Diagnostic. Leftmost ear under left leg of A; other ear under right leg of A. Left side of N lower than top of upper plow handle. Beam and singletree close to A. The 1 high. *Used for:* W-5400, 1787 Maris 68-w.

1787 · Maris 73.5 · Leftmost ear under right leg of first E. Five-pointed stars before and after CÆSAREA. *Used for:* W-5435, 1787 Maris 73.5-jj.

1787 · Maris 81 · The 1 is at far left of edge of plow. No tufts below horse's head. Diagnostic. Handles widely separated. Second 7 low. *Used for:* W-5440, 1787 Maris 81-ll.

New Jersey Obverse Dies (continued)

1788 Horse's Head Left

1788 · Maris 49 · Second 8 leans right and is completely under plow. Diagnostic. Leftmost ear under C and points to left of C. Plow handle ends near right foot of A. *Used for:* W-5470, 1788 Maris 49-f.

1788 · Maris 50 · Plow beam close to upper left of N. Diagnostic. Leftmost ear slightly right of C and points to C. N is low and is slightly closer to plow beam than to O. *Used for:* W-5475, 1788 Maris 50-f.

1788 · Maris 51 · Second 8 centered slightly right of back corner of plow. Diagnostic. Leftmost ear under space between C and A and points to C. Upper handle close to rightmost serif of A. *Used for:* W-5480, 1788 Maris 51-g.

1788 Horse's Head Right

1788 · Maris 65 · No punctuation. Leftmost ear touches C. Diagnostic. Heavy sawtooth dentils around border. *Used for:* W-5495, 1788 Maris 65-u.

1788 · Maris 66 · Star before and after each word. Leftmost ear under middle of C. Diagnostic. Front of neck and chest outlined. Mane braided vertically like a pigtail. *Used for:* W-5500, 1788 Maris 66-u. W-5505, 1788 Maris 66-v.

1788 · Maris 67 · Star before and after each word. Leftmost ear under right edge of C. Diagnostic. *Used for:* W-5510, 1788 Maris 67-v.

1788 · Maris 74 · Star after first A, quatrefoil after second A. No coulter or singletree. Diagnostic. Rightmost ear much larger and under S. *Used for:* W-5515, 1788 Maris 74-bb.

1788 · Maris 75 · Quatrefoils before and after each word. Quatrefoil above tip of singletree. Diagnostic. Leftmost ear under S. Diagnostic. *Used for:* W-5520, 1788 Maris 75-bb.

1788 · Maris 76 · Star after first A, quatrefoil after second A. With coulter and singletree. Diagnostic. Leftmost ear much larger and under E. *Used for:* W-5525, 1788 Maris 76-cc.

1788 · Maris 77 · Quatrefoils before and after each word. Tip of singletree opposite quatrefoil. Diagnostic. Leftmost ear under Æ. *Used for:* W-5530, 1788 Maris 77-cc. W-5535, 1788 Maris 77-dd.

New Jersey Obverse Dies (Unknown Dates)

Maris 79 · Head tilted backward to left. Date starts as 113. Diagnostic. Die completely hand-engraved. *Used for:* W-5550, 178? Maris 79-ee.

American Coins and Tokens, 1783–1788 ◆ New Jersey Coppers

Maris 80 · A (NOVA) close to C. Diagnostic. *Used for:* W-5560, 178? Maris 80-ff.

Easy Finding Guide
New Jersey Reverse Dies

Maris C · *Used for:* W-4700, 1786 Maris 7-C. W-4730, 1786 Maris 8.5-C. W-4765, 1786 Maris 10.5-C. W-5040, 1787 Maris 6-C.

Maris D · *Used for:* W-5050, 1787 Maris 6-D.

Maris E · *Used for:* W-4710, 1786 Maris 7-E.

Maris F · *Used for:* W-4720, 1786 Maris 8-F.

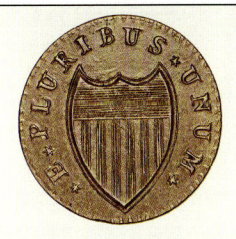

Maris G · *Used for:* W-4735, 1786 Maris 9-G. W-4740, 1786 Maris 10-G. W-4770, 1786 Maris 11-G. W-4785, 1786 Maris 11.5-G. W-4790, 1786 Maris 12-G.

Maris H · *Used for:* W-4775, 1786 Maris 11-H.

Maris I · *Used for:* W-4795, 1786 Maris 12-I. W-4955, 1786 Maris 24-I.

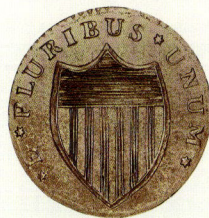

Maris J, "Square" M · *Used for:* W-4800, 1786 Maris 13-J. W-4810, 1786 Maris 14-J. W-4815, 1786 Maris 15-J. W-4835, 1786 Maris 16-J. W-4860, 1786 Maris 17-J. W-4875, 1786 Maris 18-J. W-5115, 1787 Maris 34-J. W-5125, 1787 Maris 35-J. W-5135, 1787 Maris 36-J. W-5140, 1787 Maris 37-J.

Maris K · *Used for:* W-4865, 1786 Maris 17-K.

Maris L · *Used for:* W-4820, 1786 Maris 15-L. W-4840, 1786 Maris 16-L. W-4880, 1786 Maris 18-L. W-5065, 1787 Maris 28-L. W-5075, 1787 Maris 29-L. W-5090, 1787 Maris 30-L. W-5095, 1787 Maris 31-L. W-5160, 1787 Maris 38-L.

New Jersey Reverse Dies (continued)

Maris M, Wide Shield · *Used for:* W-4890, 1786 Maris 18-M. W-4900, 1786 Maris 19-M. W-4960, 1786 Maris 24-M.

Maris N, Wide Shield · *Used for:* W-4895, 1786 Maris 18-N. W-4905, 1786 Maris 20-N. W-4910, 1786 Maris 21-N.

Maris O, Wide Shield · *Used for:* W-4915, 1786 Maris 21-O.

Maris P · *Used for:* W-4920, 1786 Maris 21-P. W-4935, 1786 Maris 22-P. W-4940, 1786 Maris 23-P. W-4965, 1786 Maris 24-P.

Maris Q · *Used for:* W-4970, 1786 Maris 24-Q.

Maris R · *Used for:* W-4925, 1786 Maris 21-R. W-4930, 1786 Maris 21.5-R. W-4945, 1786 Maris 23-R. W-4950, 1786 Maris 23.5-R. W-4975, 1786 Maris 24-R.

Maris S · *Used for:* W-4845, 1786 Maris 16-S. W-4980, 1786 Maris 25-S. W-4995, 1786 Maris 26-S. W-5055, 1787 Maris 27-S. W-5070, 1787 Maris 28-S.

Maris T, "Square" M · *Used for:* W-4825, 1786 Maris 15-T. W-5100, 1787 Maris 32-T.

Maris U · *Used for:* W-4830, 1786 Maris 15-U. W-5110, 1787 Maris 33-U.

Maris V · *Used for:* W-5120, 1787 Maris 34-V.

Maris W · *Used for:* W-5130, 1787 Maris 35-W.

Maris X · *Used for:* W-5145, 1787 Maris 37-X. W-5265, 1787 Maris 48-X.

Maris Y · *Used for:* W-5150, 1787 Maris 37-Y. W-5170, 1787 Maris 38-Y. W-5220, 1787 Maris 43-Y.

Maris Z · *Used for:* W-5175, 1787 Maris 38-Z.

Maris a · *Used for:* W-5180, 1787 Maris 38-a. W-5195, 1787 Maris 39-a.

Maris b, PLUKIBUS · *Used for:* W-4870, 1786 Maris 17-b. W-5185, 1787 Maris 38-b. W-5200, 1787 Maris 40-b.

Maris c · *Used for:* W-5190, 1787 Maris 38-c. W-5205, 1787 Maris 41-c. W-5210, 1787 Maris 42-c. W-5215, 1787 Maris 42.5-c. W-5230, 1787 Maris 44-c.

Maris d · *Used for:* W-4850, 1786 Maris 16-d. W-4990, 1786 Maris 26-d. W-5225, 1787 Maris 43-d. W-5235, 1787 Maris 44-d. W-5240, 1787 Maris 45-d.

Maris e · *Used for:* W-5245, 1787 Maris 45-e. W-5250, 1787 Maris 46-e. W-5255, 1787 Maris 47-e. W-5260, 1787 Maris 47.5-e.

Maris f · *Used for:* W-5155, 1787 Maris 37-f. W-5270, 1787 Maris 48-f. W-5470, 1788 Maris 49-f. W-5475, 1788 Maris 50-f.

Maris g, Outline to Shield · *Used for:* W-5275, 1787 Maris 48-g. W-5480, 1788 Maris 51-g.

Maris h · *Used for:* W-4745, 1786 Maris 10-h.

Maris i · *Used for:* W-5280, 1787 Maris 52-i.

New Jersey Reverse Dies (continued)

Maris j · *Used for:* W-5060, 1787 Maris 27-j. W-5290, 1787 Maris 53-j.

Maris k · *Used for:* W-5295, 1787 Maris 54-k.

Maris l, PLURIRUS · *Used for:* W-5300, 1787 Maris 55-l.

Maris m, U over S in PLURIBUS · *Used for:* W-5305, 1787 Maris 55-m.

Maris n · *Used for:* W-5310, 1787 Maris 56-n. W-5315, 1787 Maris 57-n. W-5320, 1787 Maris 58-n.

Maris o · *Used for:* W-5325, 1787 Maris 59-o.

Maris p, PLURIBS · *Used for:* W-5340, 1787 Maris 60-p. W-5345, 1787 Maris 61-p.

Maris q · *Used for:* W-5350, 1787 Maris 62-q. W-5365, 1787 Maris 63-q.

Maris r · *Used for:* W-5355, 1787 Maris 62-r. W-5360, 1787 Maris 62.5-r. W-5370, 1787 Maris 63-r. W-5395, 1788 Maris 64.5-r.

Maris s · *Used for:* W-5375, 1787 Maris 63-s.

Maris t · *Used for:* W-5380, 1787 Maris 64-t.

Maris u · *Used for:* W-5390, 1787 Maris 64-u. W-5495, 1788 Maris 65-u. W-5500, 1788 Maris 66-u.

Maris aa · *Used for:* W-5430, 1787 Maris 73-aa.

Maris v · *Used for:* W-5505, 1788 Maris 66-v. W-5510, 1788 Maris 67-v.

Maris bb, Running Fox · *Used for:* W-5515, 1788 Maris 74-bb. W-5520, 1788 Maris 75-bb.

Maris w · *Used for:* W-5400, 1787 Maris 68-w. W-5405, 1787 Maris 69-w.

Maris cc, Running Fox · *Used for:* W-5525, 1788 Maris 76-cc. W-5530, 1788 Maris 77-cc.

Maris x · *Used for:* W-5410, 1787 Maris 70-x.

Maris dd, Running Fox · *Used for:* W-5535, 1788 Maris 77-dd.

Maris y · *Used for:* W-5415, 1787 Maris 71-y.

Maris ee · *Used for:* W-5550, 178? Maris 79-ee.

Maris z · *Used for:* W-5420, 1787 Maris 72-z.

New Jersey Reverse Dies (continued)

Maris gg · *Used for:* W-4750, 1786 Maris 10-gg.

Maris hh · *Used for:* W-4780, 1786 Maris 11-hh.

Maris ii · *Used for:* W-5445, 1787 Maris 83-ii.

Maris kk · *Used for:* W-5455, 1787 Maris 84-kk.

Maris mm · *Used for:* W-5335, 1787 Maris 59-mm.

1786 New Jersey Coppers

1786 Date Under Plow Beam

W-4700 · 1786 · Maris 7-C

Notes: Discovered by James F. Ruddy in the late 1950s; sold to Edward R. Barnsley, to William T. Anton Jr. Unique. Maris called the C reverse the "pattern shield," as it is found combined with Immunis Columbia, Eagle, and Washington obverses, each of which is exceedingly rare. Indeed, any coin using this die is a rarity, save for New Jersey 1787 6-C. William T. Anton Jr. considers this to be the first New Jersey copper struck, followed by the Maris 8.5-C. Walter Breen's statement (*Encyclopedia*, 1988) that the C reverse as well as the Date Under Plow Beam and Coulterless varieties were made at "Wyon's Mint" in Birmingham can be dismissed. *Rarity:* URS-1.

W-4710 · 1786 · Maris 7-E

Notes: Five are believed to be known, the finest the Ford About Uncirculated. First auction appearance in the William J. Jenks Collection sale (Edward D. Cogan, April 1877). Any variety of the Date Under Plow Beam is a classic rarity, one of the most famous and most desired types in the state coinage series. *Rarity:* URS-4.

Selected auction price(s): Norweb I Sale (B&M 10/1987), VF, porous, $41,800. John J. Ford Jr. I Sale (Stack's 10/2003), Choice AU, $322,000.

W-4720 · 1786 · Maris 8-F

Notes: Three known; two finest are Extremely Fine or slightly higher in the Anton Collection. A Very Good is owned by the New Jersey Historical Society, ex Canfield Collection. *Rarity:* URS-3.

Selected auction price(s): Garrett III Sale (B&R 10/1980), EF, $52,000. Roper Sale (Stack's 12/1983), EF, $41,800.

1786 Coulterless

W-4730 · 1786 · Maris 8.5-C

Notes: The first of the Coulterless varieties. "Micro" date digits. Three known, the two finest being the Taylor coin and another, all in the Anton Collection. *Rarity:* URS-3.

Selected auction price(s): Garrett III Sale (B&R 10/1980), F, striated planchet, $1,700. O'Donnell Collection (Stack's 1/2001), VF, $41,400.

W-4735 · 1786 · Maris 9-G

Notes: Six known, the three finest each being Very Fine, two of these in the Anton Collection. *Rarity:* URS-4.

Selected auction price(s): O'Donnell Collection (Stack's 1/2001), VF, $27,600. John J. Ford Jr. I Sale (Stack's 10/2003), F/VG, rough, $8,337.50.

W-4740 · 1786 · Maris 10-G

Notes: Some 16 or so pieces recorded, probably others as well. Perhaps a candidate for URS-6. One of only a few collectible Coulterless varieties, although market appearances are infrequent. *Rarity:* URS-5.

G-4	VG-8	F-12	VF-20	EF-40
$900	$1,500	$5,000	$8,250	$20,000

W-4745 · 1786 · Maris 10-h

Notes: Eight known. *Rarity:* URS-4.

Selected auction price(s): Norweb I Sale (B&M 10/1987), AU, $55,000. O'Donnell Collection (Stack's 1/2001), VF, $36,800. John J. Ford Jr. I Sale (Stack's 10/2003), About VF, $9,200.

W-4750 · 1786 · Maris 10-gg

Notes: Four known, the best Extremely Fine. One was found on eBay in 2007. *Rarity:* URS-3.

Selected auction price(s): O'Donnell Collection (Stack's 1/2001), VF, $43,700. John J. Ford Jr. I Sale (Stack's 10/2003), VF, $19,550.

W-4760 · 1786 · Maris 10-oo

Notes: Found in a flea market by Texas dealer Michael Brownlee. Very Fine or so. Later owned by Henry Garrett, then in the B&M Spring Quartette sale, now in a Long Island, New York, collection. *Rarity:* URS-1.

W-4765 · 1786 · Maris 10.5-C

Notes: Found by a dealer in New Jersey. Authenticated by Michael J. Hodder; described in *CNL*, July 1992. *Rarity:* URS-1.

Selected auction price(s): O'Donnell Collection (Stack's 1/2001), Choice F, $36,800.

W-4770 · 1786 · Maris 11-G

Notes: William S. Appleton Collection to the Massachusetts Historical Society, Stack's auction in October 1970, now in the Anton Collection. While each die can be found on other varieties, in this combination the variety is unique. *Rarity:* URS-1.

W-4775 · 1786 · Maris 11-H

Notes: Ford's Extremely Fine may be the finest. *Rarity:* URS-6.

G-4	VG-8	F-12	VF-20	EF-40
$900	$1,500	$2,750	$8,250	$20,000

W-4780 · 1786 · Maris 11-hh

Notes: Discovered by Walter H. Breen circa 1952. Jacob Spiro Collection to Boyd to Ford. Good grade. Now in a collection in Washington state. *Rarity:* URS-1.

Selected auction price(s): John J. Ford Jr. I Sale (Stack's 10/2003), G, scratched, $21,850.

W-4785 · 1786 · Maris 11.5-G

Notes: Eleven recorded by Ray Williams, the finest being an especially nice Very Fine in the O'Donnell Collection. *Rarity:* URS-5.

G-4	VG-8	F-12	VF-20	EF-40
$900	$1,500	$2,750	$15,000	$25,000

W-4790 · 1786 · Maris 12-G

Notes: The most widely available of the Coulterless varieties. Breen mentioned an "MS-65" in an Ohio collection (*CNL*, February 1974). A fine collection in New Jersey contains an Extremely Fine to About Uncirculated example, ex Jacob Spiro Collection, with some mint color. *Rarity:* URS-7.

G-4	VG-8	F-12	VF-20	EF-40
$900	$1,500	$2,750	$8,250	$15,000

W-4795 · 1786 · Maris 12-I

Notes: Three Extremely Fine coins recorded (including one ex Ford, thought to have been conservatively graded); one is slightly retooled at the horse's eye. Shield details usually weak. *Rarity:* URS-6.

G-4	VG-8	F-12	VF-20	EF-40
$900	$1,500	$2,750	$7,500	$15,000

Other 1786 Issues

W-4800 · 1786 · Maris 13-J

Notes: With "square" M in UNUM. Michael J. Hodder suggests that this and the next are the first two coins made at the Rahway mint. Although both are dated 1786, likely coinage did not commence until January 1787. Breen mentioned an "MS-65" in a Plainfield, New Jersey, collection (*CNL*, February 1974); this is now evaluated as Extremely Fine, ex Spiro and Bareford collections. The finest are the Garrett and Spiro-Bareford coins, cataloged as Extremely Fine, now graded About Uncirculated. *Rarity:* URS-5.

G-4	VG-8	F-12	VF-20	EF-40
$900	$1,500	$3,000	$5,000	$20,000

W-4810 · 1786 · Maris 14-J

Notes: With "square" M in UNUM. One of the most often seen New Jersey varieties. Roger S. Siboni has examined six Mint State coins. *Rarity:* URS-12.

G-4	VG-8	F-12	VF-20	EF-40	AU-50	MS-60
$500	$750	$1,000	$3,000	$5,000	$10,000	$15,000

W-4815 · 1786 · Maris 15-J

Notes: Obverse 15 exists in several die states relating to a crack that begins at the top of EA and continues around the border through the base of the date. With "square" M in UNUM. The finest is the Maris to Garrett to O'Donnell coin. Extremely Fine coins abound. *Rarity:* URS-11.

G-4	VG-8	F-12	VF-20	EF-40	AU-50	MS-60
$500	$750	$1,000	$3,000	$5,000	$12,500	$30,000

W-4820 · 1786 · Maris 15-L

Notes: The Garrett coin is Mint State and may be the finest, followed by three About Uncirculated, then Extremely Fine. *Rarity:* URS-10.

Selected auction price(s): John J. Ford Jr. I Sale (Stack's 10/2003), EF, $3,450. Requa Collection (Stack's [ANR] 9/2006), VF-35, $1,265.

W-4825 · 1786 · Maris 15-T

Notes: With "square" M in UNUM. At least three Mint State and a handful of Extremely Fine coins are known. Maris called the variety "rather scarce." *Rarity:* URS-8.

G-4	VG-8	F-12	VF-20	EF-40	AU-50	MS-60
$500	$750	$1,000	$2,500	$5,000	$7,500	$30,000

W-4830 · 1786 · Maris 15-U

Notes: The finest is Extremely Fine. Michael J. Hodder determined that most Maris 15-U coppers were struck after the 1787-dated 33-U. Maris thought the die combination to be unique. *Rarity:* URS-6.

G-4	VG-8	F-12	VF-20	EF-40	AU-50	MS-60
$500	$1,000	$2,000	$3,500	$5,000		

W-4835 · 1786 · Maris 16-J

Notes: With "square" M in UNUM. Same obverse die as the following, but struck before the die crack occurred. Two Extremely Fine coins may be the best. *Rarity:* URS-6.

G-4	VG-8	F-12	VF-20	EF-40	AU-50	MS-60
$600	$1,200	$2,000	$5,000			$35,000

W-4840 · 1786 · Maris 16-L · Protruding Tongue variety

Notes: Nicknamed for a die crack at the horse's mouth (present on all but a few specimens). This is one of the more plentiful New Jersey varieties. Several are Mint State, followed by About Uncirculated and Extremely Fine examples. *Rarity:* URS-12.

G-4	VG-8	F-12	VF-20	EF-40	AU-50	MS-60
$350	$500	$2,000	$3,000	$5,000	$10,000	$15,000

W-4845 · 1786 · Maris 16-S

Notes: Discovered by William Pullen; now in the Anton Collection. Very Fine. *Rarity:* URS-1.

W-4850 · 1786 · Maris 16-d

Notes: Discovered by Thomas Hall in 1893 and recorded in his copy of Maris's text. Four reported, the finest Choice Extremely Fine (Ford, ex Brand, earlier called Unc.), a figure also agreed to by William T. Anton Jr. *Rarity:* URS-3.

Selected auction price(s): John J. Ford Jr. I Sale (Stack's 10/2003), Choice EF, $80,500.

W-4860 · 1786 · Maris 17-J

Notes: With "square" M in UNUM. Usually found in low grades, and often struck over another coin, especially Connecticut coppers. The finest recorded by Ray Williams is About Uncirculated, followed by several at the Extremely Fine level. *Rarity:* URS-8.

G-4	VG-8	F-12	VF-20	EF-40	AU-50	MS-60
$200	$500	$1,000	$3,000	$5,000	$8,000	

W-4865 · 1786 · Maris 17-K

Notes: Maris suggests these were struck prior to Maris 17-J and b as the obverse die state is earlier. Breen suggests that this die pair was first used at the Rahway mint on regulation planchets, and later by Matthias Ogden in Elizabethtown, with lighter stock, often overstruck on Machin's Mills and Connecticut coppers. *Rarity:* URS-10.

G-4	VG-8	F-12	VF-20	EF-40	AU-50	MS-60
		$3,000				

W-4870 · 1786 · Maris 17-b · PLUKIBUS reverse

Notes: Nicknamed the PLUKIBUS as the R is open at the top (so designated by Crosby). Ford's Mint State might be the best. Three production runs of these, the first mostly overstruck on 1787 Connecticut coppers (also on Nova Constellatio coppers and one on a Vermont RR-9) and lightweight, the second on better planchets generally 28 mm and plus or minus 150 grains, the third on small "dumpy" planchets, per Ray Williams. *Rarity:* URS-10.

G-4	VG-8	F-12	VF-20	EF-40	AU-50	MS-60
$575	$1,500	$2,000	$5,000	$7,500	—	

W-4875 · 1786 · Maris 18-J · Bridle variety

Notes: With "square" M in UNUM. This obverse die, also used on the next several varieties, has a small extraneous 6 above regular 6 in date, embedded in the plowshare; discovered by Buell Ish and published in the *C4 Newsletter*. The "Bridle" obverse die, from a crack. Two About Uncirculated coins may be the finest. Breen mentioned an impression in brass. (*CNL*, February 1974). *Rarity:* URS-7.

G-4	VG-8	F-12	VF-20	EF-40	AU-50	MS-60
$100	$250	$750	$1,000	$4,000	$10,000	—

W-4880 · 1786 · Maris 18-L

Notes: Unique. Maris to Garrett to Picker to Anton. Very Good. *Rarity:* URS-1.

W-4890 · 1786 · Maris 18-M · Wide Shield reverse

Notes: First of the varieties with "Wide Shield" reverse. One of the more plentiful New Jersey varieties. Several Mint State coins known. *Rarity:* URS-12.

G-4	VG-8	F-12	VF-20	EF-40	AU-50	MS-60
$70	$85	$240	$675	$2,400	$4,000	

W-4895 · 1786 · Maris 18-N · Wide Shield reverse

Notes: The finest are Extremely Fine. *Rarity:* URS-7.

G-4	VG-8	F-12	VF-20	EF-40	AU-50	MS-60
$150	$400	$900	$2,500	$6,000		

W-4900 · 1786 · Maris 19-M · Wide Shield reverse

Notes: The 1 in date too far left and tilted sharply left; very distinctive. Two Mint State coins exist. *Rarity:* URS-7.

G-4	VG-8	F-12	VF-20	EF-40	AU-50	MS-60
$150	$400	$900	$2,500	$6,000		

W-4905 · 1786 · Maris 20-N · Wide Shield reverse · Drunken Die Cutter obverse

Notes: Ray Williams: "Named for the misplaced horse head, rotated counterclockwise and positioned high and to the left. The '1' in the date is angled up and to the left and looks more like a gouge than a numeral." *Rarity:* URS-8.

G-4	VG-8	F-12	VF-20	EF-40	AU-50	MS-60
$70	$85	$240	$675	$2,400	$4,000	

W-4910 · 1786 · Maris 21-N · Wide Shield reverse

Notes: Finest are two Mint State (as reported by William T. Anton Jr.), most of the other high-grade examples are Very Fine or Extremely Fine. *Rarity:* URS-11.

G-4	VG-8	F-12	VF-20	EF-40	AU-50	MS-60
$70	$85	$240	$675	$2,400	$4,000	

W-4915 · 1786 · Maris 21-O · Wide Shield reverse

Notes: Finest is Mint State, followed by several graded Extremely Fine. *Rarity:* URS-7.

G-4	VG-8	F-12	VF-20	EF-40	AU-50	MS-60
$70	$85	$240	$675	$2,400	$4,000	

W-4920 · 1786 · Maris 21-P

Notes: With a bulged obverse die and a crack at E, and thus struck later than Maris 21-O. William T. Anton Jr. reports two Mint State (not including the Ford coin, scratched and perhaps recolored). *Rarity:* URS-7.

G-4	VG-8	F-12	VF-20	EF-40	AU-50	MS-60
$80	$185	$275	$750	$2,700	$4,500	

W-4925 · 1786 · Maris 21-R

Notes: Rare combination of two dies that are common on other varieties. Unknown to Maris. Discovered by Dr. Hall circa 1892. Finest Very Fine or so. *Rarity:* URS-4.

Selected auction price(s): O'Donnell Collection (Stack's 1/2001), VG, $7,475. John J. Ford Jr. I Sale (Stack's 10/2003), VF, $17,250.

W-4930 · 1786 · Maris 21.5-R

Notes: Discovered by Henry Chapman in 1903 and sold to Ryder; the Ford coin. Another is in the Anton collection ex Richard Picker. Illustrated in the 1914 ANS Exhibition catalog. A third, in Fine grade, surfaced on eBay. *Rarity:* URS-3.

Selected auction price(s): John J. Ford Jr. I Sale (Stack's 10/2003), VF, microgranular, $51,750.

W-4935 · 1786 · Maris 22-P · Coulterless

Notes: Coulterless obverse far out of numerical sequence with other varieties lacking this plow element. The 6 in date punched over a smaller 6. Finest is the Ford coin, which Roger Siboni and Ray Williams grade as Very Fine. Maris's assigning of the 22 number to a Coulterless obverse was out of step with his other listings. *Rarity:* URS-4.

Selected auction price(s): John J. Ford Jr. I Sale (Stack's 10/2003), F, scratched, $46,000.

W-4940 · 1786 · Maris 23-P

Notes: One About Uncirculated is known, followed by several in Very Fine grade. *Rarity:* URS-10.

G-4	VG-8	F-12	VF-20	EF-40	AU-50	MS-60
$60	$150	$250	$800	$2,000	$4,000	

W-4945 · 1786 · Maris 23-R

Notes: Finest is Mint State, followed by several About Uncirculated. *Rarity:* URS-10.

G-4	VG-8	F-12	VF-20	EF-40	AU-50	MS-60
$60	$150	$250	$800	$2,000	$4,000	

W-4950 · 1786 · Maris 23.5-R

Notes: Discovered by Dr. Hall in April 1895. Rare variety. Ray Williams knows of only three. *Rarity:* URS-3.

Selected auction price(s): Norweb I Sale (10/1987), VF, $13,200. John J. Ford Jr. I Sale (Stack's 10/2003), Choice VF, $51,750.

W-4955 · 1786 · Maris 24-I

Notes: Rare. Two Very Fine coins tied for finest, followed by a single Very Good with scratches. *Rarity:* URS-3.

W-4960 · 1786 · Maris 24-M · Wide Shield reverse

Notes: Discovered by William T. Anton Jr. in 1969 and acquired by him in the Harmer Rooke sale of November in the same year. Finest is Extremely Fine, then a sharp drop to Fine and Very Good. Total of four known. *Rarity:* URS-3.

Selected auction price(s): C4 Convention (M&G 11/2001), VG-8, $8,000.

W-4965 · 1786 · Maris 24-P

Notes: At least two Mint State known. *Rarity:* URS-11.

G-4	VG-8	F-12	VF-20	EF-40	AU-50	MS-60
$60	$150	$250	$800	$2,000	$4,000	

W-4970 · 1786 · Maris 24-Q

Notes: Extremely Fine finest, then a drop to Very Good and Fine to Very Fine (William T. Anton Jr. survey). The Q reverse is remarkable for the depth of the shield in the reverse die. *Rarity:* URS-3.

W-4975 · 1786 · Maris 24-R

Notes: Maris knew of only one, but modern-day scholar Michael J. Hodder has seen 24—an interesting reflection of how rarity estimates can change. Finest is Mint State. *Rarity:* URS-7.

Selected auction price(s): O'Donnell Collection (Stack's 1/2001), VF, $1,035. John J. Ford Jr. I Sale (Stack's 10/2003), Choice F, $2,530.

W-4980 · 1786 · Maris 25-S

Notes: Scarce. The S reverse was studied in *CNL*, January 1991. Usually in low grades. *Rarity:* URS-8.

G-4	VG-8	F-12	VF-20	EF-40	AU-50	MS-60
$80	$185	$300	$1,000	$5,000		

W-4995 · 1786 · Maris 26-S

Notes: Two Extremely Fine coins are the finest. Some were used as undertypes for 1787 Immunis Columbia coppers (*CNL*, Spring 1997); at least four of these are known today. *Rarity:* URS-7.

G-4	VG-8	F-12	VF-20	EF-40	AU-50	MS-60
$100	$300	$750	$2,000	$5,000		

W-4990 · 1786 · Maris 26-d
Notes: Discovered by Richard August in 1973. One in the Anton Collection, another in the M.D. Collection. One holed, the other a multiple strike. *Rarity:* URS-2.

1787 New Jersey Coppers

W-5040 · 1787 · Maris 6-C
Notes: Earlier states seen on large planchets. S (CÆSAREA) too large. The only readily collectible variety with reverse C. As such, it is in especially strong demand. Finest is Mint State. *Rarity:* URS-8.

G-4	VG-8	F-12	VF-20	EF-40	AU-50	MS-60
$60	$150	$200	$1,500	$4,000	$8,500	

W-5050 · 1787 · Maris 6-D
Notes: All seen are on large planchets. Always with thin, weak date. Three Mint State coins are known to William T. Anton Jr. *Rarity:* URS-12.

G-4	VG-8	F-12	VF-20	EF-40	AU-50	MS-60
$60	$150	$200	$600	$1,400	$3,000	

W-5055 · 1787 · Maris 27-S
Notes: Final A in CÆSAREA punched over an erroneous I. First of the "ball handles" dies comprising Maris 27, 28, 29, 30, and 55 obverses. *Rarity:* URS-7.

G-4	VG-8	F-12	VF-20	EF-40	AU-50	MS-60
$70	$175	$300	$1,000	$3,500	$7,000	

W-5060 · 1787 · Maris 27-j
Notes: Discovered by Dr. Hall in the 1890s. First A over erroneous I. Knob handles to plow (see W-5055, Maris 27-j for list). Finest two are tied for Extremely Fine (per Roger Siboni and Ray Williams). *Rarity:* URS-5.

G-4	VG-8	F-12	VF-20	EF-40	AU-50	MS-60
$900	$1,500	$2,700	$5,000	$15,000		

W-5065 · 1787 · Maris 28-L
Notes: Knob handles to plow. Finest is Mint State. Ford's was Extremely Fine. *Rarity:* URS-10.

G-4	VG-8	F-12	VF-20	EF-40	AU-50	MS-60
$60	$150	$200	$600	$1,400	$3,000	

W-5070 · 1787 · Maris 28-S
Notes: Knob handles to plow. Die crack from V into the neck. William T. Anton Jr. considers the Garrett coin to be the very finest known of any New Jersey copper. *Rarity:* URS-7.

G-4	VG-8	F-12	VF-20	EF-40	AU-50	MS-60
$80	$185	$275	$750	$2,700	$4,500	

W-5075 · 1787 · Maris 29-L
Notes: Knob handles to plow. Usually found with obverse weakness, without a full outline to the horse's head. Finest are two About Uncirculated. *Rarity:* URS-8.

G-4	VG-8	F-12	VF-20	EF-40	AU-50	MS-60
$60	$150	$200	$800	$2,000	$5,000	

W-5085 · 1787 · Maris 29.5-L
Notes: The singletree leans to the left. All other New Jersey singletrees are either straight up or lean to the right. No knobs on plow handles. Discovered by Lawrence Stack and William T. Anton Jr. in a group of miscellaneous coins at Stack's, lot 2284 in the Coin Galleries sale of July18, 1990. Described by Anton at the New Jersey Copper Symposium in 1991: "I designated it a 29 1/2-L. . . . The head on the coin is identical to the Maris 70 obverse. It's a thick moppy looking head. Last but not least, the plow handles point all the way down like an obverse Maris 79. It's the regular L reverse, it has an S letter punched in CAEsAREA like no other New Jersey copper, it is about half the size." Not examined by the author or other consultants to this book. *Rarity:* URS-1.

W-5090 · 1787 · Maris 30-L
Notes: Knob handles to plow. William T. Anton Jr. estimates that five Mint State coins exist. *Rarity:* URS-10.

G-4	VG-8	F-12	VF-20	EF-40	AU-50	MS-60
$60	$150	$200	$600	$1,400	$3,000	

W-5095 · 1787 · Maris 31-L
Notes: Usually with multiple die cracks on the obverse. Finest is Mint State. *Rarity:* URS-11.

G-4	VG-8	F-12	VF-20	EF-40	AU-50	MS-60
$60	$150	$200	$600	$1,400	$3,000	

W-5100 · 1787 · Maris 32-T
Notes: With "square" M in UNUM. Common variety. Two Mint State coins are the finest. *Rarity:* URS-12.

G-4	VG-8	F-12	VF-20	EF-40	AU-50	MS-60
$60	$150	$200	$600	$1,400	$3,000	

W-5110 · 1787 · Maris 33-U
Notes: Maris: "Quite scarce. Both dies badly broken." In actuality, the reverse die shows cracks. Only three (see William T. Anton Jr.) have been seen with a chip out of the die within the shield, as always seen on Maris 15-U. *Rarity:* URS-8.

G-4	VG-8	F-12	VF-20	EF-40	AU-50	MS-60
$70	$175	$225	$700	$1,550	$3,500	

W-5115 · 1787 · Maris 34-J
Notes: Sometimes called the Deer Head variety. With "square" M in UNUM. A die crack begins at the rim and

develops to extend upward between 7 and 8, and to become very large. Sometimes overstruck on other coins. Finest grade is About Uncirculated. *Rarity:* URS-10.

G-4	VG-8	F-12	VF-20	EF-40	AU-50	MS-60
$60	$150	$200	$600	$1,400	$3,000	

W-5120 · 1787 · Maris 34-V
Notes: Reverse with small shield, and with legend punctuated by a five-pointed star instead of the normal six points. Shield typically weak; with full shield the variety is a rarity. Finest is About Uncirculated. *Rarity:* URS-6.

G-4	VG-8	F-12	VF-20	EF-40	AU-50	MS-60
$800	$1,200	$2,000	$4,000	$6,500	$9,000	

W-5125 · 1787 · Maris 35-J · 1787 Over 1887
Notes: First 7 engraved as an 8, then corrected. Reverse die usually slightly rotated from the normal 180°. With "square" M in UNUM. Finest is Extremely Fine. Known struck over English halfpence. One is known overstruck on a Maris 34-V in turn overstruck on a 1788 RR-16 (not RR-12 as once reported) Vermont. *Rarity:* URS-6.

G-4	VG-8	F-12	VF-20	EF-40	AU-50	MS-60
		$3,500	$8,000	$20,000		

W-5130 · 1787 · Maris 35-W
Notes: Finest is Very Fine or better coin in the New Jersey Historical Society, overstruck on an Irish halfpenny. Ford's is second finest. *Rarity:* URS-4.

Selected auction price(s): John J. Ford Jr. I Sale (Stack's 10/2003), VF, some minor problems, "finest available to collectors," $46,000.

W-5135 · 1787 · Maris 36-J
Notes: The obverse lettering was engraved into the die, not punched; curious die of numismatically unfortunate rarity. With "square" M in UNUM. Finest is Mint State, next are two at the Very Fine level. *Rarity:* URS-4.

Selected auction price(s): Garrett III Sale (B&R 10/1980), EF–AU, $9,000. John J. Ford Jr. I Sale (Stack's 10/2003), AG, flaws, $6,900.

W-5140 · 1787 · Maris 37-J · Goiter variety
Notes: Goiter-like die break under horse's chin; no other state of this die seen. With "square" M in UNUM. Finest is About Uncirculated. *Rarity:* URS-7.

G-4	VG-8	F-12	VF-20	EF-40	AU-50	MS-60
$100	$200	$450	$1,000	$2,500		

W-5145 · 1787 · Maris 37-X · Goiter variety
Notes: Finest is Very Fine. *Rarity:* URS-4.

Selected auction price(s): O'Donnell Collection (Stack's 1/2001), VF, $43,700. John J. Ford Jr. I Sale (Stack's 10/2003), F–VF, $29,900. Public Auction Sale (Stack's 9/2006), F, $20,700.

W-5150 · 1787 · Maris 37-Y · Goiter variety
Notes: Reverse often weak. Finest is About Uncirculated. *Rarity:* URS-8.

G-4	VG-8	F-12	VF-20	EF-40	AU-50	MS-60
$150	$275	$500	$1,000	$2,500	$5,000	

W-5155 · 1787 · Maris 37-f · Goiter variety
Notes: Maris noted that the reverse of 1787 Maris 37-f is found with die cracks, unlike the later-dated 1788 Maris 49-f and 50-f without the break, a commentary that dating of a die can be one thing and the date of striking different. Finest is Extremely Fine or so. *Rarity:* URS-8.

G-4	VG-8	F-12	VF-20	EF-40	AU-50	MS-60
$150	$275	$500	$1,000	$2,500	$5,000	

W-5160 · 1787 · Maris 38-L · Small Head
Notes: This obverse is sometimes called the Small Head. Discovered in 1969 by Robert Lindesmith and sold into the Anton Collection (*CNL*, September 1969). *Rarity:* URS-1.

W-5170 · 1787 · Maris 38-Y · Small Head
Notes: Finest is Mint State. *Rarity:* URS-8.

G-4	VG-8	F-12	VF-20	EF-40	AU-50	MS-60
$60	$150	$200	$600	$1,400	$3,000	

W-5175 · 1787 · Maris 38-Z · Small Head
Notes: Found on large and small planchets. Struck from cracked obverse and reverse dies. Finest is Mint State. *Rarity:* URS-8.

G-4	VG-8	F-12	VF-20	EF-40	AU-50	MS-60
$60	$150	$200	$600	$1,400	$3,000	

W-5180 · 1787 · Maris 38-a · Small Head
Notes: Maris thought this variety to be common. Today, examples are met with on occasion, but examples with a full date are elusive. Finest is Extremely Fine. *Rarity:* URS-7.

Selected auction price(s): John J. Ford Jr. I Sale (Stack's 10/2003), EF, $8,050.

W-5185 · 1787 · Maris 38-b · Small Head
Notes: Finest is About Uncirculated, cherrypicked by Henry Garrett from an auction held by a Midwest firm. *Rarity:* URS-6.

G-4	VG-8	F-12	VF-20	EF-40	AU-50	MS-60
$800	$1,200	$2,000	$4,000	$6,500	$9,000	

W-5190 · 1787 · Maris 38-c · Small Head
Notes: This is the only reverse with seven vertical pales in the shield. Broken outline to the shield, in contrast to Maris 44-c, with a complete outline. The finest pieces grade About Uncirculated. *Rarity:* URS-10.

G-4	VG-8	F-12	VF-20	EF-40	AU-50	MS-60
$60	$150	$200	$600	$1,400	$3,000	

W-5195 · 1787 · Maris 39-a

Notes: Several Mint State coins are known to William T. Anton Jr. Multiple-strike examples are seen with some frequency. *Rarity:* URS-11.

G-4	VG-8	F-12	VF-20	EF-40	AU-50	MS-60
$60	$150	$200	$600	$1,400	$3,000	

W-5200 · 1787 · Maris 40-b

Notes: Finest is About Uncirculated. Known struck over Irish halfpence. *Rarity:* URS-7.

G-4	VG-8	F-12	VF-20	EF-40	AU-50	MS-60
$200	$600	$1,800	$4,000	$10,000		

W-5205 · 1787 · Maris 41-c

Notes: Finest is About Uncirculated in a New York collection. *Rarity:* URS-6.

G-4	VG-8	F-12	VF-20	EF-40	AU-50	MS-60
$300	$700	$2,000	$4,500	$12,000		

W-5210 · 1787 · Maris 42-c

Notes: Some with die crack from dentils to top of second 7. Some later-state coins show reengraving of reverse details. Finest are Very Fine to Extremely Fine. *Rarity:* URS-6.

G-4	VG-8	F-12	VF-20	EF-40	AU-50	MS-60
$80	$185	$300	$1,000	$4,000	$7,000	

W-5215 · 1787 · Maris 42.5-c

Notes: Discovered by Ed Kucia in 1995 and made public in a *Rare Coin Review* article authored by Michael Hodder. The unique example grades Very Good by today's interpretations. *Rarity:* URS-1.

W-5220 · 1787 · Maris 43-Y

Notes: Shield usually weak. Best are Extremely Fine. *Rarity:* URS-8.

G-4	VG-8	F-12	VF-20	EF-40	AU-50	MS-60
$65	$160	$225	$650	$2,000	$4,500	

W-5225 · 1787 · Maris 43-d

Notes: At least a half dozen Mint State coins exist, per William T. Anton Jr., the finest being the Garrett specimen. *Rarity:* URS-12.

G-4	VG-8	F-12	VF-20	EF-40	AU-50	MS-60
$60	$150	$200	$600	$1,400	$3,000	

W-5230 · 1787 · Maris 44-c

Notes: The only reverse with seven vertical pales to the shield. Complete outline to shield, and thus struck before any other varieties with the c reverse. Finest is Extremely Fine. *Rarity:* URS-4.

Selected auction price(s): John J. Ford Jr. I Sale (Stack's 10/2003), EF, $25,300.

W-5235 · 1787 · Maris 44-d

Notes: Called the "Sleigh Runner" variety by Montroville W. Dickeson in the *American Numismatical Manual*, 1859. Breen mentioned an impression in brass. (*CNL*, February 1974). A half dozen or so Extremely Fine coins are the finest. *Rarity:* URS-8.

G-4	VG-8	F-12	VF-20	EF-40	AU-50	MS-60
$60	$150	$200	$600	$1,400	$3,000	

W-5240 · 1787 · Maris 45-d

Notes: Extremely Fine is the finest. Scarce in high grades. *Rarity:* URS-7.

G-4	VG-8	F-12	VF-20	EF-40	AU-50	MS-60
$80	$200	$300	$1,000	$2,700		

W-5245 · 1787 · Maris 45-e

Notes: The 1 in date is the Roman numeral I, and the uprights of the 7's are curved at the bottom—very distinctive. The finest is Mint State in the cabinet of a collector in New Jersey. *Rarity:* URS-7.

G-4	VG-8	F-12	VF-20	EF-40	AU-50	MS-60
$80	$200	$300	$900	$2,500	$7,000	

W-5250 · 1787 · Maris 46-e

Notes: An easily found variety. William T. Anton Jr. has recorded a half-dozen Mint State coins. Always seen with multiple die clashes on the obverse; unless this happened when the dies first were used, a perfect-die coin remains a possibility. *Rarity:* URS-12.

G-4	VG-8	F-12	VF-20	EF-40	AU-50	MS-60
$60	$150	$200	$600	$1,400	$3,000	

W-5255 · 1787 · Maris 47-e

Notes: A scarce variety marking the only use of this obverse die. Finest is About Uncirculated. *Rarity:* URS-6.

G-4	VG-8	F-12	VF-20	EF-40	AU-50	MS-60
$800	$1,200	$2,000	$4,000	$6,500	$12,000	

W-5260 · 1787 · Maris 47.5-e

Notes: Discovered by Walter Breen in Baltimore in 1951. The finest, Very Fine, is in the Anton Collection. *Rarity:* URS-3.

Selected auction price(s): John J. Ford Jr. I Sale (Stack's 10/2003), VG/AG, granular, discovery coin, $13,800.

W-5265 · 1787 · Maris 48-X

Notes: Discovered by Jacob Spiro in 1950. Finest examples are Very Fine. Four are known to William T. Anton Jr., some overstruck on other coins. *Rarity:* URS-4.

Selected auction price(s): John J. Ford Jr. I Sale (Stack's 10/2003), VF, rough and granular, $9,200. Lorenzo Collection (Stack's 1/2008), VF-20, $43,125.

W-5270 · 1787 · Maris 48-f

Notes: Struck later than the 1788 Maris 50-f, per die-state evidence. Finest examples are About Uncirculated. *Rarity:* URS-10.

G-4	VG-8	F-12	VF-20	EF-40	AU-50	MS-60
$60	$150	$200	$600	$1,400	$3,000	

W-5275 · 1787 · Maris 48-g · Pronounced Outline to Shield

Notes: Most prominent outline of the Outline to Shield dies. Common variety. Struck after the 1788 Maris 51-g, per die-state evidence. Most exhibit a die crack across the shield. There are at least three distinctively different reverse die states. Several Mint State coins are known. *Rarity:* URS-12.

G-4	VG-8	F-12	VF-20	EF-40	AU-50	MS-60
$60	$150	$220	$650	$1,400	$2,500	

W-5280 · 1787 · Maris 52-i

Notes: Easily enough found in the marketplace. Finest is Mint State; second-finest are several at the About Uncirculated level. *Rarity:* URS-10.

G-4	VG-8	F-12	VF-20	EF-40	AU-50	MS-60
$60	$150	$200	$600	$1,400	$3,000	

W-5290 · 1787 · Maris 53-j · Period After CÆSAREA

Notes: Tiny 8 in date, period after CÆSAREA. Several Mint State coins are known. *Rarity:* URS-8.

G-4	VG-8	F-12	VF-20	EF-40	AU-50	MS-60
$70	$160	$220	$650	$1,500	$3,500	

W-5295 · 1787 · Maris 54-k · Serpent Head

Notes: So called from the shape of the neck and head. Popular from its availability and wide listings. "It does look as though it should reside at Loch Ness," commented Ray Williams. Finest may be the Ford Mint State. *Rarity:* URS-10.

G-4	VG-8	F-12	VF-20	EF-40	AU-50	MS-60
$85	$190	$375	$1,550	$3,500	$5,750	

W-5300 · 1787 · Maris 55-l · PLURIRUS

Notes: So-called PLURIRUS from a broken B punch. Knob handles to plow (see W-5055, Maris 27-j for list). Finest is Mint State, followed by several Extremely Fine coins. *Rarity:* URS-7.

G-4	VG-8	F-12	VF-20	EF-40	AU-50	MS-60
$170	$300	$475	$1,100	$3,200	$5,000	

W-5305 · 1787 · Maris 55-m

Notes: Knob handles to plow. PLURIBS misspelling corrected to PLURIBUS, with second U over an erroneous S. *Rarity:* URS-8.

G-4	VG-8	F-12	VF-20	EF-40	AU-50	MS-60
$60	$150	$200	$600	$1,400	$3,000	

W-5310 · 1787 · Maris 56-n · Camel Head

Notes: Knob handles to plow. This may be the most common of all New Jersey coppers. Most of these were overstruck on other coins, the undertypes including Connecticut, Machin's Mills, Vermont, Nova Eborac, Nova Constellatio, English, and Irish coppers—a wider variety of undertypes than found on any other state copper coin (Philip L. Mossman, p. 237, gives a detailed list, updated in *CNL*, 130). William T. Anton Jr. has recorded eight Mint State examples. *Rarity:* URS-13.

G-4	VG-8	F 12	VF 20	EF-40	AU-50	MS-60
$70	$170	$230	$800	$1,500	$2,750	

W-5315 · 1787 · Maris 57-n · Camel Head

Notes: Nickname occasionally used. Maris knew of only two. Often overstruck on other coins including Machin's Mills, Connecticut, and Vermont coppers. One has been seen with a shattered obverse die. The finest is About Uncirculated, in the Richard August Collection. *Rarity:* URS-5.

G-4	VG-8	F-12	VF-20	EF-40	AU-50	MS-60
$800	$1,600	$3,500	$8,000	$18,000		

W-5320 · 1787 · Maris 58-n · Star Below Plow Handles · Camel Head

Notes: Unique die with a perfectly formed five-pointed star, with "tail" extending downward, positioned below the plow handles; the significance of this is unknown today (not all pieces show this feature). Some are overstruck on other coins. Several About Uncirculated coins exist. *Rarity:* URS-7.

G-4	VG-8	F-12	VF-20	EF-40	AU-50	MS-60
$100	$200	$500	$1,200	$3,000		

W-5325 · 1787 · Maris 59-o · Sawtooth variety

Notes: Especially prominent, sawtooth-like dentils on the obverse, prompting Maris to assign this nickname. Obverse and reverse typically light at the centers. Two Mint State coins are known to William T. Anton Jr., both double struck (ex Spiro and Bareford collections). *Rarity:* URS-7.

G-4	VG-8	F-12	VF-20	EF-40	AU-50	MS-60
$150	$300	$600	$1,800	$4,000		

W-5335 · 1787 · Maris 59-mm · Sawtooth variety

Notes: Discovered by Roger Moore on eBay and captured by him. Very Good. *Rarity:* URS-1.

W-5340 · 1787 · Maris 60-p · PLURIBS

Notes: Everlastingly popular variety due to the misspelling on the reverse. Also used with obverse 61. Finest examples are About Uncirculated. (Also see Maris 55-m.). *Rarity:* URS-8.

G-4	VG-8	F-12	VF-20	EF-40	AU-50	MS-60
$125	$250	$500	$1,600	$3,750	$7,400	

W-5345 · 1787 · Maris 61-p · PLURIBS

Notes: Another iteration of this popular reverse. Die crack behind the mane. Finest is About Uncirculated. *Rarity:* URS-7.

G-4	VG-8	F-12	VF-20	EF-40	AU-50	MS-60
$125	$250	$500	$1,600	$3,750	$7,400	

W-5350 · 1787 · Maris 62-q

Notes: One of the most plentiful New Jersey varieties. Die cracks are found under the plow beam. Usually with weakness at the centers of both sides. Several Mint State coins are reported. Obverse 62 is of special interest as the initials WM (for "Walter Mould") can be seen under the left and right leaves below the horse's head on early-die-state examples in high grades. *Rarity:* URS-12.

G-4	VG-8	F-12	VF-20	EF-40	AU-50	MS-60
$60	$150	$200	$600	$1,400	$3,000	$9,000

W-5355 · 1787 · Maris 62-r
Notes: Discovered by Richard August in 1974. Ray Williams records four, the finest Fine to Very Fine. *Rarity:* URS-3.

W-5360 · 1787 · Maris 62.5-r · WM on obverse
Notes: Dramatic new variety with WM (most certainly for "Walter Mould") in relief on the obverse. Authenticated and published by Michael J. Hodder. Brought to market by B&M in August 1996, now in a Long Island, New York, collection. Very Fine to Extremely Fine. *Rarity:* URS-1.

W-5365 · 1787 · Maris 63-q
Notes: Plentiful in most grades, with multiple Extremely Fine coins, several About Uncirculated, and two Mint State. *Rarity:* URS-12.

G-4	VG-8	F-12	VF-20	EF-40	AU-50	MS-60
$100	$200	$550	$1,250	$3,500		

W-5370 · 1787 · Maris 63-r
Notes: Large planchet adds a degree of popularity. Finest are at the Extremely Fine to About Uncirculated level. *Rarity:* URS-7.

G-4	VG-8	F-12	VF-20	EF-40	AU-50	MS-60
$80	$170	$220	$650	$1,500	$3,500	

W-5375 · 1787 · Maris 63-s
Notes: Plentiful in most grades. Three recorded as Mint State. *Rarity:* URS-12.

G-4	VG-8	F-12	VF-20	EF-40	AU-50	MS-60
$60	$150	$200	$600	$1,400	$3,000	

W-5380 · 1787 · Maris 64-t
Notes: Large and small planchets. Readily available in most grades. The Kissner sale coin (Stack's, June 1975) weighed a remarkable 192 grains. Large-planchet examples with no roughness at the center are extremely rare. Finest are two Mint State, including one sold earlier (before the Stack's sale) by John J. Ford Jr. (per William T. Anton Jr.). *Rarity:* URS-12.

G-4	VG-8	F-12	VF-20	EF-40	AU-50	MS-60
$60	$150	$200	$600	$1,400	$3,000	

W-5390 · 1787 · Maris 64-u
Notes: Large planchet. Finest is About Uncirculated. *Rarity:* URS-7.

G-4	VG-8	F-12	VF-20	EF-40	AU-50	MS-60
$150	$300	$800	$1,800	$4,000		

W-5400 · 1787 · Maris 68-w
Notes: Rare if on a good planchet and well struck. Reverse shield somewhat casually engraved and not quite symmetrical, not unlike the Maris 83-ii reverse shield. Finest is Mint State or close. *Rarity:* URS-7.

G-4	VG-8	F-12	VF-20	EF-40	AU-50	MS-60
$150	$300	$800	$1,600	$3,500		

W-5405 · 1787 · Maris 69-w
Notes: Ray Williams records two, in just Fair (Garrett to Anton) and Fair. Counterfeit obverse die muled with an apparently discarded genuine reverse die. *Rarity:* URS-2.

Selected auction price(s): John J. Ford Jr. I Sale (Stack's 10/2003), AG–G, poorly struck as always, $25,300.

W-5410 · 1787 · Maris 70-x
Notes: Maris's coin struck over a 1786 Connecticut copper. Also known over English halfpence. Finest are several Very Fine. *Rarity:* URS-4.

Selected auction price(s): John J. Ford Jr. I Sale (Stack's 10/2003), F–VF, granular, $14,950.

W-5415 · 1787 · Maris 71-y
Notes: Usually struck over another coin, including Connecticut coppers and English halfpence. One over a 1787 RR-24 Vermont was featured in the *C4 Newsletter*, Christmas 1994. Finest is About Uncirculated or better. *Rarity:* URS-6.

G-4	VG-8	F-12	VF-20	EF-40	AU-50	MS-60
$800	$1,200	$2,000	$4,000	$9,000	$12,000	

W-5420 · 1787 · Maris 72-z
Notes: Finest is About Uncirculated. Known struck over Connecticut, English counterfeit, and Irish coppers. *Rarity:* URS-7.

G-4	VG-8	F-12	VF-20	EF-40	AU-50	MS-60
$300	$700	$800	$3,800	$8,000		

W-5430 · 1787 · Maris 73-aa
Notes: One is struck over a 1783 Georgivs Triumpho copper. Others are over Connecticut, English, and Irish coppers. One reported over a Spanish 4 maravedis. The annealing of these undertypes prior to using them as planchets was done poorly, if at all. Accordingly, the undertypes are typically very prominent on the finished coins, making evaluation of the New Jersey die features difficult in some instances. The finest is About Uncirculated. *Rarity:* URS-7.

G-4	VG-8	F-12	VF-20	EF-40	AU-50	MS-60
$70	$220	$300	$900	$2,000	$4,000	

W-5435 · 1787 · Maris 73.5-jj
Notes: Discovered by Richard August in 1979; discussed in the *C4 Newsletter*, Spring 2001. *Rarity:* URS-1.

W-5440 · 1787 · Maris 81-ll
Notes: Contemporary counterfeit. Ray Williams and William T. Anton Jr. record two, the Spiro-Oechsner coin and the Ford example. *Rarity:* URS-2.

Selected auction price(s): John J. Ford Jr. I Sale (Stack's 10/2003), Miller 81-ll, VG, $40,250.

W-5445 · 1787 · Maris 83-ii

Notes: Contemporary counterfeit with crude die work. Finest are three Fine or better coins, followed by Very Good to Fine, and Good. Save for the Garrett coin, all known pieces are porous and very dark. One is known over a Nova Constellatio copper. *Rarity:* URS-4.

Selected auction price(s): Garrett III Sale (B&R 10/1980), F, weak in areas, $7,750. O'Donnell Collection (Stack's 1/2001), Choice F, $18,400.

W-5455 · 1787 · Maris 84-kk

Notes: Contemporary counterfeit. On the reverse the R and B are engraved in mirror image. Two coins, both Very Good, recorded by Ray Williams, one ex Spiro and Oechsner collections, the other ex Ford. William T. Anton Jr. reports a third, which he purchased privately. *Rarity:* URS-3.

Selected auction price(s): John J. Ford Jr. I Sale (Stack's 10/2003), VG, overstruck, $20,700.

1788 New Jersey Coppers

1788 Horse Head Left

W-5470 · 1788 · Maris 49-f

Notes: The reason for the dramatic change of direction of the horse's head for this and the next two obverse dies is not known today, but it must have been significant in its time. This orientation matches the state arms, as does the intricate design of the plow, while the head facing right does not. Finest are a group of About Uncirculated coins (Anton, O'Donnell, and New Jersey Historical Society, although the last has also been graded Extremely Fine). *Rarity:* URS-7.

G-4	VG-8	F-12	VF-20	EF-40	AU-50	MS-60
$450	$850	$1,750	$4,750	$12,500		

W-5475 · 1788 · Maris 50-f

Notes: Struck after the 1787 Maris 48-f, per die-state evidence. Found on large and small planchets. Finest is the Garrett coin, now in a New York collection. *Rarity:* URS-10.

G-4	VG-8	F-12	VF-20	EF-40	AU-50	MS-60
$450	$850	$1,750	$4,750	$12,500		

W-5480 · 1788 · Maris 51-g · Outline to Shield

Notes: Most prominent outline of the Outline to Shield dies. Struck before the 1787 Maris 48-g, as evidenced by the reverse die state. Rarest variety of the Head Left type. Finest is Mint State, followed by a half dozen or more Extremely Fine. *Rarity:* URS-7.

G-4	VG-8	F-12	VF-20	EF-40	AU-50	MS-60
$450	$850	$1,750	$4,750	$12,500		

1788 Horse Head Right · Standard Reverse Type

W-5490 · 1788 · Maris 64.5-r

Notes: Discovered by Lyman H. Low in the 1920s, to W.W.C. Wilson, Newcomer, J.W. Garrett, now in the Anton Collection. One reported to be in the New Jersey Historical Society turned out to be a photograph. *Rarity:* URS-1 or 2.

Selected auction price(s): Garrett III Sale (B&R 10/1980), EF–AU, $11,000.

W-5495 · 1788 · Maris 65-u

Notes: One of the more readily available 1788 issues. Usually on a small planchet, occasionally large. Finest two are Extremely Fine. *Rarity:* URS-10.

G-4	VG-8	F-12	VF-20	EF-40	AU-50	MS-60
$60	$150	$200	$750	$1,400	$3,000	

W-5500 · 1788 · Maris 66-u · Braided Mane

Notes: Nickname from the weaving of the hair. Maris thought this unique. William T. Anton Jr. reports four known today, the finest being the Newcomer-to-Garrett-to-Anton Very Fine coin, closely followed by another nearly as nice. *Rarity:* URS-4.

Selected auction price(s): John J. Ford Jr. I Sale (Stack's 10/2003), F, $19,550. Public Auction Sale (Stack's 5/2005), F, $20,700.

W-5505 · 1788 · Maris 66-v · Braided Mane

Notes: William T. Anton Jr. reports several Mint State coins, one ex Roper collection. The 1914 ANS Exhibition coin went to the Ford collection, there as Extremely Fine. *Rarity:* URS-7.

G-4	VG-8	F-12	VF-20	EF-40	AU-50	MS-60
$60	$150	$200	$750	$1,400	$3,000	

W-5510 · 1788 · Maris 67-v

Notes: The most widely available 1788 issue and thus ideal for a date collection. The reverse is typically very sharp. Finest is the Mint State Roper-to-Anton coin. *Rarity:* URS-12.

G-4	VG-8	F-12	VF-20	EF-40	AU-50	MS-60
$60	$150	$200	$750	$1,400	$3,000	

1788 Horse Head Right · Running Fox Reverse Type

W-5515 · 1788 · Maris 74-bb · Running Fox

Notes: Reverses bb, cc, and dd have a running animal, popularly called a fox, although Maris considered it to be a horse (see correspondence with T. Harrison Garrett, quoted by Bowers in *The History of United States Coinage*, 1979), as did Walter Breen. Others suggest that John Bailey may have coined this; the running fox was his hallmark. On bb and dd it is on the left, on cc on the right. Decorative wreath at base of shield. Most do not show the coulter or the singletree, but well-struck examples have it. A very popular variety in any grade. Finest is Extremely Fine. *Rarity:* URS-6.

G-4	VG-8	F-12	VF-20	EF-40	AU-50	MS-60
$150	$300	$575	$2,200	$4,600	$9,000	

W-5520 · 1788 · Maris 75-bb · Running Fox

Notes: Always with a die crack at the lower left of the obverse, which enlarges to form a cud (piece out of the die). Finest is Mint State, followed by a couple of About Uncirculated. *Rarity:* URS-8.

G-4	VG-8	F-12	VF-20	EF-40	AU-50	MS-60
$150	$300	$575	$2,200	$4,600	$9,000	

W-5525 · 1788 · Maris 76-cc · Running Fox

Notes: Obverse punctuated by a star and a quatrefoil. Reverse cc has the fox on the right side. Finest is Extremely Fine. William T. Anton Jr. reports that four are known. *Rarity:* URS-3.

Selected auction price(s): Garrett III Sale (B&R 10/1980), VF–EF, $15,000. O'Donnell Collection (Stack's 1/2001), Choice VF, ex Garrett, $57,500. John J. Ford Jr. I Sale (Stack's 10/2003), VF, some flaws, $57,500.

W-5530 · 1788 · Maris 77-cc · Running Fox

Notes: In a way this variety was "discovered" by John West, who sent a pencil rubbing of it and other coins to the American Numismatic Society, December 27, 1858. However, varieties of New Jersey coppers had not been studied in detail by that time. In 1881, Maris did not know of it. In modern times another example (in Very Good grade) was identified as an unlisted variety by George Lyman and published by Roger Siboni in *CNL*, April 2007. Upon reading the article, Buell informed Ray Williams that he owned a Very Fine that he had identified earlier, but had not published it as he hoped to bring it to a convention and show it to others to confirm. This new information was published in the *C4 Newsletter*, Summer 2007. Ray Williams records just two, Very Fine and Very Good. The West coin (1858 rubbing) is not accounted for. Rarest of the Running Fox varieties. *Rarity:* URS-2.

W-5535 · 1788 · Maris 77-dd

Notes: This variety is sometimes described with roman-numeral suffixes, as Maris 77-dd I, II, or III, to denote die states. Maris was confused on this and separated one as 78-dd, no longer recognized. Breen mentioned an impression in brass (*CNL*, February 1974). Finest are three Mint State coins. *Rarity:* URS-11.

G-4	VG-8	F-12	VF-20	EF-40	AU-50	MS-60
$150	$300	$575	$2,200	$4,600	$9,000	

New Jersey Coppers (Unknown Date)

W-5550 · 178(?) · Maris 79-ee · Frightened Head

Notes: Three known, About Uncirculated (Ford), Very Fine, and Very Good. Called the "Frightened Head" by Michael J. Hodder in his cataloging of the Ford coins. Dies completely hand engraved, without the use of punches. *Rarity:* URS-3.

Selected auction price(s): John J. Ford Jr. I Sale (Stack's 10/2003), AU, $80,500.

W-5560 · 178(?) · Maris 80-ff

Notes: Maris thought this to be unique and a contemporary counterfeit. The die work is crude, completely hand engraved. On the obverse the N is backward, and the C is very close to the to A (NOVA). On the reverse, B and N are both backward. The Maris plate coin went to T. Harrison Garrett, to the Johns Hopkins University, then to Richard Picker, now in the Anton collection. Graded Very Good by current specialists. *Rarity:* URS-1.

Immunis Columbia, Confederatio, and Related Coppers
1785–1787

History

The CONFEDERATIO legend appears on an interesting series of coins, all extremely rare, dated in the 1780s. There have been many theories about the makers of these dies and places of coinage, but facts are scarce. It has been suggested that these are mostly patterns. The average condition of most examples would seem to belie this, for well-worn coins are the norm. Perhaps the explanation is more simple: by 1785, regal halfpence had not been made for a decade, and, in any event, America was now independent. The need for circulating coppers for small change was filled by many different issues, the Nova Constellatios being examples. American manufacturers made tokens from a profit motive, choosing interesting and often patriotic designs such as General Washington—a scenario no different from what happened in 1837 during the Hard Times era, when dozens of different interesting designs were produced and placed into circulation. Similarly, in the late 1780s in England, the need for circulating halfpence was filled by tokens with different motifs. As to the suggestion, "because some of these are so rare, they must be patterns," it is easily pointed out that any number of die combinations of state copper coins range in rarity from unique to just a handful known, but are not patterns.

Combinations with the CONFEDERATIO dies were made in different formats, including with the standing figure of an Indian surrounded by the legend INIMICA TYRANNIS AMERICANA, a die featuring George Washington, a die with the seated figure of Columbia and with the legend IMMUNIS COLUMBIA, and others. Maris's reverse C for New Jersey coppers was used for certain mulings. No doubt, recipients found the designs to be interesting and meaningful in their time.

Of all early American coppers, coins in this series are among the most enigmatic. Also see New York and Related Coppers in the next section.

1785 Inimica Tyrannis Coppers

W-5630 · 1785 Inimica Tyrannis America / Confederatio · large stars

Obverse: Indian standing near pedestal, arrow in right hand, bow in left. End of arrow below A. INIMICA TYRANNIS to left and right, AMERICA below. *Reverse:* Large circle at center enclosing 13 large stars, Rays around circle. CONFEDERATIO around border, 1785 below. *Notes:* Breen-1123. *Rarity:* URS-4.

Selected auction price(s): Garrett III Sale (B&R 10/1980), VG, weak at reverse center, $9,500. Roper Sale (Stack's 12/1983), F, $18,750. Norweb II Sale (3/1988), VF, weak at reverse center, $8,250.

W-5635 · 1785 Inimica Tyrannis Americana / Confederatio · small stars

Obverse: Indian standing near pedestal, arrow in right hand, bow in left. End of arrow below IC. INIMICA TYRANNIS to left and right, AMERICANA below. *Reverse:* Small circle at center enclosing 13 small stars, Rays around circle. CONFEDERATIO around border, 1785 below. *Notes:* 27.9 mm. Breen-1124. *Rarity:* URS-5.

G-4	VG-8	F-12	VF-20	EF-40
		$42,000	$68,000	

Coppers With Gen. Washington Die

W-5645 · Gen. Washington / 1785 Confederatio, large stars

Obverse: Head and shoulders portrait facing right. GEN. WASHINGTON around border. *Reverse:* Confederatio Large Stars die. *Notes:* This is one of earliest struck coins or tokens with a portrait of Washington, antedated only by the 1784 "Ugly Head" token (W-10590). Baker-9, Breen-1125. *Rarity:* URS-5.

Selected auction price(s): Garrett III Sale (B&R 10/1980), F, some marks, $6,500. Roper Sale (Stack's 12/1983), VF, edge damage, $8,800. John J. Ford Jr. II Sale (5/2004), Choice VF, $63,250.

W-5650 · Gen. Washington / 1786 Heraldic Eagle · E PLURIBUS UNUM

Obverse: Same as preceding. *Reverse:* Heraldic eagle with stars surrounding head. Arrows at left, olive branch at right E PLURIBUS / UNUM to left and right, 1786 below. *Notes:* Baker-10, Breen-1130. *Rarity:* URS-2.

W-5655 · (1786) Undated Gen. Washington / New Jersey shield

Obverse: Same as preceding. *Reverse:* Die normally used on New Jersey coppers, Maris reverse C. *Notes:* Baker-11, Breen-1126, Maris 4-C. *Rarity:* URS-3.

Selected auction price(s): Garrett III Sale (B&R 10/1980), EF, $50,000. John J. Ford Jr. I Sale (Stack's 10/2003), AU, $253,000.

1786–1787 Coppers With Immunis Columbia Dies

W-5665 · 1786 Immunis Columbia / Confederatio · Large Stars

Obverse: Seated Liberty or Columbia to the right, with pole and cap and scales of justice. IMMUNIS / COLUMBIA left and right, 1786 below; 86 high. First 1786 Immunis Columbia die. *Reverse:* Confederatio Large Stars die. *Notes:* Breen-1128. *Rarity:* URS-3.

W-5670 · 1786 Immunis Columbia / New Jersey shield

Obverse: Same as preceding. *Reverse:* Die normally used on New Jersey coppers, Maris reverse C. *Notes:* Breen-1129, Maris 3-C. *Rarity:* URS-4.

G-4	VG-8	F-12	VF-20	EF-40	AU-50	MS-60
—	—	$24,000	$60,000	$80,000	$110,000	$140,000

W-5675 · 1786 Immunis Columbia / Large Eagle

Obverse: Seated Liberty or Columbia to the right, with pole and cap and scales of justice. IMMUNIS / COLUMBIA left and right, 1786 below; 6 low. Second 1786 Immunis Columbia die. *Reverse:* Heraldic eagle, arrows to left, olive branch to right. E PLURIBUS UNUM at top and side border. Beak of eagle under second U (PLURIBUS). Walter Breen's notion that these dies were by "Wyon" in England, a questionable assumption reiterated as fact by Don Taxay and Breen alike, has been dismissed by many modern scholars. See the Frederick Taylor catalog, lot 2085, for related commentary. *Notes:* 28.5 mm. Breen-1135. *Rarity:* URS-2.

Selected auction price(s): Roper Sale (Stack's 12/1983), EF, $28,000. John J. Ford Jr. II Sale (5/2004), Choice VF, $60,375.

W-5680 · 1787 Immunis Columbia / Large Eagle · plain edge

Obverse: Seated Liberty or Columbia to the right, with pole and cap and scales of justice. IMMUNIS / COLUMBIA left and right, 1787 below. *Reverse:* Heraldic eagle, olive branch to left, arrows to right. E PLURIBUS UNUM at top and side border. Beak of eagle under S (PLURIBUS). *Notes:* This is the only readily collectible variety in the Immunis Columbia series. Breen-1136 (wide planchet, about 29 mm, very rare) and 1137 (narrow planchet, about 26.5 mm). *Rarity:* URS-8.

VG-8	F-12	VF-20	EF-40	AU-50	MS-60	MS-63
$850	$2,000	$4,500	$8,500	$12,500	$21,000	$30,000

W-5685 · 1787 Immunis Columbia / Large Eagle · ornamented edge

As preceding but ornamented edge. *Rarity:* URS-1.

Selected auction price(s): Garrett I Sale (B&R 11/1979), VF-20, copper, $2,400.

Confederatio / Heraldic Eagle Dies

W-5690 · 1785 Confederatio, Large Stars / 1786 Heraldic Eagle · E PLURIBUS UNUM

Obverse: 1785 Confederatio die with Large Stars. *Reverse:* Heraldic eagle with stars surrounding head. Arrows at left, olive branch at right E PLURIBUS / UNUM to left and right, 1786 below. *Notes:* Breen-1131. *Rarity:* URS-2.

W-5695 · 1785 Confederatio, Small Stars / 1787 Heraldic Eagle · arrows at right

Obverse: 1785 Confederatio die with Small Stars. *Reverse:* Heraldic eagle with stars surrounding head. Olive branch at left, arrows at right. E PLURIBUS / UNUM to left and right, 1787 below. This die is best known in connection with the New York Excelsior coinage. *Notes:* Breen-1133. *Rarity:* URS-1 (Breen mentions a second is "reported").

Selected auction price(s): Norweb II Sale (3/1988), F, $7,480.

Heraldic Eagle / New Jersey Muling

W-5700 · 1786 Heraldic Eagle · New Jersey shield

Obverse: Heraldic eagle with stars surrounding head. Arrows at left, olive branch at right. E PLURIBUS / UNUM to left and right, 1786 below. *Reverse:* Die normally used on New Jersey coppers, Maris 5-C. *Notes:* Breen-1132. *Rarity:* URS-1.

Selected auction price(s): Garrett III Sale (B&R 10/1980), MS, $37,500.

New York and Related Coppers
1786–1787

History

Although no official state authorization relating to a native New York coinage is known, a number of issues were made with legends relating to that state. On March 29, 1786, *The Massachusetts and New Hampshire Advertiser* contained this notice:

> New York, Connecticut, and Vermont have authorized a person in each of those states to coin coppers; numbers of them are now in circulation; they are in general well made, and of good copper, those of New York in particular.

Under what authorization the New York pieces referred to were coined is not known today.

1787 NOVA EBORAC copper related to the state of New York. (Engraving by John Gavit for O'Callaghan, *The Documentary History of the State of New-York*, 1850)

In petitions said to have been dated February 11, 1787, Ephraim Brasher and John Bailey appealed to the New York State Assembly for the right to produce copper coins. The *Assembly Journal* records that "the several petitions of John Bailey and Ephraim Brasher, relative to the coinage of copper within the state were read and referred (to committee)." The original petition can no longer be traced. It is not known whether separate petitions were presented by Brasher and Bailey or whether they combined their efforts. Brasher did not always work alone, and at one time John Bailey was associated with him, as were his brother Abraham and George Alexander at various times. In 1787 the city directory lists Brasher's address as 77 Queen Street and Bailey's residence as 22 Queen Street, which indicates the possibility of a close relationship at the time.

On March 3, 1787, Captain Thomas Machin presented his own petition to the assembly. Neither proposal was acted upon favorably. In the same year the legislature studied money in circulation and endeavored to regulate existing coinage, which came from many different sources domestic and foreign. It was reported at the time that the principal copper coins circulating within the state of New York were composed of

> a few genuine British half-pence of George the Second, and some of an earlier date, the impressions of which are generally defaced. A number of Irish half-pence, with a bust on the one side, and a harp on the other. A very great number of pieces in imitation of British halfpence, but much lighter, of inferior copper, and badly executed. These are generally called by the name of "Birmingham Coppers," as it is pretty well known that they are made there, and imported in casks, under the name of Hard Ware, or wrought copper.
>
> There has lately been introduced into circulation a very considerable number of coppers of the kind that are made in the State of New Jersey. Many of these are below the proper weight of the Jersey coppers and seem as if designed as a catch-penny for this market.

It was further noted that it took 48 genuine British halfpence, when new, to weigh one pound avoirdupois, but of the imitation or counterfeit pieces believed to be made in Birmingham, it took 60 to compose one pound weight. The genuine New Jersey coppers, at six pennyweights, six grains each, equalled 46 and 2/5 pieces to the pound, or a slightly heavier standard than the British. It was noted at the time that all of these coppers passed without discrimination at 14 pieces to a shilling, or slightly less than the value of a penny, a shilling being composed of 12 pence. It was noted that at this rate a 57 percent profit would go to coiners of genuine British halfpence, a 96 percent profit to makers of imitation "Birmingham" halfpence, and a 65 percent profit to those who made New Jersey coppers.

To remedy these inequities, on April 20, 1787, an act was passed to provide that after August 1,

> no copper shall pass current in this State except such as are of the standard weight of one third part of an ounce avoirdupois, of pure copper, which copper shall pass current at the rate of 20 to a shilling of the lawful current money of this state, and not otherwise.

An extensive issue of 1787-dated copper coins, each with a bust on the obverse surrounded by NOVA EBORAC ("New York") appeared. The reverse of these issues depicted a seated goddess with a sprig in one hand and a liberty cap on a pole in the other hand, with the legend VIRT. ET. LIB. ("virtue and liberty") surrounding, and the date 1787 below. The letter punches used on this issue are identical to those used on the Brasher doubloon die. It seems likely that John Bailey and Ephraim Brasher operated a minting shop in New York City and produced these and possibly other issues.

Machin's Mills appears to have been the most prolific coiner, albeit without any known authorization, of New York–related coinage. As noted, Thomas Machin attempted unsuccessfully to acquire an official patent from the New York legislature. This failure apparently mattered little, for at the time Machin was busily engaged in the coining enterprise and was producing issues of Vermont (with authorization), imitation English halfpence, counterfeit Connecticut coppers, and others, as described separately in this text.

Walter Breen suggests that certain dies associated with Machin's Mills and with New York may have been made in Birmingham, England, although facts are scarce. Breen's logic is that they were used to strike certain pieces in Birmingham and were later shipped to the United States for continued use. There are many die combinations among these issues, some of which are not logical, and nearly all are of great rarity.

Among other pieces that have been associated with New York, directly or through die linkages, are certain issues bearing the figure of Liberty seated on a globe with the legend IMMUNIS COLUMBIA surrounding. Another issue depicts George Clinton on the obverse and the New York State seal on the reverse. Still another illustrates the standing figure of an Indian.

Another issue features on the obverse a crude bust of George Washington with the legend NON VI VIRTUTE VICI. The reverse contains a Latinization of New York, NEO EBORACENSIS, surrounding a seated figure of Liberty holding the scales of Justice and a liberty cap, with the date 1786 below.

With the exception of the Nova Eborac coppers, which are scarce, most copper pieces bearing legends relating to New York and all die combinations of such pieces range from rare to very rare today.

1786 Non Vi Virtute Vici Coppers

W-5720 · Large Head · Neo-Eboracensis

Obverse: Large bust of Washington(?) right. NON VI VIRTUTE VICI around border. *Reverse:* Seated Liberty facing right, with scales and liberty cap on a pole, and 1786 below. *Notes:* 29.1 mm. Minter and location unknown. Breen calls this a pattern (a term he often assigned to rare coppers). Two known: Ford's About Uncirculated and Parmelee's coin called "Fair" in 1890, perhaps today's Good or Very Good. Breen-976. *Rarity:* URS-2.

Selected auction price(s): Ford II Sale (5/2004), Choice AU, $218,500.

W-5730 · Small Head

Designs similar to the preceding, but smaller bust. Both dies are different. *Notes:* 28.5 mm. Minter and location unknown. Breen-977. *Rarity:* URS-6.

G-4	VG-8	F-12	VF-20	EF-40	AU-50
—	$10,500	$21,000	$45,000	$80,000	$120,000

W-5740 · (1786) Undated · Small Head · Shield reverse

Obverse: Large bust of Washington(?) right. NON VI VIRTUTE VICI around border. *Reverse:* Shield with E PLURIBUS UNUM in the style of a New Jersey copper, but not known to have been used for New Jersey coinage. *Notes:* 29.1 mm. Unique. Parmelee collection, 1890. Breen-1134. *Rarity:* URS-1.

Selected auction price(s): Garrett III Sale (B&R 10/1980), G–VG, double struck, weak in areas, $16,500.

1787 Nova Eborac Coppers

W-5750 · Large Bust

Obverse: Large bust (often called "Large Head") facing right. NOVA / EBORAC to right and left. Quatrefoils distant before N and close after C. *Reverse:* VIRT • ET / LIB to left and right. Quatrefoil close before V and distant after B. Seated liberty figure facing left, holding pole with cap and branch. Branch hand opposite right leg of R. *Notes:* 28.3 to 29 mm. Typically in lower grades, but three About Uncirculated and one Mint State exist. Breen-985. *Rarity:* URS-6.

G-4	F-12	VF-20	EF-40	AU-50	MS-60	MS-63
$950	$3,700	$10,500	$25,000	$50,000	—	

W-5755 · Medium Bust · Seated Figure Facing Left

Obverse: Medium bust facing right. NOVA / EBORAC to right and left. Quatrefoils near N, A, and C. *Reverse:* VIRT • ET / LIB to left and right. Quatrefoil close before V and after B. Seated liberty figure facing left, holding pole with cap and branch. Branch hand opposite space between dot and E. *Notes:* The dies seem to be by the same hand as the 1788 Vermont Mailed Bust Right dies (W-2205). Usually with date partly off the planchet; probably only about 20 percent show the full date boldly visible. Two known struck over Irish halfpence. Breen-986. *Rarity:* URS-10.

G-4	VG-8	F-12	VF-20	EF-40	AU-50	MS-60
$210	$400	$650	$1,250	$4,000	$7,500	

W-5760 · Seated Figure Facing Right

Obverse: Same as preceding, but later state with a break at the quatrefoil after EBORAC. *Reverse:* VIRT / ET • LIB to left and right. Quatrefoil close before V and after B. Seated liberty figure facing right, holding pole with cap and branch. Branch hand opposite L. *Notes:* 28.3 mm. Usually lightly struck in the center of the reverse. Known in transitional die states, developing a crack at the lower right which expands to cause a piece to fall from the die, creating a large cud (this is the state most often found). One known overstruck on an Irish halfpenny and two on Nova Constellatio coppers. Breen-987. *Rarity:* URS-9.

G-4	VG-8	F-12	VF-20	EF-40	AU-50	MS-60
$275	$450	$700	$1,500	$5,000	$9,000	

W-5765 · Small Bust

Obverse: Smaller bust facing right. NOVA / EBORAC to left and right. Star before N and after C. *Reverse:* Small seated liberty figure. VIRT ET LIB around, including over head, 1787 below. *Notes:* 28.7 mm. Die workmanship cruder than on the other Nova Eborac coppers, and probably made by another hand, possibly the maker of the 1787 Connecticut "Muttonhead" copper (W-2720). Typically in low grades. Breen-988. *Rarity:* URS-5.

G-4	VG-8	F-12	VF-20	EF-40
$5,000	$8,500	$14,000	$36,000	$60,000

Excelsior Coppers

W-5775 · Eagle Facing Right / 1787 Heraldic Eagle · E PLURIBUS UNUM · arrows at left

Obverse: State arms of New York, eagle facing to observer's right, 1787 / EXCELSIOR below. *Reverse:* Heraldic eagle with stars surrounding head. Arrows at left, olive branch at right. E PLURIBUS / UNUM to left and right, 1787 below. *Notes:* 28.7 mm. Breen-978. *Rarity:* URS-4.

G-4	VG-8	F-12	VF-20	EF-40
—	—	—	—	—

W-5780 · arrows at right

Obverse: Same as preceding. *Reverse:* Heraldic eagle with stars surrounding head. Olive branch at left, arrows at right. E PLURIBUS / UNUM to left and right, 1787 below. *Notes:* 28.2 mm. Breen-979. *Rarity:* URS-5.

G-4	VG-8	F-12	VF-20	EF-40	AU-50	MS-60
						$150,000

W-5785 · Eagle Facing Left

Obverse: State arms of New York, eagle facing to observer's left, 1787 / EXCELSIOR below. *Reverse:* Same as preceding. *Notes:* 28.4 mm. Breen-980. *Rarity:* URS-6.

G-4	VG-8	F-12	VF-20	EF-40	AU-50	MS-60
$2,200	$4,250	$7,000	$16,000	$32,500	$75,000	$125,000

W-5790 · 1787 George Clinton / Excelsior · Eagle Facing Right

Obverse: Head right. GEORGE / CLINTON to left and right. Star above head and after N. *Reverse:* State arms of New York, eagle facing to observer's right, 1787 / EXCELSIOR below. *Notes:* Breen-989. *Rarity:* URS-5.

G-4	VG-8	F-12	VF-20	EF-40
$18,000	$28,000	$55,000	$140,000	$300,000

W-5795 · 1787 Liber Natus Libertatem Defendo · Indian / Excelsior · Eagle Facing Right

Obverse: LIBER NATUS LIBERTATUM DEFENDO around border. At center, standing Indian, tomahawk to the left, bow to the right, star below feet. *Reverse:* Same as preceding. *Notes:* 27.4 mm. Breen-990. *Rarity:* URS-5.

G-4	VG-8	F-12	VF-20	EF-40
$20,000	$45,000	$70,000	$180,000	$250,000

W-5800 · Indian / Neo-Eboracus · Eagle on Globe

Obverse: Same as preceding. *Reverse:* Eagle with wings outstretched, standing on top of the upper part of a globe. NEO-EBORACUS above, 1787 at border to the right. EXCELSIOR below. *Notes:* 27.1 mm. Breen-991. *Rarity:* URS-5.

G-4	VG-8	F-12	VF-20	EF-40
$20,000	$55,000	$85,000	$150,000	$350,000

(W-7880) · Indian / George III

Machin's Mills counterfeit. See listing under Machin's Mills, W-7880.

BRASHER GOLD COINAGE 1786–1787

1787 gold doubloon by Ephraim Brasher. (Early Coins of America, 1875)

Ephraim Brasher

One of the most famous of all American coin issues is the 1787 gold doubloon issued by Ephraim Brasher (pronounced as *bray-zher*), a New York goldsmith, silversmith, and jeweler who may have been associated with New York copper coinage as well (see above). In the few instances that specimens have appeared in auction catalogs during the past century, great acclaim and publicity has been given to them.

Brasher was born in 1744 of Huguenot stock. He probably entered silversmithing in his teens, completing his apprenticeship in his early 20s. About this time, in 1766, he married Anne Gilbert. Little is known about her other than that her brother was a silversmith. During the Revolutionary War, Brasher served as grenadier in the Provincial Army, 1775 to 1776. In 1783 he was part of the Evacuation Day Committee, which celebrated the departure of British troops from New York City.

On August 31, 1785, Brasher petitioned the Common Council that "he may be permitted to convert the fire Engine House in St. George's Square into a Place of Business on his erecting a fire Engine House on his own ground." Although several local proprietors objected to the petition, it was granted on September 29, 1785. Perhaps it was intended to use the structure as a smithing location. St. George's Square was located at the intersection of Pearl and Cherry streets. The first directory of the city, published in 1786, gave 1 Cherry Street as Brasher's address. In the next year he petitioned the New York State Assembly for the right to make copper coins (see New York coinage above), but his request was denied.

Coins Proposed and in Circulation

The Articles of Confederation, adopted in 1781 and continued in effect until 1789, stipulated that Congress had the power to regulate the value and alloy of coins struck, although the various states had authority to coin money. As Congress had not implemented a framework for federal production of coins, specimens in circulation continued to be a varied mixture that included much foreign coinage. Coppers of varying sorts served as small change, while silver and gold coins formed the sinews of trade. Gold coins of Spanish America, Brazil, and Portugal were in wide circulation. Many were underweight due to clipping, and some were lightweight counterfeits.

Due to their different values, the Bank of New York (established in 1784) distributed a list of coins, their weights, and the accepted values at which various foreign gold coins would be received in payment. In stores and counting-houses it was considered unwise to accept a coin until it was pronounced genuine. Confusion arising from a wide variety of denominations, designs, and countries of origin aided counterfeiters. To this was added the problem of clipping (the removal of small amounts of metal from a coin's edge) and sweating (the use of a nitric acid wash to remove a small layer of metal) gold coins.

It is believed that Ephraim Brasher was called upon to regulate foreign gold coins as well as certain silver issues. This was done by clipping or plugging gold coins in circulation to bring them up or down to the standard of gold coins published by the Bank of New York in 1784, after which appropriate hallmarks would be added. Other goldsmiths active in this trade included Standish Barry, John Burger, Jacob Boelen III, Fletcher & Gardiner, John Letellier, and Thomas Underhill, per research by William Swoger and John Kraljevich.

For Brasher, a counterstamp, usually in the form of the letters EB in an oval, was impressed upon each as a permanent identification. Specimens of EB-marked foreign gold coins are known today, a short list of which includes a rose guinea of George III, a quarter guinea of George I, and a half joe of Joseph I, which appeared in the James Ten Eyck collection sale held by B. Max Mehl in 1922. Brasher was not the only metalsmith with EB initials, so hallmarks need to be studied for proper attribution.

That Brasher was hired to evaluate gold coins is confirmed by his having served at one time as an assayer in this regard for the United States Mint. *The American State Papers, Finance*, volume 1, "Estimated Expenditures for the Year 1796," notes that a $27 Treasury warrant was made out in favor of John Shield, assignee of Ephraim Brasher; being for assays made by said Brasher, in the year 1792, for the Mint on sundry coins of gold and silver, pursuant to instructions from the then Secretary of the Treasury.

Brasher Doubloons

During this era Brasher struck two styles of gold doubloons, his coins being valued at $15. The first, antedated 1742 and bearing the date 1786 partially visible in the border, is of the so-called Lima style, loosely copied from a much earlier doubloon design used at the mint in Lima, Peru. These are signed BRASHER on the obverse. Apparently, it was thought that this familiar motif would aid in the circulation of the coins. Again, facts are scarce and theories abound. Next came the 1787-dated doubloon, showing a sun rising over a mountain on one side and an eagle on the other, also signed with full surname. Both have the counterstamp EB. Inscriptions include the state motto of New York. A lighter-weight half-doubloon was made from the same 1787 die pair.

It seems likely that these were routinely coined by Brasher from gold received and assayed by him and were paid out in commerce. The 1742 to 1786 and the 1787 doubloons bear Brasher's surname in full as BRASHER. There is no mark of value or denomination expressed. This was not an unusual situation, for when the United States Mint first produced gold coins in the following decade the pieces bore no denomination. The same characteristics extended to numerous foreign gold coins then in circulation. The value of gold coins was determined by the metallic purity and weight. For this reason the countermark EB, which appears on all known examples of the Brasher doubloon, would have been a further indication of quality.

Before and after his doubloon production, Brasher was active in New York City civic affairs, holding several offices. He died in 1810.

Numismatic Accounts

Brasher doubloons first achieved numismatic recognition in 1838 when Adam Eckfeldt discovered a piece among gold coins that were sent to the Mint for assay and melting. He withdrew the piece and gave it to the Mint Cabinet, which at that time was in its early state of formation. In 1846, W.E. DuBois, in *Pledges of History*, referred to the mint example as "a very remarkable gold coin, equal in value to a doubloon, coined at New York in 1787."

A dozen years later the obverse and reverse of the 1787 doubloon were described by J.H. Hickcox in *An Historical Account of American Coinage*, 1858. Montroville W. Dickeson's *American Numismatical Manual*, 1859, contained an illustration of the piece and noted that the author had personally seen four specimens. The first 1787 Brasher doubloon scheduled to appear at auction was the Seavey-collection specimen cataloged by W.H. Strobridge in 1873. However, Lorin G. Parmelee bought the entire collection intact before the sale took place, so the event was cancelled.

Crosby's *Early Coins of America*, 1875, contained an illustration of the Brasher doubloon. The author noted that "four of these doubloons have come to our knowledge; they are owned by Mr. Bushnell, Mr. Parmelee, Mr. Stickney, and the United States Mint at Philadelphia; the first has the punch-mark on the breast of the eagle."

The first Brasher doubloon to actually be sold at public auction was the Charles I. Bushnell specimen sold by the Chapman brothers in 1882. It realized $505 and was subsequently sold to T. Harrison Garrett through Édouard Frossard. This remains today the only known specimen of the variety with the EB punch mark on the eagle's breast rather than the wing, and it was one of three doubloons the Garrett collection eventually contained (the others being a punch-on-wing issue and a 1742).

In 1890 the Robert Coulton Davis specimen was the second to be auctioned and became the fifth example known to exist. Today five specimens of the 1787 doubloon with a punch mark on the eagle's wing can be traced.

The 1992 study by Michael J. Hodder, "Brasher's Lima Style Doubloon," disproved much of what was earlier printed, and established that the date 1786 appears on the rim of this "1742" coin, although only the bottoms of the numerals are visible.

1742 Brasher Lima-Style Doubloon

W-5820 · 1742 (1786) Lima-style gold doubloon

Obverse: Imitation of a Lima, Peru, gold doubloon. Pillars on obverse, date as 1742, BRASHER in small letters below. PHILIP V D G REX ANO 1786 around border, with ornaments (as given by Michael J. Hodder), letters only partially visible on the best known example. *Reverse:* Cross, ornaments, and inscription, the last incomplete on the finest specimen, but including I HISPAN . . . IND REX, and ornaments. *Notes:* Weight about 408 grains. Two known, finest in the Garrett collection, the other the "Paris" specimen. Breen-984. *Rarity:* URS-2.

Selected auction price(s): Gold Rush Collection (Heritage 1/2005), EF-40 (NGC), $690,000.

1787 Brasher Half Doubloon

W-5830 · 1787 Brasher half doubloon

Obverse: Mountain surmounted with sun, rays emanating; in the foreground, open sea, BRASHER below. Around the border, a circle of beads, outside which is NOVA EBORACA COLUMBIA / EXCELSIOR and ornaments. *Reverse:* Heraldic eagle at the center, olive branch in talons at left, arrows at right; 13 stars near eagle's head. Around the border, a circle of double leaves, outside which is UNUM E PLURIBUS / 1787 and ornaments. *Notes:* Dubbed the "half doubloon" as it weighs about 204 grains, or slightly less than half of a full doubloon. Small planchet with incomplete inscriptions at the borders. Lilly Collection in the Smithsonian Institution. Breen-784. *Rarity:* URS-1.

1787 Brasher Doubloons

W-5840 · **Hallmark on Wing**

Design as preceding, but full inscriptions. Weight 408 to 411 grains. *Notes:* Five known, three in private hands. Roster: Brand-Yale University, Garrett (the only Mint State coin), Smithsonian, American Numismatic Society, and Brand-Friedberg specimens. Breen-981. *Rarity:* URS-5.

Selected auction price(s): Garrett I Sale (B&R 11/1979), MS-63, $725,000 (a world-record price for *any* coin at the time). Gold Rush Collection (Heritage 1/2005), AU-55 (NGC), $2,415,000.

W-5845 · **Hallmark on Breast**

As preceding, but hallmark stamped on eagle's breast. *Notes:* Breen-982. *Rarity:* URS-1. Garrett collection.

Selected auction price(s): Gold Rush Collection (Heritage 1/2005), EF-45 (NGC), $2,990,000.

MASSACHUSETTS COPPERS 1787–1788

Massachusetts copper cent of 1788. (Engraving by John Gavit for Hickcox, *An Historical Account of American Coinage*, 1858)

Desire for a Copper Coinage

In 1786 the Massachusetts government gave serious consideration to the production of copper coins. In March of that year Seth Reed of Uxbridge in that state petitioned the Senate and House of Representatives of Massachusetts for the right to produce copper and silver coins made from metal extracted from native ore. The legislators, who heard the proposal on March 8 and 9, were skeptical and requested that Reed bring evidence that the metal was indeed the product of mines located within the geographical confines of the state.

On March 15, 1786, a week after the Reed petition, another proposal was entered, this one by James Swan, who recognized the "want of a circulating medium, which may neither depreciate, be exported, or hoarded by the rich." He asked for a patent or license to coin £20,000 value in copper.

While neither the Reed nor the Swan petitions received favorable action, they did serve to stimulate interest in a state coinage. Accordingly, on March 23, 1786, a committee was formed

> to consider the best method to be adopted by this Commonwealth for the coining of silver and copper, to determine the value of the several sorts of coin, together with the quantity that it will be expedient to issue, with proper devices therefore, and what advantages may accrue to the Commonwealth thereby.

In the same month the committee recommended that the Massachusetts government itself should establish a mint to manufacture copper pieces. It was estimated that coining £20,000 in coppers would require a cost of £8,250 worth of copper metal plus £1,950 for the workhouses, presses, plating (strip-producing) mill, and other apparatus, together with the fuel, wages of the workmen, and other costs, for a total expenditure of £10,200, returning to the Commonwealth of Massachusetts a profit of £9,800.

The committee further reported:

> The government will not be obliged to advance a great sum to set it a going as the public hath a large quantity of copper ore suitable for the business by them, if they choose to employ it that way, but if they should not incline to do that, they may purchase old copper enough at two or three months' credit, to be paid for in copper as soon as it is coined.

It was also recommended that copper should be coined in the denominations of the penny, halfpenny, and farthing.

In June 1786 the governor requested that proposals for the mint be suspended pending the outcome of the action of the United States government in the matter of coinage. It was thought that the U.S. Congress, if it were to issue coins, would provide pieces that would have uniform value throughout the different states and would be more convenient to commerce than specific Massachusetts coins. In July, in disregard of the governor's wishes, the state House of Representatives prepared a bill for the coinage of copper and erecting a mint. On October 17, 1786, legislation was passed providing

> that there be a mint erected within this Commonwealth, for the coining of gold, silver, and copper; and that all the coin that shall be struck therein shall be of the same weight, alloy, and value, and each piece bear the same name....
>
> There shall be a quantity of copper coins struck, equal to the amount of 70,000 dollars, in pieces of the two different denominations mentioned in the said resolve, and in convenient proportions; one of which to have the name Cent stamped in the center thereof, and the other Half Cent, with such inscriptions or devices as

the governor with the advice of Counsel may think proper; and the said coin, when struck, shall be received in all payments in this Commonwealth.

It was further provided that a mint be established and that an assayer, workmen, supplies, and other accessories be obtained for the purpose of coining. On May 2, 1787, the coinage committee reported that subsequent investigation found it necessary to erect a furnace made of special fire brick, the clay for which could not be obtained until that spring. Conversations were held with Captain Joshua Witherle (as he signed his name; also given as Wetherle, Wetherly, and Wetherlee in early accounts), and the committee found that he was suited to superintend the setting up and conducting of the business. During the same month copper suitable for coining was located, including 3,434 pounds weight of copper and 650 pounds of "sprews," belonging to the Commonwealth, as well as several mortars and cannon suitable for melting down for use in coinage. On June 27, 1787, the designs were established:

> The device on the copper coin to be emitted in this Commonwealth to be the figure of an Indian with a bow and arrow and a star on one side, with the word COMMONWEALTH, and on the reverse a spread eagle with the words OF MASSACHUSETTS AD 1787.

When coinage did materialize, "OF" and "AD" were omitted.

The Mint in Operation

In a speech on October 18, 1787, the governor noted that "in consequence of an act made October 1786, a mint has been erected for coining cents, and a very considerable quantity of copper will soon be ready for circulation." It seems that some had been struck by this time, as the manifest dated September 2, 1787, for the consort sloop *Lady Washington*, departing Boston on a voyage of exploration to the Pacific Northwest coast, included "300 medals, 500 cents, and 500 half cents," and an unspecified quantity of the same items aboard the flagship *Columbia*. In the legislative halls there was much interest and discussion that autumn of making silver coins as well, but nothing came of the proposals.

The *New-Haven Gazette, and the Connecticut Magazine*, Thursday, November 1787, included this item from Massachusetts:

> Springfield, November 13. We are informed, on authority not to be doubted that the copper coin of this Commonwealth, struck by order of the General Court, will, in a very few days, be in circulation, when, after that time, the coinage of any state, with the base metal imported from Birmingham, will not be a currency among us.

Problems developed with producing the half cents and cents. On January 16, 1788, the government expressed its concern with the slowness in mintage operations and ordered an investigation. On the next day, Joshua Witherle submitted a report that noted:

> In May 1787 I received orders from the government to erect necessary buildings and to prepare machines suitable for the purpose of coining copper cents, etc., agreeable to an act of this Commonwealth, which was immediately begun to be put into execution, and no pains were spared to procure every article that was thought necessary. The iron furnaces which I was obliged to depend on for several articles which I could not do without were so nearly out of blast that I could not get the patterns made for the rollers and sundry other articles that were necessary, done so as to answer the purpose intended in the spring, therefore was obliged to go on as well as I could, and after spending some time and great pains in making the rollers, which I had cast, answer the purpose expected, was obliged to have a pair of rollers made of wrought iron, which have been made use of to this time, and are yet good.
>
> The dies, with which the coin is struck, have been the means of great delay in the business, as it was not in my power to procure steel of a proper quality to receive the proper degree of hardness which is so absolutely necessary to sustain the great force of the machine in making the impression on the coin. I have now procured steel of that quality, which appears to answer the purpose very well. In addition to this, it must be supposed that some time would be spent to instruct persons in a business which has not been practiced in this country.
>
> The moulds which I proposed to cast the copper into when melted, so as to have it in a proper situation for the rolling mill, without any further expense or trouble, was a matter of great consequence in the business; therefore I took the advice of all those persons that might be supposed to have good judgment in a matter of this kind; who unanimously agreed that it was not only a cheap but a very expeditious way of doing the business; therefore I pursued the plan, as soon as the first furnace that I could hear of was in blast, to get such a number of them as would be sufficient to prove the experiment which took some time and trouble to have them in proper order for the business proposed; when this was done it appeared that the above plan would not be a means of saving money and expediting business as was expected, but would really injure the metal, employ more hands, and destroy more fuel, than casting it in much larger pieces, and drawing it with a trip hammer, which might be made, and fixed to the Mill at Dedham, which is now almost ready to operate; but before I began to fix the above hammers, I fully proved the experiment by having about a thousand-weight drawn at Newton.
>
> Thus far I have given a general account of the matter to this time, and have surmounted every difficulty that commonly occurs in any new business, more especially in one of this nature, without any expense to, or assistance from government other than thirty-five hundred pounds of rough copper, received from Hugh Orr, Esq.; and at your next meeting shall lay before you a more particular account of the state of the mint.

Dies by Callender and Perkins

Most of the dies for Massachusetts half cents and cents were made by Joseph Callender, an engraver located at Half-Square, State Street in Boston. These dies were prepared at a cost to Massachusetts of £1 4s each. His invoices reflected the making of 39 new dies and the repair of three dies.

This was considered excessive, so Jacob Perkins, a young silversmith of Newburyport, was engaged to produce additional dies at a payment of one percent of the value of the coins to be struck from the dies. It is believed that the shape of the letter S on the coins was distinctive with each engraver. In all issues of 1787 and in some of 1788, the S is open at the top and bottom, these being attributed to Callender. In both half-cent die varieties of 1788 as well as several of the cents of the same year, the S is narrow and the serifs at the upper and lower part are close to the curves, resembling somewhat a figure 8, these considered to be the work of Perkins. A later review disclosed that during the operation of the mint, £3 18s 10d had been paid to Perkins for dies, as compared to, under a different arrangement, £48 12s paid to Callender.

Perkins would later gain fame as the maker of the HE IS IN GLORY, THE WORLD IN TEARS Washington funeral medal widely distributed in 1800, for his Patent Stereotype Steel Plate paper-money innovation, and as the inventor of the siderographic process for multiplying engraved printing plates.

In addition to the foregoing, some contemporary counterfeit Massachusetts cents are attributed to Machin's Mills.

Continuing Business

Problems continued at the mint, and on June 17, 1788, Joshua Witherle reported that many other unfortunate circumstances, including particularly harsh weather the preceding winter, caused additional difficulties and delays. It was stated that $2,500 in coins had already been struck and had been deposited to the account of the Commonwealth. It was anticipated that if the government could supply the proper amount of copper, the mint would be able to have a continuing output on the order of about $50 per day in half cents and cents. An additional £600 was requested in operating expenses so that work could continue. While the output of the mint was in half cents and cents, part of a decimal system with fractional parts of a dollar, the prevailing money of account in Massachusetts at the time was based upon the English pound sterling.

As of that time £2,136 5s 7d had been expended in the operation of the mint, for which just £939 value of copper coins had been struck, leaving a loss of £1,197 5s 7d. On November 22, 1788, realizing that each half cent and cent cost more than twice its face value to produce, the Commonwealth decided to receive proposals "from any person who may offer a contract to carry on the coinage of copper within this Commonwealth." It was further resolved to coin all of the copper metal presently on hand at the mint and, when this was completed, to discharge all persons associated with the facility. On December 29, 1788, Witherle reported that about 350 pounds' weight of processed copper, apparently in disc or planchet form, was ready. "As soon as the above copper in hand to be coined is finished, I shall immediately render in the whole accounts of the mint."

Accounts of the Mint

In January 1789 the mint accounts were closed, and employees were dismissed. An inventory taken by Witherle on January 21 showed these assets, with building number 1 on Witherle's property in Boston and number 2 at a distance in the community of Dedham.

> Building No. 1 [the mint]: 1 machine for coining cents, etc.; 1 ditto for stamping [cutting planchets]; 1 cast iron frame for cutting machine; 1 iron stove and funnel; 537 pounds of copper scraps.
>
> Building No. 2 [the rolling mill, as it was called]: 1 plating machine; 1 triphammer and stake; 4 tongs; 2 iron rollers; 1 set of iron bed pieces; 1 forge; 1 annealing furnace; 50 white bricks.
>
> Building No. 2a: A small coal house containing about 50 bushels of charcoal.

Witherle petitioned the government to allow him to use the buildings and mint apparatus until the government had further use for them, for they were erected on Witherle's property and no rent had been charged. Apparently he conducted a coppersmithing business there. In *The Early Coins of America*, 1875, Sylvester S. Crosby related that Witherle's house stood on a site later occupied by houses numbered from 1132 to 1144 Washington Street, with East Waltham Street dividing Witherle's property near its southerly line.

Charles I. Bushnell's "Numismatic Notes," as quoted by Crosby, state:

> The mint house stood directly in the rear of Joshua Witherle's house, now three stories high, of wood, number 910 Washington Street, and has been occupied for several years as a lying-in hospital at Boston Neck.
>
> The building used as a mint house was a wooden one, one story in height, of high stud, about 20 feet wide by 40 feet in length. Mr. Witherle had probably occupied the building previous to the period of the state coinage. He was a copper smith by trade, and was commonly known among the boys of Boston as "the cent maker."

Crosby stated:

> The copper for the coins of Massachusetts (excepting a small quantity which was drawn at Newton), after being cast into ingots at the mint in Boston, was carted to the mill at Dedham, where it was drawn under a triphammer, and rolled into sheets, when it was returned to the mint, where the blanks were prepared and the coin stamped.

After the mint closed, the state reviewed other proposals to make coins for the state on a contractual or royalty basis, but none were adopted. As was true of other state coinages, likely the coppers panic of 1789 dimmed the possibility of any profits being made from such a venture. As evidenced by wear, these coins circulated for many years afterward.

Descriptions of the Coins

Half cents and cents were struck bearing the dates 1787 and 1788. As the preceding text relates, most coinage materialized after late 1787, so most of the 1787-dated pieces were probably struck in 1788. The Massachusetts copper coins were well received in the channels of commerce and saw active circulation for several decades following their issue.

Coined in large quantities, Massachusetts half cents and cents of 1787 and 1788 are fairly plentiful today. Numerous die varieties exist. All have a plain edge.

The obverse of each half cent and cent depicts a standing Indian, facing to the viewer's left, with a bow in his right hand and an arrow in his left. Between the top of the bow and the Indian's face is a five-pointed star (called a *mullet* by Crosby). To the left and right is lettered COMMON / WEALTH. The relative positions of the bow, arrow, and star are keys to identifying die varieties.

The reverse of each half cent and cent displays a heraldic eagle with an olive branch to the viewer's left and a bundle of arrows to the right. On its breast is a shield, with HALF / CENT in incuse letters on the smaller denomination, and CENT on the larger. An exception is Ryder 2-F, the most desired collectible die variety in the series, which has the arrows and branch transposed left to right, and CENT in raised letters. Around the top and side border is MASSACHUSETTS. The date 1787 or 1788 is under a horizontal line below the eagle. Sometimes the line (called a *dash* by Crosby) is single; other times it is double.

These copper coins represent the first appearance of the word CENT on a coin made within the United States. The denomination was intended to refer to a "cent" or 1/100th part of a Spanish milled dollar, the same money of account used on Continental Currency bills issued from 1775 to 1779.

Numismatic Aspects

The first American book on numismatics, *An Historical Account of Massachusetts Currency*, by Joseph B. Felt, 1839, took notice of the Massachusetts copper coinage of the 1780s, but described it only in the briefest terms. "It is familiar with the earliest remembrances and enjoyments of many who yet survive," perhaps the earliest mention of the charm that old copper coins can have. John H. Hickcox, in *An Historical Account of American Coinage*, 1858, recited certain legislation, but added little of use to anyone collecting the coins. Montroville W. Dickeson's *American Numismatical Manual*, 1859, treated them briefly, but did not find "the slight differences in the die" to be important.

It devolved upon Sylvester S. Crosby, in *The Early Coins of America*, 1875, to describe the dies in detail. This information was expanded by Hillyer C. Ryder and issued in 1920 by the American Numismatic Society as part of *The State Coinages of New England*.

Among the various issues of 1787 and 1788, die varieties range from common to very rare or even unique. The Ryder collection, which included many duplicates, was acquired intact by Wayte Raymond, who sold it to F.C.C. Boyd in 1948. The new owner added one coin prior to his death in 1958. John J. Ford Jr. had his pick of the Boyd coins from the estate, through widow Helen Boyd, and cherrypicked anything of interest, allowing the residue to be auctioned through New Netherlands Coin Co., in which Ford had been a partner since 1950. The writer recalls that Ford was not particularly interested in state copper coins, but prized the ownership of them. Just one coin was added to the Massachusetts holdings, a remarkable Mint State 1787 Transposed Arrows cent. The Ford coins from this state, elegantly cataloged by Michael J. Hodder, were auctioned in Ford Sale V, October 12, 2004, the finest-ever sale of this specialty.

When the Ryder collection was being assembled, and also during its later ownership changes, numismatic interest in Massachusetts coppers was mainly limited to basic types: one of each half cent and cent dated 1787 and 1788, plus the Horned Eagle cent of 1787. The Transposed Arrows 1787 cent was desired by those who could find and then afford to pay for one. Empire Coin Company hired young Massachusetts collector Phil Greco to spend a summer gathering photographs and information about state copper coins, with particular emphasis on Massachusetts issues, as they often differed but slightly and were hard to tell apart by using printed descriptions. Sets of photographic plates were made up and distributed, a venture later expanded by Robert A. Vlack. These catalyzed interest, as did the advent of the *Colonial Newsletter*. Still, the general uniformity of the dies did not have the appeal that Vermont, Connecticut, and New Jersey coppers offered numismatists. Massachusetts coppers have remained a niche interesting to investigate. As the series is not as widely studied as other state coinage, there is the potential to find rare die combinations at common-type prices. The ANS has a fine reference collection of these, largely built upon the collection purchased from Carl Würtzbach in the 1940s.

Among all copper coins issued by the different states during the 1780s, the Massachusetts pieces were the best struck and of the most uniform weight. The typical coin encountered today is apt to be in a grade of Fine to Very Fine or Extremely Fine, well struck, and on a high-quality planchet. Certain cents of 1787 and 1788 have been designated as contemporary counterfeits by Robert A. Vlack (plates, 1978), Walter Breen (*Complete Encyclopedia*, 1988), and some others. These are eagerly collected along with the official issues.

As the die differences are usually slight and require careful study to differentiate, collecting Massachusetts coppers by varieties has had a limited following over the years, but those who do collect them are very enthusiastic. In recent years Mike Packard has been in the forefront of study in this series, working with other members of the Colonial Coin Collectors Club. Much of the following information concerning grade availability is from his research.

Easy Finding Guide
1787 Half Cent Obverse Dies

Ryder 1 · Top of arrow shaft centered under W. Diagnostic. *Used for:* W-5900, Ryder 1-D.

Ryder 2 · Top of arrow shaft under right foot of W. One ray of star points at eyebrow. Diagnostic. String clear of bow at center. *Used for:* W-5910, Ryder 2-A.

Ryder 3 · Top of arrow shaft under space between W and E. Arrowhead small and distant from tunic. Diagnostic. *Used for:* W-5920, Ryder 3-A.

Ryder 4 · Top of arrow shaft under lower left of E and barely touches it. Diagnostic. *Used for:* W-5930, Ryder 4-B. W-5940, Ryder 4-C. W-5950, Ryder 4-D.

Ryder 5 · Top of arrow shaft under right foot of W. One ray of star points above collar. Diagnostic. String very close to or touches bow at center. *Used for:* W-5960, Ryder 5-A.

Ryder 6 · Top of arrow shaft under space between W and E. Arrowhead large and very close to tunic. Diagnostic. *Used for:* W-5970, Ryder 6-A. W-5980, Ryder 6-D.

Easy Finding Guide
1787 Half Cent Reverse Dies

DOUBLE DATE LINE

Ryder A · Arrows distant from period after S. Diagnostic. *Used for:* W-5910, Ryder 2-A. W-5920, Ryder 3-A. W-5960, Ryder 5-A. W-5970, Ryder 6-A.

Ryder B · One arrow points to and is close to period. Diagnostic. *Used for:* W-5930, Ryder 4-B.

SINGLE DATE LINE

Ryder C · Rightmost arrowhead overlaps period. Diagnostic. *Used for:* W-5940, Ryder 4-C.

Ryder D · Arrowheads distant from period. Diagnostic. *Used for:* W-5900, Ryder 1-D. W-5950, Ryder 4-D. W-5980, Ryder 6-D.

Easy Finding Guide
1788 Half Cent Obverse Dies

Ryder 1 · Only one die. Diagnostic. *Used for:* W-7000, Ryder 1-A. W-7010, Ryder 1-B.

Easy Finding Guide: 1788 Half Cent Reverse Dies

Ryder A · Both 8's high. Diagnostic. *Used for:* W-7000, Ryder 1-A.

Ryder B · First 8 low, second 8 high. Diagnostic. *Used for:* W-7010, Ryder 1-B.

1787 Massachusetts Half Cents

Crosby records average weights of 75 to 83 grains.

W-5900 · Ryder 1-D

Grade availability: Difficult to find above Very Fine. Ford's was choice Uncirculated. *Rarity:* URS-9.

G-4	VG-8	F-12	VF-20	EF-40
$125	$200	$350	$800	$1,500

W-5902 · Ryder 1-D · white metal

In the Richard August collection is a trial striking in white metal on a large planchet that was struck from an early die state of this pairing, probably as a test piece. Mint State; unique. *Rarity:* URS-1.

W-5910 · Ryder 2-A

Grade availability: Difficult to find above Extremely Fine. Ford's was Uncirculated. *Rarity:* URS-9.

G-4	VG-8	F-12	VF-20	EF-40
$125	$200	$350	$800	$1,500

W-5920 · Ryder 3-A

Grade availability: Difficult to find above Extremely Fine. *Rarity:* URS-7.

G-4	VG-8	F-12	VF-20	EF-40
$100	$160	$250	$625	$1,200

W-5930 · Ryder 4-B

Grade availability: Mint State coins are readily found in the context of this series. *Rarity:* URS-7.

G-4	VG-8	F-12	VF-20	EF-40
$150	$250	$375	$900	$1,800

W-5940 · Ryder 4-C

Grade availability: Mint State coins are plentiful in the context of this series. *Rarity:* URS-11.

G-4	VG-8	F-12	VF-20	EF-40
$100	$160	$250	$625	$1,200

W-5950 · Ryder 4-D

Grade availability: Four known, one of which is holed. *Rarity:* URS-3.

W-5960 · Ryder 5-A

Grade availability: Several Mint State coins known. *Rarity:* URS-10.

G-4	VG-8	F-12	VF-20	EF-40
$100	$160	$250	$625	$1,200

W-5970 · Ryder 6-A

Grade availability: Difficult to find better than Very Fine. No Mint State coins have been recorded. *Rarity:* URS-6.

G-4	VG-8	F-12	VF-20	EF-40
$500	$750	$1,200	$3,000	$6,500

W-5980 · Ryder 6-D

Grade availability: Difficult to find better than Very Fine. *Notes:* Most examples of Ryder 6-D have the Indian's right leg ending above the moccasin, and the left elbow very weak. *Rarity:* URS-6.

G-4	VG-8	F-12	VF-20	EF-40	AU-50
$500	$800	$1,600	$3,500	$8,000	

1788 Massachusetts Half Cents

Crosby records the average weight as about 76 grains, or slightly lighter than the typical 1787 half cent.

W-6000 · Ryder 1-A

Notes: This scarce variety is easy to memorize, as both 8's are high. As this is the key to forming a "set" of half cents of this date, it has acquired a measure of fame over the years. Often described as very rare. Mike Packard suggests it is overrated, noting the URS-7 is reasonable, "although I would not be uncomfortable with URS-8." *Grade availability:* Difficult to find better than Extremely Fine. Ford's was Uncirculated. *Rarity:* URS-7 or 8.

G-4	VG-8	F-12	VF-20	EF-40	AU-50	MS-60
$200	$350	$600	$1,200	$2,600	$5,200	$9,000

W-6010 · Ryder 1-B

Grade availability: Plentiful in Mint State in the context of the series. *Rarity:* URS-11.

G-4	VG-8	F-12	VF-20	EF-40	AU-50	MS-60
$125	$175	$300	$625	$1,300	$2,600	$4,500

Easy Finding Guide
1787 Cent Obverse Dies

Check the star point first, then the other features.

TOP OF ARROW SHAFT UNDER CENTER OF "E"

Ryder 1 · Aged Face · One ray of star points at chin. Point of arrow below tunic is twice the length of the arrowhead. Top of bow rises to 3/4 of the height of the letters. Diagnostic. Contemporary counterfeit. *Notes:* Sometimes called "Aged Face," from the visage. *Used for:* W-7030, Ryder 1-B.

Ryder 8 · One ray of star points over head. Star is lower on its left side. Diagnostic. Tunic has seven pleats, with the one closest to the arrow being particularly thick. Bottom of bow ends well above the moccasin and the mound. End of the collar extends into the field below the chin. (see Mike Packard and Tom Rinaldo, *C4 Newsletter*, Winter 1997). Diagnostic. *Used for:* W-7160, Ryder 8-G.

TOP OF ARROW SHAFT UNDER UPRIGHT OF E

Ryder 2 · One ray of star points at collar. Diagnostic. Point of arrow below tunic is twice the length of the arrowhead. Top of bow rises to 2/3 of the height of the letters. *Notes:* This obverse sometimes has been called 2a in combination with reverse F and 2b (slightly repunched) in combination with other dies. *Used for:* W-7040, Ryder 2-A. W-7050, Ryder 2-C. W-7060, Ryder 2-E. W-7070, Ryder 2-F. W-7080, Ryder 2-G. Also used for 1788 Ryder 18-M.

Ryder 3 · One ray of star points at forehead. Diagnostic. Point of arrow below tunic is twice the length of the arrowhead. Top of bow rises to one-half of the height of the letters. *Used for:* W-7090, Ryder 3-G.

Ryder 4 · Bowed Head · One ray of star points below collar. Diagnostic. Point of arrow below tunic is slightly more than twice the length of the arrowhead. Top of bow rises to half of the height of the letters. *Notes:* "Bowed Head" as the Indian looks downward. *Used for:* W-7100, Ryder 4-C. W-7110, Ryder 4-D. W-7120, Ryder 4-J.

Ryder 5 · One ray of star points at chin. Diagnostic. Point of arrow below tunic is one-and-a-half times the length of the arrowhead. Top of bow rises to one-third of the height of the letters. *Notes:* Left side of arrowhead larger. Top of arrow shaft under left serif of E. *Used for:* W-7130, Ryder 5-I.

Ryder 6 · Stout Indian · One ray of star points above collar. Diagnostic. Point of arrow below tunic is about the length of the arrowhead. Top of bow rises to half of the height of the letters. *Notes:* The Indian is somewhat heavy. Same as obverse 12 of 1788. *Used for:* 1787—W-7140, Ryder 6-G. Also used for 1788— W-7320, Ryder 12-H. W-7330, Ryder 12-I. W-7340, Ryder 12-K. W-7350, Ryder 12-M. W-7360, Ryder 12-O.

Ryder 7 · Stout Indian · One ray of star points at mouth. Diagnostic. Point of arrow below tunic is very slightly more than the length of the arrowhead. Top of bow rises to 3/4 of the height of the letters. *Notes:* Similar to obverse 6, the Indian is somewhat heavy. Irregular cud break develops left of ground under Indian. *Used for:* W-7150, Ryder 7-H.

Easy Finding Guide
1787 Cent Reverse Dies

DATE LINE DOUBLE, FOUR LEAVES IN BRANCH

Ryder A · Horned Eagle with break over head. The 1 is upright. Diagnostic. Lowest left leaf opposite left upright of M. Arrows close to S. *Used for:* W-7040, Ryder 2-A.

Ryder B · No break above eagle's head. The 1 leans to right. Diagnostic. Lowest left leaf opposite center of M. Arrows distant from S. *Used for:* W-7030, Ryder 1-B.

DATE LINE DOUBLE, FIVE LEAVES IN BRANCH

Ryder C · Lowest arrow points at dot. Tip of lowest outside leaf points to inside of left foot of M; thorn from tip of leaf. Diagnostic. *Used for:* W-7050, Ryder 2-C. W-7100, Ryder 4-C.

Ryder D · Lowest arrow points below dot. Tip of lowest outside leaf points to left foot of M. Diagnostic. *Used for:* W-7110, Ryder 4-D.

Ryder E · Lowest arrow points above dot. Tip of lower left leaf distant from M. Diagnostic. Branch end close to or touches feather, 17 low. *Used for:* W-7060, Ryder 2-E.

Ryder J · Lowest arrow points above dot. Tip of lower left leaf close to M. Diagnostic. Date slopes down to left. Tip of lowest outside leaf opposite left stand of M. Date slopes down to left; 1 lowest. *Used for:* W-7120, Ryder 4-J.

TRANSPOSED ARROWS

Ryder F · Transposed Arrows (Arrows on Left Side), CENT in raised letters. Diagnostic. Arrows on left side of coin (held in eagle's right claw). *Used for:* W-7070, Ryder 2-F.

DATE LINE SINGLE

Ryder G · Arrow pierces tip of wing. Diagnostic. *Used for:* W-7080, Ryder 2-G. W-7090, Ryder 3-G. W-7140, Ryder 6-G. W-7160, Ryder 8-G.

Ryder H · Highest outside leaf points to right foot of M. Diagnostic. *Used for:* W-7150, Ryder 7-H.

Ryder I · Highest outside leaf points to and touches lowest wing feather. Diagnostic. *Used for:* W-7130, Ryder 5-I.

Easy Finding Guide
1788 Cent Obverse Dies

Check the star point first, then the other features.

TOP OF ARROW SHAFT UNDER UPRIGHT OF "E"

Ryder 1 · One ray of star points below collar. Diagnostic. Point of arrow below tunic is fully two lengths of the arrowhead. Top of bow rises to the top of the letters. *Used for:* W-7190, Ryder 1-D.

Ryder 3 · One ray of star points at throat. Point of arrow below tunic is more than two lengths of the arrowhead. MM widely spaced. Diagnostic. *Used for:* W-7210, Ryder 3-A. W-7220, Ryder 3-E.

Ryder 6 · One ray of star points at collar. MM wide at base. Tip of arrow under below tunic. Diagnostic. Point of arrow below tunic is slightly more than one-and-a-half times the length of the arrowhead. Top of bow rises to one-fourth of the height of the letters. *Used for:* W-7240, Ryder 6-N.

Ryder 7 · One ray of star points to above collar. At right, sixth pleat half over leg, seventh clear of leg. Diagnostic. Point of arrow below tunic is about one-and-a-half times the length of the arrowhead. Top of bow rises to 3/4 the height of the letters. *Used for:* W-7250, Ryder 7-M.

Ryder 8 · One ray of star points at mouth. Diagnostic. Point of arrow below tunic is about one-and-a-half times the length of the arrowhead. Top of bow rises to the top of the letters. *Used for:* W-7260, Ryder 8-C.

Ryder 9 · One ray of star points at forehead. Spine extends upward from top of arrow shaft. Barb of arrowhead close to tunic. Diagnostic. Point of arrow below tunic is about one-and-a-half times the length of the arrowhead. Top of bow rises to half of the height of the letters. *Used for:* W-7270, Ryder 9-M.

Ryder 10 · One ray of star points to above collar. String separated from center of bow. Two tunic pleats left of leg (one of them touching leg); seventh pleat clear of leg. Diagnostic. Point of arrow below tunic is about one-and-a-half times the length of the arrowhead. Top of bow rises to 3/4 the height of the letters. Minimal feathers on right side of shaft. *Used for:* W-7280, Ryder 10-L.

Ryder 11 · One ray of star points at throat. Point of arrow below tunic is about one-and-a-half times the length of the arrowhead. MM close. Arrowhead is almost an equilateral triangle. Diagnostic. *Used for:* W-7290, Ryder 11-C. W-7300, Ryder 11-E. W-7310, Ryder 11-F.

Ryder 12 (Same as Ryder 6 of 1787) · **Stout Indian** · One ray of star points above collar. At right, sixth pleat on leg, seventh clear of leg. Diagnostic. Point of arrow below tunic is about the length of the arrowhead. Top of bow rises to half of the height of the letters. *Used for:* 1787—W-7140, Ryder 6. Also used for 1788—W-7320, Ryder 12-H. W-7330, Ryder 12-I. W-7340, Ryder 12-K. W-7350, Ryder 12-M. W-7360, Ryder 12-O.

Ryder 13 · One ray of star points at collar. MM wide at base. Tip of arrow to right of tunic. Diagnostic. Point of arrow below tunic is about one-and-a-half times the length of the arrowhead. Top of bow rises to slightly more than one-fourth the height of the letters. *Used for:* W-7370, Ryder 13-I. W-7380, Ryder 13-N. W-7390, Ryder 13-P.

Ryder 14 · Stout Indian · One ray of star points at neck below chin. Diagnostic. Point of arrow below tunic is about twice the length of the arrowhead. Top of bow rises to nearly half the height of the letters. *Notes:* Counterfeit from dies showing crude workmanship. *Used for:* W-7395, Ryder 14-J.

Ryder 15 · One ray of star points at or slightly above collar. MM close at base. Sixth and seventh pleats right of leg. Diagnostic. Point of arrow below tunic is almost twice the length of the arrowhead. Top of bow rises to nearly the top of the letters. COM widely spaced. *Used for:* W-7400, Ryder 15-M.

Ryder 16 · One ray of star points at forehead, another to below collar. Barb of arrowhead distant from tunic. Diagnostic. Point of arrow below tunic is nearly twice the length of the arrowhead. Top of arrow shaft ends in a thorn. Top of bow rises to half the height of the letters; top slightly double cut. Small shrub or bush at right end of ground. *Used for:* W-7410, Ryder 16-M.

Ryder 17 · One ray of star points to collar or slightly below. Diagnostic. Point of arrow below tunic is more than twice the length of the arrowhead. Top of bow rises to half the height of the letters. *Used for:* W-7420, Ryder 17-I.

Ryder 18 (Same as Ryder 2 of 1787) · One ray of star points at collar. MM close at base. Sixth pleat half on leg, seventh right of leg. Diagnostic. Point of arrow below tunic is twice the length of the arrowhead. Top of bow rises to half of the height of the letters. COM closely spaced. *Used for:* W-7430, Ryder 18-M of 1788 as here and illustrated by the unique example (also see illustration of obverse 2 of 1787); also these 1787 cents: W-7040, Ryder 2-A. W-7050, Ryder 2-C. W-7060, Ryder 2-E. W-7070, Ryder 2-F. W-7080, Ryder 2-G.

TOP OF ARROW SHAFT UNDER RIGHT PART OF "E"

Ryder 2 · One ray of star points to above collar. Diagnostic. Point of arrow below tunic is fully two lengths of the arrowhead. Top of bow rises to 3/4 the height of the letters. *Used for:* W-7200, Ryder 2-B.

Ryder 4 · One ray of star points at nose. Diagnostic. Point of arrow below tunic is fully two lengths of the arrowhead. Top of bow rises to the top of the letters. *Used for:* W-7230, Ryder 4-G.

EASY FINDING GUIDE
1788 CENT REVERSE DIES

S NARROW (RESEMBLES A FIGURE 8, PERKINS STYLE)

Ryder A · In date, 17 and second 8 high, first 8 low. S below tip of wing. Diagnostic. Highest outside leaf opposite center of M; top leaf grazes right side of tip of second feather. *Used for:* W-7210, Ryder 3-A.

Ryder B · In date, 1 slightly low, second 8 slightly high. Diagnostic. S below tip of wing. Highest outside leaf opposite right upright of M; top leaf below second feather. In date all figures widely spaced and lower than usual. *Used for:* W-7200, Ryder 2-B.

1788 CENT REVERSE DIES (continued)

Ryder C · In date, 1 high, 788 lower. Diagnostic. Highest outside leaf opposite center of M; top leaf close to or barely touches second feather. *Used for:* W-7260, Ryder 8-C. W-7290, Ryder 11-C.

Ryder D · S below tip of wing. Diagnostic. Highest outside leaf opposite inside of left upright of M; top leaf below second feather. In date, 1 and second 8 very high; 78 low. *Used for:* W-7190, Ryder 1-D.

Ryder E · In date, 1 and 8 high, 78 low. S opposite wing. Diagnostic. Highest outside leaf opposite right upright of M; top leaf below second feather. In date, 78 low, second highest. *Used for:* W-7220, Ryder 3-E. W-7300, Ryder 11-E.

Ryder F · Rightmost arrow points to tip of wing. Diagnostic. Highest outside leaf opposite slightly right of center of M; top leaf ends at junction of first and second feathers. In date, 1 high, First 8 low, second 8 high. *Used for:* W-7310, Ryder 11-F.

S WIDE AND OPEN (CALLENDER STYLE)

Ryder G · Only the rightmost arrow points past tip of feather. Diagnostic. Highest outside leaf opposite center or slightly right of center of M; top leaf touches right side of tip of second feather. In date, second 8 low. Arrow touches wingtip. *Used for:* W-7230, Ryder 4-G.

Ryder H · Highest outside leaf opposite slightly right of center of M. Digits 78 closer than are 88. Diagnostic. Top leaf ends between first and second feather tips. Bottom of close to date line. Arrows close to wing. *Used for:* W-7320, Ryder 12-H.

Ryder I · Highest outside leaf opposite right upright of M; top leaf points to inside right of tip of first feather. Diagnostic. Digits 17 close; 7 slightly high; 8's lean left. Arrow touches tip of wing. *Used for:* W-7330, Ryder 12-I. W-7370, Ryder 13-I. W-7420, Ryder 17-I.

Ryder J · Rightmost arrow points to right side of period. No arrows touch feather. Diagnostic. Highest outside leaf opposite inside left foot of M; top leaf curves to the right and points to third and fourth feathers. In date, 178 wide, 88 close. *Notes:* Contemporary counterfeit with crude die work. *Used for:* W-7395, Ryder 14-J.

Ryder K · Highest outside leaf opposite right foot of M; top leaf thin and below second feather; arrowhead distant below feather tip. Diagnostic. The 1 with top serif slanting up to left; 17 close; 7 high. *Used for:* W-7340, Ryder 12-K.

Ryder L · Highest outside leaf opposite slightly left of center of M. The 1 and 7 are close. The 7 and 8 are widely separated, the 8's are of medium separation. Diagnostic. Top leaf below second feather. Bottom of branch distant from date line. Arrows distant from wing. *Used for:* W-7280, Ryder 10-L.

Ryder M · Rightmost arrow points to slightly left of period. One arrow close to or barely touches feather. *Diagnostic.* Highest outside leaf opposite center of M; top leaf is below junction of first and second feathers and points to second feather. The seven barbed arrows are widely spread, the last pointing to above the period. *Used for:* W-7250, Ryder 7-M. W-7270, Ryder 9-M. W-7350, Ryder 12-M. W-7400, Ryder 15-M. W-7410, Ryder 16-M. W-7430, Ryder 18-M.

Ryder N · No period after Massachusetts. *Diagnostic.* Highest outside leaf opposite center of M; top leaf below second feather. In date, 17 very close; second 8 high. No period after MASSACHUSETTS. *Diagnostic. Used for:* W-7240, Ryder 6-N. W-7380, Ryder 13-N.

Ryder O · Rightmost arrow points to period. Several arrows touch feather. *Diagnostic.* Highest outside leaf opposite center of M; top leaf close to inside of very long tip of first feather. In date, 7 high; second 8 low. Arrows touch wing tip. *Used for:* W-7360, Ryder 12-O.

Ryder P · Top leaf heavy and below second feather. Arrow close below feather tip; arrowhead points to lower right of S. The 7 and second 8 high. *Used for:* W-7390, Ryder 13-P.

1787 Massachusetts Cents

Crosby records average weights of 146 to 165 grains.

W-6030 · Ryder 1-B · Aged Face

Contemporary counterfeit attributed to Machin's Mills. *Notes:* Light weight. Two of Ford's three worn examples weighed 123.6 and 112.7 grains, as compared to about 140 grains or so for comparably worn genuine issues; the third Ford coin was on a clipped planchet. Per contra, Breen-969 (*Encyclopedia*, 1988) states that these weigh 146 to 149.9 grains; Breen never had the opportunity to examine Ford's collection. Crosby wrote, "Among the most peculiar coins of this state. The Indian has an aged face, a prominent chin, and his body is slightly bowed. It is on a small planchet." It seems that quite a few were used as undertypes for Connecticut 1788 Miller 16.3-N coppers (see W-4610). *Grade availability:* Mike Packard records 10 pieces, the finest of which is Extremely Fine. Ford had three, the best Very Fine on a clipped planchet. *Rarity:* URS-5.

G-4	VG-8	F-12	VF-20	EF-40
$2,000	$3,200	$5,000	$15,000	$30,000

W-6040 · Ryder 2-A · Horned Eagle

Notes: Also known as 2b-A. Popular variety due to the nickname, from a die break on the top of the eagle's head. One of the most plentiful issues in the series. *Grade availability:* Scarce above Extremely Fine, although Mint State coins exist. *Rarity:* URS-11.

G-4	VG-8	F-12	VF-20	EF-40	AU-50	MS-60
$110	$170	$275	$800	$1,600	$3,500	$9,000

W-6050 · Ryder 2-C

Notes: Also known as 2b-C. Known with a very late state of the reverse die (Taylor-2124) with a large crack from the border through the top of M to the left side of the date line through the first two digits to the border. *Grade availability:* Scarce above Very Fine. No Mint State coins have been recorded. Ford's, the Ryder plate coin, was graded choice About Uncirculated. *Rarity:* URS-8.

G-4	VG-8	F-12	VF-20	EF-40	AU-50
$200	$350	$500	$1,500	$3,250	$6,000

W-6060 · Ryder 2-E

Notes: Also known as 2b-E. Known with a late die state (Taylor 2125) with crack from the wing through the last E to the border. *Grade availability:* Scarce above Very Fine. No Mint State coins have been recorded. Ford's two coins, both Very Fine, weighed 185 and 186 grains. *Rarity:* URS-8.

G-4	VG-8	F-12	VF-20	EF-40	AU-50
$200	$350	$500	$1,500	$3,250	$6,000

W-6070 · Ryder 2-F · Transposed Arrows

Notes: This is the most famous single issue in the Massachusetts copper series. Ryder designated the variety as 2a-F. This is the only reverse with CENT raised rather than incuse. *Grade availability:* About 15 known. Rare variety, especially above Fine. Michael J. Hodder wrote in the Ford V catalog: "According to colonials maven Bill Anton, there were two gem Uncirculated Transposed Arrows 1787 cents found in Europe early in 1976. John Ford bought one and Bill bought the other." The Ford coin was graded choice Uncirculated in the auction. The Newcomer coin, now in the Eric P. Newman collection, has traces of mint red. *Rarity:* URS-5.

G-4	VG-8	F-12	VF-20	EF-40	AU-50	MS-60
$15,000	$25,000	$35,000	$75,000	—	—	

W-6080 · Ryder 2-G
Grade availability: About 14 known. The finest is Very Fine. *Rarity:* URS-5.

G-4	VG-8	F-12	VF-20	EF-40
$850	$1,500	$2,500	$5,000	—

W-6090 · Ryder 3-G
Grade availability: Several Mint State examples have been recorded. *Rarity:* URS-10.

G-4	VG-8	F-12	VF-20	EF-40	AU-50	MS-60
$100	$160	$250	$750	$1,500	$3,300	$9,000

W-6100 · Ryder 4-C · Bowed Head
Notes: Same obverse die used for 1788 Ryder 17-I. *Grade availability:* Rare above Extremely Fine. *Rarity:* URS-9.

G-4	VG-8	F-12	VF-20	EF-40	AU-50	MS-60
$125	$200	$350	$900	$2,000	$4,000	—

W-6110 · Ryder 4-D
Notes: Same obverse die used on 1788 Ryder 17-I. *Grade availability:* Rare above Extremely Fine. *Rarity:* URS-9.

G-4	VG-8	F-12	VF-20	EF-40	AU-50	MS-60
$100	$160	$250	$750	$1,500	$3,300	$9,000

W-6120 · Ryder 4-J
Notes: Same obverse die used on 1788 Ryder 17-I. *Grade availability:* Rare in any grade. Five pieces recorded by Mike Packard. Discovered by Q. David Bowers in March 1958 (*Rare Coin Review*, May–June 1958). Finest is Very Fine to Extremely Fine, in the Richard August collection. *Rarity:* URS-4.

Selected auction price(s): Norweb II Sale (3/1988), F, $2,420.

W-6130 · Ryder 5-I
Contemporary counterfeit attributed to Machin's Mills. *Notes:* Crosby wrote, "We have seen only in the cabinet of Charles I. Bushnell. The Indian is stout and slightly bowed." Breen-960 description stated he had never seen one. Taylor-2130 was lightly struck on the right side of the obverse and corresponding area of the reverse; reverse die shattered. *Grade availability:* Mike Packard records four pieces, the finest of which is Very Fine. *Rarity:* URS-3.

W-6140 · Ryder 6-G · Stout Indian
Notes: The Indian is somewhat heavy. Same obverse as 12 of 1788. *Grade availability:* Rare above Extremely Fine. *Rarity:* URS-9.

G-4	VG-8	F-12	VF-20	EF-40	AU-50	MS-60
$100	$160	$250	$1,000	$1,800	$3,300	$9,000

W-6150 · Ryder 7-H · Stout Indian
Contemporary counterfeit attributed to Machin's Mills. *Notes:* Similar to obverse 6, the Indian is somewhat heavy. Crosby: "Another stout Indian. The die badly broken." Breen-960 description gave the weight as 155.8 to 158.9 grains; he attributes Ryder 5-I and 7-H to the same maker, different from the unknown maker of 1-B. *Grade availability:* Mike Packard records about 12 pieces, including several Mint State. *Rarity:* URS-4.

Selected auction price(s): John J. Ford Jr. V Sale (Stack's 10/2004), VF, $16,100; Gem MS, $20,700.

W-6160 · Ryder 8-G
Grade availability: Mike Packard has recorded 13 pieces. Rare above Fine. *Rarity:* URS-5.

G-4	VG-8	F-12	VF-20	EF-40	AU-50
$850	$1,500	$2,500	$5,000	$10,000	—

1788 Massachusetts Cents
Crosby records average weights of 146 to 165 grains.

W-6190 · Ryder 1-D
Grade availability: Several Mint State coins are known. *Rarity:* URS-10.

G-4	VG-8	F-12	VF-20	EF-40	AU-50	MS-60
$100	$160	$250	$600	$1,200	$2,750	$6,000

W-6200 · Ryder 2-B
Grade availability: Rare above Extremely Fine. Ford had an About Uncirculated. *Rarity:* URS-9.

G-4	VG-8	F-12	VF-20	EF-40	AU-50
$125	$200	$300	$750	$1,500	$3,300

W-6210 · Ryder 3-A
Grade availability: Rare above Extremely Fine. *Rarity:* URS-9.

G-4	VG-8	F-12	VF-20	EF-40	AU-50	MS-60
$100	$160	$250	$600	$1,200	$2,750	$7,500

W-6220 · Ryder 3-E
Grade availability: Rare above Very Fine. Ford's choice Uncirculated is the finest recorded. *Rarity:* URS-9.

G-4	VG-8	F-12	VF-20	EF-40	AU-50	MS-60
$125	$200	$300	$750	$1,500	$3,500	$7,500

W-6230 · Ryder 4-G
Grade availability: Rare above Very Fine. *Rarity:* URS-8.

G-4	VG-8	F-12	VF-20	EF-40	AU-50
$150	$250	$375	$900	$2,200	$4,500

W-6240 · Ryder 6-N · No Period After Massachusetts
Grade availability: Rare above Extremely Fine. Several Mint State coins are known. *Rarity:* URS-10.

G-4	VG-8	F-12	VF-20	EF-40	AU-50	MS-60
$115	$170	$275	$800	$1,800	$3,500	$7,500

W-6250 · Ryder 7-M
Grade availability: Rare above Extremely Fine. Ford had three Uncirculated coins, including one misattributed as Ryder 9-M. *Rarity:* URS-8.

G-4	VG-8	F-12	VF-20	EF-40	AU-50	MS-60
$150	$250	$375	$900	$1,800	$4,000	$7,500

W-6260 · Ryder 8-C
Grade availability: Rare above Extremely Fine. *Rarity:* URS-10.

G-4	VG-8	F-12	VF-20	EF-40	AU-50	MS-60
$100	$160	$250	$600	$1,500	$3,000	$6,000

W-6270 · Ryder 9-M
Grade availability: Rare above Fine. *Rarity:* URS-6.

G-4	VG-8	F-12	VF-20	EF-40	AU-50
$500	$800	$1,250	$3,000	$5,000	$10,000

W-6280 · Ryder 10-L
Grade availability: Several Mint State coins are known. *Rarity:* URS-11.

G-4	VG-8	F-12	VF-20	EF-40	AU-50	MS-60
$100	$160	$250	$600	$1,200	$2,750	$5,500

W-6290 · Ryder 11-C
Grade availability: Rare above Very Fine. None known in Mint State. *Rarity:* URS-8.

G-4	VG-8	F-12	VF-20	EF-40	AU-50
$150	$250	$375	$900	$2,000	$4,000

W-6300 · Ryder 11-E
Grade availability: Rare above Extremely Fine. Ford's was About Uncirculated. None known in Mint State. *Rarity:* URS-9.

G-4	VG-8	F-12	VF-20	EF-40	AU-50
$100	$160	$250	$600	$1,200	$2,750

W-6310 · Ryder 11-F · Slim Indian
Notes: Nickname in Ford catalog, but not widely used. *Grade availability:* Rare above Very Fine. *Rarity:* URS-7.

G-4	VG-8	F-12	VF-20	EF-40	AU-50
$150	$250	$375	$900	$2,000	$4,000

W-6320 · Ryder 12-H · Stout Indian
Notes: Same obverse as 6 of 1787. *Grade availability:* Mike Packard records eight coins, the finest of which is Extremely Fine. *Rarity:* URS-4.

W-6330 · Ryder 12-I · Stout Indian
Notes: Same obverse as 6 of 1787. *Grade availability:* Rare above Very Fine. None known in Mint State. *Rarity:* URS-9.

G-4	VG-8	F-12	VF-20	EF-40	AU-50
$125	$200	$300	$750	$1,500	$3,500

W-6340 · Ryder 12-K · Stout Indian
Notes: Same obverse as 6 of 1787. *Grade availability:* Rare above Fine. Finest known is About Uncirculated. *Rarity:* URS-7.

G-4	VG-8	F-12	VF-20	EF-40	AU-50
$400	$800	$1,250	$2,750	$5,000	$12,500

W-6350 · Ryder 12-M · Stout Indian
Notes: Same obverse as 6 of 1787. *Grade availability:* Rare above Extremely Fine, Ford offerings excepted. *Rarity:* URS-9.

G-4	VG-8	F-12	VF-20	EF-40	AU-50	MS-60
$125	$200	$300	$750	$1,500	$2,750	$7,500

W-6360 · Ryder 12-O · Stout Indian
Notes: Same obverse as 6 of 1787. *Grade availability:* Discovered in October 1951 by W.P. Keller; reported in *CNL*, January 1961. Mike Packard records five known, the finest being Very Fine. *Rarity:* URS-4.

W-6370 · Ryder 13-I
Grade availability: Mike Packard records six known, the finest being Very Fine. *Rarity:* URS-4.

W-6380 · Ryder 13-N · No Period after Massachusetts
Grade availability: Rare above Very Fine. *Rarity:* URS-8.

G-4	VG-8	F-12	VF-20	EF-40	AU-50	MS-60
$180	$250	$400	$1,200	$2,700	$5,000	$8,500

W-6390 · Ryder 13-P
Grade availability: Only one known. Discovered by Richard August. Fine obverse, Very Good reverse. *Rarity:* URS-1.

W-6395 · Ryder 14-J · Stout Indian
Contemporary counterfeit attributed to Machin's Mills. *Notes:* Indian appears somewhat stocky. *Grade availability:* At least one Uncirculated coin (Picker to Vlack) is known. *Rarity:* URS-4.

Selected auction price(s): John J. Ford Jr. V Sale (Stack's 10/2004), F, $32,200; Choice VF, $57,500.

W-6400 · Ryder 15-M
Notes: This and later obverses not known to Ryder. *Grade availability:* Rare above Very Fine. None known in Mint State. *Rarity:* URS-6.

G-4	VG-8	F-12	VF-20	EF-40	AU-50
$400	$600	$1,000	$2,400	$4,800	$9,000

W-6410 · Ryder 16-M
Notes: Discussed by W.P. Keller in *CNL*, January 1961, at which time he was aware of three, including one in ANS. "It is difficult to understand why Ryder missed this variety since Crosby specifically mentioned the double bow end which occurs on no other variety." *Grade availability:* Rare above Very Fine. *Rarity:* URS-6.

G-4	VG-8	F-12	VF-20	EF-40	AU-50
$400	$600	$1,000	$2,400	$4,800	$9,000

W-6420 · Ryder 17-I
Notes: S This die is the same as obverse 4 of 1787; used on 1787 Ryder 4-C, 4-D, and 4-J. Discovered by Phil Greco and announced in the first issue of *CNL*, October 1960. Greco knew of two, one in the Massachusetts Historical

Society. *Grade availability:* Mike Packard records seven known. The finest is the Mint State in the Richard August collection. *Rarity:* URS-4.

Selected auction price(s): Smith & Youngman Collections (B&M 3/2003), G-5, $1,840.

W-6430 · Ryder 18-M

Grade availability: Discovered by Mike Packard in 2004. Obverse same as the durable die 2 of 1787. Extensively oxidized. *Rarity:* URS-1.

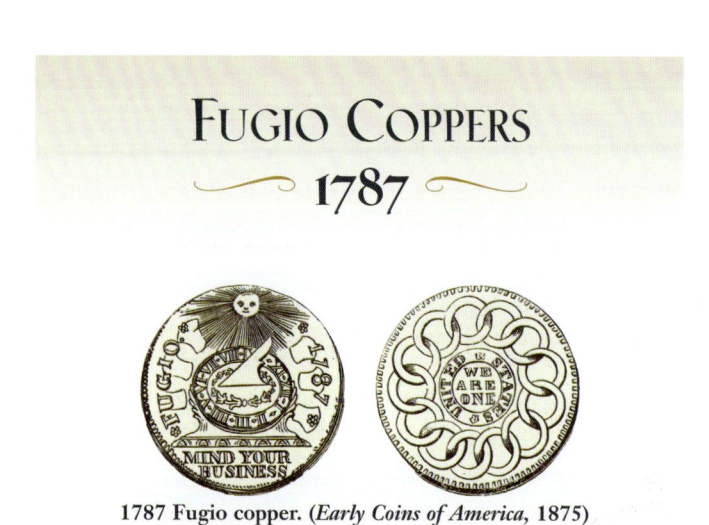

Fugio Coppers 1787

1787 Fugio copper. (*Early Coins of America*, 1875)

Background of the Coinage

Fugio coppers, often referred to as "cents" in numismatic circles, were authorized by the American Congress. Produced on contract, they are the first widely circulated coin of the federal government. Their obverse depicts a sundial with the inscription FUGIO ("I Fly," a reference to the passage of time; a motif borrowed from the earlier Continental Currency fractional notes dated February 17, 1776, and also used on the 1776 Continental dollar coins), and MIND YOUR BUSINESS, aphorisms suggested by Benjamin Franklin. On the reverse a circle of links represents the colonies, with the inscription UNITED STATES / WE ARE ONE at the center.

Minting apparently occurred in several different locations, including New Haven, Connecticut, and possibly New York City. It has been suggested that Reuben Harmon's mint in Rupert, Vermont also struck these pieces, but modern scholars discount the idea. The dies were engraved by Abel Buell, who was associated with other coinages, most notably Connecticut, but also Vermont.

The *Journal of Congress* reported on April 21, 1787, that a committee recommended that

> the Board of Treasury be authorized to contract for 300 tons of copper coin of the federal standard, agreeably to the proposition of Mr. James Jarvis, provided that the premium to be allowed to the United States on the amount of copper coin contracted for be not less than fifteen percent, that it be coined at the expense of the contractor, but under the inspection of an officer appointed and paid by the United States.

On Friday, July 6, 1787, a resolution provided that

> the Board of Treasury direct the contractor for the copper coinage to stamp on one side of each piece the following device: 13 circles linked together, a small circle in the middle, with the words UNITED STATES around it; and in the center, the words WE ARE ONE; on the other side of the same piece the following device: a dial with the hours expressed on the face of it, a meridian sun above, on one side of which is to be the word FUGIO, and on the other the year in figures 1787, below the dial, the words MIND YOUR BUSINESS.

Minting and Distribution

The initial production apparently commenced in New Haven, Connecticut, under the supervision of James Jarvis. By June 1, 1788, coinage was halted. Abel Buell went to Europe, leaving the dies and other apparatus to others, to whom various accounts refer as William and Benjamin. It is believed that Samuel Broome and Jeremiah Platt (Jarvis's father-in-law), associated with copper coinage for the state of Connecticut, continued to make Fugio coppers on a sub-contract basis at mints located near New Haven at Westville and Morris Cove.

On September 30, 1788, it was reported that

> there are two contracts made by the Board of Treasury with James Jarvis, the one for coining 300 tons of copper of the federal standard, to be loaned to the United States, together with an additional quantity of 45 tons, which he was to pay as a premium to the United States for the privilege of coining; no part of the contract has been fulfilled. A particular statement of this business, so far as relates to the 300 tons, has lately been reported to Congress. It does not appear to your committee that the Board was authorized to contract for the privilege of coining 45 tons as a premium, exclusive of the 300 mentioned in the Act for Congress.
>
> The other contract with said Jarvis is for the sale of a quantity of copper amounting, as per account, to 71,174 pounds; this the said Jarvis has received at the stipulated price of 11 pence farthing, sterling, per pound, which he contracted to pay in copper coin, the federal standard, on or before the last day of August 1788, now past; of which but a small part has been received. The remainder it is presumed, the Board of Treasury will take effectual measures to recover as soon as possible.

By September 30, 1788, very little of the huge anticipated coinage had materialized. Apparently somewhat fewer than 400,000 Fugio coppers were actually struck, instead of several million. An entrepreneur, Royal Flint, took over the enterprise, but seems to have accomplished very little.

Numismatic Aspects

The new standard reference on the series is by Eric P. Newman: *United States Fugio Copper Coinage of 1787*, an expansion and updating of his groundbreaking "Varieties of the Fugio Cent," published in *The Coin Collector's Journal*, July-August 1952. Alan Kessler updated the 1952 Newman work in 1976 and added new varieties. Fugio coppers have been a popular subject in recent years for contributors to the *Colonial Newsletter* and the *C4 Newsletter*.

A large quantity of original 1787 Fugio coppers, estimated at several thousand pieces, was for many years in the vault of the Bank of New York. Tony Terranova reported that 712 remained as of 1998. Most Mint State pieces known today trace their origin to this particular group.

The typical Fugio copper has some areas of lightness due to casual striking. This is often seen at the bottom of the obverse and on the reverse toward the outside of the rings. Dentils are usually incomplete. Planchet rifts or fissures are not uncommon. More often than not, these problems are overlooked in descriptions, and certified holders don't mention them. These defects are to be expected and add to the "personality" of each coin.

In recent years grading interpretations have become very lax in my opinion, with the result that what was Fine in 1960 may be called Very Fine or even Extremely Fine today. Because of this, it is not possible to compare market-price movements unless the coins themselves are inspected and older photographs compared. While collecting by Newman varieties appeals to specialists, most numismatists seek either a single representative example or the various major styles listed in the Red Book.

Obverse and reverse dies were made from hubs that included major features. Details were then added by hand. On the obverse, the eyes of the sun, floral ornaments at the base of the sundial gnomon, FUGIO, 1787, cinquefoils (five-lobed decorations), MIND YOUR BUSINESS, and border dentils were all added, creating variations that identify the varieties. On the reverse, the letters WE ARE ONE and the dentils were added by hand.

While Abel Buell is credited with making the hubs, inspection the coins reveals that workmanship on the details of the coining dies varied widely. Some are done skillfully with the letters well aligned, while others are amateurish. These differences add greatly to their numismatic appeal. The pages of the *Colonial Newsletter* are rich with Fugio information from Damon G. Douglas, James C. Spilman, and others, and are highly recommended for anyone with a deep interest in this series.

Cross-references are given below to the popular Newman numbers. For the so-called New Haven restrikes and fantasy issues, see chapter 12. The two most important auction offerings of Fugio coppers, the Norweb III sale (1988) and the Ford sale (1993), are selectively cited below.

Easy Finding Guide
Fugio Obverse Dies

CROSS AFTER DATE, NO CINQUEFOILS ON OBVERSE

Newman 1 · *Notes:* This is the only obverse without cinquefoils. The die sinking was incomplete, necessitating retouching of various features, especially evident upon close examination of the Roman numerals on the sun dial. The rays are a combination of thin and somewhat thick (but not heavy enough to be called "club"). The ornament (misnamed a "cross") after the date was made by hand, not with a separate punch, and consists of an X crudely formed with dots in the interstices. Most of the letters in MIND YOUR BUSINESS are horizontally shaded. *Used for:* W-6600, Newman 1-B. W-6605, Newman 1-L. W-6610, Newman 1-Z. W-6615, Newman 1-CC.

CROSS AFTER DATE, "FUCIO" SPELLING (CLUB RAYS, CONVEX ENDS)

Newman 2 · Ray points below cinquefoil before 1 (1787). Dies 5, 24, and 25 were similar at the outset, but the engraver added a crossbar to the C. *Used for:* W-6630, Newman 2-C.

Newman 23 · Ray points at cinquefoil before 1 (1787). *Used for:* W-6650, Newman 23-ZZ.

209

FUGIO OBVERSE DIES (continued)

CLUB RAYS, CONCAVE OR ROUNDED ENDS

Newman 3 · Ray touches center of cinquefoil before 1 (1787). O (YOUR) centered over upper right of E. *Used for:* W-6680, Newman 3-D.

Newman 4 · Ray close to lower part of cinquefoil before 1 (1787) but does not touch. O above S. *Used for:* W-6685, Newman 4-E.

CLUB RAYS, CONVEX ENDS

Newman 5 · D (MIND) centered over S; 2 lobes point to F (FUGIO). Ray points to third cinquefoil. *Notes:* G (FUGIO) altered from a C by adding a crossbar. *Used for:* W-6640, Newman 5-F. W-6645, Newman 5-HH.

Newman 24 · Center of D (MIND) slightly left of center of S; 1 lobe points to F. Ray points to just below cinquefoil before 1. *Notes:* G (FUGIO) altered from a C by adding a crossbar. *Used for:* W-6655, Newman 24-MM.

Newman 25 · Center of D (MIND) over right side of S; 1 lobe points to base of O. Last S very low. *Notes:* G (FUGIO) altered from a C by adding a crossbar. *Used for:* W-6660, Newman 25-PP.

1 OVER HORIZONTAL 1, POINTED RAYS

Newman 10-G · *Notes:* The first digit of the date was first punched sideways, then corrected. The undertype 1 remains distinct. Amateurish die work is also evident in the poorly aligned letters in MIND YOUR BUSINESS. *Used for:* W-6700, Newman 10-G. W-6705, Newman 10-T. W-6710, Newman 10-OO.

POINTED RAYS

All of the varieties in this section have pointed rays. As a starting point, note position of center of ornament over I (BUSINESS), which for Newman 6 through 21 moves from left to right. Obverse 22 is an exception and was numbered after the Newman text was completed.

Newman 6 · Center of ornament over space between S and I. Center of upright of R (YOUR) under left edge of bead or left of it. Nearest lobes of cinquefoil point to O (FUGIO). *Used for:* W-6730, Newman 6-W.

Newman 7 · Center of ornament over upper left corner of I. Center of upright of R (YOUR) under bead. Lobe of cinquefoil points to O (FUGIO). D (MIND) touches S; E lower than S. Eyes, nose, and mouth of the sun are heavy raised pellets. *Used for:* W-6735, Newman 7-T.

Newman 8 · Center of ornament over left edge of upright of I. Center of upright of R (YOUR) under bead. Lobes of cinquefoil point to above and below O (FUGIO). Right upright of N (MIND) over center of U. *Used for:* W-6740, Newman 8-B. W-6750, Newman 8-X.

210

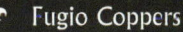

Newman 9 · Center of ornament over left edge of upright of I. Center of upright of R (YOUR) under left edge of bead or left of it. Nearest lobe of cinquefoil points to above and below O. The eyes of the sun are raised horizontal pellets. *Used for:* W-6755, Newman 9-P. W-6760, Newman 9-Q. W-6765, Newman 9-S. W-6770, Newman 9-T.

Newman 11 · Center of ornament over center of I. Center of upright of R (YOUR) under bead. Lobes of cinquefoil point to above and below O (FUGIO). Lobe of third cinquefoil points to base of 1; fourth cinquefoil closer to 7 than to base of sundial. Eyes of the sun in the form of horizontal pellets, the one on the left smaller and more nearly round. *Used for:* W-6780, Newman 11-A. W-6785, Newman 11-B. W-6790, Newman 11-X.

Newman 12 · Center of ornament over center of top of I which tilts slightly to the left. Center of upright of R (YOUR) under bead. Lobes of cinquefoil point to above and below O (FUGIO). Two lobes of cinquefoil point to F (FUGIO). At least two die variations exist, differing slightly in the relationship of B (BUSINESS) to the dentils and the shape and size of the eyes of the sun, no doubt from reworking the die. *Used for:* W-6800, Newman 12-M. W-6805, Newman 12-S. W-6810, Newman 12-U. W-6820, Newman 12-X. W-6830, Newman 12-Z. W-6835, Newman 12-KK. W-6840, Newman 12-LL.

Newman 13 · Center of ornament over center of I. Center of upright of R (YOUR) under bead. Lobe of cinquefoil points to O (FUGIO). U centered over S; R close to or touches base of sundial. Face of sun appears "sleepy." *Used for:* W-6845, Newman 13-N. W-6850, Newman 13-R. W-6855, Newman 13-X. W-6858, Newman 13-JJ. W-6860, Newman 13-KK.

Newman 14 · Center of ornament over center of I. Center of upright of R (YOUR) under bead. Lobes of cinquefoil point to above and below O (FUGIO). Lobe of third cinquefoil points to top of 1; fourth cinquefoil centered between 7 and base of sundial. Letters of aphorism irregularly aligned. The sun is bug-eyed. *Used for:* W-6870, Newman 14-H. W-6875, Newman 14-O. W-6880, Newman 14-X.

Newman 15 · Center of ornament over right edge of upright of I. Center of upright of R (YOUR) under bead. Lobes of cinquefoil point to above and below O (FUGIO). U touches S below it. YO (YOUR) high. Prominent eyes on sun. *Used for:* W-6890, Newman 15-H. W-6900, Newman 15-K. W-6910, Newman 15-V. W-6915, Newman 15-Y.

Newman 16 · Center of ornament over right edge of upright of I. Center of upright of R (YOUR) under right edge of bead. D (MIND) low. Top of O (YOUR) broken. *Used for:* W-6920, Newman 16-H. W-6925, Newman 16-N.

Newman 17 · Center of ornament over right edge of upright of I. Center of upright of R (YOUR) under bead. Lobes of cinquefoil point to above and below O (FUGIO). Right edge of S slightly right of edge of D above it; letters in aphorism irregularly aligned. *Used for:* W-6930, Newman 17-I. W-6935, Newman 17-S. W-6940, Newman 17-T. W-6945, Newman 17-WW.

Newman 18 · Center of ornament over upper right corner of I. Center of upright of R (YOUR) under bead. Lobe of cinquefoil points to O (FUGIO). Third cinquefoil low; bottom lower than base of 1. Eye of sun on right more prominent. Letters in aphorism crudely aligned. *Used for:* W-6950, Newman 18-H. W-6960, Newman 18-U. W-6965, Newman 18-X.

211

Fugio Obverse Dies (continued)

Newman 19 · Center of ornament over space between I and N. Center of upright of R (YOUR) under bead. Lobes of cinquefoil point to above and below O (FUGIO). Upright of R over upper right of S. Eye of sun on left larger. Letters in aphorism crudely aligned. *Used for:* W-6970, Newman 19-M. W-6975, Newman 19-Z. W-6980, Newman 19-SS.

Newman 20 · Center of ornament over space between I and N. Center of upright of R (YOUR) under bead. Lobe of cinquefoil points to top of O (FUGIO). Third cinquefoil higher and above base of 1. Sun eyes especially prominent. *Used for:* W-6990, Newman 20-R. W-7000, Newman 20-X.

Newman 21 · Center of ornament over upper left corner of N. Center of upright of R (YOUR) under bead. Lobe of cinquefoil points to O (FUGIO). D very close to S with S tilted; N (BUSINESS) high and tilted left. Prominent sun eyes. *Used for:* W-7010, Newman 21-I.

Newman 22 · Center of ornament over slightly right of the center of I. Center of upright of R (YOUR) under bead. Lobe of cinquefoil points to O. U centered over S; R distant from base of sundial. *Used for:* W-7020, Newman 22-M.

Easy Finding Guide Fugio Reverse Dies

AMERICAN CONGRESS ON LABEL

Newman CC · Links with state names, AMERICAN CONGRESS on label. *Notes:* AMERICAN CONGRESS on label, enclosing WE ARE ONE in three lines at the center. Rays emanate from label. Around are 13 rings, each with the abbreviated name of a state, with N HAMP at top, continuing clockwise to GEORGI. For fantasy issues with AMERICAN CONGRESS see "'New Haven Restrike' Copies" in chapter 12. *Used for:* W-6615, Newman 1-CC.

RAISED RIMS ON CENTER LABEL

Newman Z · *Notes:* This is one of the most curious and distinctive of the reverses. "Not only are the inside and outside edges of the bands 'raised,' but the edges of the letters in STATES UNITED are also 'raised.' On close examination it is found that neither edges nor rims are in fact raised, but only appear as such because of the effective removal of material between the edges of the letters and the rims. . . . The cinquefoils do *not* have raised edges but do have additional ornamentation at each side, a feature which does not appear on any other variety. This consists of four dashes in a diamond or cruciform configuration at each side of each cinquefoil, for a total of 16 dashes. . . . The letters in WE ARE ONE are hand cut and are exceptionally large in comparison with the punched letters on the other reverses." (*CNL*, April–June 1962, James C. Spilman study). *Used for:* W-6610, Newman 1-Z. W-6830, Newman 12-Z. W-6975, Newman 19-Z.

8-POINTED STARS ON CENTER LABEL

Newman Y · Stars are in relief within a depressed area. The only reverse with this curious feature. *Used for:* W-6915, Newman 15-Y.

UNITED ABOVE, STATES BELOW

Newman A · Distinctive and easy to read arrangement of UNITED STATES found on no other die. *Used for:* W-6780, Newman 11-A.

UNITED LEFT, STATES RIGHT · CINQUEFOILS INCUSE ON LABEL EXCEPT PP

Descriptions quoted or adapted from Newman.

Newman B · W tilts right. Base of each E is low, particularly the first. Last E slightly farther to right than second E. Cinquefoil in band under left foot of N. W and second E are light. Die crack develops from 10th link to edge. *Used for:* W-6600, Newman 1-B. W-6740, Newman 8-B. W-6785, Newman 11-B.

Newman C · W and E widely separated. Upper left of W pierces label and extends into D. First E tilts left and is incomplete at bottom. Cinquefoil in label under left foot of N. Inner outline of label irregular above WE. *Used for:* W-6630, Newman 2-C.

Newman D · Letters punched very deeply into the die. W touches D (UNITED). Bottom right of first E is short. Top of second E is very low. O is large and low; right side is misshapen. Right side of N is thin. Cinquefoil in band under center of N. Second, third, sixth, and seventh links show double punching. Diagnostic. *Used for:* W-6680, Newman 3-D.

Newman E · Letters punched very deeply into the die. W does not touch D (UNITED). O is irregular on right side. Right side of N is thin. Cinquefoil on label under left foot of N. *Used for:* W-6685, Newman 4-E.

Newman F · ARE is much nearer to WE than to ONE. W, A, and O each lean to the right. Last E pierces label and is over right end of base of E (UNITED). *Used for:* W-6640, Newman 5-F.

Fugio Reverse Dies (continued)

Newman G · ARE is much nearer to WE than to ONE. W pierces label and touches lower left of D (UNITED). Base of first E slants down. Base of O is defective. N and second E are low. Cinquefoil in label under left side of N. *Used for:* W-6700, Newman 10-G.

Newman H · Top of W much lower than top of E, upper left pierces label and is opposite right part of D. R tilts left and barely touches second E. O is low. N and last E touch. Cinquefoil in label under right side of N. Die cracks develop between seventh and eighth links to edge and from 12th link to edge. *Used for:* W-6870, Newman 14-H. W-6890, Newman 15-H. W-6920, Newman 16-H. W-6950, Newman 18-H.

Newman I · ARE is much nearer to WE than to ONE. W under D (UNITED). ONE slopes down to right; E pierces label at upright of E (STATES). *Notes:* Reverse J, earlier assigned, was found to be the same as Reverse I (*CNL*, April 1961 superseded by April–June 1962). Dramatic incusation marks from the obverse include the date. The die must have clashed early in its life. *Used for:* W-6930, Newman 17-I. W-7010, Newman 21-I.

Newman HH · W pierces label and extends through bottom of D (UNITED). A and R widely separated. R leans right. O leans right. N low and leans left. *Used for:* W-6645, Newman 5-HH.

Newman JJ · R (ARE) touches bottoms of W and E above. Base of first E nearly touches top of E below it. A has an exceptionally long lower left serif. *Notes:* This is the only UNITED (left) STATES (right) reverse combined with the popular 13 obverse. *Used for:* W-6858, Newman 13-JJ.

Newman PP · *Raised* cinquefoils on label. *Notes:* Distinctive die with W and E the farther apart than on any other die; E high. *Used for:* W-6660, Newman 25-PP.

Newman ZZ · W small and distant from E; W and E each touch label. Letters in ARE progressively lower. Base of O slightly low. *Used for:* W-6650, Newman 23-ZZ.

STATES LEFT, UNITED RIGHT • CINQUEFOILS INCUSE ON LABEL EXCEPT MM

Descriptions quoted or adapted from Newman.

Newman K · First E low and clear of label. Second E low. Top of N touches last E. Cinquefoil in label under center of last E. Die crack develops from outside of juncture of 10th and 11th links to border. *Used for:* W-6900, Newman 15-K.

Newman L · Tops of W and E each intrude into label. First E low. A distant from R and is very close to label. Base of O is low. Cinquefoil in label under space between N and E. *Used for:* W-6605, Newman 1-L.

Newman M · A directly under O. A and R widely separated. R leans slightly left and is farther to the right then is the N below it. Tops of NE do not touch. Cinquefoil in label under the middle of last E. *Used for:* W-6800, Newman 12-M. W-6970, Newman 19-M. W-7020, Newman 22-M.

Newman N · W and E touch and intrude into the label. Letters in ARE well spaced. Top of O slightly high. Cinquefoil in label under space between N and last E. Die cracks develop from label through the third link to the edge, and through the eighth link to the edge. *Used for:* W-6845, Newman 13-N. W-6925, Newman 16-N.

Newman O · ARE well spaced and much closer to ONE than to WE. Base of O slightly low. Cinquefoil in label under center of last E. *Used for:* W-6875, Newman 14-O.

Newman P · Letters punched very deeply into the die. First E tilts slightly left. A touches label and is distant from R. O low and open at bottom. Cinquefoil in label under left side of final E. *Used for:* W-6755, Newman 9-P.

Newman Q · W touches label. W and E are widely spaced. First E slightly low and close to or touching RE below. A touches label and is distant from R. Base of O slightly low. N and E do not touch. Cinquefoil in label under right side of N. (This reverse is misdescribed in the Newman text.) *Used for:* W-6760, Newman 9-Q.

Fugio Reverse Dies (continued)

Newman R · WE too far to the left. W touches label. Second E directly over last E, but center of R is slightly left of center of N below. O is low. N leans slightly right. Last E low. *Used for:* W-6850, Newman 13-R. W-6990, Newman 20-R.

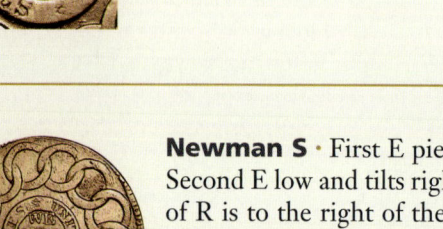

Newman S · First E pierces label. Second E low and tilts right. Center of R is to the right of the center of N below. Last E leans slightly right. Cinquefoil in label under center of last E. Die cracks develop from the second and from the third links to the label and from between the sixth and seventh links across the seventh link to the edge. *Used for:* W-6765, Newman 9-S. W-6805, Newman 12-S. W-6935, Newman 17-S.

Newman T · Letters punched very deeply into the die. WE too far to left. W pierces label and touches last S (STATES). First E slightly low. R high. Second E very low. Cinquefoil in label under space between N and last E. Some ring intersections are weak. *Used for:* W-6705, Newman 10-T. W-6735, Newman 7-T. W-6770, Newman 9-T. W-6940, Newman 17-T.

Newman U · W touches label. Center of second E is to the left of the center of last E below it. Cinquefoil in label under left side of last E. In combination 12-U prominent clash marks from the obverse die include part of the date. *Used for:* W-6810, Newman 12-U. W-6960, Newman 18-U.

Newman V · Letters in ARE and in ONE are progressively lower. Last E large and low. Cinquefoil in label below space between N and E. *Used for:* W-6910, Newman 15-V.

Newman W · W pierces label and also tilts right. Second E is low and directly over last E. Last E low and pierces band and touches E and D (UNITED). Cinquefoil in label under right upright of N. Die crack develops from label through ninth link to edge. *Used for:* W-6730, Newman 6-W.

Newman X · W and E touch each other and also piece the label. Top of first E slants upward. A is distant from R. Second E low. N is small and base is above those of adjacent letters. Cinquefoil in label under space between N and last E. Die cracks develop from label passing through seventh and eighth links to edge and across the inside of the ninth link. *Used for:* W-6750, Newman 8-X. W-6785, Newman 11-B. W-6820, Newman 12-X. W-6855, Newman 13-X. W-6880, Newman 14-X. W-6965, Newman 18-X. W-7000, Newman 20-X.

Newman KK · W slightly high. R and E wide; E leans slightly right. Lower right of N heavy. Cinquefoil in label under third E. *Used for:* W-6835, Newman 12-KK. W-6860, Newman 13-KK.

Newman LL · WE high; ends pierce label. ARE widely spaced, AR widest; E low. Top of third E high. Cinquefoil in label under space between N and last E. Some hub doubling on links. Discovered by Richard Picker in 1974 (*CNL*, January 1976). *Used for:* W-6840, Newman 12-LL.

Newman MM · *Raised* cinquefoils on label. Unique as such. Otherwise with letter arrangements somewhat similar to Reverse OO. Discovered by Anthony Terranova (*CNL*, July 1979). *Used for:* W-6655, Newman 24-MM.

Newman OO · W small, pierces label, and leans right; distant from E. ARE well spaced. O with thin right side; open at bottom. Cinquefoil on label under right upright of N. Discovered by Mike Ringo (*CNL*, June 1988). *Used for:* W-6710, Newman 10-OO.

Newman SS · Left part of W short. A leans slightly right. Second E low and leans right. NE touch with E lower. Cinquefoil in label under center of last E. *Used for:* W-6980, Newman 19-SS.

Newman WW · W leans right. R high and leans right. O heavy; ON closer than are NE. Last E pierces label. Cinquefoil in label under right upright of N. *Used for:* W-6945, Newman 17-WW.

1787 Fugio Coppers

Cross After Date, No Cinquefoils

W-6600 · Newman 1-B
Notes: The "cross" is actually a four-lobed decoration, a quatrefoil, when viewed closely on high-grade coins. This ornament is found on no other die. Usually on a planchet with few if any problems, this being true of other varieties of this configuration. All Cross After Date varieties are in strong demand due to their distinctive style and their listing in the Red Book. *Rarity:* URS-7.

G-4	VG-8	F-12	VF-20	EF-40	AU-50
	$1,200	$2,400	$6,000	$10,500	$17,500

W-6605 · Newman 1-L
Notes: Finest is Ford's About Uncirculated. *Rarity:* URS-6.

G-4	VG-8	F-12	VF-20	EF-40	AU-50
	$1,800	$4,000	$8,500	$20,000	

W-6610 · Newman 1-Z · Raised Rims on center label
Notes: Rare. Always an attention-getter due to the fact that both the obverse and the reverse are distinctive. *Rarity:* URS-5.

G-4	VG-8	F-12	VF-20	EF-40	AU-50
	$4,000	$8,000	$16,000	$30,000	$45,000

W-6615 · Newman 1-CC · AMERICAN CONGRESS on label
Notes: Three confirmed. Conspicuously absent from the Ford collection. *Rarity:* URS-3.

G-4	VG-8	F-12	VF-20	EF-40	AU-50
			—	$350,000	$750,000

Club Rays, Concave Ends, Cinquefoils

W-6630 · Newman 2-C · FUCIO
Notes: Rare. Immensely popular due to its listing in the Red Book and other popular sources. At least two Extremely Fine known. *Rarity:* URS-4.

G-4	VG-8	F-12	VF-20	EF-40
		$5,500	$20,000	$45,000

W-6640 · Newman 5-F · FUGIO
Rarity: URS-4.

Selected auction price(s): Smith & Youngman Collections (B&M 3/2003), VF-20 (PCGS), $10,350. John J. Ford Jr. I Sale (Stack's 10/2003), EF, perhaps finest known, $17,250.

W-6645 · Newman 5-HH · FUGIO spelling
Notes: Reported by Richard Picker in the *Colonial Newsletter*, March 1965. Called unique by Alan Kessler (1976); more found since, but still extremely rare. None in the Ford collection. *Rarity:* URS-4.

W-6650 · Newman 23-ZZ · FUCIO
Rarity: URS-1.

W-6655 · Newman 24-MM · FUGIO
Notes: Discovered by Anthony Terranova (*CNL*, July 1979). *Rarity:* URS-1.

W-6660 · Newman 25-PP
Notes: Discovered by Anthony Terranova (*CNL*, December 1997). *Rarity:* URS-1.

Club Rays, Convex Ends, Cinquefoils

W-6680 · Newman 3-D
Rarity: URS-10.

G-4	VG-8	F-12	VF-20	EF-40	AU-50
$575	$1,500	$3,000	$5,700	$12,500	

W-6685 · Newman 4-E
Rarity: URS-10.

G-4	VG-8	F-12	VF-20	EF-40	AU-50
$575	$1,300	$3,000	$5,700	$12,500	

1 Over Horizontal 1, Cinquefoils

W-6700 · Newman 10-G
Notes: Rare in any grade. Typically Very Good or Fine, sometimes overgraded. *Rarity:* URS-4.

Selected auction price(s): CSNS Sale (Heritage 4/2002), VF-25 (PCGS), $2,070. John J. Ford Jr. I Sale (Stack's 10/2003), EF, $1,495; About F, $4,600.

W-6705 · Newman 10-T
Notes: Rare. Ford's was graded Extremely Fine, probably equivalent to Very Fine of a generation earlier. Some lightness of strike on the obverse. Usually on a decent planchet. *Rarity:* URS-6.

G-4	VG-8	F-12	VF-20	EF-40	AU-50
$750	$1,600	$4,000	$8,500	$17,500	

W-6710 · Newman 10-OO
Notes: Discovered by Mike Ringo (*CNL*, June 1988). *Rarity:* URS-1.

Pointed Rays, Cinquefoils

W-6730 · Newman 6-W
Notes: Scarce in all grades. Multiple Very Fine and Extremely Fine coins of nice quality exist, the latter grade being rare. *Rarity:* URS-9.

G-4	VG-8	F-12	VF-20	EF-40	AU-50
			$5,000	$7,500	

W-6735 · Newman 7-T
Notes: The obverse die was used only in this combination. Progressive die states exist. *Rarity:* URS-11.

G-4	VG-8	F-12	VF-20	EF-40	AU-50	MS-60
$450	$700	$1,250	$2,000	$3,500		—

W-6740 · Newman 8-B

Notes: Some 246 remained in the Bank of New York hoard in 1948 (when inventoried by Damon G. Douglas). Readily available in Mint State, usually with some problems—as expected, and often overlooked in catalog descriptions. *Rarity:* URS-12.

VG-8	F-12	VF-20	EF-40	AU-50	MS-60	MS-63
$300	$500	$1,000	$1,750	$2,000	$5,000	

W-6750 · Newman 8-X

Notes: In 1948, there remained 189 in the Bank of New York hoard. A massive crack developed on the obverse, resulting in weakness on the corresponding part of the reverse. *Rarity:* URS-11.

VG-8	F-12	VF-20	EF-40	AU-50	MS-60	MS-63
$300	$500	$1,000	$1,600	$2,000	$5,000	$7,500

W-6755 · Newman 9-P

Notes: Twelve remained in the Bank of New York hoard in 1948. Late die states show a bisecting crack on the obverse. *Rarity:* URS-10.

VG-8	F-12	VF-20	EF-40	AU-50	MS-60	MS-63
$500	$800	$1,500	$4,000	$5,000	$9,500	$15,000

W-6760 · Newman 9-Q

Notes: Rare at any level. Usually seen well worn. Ford's (ex Ryder) was graded Very Fine. *Rarity:* URS-7.

G-4	VG-8	F-12	VF-20	EF-40
	$450	$850	$2,400	$7,500

W-6765 · Newman 9-S

Notes: One remained in the Bank of New York hoard in 1948. None in the Ford collection. *Rarity:* URS-4.

VG-8	F-12	VF-20	EF-40	AU-50	MS-60	MS-63
$650	$1,200	$2,000	$4,000	$6,500	—	—

W-6770 · Newman 9-T

Notes: Finest is About Uncirculated. *Rarity:* URS-6.

G-4	VG-8	F-12	VF-20	EF-40	AU-50
	$650	$1,500	$2,000	$5,000	

W-6780 · Newman 11-A · UNITED above, STATES below

Notes: Only variety with this reverse lettering arrangement. Ten remained in the Bank of New York hoard in 1948. Michael J. Hodder estimated a population of about 25 in the Ford catalog narrative. As Mint State is par for these, it is likely that those in numismatic hands originated from the same hoard. *Rarity:* URS-6.

VG-8	F-12	VF-20	EF-40	AU-50	MS-60	MS-63
—	—	$10,000	$17,500	$20,500	—	—

W-6785 · Newman 11-B

Notes: Sixty remained in the Bank of New York hoard in 1948. Planchet quality varies, but is often free of flaws. Distinguished by prominent clash marks in the right obverse field. *Rarity:* URS-9.

VG-8	F-12	VF-20	EF-40	AU-50	MS-60	MS-63
$300	$500	$1,000	$1,600	$2,000	$5,000	$7,500

W-6790 · Newman 11-X

Notes: Some 132 remained in the Bank of New York hoard in 1948. One of the more readily available varieties. Typically with areas of light striking, or planchet problems, or both. Distinguished by prominent clash marks in the right obverse field. *Rarity:* URS-9.

VG-8	F-12	VF-20	EF-40	AU-50	MS-60	MS-63
$300	$500	$1,000	$1,600	$2,000	$5,000	$7,500

W-6800 · Newman 12-M

Notes: Rare in high grades. Extremely Fine and About Uncirculated are top of the line. *Rarity:* URS-9.

G-4	VG-8	F-12	VF-20	EF-40	AU-50
	$450	$800	$2,000	$4,000	$8,500

W-6805 · Newman 12-S

Notes: Fairly scarce. Planchet flaws are typical. Low grades are the norm. *Rarity:* URS-9.

G-4	VG-8	F-12	VF-20	EF-40
	$500	$750	$3,000	$5,500

W-6810 · Newman 12-U

Notes: Reverse typically with heavy clash marks. *Rarity:* URS-9.

G-4	VG-8	F-12	VF-20	EF-40	AU-50
	$400	$600	$1,700	$2,400	$4,500

W-6820 · Newman 12-X

Notes: In 1948, 264 remained in the Bank of New York hoard. Signature die crack from border downward past right of sun. Usually with planchet problems and localized areas of light striking. *Rarity:* URS-12.

G-4	VG-8	F-12	VF-20	EF-40	AU-50	MS-60
	$300	$500	$1,000	$1,600	$2,000	$5,000

W-6830 · Newman 12-Z · Raised Rims on center label

Notes: Usually with lightness of strike at the center right of the obverse. *Rarity:* URS-5.

G-4	VG-8	F-12	VF-20	EF-40	AU-50
	$1,000	$2,000	$4,500	$10,500	

W-6835 · Newman 12-KK

Notes: First described by Edward R. Barnsley in *CNL*, October–December 1961. *Rarity:* URS-6.

G-4	VG-8	F-12	VF-20	EF-40	AU-50
		—	—	—	

W-6840 · Newman 12-LL

Notes: Discovered by Richard Picker in 1974 (*CNL*, January 1976). *Rarity:* URS-4.

W-6845 · Newman 13-N

Notes: None in the Ford collection. After acquiring the Boyd collection of Fugios, Ford made little effort to add to or upgrade the set, the same being true of other copper series of the 1790s. *Rarity:* URS-6.

G-4	VG-8	F-12	VF-20	EF-40	AU-50
—	—	—	—	—	—

W-6850 · Newman 13-R

Notes: Rare. Usually on good planchet stock. Typically with clashmarks. *Rarity:* URS-7.

G-4	VG-8	F-12	VF-20	EF-40
			—	

W-6855 · Newman 13-X

Notes: In 1948, 726 remained in the Bank of New York hoard. Another readily available issue, ideal for a type set. Planchet and striking problems are typical. *Rarity:* URS-12.

G-4	VG-8	F-12	VF-20	EF-40	AU-50	MS-60
		$750	$1,500	$2,500	$4,000	$7,500

W-6858 · Newman 13-JJ

Notes: New die combination and reverse discovered by Scott Mitchell of Stack's in autumn 2007 while cataloging coins for the sale noted below. *Rarity:* URS-1.

Selected auction price(s): Americana Sale (Stack's 1/2008), F-15, $109,250.

W-6860 · Newman 13-KK

Notes: Rare in any grade. Not in the Ford collection. *Rarity:* URS-4.

Selected auction price(s): Norweb III Sale (1988), VF, $2,970. Pre–Long Beach Sale (I. & L. Goldberg 2/2007), F-15, $5,463.

W-6870 · Newman 14-H

Notes: Called unique by Alan Kessler (1976). Discovered by Richard August. Very Fine to Extremely Fine. August believes a second has been found. *Rarity:* URS-1 or 2(?)

W-6875 · Newman 14-O

Notes: Most are well worn. *Rarity:* URS-9.

G-4	VG-8	F-12	VF-20	EF-40	AU-50
		$750	$1,500	$3,500	$5,000

W-6880 · Newman 14-X

Notes: Not listed by Kessler. Discovered by Richard August. Extremely Fine. *Rarity:* URS-1.

W-6890 · Newman 15-H

Notes: Not listed by Kessler. Now collectible, but scarce. Typically with extensive wear. *Rarity:* URS-7.

G-4	VG-8	F-12	VF-20	EF-40
		$900	$1,700	$3,000

W-6900 · Newman 15-K

Notes: Ford's Extremely Fine, dark and with some roughness, was billed as "technically the finest known." *Rarity:* URS-4.

Selected auction price(s): CSNS Sale (Heritage 4/2002), EF-45 (PCGS), $1,725. John J. Ford Jr. I Sale (Stack's 10/2003), EF, $2,990.

W-6910 · Newman 15-V

Rarity: URS-6.

G-4	VG-8	F-12	VF-20	EF-40	AU-50
	$950	$1,750	$4,500	$8,000	

W-6915 · Newman 15-Y · 8-Pointed Stars on label

Notes: Only use of this distinctive reverse die. Readily available in the marketplace, usually showing significant wear. The top star is usually the sharper of the two. *Rarity:* URS-10.

VG-8	F-12	VF-20	EF-40	AU-50
$700	$1,000	$2,400	$5,200	$8,000

W-6920 · Newman 16-H

Notes: Extremely Fine and About Uncirculated coins are top of the line. *Rarity:* URS-6.

G-4	VG-8	F-12	VF-20	EF-40
			$2,000	$5,000

W-6925 · Newman 16-N

Notes: Rare. Usually seen in low grades. Planchet quality varies. *Rarity:* URS-7.

G-4	VG-8	F-12	VF-20	EF-40	AU-50
			$2,000	$4,000	$6,000

W-6930 · Newman 17-I

Notes: Called unique by Alan Kessler (1976). By 2007 at least six had been found; the best may be Very Fine to Extremely Fine (August collection). *Rarity:* URS-4.

Selected auction price(s): Norweb III Sale (1988), F, the discovery coin, $3,300. C.L. Lee Sale (Stack's [ANR] 9/2005), VF-25 (NGC), $18,400.

W-6935 · Newman 17-S

Notes: Very Fine and Extremely Fine are par for high-grade coins, with few exceptions. *Rarity:* URS-9.

G-4	VG-8	F-12	VF-20	EF-40	AU-50
			$1,800	$3,000	$5,500

W-6940 · Newman 17-T

Notes: Not listed by Alan Kessler. *Rarity:* URS-4.

W-6945 · Newman 17-WW

Notes: Not in the Ford collection. *Rarity:* URS-4.

Selected auction price(s): Norweb III Sale (1988), EF, $2,860. Americana Sale (Stack's 1/2005), VG, $4,025.

W-6950 · Newman 18-H

Notes: With areas of light striking. *Rarity:* URS-6.

G-4	VG-8	F-12	VF-20	EF-40
	$750	$1,500	$4,000	$6,000

W-6960 · Newman 18-U

Notes: Several About Uncirculateds top the condition census. *Rarity:* URS-9.

G-4	VG-8	F-12	VF-20	EF-40	AU-50
	$600	$1,000	$1,500	$3,500	$5,000

W-6965 · Newman 18-X

Notes: Not in the Ford collection. *Rarity:* URS-4.

Selected auction price(s): Norweb III Sale (1988), VF, $1,045.

W-6970 · Newman 19-M

Notes: Extremely Fine and About Uncirculated seem to be the best. *Rarity:* URS-4.

Selected auction price(s): John J. Ford Jr. I Sale (Stack's 10/2003), EF, $13,800. Henry Leon Sale (Stack's 5/2007), F-15, $2,185.

W-6975 · Newman 19-Z · Raised Rims on center label

Notes: Rare. Popular by virtue of the distinctive reverse. *Rarity:* URS-6.

G-4	VG-8	F-12	VF-20	EF-40	AU-50
	$550	$1,000	$3,000	$6,000	$12,000

W-6980 · Newman 19-SS

Notes: Not in the Ford collection. *Rarity:* URS-6.

G-4	VG-8	F-12	VF-20	EF-40
		$3,500	$5,700	$9,000

W-6990 · Newman 20-R

Notes: Not in the Ford collection. *Rarity:* URS-6.

G-4	VG-8	F-12	VF-20	EF-40
			—	

W-7000 · Newman 20-X

Notes: Typically well worn. *Rarity:* URS-6.

G-4	VG-8	F-12	VF-20	EF-40
			$3,500	$5,000

W-7010 · Newman 21-I

Notes: Some with dramatic clash marks on the reverse. *Rarity:* URS-7.

G-4	VG-8	F-12	VF-20	EF-40
	$475	$900	$1,750	$4,000

W-7020 · Newman 22-M

Notes: Not in the Ford collection. *Rarity:* URS-6.

G-4	VG-8	F-12	VF-20	EF-40
	$475	$900	$1,750	$4,000

Machin's Mills Coppers
1780's

An Impressive Mint Planned

In 1787 Reuben Harmon Jr., holder of the franchise to coin Vermont coppers, entered into a partnership with a number of other individuals involved in minting. Ownership interests were formed between Harmon and Machin's Mills, a private mint, located on the shore of Orange Pond near Newburgh, New York.

Machin's Mills was established by an agreement dated April 18, 1787, which united the interests of Samuel Atlee, James F. Atlee, David Brooks, James Grier, and James Giles, all of New York City, with Thomas Machin of Ulster County, New York.

Captain Machin was of English birth. Prior to the Revolution he served as an officer with the British forces. During the war he entered the American Army as an engineer and in 1777 was employed by Congress to erect fortifications along the Hudson River and to stretch an iron chain across the river at West Point to prevent the passage of British ships. Following the war, Machin located near Newburgh, where he erected buildings subsequently used for the coinage venture.

The agreement provided that the profits from the coining enterprise should be split six ways, directly in proportion to the original stock, which consisted of £300 of capital, split into six shares valued at £50 each. It was stated that Samuel Atlee and James F. Atlee, "being possessed of certain implements for carrying on said trade, do agree to lend them to the parties to these presents for and during the continuance of their co-partnership without any fee or reward for the same." What these "certain implements" were is not known today.

In the Machin's Mills agreement it was further provided that "Thomas Machin, being possessed of certain mills, doth hereby agree to let the parties have free use of them for and during the continuation of their co-partnership." Brooks, Grier, and Giles agreed to pay an additional £10 each toward readying Machin's Mills, as the facility is referred to by numismatists today, to make it suitable for coinage. The management was to be by James F. Atlee and Thomas Machin.

On June 7, 1787, another agreement was drawn up. Ten partners participated, including the original six involved in the Machin's Mills enterprise, plus four others: Reuben Harmon Jr. (the Vermont coiner); William Coley (the New York City silversmith and engraver, also associated with Harmon in Vermont); Elias Jackson (of Litchfield County, Connecticut); and Daniel Van Voorhis (New York City silversmith and partner of Coley). It was noted in the agreement that Harmon, after obtaining the coinage privilege from the legislature of Vermont, took in Coley, Jackson, and Van Voorhis as equal partners.

It was proposed that coinage be conducted in two locations: Machin's Mills, then in the process of readying for coinage; and in the existing facilities in Rupert, Vermont. Duties were divided among the various partners, with provisions being made for audits, settling accounts, and other business necessities. Whether much if any coinage under the new agreement was done at Rupert is questionable, in the view of the author. Any statements of a coinage at Rupert from dies attributed to Machin's Mills has no foundation in any hard evidence. The entire matter seems to be a web of ideas that evolved into theories that were later presented as fact.

Description of Machin's Mills

Machin's Mills was located on Orange Pond, which at one time was also called Machin's Pond. A new outlet, which provided water to a large extent for Chambers Creek, was tapped, and at the outlet the minting structure was erected. Originally this outlet was an overflow for times of high water, the natural one being farther west at a place called Pine Point.

The business of Machin's Mills was conducted with secrecy. Tradition holds that a guard with a hideous mask was employed to frighten away the curious. In *An Outline History of Orange County, New York*, Samuel W. Eager noted that "operations there, as they were conducted in secret, were looked upon at that time with suspicion, as illegal and wrong."

To aid in their acceptance into commercial channels, the counterfeit English halfpence were struck from dies deliberately made to produce coins that looked weak, as if they had been in circulation for a long time. Presumably the coins were toned or darkened to aid in the deception. At the time, America, newly independent from England, probably had little incentive to punish American citizens who counterfeited English coins, although some cases can be found in the annals of law, none involving the Machin's Mills coiners.

It was related that in the year 1789, one thousand pounds of copper coins saw production. This relatively small amount may have represented the tail end of the operation. Although no figures survive, it is likely that the total mintage ran into the hundreds of thousands of coins, if not more. On October 14, 1790, James F. Atlee wrote to Thomas Machin to request that the partners dissolve the enterprise on suitable terms so as to avoid a tedious and expensive lawsuit.

Machin's Mills Coinage

Numismatists today believe that Machin's Mills coined a wide variety of coppers, probably anything that they thought could be circulated at a profit. Included were numerous counterfeits of contemporary English halfpence. As noted by Crosby, these bore on the obverse the portrait of George III with GEORGIUS III REX surrounding. The reverse depicted the seated figure of Britannia. At the same time it is virtually certain that pieces bearing legends relating to Connecticut, Vermont, New York, and possibly other coinages were made as well. The Vermont coins were perfectly legal, as partner Harmon held the contract. Other coinages were unofficial, this meaning counterfeit. In some instances the dies were mixed, probably inadvertently, resulting in illogical combinations (e.g., a 1787 copper coin with a Vermont inscription on the obverse and with a reverse showing Britannia—a style intended for use on a counterfeit English halfpenny).

Many 1787 Vermont coppers and probably all of those dated 1788 were struck at Machin's Mills. Nearly all of these are lighter in weight than the earlier 1785 and 1786 Vermont issues, are less carefully engraved, and are often carelessly struck. Among counterfeit issues, those with Connecticut inscriptions are nearly always lightweight and on high-quality planchets. Features are often indistinct, as made, to facilitate their circulation. Coins with IMMUNE COLUMBIA and various New York–related inscriptions were made. It is likely that counterfeit silver coins were struck there as well, but this probability has had no more than casual study. The coins cited by Crosby as having a "figure of a plough on one side" were probably not Vermont coppers, as none of these exist today with the general fabric or appearance of a Machin's Mills product. Counterfeit New Jersey coppers may have been intended, or the recollection, dating from 1855, may have been incorrect.

Numismatic Aspects of Machin's Mills Coppers

C. Wyllys Betts, in *Counterfeit Half-Pence Current in the American Colonies*, 1886, pioneered the serious study of Machin's Mills counterfeits, considerably expanding upon the Crosby text. In *The Numismatist*, February 1942, Howard Kurth's "Connecticut and Vermont Coppers of British Type" told of the relationship between American state coinage and designs found on English halfpence. A follow-up appeared in the July issue.

Robert A. Vlack listed varieties in his *Early American Coins*, 1965. In 1974 he published two photographic plates illustrating coins from his own collection as well as those from the ANS, Eric P. Newman, and Ted Craige. Today Vlack numbers are used in attributions, including for new discoveries. Machin's Mills has been the focal point of study by several other numismatists besides Vlack, including William T. Anton Jr., Richard August, Walter Breen, Kenneth E. Bressett, Bruce Kesse, Eric P. Newman, Mike Ringo, Edwin Sarrafian, Gary Trudgen, and others. An updating and overview by Richard August and Edwin Sarrafian, "Machin's Mills Coins: Condition Census, Die States, Discoveries, and Estimated Rarity by Grades," was published in the *C4 Newsletter*, Spring 1998.

Counterfeits *specifically attributable to Machin's Mills* are in great demand today. These are identifiable by having letter, numeral, or device punches connected with Vermont coppers and counterfeits of Connecticut and other state coinages, although with unrelated inscriptions. Certain of these are quite distinctive in their appearance: George III almost appears as if wearing lipstick, from some sort of an "apostrophe" punch used to make the lips. As a general guideline, this includes many English halfpence with a date of 1778, 1787, or 1788. No regal (authentic, made in England) halfpence were struck after 1775. For counterfeits dated from 1747 to 1778, guidelines are more challenging.

To be attributed to Machin's Mills, a coin must have sawtooth dentils; the 1 in the date must not be a "J"; there must be no berries in the obverse wreath; the shield lines must be unfimbriated (i.e., must not have outlines to the solid shield lines); and the lips must be distinctive.

Those listed in this section are copies of English halfpence and variations thereof, many (but not all) of which can be specifically attributed to Machin's Mills, although opinions can vary. These have been especially popular since their listing in the Red Book. One caveat: many counterfeit English halfpence that are offered as "Machin's Mills" coins on the Internet were *not* made in America.

See "Other 'Evasion' or 'Bungtown' Coppers" for certain items listed by Robert A. Vlack that are no longer considered to be products of Machin's Mills. The presentation of the Mike Ringo collection of counterfeit halfpence in Stack's January 2008 Americana Sale, cataloged by John Kraljevich, is a particularly valuable source for information on pieces by various coiners on both sides of the Atlantic. "James Atlee's Imitation British Halfpence," in the *Colonial Newsletter*, March 1987, is a rich resource that divides the issues into several groups. As noted elsewhere, today it is thought that Atlee, while he was the *coiner* at Machin's Mills, was not necessarily the engraver of dies. Trudgen's Group III comprises pieces he attributes specifically to this mint.

Edwin Sarrafian has been the primary contributor to this section, with nods to Richard August and Jack Howes. The condition census gives the top and bottom grade range for the finest six examples known to Edwin Sarrafian. In instances in which the population is fewer than six, the condition census includes the range of all known pieces. This is hardly an exact science, and the information should be viewed as approximate.

Machin's Mills Counterfeit English Halfpence

W-7660 · 1747 Vlack 1-47A

Obverse: GEORGIVS II head left. The only obverse with head facing left. Heavy dots instead of periods for punctuation. Usually found with a softly struck profile. *Reverse:* Branch hand opposite T. Both 7's in the date lean to the right; second 7 very high. *Notes:* Has very heavy obverse punctuation and solid shield lines. Difficult to find with choice color and surfaces. Breen-1002. *Condition census:* VF-35 to MS-60. *Rarity:* URS-7.

G-4	VG-8	F-12	VF-20	EF-40	AU-50	MS-60
$600	$950	$1,400	$3,500	$8,000		

W-7670 · 1771 Vlack 2-71A

Obverse: GEORGIVS III head to right, as on all to follow (except those with state obverses). Shallowly cut dies. Wreath is often indistinct and blended in with the head. *Reverse:* Branch hand opposite right part of T. Britannia figure leaning slightly forward. *Notes:* Sawtooth borders. The 1 in date is not a J. No berries in the obverse wreath. Breen-1003. *Condition census:* VF-30 to About Uncirculated. *Rarity:* URS-8.

G-4	VG-8	F-12	VF-20	EF-40
$200	$350	$1,000	$1,800	$4,500

W-7680 · 1771 Vlack 3-71B

Obverse: Large, bulbous head. Die used with Vlack 71B and 74A. *Reverse:* Branch hand opposite space between T and A. The hand holding the staff has elongated fingers not found on any other reverse in the series. *Notes:* Normally found better struck than 2-71A. Breen-1003. *Condition census:* VF-25 to MS-60. *Rarity:* URS-7.

G-4	VG-8	F-12	VF-20	EF-40
$300	$550	$1,200	$2,500	$6,000

W-7690 · 1771 Vlack 4-71C

Obverse: Deeply cut obverse die that almost gives the illusion that George is wearing a helmet. This die also used for Vlack 71D and 75A. *Reverse:* Branch hand opposite left leg of A. The second 1 in the date leans right. Die crack from the neck of Britannia toward the wreath. Die crack above IA (BRITANNIA). *Notes:* Discovered by Richard August in 1964. Breen-1003. *Condition census:* VG-8 to VF-20. *Rarity:* URS-4.

W-7700 • 1771 Vlack 4-71D

Obverse: Same as preceding. *Reverse:* Branch hand opposite space between I and T. All digits in the date are upright. Pole points to left of first 1. *Notes:* Not on 1974 Vlack photo sheet. Discovered by Frank Steimle (*CNL*, October 1990). Three known, all in low grades. *Rarity:* URS-3.

W-7710 • 1772 Vlack 5-72A

Obverse: Large head, though not quite as large as obverse 3. This die is the same as Vlack's obverse 8 (corrected here to obverse 5; obverse 8 is the heavily lapped version). Die used on 1772 Vlack 5-72A and 1774 Vlack 5-74A. *Reverse:* Branch hand opposite left leg of A. Digits in the date are very small. The reverse is also used on the next. *Notes:* Breen-1004. *Condition census:* VF-30 to About Uncirculated. *Rarity:* URS-6.

G-4	VG-8	F-12	VF-20	EF-40
$300	$550	$1,250	$2,700	$5,500

W-7720 • 1772 Vlack 6-72A

Obverse: Tall head. The die was cut deeply so it is almost never found with any wreath detail. Die also used for Vlack 6-72B and 6-76A. *Reverse:* Same as preceding. Breen-unlisted. *Condition census:* VF-30 to About Uncirculated. *Rarity:* URS-6.

G-4	VG-8	F-12	VF-20	EF-40
$350	$650	$1,500	$3,000	$7,500

W-7730 • 1772 Vlack 7-72B

Obverse: Obverse 7 has U instead of V in the obverse legend, diagnostic. Also used for Vlack 74A. Usually well struck. *Reverse:* Branch hand opposite left foot of A. Date digits small and high. *Notes:* Breen-1004. *Condition census:* VF-25 to About Uncirculated. *Rarity:* URS-5.

G-4	VG-8	F-12	VF-20	EF-40
$350	$650	$1,500	$3,400	$8,500

W-7740 • 1772 Vlack 24-72C

Obverse: With just a trace of the bottoms of a few letters remaining, as the die was ground down. *Reverse:* Branch hand points to T. Last two digits of the date are always weak. *Notes:* Not on 1974 Vlack photo sheet. Discovered by Richard August (*CNL*, June 1985). Only use of these dies. Breen-1004. *Condition census:* VF-30 to EF-45. *Rarity:* URS-5.

Selected auction price(s): Public Auction Sale (Stack's 9/2006), F, $1,840. Henry Leon Sale (Stack's 5/2007), VF-30, $13,800.

W-7750 • 1774 Vlack 3-74A

Obverse: Large, bulbous head. Die also used for Vlack 71B. *Reverse:* Branch hand opposite right part of T. Tops of 7's parallel and close under date line. Only reverse for this year. Also used on the next two varieties. Die crack from date line to tops of BRI (BRITANNIA). *Notes:* Breen-1005. *Condition census:* VF-30 to MS-60. *Rarity:* URS-8.

G-4	VG-8	F-12	VF-20	EF-40
$300	$600	$1,300	$3,000	$7,000

W-7760 • 1774 Vlack 5-74A

Obverse: Die also used on 1772 Vlack 5-72A. *Reverse:* Same as preceding. *Notes:* This is Vlack's 8-74A, now corrected to 5-74A. *Notes:* Breen-1005. *Condition census:* VF-30 to About Uncirculated. *Rarity:* URS-8.

G-4	VG-8	F-12	VF-20	EF-40
$150	$200	$450	$1,400	$4,500

W-7770 · 1774 Vlack 7-74A

Obverse: Obverse 7 has U instead of V in the obverse legend. Diagnostic. Also used with Vlack 7-72B, but 7-74A was struck first. Usually well struck. *Reverse:* Same as preceding, but not with die crack. *Notes:* Breen-1006. *Condition census:* VF-20 to VF-30. *Rarity:* URS-8.

G-4	VG-8	F-12	VF-20	EF-40
$300	$550	$800	$2,600	$5,700

W-7780 · 1775 Vlack 4-75A

Obverse: Deeply cut obverse die that almost gives the illusion that George is wearing a helmet. This die also used for used for Vlack 71C and 71D. *Reverse:* Branch hand opposite left foot of A. The 1 in the date leans right. *Notes:* Only one known variety with this date. NIA very close to the date line. Both the obverse head style and the positioning of NIA of BRITANNIA make it an easy attribution. Breen-1007. *Condition census:* VF-35 to EF-40. *Rarity:* URS-9.

G-4	VG-8	F-12	VF-20	EF-40	AU-50
$190	$250	$600	$1,400	$3,600	$6,500

W-7790 · 1776 Vlack 6-76A

Obverse: Tall head. The die was cut deeply so it is almost never found with any wreath detail. Die also used with Vlack 6-72B. *Reverse:* Branch hand opposite space between I and T (BRITANNIA). Larger date than on following. The 7's are widely separated. *Notes:* One known overstruck on a 1785 Immune Columbia copper (*C4 Newsletter*, Summer 2006), two others on counterfeit pistareens of 1709 (misattributed in the Breen *Encyclopedia* as a Spanish 8-maravedis; the coins are in the ANS). There are other evasion halfpence dated 1776, but those attributed to Machin's Mills have either Vlack reverse 76A or B. Breen-1008. *Condition census:* EF-45 to MS-60. *Rarity:* URS-8.

G-4	VG-8	F-12	VF-20	EF-40
$300	$650	$1,500	$3,600	$7,000

W-7800 · 1776 Vlack 9-76B

Obverse: CEORCIVS spelling. S touches head, period on head. Some with a die crack above head. Die also used on Vlack 15-86NY. *Reverse:* Branch hand opposite and very close to upright of T. Small date with figures widely separated, 76 closest. The seated figure punch was also used on Vermont W-2205. *Condition census:* VF-20 to Extremely Fine. *Notes:* Most are on small planchets, but there are at least two exceptions. Breen-992. *Rarity:* URS-5.

G-4	VG-8	F-12	VF-20	EF-40
$3,000	$6,500	$10,500	$20,000	

W-7820 · 1778 Vlack 11-78A

Obverse: R (REX) opposite nose. Ribbons point to the first G. *Reverse:* Date numerals are large. Pole points to the right part of the first 7. *Notes:* Usually well struck on a quality planchet. Breen-994. *Condition census:* EF-40 to MS-60. *Rarity:* URS-10.

G-4	VG-8	F-12	VF-20	EF-40
$100	$270	$350	$1,600	$4,000

W-7830 · 1778 Vlack 12-78B

Obverse: Fillets (ribbons) point to E. *Reverse:* Branch hand opposite left side of T. The 8 is very small. Pole points between 1 and 7. *Notes:* Usually on a rough planchet. Breen-993. *Condition census:* EF-45 to MS-60. *Rarity:* URS-9.

G-4	VG-8	F-12	VF-20	EF-40
$160	$270	$550	$1,700	$5,000

W-7840 · 1778 Vlack 13-78B

Obverse: Fillets point downward toward G. Smallest head of this year. Also used on Vlack 13-87CT and 13-88CT. *Reverse:* Same as preceding. Breen-993. *Condition census:* VF-30 to About Uncirculated. *Rarity:* URS-7.

G-4	VG-8	F-12	VF-20	EF-40
$160	$270	$550	$1,600	$4,000

W-7845 · 1778 Vlack 13-78C

Obverse: Same as preceding. *Reverse:* BRI visible, as well as the head. The line above the date and the date 1778 are quite sharp. The 1 is heavy, without serifs, has the top slanting down slightly to the left; the entire figure leans slightly right. The 8 is distinctive, is significantly smaller than the adjacent 7, and leans right. The pole end is over the first 7, slightly right of its center. Prominent dentils are seen below the date, with one pointing to the lower right of the 1, the second pointing just left of the base of the first 7, and another pointing directly at the base of the second 7. *Notes:* From *CNL* 138: "The weight of the coin is 101.2 grains, and the diameter is 27.2 mm. The reverse die is rotated approximately 135° clockwise instead of the normal 'coin turn' rotation of 180°." Discovered in 2008 and first published in the *C4 Newsletter*. *Rarity:* URS-1.

(W-1995) · 1785 Vlack 15-85NY · Immune Columbia

See listing for W-1995 in the Immune Columbia coppers section.

W-7880 · 1787 Vlack 9-87NY · Liber Natus Libertatem Defendo · Indian

Obverse: CEORCIVS spelling. *Reverse:* Indian and arms. *Notes:* This variety is always found unevenly struck. As obverse 9 developed a cud break the coiners misaligned the dies so that the cud area would not strike up, thus getting more life out of the die. Three known. Breen-1001. *Rarity:* URS-3.

Selected auction price(s): Garrett I Sale (B&R 11/1979), EF or better, weakly struck in areas, $20,000.

W-7890 · 1787 Vlack 13-87CT · Connecticut

Obverse: Small head. Also used on 1778 Vlack 13-78B and 13-88CT. *Reverse:* Connecticut Miller G.2. *Notes:* Four known: ANS collection (ex Richard August to Edward Barnsley); ex Ted Craige collection; ex Stack's John Ford collection, May 2005; and the Very Fine to Extremely Fine in the Richard August collection. Breen-998. *Rarity:* URS-3.

Selected auction price(s): John J. Ford Jr. IX Sale (Stack's 5/2005), VF, rough, $40,250.

W-7900 · 1787 Vlack 17-87A

Obverse: Tall head with a long, thin nose. Used on Vlack 17-87A, B, and E. *Reverse:* Branch hand opposite right part of A. The 1 in the date is very high. Pole points between 1 and 7. *Condition census:* AU-50 to MS-60. *Notes:* Usually on quality planchets. Breen-996. *Rarity:* URS-11.

G-4	VG-8	F-12	VF-20	EF-40
$120	$250	$400	$1,300	$3,500

W-7910 · 1787 Vlack 17-87B

Obverse: Same as preceding. *Reverse:* Branch hand opposite T. Pole points to right element of first 7. *Notes:* Usually on quality planchets. Breen-996. *Condition census:* EF-40 to MS-60. *Rarity:* URS-11.

G-4	VG-8	F-12	VF-20	EF-40
$120	$250	$400	$1,300	$3,500

W-7920 · 1787 Vlack 17-87E

Obverse: Same as preceding. *Reverse:* Branch hand opposite left leg of A. Pole points between 7 and 8, closer to 8. Die crack from TA to shield. Later states of the die have the first N and the head of Britannia missing due to a die break. *Notes:* Discovered by David Sonderman (*CNL*, April 1978). Six known, the finest the Mint State coin in the Richard August collection. Breen-996. *Condition census:* VG-10 (holed) to MS-60. *Rarity:* URS-4.

W-7930 · 1787 Vlack 18-87C

Obverse: Round head. Period after S. R (REX) is large and misshapen; its left stand is opposite the tip of the nose. *Reverse:* Die used on Vlack 18-87C, 19-87C, 20-87C, 21-87C, and 23-87C, and (in a much later state) Vermont RR-13. Branch hand opposite right part of T. The 1 and 8 lean right. Single date line. Die crack above head. Breen-995. *Condition census:* AU-50 to MS-65. *Rarity:* URS-8.

G-4	VG-8	F-12	VF-20	EF-40
$120	$270	$425	$1,300	$3,500

W-7940 · 1787 Vlack 19-87C

Obverse: Round head. No period after S. First G low relative to the uppermost armor plate. Letters III lean slightly right, with the second I slightly lower than the others. Armor has a steep decline when viewed from left to right. *Reverse:* Same as preceding. Breen-995. *Condition census:* EF-40 to MS-60. *Rarity:* URS-11.

G-4	VG-8	F-12	VF-20	EF-40
$120	$270	$425	$1,300	$3,500

W-7950 · 1787 Vlack 20-87C

Obverse: Round head. No period after S. The G is high relative to the uppermost armor plate. Letters in III aligned properly. The slope of the lower armor is much flatter than on obverse 19. *Reverse:* Same as preceding, but without break over head. *Notes:* Breen-995. *Condition census:* VF-20 to MS-60. *Rarity:* URS-5.

G-4	VG-8	F-12	VF-20	EF-40
$250	$500	$1,200	$2,500	$3,500

W-7960 · 1787 Vlack 21-87C

Obverse: Round head. No period after S. III widely spaced. Period after III is opposite nose. *Reverse:* Same as preceding, but late die state with weak legends. *Notes:* Discovered by Richard August in 1962. Breen-995. *Condition census:* VF-20 to EF-40. *Rarity:* URS-5.

G-4	VG-8	F-12	VF-20	EF-40
$250	$500	$1,200	$2,500	$3,500

W-7970 · 1787 Vlack 21-87D

Obverse: Same as preceding. *Reverse:* Branch hand opposite right leg of A. Pole points between 1 and 7. Double date line. *Notes:* Two die states, early and late, the last with tops of the obverse letters missing as well as most of the date and BRITANNIA on the reverse. These are sometimes collected separately. Breen-996. *Condition census:* EF-40 to Mint State. *Rarity:* URS-9.

G-4	VG-8	F-12	VF-20	EF-40
$150	$275	$450	$1,350	$3,500

W-7980 · 1787 Vlack 23-87C

Obverse: No period after S; period before III. Large triangular bow attached to wreath. The obverse die is the latest state of obverse 23 which is normally found with reverse 88A. Die used on Vlack 23-87C and 23-88A. *Reverse:* See earlier description. *Notes:* Discovered by Michael Ringo (*CNL*, June 1988). This is most likely the last Machin's Mills halfpenny variety struck. Seven known, finest About Uncirculated. Breen-995. *Condition census:* VG-8 to AU-50. *Rarity:* URS-4.

W-8070 · 1787 Vlack VT-87C · Vermont

Same as Vermont RR-13. See entry for W-2255.

227

W-8080 · 1788 Vlack 13-88CT · Connecticut

Obverse: Described with W-7840 (1778 Vlack 13-78B). *Reverse:* Miller Connecticut reverse D. Breen-999. *Condition census:* VF-35 to AU-50. *Rarity:* URS-7.

G-4	VG-8	F-12	VF-20	EF-40
$120	$225	$600	$1,650	$3,500

W-8090 · 1788 Vlack 22-88VT · Vermont

Same as Vermont RR-31. See entry for W-2260.

W-8100 · 1788 Vlack 23-88A

Obverse: Die used on Vlack 23-87C and 23-88A. *Reverse:* Branch hand opposite T. Double date line. Pole points to right element of 7. *Notes:* Toward the end of its life it develops a bulge by the bow and fillets and shortly after is muled with reverse C. Breen-997. *Condition census:* AU-50 to MS-60. *Rarity:* URS-11.

G-4	VG-8	F-12	VF-20	EF-40
$150	$300	$475	$1,500	$3,500

Other Counterfeits or "Bungtown" Coppers

There are many other varieties of counterfeit English halfpence and other coins that were made other than at Machin's Mills, most notably by the token manufacturers in Birmingham and elsewhere in England. Generally, these are called "evasion" or "bungtown" coppers by collectors, although "evasion" is more applicable to English-made counterfeits with inscriptions that are deliberately misspelled or use other wording, to evade counterfeiting laws. Many were close copies of contemporary English halfpence, bore the portraits of George II or III, and incorporated the Britannia motif on the reverse. Others, these being "evasions," were deliberately different in certain characteristics from the regular issues, the word REX being spelled ROX, for example, perhaps in an effort to evade counterfeiting laws. Still others are of a satirical nature and relate to persons, places, and events of the time.

Thomas L. Elder, writing in his May 1920 catalog of the Henry C. Miller collection, noted the following concerning false halfpence:

They circulated largely among the early German colonists in the eastern part of the state [Pennsylvania]; in fact, the cataloger has hardly met with a single example in western Pennsylvania, where he resided for many years. And a good many of them never left England. In Pennsylvania the problem of counterfeit coppers was so intense that on July 14, 1781, Joseph Reed, president of the Supreme Executive Council of the Commonwealth, issued a proclamation stating that:

"Diverse ill-disposed persons have manufactured or imported into this state quantities of base metal, in the similitude of British half pence, but much inferior in value and weight to the genuine British halfpence, to the great depreciation of that coin, the injury of the community in general, and the poor in particular, and we have, therefore, thought proper to prohibit, and do hereby strictly enjoin all officers—not to receive such base coin in any payments whatsoever—and do earnestly recommend to all the faithful inhabitants of this state to refuse it in payment—and to make due inquiry after offenders in the premises, that they may be brought to speedy and condign punishment."

The origin of the term "bungtown" has been debated by numismatists for many decades. One theory is that it may have been derived from a corruption of "Barneysville," a Massachusetts town where certain imitation halfpence may have been made, although North Swansea (Massachusetts) and Westerly (Rhode Island) have also been proposed as sources. The idea that "bungtown" may have come from the slang term "to bung," meaning to cheat or deceive, has also been suggested. *Bung* also means "hole," as in a barrel, or, vulgarly, "anus." By any reading it was a pejorative word.

The following listings are out-takes from the Vlack plates for Machin's Mills coins, as they are no longer attributed to that mint. Several pieces related to Connecticut are counterfeits from unknown mints (not Machin's Mills) and are highly sought and are listed in the Connecticut coppers section of this book, under the year 1786. The listing of other evasion halfpence is extensive and is beyond the scope of the present work.

Vlack Machin's Mills Out-Takes (Formerly Attributed to Machin's Mills)

W-8125 · 1777 Vlack 10-77A

Obverse: Tall head. Long nose points to center of R. Only use of this die. *Reverse:* Pole points to first 7. Double date line. Only use of this die. *Notes:* Listed by Robert A. Vlack on his early plate of Machin's Mills coppers, but now thought to be made elsewhere, possibly a counterfeit of obverse 17. Generally found well struck on a quality planchet. Four known. Breen-1009. *Rarity:* URS-3.

Selected auction price(s): Americana Sale (Stack's 1/2008), Fair-2, $2,760.

W-8130 · 1784 Vlack 14-84A

Obverse: Somewhat frail-looking head with a long neck. Letters in GEORGIVS widely spaced. III and REX are close to each other; E at approximately 3 o'clock. *Reverse:* Letters in BRITANNIA normally spaced. The 1 in date is a J. Shield lines are outlined (not always visible due to striking), not found on Machin's Mills coins. *Notes:* Not a Machin's Mills coin. Usually irregularly struck. A "counterfeit of a counterfeit" is known—a contemporary imitation of this counterfeit! Mike Ringo and Richard August collections. Breen-974. *Condition census:* VF-30 to AU-50. *Rarity:* URS-7.

Selected auction price(s): Baltimore Sale (B&M 6/2007), VG, $1,380.

G-4	VG-8	F-12	VF-20	EF-40
$850	$1,400	$2,500	$6,500	

W-8140 · 1786 Vlack 16-86A

Obverse: Head in fairly high relief, collar bold with six interior elements, prominent highest leaf in wreath, lettering irregular. *Reverse:* BRITA left, NNIA right; second A very low. Branch hand opposite first A. Two heavy date lines. The digit 6 high and pierces lines. *Notes:* Three known, one in ANS. Breen-975. *Condition census:* G-4 (counterstamped; in ANS) to AU-50. *Rarity:* URS-3.

8

OTHER EARLY AMERICAN PIECES

GLOUCESTER TOKENS
1714

One of the most curious of all early American issues is the so-called "Gloucester shilling." In *Early Coins of America*, 1875, Sylvester S. Crosby noted in part:

> Of the history . . . of the Gloucester token, nothing is known. It appears to have been intended as a pattern for a shilling of a private coinage, by Richard Dawson of Gloucester (county?), Virginia. But two specimens of this are known, both struck in brass. A full description cannot be given of it, as both impressions are very imperfect, and together they do not supply the entire legends with certainty.
>
> The house upon this token may have been design to represent a warehouse, but is of a style corresponding more closely to that of some of the public buildings of olden times. Possibly it may have represented the court house of Gloucester County, and the legend, should any specimen fortunately be discovered to supply the missing portions, may prove to be GLOVCESTER CO HOUSE VIRGINIA.

Only three specimens, each struck in brass, are known to exist today, including two sold decades ago in the Roper and Garrett collections. Crosby's two were the Garrett and Appleton coins, but the latter was found to be a cast. Today, the reverse inscription is thought to read RIGHAVLT DAWSON ANNO DOM 1714. The Righault and Dawson families were landowners in Gloucester County. The description of Garrett-collection coin in 1980 speculated that the XII denomination, in combination with the use of brass (instead of silver), may indicate this was not intended to be a coin, but instead a check for tobacco, which was legal tender in the colony at the time. Or it may have been a store card issued by a Righault-Dawson partnership. The depiction of a courthouse may refer to the nearest business and judicial center.

In 1979, Anthony German, using a metal detector, located a 1715-dated Gloucester token not far from the site of the courthouse. The coin is extensively oxidized and is graded About Good. Enough lettering remains to indicate that the inscriptions differ from those on the 1714 version.

Numismatic Aspects

1714 Gloucester Token or Shilling

W-8180 · brass

Obverse: Rectangular building; XII (for 12 pence, or 1 shilling) below. GLOUCESTER CO [illegible mark] VA around border. *Reverse:* Five-pointed geometric star. RIGHAVLT DAWSON ANNO DOM 1714 around border. Edge plain. *Notes:* Breen-237. Two known (both 24 mm): one in the Garrett collection and one held by Gerry Nelson, weights 61.1 and 43.4 grains, respectively. *Rarity:* URS-2.

F-12
$120,000

1715 Gloucester Token (?)

W-8185

Notes: Inscriptions incomplete, but different from the preceding. Possibly a sixpence? Heavily oxidized. 18.2 mm. 25.3 grains. See Michael J. Hodder, "The Gloucester County, Virginia Courthouse Tokens" (*CNL*, April 1997). Although opinions concerning the status of this coin are divided due to the lack of information obtainable from the low-grade coin, Hodder suggests that "the 1715 token deserves more study than it has so far received." John Kleeberg wrote, in correspondence, "I'm not convinced by the 1715 piece. The only parts visible on it are a numeral '5,' one letter, and what might be the point of the star. It really could be anything from a Swedish 18th-century coin to a Masonic chapter penny." *Rarity:* URS-1.

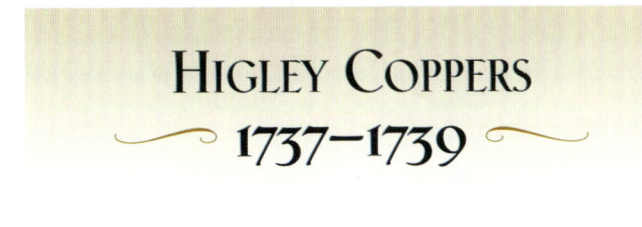

HIGLEY COPPERS
1737–1739

Higley copper of 1737 with three crowned hammers. (*Early Coins of America*, 1875)

Among the most interesting of all early American issues are the copper tokens struck circa 1737 to 1739 by Dr. Samuel Higley of Granby, Connecticut. Higley, a medical doctor with a degree from Yale College, also practiced blacksmithing and performed many experiments in metallurgy. In 1727 he devised a practical method of producing steel.

In 1728 Higley purchased acreage on a hill in Simsbury (the area later known as Granby). The area was the site of many copper mines, which were worked extensively during the early and middle 18th century. Years later, in October 1773 the Connecticut General Assembly voted to convert the subterranean caverns and external buildings of the Simsbury mines for use as a public jail and workhouse. Phelps, in his *History of the Copper Mines in Newgate Prison at Granby, Connecticut*, noted:

> The prisoners were to be employed in mining. The crimes, by which the acts subjected offenders to confinement and labor in the prison, were burglary, horse stealing, and counterfeiting the public bills or coins, or making instruments and dies therefore.
>
> By the time Newgate Prison was abandoned in 1827, the buildings had been destroyed by fire three times. The cruel, dark, damp conditions precipitated numerous revolts and violent incidents. Escapes were frequent.

Following his 1728 purchase, Higley operated a small but thriving mining business that extracted exceptionally rich copper. Much if not most of the metal was exported to England. Sometime around the year 1737 Higley is thought to have produced a copper token, perhaps using his own copper, but this is not verified. The obverse depicted a standing deer with the legend THE VALUE OF THREE-PENCE. The reverse showed three crowned hammers (derived from the arms of the English blacksmiths' guild) with the surrounding legend CONNECTICUT and the date 1737.

Legend tells us that drinks in the local tavern sold at the time for three pence each, and Higley was in the habit of paying his bar bill with his own coinage. There was a cry against this, for in diameter the Higley copper threepence was no larger than the contemporary (and locally circulated) English halfpence, which had a value just one-sixth of that stated on the Higley coin. Accordingly, Higley redesigned his coinage so that the obverse legend read VALUE ME AS YOU PLEASE. The pieces still bore an indication of value: the roman numeral III below the standing deer. Two new reverses were designed, one of which pictured three hammers with the inscription I AM GOOD COPPER. The other reverse, picturing a broad axe, bore the legend I CUT MY WAY THROUGH. The third obverse design, of which only a single specimen is known, depicted a wagon wheel with the legend THE WHEELE GOES ROUND.

Samuel Higley died on a voyage to England in May 1737, on a ship loaded with copper from his own mine. His oldest son, John, together with Rev. Timothy Woodbridge and William Cradock, probably engraved and struck the issues of 1739. Facts are scarce, while numismatic tradition is strong. In the same year, John Read of Boston proposed to the Connecticut General Court assembled in New Haven that he be granted a patent to produce copper halfpence and farthings from native Connecticut ore mined in the Simsbury-Granby area. Cradock and Woodbridge joined him in the proposal.

Read's petition came to naught, so the first *authorized* coinage did not occur until several decades later with the Connecticut coppers of 1785, by different principals and in another location.

In a communication, numismatic historian David Gladfelter noted:

> The problem in ascribing the 1737-dated tokens to Samuel Higley is the lateness of their dates. The date 1737 would not have been used in Connecticut until March 25, 1737 (then New Year's Day) and thereafter. Samuel Higley lost his life at sea in May 1737, so he would have had only a few weeks to prepare dies and strike tokens dated 1737.

Apparently the original Higley coinage was small, circulating mainly in Granby and its environs. Crosby relates that a goldsmith who served his apprenticeship around 1810 said that Higley pieces were hard to find at the time and were in demand to use as an alloy for gold. The goldsmith related that his master had delayed the completion of a string of gold beads because he was unable to find a copper Higley threepence with which to alloy the metal.

Numismatic Aspects

Today, Higley issues of all types are exceedingly rare, and often a span of years will occur between offerings. Nearly all pieces show very extensive evidence of circulation, with most grading in the range of Good or Very Good, although a Fair or About Good coin would be desirable and highly collectible. Most collectors would do well to have even a single example to illustrate the Higley series. Cabinets with as many as four or five coins have been few and far between in the annals of the hobby. Remarkably, in the 18th century, pioneer American numismatist Pierre Eugène Du Simitière had seven specimens.

Crosby's *Early Coins of America* gives basic information on the Higley series. *Walter Breen's Complete Encyclopedia of U.S. and Colonial Coins* offers an expanded view. Most useful today is the carefully researched study on "The History and Die Varieties of the Higley Coppers," by Daniel Freidus, based on his presentation at the Coinage of the Americas Conference held by the ANS in 1994 (text published in 1995). The text assigns whole numbers to types and decimal parts to varieties; for example, obverse Type 1, variety 1.1, with reverse A, translates to 1.1-A. These are cross-referenced as "Freidus numbers" below. The average diameter of a Higley copper is about 28.6 mm. All have a plain edge.

Standing Deer, THE VALVE OF THREE PENCE

W-8190 · Freidus 1.1-A · Crosby 17 · 3 Hammers · CONNECTICVT 1737

Obverse: Upper date line points to lower right of N (PENCE). *Reverse:* Three crowned hammers at the center. CONNECTICVT 1737 around the border. *Notes:* Two known. Newman Collection, Stack's, sale of October 1987. *Rarity:* URS-2.

W-8200 · Freidus 1.2-A · Crosby 18 · 3 Hammers · CONNECTICVT 1737

Obverse: Upper date line touches bottom of C (PENCE). Leftmost antler is under left side of O (OF). Dot between VALVE and OF is closer to O. *Reverse:* Same as preceding. *Notes:* 28.7 mm. One is held by the Connecticut Historical Society. *Rarity:* URS-4.

G-4	VG-8	F-12	VF-20	EF-40
$14,000	$30,000	$55,000	$110,000	$225,000

W-8205 · Freidus 1.2-B.a · Crosby 19 · I AM GOOD COPPER 1737

Obverse: Same as preceding. *Reverse:* Head of third hammer is over 3 (1737). Diagnostic. *Notes:* 28 mm. Two known: Bushnell to Parmelee to Ford; Norweb collection. *Rarity:* URS-2.

Selected auction price(s): Ford II Sale (5/2004), EF, $218,500.

W-8215 · Freidus 1.3-A · 3 Hammers · CONNECTICVT 1737

Obverse: Upper date line points to bottom of C (PENCE). Leftmost antler is under O (OF). Dot between VALVE and OF is closer to E. *Reverse:* Three crowned hammers at center. CONNECTICVT 1737 around the border. *Notes:* Discovered by Henry Chapman prior to 1916. Among the owners are the Connecticut State Library (coin has two holes) and the Newman collection. *Rarity:* URS-4.

Standing Deer, VALVE ME AS YOU PLEASE III

W-8225 · Freidus 2-B.a · I AM GOOD COPPER 1737

Obverse: VALVE spelling is diagnostic. *Reverse:* Top edge of head of third hammer is over 3 (1737). Diagnostic. *Notes:* Three known, one in the Newman collection. *Rarity:* URS-3.

W-8230 · Freidus 2-B.b · Crosby 20 · I AM GOOD COPPER 1737

Obverse: Same as preceding. *Reverse:* Head of third hammer is over second 7 (1737). Diagnostic. *Notes:* Unique. Connecticut State Library, ex J.C. Mitchelson collection. *Rarity:* URS-1.

Standing Deer, VALUE ME AS YOU PLEASE III

W-8240 · Freidus 3.1-B.a · Crosby 21 · I AM GOOD COPPER 1737

Obverse: Leftmost antler barely left of A (AS), rightmost antler under right foot of A. Diagnostic. *Reverse:* Head of third hammer is over 3 (1737). Diagnostic. *Notes:* Although it is rare, this is still one of the more widely available varieties. *Rarity:* URS-5.

G-4	VG-8	F-12	VF-20
$15,000	$30,000	$50,000	$110,000

W-8245 · Freidus 3.1-C · Crosby 23 · Broad Axe · J CUT MY WAY THROUGH

Obverse: Same as preceding. *Reverse:* Broad axe with blade of axe adjacent to inner circle. No date. *Notes:* One is in the Connecticut State Library, ex J.C. Mitchelson collection. *Rarity:* URS-4.

G-4	VG-8	F-12	VF-20
$14,000	$30,000	$55,000	$110,000

W-8255 · Freidus 3.2-B.a · Crosby 22 · I AM GOOD COPPER 1737

Obverse: Leftmost antler under A; rightmost antler under S. Diagnostic. *Reverse:* Head of third hammer is over 3 (1737). Diagnostic. *Notes:* One is held by the American Numismatic Society. *Rarity:* URS-4.

G-4	VG-8	F-12	VF-20
		$55,000	$200,000

W-8260 · Freidus 3.2-C · Crosby 24 · Broad Axe · J CUT MY WAY THROUGH

Obverse: Same as preceding. *Reverse:* Broad axe with blade of axe adjacent to inner circle. No date. *Notes:* Although rare, this is still one of the more widely available varieties. *Rarity:* URS-5.

G-4	VG-8	F-12	VF-20	EF-40
$14,000	$30,000	$55,000	$110,000	$240,000

W-8265 · Freidus 3.2-D · Broad Axe · J CUT MY WAY THROUGH 1739

Obverse: Same as preceding. *Reverse:* Broad axe with blade of axe distant from inner circle. Date 1739 in border at lower left. *Notes:* Discovered by Daniel Freidus in 1985. *Rarity:* URS-4.

Selected auction price(s): Norweb I Sale (B&M 10/1987), G, $4,070. Classics Sale (Stack's [ANR] 6/2004), VF, $40,250.

W-8275 · Freidus 3.3-B.a · I AM GOOD COPPER 1737

Obverse: Leftmost antler under A; rightmost antler under space between A and S but closer to A. Diagnostic. *Reverse:* Head of third hammer is over 3 (1737). Diagnostic. *Notes:* Discovered by Thomas Hall. Daniel Freidus traces only two. *Rarity:* URS-2.

W-8280 · Freidus 3.3-C · Crosby 25 · Broad Axe · J CUT MY WAY THROUGH

Obverse: Same as preceding. *Reverse:* Broad axe with blade of axe adjacent to inner circle. No date. *Rarity:* URS-3.

Selected auction price(s): Ford II Sale (5/2004), VF, flawed and with cut on reverse, $34,500; VF, $97,750.

W-8285 · Freidus 3.3-D · Crosby 26 · Broad Axe · J CUT MY WAY THROUGH 1739

Obverse: Same as preceding. *Reverse:* Broad axe with blade of axe distant from inner circle. Date 1739 in border at lower left. *Notes:* Although it is rare, this is still one of the more widely available varieties. Owners include the Connecticut State Library and the Newman collection. *Rarity:* URS-4.

G-4	VG-8	F-12	VF-20
$18,000	$36,000	$65,000	$150,000

THE WHEELE GOES ROUND

W-8295 · Freidus 4-C · Broad Axe · J CUT MY WAY THROUGH

Obverse: Spoked wheel at the center. THE WHEELE GOES ROUND at border. *Reverse:* Broad axe with blade of axe adjacent to inner circle. No date. *Notes:* Discovered by Howland Wood and published in *The Numismatist*, July 1913. Unique. John W. Ellsworth, John W. Garrett, John L. Roper, to New York collector. *Rarity:* URS-1.

Selected auction price(s): Garrett III Sale (B&R 10/1980), F–VF, some weakness of striking, $45,000, to the following. Roper Sale (Stack's 12/1983), F, $60,500.

PITT TOKENS
1766

The so-called Pitt tokens, issued in "halfpenny" and "farthing" sizes, typically made of brass or copper, bear on the obverse a portrait of William Pitt with surrounding legend, and on the reverse a ship and the words AMERICA / THANKS TO THE FRIENDS OF LIBERTY AND TRADE. The reference is to the Stamp Act of March 22, 1765, and detested by American colonists. Through the efforts of William Pitt, an English statesman, it was repealed on March 18, 1766. Pitt stated that English control over the American colonies did not include the right of taxation. For this he was admired by the colonists.

While the pieces probably were intended as commemorative medalets, the larger-size copper issues are referred to as halfpence (as in this text) or halfpennies by numismatists today. Some of these circulated in the colonies, as evidenced by metal-detector finds. The smaller brass issues, the "farthings," bear a differently styled portrait and appear to be struck on thicker planchets that were cast prior to striking.

Little is known concerning the circumstances of issue. Robert Vlack suggests that the pieces may have been designed by Paul Revere. Striking may have been accomplished around 1769 by James Smither (or Smithers) of Philadelphia. Louis E. Jordan (correspondence) gives this view:

> The Smither and Revere connection are from Montroville Dickeson (*The American Numismatic Manual*, 1859), and the James Smither attribution for the dies has continued in the numismatic literature. Smither was an English born gunsmith and engraver who worked in Philadelphia during the 1760s–1770s. He is known for engraving the border cuts for the April 3, 1772, emission of Pennsylvania currency.

> Michael Hodder mentions it is uncertain if the Pitt tokens were manufactured in England or America but does not elaborate on this statement. An English origin for the token is possible since English merchants, and specifically London merchants, protested loudly as to how the stamp tax would adversely affect trade. They praised Pitt and encouraged the king to support him in repealing the Stamp Act.

> Indeed, we know several medals commemorating Pitt's role in the repeal of the Stamp Act were struck in England. Thomas Pingo, an engraver at the Royal Mint, created two different medals (Brown, 100–101), while three other English Pitt medals cannot be attributed to a specific engraver (Brown, 102 and 104–105).

> In addition to the fact that all other known Pitt medals are from England, the legends and images on the RESTORER OF COMMERCE token seem to reflect an English point of view. The obverse hails Pitt as the restorer of commerce while the reverse shows a

ship headed toward America (based on the way the flags are flying in the wind, the ship appears to be heading toward the word "America"). This emphasis on commerce and trade to America precisely reflects the attitude of the English merchants, rather than the attitude of the New York-based Sons of Liberty, which protested the stamp act in America primarily as a repression of freedom rather than as a hindrance to English-American trade. Interestingly, Laurence Brown in his *Catalogue of British Historical Medals 1760–1960* includes the Restorer of Commerce medal (Brown 103) as one of several Pitt medals produced in England commemorating the repeal of the Stamp Act.

Numismatic Aspects

Pitt "Farthing" Token

W-8345 · brass
Obverse: Bust of Pitt facing left. THE RESTORER OF COMMERCE 1766 / NO STAMPS around border. *Reverse:* Ship sailing to the left; AMERICA in field near stern. THANKS TO THE FRIENDS OF LIBERTY AND TRADE around most of border. Edge plain. *Notes:* Betts-520, Breen-248. Brass. About 25 mm. Usually porous. Thought to have been struck on cast planchets. Sometimes with crude "reeding," as if filed (per Breen). No copper impressions confirmed. *Rarity:* URS-5.

G-4	VG-8	F-12	VF-20	EF-40
$4,000	$8,000	$15,000	$35,000	$50,000

W-8347 · white metal
As preceding, but in white metal. *Notes:* Breen-250. One reported in the William T. Anton Jr. collection. *Rarity:* URS-2.

W-8348 · silver
As preceding, but in silver. *Notes:* Breen-249, reported, not verified. *Rarity:* URS-1(?).

Pitt "Halfpenny" Token

W-8350 · copper
Designs similar to preceding, but different dies, larger, with Pitt in a bulkier wig (among other differences). Edge plain. *Notes:* Betts-519, Breen-251. Copper. About 28 mm. Some were issued lightly silvered (coated with tin). For these, if in high grade and with original silvering, add 40 percent to the values. Beware of pieces that were silvered later. *Rarity:* URS-10.

VG-8	F-12	VF-20	EF-40	AU-50	MS-60	MS-63
$650	$1,200	$2,400	$4,500	$7,000	$8,500	$11,500

W-8354 · brass
Same as preceding, but struck in brass. *Notes:* Breen-252. *Rarity:* URS-4.
Selected auction price(s): Long Beach Sale (Superior 2/2005), AU-55 (PCGS), $4,500.

W-8358 · tin
Same as preceding, but struck in tin. *Notes:* Betts-519, Breen-254. *Rarity:* URS-3.
Selected auction price(s): John J. Ford Jr. VII Sale (Stack's 1/2005), AU, dark, $6,037.50.

W-8360 · silver
Same as preceding, but in silver. *Notes:* Betts-519, Breen-253. Reported by Betts. Not traced. *Rarity:* URS-1(?).

MASSACHUSETTS COPPER COINAGE 1776

While silver coins were produced by the Massachusetts Bay Colony beginning in 1652 (and extending until 1682), it was not until nearly a century later, in 1776, that copper pieces were made. In the latter year at least three varieties of coins, all presumably patterns, were struck. Very little is known today about their origin or the circumstances under which they were made.

A 1776 Massachusetts copper "penny" bears on the obverse the representation of a pine tree. Crosby told of its provenance:

> Now in the collection of Mr. William F. Appleton, it was formerly owned by Mr. J. Colburn, of Boston, who obtained it about 1852, from Mr. Edward W. Hooper, then a schoolboy collector of coins. Mr. Hooper purchased it from a grocer at the northerly part of the city, who found it many years before while excavating on his premises, in the vicinity of Hull or Charter Street for the purpose of making an addition to his dwelling. He had long preserved it as a curiosity. We take this to be the first pattern for a Massachusetts cent.

Another curious 1776 Massachusetts copper is of a different design and features on the obverse the standing figure of an Indian. The reverse depicts a goddess seated. The third 1776 pattern issue of Massachusetts has been known as the

235

"Janus copper" and on the obverse has three heads in one. Of the coin, M.W. Dickeson notes in his *American Numismatical Manual*, 1859:

> This coin is in the collection of M.A. Stickney, Esq., of Salem, Massachusetts, to whom we are indebted for a facsimile, and who informs us that the die was gotten up and cut by the distinguished mechanic, patriot, and gentleman Col. Paul Revere of Boston; that he thinks it was designed for currency, the value, half-pence, being impressed upon it, and that the head on the obverse was supposed to refer to the Whig and Tory parties of 1776. This is probably the only specimen of this coin to be found in our country, and it is consequently very rare and valuable.
>
> Janus upon an American coin invites speculation. As representing the Whig and Tory parties, it was truthful, for they looked at different ways. Could the idea have been suggested, however, from the planting a colony and founding a town? The principals of liberty at this time—1776—were planted, which resulted in the founding of an independent nation. This may have induced the idea, though we are inclined to think its application was exclusively to the Tories; as they looked one way, and thus attempted to disguise the fact that they were operating in a contrary direction; so that with fair protestations in behalf of the liberty of the colonies, that sterling patriot, Col. Revere, saw that Janus was their prototype, and hence his effigy was a fit emblem for a device illustrative of the fact, and the Goddess of Liberty on the reverse, as the antidote our true symbol of devotion.

Crosby offered this:

> This piece, which has been known as the "Janus Copper," we think may more properly be called the Massachusetts Halfpenny. It has three heads combined instead of two as in a Janus head. This device resembles the Brahma of Hindoo mythology, which represents the past, the present, and the future.
>
> The only specimen known of this curious pattern is in the collection of Matthew A. Stickney, Esq., and was found with an engraved piece and some proof impressions from plates for Continental paper money engraved by Paul Revere; from this circumstance Mr. Stickney is inclined to the opinion that they were the work of that engraver. However this may be, the pine tree cent and this halfpenny sufficiently resemble each other in their workmanship to be considered the work of the same artist. They were probably private enterprises, as no mention of them is found upon any records.

Numismatic Aspects

W-8375 · "Pine Tree" penny
Obverse: Pine tree. MASSACHUSETTS STATE around the border. "IdLM" under the tree, assumed to be the denomination. *Reverse:* Goddess seated on a globe. LIBERTY AND VIRTUE / 1776 around the border. Edge plain. *Notes:* Breen-704; Crosby Plate VII, 7; 32 mm, hence assigned the "penny" value. Anne Bentley, *Witness to America's Past*. Massachusetts Historical Society. *Rarity:* URS-1.

W-8380 · "Province" copper
Obverse: Standing figure of an Indian. Inscription may read PROVINCE OF MASSA, or similar. *Reverse:* Goddess seated on globe. Date 1776 below. LIBERTATIS is part of the inscription. *Notes:* Breen-702. Diameter 27 mm. Overstruck on a 1747 English halfpenny. The only known specimen is very worn, with incomplete inscriptions, and is holed. American Numismatic Society. *Rarity:* URS-1.

W-8385 · "Janus" copper
Obverse: Three heads in one, facing forward. STATE OF MASSA 1/2 D around border, the D for denarium or penny. *Reverse:* Seated figure with staff and globe. GODDESS LIBERTY / 1776 around border. Edge plain. *Notes:* Breen-703, Crosby Plate VII, 8. Massachusetts proclaimed itself a state, no longer a colony, in 1776. Conventional wisdom has it that this was found with papers of Paul Revere, but the custodian of the papers, the Massachusetts Historical Society, has no confirmation of this. *Rarity:* URS-1.

Selected auction price(s): Garrett I Sale (B&R 11/1979), F-12, $40,000.

New Hampshire Copper Coinage
1776

On March 13, 1776, the New Hampshire House of Representatives established a committee to consider the production of copper coinage. The members reported that it would be beneficial to produce copper issues as the Continental currency since other paper-money issues in circulation were too large for use in small transactions. William Moulton, an accomplished silversmith, was recommended for the franchise to produce up to 100 pounds' weight of coppers to be submitted to the General Assembly prior to circulation. It was further recommended that 108 of these pieces be equal to one Spanish milled dollar, with the weight of each individual coin being equal to that of the current English halfpenny.

A design was submitted showing on the obverse a tree and the words AMERICAN LIBERTY, emblematic of the revolutionary spirit prevailing at the time. The reverse was to depict a harp and the date 1776. On June 28, 1776, the House of Representatives' vote is recorded as follows:

> That the treasurer of this colony receive into the treasury, in exchange for paper bills of this colony, any quantity of copper coin, made in this colony, of the weight of five pennyweight and ten grains each, to the amount of any sum or sums not exceeding 1,000 pounds lawful money, which coppers shall have the following device: a pine tree with the words American Liberty on one side and a harp and the figure 1776 on the other side.

Known facts end here.

Numismatic Aspects

Walter Breen (*Encyclopedia*, 1988) suggests that Moulton made about 4,600 of these coppers, each cast by hand—an unlikely scenario for such a seemingly formidable task. The style with pine tree, AMERICAN LIBERTY, and a harp with the 1776 date is Breen-708.

No contemporary records of coinage have been found. Crosby (1875) mentioned a piece with the initials W • M recently discovered in Portsmouth in that state. This does not conform to the original legislation and may be a fantasy, or at least an unresolved mystery. Other coins with W • M and part of the design have surfaced, some of these unquestionably later casts and novelties.

Until better evidence is found, it is probably wise to treat "1776 New Hampshire" coins with W • M as curiosities. As to the cast-copper types with a pine tree, AMERICAN LIBERTY, and a harp, at least these follow the authorization. Some date back to the 19th century, but again, no facts are at hand.

Pine Tree

W-8395 · Harp · copper

Obverse: Large pine tree with AMERICAN to the left and LIBERTY to the right. *Reverse:* A harp. Date 1776 at border at top right. *Notes:* Breen-708. About 28.5 mm. The Crosby-Garrett coin is illustrated. Breen states eight or nine are known. It is unknown whether such pieces are contemporary with the 1776 legislation. *Rarity:* URS-5 or 6.

Selected auction price(s): Garrett III Sale (B&R 10/1980), VG, ex Stickney, Crosby plate coin, $13,000.

W-8400 · W • M · copper · possible fantasy issue

Obverse: Pine tree on mound with 17 76 divided by the trunk. Beads around border. *Reverse:* W • M at center. AMERICAN LIBERTY around border. *Notes:* Breen-706. About 28 mm. Illustrated is a composite of sketches from Crosby, 1875. Actual coins vary from these sketches. Breen states three to five known. They have no basis in any contemporary legislation or history thus far encountered. It is possible these are 19th-century fantasies, to which population many more recent copies have been added. *Rarity:* URS-3 per Breen, although not reliable as a basis today.

Selected auction price(s): Garrett III Sale (B&R 10/1980), AG, $7,500.

Continental Dollars
1776

One of the most significant early American issues is the 1776 Continental dollar. Bearing devices and inscriptions taken from paper Continental Currency (authorization February 17, 1776), these bear on the obverse the 1776 date and, surrounding, the inscription CONTINENTAL CURRENCY. Within is a sundial, below which is MIND YOUR BUSINESS, with FUGIO ("I fly," a reference to the passage of time) to the left. The reverse displays 13 intertwined circles, each with the name of a state, joined to form a linked-chain border. Within the center is the inscription AMERICAN CONGRESS—WE ARE ONE.

1776 Continental dollar, variety with CURENCY spelling. (Prime, *Coins, Medals, and Seals*, 1861)

No specific documentation has been found regarding the origin of the Continental dollar. The resolution of February 1776, pertaining to the issuance of paper money, resulted in the production of different denominations from the one-sixth dollar through $8, including the $1 denomination. The resolution of May 9, 1776, provided for various denominations from $1 through $8. However, the resolution of July 22, 1776, omitted the $1 denominations and contained others from $2 through $30. Likewise, the final resolution of that year, November 2, 1776, omitted the $1 note and began with the $2.

It was likely intended that the pewter Continental dollar coin serve in place of the $1 note during the latter part of 1776. The reason for striking brass impressions is not known. A few silver examples are known, of full intrinsic worth at the time, and may represent the intention for all of the coinage. The Continental Congress was short of funds, and the amount of silver on hand was insufficient for quantity production.

Certain varieties have the inscription EG FECIT, meaning "E.G. made it." Eric P. Newman, who has studied the series extensively, identified the Continental-dollar dies as the work of Elisha Gallaudet, of Freehold, New Jersey, who also engraved plates for printing Continental Currency. The same engraver cut all the dies for this series, as evidenced by the craftsmanship.

Several different die varieties were made. "Currency" was spelled three ways: CURRENCY, CURENCY, and CURRENCEY, the latter being imitative of an error found on the one-sixth-dollar note of February 17, 1776, indicating that the engraver may have copied the specific legends on this particular design while making the dies. The typical pewter strike is about 41 mm diameter and has the edge ornamented with twin olive leaves.

A commentary by Michael J. Hodder, cataloger of the John J. Ford Jr. collection catalog (Stack's, part 1, October 2003), includes this:

> It is almost certain that the first 1776 Continental dollars were struck in New York City in the summer of 1776, just before the British captured the city in September. This fits with Ford's observation that New York state omitted the $1 denomination from the currency issue of August 13.

This agrees with an article in the *New-York Journal*, June 27, 1776, which printed a rumor that in three months a new Continental coin in *copper* would be struck, to be current at the rate of 12 for an eighth of a Spanish dollar, or about one cent. No such copper coinage is known to have been made, however. Further from the Hodder narrative:

> The New York mint may not have had enough time to strike all the 1776 Continental dollars before the British captured the city. The coiners probably packed what they could and smuggled themselves and whatever machinery they could conveniently carry out of the city just before it fell to the enemy. Since the coinage was official Continental Congress business, the mint traveled with the Congress wherever it went. The second group of Continental dollars was struck after the Mint left New York, when the Congress settled in Pennsylvania. Philadelphia and Lancaster have been proposed as mint sites for the E.G. FECIT, CURRENCY, and floral cross varieties.

Numismatic Aspects

Specimens of the Continental dollar struck in pewter, while elusive, do appear on the market with regularity, indicating that the original coinage must have been extensive. A few brass and silver examples are extant and are exceedingly rare. Attributions are to Eric P. Newman, "The 1776 Continental Currency Coinage," 1952. A notable auction offering of these was in the Ford collection in 2003.

W-8430 · Newman 1-A · CURENCY misspelling · brass

Obverse: CURENCY misspelling. *Reverse:* Rings as dotted lines. N. HAMPS right of MASSACHS *Notes:* Breen-1085. Michael Hodder estimated 12 to 15 known. *Rarity:* URS-5.

F-12	VF-20	EF-40	AU-50	MS-60
				—

W-8435 · Newman 1-B · pewter

Obverse: Same as preceding. *Reverse:* Dots partly cut into lines. *Notes:* Breen-1086. Not known to Newman. Pewter. *Rarity:* URS-2.

W-8440 · Newman 1-B · brass

Obverse: Same as preceding. *Reverse:* Dots partly cut into lines. *Notes:* Breen-1087. Brass. *Rarity:* URS-4.

F-12	VF-20	EF-40	AU-50
$47,000	$110,000	$170,000	$300,000

W-8445 · Newman 1-C · pewter

Obverse: Same as preceding. In its late state, often seen, the obverse die has a break over GI (FUGIO); Newman calls this 1.1-C. *Reverse:* The preceding die was heavily lapped and reworked. The rings are now circles composed of thick lines. The comma after AMERICAN is now a period. *Notes:* Breen-1089. Ford's finest was "nearly choice brilliant Uncirculated." One is on an overly large planchet. Pewter. *Rarity:* URS-10.

F-12	VF-20	EF-40	AU-50	MS-60	MS-63
$12,000	$21,000	$34,000	$45,000	$100,000	$175,000

W-8450 · Newman 1-C · silver

Same as preceding, but struck in silver. *Notes:* Breen-1091. Two known, the Garrett coin and one in the Don Corrado Romano collection sale (Stack's, 1987). *Rarity:* URS-2.

Selected auction price(s): Garrett III Sale (B&R 10/1980), VG, $95,000; later in the John J. Ford Jr. I Sale (Stack's 10/2003), $287,500. John J. Ford Jr. VII Sale (Stack's 1/2005), VF, $345,000.

W-8455 · Newman 2-C · CURRENCY · pewter

Obverse: CURRENCY spelled correctly. *Reverse:* Same as preceding. *Notes:* Breen-1092. Ford's finest was a prooflike gem Mint State. *Rarity:* URS-10.

F-12	VF-20	EF-40	AU-50	MS-60	MS-63	MS-65
$12,000	$21,000	$34,000	$45,000	$75,000	$150,000	$250,000

W-8460 · Newman 3-D · EG FECIT · pewter

Obverse: EG FECIT added to band around central image. *Reverse:* N. HAMPS left of MASSACHS. *Notes:* Breen-1095. This variety is typically seen well struck, as all features were cut deeply into the dies. *Rarity:* URS-9 or 10.

F-12	VF-20	EF-40	AU-50	MS-60	MS-63	MS-65
$13,000	$23,000	$35,000	$47,000	$75,000	$150,000	$250,000

W-8465 · Newman 3-D · brass

Same as preceding, but struck in brass. *Notes:* Listed as Breen-1094 with the notation "unique?" Listed by Eric P. Newman as R-8 on the Sheldon scale (two or three known). *Rarity:* URS-2 or 3.

W-8470 · Newman 3-D · silver

Same as preceding, but struck in silver. *Notes:* Breen-1096. *Rarity:* URS-2.

Selected auction price(s): John J. Ford Jr. I Sale (Stack's 10/2003), EF, $425,500.

W-8475 · Newman 4-D · CURRENCEY misspelling · pewter

Obverse: CURRENCEY misspelling. *Reverse:* Same as preceding. *Notes:* Breen-1097. Michael J. Hodder estimates four known. Finest is the Newman Mint State coin (illustrated). *Rarity:* URS-3.

Selected auction price(s): Roper Sale (Stack's 12/1983), EF, $6,050. John J. Ford Jr. I Sale (Stack's 10/2003), Choice EF, $74,750.

W-8480 · Newman 5-D · corrected to CURRENCY · pewter

Obverse: CURRENCEY die with Y added over second E and ornament added over original Y. *Reverse:* Same as preceding. *Notes:* Breen-1098. Three verified: Norweb collection (now in a New York collection); Very Fine example, ex Newcomer, later sold by Spink America, June 1997; Very Fine coin discovered in April 1990. *Rarity:* URS-3.

Selected auction price(s): Norweb II Sale (3/1988), AU, $50,600.

ALBANY CHURCH PENNIES
1790

In the 18th century, just as today, churches depended upon the contributions of members to remain in operation. The problem for the First Presbyterian Church of Albany, New York, was the scarcity of small change in the area, this following the coppers panic of 1789. Many parishioners had either no change at all or only worn-out coppers and counterfeit cents to drop into the Sunday offering plate. On January 4, 1790, the elders hit on a novel solution:

> Resolved: That one thousand coppers be stamped *Church Penny*, and placed with the treasurer to exchange with members of the congregation, at the rate of twelve for one shilling, in order to add respect to the weekly collections.

Two different variations were produced. The first has CHURCH in block letters with "Penny" in script. The second variety is the same but with the script letter D above CHURCH, "D" perhaps being the abbreviation for penny, or denarium, in the English monetary system. These pieces are exceedingly rare. Fewer than a dozen exist of each variety. The inaugural appearance at auction for each may have been W.E. Woodward's second Semi-Annual Sale in April 1863, lots 2079 and 2080.

W-8495 · Without D

Obverse: CHURCH / Penny in two lines, within crenellated border, stamped on a copper blank, some on worn coppers. *Reverse:* Blank. *Edge:* Plain. *Notes:* Breen-1169, 28 to 29 mm. *Rarity:* URS-4.

VG-8	F-12	VF-20
$10,000	$26,000	$70,000

W-8500 · With D

Obverse: Same as preceding, but script D added above CHURCH. *Reverse:* Same as preceding. *Edge:* Plain. *Notes:* Breen-1170. *Rarity:* URS-4.

VG-8	F-12	VF-20
$10,000	$26,000	$70,000

STANDISH BARRY COINAGE
1790

Standish Barry, a Baltimore silversmith, struck a distinctive silver threepence token in 1790. Barry, then 27 years old, may have intended the piece to commemorate the anniversary of American independence, or perhaps some special celebration was held in Baltimore to occasion its issue. The piece bears a male portrait on the obverse, perhaps Barry himself. The specific day, July 4, in addition to the year (expressed as 90) is a distinctive feature. Coinage apparently was quite limited, for his threepence are exceedingly rare today.

About this time he is believed to have made imitation Spanish-American gold doubloons hallmarked SB (a scenario similar to Ephraim Brasher's imitation 1742 Lima gold doubloon), per the research of John Kraljevich in the description of a coin in the Eliasberg collection sale, 2005, lot 3012.

Barry was born in Baltimore on November 4, 1763. By the age of 16 he had developed patriotic fervor and enlisted in the Revolutionary War. Afterward he set up business in the city of his birth and tried on a variety of vocational hats, including silversmith, watchmaker, and jeweler. He first advertised as a watch and clock maker and engraver in the *Maryland Journal* on November 26, 1784, having completed his apprenticeship in the trade with David Evans. Not long afterward he became a partner with Joseph Rice, an arrangement that continued until June 1787. His memorable threepence pieces were issued several years later. In the meantime it seems that he was involved in the assaying of gold coins, creating his own imitations of Spanish-American pieces. In New York City his contemporary, Ephraim Brasher, did the same thing. On October 10, 1788, Barry married Agnes Thompson. The couple had six children, one of whom, Standish Jr., served as an assistant treasurer of the United States.

Barry maintained his interest in the military, and by 1798 he was a lieutenant in the Baltimore Independent Blues (earlier called the Sans Culotte), organized to defend the city should a war develop with France. At that time the French were seizing American ships on the high seas, and tensions ran high. In the early 19th century he was listed in directories as a watchmaker and silversmith at 20 North Gay Street. In 1808 he was requested to submit a quote for supplying 3,000 gross each of coat and vest buttons with insignia of the First and Second regiments.

During the War of 1812 he served in the battle with the British at Bladensburg, Maryland, on August 24, 1814. The next month Barry was in Baltimore, when the British attempted to land after they had sacked Washington, but were repulsed by "the rockets' red glare, the bombs bursting in air" fired by troops manning Fort McHenry in the harbor. Later accounts have Barry, or someone with a similar name, living as a grocer and holding minor public offices.

In 1838 he moved to Newport, New York, to live with his son, Standish Jr. He died in Newport on November 6, 1844.

Nearly all examples of the silver threepence show significant wear, indicating that these must have circulated for a long time. The gold doubloon, a recent discovery, is unique.

Numismatic Aspects

W-8510 · 1790 threepence

Obverse: Male portrait facing left, possibly of Barry. BALTIMORE TOWN JULY 4 90 around border, with ring separating it from the portrait. *Reverse:* THREE / PENCE in two lines at the center. STANDISH BARRY among ornaments at border, with a ring separating the inscription from the central denomination. *Edge:* Plain. *Notes:* Breen-1019, 14.5 mm. Typically on a small planchet, with rim incomplete. Obverse die buckled on some impressions. Reverse die with border-to-border crack at left on some specimens. *Rarity:* URS-6.

F-12	VF-20	EF-40	AU-50
$26,000	$55,000	$110,000	$185,000

W-8515 · imitation Lima 1735 doubloon

Cast-gold imitation of a 1735 Lima (Peru) 8 escudos. Identified by John Kraljevich in the Eliasberg collection of world gold coins (Stack's [ANR], 2006). From the catalog (excerpt):

26.42 grams, 28.70 mm. Reverse counterstamped SB in oval at center of cross and again near edge at 3:00 on cast imitation Peru host (Friedberg-7). Edge hand-reeded to prevent clipping. Mark attributed to Baltimore silversmith Standish Barry in American Silver: Garvan and Other Collections in the Yale University Art Gallery, 1970, which illustrates this precise mark on a circa 1790 to 1800 Standish Barry teapot stand. Yale's attribution of dates is, of necessity, speculative but Barry's independent workshop opened in 1787. A previously unpublished American counterfeit from the earliest days of the Republic, most closely analogous to the 1742-dated struck counterfeits produced by Standish Barry's contemporary Ephraim Brasher of New York. Pale yellow gold, smooth, and somewhat polished near the rims but rough and granular among the central details, consistent of a piece produced by a casting process. Some tiny pits near the rims are likewise consistent, as are the file marks on the edge. After filing, the edges of this piece were carefully decorated with 41 distinct impressions of a flower-like prepared punch that would act as reeding. Marked twice by Barry, once at center and once at an angle near 3:00 on the reverse.

Rarity: URS-1.

Bar Coppers (undated)

The *New Jersey Gazette* of November 12, 1785, told of the advent of this token:

A new and curious kind of coppers have lately made their appearance in New York. The novelty and bright gloss of which keeps them in circulation. These coppers are in fact similar to Continental buttons without eyes; on the one side are thirteen stripes and on the other U.S.A., as was usual on the soldiers' buttons.

It is believed that these were produced in Birmingham, England, by a Thomas Wyon, according to researcher Russell Rulau (although facts are scarce). The obverse is a simple monogram formed by the intertwined letters USA. The reverse consists of a series of 13 parallel bars. The design is the same as on certain Revolutionary War uniform buttons, as noted in the above account.

Although they are scarce, examples come on the market with regularity. Nearly all are in higher grades.

W-8520

Obverse: USA monogram. S under left side of A. *Reverse:* Thirteen parallel bars with tiny thorn or spur extending upward from the leg of the 12th bar. *Edge:* Plain. *Notes:* Breen-1145, Crosby Plate IX, 25. Originals date from circa 1785. In the 1860s John A. Bolen made a clever copy (W-14200), but with the S (USA) over the left side of the A. *Rarity:* URS-9.

EF-40	AU-50	MS-60	MS-63	MS-65
$12,500	$17,500			

New Spain Jolas
1818

In 1818, the entire southwestern United States was part of the Viceroyalty of New Spain. Starting in the late 17th century, Franciscan Catholic missionaries began to colonize the territory, beginning with a chain of missions in the fertile valley of the San Antonio River. The Alamo, erected in 1718, was the first built. Over the next century, the area's population of missionaries, Native Americans, Spanish soldiers, ranch workers, and other newcomers grew to such an extent that a local coinage became necessary. The military governor lieutenant in San Antonio, Colonel Manuel Prado, authorized one of the six-member *ayuntamiento* (city council) to arrange for the striking of copper tokens of the value of one-half real. Over an 18-month period, in a building on the corner of what are now called Houston and Soledad streets, "JAG" minted 8,000 jolas bearing his own initials on the obverse. The reverse was blank except for a small, five-pointed star at the center, which some say constitutes the earliest use of the Lone Star of Texas.

"JAG" was José Antonio de la Garza, a San Antonian by birth and a widely respected gentleman "don" who, in 1823, during the government-mandated secularization of mission estates, managed to obtain for himself the Mission San Francisco de la Espada with its two-league tract of ranchland. It is quite likely that Don José paid his workers with jolas. Certainly he retained his high status in the region until his death in 1851, because eventually a Texas county was named after him.

In 1958, the 18-year-old James J. Zotz Jr. and two family members unearthed 60 or so pieces at a site being excavated for a flood-control project. His father, a part-time coin dealer, recognized the coins' possible importance and researched their history. Details are given by Katherine M. Jaeger in *100 Greatest American Medals and Tokens*, 2007. It is estimated that fewer than 100 are known today. The first publication of the token may have been in *The Numismatist* in 1903. These tokens became especially popular after they were listed in the Red Book.

Numismatic Aspects

W-8540 • Small Planchet

Designs as below. *Notes:* Breen-1081, copper, 17 mm. Small planchet. Usually with porous surfaces, sometimes conserved to give a glossy appearance. *Rarity:* URS-6.

VF-20	EF-40
$12,000	$22,000

W-8542 • Large Planchet

Obverse: JAG / 2 / 1 [2 and 1 horizontal] / 1818, all letters and numbers very crude. Crude spikes around the edge as dentils. *Reverse:* Five-pointed star stamped on the finished coin (and thus recessed). *Edge:* Plain. *Notes:* Breen-1082, copper, 19 mm. Large planchet. Usually with porous surfaces, sometimes conserved to give a glossy appearance. *Rarity:* URS-6.

VF-20	EF-40	AU-50
$12,000	$22,000	

9

EUROPEAN COINS AND TOKENS FOR AMERICA, LATER ISSUES

INTRODUCTION

British Conder Tokens With American Themes

From about 1787 to the turn of the 19th century, millions of copper tokens were struck in England in Birmingham (mainly) and London, circulating at the value of a halfpenny. Many of these served as a medium of exchange in England at a time when official halfpence were scarce, for official coinage of regal halfpence ceased after 1775. Soon it became a popular pursuit to collect them. A passion arose, and private mints tried to outdo each other in the creation of unusual motifs and varieties, as well as dies illogically combined with each other. Variations in edge lettering added other possibilities.

Certain of these tokens have American themes and are widely collected on this side of the Atlantic. Included are a handful of issues listed in the Red Book, among which are the 1787 Auctori Plebis, 1794 Franklin Press, circa 1792 to 1794 Kentucky token, 1796 Myddelton token, and others, including some with Washington's portrait. The circa 1798 Theatre at New York copper token, about the size of a English penny, is eagerly sought as well. In the same family as the halfpence are the 1794 and 1795 Talbot, Allum & Lee cents, made in Birmingham and exported to America to serve in circulation, although English collectors took notice of them as well, and some illogical combinations were made for their pleasure.

Today, specialists usually refer to the copper issues of this period as Conder tokens, because English collector James Conder prepared a listing of them in 1798. Conder's was not the first listing but happened to be the one posterity smiled upon. Conder lived in Ipswich, Suffolk. His book was titled *An Arrangement of Political Coins, Tokens, and Medalets, issued in Great Britain, Ireland, and the Colonies, within the last 20 years, from the farthing to the penny size.* Conder was born in 1761. He issued tokens on his own, some of which depicted Cardinal Thomas Wolsey. One of his tokens has the edge lettered PAYABLE AT CONDER'S DRAPERY WAREHOUSE, IPSWICH and was produced in 1796. Conder's cabinet was auctioned in 1855 by Sotheby and Wilkinson in London.

A predecessor to Conder was Thomas Spence, a prolific issuer of tokens who in 1795 published *The Coin Collector's Companion. Being a Descriptive Alphabetical List of the Modern Provincial, Political, and Other Copper Coins.* The text was up to date and included several tokens collected by Americans today. Second on the list was what is known today as the Kentucky token.

In 1910, *The Provincial Coinage of the Eighteenth Century*, written by Richard Dalton and S.H. Hamer and nearly 570 pages in length, updated and vastly expanded the Conder effort.

In addition to those issues properly counted as part of the Conder token series, many "evasion halfpence" were issued. These had designs similar to the regal issues, but with some differences in the lettering to evade counterfeiting laws.

The Bushnell Commentary

In 1859 Charles I. Bushnell, one of the leading numismatists and researchers of the time, published *An Historical Account of the First Three Business Tokens Issued in the City of New York, N.Y.* The book discussed Talbot, Allum & Lee cents, offering this about illogical combinations in the Conder token series:

> These mules were struck for exclusive circulation in England and were issued at a time when the rage for provincial half-pence extended to a degree almost incredible, threatening at one time even to supersede the national currency. Patronized by the nobility, and encouraged by the wealthy, die sinkers vied with each other in the number they produced.
>
> Obverses and reverses bearing no relation to each other were used for the production of illegitimate varieties, whose only value was their novelty, while impressions even from unfinished dies were bought at extravagant sums, merely for the selfish gratification of having what others had not. Varieties of collar were made to produce varieties of edge; old hubs were ferreted out to multiply specimens supposed to be unique, while worn-out and discarded dies were lapped, and impressions therefrom palmed off upon inexperienced but enthusiastic young collectors as Proofs.
>
> Tokens ridiculing even the collectors themselves were put forth and eagerly bought up as soon as issued by a throng of voracious antiquarians. Of these caustic emissions, the most celebrated was the collectors' half-penny token, by [Obediah] Westwood, of two varieties of reverse. One of them, bearing a representation of a race between two persons mounted on asses, ridiculed the reckless passion for collecting, in the legend *"Asses Running for Half Pence,"* while the other, being intended as a sarcasm upon the encouragement shown to the production of ridiculous combinations, bore the representation of an ass and a mule in private consultation, with the legend emanating from the mouth of the former, *"Be assured, friend Mule, you never shall want my protection."*
>
> So great was the demand for copper tokens that no less than 600 tons' weight were coined in Birmingham alone from the year 1787 to the year 1797. The profit to the publisher on one ton alone, as shown by an estimate furnished by a manufacturer, was no less a sum than £64/13/4. It is not surprising, therefore, that the sale of these pieces was a source of great profit to dealers, and that many of them soon retired with means not only adequate for their support through life, but also amply sufficient for the enjoyment of almost every luxury which they might or could desire.
>
> This mania in England for tokens, which commenced in 1787 and continued until the year 1797, received in that year an effectual check in the issue by the [English] government of 500 tons of copper coined into pennies of an ounce weight each, pursuant to a contract made with the ingenious Mr. [Matthew] Boulton, of Soho.

In 1797 a flood of official copper farthings, halfpence, pence, and twopence pieces struck at the Soho Mint was placed into circulation, easing the shortage of coppers. This spelled the end of issuing private halfpence in volume, although pieces continued to be made later.

In the second half of the 20th century it was popular for numismatic writers, Walter Breen in particular, to attribute to specific English engravers and mints the various Conder and other pieces (such as Nova Constellatio coppers, Immune Columbia coppers, etc.) with American inscriptions or connections. Sometimes this was pure speculation. Other times it hinged on a related die being combined with a store card of an English token manufacturer. The assumption did not include the possibility that dies were exchanged among manufacturers. Many attributions should be taken with a grain of salt today, unless there is documentary evidence.

While the Soho Mint made some "evasion halfpence," shops such as those of Peter Kempson and, in particular, William Lutwyche turned out large quantities. R.N.P. Hawkins, in *A Dictionary of Makers of British Metallic Tickets, Checks, Medalets, Tallies, and Counters 1788–1910*, states that Lutwyche utilized the engraving talents of Roger Dixon, Francis Arnold, Peter Wyon, Noel Alexandre Ponthon, and, in London, Benjamin Jacobs and Charles James. Hawkins wrote that none of the Lutwyche dies are known combined with those of any other manufacturer.

Talbot, Allum & Lee Cents 1794–1795

Talbot, Allum & Lee cent of 1794. (Engraving by John Gavit for O'Callaghan, *The Documentary History of the State of New-York*, 1850)

History of the Company

On the American numismatic scene the most widely known Conder tokens are those imported by Talbot, Allum & Lee in 1794 and 1795, to be placed into circulation to advertise the business. At 241 Water Street in lower New York City, the firm engaged in the India trade, importing goods by ship. The partnership operated only two years, from 1794 to 1796. Principals included William Talbot, William Allum, and James Lee. This particular district of the city was a beehive of activity, with vessels continually arriving and departing. Numerous ships' chandlers, grog houses, cheap lodging places, and other establishments for the convenience of sailors did a lively business.

Copper tokens dated 1794 and 1795, bearing the image of the standing goddess of Liberty with a bale representing commerce on the obverse and a fully rigged sailing ship on the reverse, were struck to the order of Talbot, Allum & Lee by Peter Kempson & Co., Birmingham, and imported into America by the partners. Their quantity has been estimated at over 200,000 coins, but no original records have been located.

Tokens dated 1794 were put into circulation, at the value of one cent, in local and regional commerce, alongside coppers bearing imprints of the various states, Nova Constellatio, and other inscriptions, as well as federal copper cents first struck at the Philadelphia Mint in 1793. Talbot, Allum & Lee tokens dated 1795 seem to have been less popular. Apparently, undistributed tokens piled up at the waterfront store. What should be done with the hoard?

To the Philadelphia Mint

The answer came quickly. On April 23, 1795, the firm sold 1,076 pounds of the tokens to the Philadelphia Mint for 18¢ per pound, or $193.68. On December 10, 1796, the Mint purchased the remainder, amounting to 1,914 pounds of copper, from William Talbot for $319, or 16.6¢ per pound. These tokens weighed in at about 46 to 50 to the pound, equivalent to around 140,000 to 150,000 pieces acquired in the Mint's two purchases.

The coins were a godsend to the Mint, which had been experiencing severe difficulties obtaining copper stock from which to strike half cents and cents. Cooper supplies were erratic, of uncertain quality and included such varied sources as copper sheet for roofing and the protection of ships' hulls, barrel hoops, and old pots and kettles.

Planchets for U.S. half cents were cut by punching discs from the Talbot, Allum & Lee tokens, most of which were probably in mint condition. Today it is not unusual to find a 1795 or 1797 U.S. half cent (but none dated 1796) with faint traces remaining of the token undertype—usually some of the ship's rigging and/or some of the letters around the border of the token. Such half cents are highly prized by numismatists as they are literally two coins in one. Two 1795 cents are known overstruck on these tokens, one owned by Dan Holmes, the other by John Wright.

Description of the Tokens

Talbot, Allum & Lee tokens dated 1794 and 1795 bear the standing figure of Liberty (holding a pole with a liberty cap) on the obverse, with LIBERTY & COMMERCE surrounding, and the date at the bottom border. On the reverse is a sailing ship. Those of 1794 have ONE CENT as part of the inscription on the reverse and PAYABLE AT THE STORE OF lettered on the edge. Those dated 1795 have the denomination on the lettered edge: WE PROMISE TO PAY THE BEARER ONE CENT. Details are given below.

Certain other odd die combinations and unusual styles of edge lettering were made for numismatists in England, who collected them with a passion, per the Bushnell commentary. Talbot, Allum & Lee obverse dies (featuring the goddess of Liberty) were muled with completely irrelevant reverses, such as one picturing a bird and the inscription PROMISSORY HALFPENNY, another pertaining to the Blofield Cavalry, and another depicting the York Cathedral.

Numismatic Aspects

In 1859 Bushnell considered the 1795 Talbot, Allum & Lee cent to be "by far the rarest, fewer from that die having been struck." This would seem to indicate that 1795 tokens, considered to be fairly plentiful in high grades by numismatists today, were scarce in America in 1859. When Talbot, Allum & Lee tokens and other Conder tokens bearing inscriptions relating to America started having significant value to collectors in the United States, beginning in the 1930s and 1940s, numismatists found that London dealers (primarily Spink & Son, A.H. Baldwin & Sons, and B.A. Seaby, Ltd.) had such pieces in inventory among regular English tokens. Thus, many were sold to Americans. After this time examples of Uncirculated 1795 tokens became readily available in U.S. collector and dealer holdings.

In a related work, *Early New York Tokens*, 1858, Bushnell described four obverse and two reverse dies for 1794 tokens, but just one pair for those dated 1795. In addition, six mulings were listed. In 1875's *Early American Coins*, Sylvester S. Crosby commented on the Bushnell study, concluding: "Six 'mules' with reverses of these tokens are described in Bushnell's work, but as they bear no evidence of having been intended for America, we omit them."

From the mid-19th century to the present, the Talbot, Allum & Lee tokens have been featured in virtually every comprehensive reference work on American coins and in countless auction and sale catalogs. Emphasis has been on the regular issues intended for circulation in America. While certain die varieties and mulings are rare, common issues of 1794 or 1795 are inexpensive on the numismatic market. Those dated 1794 are usually seen with light wear, while it is not unusual to encounter Mint State specimens dated 1795. Many of the latter have prooflike fields and are marketed as "Proofs." Most are fairly well struck, especially 1795 issues. As for the mulings, these are not widely known; they are not listed in the Red Book. Help is provided by *Walter Breen's Complete Encyclopedia of U.S. and Colonial Coins*, 1988, which gives detailed descriptions. A basic set of mulings forms a nice display. The rarest is the York Cathedral variety.

1794 Without NEW YORK

W-8560 · copper

Obverse: Liberty standing with pole and cap. LIBERTY & COMMERCE / 1794 around border. Peak of cap at left side of & [ampersand]. Large "&:" top of & far above tops of nearby letters. *Reverse:* Sailing ship headed to the right. TALBOT ALLUM & LEE. / ONE CENT around border. Without NEW YORK above ship. *Edge:* PAYABLE AT THE STORE OF. *Notes:* Fuld-1, Breen-1028. The is the famous rarity in the series. Usually seen well worn. This early issue seems to have been nearly entirely placed into circulation. The obverse die failed at the right and was probably used for only a short time. Five were in the Ford collection, the finest About Uncirculated. *Rarity:* URS-7.

G-4	VG-8	F-12	VF-20	EF-40	AU-50
	$600	$1,500	$3,500	$6,500	$11,000

W-8565 · silver
As preceding, but in silver. *Rarity:* URS-3.

1794 With NEW YORK

W-8570 · Large "&" on reverse · lettered edge
Obverse: Same as preceding. *Reverse:* Sailing ship headed to the right. With NEW YORK above ship. On die 1, upper left of N (NEW) is below lower right tip of T (TALBOT). Rare die. *Edge:* PAYABLE AT THE STORE OF. *Notes:* Fuld-2, Breen-1029 (thick planchet) and 1030 (thin). High-grade coins are usually prooflike, often classified as Proof. *Rarity:* URS-12.

VG-8	F-12	VF-20	EF-40	AU-50	MS-60	MS-63
$85	$150	$275	$525	$900	$1,400	$2,000

W-8575 · plain edge
Design as above. *Edge:* Plain. *Notes:* Breen-1031. *Rarity:* URS-4.

Selected auction price(s): Ford II Sale (5/2004), VF, $2,530.

W-8580 · Small "&" on reverse · lettered edge · copper
Obverse: Liberty standing with pole and cap. LIBERTY & COMMERCE / 1794 around border. Peak of cap just past Y (LIBERTY). Top of "&" [ampersand] at same level as tops of nearby letters. *Reverse:* Die 1, as preceding. *Edge:* PAYABLE AT THE STORE OF. *Notes:* Fuld-3, Breen-1032. Thick planchets. None in the Ford collection. *Rarity:* URS-5.

Selected auction price(s): ANA Sale (Superior 8/2002), PF-64BD (PCGS), $3,335. Pre–Long Beach Sale (Superior 5/2003), PF-65BB (NGC), $4,025. Pre–Long Beach Sale (Superior 1/2004), MS-66BD (PCGS), $4,888. FUN No. 1 (Heritage 1/2005), PF-65BN (PCGS), $3,393. NY Signature Sale 380 (Heritage 6/2005), MS-66BN (PCGS), $4,313. Long Beach Sale (Heritage 9/2005), PF-64BN (PCGS), $2,070. FUN Sale (Heritage, 1/2007), PF-64 BN (PCGS), $3,738. Pre–Long Beach Sale (I. & L. Goldberg 2/2007), MS-64BN PL, $2,645.

W-8585 · plain edge
Design as above. *Edge:* Plain. *Notes:* Fuld 3-A, Breen-1033. *Rarity:* URS-4.

Selected auction price(s): Ford II Sale (5/2004), MS, $4,600.

W-8587 · lettered edge · silver
Design as above, but silver. *Edge:* PAYABLE AT THE STORE OF. *Notes:* Breen-1033. *Rarity:* URS-3.

Selected auction price(s): Ford II Sale (5/2004), Choice PF, $40,250.

W-8590 · Small "&" on reverse · lettered edge · copper
Obverse: Same as preceding. *Reverse:* From die 2. Upper left of N (NEW) distant from lower right tip of T (TALBOT). The most commonly seen die. *Edge:* PAYABLE AT THE STORE OF. *Notes:* Fuld-4, Breen-1032. Thick planchets. *Rarity:* URS-12.

G-4	VG-8	F-12	VF-20	EF-40	AU-50	MS-60
$200	$300	$800	$2,000	$3,500	$5,000	

W-8595 · plain edge
Design as above. *Edge:* Plain. *Notes:* Fuld 4-A, Breen-1033. *Rarity:* URS-3.

W-8600 · lettered edge · silver
Design as above, but silver. *Edge:* PAYABLE AT THE STORE OF. Breen-1034. *Rarity:* URS-3.

1795

W-8620 · WE PROMISE TO PAY THE BEARER ONE CENT
Obverse: Standing figure as used the preceding year. LIBERTY & COMMERCE / 1795 around border. Tip of cap below lower right serif of Y. Small &. In date, 7 partly under a dentil, 9 and 5 touch dentils. *Reverse:* Sailing ship. AT THE STORE OF TALBOT ALLUM & LEE NEW YORK around border. *Edge:* WE PROMISE TO PAY THE BEARER ONE CENT. *Notes:* Fuld-1, Breen-1035 (thick planchet), 1036 (thin planchet). This is far and away the most common Talbot, Allum & Lee cent. Usually seen in Mint State, often prooflike (sometimes called Proof). Just one pair of dies was used for the coinage. Thin (usual) and thick planchets. *Rarity:* URS-13.

VG-8	F-12	VF-20	EF-40	AU-50	MS-60	MS-63
$80	$140	$245	$400	$650	$1,100	$1,300

W-8630 · CURRENT EVERYWHERE
Design as above. *Edge:* CURRENT EVERYWHERE. *Notes:* Breen-1037. *Rarity:* URS-1.

Selected auction price(s): Ford II Sale (5/2004), Choice EF, $6,325.

W-8635 · CAMBRIDGE BEDFORD HUNTINGTON
Design as above. *Edge:* CAMBRIDGE BEDFORD HUNTINGTON. X.X. *Rarity:* URS-1.

W-8640 · plain edge
Design as above. *Edge:* Plain. *Rarity:* URS-1 or 2.

W-8650 · two leaves on edge
Design as above. *Edge:* With two leaves. *Rarity:* URS-1 or 2.

Talbot, Allum & Lee Mulings

W-8665 · 1794 T.A. & L. / 1793 Birmingham halfpenny · boy · lettered edge · copper
Obverse: Die of 1794 (W-8580). *Reverse:* Boy standing with vertical screw with arms above, possibly the top of a coining press. BIRMINGHAM HALFPENNY / 1793 around border. *Edge:* PAYABLE IN LONDON. *Notes:* Fuld Mule-1, Breen-1040. Plentiful in the context of mulings. *Rarity:* URS-8.

AU-50	MS-60	MS-63	MS-65
$1,000	$2,500	$4,000	

W-8501 · brass
Design as preceding, but in brass. *Notes:* Breen-1042. *Rarity:* URS-1 or 2.

W-8660 · plain edge · copper
Design as preceding, but in copper. *Edge:* Plain. *Notes:* Breen-1041. Breen calls extremely rare. Ford Proof described as possibly unique, the Fuld plate coin. *Rarity:* URS-1 or 2.

Selected auction price(s). Ford II Sale (5/2004), Choice PF, $1,610.

W-8670 · 1794 T.A. & L. / 1793 promissory halfpenny · stork · PAYABLE AT THE WAREHOUSE LIVERPOOL XXX · copper
Obverse: Die of 1794 (W-8580). *Reverse:* Stork standing, facing to right. PROMISSORY HALFPENNY / 1793 around border. *Edge:* PAYABLE AT THE WAREHOUSE LIVERPOOL XXX. *Notes:* Fuld Mule-2, Breen-1043. Double dated, 1794 on obverse, 1793 on reverse. *Rarity:* URS-9.

AU-50	MS-60	MS-63	MS-65
$1,000	$2,500	$4,000	

W-8680 · brass
Design as preceding but struck in brass. *Notes:* Breen-1046. *Rarity:* URS-1, not presently located.

W-8690 · PAYABLE IN LONDON · copper
Design as preceding. *Edge:* PAYABLE IN LONDON. *Notes:* Breen-1044. *Rarity:* URS-6.

Selected auction price(s). Ford II Sale (5/2004), Choice PF, $575; Choice PF, $603.75; Gem PF, $747.50. FUN Sale (Heritage, 1/2007), MS-64RB (PCGS), $3,450.

W-8700 · plain edge
Design as preceding. *Edge:* Plain. *Notes:* Breen-1045. *Rarity:* URS-3.

W-8710 · 1794 T.A. & L. / Earl Howe · copper
Obverse: Die of 1794 (W-8580). *Reverse:* Head and shoulders portrait facing left. EARL HOWE & THE GLORIOUS FIRST OF JUNE around border. Tip of cap points to left upright of H (THE). *Edge:* PAYABLE IN LONDON. *Notes:* Fuld Mule-3, Breen-1047. Typically lightly struck at the reverse center and with tips of reverse letters off the planchet; die often cracked; a mismatching of die diameters. Richard, Earl Howe was the same Admiral Howe noted on the 1778 and 1779 Rhode Island Ship medal. *Rarity:* URS-9.

AU-50	MS-60	MS-63	MS-65
$900	$2,000	$3,500	

W-8525 · tin
Design as preceding, but tip of hat points to E (THE). Tin. *Notes:* Fuld Mule-4, Breen-1048. Ford collection. *Rarity:* URS-1.

W-8720 · 1794 T.A. & L. / John Howard · lettered edge
Obverse: Die of 1794 (W-8580). *Reverse:* Head and shoulders portrait facing left. IOHN HOWARD F.R.S. PHILANTHROPIST. around border—Howard (1726–1790) was a fellow of the Royal Society (F.R.S.) and prominent in social reform, including improvement of conditions in prisons. *Edge:* PAYABLE IN LONDON. *Notes:* Fuld Mule-5, Breen-1049. First name with I instead of J. Reverse seen with many cracks around border. *Rarity:* URS-9.

AU-50	MS-60	MS-63	MS-65
$900	$2,000	$3,500	

W-8531 · plain edge
Design as preceding. *Edge:* Plain. *Rarity:* URS-3.

W-8725 · 1795 T.A. & L. / Blofield Cavalry
Obverse: Die of 1795 (W-8730). *Reverse:* Military gear with BLOFIELD CAVALRY above and FIFTH TROOP: on ribbon. *Edge:* Serpentine line and dots. *Notes:* Fuld Mule-6, Breen-1051. *Rarity:* URS-8.

AU-50	MS-60	MS-63	MS-65
$1,500	$3,000	$5,000	

W-8730 · 1795 T.A. & L. / 1795 York Cathedral · FEAR GOD AND HONOUR THE KING
Obverse: Die of 1795 (W-8730). *Reverse:* Angular view of cathedral with YORK 1795 below. *Edge:* FEAR GOD AND HONOUR THE KING. *Notes:* Fuld Mule-7A, Breen-1052. Rarest of the basic types of Talbot, Allum & Lee mulings. *Rarity:* URS-7.

AU-50	MS-60	MS-63	MS-65
$1,500	$3,000	$5,000	

W-8755 · PAYABLE ON DEMAND
Design as above. *Edge:* PAYABLE ON DEMAND. *Rarity:* URS-1.

W-8760 · plain edge
Design as above. *Edge:* Plain. *Rarity:* URS-1, not presently located.

AUCTORI PLEBIS TOKEN
1787

The 1787 Auctori Plebis token, struck in England, has on the obverse a draped bust facing left, very similar to the design found on Vermont and Connecticut copper cents of the same era. There is no reason to associate the production of these tokens with America other than the similarity of the obverse motif, although American catalogs have listed it for a long time. As part of the Conder token series it circulated in England at least by 1795, by which time it was listed in *The Virtuoso's Companion*. Other tokens with non-American portraits are described in *Walter Breen's Complete Encyclopedia of U.S. and Colonial Coins*, 1988.

W-8770 · 1787 Auctori Plebis
Obverse: Mailed Bust Left of King George II, of the style used on certain Connecticut and Vermont coppers. AUCTORI: PLEBIS: and cinquefoils around border. Style-wise, a close copy of a state copper of the 1786 era. *Reverse:* Seated figure with anchor, globe, and lion. INDEP ET LIBER at top and side border, 1787 at bottom. *Edge:* Plain. *Notes:* Breen-1147. Lightly struck at the obverse center. The entire obverse die is shallowly cut. Grading is best done by evaluating the reverse. The latter is only rarely found with all lettering and a full date on the planchet. Most examples show light wear. *Rarity:* URS-10.

G-4	VG-8	F-12	VF-20	EF-40	AU-50	MS-60
$100	$160	$325	$750	$1,400	$2,900	

KENTUCKY TOKENS
c. 1793–1795

The so-called Kentucky token, produced in England, was made in large quantities. The obverse illustrates a hand holding a scroll on which is imprinted the inscription OUR CAUSE IS JUST (adapted from Washington's Proclamation of Neutrality, 1793). Surrounding is the legend UNANIMITY IS THE STRENGTH OF SOCIETY. An item in the *American Journal of Numismatics*, January 1884, stated that the Most Noble Order of Bucks, location not given, in 1756 had as its motto, "Unanimity is the strength of society." Further:

> Their club room, decorated with a buck's head and antlers; and their social brotherhood, surrounded with bottles, bowls, and glasses, appear somewhat elevated with conviviality and good cheer; but they are not distinguished by any peculiarity of dress as the Freemasons are in their lodges.

The reverse depicts a pyramid of 15 stars, each with 12 points, surrounded by rays. On each star is the abbreviation of a state with K, representing Kentucky, at the top, hence the token's name; otherwise there is no connection with the 15th state, admitted to the Union on June 1, 1792. E PLURIBUS UNUM surrounds.

These are not known to have circulated in America. Rather, they were made as part of the English Conder token series, widely collected by English numismatists and others at the time. These were struck in a number of different varieties distinguished by their thickness and variations in edge lettering inscriptions. Most often seen is the Plain Edge variety. Probably well over 1,000 Kentucky tokens are in the hands of numismatists. The typical grades are rather high and range from Very Fine though Uncirculated, with Extremely Fine to About Uncirculated being about average. Often such pieces have glossy surfaces. The planchets used were of very high quality. The diagonally reeded edge style is rare, and the PAYABLE AT LANCASTER variety is scarce. Other varieties are seldom seen.

W-8800 · plain edge · copper
Obverse: Hand holding scroll inscribed OUR CAUSE IS JUST. UNANIMITY IS THE STRENGTH OF SOCIETY around border. *Reverse:* Pyramid with 15 letters representing as many different states, with K (for Kentucky) at the top, rays around. At the border is E PLURIBUS UNUM. *Edge:* Plain. *Notes:* Breen-1154 (thick) and 1155 (thin). In the 19th century this was often called the triangle cent. Thick (scarcer) and thin planchets, but not often differentiated as such. Sometimes seen with extensive wear indicated these circulated widely. *Rarity:* URS-12.

VF-20	EF-40	AU-50	MS-60	MS-63
$215	$400	$700	$900	$1,250

W-8805 · reeded edge
Design as preceding. *Edge:* Diagonally reeded (sometimes erroneously called "engrailed"). *Notes:* Usually seen in higher grades; made for collectors. Breen-1162. *Rarity:* URS-6.

F-12	VF-20	EF-40	AU-50	MS-60	MS-63	MS-65
	$550	$950	$1,600	$2,300	$3,600	

W-8810 · PAYABLE IN LONDON LANCASTER OR BRISTOL
Design as preceding. *Edge:* PAYABLE IN LONDON LANCASTER OR BRISTOL. Thick and thin planchets, so edge-lettering size can vary. *Notes:* Usually seen in higher grades; made for collectors. Breen-1156 to 1159. *Rarity:* URS-7.

AU-50	MS-60	MS-63
$800	$1,000	$1,350

W-8815 · PAYABLE AT BEDWORTH NUNEATON OR HINKLEY
Design as preceding. *Edge:* PAYABLE AT BEDWORTH NUNEATON OR HINKLEY. *Notes:* Breen-1159. Norweb collection. *Rarity:* URS-1.

W-8818 · PAYABLE AT I. FIELDINGS MANCHESTER
Design as preceding. *Edge:* PAYABLE AT I. FIELDINGS MANCHESTER (relates to John Fieldings of Manchester). *Notes:* Discovered by Richard Picker; published in 1962 in the *Colonial Newsletter*. Breen-1161. *Rarity:* URS-1.

W-8820 · AN ASYLUM FOR THE OPPRESS'D OF ALL NATIONS
Design as preceding. *Edge:* AN ASYLUM FOR THE OPPRESS'D OF ALL NATIONS. *Notes:* Breen-1160. Reported by James Atkins, *Coins and Tokens of the Possessions and Colonies of the British Empire*, 1889. *Rarity:* Not traced.

W-8822 · BIRMINGHAM LONDON OR BRISTOL
Design as preceding. *Edge:* BIRMINGHAM LONDON OR BRISTOL. *Rarity:* URS-1 or 2.
Selected auction price(s): John J. Ford Jr. VII Sale (Stack's, 1/2005), Choice EF, $3,450.

W-8825 · lines and dots
Design as preceding. *Edge:* No lettering; ornamented with series of lines and dots. *Notes:* Breen-1163. Eric P. Newman collection. *Rarity:* URS-1.

W-8828 · silver
Design as preceding, but struck in silver. *Notes:* Breen-1164. *AJN*, October 1870, reported that in 1843, Blick's sale in London included a "Kentucky token struck in silver." *Rarity:* Not traced.

W-8835 · LANCASTER · white metal
Obverse die trial in white metal. *Edge:* LANCASTER. Sydney Miller collection. *Rarity:* URS-1.

Franklin Press Tokens
1794

The Franklin Press token, struck in England, pictures on the obverse a hand press. Its association with a shop in London where Benjamin Franklin once worked has made this 1794 issue popular with American numismatists. It is a part of the Conder token series, in this instance a variety that circulated widely, and attributed by Walter Breen to Lutwyche's mint in Birmingham.

W-8850 · plain edge
Obverse: Wood-frame hand printing press of the type operated by Benjamin Franklin, date 1794 below. SIC ORITOR DOCTRINA SURGETQUE LIBERTAS ("Thus learning

advances and liberty grows") around border. *Reverse:* PAYABLE / AT / THE FRANKLIN / PRESS / LONDON. *Edge:* Plain. *Notes:* Breen-1165. One of the more plentiful Conder tokens associated with America. Usually seen with a heavy horizontal die break at the center and slightly right on the obverse, within the press; also with a bulge at T (LIBERTAS). Rarely seen with any significant amount of original mint red-orange color. *Rarity:* URS-13.

F-12	VF-20	EF-40	AU-50	MS-60	MS-63	MS-65
	$275	$450	$800	$1,050	$1,400	

W-8855 · AN ASYLUM FOR THE OPPRESS'D OF ALL NATIONS

Design as preceding. *Edge:* AN ASYLUM FOR THE OPPRESS'D OF ALL NATIONS (as regularly used on the 1795 Liberty and Security halfpenny). *Notes:* Breen-1166. In English collection. *Rarity:* URS-1.

W-8860 · reeded edge

Design as preceding. *Edge:* Diagonally reeded. *Notes:* John J. Ford Jr. collection. *Rarity:* URS-1.

W-8865 · British East India Company emblem

Obverse: Design as preceding. Struck on crude planchet. *Reverse:* Impression of British East India Company emblem. *Notes:* Discovered by Howland Wood. American Numismatic Society. *Rarity:* URS-1.

P.P.P. MYDDELTON TOKENS 1796

P.P.P. Myddelton token, 1796. (A.M. Smith, *Visitor's Guide & History of the United States Mint*, 1885)

In 1875, in *The Early Coins of America*, Sylvester S. Crosby paid this piece the ultimate compliment: "In beauty of design and execution, the tokens are unsurpassed by any piece issued for American circulation." Today, the Myddelton tokens are still considered to be among the most attractive early issues. In reality, these were not issued for American circulation, although it was the intention of their originator, Philip Parry Price (a.k.a. Philip Parry Price Myddelton), to do so. Instead, circumstances intervened. Today, examples of this token are known in silver and the slightly scarcer copper, all with Proof finish, and distributed to dealers in and collectors of Conder tokens.

The obverse is inscribed BRITISH SETTLEMENT KENTUCKY and illustrates Hope (representing Britain) presenting two of her children to the goddess Liberty who welcomes them with an outstretched arm, behind her a cornucopia of plenty representing the bounty of America. The reverse shows the goddess Britannia, dejected and defeated, her tyranny against America having been thwarted by losing the Revolutionary War.

Myddelton, an Englishman, acquired a tract of land in northern Kentucky along the Ohio River and sought to create an extensive settlement there to be populated by his countrymen. On August 24, 1796, it was reported that "Middleton" had been convicted in London, under the provisions of an act of 1783, of enticing English "artificers" (craftsmen and artistic workers) to emigrate there, for which offense he was sentenced to a year in Newgate prison. By that time he had convinced "the greater part of 1,200" laborers and cultivators to go to America, "the greater part of whom have since arrived in several parts of the United States." (*CNL*, December 1963, contribution by Richard Picker; December 1999, Richard Margolis) His time in Newgate was actually three-and-a-half years, effectively ending Myddelton's dream of further colonization.

The dies for this beautiful token were cut by Conrad Küchler, a gifted artist who about the same time prepared the three different Washington Seasons medal motifs (The Farmer, The Shepherd, The Home). On January 24, 1796, Myddelton wrote to Matthew Boulton, partner in the Soho Mint in Birmingham, requesting these motifs for the obverse and reverse.

> The figure of Liberty holding out her hand to welcome two little genii presented to her by Hope, at the feet of the figure of Liberty the Emblems of Peace and Plenty. Legend "British Settlement Kentucky 1796."
>
> Britannia with her head pendant, her spear reversed and leaning on her shield, before her the demons of Discord and Tyranny treading under foot the Emblems of Liberty and Justice. Legend "Payable by P.P.P. Myddelton."

Likely, any loyal Britisher would consider the reverse emblems seditious. On March 8, 1796, the first silver pieces, thought to have numbered 53, were delivered to Myddelton at a cost of 2 shillings sixpence each (about 50¢). On the 19th of the same month, 11 copper examples with bronzed finish (toned brown to highlight the artistry) were delivered at sixpence each. Myddelton intended to order a large quantity of copper pieces to take to America the same year. This further amount was never made. Most of the silver coins were returned by the buyer. It is likely that additional pieces in both metals were struck for collectors sometime afterward, the copper pieces lacking the bronzed finish. Early in the 19th century the obverse of the Myddelton token was muled with an unrelated reverse die pertaining to the Copper Company of Upper Canada.

W-8900 · bronzed copper

Obverse: Standing figure of Liberty welcomes two British youth presented to her by Hope. Emblems of peace and plenty. BRITISH SETTLEMENT KENTUCKY / 1796 around border. *Reverse:* Seated Britannia, head downward, treading on emblems of peace and justice. PAYABLE BY P.P.P. MYDDELTON around border. *Edge:* Plain. *Notes:* Breen-1074. Part of the Conder token series. Not a circulating issue. Scarcer than the silver issue. *Rarity:* URS-5.

PF-63
$30,000

W-8905 · silver
Designs and edge as preceding. Struck in silver. *Notes:* Breen-1073. *Rarity:* URS-6.

PF-63
$35,000

W-8910 · muling with Copper Company of Upper Canada halfpenny
Obverse: Same as W-8900. *Reverse:* Lettering at center in four lines: COPPER / COMPANY / OF UPPER / CANADA, with ONE HALF PENNY around border. *Edge:* Plain. *Notes:* Breen-1096. Struck in copper. A muling made for the numismatic trade. John J. Ford Jr. (communication) believed that all these tokens were made as numismatic souvenirs or samples, and that none were ever used in Canada. *Rarity:* URS-4.

PF-63
$16,500

THOMAS PAINE TOKENS
c. 1794–1797

American Patriot
The writings of Thomas Paine helped to inspire the American Revolution by bringing thoughts of liberty and freedom to American colonists. His views on human rights made him both admired and hated in his native England, and even to some degree in America. His famous pamphlets, *The Rights of Man* and *Common Sense*, brought him to prominence in both countries and made him the theme of numerous English political and satirical tokens linking him with fellow revolutionary activists Thomas Spence and Thomas More.

Paine was born in England in 1737 and died in New York City in 1809. He was invited to emigrate to the English colonies in America by Benjamin Franklin and arrived in Philadelphia in 1774 in time to take part in the American Revolution. It was Paine who proposed the name "United States of America" for the new nation.

Numismatic Aspects
This study, a new area for most specialists in American-related early coins, is largely the work of Kenneth Bressett, editor of the Red Book. "Listing these will be a radical departure from tradition, but I think these pieces are as meaningful as many of the other similar items that have been part of the colonial scene for decades," he commented. Had there been space in his Red Book, they would have been included there!

Made for collectors, many of the tokens are mulings of similar dies. The typical grades for these pieces are rather high and range from Very Fine though Uncirculated, with Extremely Fine to About Uncirculated being about average. A brief overview of Paine-related tokens is given here. Cross-references are to R. Dalton and S.H. Hamer ("D&H") in the "Middlesex" section of their text, *English Provincial Token Coinage of the 18th Century*. The following have been divided into categories by inscriptions. Whitman numbers have been assigned to these. Expanded descriptions of appearance and rarity may appear in a future edition of this book should Paine tokens become popular with American collectors.

Farthings

W-8920 · D&H 1105   **W-8926 · D&H 1107**

W-8932 · D&H 1109   **W-8934 · D&H 1110**

End of Pain. The "End of Pain" inscription has a double meaning—the end of suffering, as well as the end of Thomas Paine (although he lived for many years afterward). *Other End of Pain token varieties:* W-8922 (D&H 1106); W-8924 (D&H 1106a); W-8926 (D&H 1107); W-8928 (D&H 1108); W-8930 (D&H 1108a); W-8932 (D&H 1109); W-8934 (D&H 1110); W-8936 (D&H 1111); W-8938 (D&H 1111a).

VG-8	F-12	VF-20	EF-40	AU-50	MS-60	MS-63
	$80	$125	$200	$300	$550	$700

Advocates for the Rights of Man. Three advocates are referred to: Thomas Spence, Sir Thomas More, and Thomas Paine, all of whom were prosecuted or censured for their writings. *Other Advocates token varieties:* W-8950 (D&H 1112); W-8952 (D&H 1113); W-8954 (D&H 1114); W-8956 (D&H 1115); W-8958 (D&H 1116); W-8962 (D&H 1117); W-8964 (D&H 1118); W-8966 (D&H 1119).

VG-8	F-12	VF-20	EF-40	AU-50	MS-60	MS-63
	$70	$100	$150	$200	$400	$500

The Three Thomases. With inscriptions pertaining to Spence, More, and Paine. *Other Three Thomases token varieties:* W-8974 (D&H 1120); W-8978 (D&H 1120a); W-8980 (D&H 1121); W-8982 (D&H 1122); W-8984 (D&H 1123); W-8986 (D&H 1123a).

VG-8	F-12	VF-20	EF-40	AU-50	MS-60	MS-63
	$70	$100	$150	$200	$400	$500

Halfpence

Most motifs are similar to those found on farthings.

End of Pain. W-8980 (D&H 827); W-8982 (D&H 828); W-8984 (D&H 829); W-8986 (D&H 829a); W-8988 (D&H 830); W-8990 (D&H 830a); W-8992 (D&H 831); W-8994 (D&H 831a); W-8996 (D&H 832); W-8998 (D&H 833); W-9000 (D&H 833a); W-9002 (D&H 834); W-9004 (D&H 835); W-9006 (D&H 835); W-9010 (D&H 836).

VG-8	F-12	VF-20	EF-40	AU-50	MS-60	MS-63
	$80	$125	$200	$300	$550	$700

Noted Advocates for the Rights of Men [plural]. W-9020 (D&H 837); W-9022 (D&H 837); W-9024 (D&H 838); W-9026 (D&H 837).

VG-8	F-12	VF-20	EF-40	AU-50	MS-60	MS-63
	$70	$100	$150	$200	$400	$500

W-9060 · D&H 677

Noted Advocates for the Rights of Man [singular]. W-9030 (D&H 677); W-9040 (D&H 677); W-9043 (D&H 716); W-9046 (D&H 725); W-9049 (D&H 798); W-9052 (D&H 811); W-9055 (D&H 818); W-9060 (D&H 677); W-9063 (D&H 842); W-9066 (D&H 842a); W-9069 (D&H 842).

VG-8	F-12	VF-20	EF-40	AU-50	MS-60	MS-63
	$70	$100	$150	$200	$400	$500

THEATRE AT NEW YORK TOKEN
c. 1798

The Theatre at New York token has been popular in American circles for a long time. The *American Journal of Numismatics*, April 1868, noted "This rare and interesting token represents the Park Theatre, destroyed by fire [on] May 25, 1820, but afterwards rebuilt in a style somewhat different from that of the building exhibited on the coin."

The cornerstone was laid on May 5, 1795, on Chatham Row, New York City. At first called the New Theatre, the 2,300-seat facility officially opened on January 29, 1798. Featured was Shakespeare's *As You Like It*, preceded by an address by Mr. Hodgkinson and a prelude by Mr. Milne, and followed by "Purse, or American Tar," a musical entertainment. In 1806 the building was sold to John Jacob Astor and John K. Beekman for $50,000. They were the owners at the time of the fire.

It is presumed that this token was issued about 1798, when the popular passion in England for collecting Conder tokens was fading rapidly. Dies by Benjamin Jacob, a Birmingham engraver, auctioneer, and ironmonger, were used to create these pieces. Coining was done at a factory operated by Peter Skidmore, in partnership with his father John, at 15 Coppice Row, Clerkenwell, London, from 1797 to 1809. For years the elder Skidmore operated a London iron smithy, grate shop, and furniture store at 123 High Holborn Street.

The penny size is unusual in the context of Conder-style tokens and was part of a series of Skidmore issues of this format illustrating various buildings. All known examples are struck in copper and have Proof finish. These were made for collectors, not for use as advertising. Today, examples are scarce. About 20 are known.

W-9080 · penny token

Obverse: View of the theater copied from Longworth's *American Almanack, New-York Register, and City Directory*, 1797, a sketch by Elkanah Tisdale. The signature of Jacobs (sic) is below the building. THE THEATRE AT NEW YORK / AMERICA is around the border. *Reverse:* Dock with bales, anchor, and overflowing cornucopia in the foreground, two sailing ships in the distance. MAY COMMERCE FLOURISH at top and side border. *Edge:* I PROMISE TO PAY ON DEMAND THE BEARER ONE PENNY x.

Notes: Breen-1055. Copper. A Conder series–related token made for English collectors, but of American interest due to the obverse subject. John Kleeberg, in *The Theatre at New York: Coinage of the Americas Conference*, 1995, gives extensive details of the building and its history. *Rarity:* URS-6.

EF-40	PF-63
$15,000	$27,500

W-9085 · ANTIENT SCOTTISH WASHING muling
Muling with an irrelevant die for a token depicting "ANTIENT SCOTTISH WASHING," Dalton & Hamer Kinrosshire 1. Struck in white metal. *Notes:* Breen-1057. Existence not confirmed. *Rarity:* URS-1.

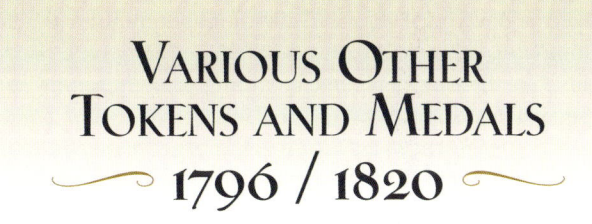

Various Other Tokens and Medals 1796 / 1820

Silver Castorland medal or jeton of 1796, a French issue. (Engraving by John Gavit for Hickcox, *An Historical Account of American Coinage*, 1858)

A French Colony in New York State

The 1796 Castorland jeton or "half dollar" medal pertains to a French settlement of that name proposed during the 1790s on the Black River, about 20 miles from the present-day city of Watertown in northern New York. Peter Chassanis of Paris purchased in August 1792 a tract of sugar maple forest in what is now Jefferson and Lewis counties, expected to be divided into 4,000 farms of 50 acres each, along the watershed of the Beaver River. The Compagnie de New York drew up an elaborate constitution designating Chassanis as head of the government, to be assisted by six commissaries. Two of the six would reside at the settlement seat, known as Castorville (*castor* is the French word for beaver). Four would remain in Paris. Chassanis and commissary Rodolphe Tillier were the only members to receive a salary; those remaining in France would be paid in silver tokens:

> In recognition of the care which they may bestow upon the common concerns, there shall be given them an attendance fee for each Special or General Assembly where they may meet on the affairs of the Company. The fee is fixed at two jetons of silver, of the weight of four or five gros. They shall be made at the expense of the company, under the direction of the commissaries, who shall decide on their form and design.

The *History of Lewis County* (New York) includes this poem by Caleb Lyon of Lyonsdale, concerning the Castorland piece:

> Then was struck a classic medal by this visionary band:
>> Sybele was on the silver, and beneath was Castorland;
>> The reverse a tree of maple, yielding forth its precious store,
>> Salve magna parens Frugum was the legend that it bore.

Castorland never lived up to expectations. Harsh winters, theft of company funds, inaccurate surveying mapping, and other difficulties ended the dream. The district remained thinly populated for years afterward.

Benjamin Duvivier, a stockholder in the company, is believed to have engraved the dies. The 1796 Castorland pieces were possibly intended to circulate at the value of a half dollar, for the size and weight is similar to the standard U.S. issue of the time. It is unlikely these ever saw use as money in the United States, as the settlement was not formed at the time.

Originals in silver and copper are elusive. Restrikes and copies were later made in silver, copper, and gold; today modern copies are available from the Paris Mint.

1796 Castorland Medals or Jetons

Original Castorland Medals

W-9100 · silver
Obverse: Crowned head of goddess Cybele, with CASTORLAND below head. FRANCO-AMERICANA COLONIA / 1796 around border. In date, 1 runs into a border bead. *Reverse:* Standing goddess, possibly Ceres, holding a cornucopia, with a rock maple tree nearby. A tap in the tree, complete with spigot, yields sap into a bucket below. At the bottom is a recumbent beaver. SALVE MAGNA PARENS FRUGUM at the border left and right. UG (FRUGUM) touch; no bulge at PARENS and no crack at the S of that word. *Notes:* Breen-1058. A small hoard of 14 pieces existed in the late 19th century, descended in a family connected with Castorland. One of these was studied by Michael J. Hodder in 1993 and found to be an impression from the early state of the die. *Edge:* Reeded. *Rarity:* URS-7, including hoard examples.

VF-20	EF-40	AU-50	MS-60	MS-63
	$7,000	$10,500	$12,000	$16,500

W-9110 · copper · reeded edge
Design as preceding, but struck in copper. *Edge:* Reeded. *Notes:* Breen-1059. *Rarity:* URS-4.

EF-40	AU-50	MS-60	MS-63
$8,500	$14,000	$25,000	

W-9115 · plain edge
Design as preceding. *Edge:* Plain. *Notes:* Thick planchet. *Rarity:* URS-2.

W-9120 · brass
Design as preceding, but struck in brass. *Notes:* Breen-1060. Garrett collection. At least two clichés or splasher impressions exist of the reverse die; one was in the Ford VII sale, lot 150. *Rarity:* URS-1.

Restrike Castorland Medals

W-9130 · early restrike · reeded edge · gold
As preceding, but with die defects at PARENS. *Edge:* Reeded. *Notes:* Breen-1058. Differences among early restrikes admit of differing numismatic opinions. See Breen's *Encyclopedia*, 1988, for expanded discussion. *Rarity:* URS-1, not traced today.

W-9135 · silver
Design as preceding, but struck in silver. *Notes:* Breen-1062. *Rarity:* URS-5.

EF-40	AU-50	MS-60	MS-63
	$30	$50	$70

W-9140 · copper
Design as preceding, but struck in copper. *Notes:* Breen-1063. *Rarity:* URS-6.

EF-40	AU-50	MS-60	MS-63
	$20	$30	$40

W-9150 · later restrike · reeded edge · silver
Obverse from original die, reverse from copy die. *Edge:* Reeded, some with ARGENT (for "silver") stamped over reeding. *Notes:* Breen-1064. Surface styles vary. *Rarity:* URS-6.

EF-40	AU-50	MS-60	MS-63	MS-65
$18	$20	$35	$50	$200

W-9155 · copper
Dies as preceding. *Edge:* Reeded, some with CUIVRE (for "copper") stamped over reeding. *Notes:* Breen-1065. Surface styles vary. *Rarity:* URS-7.

EF-40	AU-50	MS-60	MS-63	MS-65
$18	$20	$35	$50	$200

W-9160 · plain edge · gold
Copy dies. *Edge:* Plain, some with OR (for "gold") stamped. *Notes:* Breen-1069. Modern restrikes available today from the Paris Mint. Currently available. Prices vary. *Rarity:* Unlimited.

W-9165 · silver
Dies as preceding. *Edge:* Plain, some with ARGENT stamped. *Notes:* Breen-1070. Modern restrikes available today from the Paris Mint. Prices vary. *Rarity:* Unlimited for modern issues, earlier issues scarcer.

W-9170 · copper
Dies as preceding. *Edge:* Plain, some with CUIVRE stamped. *Notes:* Breen-1071, 1072. Earlier examples in this category are chocolate bronze, later are a lighter color. Modern restrikes available today from the Paris Mint. Prices vary. *Rarity:* Unlimited for modern issues, earlier issues scarcer.

1820 North West Company Token

The North West Company token, dated 1820 and depicting George IV on the obverse and a beaver on the reverse, is believed to have been struck in Birmingham by John Walker & Company. These were used in the Indian trade in the Pacific Northwest, particularly along the Columbia and Umpqua river valleys.

In 1821 the North West Company merged with the Hudson's Bay Company, and business continued under the latter name. Likely, these tokens were used through the 1820s to pay Indians in exchange for one beaver pelt. The tokens could be redeemed for merchandise.

W-9250 · brass
Obverse: Portrait of King George IV (crowned this year) facing right. TOKEN at top border, 1820 below portrait. *Reverse:* Beaver facing right. NORTH WEST at edge above, COMPANY below. *Edge:* With diagonally incuse "reeding" at the center part of the edge (not extending to the rims). *Notes:* Breen-1083. Brass. 28.6 mm. Nearly always seen with surface oxidation. Exceptions with smooth surfaces are worth a premium. Examples actually used in trade are holed at top for suspension on a cord. Two without holes have been reported. *Rarity:* URS-9.

F-12	VF-20	EF-40
$8,750	$15,000	

W-9252 · copper
Design as preceding, but struck in copper. *Notes:* Breen-1084. *Rarity:* URS-5.

Selected auction price(s): Long Beach Auction (Heritage 9/2007), F-15 (NGC), $11,500.

W-9255 · brass · security edge
Design as preceding, but struck in brass. *Edge:* Lightly impressed engrailed or security edge. *Notes:* Two reported, one in the Sydney Martin Collection. *Rarity:* URS-2.

10

Early Washington Coins and Tokens

The Life of Washington

George Washington, our first and most famous president, was born in Wakefield on Pope's Creek, Virginia, son of Augustine and Mary Ball Washington. His father died when he was 11. At age 16 he went to live with his brother Lawrence, who built the Mount Vernon estate (which George later inherited) on the Potomac River. He learned surveying, then served with English forces in the French and Indian War. In the American Revolutionary War he served as commander in chief of the U.S. Army. His forcing of the British to evacuate Boston, the privations of the winter camp in Valley Forge, the crossing of the icy Delaware River, and other difficulties and triumphs became part of history. In 1781, with the aid of French allies and the assistance of Marquis de LaFayette, he forced the surrender of British General Cornwallis at Yorktown.

Washington was chairman of the Constitutional Convention in 1787 and 1788. After ratification of the Constitution, the Electoral College named him as our first president. It was his task and challenge to develop the first cabinet, to work with Congress and the Supreme Court, and to establish procedures for the presidency. At the time the seat of the federal government was in New York City.

When the French Revolution was followed by war between England and France, Washington ignored the recommendations of Secretary of State Thomas Jefferson and Secretary of the Treasury Alexander Hamilton and insisted upon a neutral stance. In his farewell address he recommended that in the future the country avoid entangling foreign alliances.

By the 1796 election, two political parties had developed, setting the scene for a contest. In 1797 Washington retired to his Mount Vernon estate on the banks of the Potomac River, where he lived until dying of a throat infection on December 14, 1799. In 1800, funeral medals inscribed HE IS IN GLORY, THE WORLD IN TEARS were issued in his memory by Jacob Perkins. This inaugurated well over 1,000 later varieties of coins, tokens, and medals issued after his passing, extending down to the present day.

Washington UNITY STATES cent, dated 1783. (Engraving by John Gavit for O'Callaghan, *The Documentary History of the State of New-York*, 1850)

Washington and Numismatics

On February 22, 1860, Washington's birthday (per the new calendar), the Washington Cabinet of Medals was formally inaugurated at the U.S. Mint in Philadelphia. This culminated a flurry of collecting activity by Mint officials and others, most notably director James Ross Snowden, who had been in that post since May 1853 and was interested in numismatics. Shortly after he left the Mint in 1861, Snowden's book, *A Description of the Medals of Washington*, chronicled the Mint collection. The introduction noted, in part:

> In the early part of the year 1859 it occurred to the writer that it would be interesting, and no doubt gratifying to the public taste, to collect and place in the Cabinet of the National Mint one or more specimens of all the medallic memorials of Washington which could be obtained. At that time he did not know of the existence of more than twenty of such memorials. The Cabinet of the Mint contained only four or five specimens besides the pieces known as the Washington cents. During an investigation subsequently made, it was ascertained that there were at least sixty different medals, etc., of the above character.
>
> To obtain specimens of these medals and of such others as had escaped notice, a circular was issued inviting the assistance of the public to procure them. The newspaper press seconded the effort by giving a general notice of the request, and many collectors of coins, with other gentlemen, have rendered the most valuable and efficient assistance. Under these influences, and with these advantages, we have been enabled to gather together a large and interesting collection of these medallic memorials, embracing 138 specimens.
>
> The collection thus made was arranged in an appropriate case, and formally inaugurated, as a part of the Cabinet of the Mint, on the 22d day of February, 1860, in the presence of the officers and workmen; on which occasion THE FAREWELL ADDRESS was read and remarks were made by several of the officers of the institution.

The Snowden volume, illustrated with steel plate engravings and handsomely bound, would be the standard reference for many years. Its predecessors, which were not widely known, included an essay by Joshua Francis Fisher of Philadelphia, "Medals of George Washington," part of "Description of American Medals" in *Collections of the Massachusetts Historical Society*, 1837, which described 14 varieties; and "The Washington Coins," by Augustine Shurtleff, a Boston medical doctor, which appeared in the *Boston Evening Transcript* and was later reprinted as a supplement to the Bangs, Merwin & Co. listing of the Charles H. Morse collection, October 17 and 18, 1860. This described 49 varieties.

Throughout the 1860s and the 1870s, growth years in coin collecting, Washington pieces ascended to be one of the most popular areas in the American numismatic spectrum. Tokens, medals, and other pieces bearing the portrait of Washington, some made in England and France but most made in America, were avidly sought. In 1885 the monumental work, *The Medallic Portraits of Washington*, by W.S. Baker, was published in Philadelphia, and described 651 varieties. From the mid-19th century to the present, Washington pieces have formed an important plank in the platform of numismatics. Indeed, no major reference book is complete without mention of them, and no collection can be called comprehensive without containing examples of Washington coins and medals.

In the 1950s and 1960s George J. Fuld studied Washington coins, tokens, and medals intensely. He annotated a reprint of the Baker work issued by Krause Publications, then collaborated with Russell Rulau in the present standard reference, *Medallic Portraits of Washington*, which continued and expanded the Baker numbering system. In the meantime, Walter Breen developed many theories, often presented as facts, that can be found in his writings, most particularly *Walter Breen's Complete Encyclopedia of U.S. and Colonial Coins*, 1988, but also in articles and in auction catalogs. These often dealt with attributing certain coins and dies to specific engravers and mints. As a sample, Breen stated that John Gregory Hancock, who had designed one-cent pieces in 1791 that were submitted to Congress for consideration as a contract coinage, but not accepted, then took this course:

> When news of Washington's rejection reached Birmingham, John Gregory Hancock (doubtless with Westwood's gleeful consent, possibly even at his instigation) undertook an extraordinary piece of revenge. As Washington's spokesmen had compared the idea of presidential portraits on coins to the practice of Nero, Caligula, and Cromwell, so Hancock's (and/or Westwood's) idea was to portray Washington as a degenerate, effeminate Roman Emperor.... Their existence was kept secret for over 40 years lest it become an "international incident"!

Reality is that during the honoring of Washington, there were many depictions of him in classical garb and poses, intended as a compliment. All we really know is what the Washington Roman Head token looks like (see W-10840) and that it was made from dies by Hancock, for a trial piece is known with his signature. We assume that it is simply a Conder token made for English collectors, which Don Taxay in *U.S. Mint and Coinage*, 1966, suggested. "From the imperial conception of the bust," Taxay wrote, "it seems likely that the issue was intended for 'collector consumption' in England."

All researchers stand on the shoulders of others, and today much of Breen's research remains valuable. More careful scholarship, often presented in the *Colonial Newsletter* and the *C4 Newsletter*, has presented new information of a more reliable nature.

Today, the most popular of the Washington pieces in numismatic circles are those listed in the Red Book. These are mainly of coin and token size, as also studied here, as these were the pieces made up through 1795.

Numismatic Aspects

During the 1790s, when Washington was serving as president, his image appeared on a number of coins and tokens, mostly dated 1791 to 1795. Some were produced as proposals for a federal coinage, while others were privately issued. Many were made in England as part of the Conder token series. Some were very popular in their time, as evidenced by extensive wear on surviving specimens. Generally collected with 18th century pieces are various Washington coins and tokens dated 1783, the year the peace treaty was signed to end the Revolutionary War; most of the "1783" pieces were struck after 1800, some probably into the 1820s, with the GEORGIVS TRIUMPHO token being an exception.

The following arrangement describes smaller diameter pieces generally classified as coins or tokens, including those listed in the Red Book. Most of these were either used as money, or were cabinet coins made for collectors (such as selected Conder tokens). Cross references are made to studies by Baker (as revised by Fuld and Rulau), Breen (*Encyclopedia*, 1988), and Fuld ("Coinage Featuring George Washington," 1996, the most authoritative). See the Selected Bibliography for other sources.

1783 GEORGIVS TRIUMPHO Token

It is not known if the Georgivs Triumpho token was produced in 1783, as dated, but it was at least made in that decade. The date numerals are identical in form and spacing to those used on a Nova Constellatio copper (W-1860, Crosby 1-A, thought to have been struck in 1785, although dated 1783). This is the only 1783-dated Washington token actually struck in the 1780s. A Georgivs Triumpho token was used as an undertype for a 1787 Maris 73-aa New Jersey copper (described by Dennis Wierzba in the *C4 Newsletter*).

It is generally thought that the inscriptions relate to George Washington, although what was perhaps a stock portrait of King George III (somewhat similar to that found on Irish halfpence of the decade) was used by the English die sinker. His actual image was not widely known in England, and worldwide the first medal struck with a portrait from life was the Manly medal of 1790. The Voltaire medal of Washington made in Paris in 1789 has a fictitious portrait since apparently there was no model for a true image.

The *Historical Magazine*, July 1860, contained a discussion of the GEORGIVS TRIUMPHO token by F.P.B. (Fisk Parsons Brewer, curator of the numismatic cabinet at Yale), who wondered why it was attributed by certain numismatists to George Washington, when the portrait seemed to be that of King George of England. The 13 bars on the reverse match the number of original colonies, and the French fleur-de-lis may refer to France's help in the Revolutionary War.

These tokens were made in quantity, possibly for circulation in the British Isles as well as in America. A 1787 American newspaper article refers to them as currently in use. None are known to have been struck for cabinet purposes.

W-10100 · GEORGIVS TRIUMPHO

Obverse: Portrait of English King George III with GEORGIVS TRIUMPHO to the sides. *Reverse:* Standing goddess behind a railing composed of 13 bars and fleur-de-lis. The legend VOCE POPOLI surrounds. *Edge:* Plain. *Notes:* Baker-7, Breen-1184, Fuld-WA.1783.1. All examined pieces show evidence of circulation. One served as the undertype for a New Jersey copper (Maris 73-aa, W-5430). *Rarity:* URS-10.

VG-8	F-12	VF-20	EF-40	AU-50
$125	$275	$750	$1,500	$2,750

W-10105 · muling with counterfeit skilling

Design as preceding, but muled with an irrelevant reverse die of the reverse of a counterfeit Danish West Indies XXIIII skilling coin. *Notes:* Discovered by Mike Ringo. Two known. *Rarity:* URS-2.

1783 UNITY STATES Cents

The 1783-dated Washington cents with UNITY STATES OF AMERICA reverse most certainly were produced well after the turn of the 19th century. The obverse depicts a Draped Bust portrait similar in style to other 1783-dated Washington tokens from dies cut by Thomas Wells Ingram after a portrait by Edward Savage. Production is attributed to the Soho Mint in Birmingham.

The reverse is a copy of that used on the Draped Bust large copper cent through and including 1807. Perhaps UNITY was cut into the die, instead of UNITED, to evade any charges of counterfeiting. Despite the American denomination of this piece, it is likely that they circulated in England at the value of a halfpenny, as reflected by examples being found there in quantity in later years. They were imported into the United States as well, for use as a cent, and are mentioned in several counterfeit detector publications in the 1850s. On this side of the Atlantic they circulated contemporaneously with Hard Times tokens. Some may have been distributed by James Kean of Philadelphia.

W-10130 · UNITY STATES

Obverse: Draped Bust portrait of Washington facing left. WASHINGTON & INDEPENDENCE, 1783 around border. *Reverse:* Copy of a United States large copper cent of the early 1800s, except for substitution of UNITY for the regular UNITED. Outside berry below F (OF); tops of O and E (ONE) close to or touch leaves; other differences. Compare to next. *Edge:* Plain. *Notes:* Baker-1, Breen-1188, Fuld-WA.NC.1783.1, Vlack 27-W. All examined pieces show evidence of circulation. The planchet stock was striated, probably from an incorrectly set drawing bench used to thin the strip. Copper alloy, sometimes resembling brass. *Rarity:* URS-12.

VG-8	F-12	VF-20	EF-40	AU-50
$115	$275	$600	$1,150	$2,750

W-10135 · no outside berry on reverse

Design as preceding, but from a different reverse die. *Reverse:* No outside berry below F (OF); tops of O and E (ONE) distant from leaves; other differences. Compare to above. Discovered by James D. King of Harmer-Rooke, December 5, 1972; now in the Richard August collection. Another is in the Sydney Martin collection. *Notes:* Baker-1A, Breen-1187, Fuld-WA.NC.1783.2, Vlack 27-X. *Rarity:* URS-2.

Selected auction price(s): Milwaukee ANA Sale (Heritage 8/2007), EF-45 (NGC), $17,250.

1783 Washington Military Bust Coppers

The 1783-dated Washington Military Bust coppers bear a portrait, adapted (with a different perspective on the coin and a wreath added to the head) from a painting by Edward Savage, somewhat similar to that used on the Double Head cent (W-10200). WASHINGTON & INDEPENDENCE is around the border, with 1783 below. The reverse illustrates a seated figure with UNITED STATES at the top border. The dies were cut by Thomas Wells Ingram. Reverse dies are signed T.W.I. and E.S., the last for artist Edward Savage. It is likely these were made no earlier than the 1820s.

These seem to have circulated in England as well as America. In the United States notice of them is found in counterfeit detector publications of the 1850s. In the 1960s these and the related 1783-dated Washington Draped Bust cents were studied by George J. Fuld and Robert A. Vlack, with much information published in the *Colonial Newsletter.* Many varieties exist, but they are not well known outside of a circle of specialists. Accordingly, the opportunity exists to acquire rare die combinations for little premium over a regular issue.

W-10150 · Vlack 1-A · Small Military Bust · corded or engrailed edge

Obverse: W distant from bust. Point of wreath close to, but not touching base of I. Beads are fine and close. Long crossbar on the G is close to, but not touching, left serif of T. C is defective at the top as is A at the right base. Sometimes seen with die cracks. *Reverse:* Three berries on the branch. Cap extends between T and A and touches A. I has two beads equally spaced over it; A points slightly right of a bead. The T (T.W.I.) is over the left side of a bead and the S (E.S.) is over a bead with the lower curve of the S pointing to the lower portion of the period. *Edge:* The only variety with a corded or engrailed edge—a recessed, ropelike design more or less centered around the edge (as viewed from the side, edge-on), with plain space above and below. All other Military Bust coppers have a plain edge. *Notes:* Baker-4B, Fuld-WA.NC.1783.8a. *Rarity:* URS-6.

EF-40	AU-50	MS-60
$800	$2,200	$5,000

W-10155 · plain edge

Design as preceding. *Edge:* Plain. *Notes:* Baker-4A, Fuld-WA.NC.1783.8. *Rarity:* URS-7.

EF-40	AU-50	MS-60
$550	$1,500	$5,000

W-10160 · break in obverse field

Obverse: Similar to preceding, but lacking obverse and reverse cracks. Instead there is a break in the right obverse field which follows an irregular course down from under the second E to a "thread" projecting like a short ribbon end from the bottom corner of the lower bow. A break-like defect, parallel to the middle of the crack just described; lies in the field above it adjacent to two similar, smaller and less obvious defects. The 7 has a spur projecting diagonally to the left from its top right corner. The two base points of the W are connected by a short break. These extensive breaks might account for the scarcity of this obverse die. *Reverse:* Same as preceding. *Edge:* Plain. *Notes:* Only one seen by George J. Fuld is New Netherlands' Sale 60, Lot 1968, Lot 473. Fuld-WA.NC.1783.9. Unlisted by Vlack and Baker. *Rarity:* URS-1.

W-10165 · Vlack 2-B · Large Military Bust

Obverse: W close to bust on this and all Large Military Bust coppers. On Obverse 2: Point of wreath close to, but not touching I. Upright of 7 points slightly right of bead. W is normal. A points at space between beads. Second I has a bead slightly left of its center. C is defective on top. *Reverse:* No berries on the branch, only stems. Cap very close to left tip of A, but not touching. I has a bead over its center, and A points slightly to right of a bead. Bottom of branch points straight down. The T and the S of the initials over a space between beads; curve of the S points to the center of the period which is low. Period after W is closer to I. *Notes:* Baker-4 for all Large Military Bust issues. Fuld-WA.NC.1783.10. *Rarity:* URS-7 or 8.

EF-40	AU-50	MS-60
$475	$1,000	$5,000

W-10170 · Vlack 3-C

Obverse: Point of wreath heavily touches left base of I. Seven points to a bead. A at a space between beads. First word slightly repunched. C defective at top. *Reverse:* Resembles Reverse B. One berry on branch plus 2 stems. Cap is under space between T and A and is close. Bottom of cap has pointed ends and is smaller than on any other reverse. I has a bead over its center. A points slightly right of a bead and has right leg weak. Bottom of branch points straight down. T and S of the initials over a space between beads; lower curve of S points to the center of the period. *Notes:* Fuld-WA.NC.1783.11. *Rarity:* URS-7 or 8.

EF-40	AU-50	MS-60
$475	$1,000	$5,000

W-10180 · Vlack 4-D

Obverse: Point of wreath heavily touches left base of I at about the point where the serif begins. Upright of 7 points between beads. Left crossbar of W is defective. A points to left side of a bead. Second I has a bead slightly left of center. *Reverse:* The rock under the seated figure is speckled. Branch has three berries; lowest lacks stem. Bottom of branch separated from the hand. Bead right of the center of I. A points at a bead. T of initials is over a space between beads. Period after I is larger than the others. S of initials over a bead, is higher than the distant E; lower curve of S points to period which is high. Cap distant from left leg of A. *Notes:* Fuld-WA.NC.1783.12. *Rarity:* URS-7.

EF-40	AU-50	MS-60
$475	$1,000	$5,000

W-10190 · Vlack 5-D

Obverse: Point of wreath close to but not touching base of I. Upright of 7 points to a bead. Top of 3 is straight (compare to obverse 6). Left crossbar of W defective. A points slightly right of space between beads. Second I has a bead slightly left of its center and is double punched. C defective on top. *Reverse:* Same as preceding. *Notes:* Fuld-WA.NC.1783.13. *Rarity:* URS-7.

EF-40	AU-50	MS-60
$475	$1,000	$5,000

W-10200 · Vlack 6-E

Obverse: Point of wreath close to, but not touching I. Upright of 7 points to a bead. Top of 3 is wavy. A points between beads. Second I has bead over its center and is repunched at its left bottom. Typically weakly struck at CE. *Reverse:* Three berries on branch. Beads sometimes flattened and indistinct. Center of I points at space between beads. A points slightly right of a bead. S of initials over space between beads and is about the same height as the distant E; lower curve of S points to center of the period. Cap ends under left leg of A and is distant from it. The left side of the water appears flattened. Some beads indistinct. *Notes:* Fuld-WA.NC.178314. *Rarity:* URS-8.

EF-40	AU-50	MS-60
$475	$1,000	$4,000

W-10210 · Vlack 7-E

Obverse: Point of wreath touches left base of I. Upright of 7 points at a bead. Left serif of W is defective. A points slightly left of a bead. Second I has a bead left of its center. C is defective on top. *Reverse:* Same as preceding. *Notes:* Fuld-WA.NC.1783.15. *Rarity:* URS-8 or 9.

EF-40	AU-50	MS-60
$475	$1,000	$4,000

W-10220 · Vlack 8-E

Obverse: Point of wreath touches left base of I. Upright of 7 points at a bead. Left serif of W is defective. A points at space between beads. Second I has a bead slightly left of its center. Top of C is defective. *Reverse:* Same as preceding. *Notes:* Fuld-WA.NC.1783.16. *Rarity:* URS-8 or 9.

EF-40	AU-50	MS-60
$475	$1,000	$4,000

W-10230 · Vlack 9-F

Obverse: Point of wreath close to but does not touch left base of I. Upright of 7 points very slightly right of a bead. Left serif of W defective. A points between bead. Second I has bead over its center. C defective at top. Lower serif of second E is double punched. *Reverse:* Four berries on the branch, with double berry at base of top leaf. I points left of a bead. A points right of a bead. T of the initials over a bead. S of the initials slightly right of a bead and tilts left, with lower curve pointing to the bottom of the period. Cap ends below left leg of A and is distant. *Notes:* Fuld-WA.NC.1783.17. *Rarity:* URS-8.

EF-40	AU-50	MS-60
$475	$1,000	$4,000

W-10240 · Vlack 10-G

Obverse: Point of wreath touches extreme left base of I. Upright of 7 points to space between beads. Left serif of W is defective. A points slightly right of a bead. Second I has a bead very slightly left of its center. Top of C is defective. *Reverse:* Three berries on branch. I points at space between beads. A points at a bead. T of the initials is over left side of a bead and is slightly higher than the distant E; lower curve of the S points to the enter of the period. Cap ends below left leg of A and is distant. *Notes:* Fuld-WA.NC.1783.18. *Rarity:* URS-8 or 9.

EF-40	AU-50	MS-60
$475	$1,000	$4,000

1783 Washington Draped Bust Coppers

Portrait of Washington by Edward Savage, 1789.

The Washington Draped Bust cents dated 1783 depict Washington with the top of a toga draped on his shoulders. There are two main "types" of this issue, one with a button at the folds in the front of the toga and the other without. Those without the button have the initial "I" (for Ingram) in the toga above the right side of 3 (1783). The lettering is larger than on the with-button type. The reverse combined with the no-button obverse has a female seated on a rock surrounded by water. In her right hand is an olive branch, in her left a pole with cap. There are no initials below. The reverse combined with the with-button type is similar, but the rock is squared and resembles a box. The initials T.W.I. and E.S. are below the figure on all but one die.

The portrait is adapted from the painting by Edward Savage, although in this instance the likeness is far more realistic. The reverse is essentially the same design as used on the 1783 Military Bust cents.

After the Soho Mint closed in 1848 at least four pairs of dies came under the control of William Joseph Taylor, who made new working dies to create "restrikes" marketed by W.S. Lincoln, a London coin dealer. These were offered in 1858, and possibly earlier as well, at 2 shillings 6 pence for bronzed copper Proofs and six shillings each for silver Proofs. In addition, mulings were struck with an unrelated die depicting a kangaroo, made for the London International Industrial Exhibition in London held in the Crystal Palace in 1851 (the first "world's fair").

No Button on Toga, No Initials on Reverse

W-10300 · Vlack 13-J · Draped Bust · plain edge

Obverse: With initial I (for Ingram) in toga folds, as on all without button. Main toga fold ends in a sharp point over center of 7. Upright of 7 points to a bead. A points to left of center of bead. Second I points slightly left of a bead. C "pinched" on top and bottom. Other letters sometimes appear defective. *Reverse:* Cap touches lower left of A. Second lowest left leaf has a break creating a tiny dot at the end of the leaf; a smaller break is also seen on the third leaf from the bottom on the right. Center of I and A each point to about the center of space between beads. Beads sometimes flattened when combined with Obverse 13 as here. This die was later reworked to create reverse K. *Edge:* Plain. *Notes:* Baker-2B, Fuld-WA.NC.1783.3. *Rarity:* URS-10 or 11.

VG-8	F-12	VF-20	EF-40	AU-50	MS-60
$95	$200	$450	$900		$4,000

W-10310 · Vlack 14-J · Proof restrike · plain edge · copper

Obverse: Main toga fold curves over the 7 and ends over the extreme right of the upright of 1. A points very slightly left of a bead. Second I has a bead slightly right over its center. C defective at bottom. *Reverse:* Same as preceding, but beads usually well defined. *Edge:* plain. *Notes:* Baker-3C, Fuld-WA.NC.1783.6. *Rarity:* URS-5.

PF-63
$1,000

W-10320 · Vlack 14-J · plain edge · silver
Design as preceding, but in silver. *Notes:* Baker-3F, Fuld-WA.NC.1783.6c.Ag. *Rarity:* URS-5.

PF-63
$1,000

W-10330 · Vlack 14-J · corded edge · copper
Design as preceding, but in copper with corded edge. Just one seen by Vlack. *Notes:* Baker-3D, Fuld-WA.NC.1783.6a. *Rarity:* URS-2.

Selected auction price(s): Ford II Sale (5/2004), Gem BrPF, $1,840.

W-10340 · Vlack 16-K · plain edge · silver
Obverse: Main toga fold curves over 7 and ends over center of 1. The 7 points at a bead; the 3 has a period directly in back of and very close to its apex. A and second I point very slightly left of a bead. C defective at top. *Reverse:* Reworking of reverse J, now with dot-like breaks at leaves absent and with no curls at the bottom of the neck. Chip break back of the D. Left leg of A is heavy, perhaps from die rust. Liberty cap just misses right side of base of A of STATES. Olive branch lightly engraved, dentils weak at 6 o'clock. This die reworked from reverse J with absence of period-like break at branch, and no curls along back of neck. Die break as a chip occurs in back of D. This reverse is used with the Melbourne muling. *Edge:* Plain. *Notes:* Baker-3F. *Rarity:* URS-1 or 2.

W-10350 · Vlack 16-K · corded edge
Obverse: Similar to obverse 7 in many ways. Upright of 7 points to space between beads. A has flat top and is repunched at bottom. First N repunched with base of left leg below base of I. A and second I point to a bead. *Reverse:* As preceding. *Edge:* Corded. *Notes:* Fuld-WA.NC.1783.5. *Rarity:* URS-2 or 3.

W-10360 · Vlack 17-L · Proof restrike · corded edge · copper
Obverse: Main toga fold curves over 7 and ends over extreme right edge of upright of 1. Upright of 7 points slightly right of bead. The 1 and 7 show slight repunching. A has flat top and points at a bead. O is repunched at bottom. Second I has bead over its center. *Reverse:* Cap is very close to right leg of A, but does not touch. I has a bead over its right center. A has a flat top and points between beads. Right side of U slants left. *Edge:* Corded. *Notes:* Baker-3, Fuld-WA.NC.1783.7. Proof restrike with mirrored fields. *Rarity:* URS-8 or 9.

PF-63
$850

W-10370 · Vlack 17-L · bronzed copper
Design as preceding, but with bronzed surfaces. *Notes:* Baker-3, Fuld-WA.NC.1783.7a.Bz. *Rarity:* URS-7 or 8.

PF-63
$850

W-10380 · Vlack 17-L · silver
Design as preceding, but in silver. *Notes:* Baker-3A, Fuld-WA.NC. 1783.7b.Ag. One hundred said to have been struck. *Rarity:* URS-8.

PF-63
$1,800

W-10390 · Vlack 17-L · gold
Design as preceding, but in gold. Just two said to have been struck. *Notes:* Baker-3B, Fuld-WA.NC.1783.7b.Au. *Rarity:* URS-1 or 2.

Muling With Reverse K

W-10400 · Vlack MEL-K · Melbourne kangaroo muling
Obverse: At center, kangaroo on the ground facing right. MELBOURNE above. W.J. TAYLOR, MEDALLIST / TO THE GREAT / EXHIBITION / 1851 below. *Reverse:* See above. *Notes:* Baker-3M, Fuld-1783.M1. Numismatic novelty made with Proof finish. *Rarity:* URS-7.

PF-63

Button on Toga, T.W.I. and E.S. on Reverse

W-10410 · Vlack 20-P · Draped Bust
Obverse: A points slightly right of a bead. Second I has a bead about over its center. A heavy bead sometimes shows near the rim below the 8 and another slightly right of the 1.

Reverse: Cap extends between A and T and touches T. Center of the I and A each point left of a bead. T of initials over a bead. S of initials over a bead and is slightly higher than the E; lower curve of S points to center of period. There is no period after the S. The D has a period in its center. *Notes:* Fuld-WA.NC.1783.19. Rarity: URS-4 or 5.

EF-40	AU-50	MS-60
$675	$1,200	

W-10420 · Vlack 20-Q
Obverse: Same as preceding. *Reverse:* Cap extends between A and T and is close, but does not touch the T. Center of I points to a bead. A points to right of a bead. T of initials over left edge of a bead. S of initials over space between beads, is slightly lower than the E; lower curve of S points to period. Period after S. *Notes:* Fuld-WA.NC.1783.20. Rarity: URS-2 or 3.

W-10430 · Vlack 21-Q
Obverse: Upright of 7 points left of a bead. A points slightly right of a bead. Second I points left of a bead. *Reverse:* Same as preceding. *Notes:* Fuld-WA.NC.1783.21. Rarity: URS-4 or 5.

EF-40	AU-50	MS-60
$675	$1,200	

W-10440 · Vlack 22-R
Obverse: Upright of 7 is slightly lower than 1 and 8 and points at a bead. A points at a bead. Second I points to space between beads. *Reverse:* Cap extends between A and T, and is close to but does not touch T. T of the initials over right edge of a bead; period after I rather distant. S of initials over a space between beads and is slightly lower than the E; lower curvature of S points to bottom of period. Period after S is distant from it. *Notes:* Fuld-WA.NC.1783.22. Rarity: URS-5.

EF-40	AU-50	MS-60
$675	$1,200	

W-10450 · Vlack 24-T · INDEPEDENCE misspelling
Obverse: Massive head with bull neck, large ribbon bow behind. Toga drapery low. Letters and date small. Top wreath leaf ends almost midway between & and I. Toothed rather than beaded border, and with 83 running into it. INDEPEDENCE misspelling. *Reverse:* Long cone-shaped cap on pole. No T.W.I. or E.S. initials. *Notes:* Baker-2C, Breen-1200, Fuld-WA.NC.1783.23. Only one reported; in an English collection. Either a contemporary (1820s) counterfeit, or a copycat piece made by another English token shop. Rarity: URS-1.

1784 "Ugly Head" Tokens
This medalet or token is likely of American origin, although it could have been made elsewhere. "D.G." was the common inscription on English coins at the time and was an abbreviation of "Dei Gratia," which translates to "by the grace of God." Is this a crude token created as a souvenir, or, as some suggest, was it made to satirize Washington? The 1784 date is not known to have any particular significance in Washington's life. Facts are nonexistent.

Originals were struck in copper and white metal and seem to have circulated in their time, although at a narrow 27 mm width they fell short of normal halfpenny size of 28 to 29 mm. Their edge is plain. Likely, they were struck in America, but no information has been located.

W-10590 · copper
Obverse: Fantasy profile, possibly bald (without wig) and without teeth, facing right. WASHINGTON THE GREAT D.G. around border. *Reverse:* Linked rings, similar in concept to the 1776 Continental dollar, with some different abbreviations for the colonies, and with C (Connecticut) between R.I. and N.Y., instead of to the right of M.B. (Massachusetts Bay) as seen on the dollar. At the center in two lines: 17 / 84, with the 17 hardly readable even on the better examples *Notes:* Baker-8, Breen-1185, Fuld-WA.1784.1. 27 mm. Discovered by Robert W. Gibbes and first published in the *Historical Magazine*, March 1860. Electrotype copies exist. Rarity: URS-4.

G-4	VG-8
$75,000	

W-10595 · white metal
As preceding, but struck in white metal. *Notes:* Breen-1186, Fuld-WA.1784.1.WM. Now at Colonial Williamsburg. Rarity: URS-1.

Selected auction price(s): Garrett IV Sale (3/1981), Poor, $3,600.

1791 Large Eagle and Small Eagle Cents
The 1791 Large Eagle and Small Eagle cents have been numismatic favorites for generations. Although they were struck in England, the motifs and inscriptions are pure American, giving them a particular appeal to stateside collectors. The dies are attributed to teenaged John Gregory Hancock Jr. (1775–1815), an engraver of precocious talent who also created the 1792 Washington Roman Head cent. His work is viewed as artistic and boldly executed.

In 1791, Congress and the Senate discussed the proposals for a federal coinage as forwarded by Alexander Hamilton in a report given to Congress on January 28, 1791. On March 3, 1791, Congress voted to authorize the president to establish a federal mint and to hire the necessary people to conduct it. A related proposal was made to the Senate on December 21, 1791, by Robert Morris (formerly the superintendent of finance during the Confederation) to use the president's portrait on coinage. The Mint Act of April 2, 1792, spelled out details. While this was happening, and with the realization that Congress could change its mind, coiners and entrepreneurs of Birmingham, of whom Boulton and Watt (the Soho Mint) were most important, proposed that they could supply high quality coins for less expense, which was probably true. W. and Alex. Walker of Birmingham sponsored the Large Eagle and Small Eagle cents as proposals, with designs intended to impress observers.

The Fuld "Coinage Featuring George Washington" text notes that Walker shipped a cask filled with these cents, estimated to be about 2,500 Large Eagle and 1,500 Small Eagle coins, to Thomas Ketland & Sons, a Philadelphia contact, to be distributed to legislators. The depiction of Washington was contrary to the president's own desires, who felt that having his image on coins would appear to have the "stamp of royalty." Most of the coins were released into general circulation, the same source stated. Many different patterns, uniface impressions, and other preparatory strikings are described in the Fuld and Baker (Fuld-Rulau) texts.

Examples of each are readily collectible today, usually in high grades and very attractive. English dealers and collectors had been the main source for many years.

1791 Large Eagle Cent

W-10610 · lettered edge

Obverse: Uniformed bust of Washington facing left. WASHINGTON PRESIDENT / 1791 around side and top border. From a popular portrait by Pierre Eugène Du Simitière. *Reverse:* Heraldic eagle with wings downward, ribbon inscribed UNUM E PLURIBUS [*sic*] in beak. ONE CENT at top border. *Edge:* UNITED STATES OF AMERICA X. *Notes:* Baker-15, Breen-1206, Fuld-WA.1791.1. 30 mm. Usually seen in high grades and often prooflike. Most examples in American cabinets have come from England in the past century. Usually collected as a pair with W-10630. This obverse die was also used on the 1791 Liverpool halfpenny, W-10650. *Rarity:* URS-11.

EF-40	AU-50	MS-60	MS-63	MS-65
$950	$1,750	$2,750	$4,000	$15,000

W-10615 · plain edge

Design as preceding, but plain edge. *Notes:* Baker-15 (mention), Breen-1208, Fuld-WA.1791.1b One reported in the 19th century, not confirmed or traced today.

W-10620 · Draped Bust muling

Reverse of preceding muled with an irrelevant obverse: Draped bust of facing left, GEORGIVS III DEI GRATIA at border. *Notes:* Baker-15 (mention), Breen-1216, Fuld-WA.1791.P6. Fuld: "This is quite a strange muling, probably a pièce de caprice." Private New York collection. *Rarity:* URS-1.

1791 Small Eagle Cent

W-10630 · UNITED STATES edge

Obverse: Uniformed bust of Washington facing left. WASHINGTON PRESIDENT. around side and top border. *Reverse:* Heraldic eagle with wings upraised. ONE CENT at top border, 1791 at bottom. *Edge:* UNITED STATES OF AMERICA X. *Notes:* Baker-16, Breen-1217, Fuld-WA.1791.2. 30 mm. Sometimes seen in high grades and often prooflike, but considerably harder to find in this preservation than is W-10610. Most examples in American cabinets have come from England in the past century. The obverse die was used later on the 1793/2 Ship halfpenny, W-10850. *Rarity:* URS-10.

EF-40	AU-50	MS-60	MS-63	MS-65
$1,000	$2,000	$3,250	$4,500	$15,000

W-10632 · brass

As preceding, but brass. *Rarity:* URS-2.
Selected auction price(s): Garrett IV Sale (3/1981), VF–EF, $1,600.

W-10635 · MACCLESFIELD edge

Design as preceding, but with MACCLESFIELD edge. Copper. Edge lettered PAYABLE AT MACCLESFIELD LIVERPOOL OR LONDON. *Notes:* Baker-16B, Breen-1218, Fuld-WA.1791.2a. *Rarity:* URS-3.
Selected auction price(s): Ford II Sale (5/2004), Choice MS, $5,865. Long Beach Sale (Heritage 6/2005), MS-61BN (PCGS), $8,050.

W-10640 · PAYABLE AT THE WAREHOUSE edge

Design as preceding, but with edge lettered PAYABLE AT THE WAREHOUSE OF THOS. WORSWICK & SONS. *Notes:* Baker-unlisted, Breen-1219, Fuld-WA.1791.2b. Listed as D&H Middlesex 1050a. *Rarity:* URS-2.
Selected auction price(s): Norweb Sale (11/2006), MS, $9,200.00.

W-10645 · plain edge

Design as preceding, but with plain edge. *Notes:* Baker-unlisted, Breen-1224, Fuld-WA.1791.3a. *Rarity:* URS-1.
Selected auction price(s): John J. Ford Jr. Part II (Stack's 5/2004), $2,300.

1791 Liverpool Halfpennies

The 1791 Liverpool halfpenny depicts the uniformed bust of Washington facing left, as earlier used on the Washington 1791 Large Eagle cent (W-10610), while the reverse illustrates a sailing ship from the LIVERPOOL HALFPENNY die (so lettered) that was also combined with other dies in the Conder token series. These copper pieces were made for circulation, probably around 1793, although numismatists noticed them as well. Typically encountered examples show wear and also reverse die cracks.

W-10650 · PAYABLE IN ANGELSEY edge

Obverse: Uniformed bust of Washington facing left. WASHINGTON PRESIDENT / 1791 around border. *Reverse:* Fully rigged ship sailing to the right. LIVERPOOL HALFPENNY around sides and top border. *Edge:* PAYABLE IN ANGELSEY LONDON OR LIVERPOOL X. *Notes:* Baker-17, Breen-1223, Fuld-WA.1791.3. 28.3 mm. Typically seen in worn grades and with die cracks on the reverse. *Rarity:* URS-6.

VG-8	F-12	VF-20	EF-40	AU-50
	$1,400	$2,500	$4,950	$9,000

W-10652 · plain edge

Design as preceding, but plain edge. *Rarity:* URS-1.

Selected auction price(s): Ford II Sale (5/2004), VF–EF, copper plated at one time, $2,300. EAHA Sale (6/2005), copper-plated AU, ex Ford, $14,490.

W-10654 · white metal

Different dies. White metal. *Notes:* Breen-1222. *Rarity:* URS-1.

Selected auction price(s): Norweb Sale (11/2006), AU-55, $103,500. Now in the Sydney F. Martin collection.

1792 Washington Coinage (English)

This extensive series of Washington pieces bears no denomination but is related to John Gregory Hancock's Large Eagle and Small Eagle cents of 1791, which were inscribed ONE CENT. Breen (*Encyclopedia*, 1988) suggests that these were "not fancy enough" for English collectors, and "were dumped into a keg and shipped to the USA." Be that as it may, many of these pieces now in American cabinets have been obtained from English coin dealers. Likely, collectors of Conder tokens enjoyed certain of these as well, and any that were shipped to America were appreciated as mementoes of Washington. Breen also theorizes that copper pieces could have served as cents, silver as half dollars, and the single known gold striking as a $10 coin. As to whether these are coins, tokens, or medalets, the reader can decide, but they are listed in the Red Book as coins and are collected as such. The average diameter of 31 mm does not match the common size of state coppers or English halfpence (about 29 mm). Accordingly, they would have been uneconomical to produce as such and, moreover, would have been curious to their recipients. In a way they can be likened to the Admiral Vernon medals, made in England in the 18th century to honor an admiral of commanding importance. Many varieties were struck and sold. Recipients often handled them extensively, as nearly all show significant wear today.

The skilled young engraver John Gregory Hancock no doubt cut the dies resembling the 1791 cent obverses, while others may have been done by different hands. Current wisdom is that Obediah Westwood of Birmingham was the coiner. Of particular interest are the Washington Born Virginia coppers, giving biographical dates on the reverse. These seem to have been made in small numbers, for all are elusive today. Curiously, one of these obverse dies descended in the family of Jacob Perkins of Newburyport, Massachusetts, prominent die cutter and token/medal issuer, although he may have sent it back from England (where he moved in 1818, long after he made medals in America).

1792 Washington President

W-10660 · plain edge · copper

Obverse: Uniformed bust of Washington facing left. WASHINGTON PRESIDENT / 1792 around border. T (PRESIDENT) just left of back edge of shoulder. *Reverse:* Heraldic eagle reminiscent of that used on the 1791 Large Eagle cent, with eagle holding ribbon inscribed UNUM E PLURIBUS, but here with one star above the eagle's head and 12 in an arc at the top border. *Edge:* Plain. *Notes:* Baker-21, Breen-1230, Fuld-WA.1792.4. George Fuld (communication) knows of only a single coin, the Steinberg collection piece sold by Stack's in October 1989. *Rarity:* URS-1.

VG-8	F-12	VF-20	EF-40	AU-50	MS-60	MS-63
$2,750	$7,500	$18,000	$25,000	$50,000	$100,000	$175,000

W-10665 · silver

Design as preceding, but struck in silver. *Notes:* Baker-20, Breen-1232, Fuld-WA.1792.4b.Ag. Some have called this a "half dollar." *Rarity:* URS-3 or 4.

Selected auction price(s): Roper Sale (Stack's 12/1983), EF (ex 1982 Robinson sale at $44,000), $35,200.

W-10670 · UNITED STATES OF AMERICA · copper

Design as preceding, but edge lettered UNITED STATES OF AMERICA. *Notes:* Baker-21, Breen-1229, Fuld-WA.1792.4a. *Rarity:* URS-4.

Selected auction price(s): Norweb Sale (11/2006), AU-53, $253,000.

W-10675 · silver

Design as preceding, but struck in silver. *Notes:* Baker-20, Breen-1231, Fuld-WA.1792.4c.Ag. *Rarity:* URS-3.

Selected auction price(s): Ford II Sale (5/2004), F–VF, $115,000.

W-10680 · gold
As preceding, but struck in gold. *Notes:* Baker-20A, Breen-1233, Fuld-WA.1792.4.Au. Unique. Considered by owner Eric P. Newman to have been presented to Washington for use as a pocket piece. *Rarity:* URS-1.

W-10685 · variant die · UNITED STATES OF AMERICA · copper
Obverse: Similar to preceding, but from a different die with T (PRESIDENT) below shoulder. *Reverse:* As preceding. *Edge:* UNITED STATES OF AMERICA. *Notes:* Breen-1228, Fuld-WA.1792.5 Eric P. Newman collection. Fuld, suggesting that others may be found, commented: "Not all obverse dies of this design have been checked." *Rarity:* URS-1.

W-10690 · General of the American Armies · plain edge
Obverse: Uniformed bust of Washington facing left. WASHINGTON PRESIDENT / 1792 around border. *Reverse:* Inscription in 10 lines: GENERAL / OF THE / AMERICAN ARMIES / 1775 / RESIGNED / 1783 / PRESIDENT / OF THE / UNITED STATES / 1789. The 1 (1775) under left foot of second A (AMERICAN). *Edge:* Plain. *Notes:* Baker-59, Breen-1234, Fuld-WA.1792.6. First die. *Rarity:* URS-6.

Selected auction price(s): Garrett IV Sale (3/1981), EF, $15,500. John J. Ford Jr. II Sale (5/2004), EF, $25,300, Norweb Collection (Stack's 11/2006), VF-35 (PCGS), $29,900.

W-10695 · UNITED STATES OF AMERICA
Design as preceding, but with edge lettered UNITED STATES OF AMERICA. *Notes:* Baker-59A, Breen-1235, Fuld-WA.1792.6a. *Rarity:* URS-4.

Selected auction price(s): Garrett IV Sale (3/1981), VF, $6,000. Norweb Collection (Stack's 11/2006), AU-55, (PCGS), $92,000.

1792 Washington Born Virginia

W-10710 · Eagle reverse · plain edge
Obverse: Uniformed bust of Washington facing left. GEO. WASHINGTON BORN VIRGINIA FEB. 11 1732 around border. *Reverse:* Large eagle, UNUM E PLURIBUS on ribbon, one star above head and arc of 12 stars at top border. *Edge:* Plain. *Notes:* Baker-22, Breen-1236, Fuld-WA.1792.7. Extremely rare muling of two dies. *Rarity:* URS-3.

Selected auction price(s): Norweb Collection Sale (Stack's 11/2006), AU-53, $212,750.

W-10720 · General of the American Armies reverse
Obverse: As preceding. *Reverse:* Inscription in 10 lines: GENERAL / OF THE / AMERICAN ARMIES / 1775 / RESIGNED / 1783 / PRESIDENT / OF THE / UNITED STATES / 1789. The 1 (1775) directly under left foot of second A (AMERICAN). *Edge:* Plain. *Notes:* Baker-60 obverse and Baker-59 reverse, Breen-1238, Fuld-WA.1792.10. First die. *Rarity:* URS-3.

Selected auction price(s): Norweb Collection Sale (Stack's 11/2006), VF-35 (PCGS), $12,650.

W-10730 · variant die · copper
Obverse: As preceding. *Reverse:* Inscription as preceding but the 1 (1775) directly under I (AMERICAN). *Edge:* Plain. *Notes:* Baker-60, Breen-1239, Fuld-WA.1792.9. 31 mm. Second die. This is the Washington Born Virginia cent most often seen in the marketplace. Uniface restrikes were made from the obverse die (which is now in the ANA Museum). *Rarity:* URS-7.

VG-8	F-12	VF-20	EF-40	AU-50	MS-60	MS-63
$2,400	$5,000	$8,500	$15,000			

W-10740 · silver
Design as preceding, but struck in silver. *Notes:* Baker-60A, Breen-1239, Fuld-WA.1792.9.Ag. *Rarity:* URS-4.

VG-8	F-12	VF-20	EF-40	AU-50
—	—	—	—	

W-10750 · UNITED STATES OF AMERICA

Design as preceding, but with edge lettered UNITED STATES OF AMERICA. *Notes:* Baker-60B, Breen-1241, Fuld-WA.1792.9a.Ag. Two reported, one holed and with a brass plug (Harold Whiteneck to George Fuld to Richard Picker), the other the Ford coin. *Rarity:* URS-2.

Selected auction price(s): Ford II Sale (5/2004), VF, $37,375.

1792 Washington Getz Private Pattern Coinage (American)

Peter Getz, a Lancaster, Pennsylvania silversmith, is credited as the maker of this series, likely in response to Robert Morris's proposal of December 21, 1791, suggesting that a portrait of the president be used on coinage. Walter Breen (*Encyclopedia*, 1988) developed a pseudo-history in which these pieces were struck in Philadelphia at the coach house of John Harper where equipment intended for use in the soon-to-be-built Philadelphia Mint was being stored. This coinage was done directly with the supervision of Adam Eckfeldt, chief Mint mechanic, per the same writer. Breen's account has Getz's coins ready in late 1791, with perhaps 35 to 40 samples in silver passed out to senators and dignitaries and a larger number of copper impressions going to congressmen. Further, Breen states that Getz was seeking a position as engraver at the Mint. After this didn't happen, Getz or someone made additional strikings on his own, including at least one overstruck on a federal cent of 1794 or 1795. The above scenario is not supported by any evidence seen by consultants to the present work.

The usual diameter of about 32 mm does approximate that of the 1792 Birch pattern cents made for the Mint, although some Getz pieces were made to about 35 mm with broad toothed borders.

Historical Magazine, September 1861, noted:

> John Harper, an extensive manufacturer of saws, at the corner of Sixth and Cherry streets, caused dies to be made under the direction of Robert Birch. The coins of 1791 were made in the cellar of Mr. Harper's shop on a press which it is supposed was imported from England. The coins of 1792 were struck on a press which was set up in an old coach-house in Sixth Street above Chestnut, directly opposite Jayne Street. This last described press was made by Adam Eckfeldt.

In 1861, five years before the *American Journal of Numismatics* was founded, the *Historical Magazine* served as a forum for the exchange of numismatic ideas, some of lasting worth, others made obsolete by later research. The above account states that the 1791 cents were made in Philadelphia, a scenario now considered invalid. The "coins of 1792" were likely Birch cents, not Getz pieces.

In creating the obverse of this medalet (or coin) the diecutter seems to have been inspired by the 1791 and 1792 English issues. The reverse is a rendering of the Great Seal, somewhat rustic in its workmanship. Both sides generally conform to The Mint Act of April 2, 1792, originally written in the Senate, which proposed that:

> Upon one side of each of the said coins, there shall be an impression or representation of the head of the president of the United States for the time being, with an inscription which shall express the initial or first letter of his Christian or first name, and his surname at length, the succession of the presidency numerically, and the year of the coinage.

It also provided that the reverses of the gold and silver coins were to bear the figure or representation of an eagle with the inscription THE UNITED STATES OF AMERICA, and the reverses of the copper coins were to bear the inscribed denomination. The House of Representatives, probably acceding Washington's oft-expressed wishes, deleted the portion referring to the head of the president and substituted that "upon one side of each of the said coins there shall be an impression emblematic of liberty, with an inscription of the word, LIBERTY." In the meantime, the Getz-attributed pieces may have been made. It should be noted that Getz's reverse lacked the denomination.

Montroville W. Dickeson provided a sketch of the engraver's life in the *American Numismatical Manual*, 1859, reprinting text furnished by J. Franklin Reigart of Lancaster (adapted):

> Mr. Peter Getz was born in Lancaster, Pa.; his occupation was that of a silversmith; but he was, otherwise, a very skillful mechanic and remarkable for his ingenuity. He excelled as a seal-engraver, and an engraver on steel, and was the inventor of a very ingenious hand-vise. He built the three first fire-engines for his native town, the *Active*, *Sun*, and another, which is still in existence in the county, and invented an improved printing press—noticed in the *Lancaster Journal*, January 8, 1810—worked by rollers instead of the screw, which, by printers was considered a great improvement. . . . Mr. Getz died, December 29th, 1809, at 47 years of age, leaving a large family. . . . Mr. Getz was personally complimented by Washington for his artistic skill in producing the die for what is called the "Washington Cent," and it was also officially recognized by the government.

Getz is not known to have been interviewed on the subject of speculative coinage for 1792, nor has any contemporary documentation survived.

W-10775 · plain edge · copper

Obverse: Uniformed bust of Washington facing left. G. WASHINGTON PRESIDENT. 1. / 1792 around border.
Reverse: Adaptation of the Great Seal of the United States, here with 15 stars above the eagle, olive branch to observer's left, arrows to right. UNITED STATES OF AMERICA

around border. Edge plain. *Notes:* Baker-25, Breen-1352, Fuld-WA.1792.1. 32 mm. One exists struck over a later federal cent of 1794 or 1795 (Fuld-WA.1791.1a.o), several are known on an overly large planchets of 35 mm (Fuld-WA.1792.1b). Examination of die states (rust) indicates that copper pieces preceded the silver strikings. *Rarity:* URS-6.

VG-8	F-12	VF-20	EF-40	AU-50	MS-60	MS-63
$12,000	$17,500	$35,500	$75,000			

W-10780 · silver
As preceding, but struck in silver. Edge plain. *Notes:* Baker-25, Breen-1347 and 1348, Fuld-WA.1792.1e.Ag. 32 mm. Most are overstruck on crown-size foreign coins with ground-down edge devices. *Rarity:* URS-5.

VG-8	F-12	VF-20	EF-40	AU-50	MS-60
—	—	—	$300,000		

W-10785 · circles-and-squares edge
Dies as preceding. *Edge:* First style, ornamented with circles and squares. *Notes:* Baker-25D, Breen-1357, Fuld-WA.1792.1c. 35 mm. Garrett had a choice Mint State example. A Mint State coin with much original color is in the British Museum (per George Fuld). *Rarity:* URS-4

VG-8	F-12	VF-20	EF-40	AU-50	MS-60
—	—	—	$175,000		

W-10790 · silver
Dies as preceding, but struck in silver. *Notes:* Baker-24A, Breen-1350, Fuld-WA.1792.1g.Ag. About 35 mm. *Rarity:* URS-3 or 4.

Selected auction price(s): Ford II Sale (5/2004), Gem MS, $391,000. Norweb Sale (11/2006), VF-25, $184,000.

W-10792 · vine-and-leaves edge
Dies as preceding. *Edge:* Second style, ornamented with vine and leaves. *Notes:* Baker-24B, Breen-1351, Fuld-WA.1792.1h.Ag. About 35 mm. Two known; one plugged, the other the Ford coin. *Rarity:* URS-2.

Selected auction price(s): Ford II Sale (5/2004), EF, $103,500.

W-10800 · Large Eagle reverse · plain edge
Obverse: Die as preceding. *Reverse:* Large eagle with olive branch and arrows, no stars. UNITED STATES OF AMERICA around border. Chisel cut across eagle (in die). *Edge:* Plain. *Notes:* Baker-23, Breen-1346, Fuld-WA.1792.2.Ag. 32 mm. This identical coin was believed to have a pedigree back to 1831, but recent research suggests that this is incorrect. The Large Eagle silver half dollar was first written up by Winslow J. Howard in *Norton's Literary Letter* No. 2, 1858, in which he claimed he purchased it from a shoemaker named Bossnet. This is pure fiction. An early write-up of this coin was by Augustus B. Sage in the February, 1867, *American Journal of Numismatics*. The reverse of this coin is virtually identical to that of a coin first auctioned in the Fonrobert Sale in Berlin in 1878. The obverse of the Fonrobert coin does not resemble any issue of the late 18th century and clearly dates to around 1850 or 1860. The reverses of the Large Eagle coin and the Fonrobert fantasy (Baker 26) are almost identical—they must date from the same period. The first sale of this Large Eagle coin was in Woodward's Rev. J. M. Finotti Sale on November 11 through 14, 1862. The pedigree back to 1831 plus other prior fictitious owners quoted in the Breen *Encyclopedia* back to 1792 are wholly imaginary. *Any pedigree assigned to this coin before 1858 must be considered false.* Who made this production and where it was struck is an open question. *Rarity:* URS-1.

Selected auction price(s): Garrett IV Sale (3/1981), EF, offered "as is" with comment that opinion was divided, $16,600, later in the Ford II Sale (5/2004), EF, $34,500.

1792 Roman Head Cents

The Roman Head cent depicts Washington dressed in the style of a Roman official, a popular way of honoring him, at least in memory, but these are dated during his life. The apotheosis of Washington saw many forms, most famously in Horatio Greenough's statue of epic proportions showing Washington as a Roman emperor seated on a throne. For years this was displayed on the U.S. Capitol grounds. There are many versions of similar tributes in the classic style to be found on bank note vignettes.

A member of the Conder token series, the Roman Head cent was made for cabinet purposes, with none intended for circulation. The dies were cut by young engraver John Gregory Hancock, who signed the obverse of a pattern trial impression. The coins were struck at Obediah Westwood's private mint in Birmingham.

W-10840
Obverse: Head of Washington facing right, in the style of a Roman dignitary. WASHINGTON PRESIDENT / 1792 around border. *Reverse:* Heraldic eagle holding an olive branch and arrows, six stars near head, CENT at top border. *Edge:* UNITED STATES OF AMERICA X. *Notes:* Baker-19, Breen-1249, Fuld-WA.1792.3. 29.4 mm. Nearly all are in high grades, Proof-63 being about par. *Rarity:* URS-6.

PF-63
$90,000

267

1793/2 Ship Halfpennies

The 1793/2 Ship halfpenny, from an overdated reverse die, is part of the Conder token series, but nearly all went into circulation. Most seen today are dark and show moderate wear. None are known from the 1792 state of the die, before overdating.

W-10850 · plain edge · copper

Obverse: Same as W-10630 used on the Small Eagle cent of 1791, but now with slight repunching of the letters. Portrait of Washington facing left. WASHINGTON PRESIDENT around border. *Reverse:* Ship sailing to the right. HALFPENNY at top border. Date 1793 (3 cut over 2) on cartouche at bottom border. Die usually bulged at lower right border. *Edge:* Plain. *Notes:* Baker-18A, Breen-1226, Fuld-WA.1793/2.2.1a. 28 mm. Genuine specimens with plain edge are very rare. Electrotype copies exist. *Rarity:* URS-3.

W-10855 · PAYABLE IN ANGLESEY edge

Design as preceding. Die usually bulged at lower right border. *Edge:* Lettered PAYABLE IN ANGLESEY LONDON OR LIVERPOOL and punctuation. *Notes:* Baker-18, Breen-1225, Fuld-WA.1793/2.2.1. 28 mm. This is the variety typically seen. Part of the Conder token series, but most went into circulation. High grade coins are rare. *Rarity:* URS-9.

VG-8	F-12	VF-20	EF-40	AU-50	MS-60
	$220	$450	$850	$1,500	

W-10865 · brass

Design as preceding, but struck in brass. *Notes:* Baker-18B, Breen-1227, Fuld-WA.1793.1.Br. Mickley collection, later Jack Collins. *Rarity:* URS-1.

Undated (Possibly c. 1793) Washington SUCCESS Tokens

The date and purpose of issue of the several varieties of Success tokens, small and large, is not known. Each has the portrait of Washington on the obverse and the inscription SUCCESS TO THE UNITED STATES on the reverse. W.E. Woodward in 1864 (McCoy collection sale, lot 236) suggested that they were connected with George Washington's second inauguration in March 1793, a theory seconded by W.S. Baker in 1885, J. Doyle DeWitt (*A Century of Campaign Buttons—1789–1889*) in 1959, and George J. Fuld ("Coinage Featuring George Washington"), among others. In his sale of the Matthews collection, December 1885, Woodward further noted under lot 1894:

Success to the United States. Bust; rev. sun and stars; said to have been designed and struck by Jacob Perkins for the citizens of Boston, and worn on the occasion of the second inauguration of Washington as president; brass, very fine.

The size and brass fabric of the issues does not suggest that they were made to circulate in commerce. Perhaps the tokens were souvenirs or remembrances. Whatever their intent, they seem to have been made in large quantities, as three different obverse dies were employed to strike the larger size.

The use of 15 stars, rather than 13 for the original colonies, suggests that the piece may have been made between the time Vermont joined the Union as the 14th state in 1791 and Tennessee became the 16th in 1796, as proposed by Woodward. Kentucky became the 15th state on June 1, 1792. Moreover, "Success to the United States" would have been an appropriate sentiment for young America at the time, as only about a decade had elapsed since the Confederation.

Others have suggested that these may have had a 19th century origin, resembling as they do the plentiful German brass *spielmarken* ("play money") so popular in the mid-19th century. However, they are not inscribed in the manner of coins and they lack a denomination or value. Their use as game counters has also been suggested, as these fit nicely with brass tokens, mostly made in England, that were used to keep count of progress in games and contests. The brass tokens of Kettle & Son, English makers, are particularly well known. An expansion of this idea by L. Benj Fauver appears in the *C4 Newsletter*, Spring 1999. A book of rubbings from about 1830, kept by the Portsmouth Athenaeum (New Hampshire), depicts a Success token, confirming they were in existence by that time.

For a long time these enigmatic issues have been numismatic favorites.

W-10875 · small · reeded edge · brass

Obverse: Bust of Washington facing right. GEORGE WASHINGTON at border. *Reverse:* All-seeing eye at center with 15 long rays (with shorter rays between them) separating 15 six-pointed stars toward the border. SUCCESS TO THE UNITED STATES around the border. *Edge:* Reeded. *Notes:* Baker-267, Breen-1289, Fuld-WA.1792.5.4.Br. Struck in brass. 20 mm. Some issued with silvered surfaces (worth a premium if in a high grade with much silvering intact; silver example illustrated). Usually lightly struck, with the center of the reverse appearing as a blob. *Rarity:* URS-7.

VF-20	EF-40	AU-50	MS-60	MS-63
$650	$1,200	$2,500		$4,600

W-10877 · plain edge
Design as preceding, but plain edge. *Notes:* Baker-267, Breen-1289, Fuld-WA.1792.5.4.Br. *Rarity:* URS-7.

VF-20	EF-40	AU-50	MS-60	MS-63
$650	$1,200	$2,500	$3,500	$5,000

W-10879 · copper
Design as preceding, plain edge, but struck in copper. *Notes:* Baker-267, Breen-1291, Fuld-WA.1792.5.4b. Attributions to copper are not necessarily reliable, as some brass strikes may appear to be copper. *Rarity:* URS-2 or 3.

W-10881 · pewter or white metal
Design as preceding, plain edge, but struck in pewter or white metal. Breen and Fuld suggest it may be a die trial (pattern). *Notes:* Baker-267S, Breen-1293, Fuld-WA.1792.5.4b. *Rarity:* URS-3.

W-10895 · silver
Design as preceding, but struck in silver. "Hand scalloped edge." Unique. *Notes:* Virgil Brand, New Netherlands (1952), George Fuld (1967), John L. Roper III. Baker-unlisted. Breen-1292, Fuld-WA.1792.5.4c.Ag. *Rarity:* URS-1.

W-10900 · large · reeded edge (first die) · brass
Obverse: Bust of Washington facing right. GEORGE WASHINGTON at border. Bridge of Washington's nose curves slightly inward (ski-jump style). GE (GEORGE) closely spaced; GT (WASHINGTON) closely spaced. *Reverse:* Similar to small-size issue, with all-seeing eye at center with 15 long rays (with shorter rays between them) separating 15 six-pointed stars toward the border. SUCCESS TO THE UNITED STATES around the border. *Edge:* Reeded (first die). *Notes:* Baker-265, Breen-1286, Fuld-WA.1792.5.2.Br. Struck in brass. 26 mm. Many issued with silvered surfaces (worth a premium if in a high grade with much silvering intact). Usually with a prominent die crack above center, from border, through head, nose, exiting to right. Usually lightly struck at the center of the reverse. *Rarity:* URS-7.

VF-20	EF-40	AU-50	MS-60	MS-63
$550	$1,000	$2,300	$3,500	$5,000

W-10905 · plain edge
Design as preceding, but plain edge. *Notes:* Baker-265A, Breen-1287, Fuld-WA.1792.5.2a.Br. *Rarity:* URS-4.

Selected auction price(s): Baltimore Sale (B&M 7/2004), AU-53, $1,725. Old Colony Collection Sale (Stack's [ANR] 12/2005), F-15, $1,495. Norweb Collection Sale (Stack's 11/2006), AU-50, $1,955. Dallas Coin Auction (Heritage 11/2006), MS-62 (NGC), $3,738.

W-10915 · reeded edge (second die)
Obverse: Bust of Washington facing right. GEORGE WASHINGTON at border. Bridge of Washington's nose curves slightly outward ("Roman nose"). *Reverse:* Same as preceding. *Edge:* Reeded (second die). *Notes:* Baker-266, Breen-1282, Fuld-WA.1792.5.1.Br. Struck in brass. 26 mm. Many issued with silvered surfaces (worth a premium if in a high grade with much silvering intact). Usually with a prominent die crack above center, from border, through head, nose, exiting to right. Usually lightly struck at the center of the reverse. *Rarity:* URS-6.

VF-20	EF-40	AU-50	MS-60	MS-63
$550	$1,000	$2,300	$3,500	$5,000

W-10920 · plain edge
Design as preceding, brass, but plain edge. *Notes:* Baker-266B, Breen-1283, Fuld-WA.1792.5.1a.Br. *Rarity:* URS-2 or 3.

Selected auction price(s): Long Beach Sale (Heritage 9/2005), MS-62 (PCGS), $6,038. Baltimore Sale (B&M 3/2006), MS-61 (NGC), $4,255. Dallas Sale (Heritage 7/2006), MS-61 (NGC), $4,600.

W-10925 · reeded edge · copper
Design as preceding, but struck in copper with reeded edge. *Notes:* Baker-266C, Breen-1284, Fuld-WA.1792.5.1b. *Rarity:* URS- or 3.

W-10930 · scalloped edge · silver
Design as preceding, but struck in silver with scalloped edge. *Notes:* Baker-66D, Breen-1285, Fuld-WA.1792.5.1c.Ag. *Rarity:* URS-1.

1795 Grate Halfpenny Tokens

These tokens, part of the Conder series, were made in large quantities as an advertisement for the London firm of Clark & Harris. The die work is attributed to Thomas Wyon, and the pieces are believed to have been struck in Birmingham. They were produced for circulation in the British Isles, although collectors noticed them as well. During the past century, English collectors and dealers have been a ready source for these for American cabinets.

W-10950 · Small Buttons · reeded edge

Obverse: Bust of Washington facing right, larger than on W-10955. Small buttons on coat. G. WASHINGTON: THE FIRM FRIEND TO PEACE & HUMANITY around border. N (HUMANITY) very close to coat. *Reverse:* Fireplace with coal grate, LONDON / 1795 below. PAYABLE BY CLARK & HARRIS 13. WORMWOOD St. BISHOPSGATE around border. *Edge:* Diagonally reeded, slopes down to right. *Notes:* Baker-29D, Breen-1270, Fuld-WA.1795.6. Nearly always seen with significant wear and with lightness of strike in areas, this in contrast to the Large Buttons variety that is easily available in Mint State. Late die state shows piece out of the die in the field below TON (WASHINGTON) and another after Y (HUMANITY). *Rarity:* URS-9.

VG-8	F-12	VF-20	EF-40	AU-50
		$275	$575	$1,100

W-10955 · Large Buttons

Obverse: Bust of Washington facing right, slightly smaller than on W-10950. Large buttons on coat. G. WASHINGTON: THE FIRM FRIEND TO PEACE & HUMANITY around border. Generous space between N (HUMANITY) and coat. *Reverse:* Same as preceding. *Edge:* Diagonally reeded, sloping either down to right or up to right. *Notes:* Baker-29A (reeding slopes down to right), 29AA (slopes down to left), Breen-1271 (reeding slopes down to right), Fuld-WA.1795.5a, Breen-1272 (slopes down to left), Fuld-WA.1795.5a. This is the most plentiful issue, including in Mint State. Most have a die crack on the obverse at THE FIRM. Fuld states that the variety with reeding sloping down to the left has been reported but not seen by modern numismatists, and may not exist. *Rarity:* URS-12.

VF-20	EF-40	AU-50	MS-60	MS-63	MS-65
$210	$425	$650	$750	$1,000	$5,000

W-10960 · brass

Design as preceding, but struck in brass. *Notes:* Breen-1273, Fuld-WA.1795-5.Br. *Rarity:* URS-1.

Selected auction price(s): Garrett IV Sale (3/1981), VF, $2,600.

W-10990 · lettered edge

Design as preceding, but with edge lettered PAYABLE AT LONDON LIVERPOOL OR BRISTOL. *Notes:* Baker-9, Breen-1274, Fuld-WA.1795.5b. Scarce. Usually seen in higher grades. *Rarity:* URS-6.

VF-20	EF-40	AU-50	MS-60	MS-63	MS-65
$425	$850	$1,900	$2,000	$2,700	$5,000

1795 LIBERTY AND SECURITY Issues

The Liberty and Security copper halfpence and pennies were struck in England in 1795 and circulated widely there. The penny in particular is plentiful today and nearly always shows wear, often extensive. All are part of the Conder series.

Halfpence

W-11000 · plain edge

Obverse: Bust of Washington facing right. GEORGE WASHINGTON around top and side border. *Reverse:* Heraldic eagle on spade-shaped shield. LIBERTY AND SECURITY around edge, dated at bottom, divided by shield point as 17 95. *Edge:* Plain. *Notes:* Baker-31C, Breen-1262, Fuld-WA.1795.1c. This particular variety is on a slightly smaller (about 29 mm) planchet than the others. Typically with areas of light striking. *Rarity:* URS-5.

VG-8	F-12	VF-20	EF-40	AU-50
$160	$350	$725		$1,600

W-11005 · ASYLUM edge

Design as preceding, but with edge lettered AN ASYLUM FOR THE OPPRESS'D OF ALL NATIONS. *Notes:* Baker-31A, Breen-1263, Fuld-WA.1795.1a. This is the rarest of the lettered-edge styles. Breen reported that as of 1968 he knew of only a dozen examples. *Rarity:* URS-6.

VG-8	F-12	VF-20	EF-40	AU-50
$300	$650	$1,750		$2,750

W-11010 · BIRMINGHAM edge

Design as preceding, but with edge lettered BIRMINGHAM REDRUTH & SWANSEA, after which are symbols for Mercury, Saturn, the moon, Venus, Jupiter, and Mars. *Notes:* Baker-31B, Breen-1261, Fuld-WA.1795.1b. Typically with areas of light striking. *Rarity:* URS-7.

VG-8	F-12	VF-20	EF-40	AU-50
$170	$375	$850		$1,750

W-11015 · LONDON edge

Design as preceding, but with edge lettered PAYABLE AT LONDON LIVERPOOL OR BRISTOL. *Notes:* Baker-31, Breen-1260, Fuld-WA.1795.1. Typically with areas of light striking. *Rarity:* URS-6.

VG-8	F-12	VF-20	EF-40	AU-50
	$150	$325	$700	$1,200

W-11020 · muling with IRISH HALFPENNY obverse

Reverse as preceding, muled with irrelevant die: standing goddess Hope and anchor, with IRISH HALFPENNY / 1795 around border. Conder token. Always seen with die cracks at the top of the Liberty and Security side. *Notes:* Baker-31M, Breen-1266, Fuld-WA.1795.MI. Of medium scarcity. *Rarity:* URS-6.

W-11025 · muling with FOR THE CONVENIENCE obverse

Reverse as preceding, muled with irrelevant die: Fame flying to left, blowing a trumpet. FOR THE CONVENIENCE OF THE PUBLIC / 1794 around border. Conder token. *Notes:* Baker-31P, Breen-1269, Fuld-WA.1795.M2. Reported in the 19th century. Not traced today. *Rarity:* URS-1(?).

Pennies

W-11050 · (1795) undated

Obverse: Bust of Washington facing left. GEORGE WASHINGTON around top and side border. *Reverse:* Heraldic eagle on space-shaped shield. LIBERTY AND SECURITY around edge. No date. *Edge:* AN ASYLUM FOR THE OPPRESS'D OF ALL NATIONS. *Notes:* Baker-30, Breen-1253, Dalton & Hamer Middlesex-243, Fuld-WA.1795.2. These were made in large quantities and circulated extensively in England. Most show wear. *Rarity:* URS-11 (regular rims and surfaces).

F-12	VF-20	EF-40	AU-50	MS-60	MS-63	MS-65
$300	$525	$1,100	$1,800	$2,000	$3,750	

W-11055 · ornamented rims

Design as preceding, but with rims trimmed/ornamented by engine turning after striking. Sometimes called "corded rim" or "knurled rim." Nearly always seen in higher grades. *Notes:* Baker-30D, Breen-1253, Fuld-WA.1795.5.2d. Garrett's choice Uncirculated sold about twice the price of W-11050. *Rarity:* URS-4.

Selected auction price(s): EAHA Sale (4/2004), MS-62BN (PCGS), $6,037.50. Ford II Sale (5/2004), Choice MS, $8,337.50. EAHA Sale (6/2000), AU-55 (PCGS), $2,990. Long Beach Auction (Heritage 9/2007), MS-61, $13,800. FUN Sale (Heritage 1/2008), MS-60BN (PCGS), $5,175.

W-11060 · normal rims · fire-gilt

Design as preceding, but with normal rims and fire-gilt finish having a bright gold appearance, as made for cabinet purposes. Seen in higher grades. *Notes:* Baker-30D, Breen-1254 (mention of), Fuld-WA.1795.5.2c. *Rarity:* URS-5.

Selected auction price(s): Norweb Sale (11/2006), AU-55, $6,325.

W-11065 · muling with AM I NOT A MAN obverse · plain edge

Reverse of preceding, with eagle, shield, no date, muled with irrelevant die: slave kneeling to the right, AM I NOT A MAN AND A BROTHER in small letters at top and side border; die of Dalton & Hamer Middlesex (Political and Social)-235. *Edge:* Plain. *Notes:* Copper. American Numismatic Society. *Rarity:* URS-1.

W-11080 · white metal

Obverse: Large head of Washington facing right, with tiny rays surrounding, no inscription. *Reverse:* As preceding, with eagle, shield, no date, muled with irrelevant die. *Edge:* Plain. *Notes:* White metal. May have been made later than the 1790s. Two known, American Numismatic Society (Norweb donation) and the piece illustrated in the 1965 Baker reprint (Fuld collection). *Rarity:* URS-2.

W-11085 · 1795 (dated) · LIBERTY AND SECURITY reverse · lettered edge

Obverse: As preceding. *Reverse:* Heraldic eagle on space-shaped shield. LIBERTY AND SECURITY around edge. Date at bottom, divided by shield point as 17 95. *Edge:* AN ASYLUM FOR THE OPPRESS'D OF ALL NATIONS. *Notes:* Baker-32, Breen-1258, Dalton & Hamer Middlesex-244, Fuld-WA.1795.4. This is a well-known rarity. Usually seen well worn. *Rarity:* URS-4.

VG-8	F-12	VF-20	EF-40	AU-50	MS-60
—	—	—	—		

North Wales Halfpenny Tokens

The undated North Wales halfpenny issues, believed to have been struck in England in the early 1790s (usually listed as 1795, although this may be two or three years after they were coined), are part of the "evasion halfpence" series. Accordingly, unlike Conder tokens, they were not created for collectors. None are known to have survived with sharp features and in high grades, as is characteristic of cabinet pieces. All examples are crudely struck on lightweight planchets, from dies displaying a low level of craftsmanship. They were probably made to appear as if circulated for a long time, thus aiding in the acceptance of this unofficial issue, similar to the modus operandi of Machin's Mills in America. Grading of these to reflect actual wear, rather than casual appearance, requires skill and experience.

W-11150 · Two Stars · plain edge · copper

Obverse: Bust of Washington facing left. GEORGEIVS WASHINGTON around top and side border. *Reverse:* Harp with crown, with star above the crown and one star to each side of the base of the harp for a total of two stars. NORTH WALES at border. *Edge:* Plain. *Notes:* Baker-34, Breen-1294 and 1295, Fuld-WA.1795.7. 27 mm. Very thin planchet. In brassy copper, usually dark or black. Raised-rim (usual) and flat-rim styles. *Rarity:* URS-10.

VG-8	F-12	VF-20	EF-40	AU-50
	$275	$675	$2,000	$3,600

W-11160 · Two Stars · LANCASTER LONDON OR BRISTOL edge

Design as preceding, but with edge lettered PAYABLE IN LANCASTER LONDON OR BRISTOL. *Notes:* Baker-34A, Breen-1296, Fuld-WA.1795.7a. Thick (regular) planchet. *Rarity:* URS-5.

VG-8	F-12	VF-20	EF-40
	$1,700	$5,500	$9,000

W-11065 · LANCASTER OR BRISTOL edge

As preceding, but edge lettered PAYABLE IN LANCASTER OR BRISTOL (no mention of London). Possibly a mechanical edge-lettering error? Discovered in London in 1974. *Notes:* Baker-unlisted, Breen-1297, Fuld-WA.1795.7b. *Rarity:* URS-1.

W-11190 · Four Stars

Obverse: Same as preceding. *Reverse:* Harp with crown, with fleur-de-lis above the crown and two stars to each side of the base of the harp for a total of four stars. NORTH WALES at border. *Edge:* Plain. *Notes:* Baker-35, Breen-1298. In brassy copper, usually dark or black. Crudely struck on lightweight planchet, from dies displaying a low level of craftsmanship. Only known in low grades. *Rarity:* URS-5.

VG-8	F-12	VF-20
	$8,000	$20,000

Washington Double-Head Cents

The Washington Double-Head cent is not dated, but some have assigned it the arbitrary date of 1783, as the portrait resembles the 1783 Military Bust tokens (though these were made in the early 19th century). The Military Bust tokens are attributed to dies cut by Thomas Halliday, adapting the portrait of Washington from an Edward Savage painting. This depiction was also used on 1783-dated Washington Military Bust coppers. As to the time of the Double Head cent, it is likely they were struck in Birmingham by Edward Thomason sometime in the 1820s or later. They were made in England, as evidenced by many in collections having been found there, but long after the Conder token era. The piece is denominated ONE CENT and, when exported to the United States, circulated along with Hard Times tokens of the 1830s.

W-11200 · plain edge

Obverse: "Military Bust" portrait of Washington facing to the left, star ornament below (ray points at a border bead), WASHINGTON along the border above. *Reverse:* Portrait similar to the foregoing (but with some differences), ornament below, ONE CENT along the border above. *Edge:* Plain. *Notes:* Baker-6, Breen-1204, Fuld-WA.NC.1783.24, Vlack 28-Y. 27.8 mm average. Many have edge bumps. This issue is common in worn grades but in true Mint State is a notable rarity. *Rarity:* URS-11.

F-12	VF-20	EF-40	AU-50	MS-60
$100	$275	$550	$1,150	

W-11205 · engrailed edge

Design as preceding but with engrailed (incuse reeding) edge. *Notes:* Baker-6A, Breen-1205, Fuld-WA.NC.1783.24a. *Rarity:* URS-1 or 2.

Selected auction price(s): Norweb Sale (11/2006), AU-55, $1,035.

W-11210 · altered portrait

Obverse: Different die with slightly different portrait. Ray on star ornament points between border beads. 29 mm. Flat rims. *Edge:* Plain. *Notes:* Published by Mike Ringo, *CNL 81*, April 1989. Richard August collection (discovery coin) and 2008 eBay offering. As this variety is largely unknown except to advanced specialists, an opportunity exists to look for one among regular issues. Baker-6B, Fuld-WA.NC.1783.25, Vlack 29-Y. *Rarity:* URS-1.

Washington Colonial Patterns and Die Trials

The following die trials, patterns, and related pieces have been described by George J. Fuld for inclusion in the present text. All are very rare.

W-11250 · Large Eagle cent reverse die trial · BERSHAM BRADLEY edge

Weight 190.3 grains. Very similar to adopted die, but there is no outline around the shield as on the regular issue. Top of O of ONE is closed. The reverse is blank, but rough, with scratched numbers "41474" which may refer to the job or shop number. *Edge:* lettered BERSHAM BRADLEY WILLEY SNEDSHILL. *Notes:* Baker-15G, Fuld-WA.1791.P1, Breen-1214. Unique. *Rarity:* URS-1.

Selected auction price(s): Garrett IV Sale (3/1981), EF, $1,550; later in the Ford II Sale (5/2004), $6,325.

W-11255 · SHREWSBURY edge

Weight 167.6 grains. Identical to the adopted 1791 Large Eagle Cent with a blank, irregular reverse. Open O in ONE. *Edge:* lettered PAYABLE AT SHREWSBURY, representing blanks of Salop Woolen Manufactory halfpence, D&H Shropshire (Shrewsbury) 19-21, by Hancock. *Notes:* Baker-15F, Fuld-WA.1791.P2, Breen-1215. *Rarity:* URS-2.

Selected auction price(s): Garrett IV Sale (3/1981), AU, $1,900.

W-11260 · UNUM E PLURIBUS

An early die trial of the Large Eagle cent, similar to W-10610 before lettering added and without ribbon through eagle's beak. Hand punched where ribbon would be is UNUM E PLURIBUS, with some letters reversed. *Notes:* Baker-15H, Fuld-WA.1791.P3, Breen-1213. *Rarity:* URS-1.

Selected auction price(s): Garrett IV Sale (3/1981), EF, $1,650; later in the Ford II Sale (5/2004), as struck, $6,325.

W-11265 · Small Eagle cent reverse die trial

The adopted die of the small eagle cent, struck about 5 percent off center, Kolit 12. *Reverse:* Blank with small, raised, "icicle"-shaped segment. *Notes:* Baker-unlisted, Fuld-WA.1791.P4, Breen-unlisted. *Rarity:* URS-1.

Selected auction price(s): Norweb Sale (11/2006), $9,200.

W-11270 · Large Eagle cent die trial · large thin flan

Weight 127.4 grains. An oddly struck pattern showing the regular Washington obverse date 1791, with a Large Eagle die trial reverse struck on a very large flan of 32.3 mm diameter. The flan is very thin, about 1 mm, and the edge of the beading of the obverse and reverse is at least 1 mm in from the edge. The coin has been canceled by a small burred roller, leaving about 6 mm grooves, and then apparently machine canceled. There is no trace of the shield on the eagle's breast. Traces of lettering on the edge, with only ABLE discernible. *Notes:* Baker-unlisted, Fuld-WA.1791.P5, Breen-unlisted. *Rarity:* URS-1.

W-11275 · Large Eagle / George III muling

Weight 215.4 grains. Regular Large Eagle cent reverse with obverse showing George III, the obverse of Peck-924. *Obverse:* Laureated bust of George III facing left, GEORGE III DEI GRATIA around. *Notes:* Baker-15AA, Fuld-WA.1791.P6, Breen-1216. *Rarity:* URS-1.

W-11280 · 1791 Large Eagle cent die trial

Weight 182.7 grains. The regular Large Eagle cent obverse with an unfinished reverse, lacking, ONE CENT. Edge inscribed BERSHAM BRADLEY WILLEY SNEDSHILL, on a blank for Hancock's John Wilkinson Iron Master token, D&H Warwickshire 332-445. *Notes:* Baker-15E, Fuld-WA.1791.P7, Breen-1210. *Rarity:* URS-1.

W-11285 · Uniface obverse-punch die trial

Weight 194 grains. Bust on a plain field, reverse blank. No coat buttons, queue and epaulets are unfinished. *Edge:* Lettered PAYABLE AT MACCLESFIELD LIVERPOOL OR CONGLETON X. The edge represents blanks for Roe & Co., Macclesfield halfpence, D&H Cheshire 8/60. *Notes:* Baker-unlisted, Fuld-WA.1791.P8, Breen-1211. *Rarity:* URS-1.

Selected auction price(s): Ford II Sale (5/2004), as struck, $5,520. Norweb Sale (11/2006), MS, $12,650.

W-11290 · 1791 Small Eagle Hub die trial

Weight 188.4 grains. An obverse hub punch die trial, impression similar to W-1063 s0. Reverse blank. *Edge:* BERSHAM, BRADLEY, WILLEY, SNEDSHILL. As on the coin, Washington's queue and epaulet are incomplete and there are no buttons on the coat. *Notes:* Unlisted in Baker, Fuld, Breen, and Crosby. *Rarity:* URS-1.

Selected auction price(s): Ford II Sale (5/2004), as struck, $4,370.

W-11295 · Small Eagle obverse die trial

Weight 192.4 grains. Identical to the regular issue, but there are no buttons on the jacket of Washington. Queue and epaulets are unfinished. Reverse blank. Edge inscribed PAYABLE AT THE WAREHOUSE OF THOS. &

ALEXR. HUTCHINSON. Blank originally intended for Hutchinson's 1790-1 Edinburgh halfpence by Hancock, D&H Lancashire (Edinburgh) 22-37. *Notes:* Baker-16F, Fuld-WA.1791.P9, Breen-1221. *Rarity:* URS-1.

Selected auction price(s): Ford II Sale (5/2004), as struck, $6,612.50. FUN Sale (Heritage, 1/2007), MS-63 (NGC), $12,650.

W-11300 · Small Eagle obverse die trial

Weight 193.5 grains. Same dies as previous but with different edge lettering. *Edge:* Lettered PAYABLE AT MACCLESFIELD LIVERPOOL OR CONGELTON X. *Notes:* Baker-16E, Fuld-WA.1791.P10, Breen-1212. *Rarity:* URS-1.

Selected auction price(s): Norweb Sale (11/2006), $12,650.

W-11310 · Roman Head cent uniface die trial

Weight 197.4 grains. The hub head of Washington is identical to the hub on the regular 1792 Roman head cent, W-8540. The legend WASHINGTON PRESIDENT. is the same as on the regular issue, but positioned differently. In place of the date in exergue, I. G. HANCOCK'S. The edge is lettered PAYABLE AT MACCLESFIELD LIVERPOOL OR CONGLETON. The only known specimen was stolen from Richard Picker in 1971 and has not been recovered. *Notes:* Baker-19A, Fuld-WA.1792.P1, Breen-1248. *Rarity:* URS-1.

W-11320 · PRESEDENT · white metal

The Washington hub is slightly different from the regular issue, W-8540. It does not bear a date. The obverse legend reads WASHINGTON PRESEDENT [*sic*]. The reverse is blank and slightly incuse, not sharply struck, a brockage. The only known specimen was stolen from Richard Picker in 1971 and has not been recovered. *Notes:* Baker-19C, Fuld-WA.1792.P2, Breen-1247. *Rarity:* URS-1.

11

UNRELATED FOREIGN COINS AND TOKENS

INTRODUCTION

This section is devoted to the many coins "adopted" by American collectors and listed in popular reference books the Red Book and *Walter Breen's Complete Encyclopedia of U.S. and Colonial Coins*, but not specifically related to areas now a part of the United States. Some of these pieces circulated extensively in America, as did hundreds of other types, including some designated as legal tender. However, they bear no inscriptions pertaining to what is now the United States, save for certain of the curious Elephant tokens of circa 1694, but in a different context.

In *Scott's Comprehensive Catalogue and Encyclopedia of U.S. Coins*, 1971, Don Taxay put certain of these in a section titled "Quasi Colonial and Early American Coins," noting:

> These are coins, tokens, and medals which traditionally have been included in the American series, but properly form no part of it. Some have a peripheral or oblique association, while others might well be called pseudo-colonials. The status of particular issues may be inferred from their accompanying descriptions.

Then followed listings for Sommer Islands coins, Elephant tokens, St. Patrick's coins, Wood's Hibernia coinage, Voce Populi coppers, and several medalets and tokens including the Pitt, Rhode island, Franklin Press, Theatre at New York, and North American issues. Six different French colonial coins were listed among American pieces.

Coins struck in France and used there as well as in its possessions have been popular with some American numismatists. To list them all would exceed the space available in this text. Similarly, Spain and its New World possessions made many coins with Spanish inscriptions that were widely used in the colonies and also in western districts that later became part of the United States. Spanish issues were *much* more widely circulated than French coins. It can be said that any coins or tokens struck in or for Alaska and Hawaii prior to their statehood in 1959 could be called "colonial" or "territorial" coins; ditto for gold coins struck in San Francisco prior to California statehood in 1850. Again, there are limits.

Coinage for the Sommer Islands (Bermuda) 1616

Bermuda shilling. (A.M. Smith, *Visitor's Guide & History of the United States Mint*, 1885)

Introduction

The Sommer (or Somer) Islands, or the Bermuda Islands as they are known today, are not part of what is now the United States. At one time they were under control of the Virginia Company, a joint-stock mercantile venture based in London and formed under a royal charter. There were actually two companies: the Virginia Company of Plymouth (for what today is New England) and the Virginia Company of London (for the South). The latter company established Jamestown in 1607. The mishap of George Somers on his way there in 1609 is history. Bermuda then became a separate entity of the Virginia Company of London, from November 1612 until June 29, 1615. On the latter date, "the Governour and Company of the City of London for the Plantacon of the Somer Islands," based in London and often called the Bermuda Company by historians, was officially incorporated under royal charter. This document granted the right of coinage. The coins did not arrive in the islands until May 16, 1616, at the earliest, a year after Bermuda was under its new charter.

Bermuda was never a part of Virginia. The political relationship between them is that both, for about three years and prior to the coinage, were under the umbrella of the Virginia Company. Details can be found in Louis E. Jordan's article "Somer Islands 'Hogge Money' of 1616: The Historical Context," in the *Colonial Newsletter*, August 2003. Notwithstanding this, some numismatists have adopted these interesting and rare coins into the American colonial series.

The Red Book heralds its colonial section with the Bermuda issues, in good company with Sylvester S. Crosby's magisterial *Early Coins of America*, 1875, with the same beginning. Crosby noted, "As the coinage for the Bermuda or Sommer Islands was doubtless the first ever struck for the English colonies in America, that first claims attention in the development of our plan." He then drew upon Captain John Smith's *Generall Historie of Virginia New-England and the Summer Isles*, 1624, for basic information (a source that has been tapped ever since).

An early numismatic mention of the Bermuda coinage is found in T. Snelling, *A View of the Silver Coin and Coinage of England*, 1762:

> We now come to those coins we have been able to discover, that have been struck in our West India colonies.
>
> The first of them, in order of time, appertains to the Sommer or Summer Islands, which received their name from Sir George Sommers who was shipwrecked there, anno 1609. A colony was endeavoured to be settled there under the Virginia Company in 1612, Mr. John More being sent for that purpose; he was succeeded by Capt. Daniel Tuckar, in whose time it was our piece, No. 19 [in the illustrations] had a currency, as we are informed by Capt. Smith. His words are these, "besides meat and drink, and cloaths, they had for a time a certaine kind of brass money, with a Hogge on one side, in memory of the abundance of hogges which were found at their first landing." Over the Hog on No. 19, is XII. The signification of which we do not know. It has on its reverse a Ship. We have never seen any other than this single piece, which is in the collection of Mr. Hollis.

As noted, Snelling was aware of but a single coin and denomination, a brass shilling.

While the Bermuda coins were struck for an English settlement in the Western Hemisphere, in 1616 the Bermuda Islands were not part of the Virginia colony proper. The distinction is technical, but very important.

The Sommer Islands Coinage

The Sommer (per the spelling on the coins) Islands were first visited by Englishmen when a party including Henry May and Capt. Lancaster was shipwrecked there in 1591. In 1593 a French man-of-war was wrecked there. After a six-month stint on the otherwise uninhabited islands, survivors sailed to Newfoundland in a small ship they had constructed. Earlier, circa 1505, the islands are said to have been discovered by Juan Bermudez, a Spaniard, who later was shipwrecked there in 1532. This Spanish captain gave the islands their lasting name. Alternatively, a ship may have borne the name *Bermudez* or something similar. Facts are scarce.

In July 1609, nine ships were sent from England with Sir Thomas Gates, Sir George Somers, Capt. Christopher Newport, and 500 others to establish a new government in Virginia, where Capt. John Smith was governor. The fleet ran into a fierce hurricane, and three days later was driven ashore on the Bermudez Islands, as they were known by then to some, sometimes spelled Bermoothes in English. Hogge Islands was another appellation, as was Devil Island. Capt. Smith told of the flagship, the *Sea Adventure*:

> Not long it was before they struck upon a rock, until a surge of the sea cast her from thence, and so from one to another, until most luckily at last so upright betwixt two, as if she had been in the stocks. They unshipped all of their goods, victuals, and persons into the boats, with

extreme joy, even almost to amazedness, arrived in safety, although then a league from the shore, without the loss of a man, yet were they in all 150 . . . and they found the land to be the richest, health fullest, and pleasantest they ever saw.

Shortly after their arrival the castaways killed 32 hogs and hundreds of other specimens of wildlife, mainly birds. The wild hogs, black in color and menacing in their demeanor, were in abundance, descended from stock that came ashore from Bermudez's wrecked ship. It was customary to carry livestock and fowl on ocean voyages to provide a supply of fresh meat.

By May 1610 two new ships of cedar, the *Deliverance* and the *Patience*, had been constructed, fitted with supplies from the wrecks, and stocked with provisions. On the 10th of that month, most of the refugees departed the islands and sailed to Virginia, leaving just three people behind.

On June 19, 1610, Sir George Somers, then about 60 years of age, set sail on a ship of 30-ton displacement to visit the Bermuda Islands again. Following an arduous journey, delayed by adverse weather, he finally arrived. Fortune did not attend him for long, and in the place called St. George's Island he died. In honor of Somers, the area became known as the Somer Islands.

Sensing an economic opportunity, a group of 120 persons affiliated with the Virginia Company acquired its supposed right to the islands and separately obtained a patent from the king giving them authority over the area. Richard Moore (or More) was elected governor of what was anticipated to become a thriving settlement and port of call.

On July 11, 1612, under the direction of Moore, 60 persons arrived at the south side of Smith's Island. Moore governed until 1615, at which time he was succeeded by six governors, each of whom held the position for one month in alternation. Capt. John Smith's memoirs identify four of these governors as being Charles Caldicot, John Mansfield, Christopher Carter, and Miles Kendall. Their collective rule was despotic, causing much dissatisfaction and many desertions. As noted above, on June 29, 1615, the Bermuda Company, as it was sometimes later designated, was chartered as a separate entity, based in London and no longer connected with the Virginia Company.

A new governor, Daniel Tuckar (or Tucker), a planter from the Virginia Plantation, arrived in the middle of May 1616. Tucker found that the colonists had fallen into idle ways, resenting leadership and avoiding labor. He instituted a strict administration and began the task of clearing trees, preparing timber, planting vines and fruits, and otherwise organizing the colony. His command was also viewed as despotic. It was during his two years of rule that the Bermuda coins were introduced. As they had an exchange value but little intrinsic worth, they could just as easily be called tokens. Notwithstanding the utility of these pieces, nearly all commerce was conducted in tobacco, including the payment of taxes and the loaning and repayment of money.

Coins Authorized, Struck, and Distributed

The Bermuda coins were authorized under letters patent of James I, on June 29, 1615, for the Bermuda Company, noting (edited):

> And we do further for us, our heirs and successors, that they shall and lawfully may establish and cause to be made a coin to pass current in their said Somer Islands, between the inhabitants there for the more easy of commerce and bargaining between them of such metal and in such manner and form said Governor and Company in any of their said General Courts shall limit and appoint.
>
> We have appointed a base coin which we send rated with our provisions, whereby you may give to such men their weekly wages when they work, and as you shall find them to deserve, with which coin it shall be lawful and free for them to buy any provisions out of the store, or any fish, corn, tools, or any such thing in the Islands where they can get the same. And to that end you shall proclaim the said coin to be current to pass freely from man to man, only throughout the islands, and not otherwise.

Pieces were struck in the denominations of two pence, threepence, sixpence, and shilling, bearing the denominations II, III, VI, and XII, respectively, Each of the several values depicts a wild hog on the obverse, with the denomination above, and with SOMMER I[S]LANDS within two circles of beads on the VI and XII, while the II and III values have one circle of beads and lack the name. The reverse illustrates a full-rigged sailing ship, presumably the *Sea Adventure*, with the flag of St. George. Shilling varieties have either large or small sails, and threepence and sixpence coins exist with either large or small portholes. The twopence and threepence have the location identified by an S on one side of the ship and an I on the other.

Thin brass planchets or blanks were used to strike the coins, after which many if not all of them were given a light wash or coating of silver. In an era when British silver shillings and fractions traded in commerce based on their intrinsic value, the Bermuda pieces were tokens of little value, a fiat currency that circulated in the manner that paper money would later be used worldwide—good as long as both parties had confidence in the value. As might be expected, these coins had little or no trade value other than within the islands, where they were mostly used at the company storehouse, exchanged for supplies. At the same time, various commodities, including tobacco leaves, served as mediums of exchange. The supply ship *Diana* arrived on January 15, 1618, and sold goods directly to the colonists, who paid with tobacco. After this time the Bermuda coins (or tokens) were retired.

Numismatic Aspects

Until the widespread popularity of metal detection with electronic devices in the late 20th century, all Bermuda coins were considered to be rare, and many extremely rare. In

1993 and 1994, in archaeological excavations on Castle Island, 19 Bermuda coins were found. These consisted of 17 sixpence pieces and two shillings. Others have been found by metal detectorists. This is a dramatic change from the day of Snelling when just one coin, a shilling, was known, and from Crosby, who knew of but three shillings and a solitary sixpence.

Typical grades are Good to Fine or Very Fine, often with heavy green oxidation or patination (unless cleaned), with rough surfaces, sometimes with pieces of the rim broken away. Few show traces of silvering. In recent decades, dozens more have been discovered, most showing extensive corrosion and barely identifiable as to variety. The Bermuda Maritime Museum, located in an old fort at the Royal Navy Dockyard, displays many such finds.

Choice examples in Fine or better preservation, with minimum corrosion, remain rare and typically are encountered only when important specialized collections come on the market.

Market values are for coins that show medium corrosion. Higher-grade coins, as well as coins with smooth surfaces and well-defined details, are worth more. Extensively corroded coins with major portions of the design indistinct and with incomplete rims are valued lower. *Coins of Bermuda*, issued by the Bermuda Monetary Authority in 1997, is a valuable guide to the series and has been employed in the following descriptions.

Bermuda Twopence

W-11400 · British Monetary Authority (BMA) Type I · Small Star below hog

Obverse: Hog facing left. II over bristly hairs; both I's same height. Small star (in all instances, perhaps a flower) under belly. Row of five pellets below grass, plus another pellet below the row. *Reverse:* Two-masted ship with S to the left of the bow and I to the right of the stern. Bow faces left (as on all Bermuda coins). *Notes:* Breen-7. About 16 to 17 mm. *Rarity:* URS-4.

G-4	VG-8	F-12	VF-20	EF-40	AU-50	MS-60
$7,000	$10,000	$18,000	$50,000	$80,000		

W-11410 · BMA Type II · Large Star below hog

Obverse: First I is high. Large star under belly. Pellets similar to the preceding. *Reverse:* Same die as preceding. *Notes:* Breen-6. About 16 to 17.5 mm. *Rarity:* URS-4.

G-4	VG-8	F-12	VF-20	EF-40	AU-50	MS-60
$7,000	$10,000	$18,000	$50,000	$80,000		

Bermuda Threepence

W-11420 · BMA Type I · Small Portholes

Obverse: Hog facing left. III centered over back. Pellet, with four pellets surrounding, to left of forefeet. *Reverse:* Two-masted ship with S to the left of the bow and I to the right of the stern. Smaller portholes than on the following. *Notes:* Breen-4. About 21 mm. In 1997 the BMA knew of just six; since then, others have been found. *Rarity:* URS-4 or 5.

G-4	VG-8	F-12	VF-20	EF-40	AU-50	MS-60
—	$75,000	$125,000	$175,000	—		

W-11425 · BMA-unlisted · Large Portholes

Obverse: Hog facing left. Group of five dots in field in front of snout. In denomination III each element is slightly higher from left to right. *Reverse:* Larger portholes than on the preceding. *Notes:* About 19 mm. Unique, Bowers and Merena sale of March 1999, lot 1001, Fine but holed and with two attempted puncture marks; net G-6. *Rarity:* URS-1.

Bermuda Sixpence

W-11440 · BMA Type II · Small Portholes

Obverse: SOMMER ILANDS around border. Beaded circle within, enclosing hog facing left. VI centered above back. Four pellets between legs plus a fifth pellet below grass. *Reverse:* Three-masted sailing ship with four small portholes. Row of widely spaced studs on planking over the portholes. *Notes:* Breen-4. About 25 to 27 mm. Most pieces show extensive corrosion. *Rarity:* URS-5.

G-4	VG-8	F-12	VF-20	EF-40
$5,000	$8,000	$15,000	$50,000	$75,000

W-11445 · BMA Type I · Large Portholes

Obverse: Same as preceding. *Reverse:* Four portholes slightly larger than on the preceding. *Notes:* Breen-3. About 25 to 27 mm. This is the variety found in the largest numbers in Bermuda from the 1990s to date. Most show extensive oxidation. *Rarity:* URS-6.

G-4	VG-8	F-12	VF-20	EF-40
$5,000	$8,000	$15,000	$50,000	$75,000

Bermuda Shillings

W-11460 · BMA Type I · Small Sail

Obverse: SOMMER ISLANDS within beaded border. The first S (ISLANDS) is weak. At the center a circle of beads encloses a hog facing left. XII over back. Ground below feet. *Reverse:* Outside border of beads encloses a three-masted ship. Sail slightly smaller than on the following. Leftmost sail distant from border. Number of portholes uncertain; may be as many as eight. Waves below ship. *Notes:* Breen-2. About 30 to 35 mm, most are 31 to 32 mm. The usually encountered variety of this denomination. *Rarity:* URS-7.

G-4	VG-8	F-12	VF-20	EF-40
$7,000	$12,000	$40,000	$68,000	$100,000

W-11465 · BMA Type II · Large Sail

Obverse: Similar to the preceding, but with three pellets in front of forelegs and one pellet under the hog. *Reverse:* Similar to the preceding, but with larger sail. Leftmost sail very close to border. Nine or 10 portholes. *Notes:* Breen-1. About 30 to 35 mm. This was the only variety known to Snelling in 1762. *Rarity:* URS-4.

G-4	VG-8	F-12	VF-20	EF-40
$8,000	$17,000	$50,000	$85,000	—

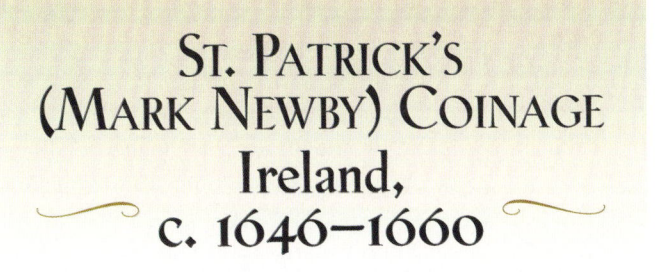

St. Patrick's (Mark Newby) Coinage
Ireland, c. 1646–1660

History

In 1881, Dr. Edward Maris, in his text on New Jersey coppers, included mention of the St. Patrick's or Mark Newby (spelled Newbie by some) coins. These pieces, listed in the Red Book, continue to be collected by some as an adjunct to the later New Jersey coppers of 1786 to 1788. Some numismatists consider them to be a basic part of the American colonial series. Opinions vary.

Newby, who had been a shopkeeper in Dublin in the 1670s, moved to Bellicane, County Wicklow, then emigrated to West Jersey (today's New Jersey), arriving on November 19, 1681, with a group of others.

He brought with him a quantity of coins of St. Patrick's halfpence. Newby, who subsequently became a member of the West Jersey Legislature, influenced the province to pass an act on May 8, 1682, which provided

> that Mark Newby's half-pence, called Patrick's [sic] half-pence, shall from and after this said 18th instant, pass for half-pence current pay of this Province, provided he, the said Mark, give sufficient security to the Speaker of this House; for the use of the General Assembly from time to time being, that he the said Mark, his executors and administrators, shall and will change the said half-pence for any pay equivalent, upon demand: and provided also that no person or persons be hereby obliged to take more than five shillings in one payment.

Thus, by legislative act, these pieces became "current pay" for small transactions in West Jersey. However, as the inscriptions do not relate at all to West Jersey, and most such pieces circulated elsewhere, there is no direct connection with America beyond that of many other foreign coins that were made legal tender by acts of various colonial governments.

The St. Patrick coppers were minted in two weights and diameters, the smaller being far more common. Because of this size differential, the natural numismatic reflex has been to consider them in a farthing/halfpenny relationship, despite the fact that the smaller is far more than half the weight of the larger. Some theories have suggested that they were minted in a combination of twopence and pennies, or as pennies and halfpence, or a currently popular concept that they were both halfpence, but of different sizes. It has been stressed that while the denomination for which either was originally struck remains unconfirmed, it remains irrelevant what value later generations may have assigned to them under the pressure of changing economic conditions. Those few that have been located in America by metal detectorists have all been the smaller-sized coin, strongly suggesting that this was the variety imported by Newby and legalized to pass for a halfpenny in West Jersey. These and related topics are well covered in the American Numismatic Society's 2006 *Coinage of the Americas Conference* anthology.

There have been many opinions and theories relating to when these coins were issued in Ireland and by whom. Research by Brian Danforth, Oliver D. Hoover, and others, published in the *Colonial Newsletter* and the *American Journal of Numismatics*, together with contributions by other scholars in recent years, has brought new information to light, illuminating a coinage for which documentation is scarce in certain aspects.

It has been suggested that these undated coins were likely struck for circulation in Ireland circa 1667 to 1669 by Pierre Blondeau to fill an order made by James Butler, the Duke of Ormonde. Again, facts are hard to come by.

The obverse of the "farthing" depicts King David, kneeling while playing an Irish harp, with a crown above. During the coinage process these pieces, made of copper, had a small piece of brass inserted at the crown point to give it a golden appearance. The reverse shows St. Patrick standing, with a church to the right.

The obverse design of the "halfpenny" is similar to the "farthing." The reverse depicts St. Patrick standing, surrounded by a group of followers, and with a shield.

St. Patrick is the ancient Episcopal patron of Ireland. While he is generally attributed as a Catholic bishop, on the coin he wears the vestments of an Anglican bishop. The writings of Hoover and Danforth beckon for anyone interested in a further explanation of the series.

Numismatic Notes

Today, copper impressions of the "farthing" and "halfpenny" are regularly encountered in collections. More than 140 die varieties of the smaller denomination have been identified, and just nine of the larger. Excavation and metal-detector finds in New Jersey have brought to light multiple "farthing" coins, suggesting that they may have been the main size used, but valued at a halfpenny in legislation. None of the "halfpenny" size have been found this way. This is in contravention to earlier conventional wisdom that the larger pieces were the ones authorized as legal tender. Silver specimens, sometimes referred to as patterns, were perhaps intended for coinage by the issuer, as many are found badly worn, including one found in New Jersey. These were not authorized by that colony, nor were gold strikings. A unique specimen of the last may have been intended for use as a sovereign in Ireland.

The typical St. Patrick's coin is likely to be a dark color, often oxidized, and to show extensive use in circulation. Die varieties exist and have attracted the attention of some specialists. Most examples have been acquired from numismatists in England during the past 150 years.

St. Patrick's "Farthing"

W-11500 · copper

Obverse: King David playing a harp. FLOREAT / REX to left and right. *Reverse:* Saint Patrick standing. Church to the right and vanquished serpents to the left, apparently a reference to the saint driving the snakes from Ireland. QVIESCAT PLEBS at the border. *Edge:* Reeded. *Notes:* Copper, often with a brass plug in the planchet in the area of the crown, to make it appear "golden." This size likely represents the coins that circulated in the colony of New Jersey. Oliver D. Hoover suggests that if FLOREAT REX and QVIESCAT PLEBS are read together, they would translate to mean that King David and his subjects are bound together in a common fulfillment of religion. Others have translated QVIESCAT PLEBS to "May the people be quiet" or "May there be peace." A contemporary counterfeit in the Richard August collection may have been made in America; if so, this would have special significance. *Rarity:* URS-13.

G-4	VG-8	F-12	VF-20	EF-40	AU-50
$125	$300	$800	$2,750	$6,000	$12,000

W-11520 · silver

Design as preceding, but struck in silver. *Notes:* Some of these may have circulated in New Jersey or in Ireland. Not specifically authorized by the colony. Multiple die combinations exist, indicating a fairly extensive coinage. *Rarity:* URS-7.

G-4	VG-8	F-12	VF-20	EF-40	AU-50
$1,800	$2,800	$5,750	$9,500	$13,500	$18,000

W-11530 · gold

Designs the same as the copper "farthing," W-11500. *Edge:* Reeded. *Notes:* Breen-209. Possibly a pattern made for an early numismatic cabinet, or possibly used in commerce as a sovereign. The Norweb coin, cataloged as controversial, was determined to be a forgery. *Rarity:* URS-1.
Selected auction price(s): John J. Ford Jr. VII Sale (Stack's 1/2005), AU, $184,000.

St. Patrick's Halfpenny

W-11540 · reeded edge · copper

Obverse: King David playing a harp. FLORE / AT / REX at border. *Reverse:* Saint Patrick standing with followers nearby. ECCE GREX at top border. *Edge:* Reeded. *Notes:* Breen-198 to 204. Copper, often with a brass plug in the planchet in the area of the crown, to make it appear "golden." This size seems to have no connection with West Jersey. Nine die varieties are known. *Rarity:* URS-10.

G-4	VG-8	F-12	VF-20	EF-40	AU-50
$400	$1,000	$1,800	$4,500	$13,000	$19,000

W-11550 · plain edge · silver

Design as preceding. *Edge:* Plain. *Notes:* Breen-205. Possibly used in Ireland as a shilling. Usually seen well worn. *Rarity:* URS-2 or 3.

French Colonial Coinage
France and America

History

On February 19, 1670, Louis XIV authorized coinage for general use in the French possessions in America, including Canada and the West Indies. Coined at the time were silver pieces denominated 5 sols and 15 sols. Of the former, 200,000 were struck, and of the latter 40,000 were coined.

In December 1716 the regent for Louis XV authorized the coinage of 6-denier and 12-denier copper pieces to be struck at the Perpignan Mint in France. Problems developed with the quality of the copper to be used, and only a few pieces were struck. Some additional pieces under this authorization are dated 1720, but the origin of these has been questioned. The 1717 to 1720 issues are of great rarity. These may have been in Louisiana.

From 1709 to 1713, coinage of billon metal (an alloy mostly composed of copper, with silver added to give it a gray color) in denominations of 15 deniers and 30 deniers were struck at mints in France, as were half sou marque and sou marquee coins later on, from 1738 to 1760. These were circulated throughout the colonies, especially Canada and the West Indies. None bore a specific legend or reference to the Americas, however.

In June 1721 Louis XV authorized a copper coinage for the colonies, with the designation COLONIES FRANÇOISES. These pieces, copper sous valued at 9 deniers, were struck at the Rouen ("B" mintmark) and La Rochelle ("H" mintmark) mints in 1721 and exclusively at La Rochelle in 1722.

While certain earlier French colonial issues could claim a relation to Louisiana, which was ceded to Spain (areas west of the Mississippi river) in 1762 and to England (areas east of the Mississippi) in 1763, another such issue struck in copper and dated 1767 is related only to the West Indies. Although they are not listed here, such pieces are described in the Red Book and elsewhere. France reacquired Louisiana in 1801 but sold the territory to the United States in 1803. No French coins were ever made specifically for the Louisiana district.

Numismatic Aspects

Robert A. Vlack in particular has popularized these coins, beginning with his *Early American Coins* book in the 1960s, continuing to his extensively researched *An Illustrated Catalogue of the French Billon Coinage in the Americas*, 2004. Vlack's *Early American Coins* lists just these specific issues made for *Canada:*

> 1670 15 sols, 1670 5 sols, 1670 double denier, and 9 deniers coppers of 1721-B, 1721-H, 1722/1-H, 1722-H, 1767-A, and 1767 with RF counterstamp.

"An American Collector's Guide to the Coins of Nouvelle France," by Michael J. Hodder, 1994 (from the 1992 Coinage of the Americas Conference) states this:

> Are there any coins that are really French-Canadian? What types can a collector include with confidence? Finding an answer is not as easy as posing the question. . . . [R.W.] McLachlan pointed out that the first coin specifically to mention Canada in its legends was the 1794 Copper Company of Upper Canada token. No other coin prior to [that] date bears the words "Canada" or "Nouvelle France" it its legends. The double of the 1670 issue is the only French colonial coin that bears the word "America" as part of its legends.

The same writer noted that no French coins were struck exclusively for circulation in Nouvelle France to the exclusion of other New World colonies. Admit "other colonies" into the evaluation, and these are included:

> The 1670 silver 5 and 15 sols, the "Gloriam Regni" issue, and the copper double de l'Amérique françoise of the same date. . . .
>
> The earlier douzains with a similar counterstamp, authorized by Louis XIII in 1640, are another probable candidate for this category. These two types are, almost certainly, the sols marquez referred to in Quebec ordinances dated prior to 1710, such as that of March 20, 1662, raising the ratings of French coins in Canada. On the strength of this proposed attribution these two types are included in this category. The billon 30 deniers of 1710–15 struck at Lyon, the so-called mousquetaires, were authorized by royal decree to circulate in Nouvelle France. Also included are the 1717-Q copper 12 and 6 deniers colonies, and the 1721-B, 1721-H, 1722/1-H, and 1722 H copper sols of 9 deniers which replaced the 1717 coins.

In the same vein, the Red Book lists certain issues made for Canada and the West Indies, but notes, "The copper coinage of 1717 to 1722 was authorized by edicts of 1716 and 1721 for use in New France, Louisiana, and the French West Indies." Many different varieties exist.

For in-depth discussions, the earlier mentioned Vlack *Illustrated Catalogue* is essential. Only a few types made especially for the French colonies are described in the present text. Paris coins have an A mintmark, Rouen a B, Lyon a D, LaRochelle an H, Perpignan a Q. There were many other mints as well, but these were not relevant to Louisiana.

Coins Struck for Nouvelle France, but Not Louisiana

W-11600 · 1670-A Double Denier · copper

Obverse: L at center, inscription around. *Reverse:* The inscription DOVBLE / DE LA / MERIQVE / FRANCOISE, three fleurs-de-lis, and mintmark A. *Notes:* Breen-257, Hodder-2. This is the only issue in the series with an inscription

281

specifically pertaining to America. At this early time, however, Louisiana had not been settled by the French. Accordingly, the relation of this and other 1670 coinage to U.S. colonial areas is debatable. Authorized by the edict of February 19, 1670. Unique. Norweb collection. *Rarity:* URS-1.

Selected auction price(s): Norweb Collection Part I (1987), VF, $65,000.

W-11605 · 1670-A 5 Sols (1/12 écu) · silver
Obverse: Bust of Louis XIV facing right, inscription around. *Reverse:* Crowned shield surrounded by inscription, including GLORIAM REGNI. *Notes:* Breen-256, Hodder-3. Die varieties exist. Authorized by the edict of February 19, 1670. *Rarity:* URS-5.

VG-8	F-12	VF-20	EF-40	AU-50	MS-60
$650	$1,200	$2,500	$4,500		

W-11610 · 1670-A 15 Sols (1/4 écu) · silver
Obverse: Bust of Louis XIV facing right, inscription around. *Reverse:* Crowned shield surrounded by inscription, including GLORIAM REGNI. *Notes:* Breen-255, Hodder-4. Authorized by the edict of February 19, 1670. *Rarity:* URS-4.

VG-8	F-12	VF-20	EF-40
$12,000	$30,000	$70,000	$100,000

Coins Specifically Relevant to Louisiana

The 1709 to 1722 issues are relevant as U.S. "colonials" in addition to use in other colonies.

W-11700 to 11745 · 1709-D to 1713-D · 30 Deniers aux 2 L Couronnes · "Mousquetaire"
Obverse: Double L's back to back, crowned. Fleurs-de-lis in field. Inscription around border. *Reverse:* Outline cross with fleurs-de-lis in angles. Inscription around border. *Notes:* Hodder-7. Hodder: "Authorized by edicts of September 26, 1709, and June 15, 1711. Forty million ordered struck, but the actual mintage exceeded 122 million. Lyon Mint issues authorized for circulation only in Nouvelle, France. Billon, 23 to 24 mm." Vlack wrote, "The chief engraver [at Lyon] was Clair I. Jacquemin, whose term lasted from approximately 1690 until December 9, 1709, when he was replaced by Bertrand Jacquemin, who apparently was his son." The term "mousquetaire" has been given to the series, as the outlined cross is similar to that used on tabards carried by French musketeers. Varieties of contemporary counterfeits exist.

W-11700 · 1709-D · 30 Deniers
Notes: Breen-278, Vlack 1. *Rarity:* Per Vlack, "None reported"; per Breen, "Extremely rare."

W-11710 · 1710-D
Notes: Breen-280, Vlack 2. *Mintage:* 16,663,941. Seven in the Ford collection. *Rarity:* URS-7 or 8.

VG-8	F-12	VF-20	EF-40	AU-50
$85	$175	$325	$700	$1,100

W-11712 · 1710-D
Piedfort (silver, double thickness). *Notes:* Vlack 2a. *Rarity:* URS-2 or 3(?).

W-11720 · 1711-D
Notes: Breen-284, Vlack-3. *Mintage:* 13,806,514. Five in the Ford collection. *Rarity:* URS-7 or 8.

VG-8	F-12	VF-20	EF-40	AU-50
$85	$175	$325	$700	$1,100

W-11720 · 1711-"G"
Notes: Vlack 4. Vlack wrote, "The mintmark G was used in place of a D. This is a truly remarkable error. At first it was believed to be a counterfeit, however, after careful examination, it was decided to be a genuine specimen made at the Lyon Mint where this G mintmark was mistakenly used for a D and issued as such. The letter punches and other features match the genuine specimens as well as the overall style. Even a counterfeiter would not have made this mistake." Later, the Poitiers Mint regularly used the G mintmark. *Rarity:* URS-4 or 5.

W-11730 · 1712-D
Notes: Breen-286, Vlack 5. *Mintage:* 26,719,786. Eight in the Ford collection. *Rarity:* URS-8.

VG-8	F-12	VF-20	EF-40	AU-50
$85	$175	$325	$700	$1,100

W-11740 · 1713-D · No Star after date
Notes: Breen-288, Vlack 5. *Mintage:* 10,381,339 (mostly comprising the following). *Rarity:* URS-3 or 4(?).

VG-8	F-12	VF-20	EF-40	AU-50
$85	$175	$325	$700	$1,100

W-11745 · 1713-D · Star after date

Notes: Breen-288, Vlack 6. Considered by Vlack to be among the more readily available issues and more plentiful than the No Star variety. Breen considered it to be "extremely rare." *Rarity:* URS-6 or 7(?).

VG-8	F-12	VF-20	EF-40	AU-50
$85	$175	$325	$700	$1,100

W-11800 · 1717-Q · 6 Deniers des Colonies · copper

Obverse: Bust of Louis XV to right, inscription around. *Reverse:* Inscription in horizontal lines. *Notes:* Breen-259, Hodder-7. Authorized for use in Canada by royal letter patent of March 9, 1717. Planned mintage at Perpignan was 3,000,000, but far fewer were struck due to the insufficient quantity of copper stock on hand. *Rarity:* URS-3 (per Breen, "Three or four reported").

W-11820 · 1717-Q · 12 Deniers des Colonies · copper

Obverse: Bust of Louis XV to right, inscription around. *Reverse:* Inscription in horizontal lines. *Notes:* Breen-258, Hodder-8. At least two die varieties exist. *Rarity:* URS-7 or 8.

VG-8	F-12	VF-20	EF-40	AU-50
			$45,000	

W-11825 to 11840 · 1721 and 1722 9 Deniers des Colonies, or Sou · copper

Obverse: Crossed L's with crown above, inscription around. *Reverse:* Inscription in several lines. *Notes:* Hodder-9. In the 19th century in American catalogs these were widely referred to as "Louisiana coppers." Die varieties exist. Individual dates and mints are given in the following listings. *Rarity:* URS-12 (as a group).

W-11825 · 1721-B

Notes: Breen-260.

VG-8	F-12	VF-20	EF-40	AU-50
$200	$500	$1,200	$3,000	

W-11830 · 1721-H

Notes: Breen-261.

VG-8	F-12	VF-20	EF-40	AU-50
$100	$225	$600	$1,000	

W-11835 · 1722/1-H

Notes: Breen-262.

VG-8	F-12	VF-20	EF-40	AU-50
$175	$300	$750	$1,400	

W-11840 · 1722-H

Notes: Breen lists three die varieties, Breen-263 to 265.

VG-8	F-12	VF-20	EF-40	AU-50
$100	$225	$600	$1,000	

Elephant Tokens
London, c. 1694

1694 New England Elephant Token. (Engraving by John Gavit for O'Callaghan, *The Documentary History of the State of New-York*, 1850)

History

The pieces known today as Elephant tokens are said by some to have been struck in England by or for the Royal African Company, but this can be dismissed since that entity was no longer active when these were made. They likely were struck at the Tower Mint in London and used as trade tokens there. Facts are scarce. Probably all were minted in or around 1694.

The most common issues today are those with inscriptions on the reverse pertaining to London. The obverse is devoid of lettering and has at the center a large and ponderous elephant. The reverse bears a shield, usually with a dagger at the upper left quadrant. The legend GOD PRESERVE LONDON surrounds it. One variety simply bears the name of the city, LONDON. The inscription is believed by some to refer to the 1665 plague and 1666 fire that ravaged London, although these events took place nearly two decades prior to the tokens' issuance.

Apart from the peripheral connection of varieties with inscriptions of "New England" and "Carolina" (see following), there is no reason to associate the London Elephant tokens in any way with America. There is no evidence that any circulated in the American colonies.

Certain distinctive reverse dies bearing the date 1694 were combined with the elephant obverse. One bears the reverse legend GOD: PRESERVE: NEW: ENGLAND: 1694. Another variety has: GOD: PRESERVE: CAROLINA: AND: THE: LORDS: PROPRIETERS: 1694. An error in spelling was realized, and the word PROPRIETERS was altered by overpunching one letter with an O so that a later variety from the same die read PROPRIETORS.

T. Snelling, in his 1769 survey, *On Coins of Great Britain*, part 5, "Pattern Pieces," did not mention the New England issues but did say of the Carolina piece:

> We cannot ourselves conceive the intent of striking it, or for what purpose it was intended; however, we think it has no claim to be admitted as a piece of money, but rather is of the ticket kind, and we are of the same opinion in regard to another piece, which is certainly of the same class with this; be it what it will, it is what we call the London halfpenny, one side of both, that is the elephant, we apprehend was struck from the same die, which is still remaining in the Tower [the Tower of London, once used as a mint], and appears to be the work of [John] Roettier; on the other side instead of GOD PRESERVE CAROLINA AND THE LORDS PROPRIETORS, 1694, as upon this; there is upon that, round the city arms, GOD PRESERVE LONDON; we have heard two or three opinions concerning the intent of uttering this piece, as that it was for the London Workhouse; also, that its inscription alludes to the plague, and it was struck whilst it raged in London; and we have likewise heard that it was intended to be made current at Tangier in Africa but never took place.

A recent theory with extraordinary merit was proposed by R. Neil Fulghum in "The Hunt for Carolina Elephants: Questions Regarding Genuine Specimens and Reproductions of the 1694 Token," 2003. These may have been used within London itself at coffee houses named New England and Carolina which were in business at that time. If so, these pieces have no direct connection at all with America. Moreover, it is unlikely that any token relating to America would be inscribed NEW ENGLAND, as the Massachusetts Bay Colony was the name of the main settlement, and Connecticut was independent from it. There was no formal or informal group of colonies acting as New England, although NEW ENGLAND did appear on certain Massachusetts silver coins. Again, facts are scarce.

Numismatic Aspects

While London Elephant tokens are seen with frequency today, the Carolina issues are exceedingly elusive, with only a half dozen known of the variety with the PROPRIETERS misspelling. Of the New England variety just three pieces are known to numismatists. The typical diameter is about 28.5 mm. All have plain edges.

There are two obverse dies, each with an elephant facing left and no inscription: the first has the tusks away from border, and the second has the tusks close to the border. For a long time the London Elephant tokens have been popular on this side of the Atlantic. As might be expected, English dealers have been the main source of supply. The best study on this is by Michael J. Hodder, "The London, Carolina, and New England Elephant Tokens," in the Norweb Collection Part I catalog, 1987, the source of the "Hodder numbers" cited below. Also provided are cross-references to Walter Breen's *Complete Encyclopedia of U.S. and Colonial Coins* and C. Wilson Peck's *English Copper, Tin and Bronze Coins in the British Museum 1558–1958*.

London Elephant Tokens

W-12000 · Hodder 1-A · God Preserve London · thin planchet

Obverse: Elephant facing to the left. Hodder's first die with tusks away from border. *Reverse:* LONDON: GOD: PRESERVE: at side and top border. Shield with dagger vertical in the first quadrant (correct placement); diagonals in center of shield. Five-pointed star below shield. *Notes:* Breen-185, Peck-501. 28.9 mm. Thin planchet. *Rarity:* URS-5.

G-4	VG-8	F-12	VF-20	EF-40	AU-50	MS-60
	$550	$1,100	$3,800	$6,500	$9,250	

W-12020 · Hodder 1-C · diagonals in center of shield

Obverse: First die as preceding. *Reverse:* LONDON: GOD: PRESERVE: at side and top border. Shield with dagger vertical in the second quadrant (incorrect placement); diagonals in center of shield. No star below shield. *Notes:* Breen-184, Peck-502. 28.5 mm. Michael J. Hodder could account for only four coins; rarest of the London elephant tokens. *Rarity:* URS-3.

G-4	VG-8	F-12	VF-20	EF-40	AU-50	MS-60
	$700	$2,500	$7,600	$12,500	$20,000	

W-12040 · Hodder 2-B · (usually) thick planchet

Obverse: Elephant facing to the left. Second die with tusks very close to border. *Reverse:* LONDON: GOD: PRESERVE: at side and top border. Shield with dagger vertical in the first quadrant (correct placement); no diagonals in center of shield. Six-pointed star below shield. *Notes:* Breen-186 to 188, Peck-503. This is the variety most often encountered. 28.3 mm (varies). Examples are found on planchets of varying thicknesses. A few are on thin, wide planchets. One is overstruck on a pattern regal halfpenny. *Rarity:* URS-11.

VG-8	F-12	VF-20	EF-40	AU-50	MS-60	MS-63
$350	$625	$1,250	$2,000	$3,000	$4,000	$10,000

W-12060 · Hodder 2-D · LON / DON

Obverse: Elephant facing to the left. Second die with tusks very close to border. *Reverse:* LON at left border, DON at right. Shield with dagger vertical in the first quadrant (correct placement); no diagonals in center of shield. Six-pointed star above and below shield. *Notes:* Breen-190, Peck-500. 28.6 mm. Thin planchet. The finest is the Mint State coin from the Roper collection. *Rarity:* URS-5.

VG-8	F-12	VF-20	EF-40	AU-50	MS-60	MS-63
$1,000	$2,500	$4,750	$7,800	$13,500	$15,000	$20,000

Elephant Tokens With American Inscriptions

W-12100 · Hodder 1-E · GOD PRESERVE CAROLINA AND THE LORDS PROPRIETERS 1694

Obverse: Elephant facing to the left. First die with tusks away from border. *Reverse:* GOD: / PRESERVE: / CAROLINA: AND / THE LORDS: / PROPRIETERS / 1694. *Notes:* Breen-191. With PROPRIETERS misspelling, later corrected (see following). 28.5 mm. Thin planchet. *Rarity:* URS-4.

F-12	VF-20	EF-40	AU-50	MS-60
$7,500	$16,000	$26,000	$45,000	$75,000

W-12120 · Hodder 2-F · PROPRIETORS (O over E)

Obverse: Elephant facing to the left. Second die with tusks close to border. *Reverse:* GOD: / PRESERVE: / CAROLINA: AND / THE LORDS: / PROPRIETORS / 1694. *Notes:* Breen-192 (thick planchet), 193 (medium planchet), 194 (thick planchet). 29.1 mm. O over erroneous E in PROPRIETORS; correction of the earlier die. For this striking the second obverse was used. *Rarity:* URS-6.

F-12	VF-20	EF-40	AU-50
$7,000	$14,000	$22,000	$35,000

W-12140 · Hodder 2-G · GOD PRESERVE NEW ENGLAND 1694

Obverse: Second die, as preceding. *Reverse:* GOD: / PRESERVE: / NEW: / ENGLAND: / 1694:. *Notes:* Breen-196 (thick planchet), 197 (thick planchet). 28.5 mm. Three known: Mickley-Roper, Garrett, and Norweb. *Rarity:* URS-3.

F-12	VF-20	EF-40
$80,000	$95,000	$130,000

Wood's Hibernia Coinage
Ireland, 1722–1724

History

Nearly concurrent with the Rosa Americana patent, William Wood obtained on June 16, 1722 (ratified on July 22, 1722), a franchise to produce coins for circulation in Ireland. Patterns were produced in several design variations of the copper halfpenny and farthing. The first adopted style depicted King George I on the obverse with the legend GEORGIUS • D:G: REX: ("George, king by the grace of God"). The

285

reverse bore the notation HIBERNIA ("Ireland") and the date. At the center was a seated goddess holding the emblem of Ireland, a harp.

Wood's coinage for Ireland, authorized to a total value of £100,000, commenced in 1722. Sir Isaac Newton was appointed comptroller to oversee the operation, but later Newton resigned and at his request Mr. Barton, his nephew, was appointed in his stead. It is believed that examples of this coinage were struck in Bristol.

By late 1723 a large furor arose in Ireland concerning the pieces. Jonathan Swift, among others, participated in a propaganda campaign, some details of which were related in his *Drapier Papers*. It was asserted that the issues for Ireland were produced without Irish advice or consent, that the arrangements were made in secret and for the private profit of Wood, and that the pieces were seriously underweight.

So great was the clamor that King George reduced the authorized coinage to a total value of £40,000. The controversy continued, and in 1725 Wood relinquished his patent in exchange for a pension of £3,000 per year for an eight-year period.

Numismatic Aspects

These pieces have no connection with America apart from their common authorship with the Rosa Americana coinage and their circulation in the colonies through informal importation (occasional coins have been found in the United States). Today, most Hibernia pieces in collectors' cabinets trace their origin to 19th- and 20th-century sources in England. It is presumed that the bulk of Wood's Hibernia coinage circulated in that country, possibly at a reduced value from that originally intended. Silver strikings were made of certain die combinations.

The new standard reference on this series, *The Hibernia Coinage of William Wood (1722–1724)*, by Sydney F. Martin, describes 57 varieties of farthings and 228 halfpence, and is highly recommended as a valuable and comprehensive resource for anyone desiring to explore the series in depth. He assigned numbers to obverse styles with decimals for varieties within those styles, such as 5.1, 5.2, and 5.3 representing three different dies of the same style. Reverses were given capital letters for major styles, lower-case letters for subsets, and decimals within those subsets for varieties, such as Gc.1, 2, and 3.

The same writer suggests that dies had a maximum life of about 50,000 strikes. Based upon the number of dies known, he posits that no more than 1,595,000 Hibernia farthings were made and no more than 6,710,000 halfpence. Farthings are about 22 mm diameter, halfpence 26 mm, but diameters can vary plus or minus a millimeter or so. All have plain edges.

Listed in the present text are basic types and a selection of notable varieties based upon obverse and reverse punctuation and harp string count. The basic Martin styles have been cross-referenced below. When there are many Martin varieties, a decimal point and further number is given, representing, for example, 3.2, 3.4, 3.5, 3.8 and others within a single Whitman listing. "Generic" prices are listed for various types. In time, as the Martin book is adopted by collectors, it is likely that certain scarce and rare varieties will achieve extra value. The Whitman numbers are "open" and widely spaced where there are many varieties, allowing for specific numbers to be assigned in future editions if demand develops.

Wood's Hibernia Farthings

1722

W-12200 · Martin 1.1-A.1 · GEORGIUS · D : G : REX · · Harp Left · 10 Strings

Obverse: Head of George facing right. GEORGIUS to the left, • D : G : REX • to the right. *Reverse:* Seated figure with harp to the left. HIBERNIA 1722 at border, with dots before and after the word and date. *Notes:* Breen-168. *Rarity:* URS-7.

VG-8	F-12	VF-20	EF-40	AU-50	MS-60	MS-63
$425	$600	$1,500	$3,200	$4,750		$9,500

1723

W-12240 · Martin 1-Bc · · D: G: REX · · 11 Strings

Obverse: Style as preceding. *Reverse:* Seated figure with harp to the right (as on all to follow). HIBERNIA 1723 at border, with dots before and after the date. *Notes:* Breen-169. *Rarity:* URS-8.

VG-8	F-12	VF-20	EF-40	AU-50	MS-60	MS-63
$125	$175	$325	$650	$850		$1,600

W-12255 to 12550 · Martin 3-Bc · GEORGIUS · DEI · GRATIA · REX ·

Obverse: Head of George facing right. Punctuation as described, with dots after each word. *Reverse:* Style as preceding except for punctuation variation on Martin 3-C. *Notes:* The Martin text lists many subvarieties beyond the basic styles given below. Breen does not classify by harp-string count. *Rarity:* URS-13.

VG-8	F-12	VF-20	EF-40	AU-50	MS-60	MS-63
$70	$100	$200	$350	$600	$750	$1,000

W-12255 · Martin 3-Ba · 9 Strings

Style as preceding. Martin lists three varieties. *Rarity:* URS-9.

W-12290 · Martin 3-Bb · 10 Strings

Style as preceding. Martin lists eight varieties. *Rarity:* URS-10.

W-12350 · Martin 3-Bc · 11 Strings · one dot after 1723

Style as preceding. Martin lists 28 varieties. *Rarity:* URS-12.

W-12500 · Martin 3.3-Bc.3 · silver

Style as preceding, but struck in silver. *Notes:* Breen-171 and 173. This is the most available silver striking in the Wood's Hibernia series. Martin lists two varieties. *Rarity:* URS-7.

VG-8	F-12	VF-20	EF-40	AU-50	MS-60	MS-63
$1,800	$2,500	$4,500	$6,000	$7,750	$10,000	$12,500

W-12520 · Martin 3.10-Bc.3 · pewter

Style as preceding, but struck in pewter. Three varieties (including one discovered in December 2007). *Rarity:* URS-3.

W-12530 · Martin 3.5-Bc.6 · 11 Strings · second G (GEORGIUS) over A

Style as preceding. Only one variety. *Notes:* Breen-174. *Rarity:* URS-8.

W-12540 · Martin 3.23-C.1 · 11 Strings · two dots after 1723 · silver

Style as preceding, but struck in silver. One variety. *Rarity:* URS-2 or 3.

W-12550 · Martin 3-Bd · 12 Strings

Style as preceding. Martin lists six varieties. *Rarity:* URS-10.

1724

W-12600 to 12620 · Martin 3.7-E.1 to 3.22-E.2

Obverse: Head of George facing right. GEORGIUS DEI GRATIA REX at border, dots after each word. *Reverse:* Seated figure with harp to the right. HIBERNIA 1724 at border, with dots before and after the word and date; one style lacks dot after date. *Notes:* Breen-175 (with period after date) and 177 (without period). *Rarity:* URS-11.

VG-8	F-12	VF-20	EF-40	AU-50	MS-60	MS-63
$130	$250	$800	$1,750	$2,500	$3,000	$4,000

W-12600 · Martin 3-D · 10 Strings · period after date

Style as preceding. Martin describes two varieties. *Notes:* Breen-175. *Rarity:* URS-9.

W-12610 · Martin 3-E · 11 Strings · no period after date

Style as preceding. Martin describes two varieties. *Notes:* Breen-177. *Rarity:* URS-9.

Wood's Hibernia Halfpence

1722

W-12650 · Martin 1-A · HIBERNIÆ

Obverse: Head of George facing right. GEORGIVS to the left, D: G: REX • to the right. *Reverse:* Seated figure with harp to the left. Rocks (per standard nomenclature; also resembles a hooded, draped figure) to the right of the figure. • HIBERNIÆ • above. 1722 at bottom border. *Notes:* Breen-143. Called the "rock halfpenny" pattern by Nelson, "this title standing quite alone in the English and Irish series, either before or since this time." *Rarity:* URS-5.

VG-8	F-12	VF-20	EF-40	AU-50	MS-60	MS-63
—	—	$8,000	$12,000	$20,000	$25,000	$35,000

W-12670 to 12790 · Martin 3-B to 5-B · Harp Left

Obverse: Head of George facing right. GEORGIUS DEI to the left, GRATIA REX to the right; dot after REX. Spacing of words and dots varies among varieties. *Reverse:* Seated figure with harp to the left. HIBERNIA 1722 at border, with dots before and after the word and date. *Notes:* Breen-144 except as listed below. Varieties with 7, 8, 9, 10, or 11 harp strings. *Rarity:* URS-11.

VG-8	F-12	VF-20	EF-40	AU-50	MS-60	MS-63
$125	$175	$350	$750	$1,200	$1,500	$1,900

W-12670 · Martin 3-Ba and 5-Ba · 7 Strings

Style as preceding. Martin describes two varieties. *Rarity:* URS-6.

W-12690 · Martin 3-Bb and 4-Bb · 8 Strings

Style as preceding. Martin describes six varieties. *Rarity:* URS-11.

W-12730 · Martin 4-Bc and 5-Bc · 9 Strings

Style as preceding. Martin describes two varieties. *Rarity:* URS-6.

W-12745 · Martin 4.3-Bc.1 · silver

Style as preceding, but struck in silver. Only one variety. *Notes:* Breen-145. *Rarity:* URS-3.

Selected auction price(s): John J. Ford Jr. VII Sale (Stack's 1/2005), VF, $31,625.

W-12755 · Martin 4-Bd · 10 Strings

Style as preceding. Martin describes four varieties. *Notes:* Martin lists 4.97-Bd.1 in an off metal, possibly Bath metal. *Rarity:* URS-8.

W-12790 · Martin 4-Be · 11 Strings

Style as preceding. Martin describes two varieties. *Rarity:* URS-8.

W-12810 · Martin 4-C and 5-C · Harp Right

Obverse: Head of George facing right. GEORGIUS • DEI • GRATIA • REX • at border. *Reverse:* Seated figure with harp to the right (as on all to follow). HIBERNIA 1722 at border, with dots before and after the word and date. Eleven harp strings. *Notes:* Breen-146 in copper. This type is one of the more elusive in the Hibernia series. Most show extensive circulation. Breen's 147, listed as DEII instead of DEI, is a repunching of the I, not a spelling error; other letters are also repunched on this die (Martin obverse 4.20). *Rarity:* URS-8.

VG-8	F-12	VF-20	EF-40	AU-50	MS-60	MS-63
$100	$135	$325	$700	$1,500	$1,750	$2,500

W-12835 · silver

Style as preceding, but struck in silver. *Notes:* Breen-148, "extremely rare." Not listed by Sydney Martin. *Rarity:* URS-(?).

1723/2

W-12850 · Martin 3-D and 4-D

Obverse: Head of George facing right. GEORGIUS • DEI • GRATIA • REX • at border. *Reverse:* Seated figure with harp to the right. HIBERNIA 1723 at border, with dots before and after the word and date. Large and small 3 varieties noted, but the difference is slight. *Notes:* Breen-152 (large 3) and 153 (small 3). *Rarity:* URS-10.

VG-8	F-12	VF-20	EF-40	AU-50	MS-60	MS-63
$80	$150	$450	$850	$1,300	$1,500	$2,400

1723

W-12880 to 13660 · Martin 4-F to 4-H and others

Designs as preceding. Standard obverse has dots after GEORGIUS, GRATIA, DEI, REX, and date. Reverses vary with one, two, or three dots. Many die varieties. Ten, 11, or 12 harp strings. Breen reports various numbers; not attributed by harp-string count. *Rarity:* URS-16.

Selected auction price(s): Prices differ among varieties; see original catalogs. O'Donnell Collection (Stack's 1/2001), AU, $1,035. Lake Geneva Sale (B&M 6/2001), MS-64BB (PCGS), $748. Pre–Long Beach Sale (Superior 5/2001), MS-65BN (PCGS), $1,610. ANA Sale (Superior 8/2002), MS-64BB (PCGS), $1,495; MS-64BD (PCGS), $2,875. Pre–Long Beach Sale (I. & L. Goldberg 9/2002), MS-65BN (PCGS), $1,840, MS-65BB (PCGS), $1,782. Pre–Long Beach Sale (I. & L. Goldberg 9/2002), MS-65BN (PCGS), $1,207. Long Beach Sale (Heritage 9/2002), MS-64BB (PCGS), $1,093, $1,150. Pre–Long Beach Sale (Superior 2/2003), Specimen-66BN (PCGS), $4,600. Long Beach Sale (Heritage 9/2003), MS-64BB (PCGS), $1,150. Rarities Sale (B&M 9/2003), MS-65BB (PCGS), $2,070. Long Beach Sale (Heritage 9/2003), MS-65BN (PCGS), $1,725; SP-65BN (PCGS), $4,025. FUN Sale (Heritage 1/2004), MS-64BB (PCGS), $1,093. CSNS Sale (Heritage 5/2004), MS-65BB (NGC), $1,380. Long Beach Sale (Heritage 6/2004), MS-65BB (PCGS), $1,553. John J. Ford Jr. VII Sale (Stack's 1/2005), MS BN, $1,150; Choice MS BN, $1,150; Choice MS BB, $2,070, $2,185, $2,300, $4,888; Gem MS BN, $2,300; Gem MS BN PL, $4,600, $5,463; Gem MS BD, $6,900. Pre–Long Beach Sale (I. & L. Goldberg 2/2005), MS-64 (PCGS), $1,495. Baltimore Sale (Stack's [ANR] 3/2005), MS-64 (NGC), $1,035, MS-65BB (PCGS), $2,588. Long Beach Sale (Heritage 6/2005), MS-64BB (PCGS), $1,150. ANA Sale (Heritage 7/2005), MS-65BN (NGC), $1,725. FUN Elite Sale (Superior 1/2006), MS-65BB (NGC), $2,300. New York City Winter

Auction (R.M. Smythe 3/2006), MS-63BB (ANACS), $1,610. Pre–Long Beach Sale (Superior 9/2006), MS-64BN (NGC), $1,553. Dallas Coin Auction (Heritage 11/2006), MS-63BN (NGC), $575. Dallas Coin Auction (Heritage 11/2006), MS-63BN (NGC), $780. FUN Sale (Heritage 1/2007), MS-63BN (PCGS), $633; MS-64BN (NGC), $863; MS-64BD (PCGS), $2,990; MS-65BB (PCGS), $2,070; SP-65BN (PCGS), $12,650; MS-65BB (PCGS), $3,450; MS-66BN (NGC), $3,738. Long Beach Sale (Heritage 2/2007), MS-64BN (PCGS), $1,093. Brooklyn Sale (Stack's 3/2007), MS-62BN (PCGS), $690; MS-63BB, $1,035. Dallas Sale (Heritage 4/2007), MS-63BN (PCGS), $748; MS-64BN $1,265. Long Beach Sale (Heritage 5/2007), MS-63BN (PCGS), $748. CSNS Sale (Heritage 5/2007), MS-62BN (NGC), $720. Baltimore Sale (B&M, 6/2007), MS-62 (PCGS), $690; MS-63BN (PCGS), $1,150. Summer Coin Sale (Lyn Knight 6/2007), MS-64BN (PCGS), $1,725. ANA Sale (Heritage 8/2007), MS-66BB (PCGS), $6,900. 72nd Anniversary Sale (Stack's 10/2007), MS-64BB (PCGS), $900. Sale No. 452 (Heritage 11/2007), MS-64BB (PCGS), $1,150.

W-12880 · Martin 4-Ga1 · 10 Strings · two dots on reverse

Style as preceding. Dots after HIBERNIA and date. Martin describes two varieties. *Rarity:* URS-10 or 11.

VG-8	F-12	VF-20	EF-40	AU-50	MS-60	MS-63
$50	$75	$200	$350	$550	$1,250	$2,000

W-12900 · Martin 4-Ha and 4-Hb · 11 Strings · one dot on reverse

Style as preceding. Dot after HIBERNIA. Martin describes two varieties. *Rarity:* URS-11.

VG-8	F-12	VF-20	EF-40	AU-50	MS-60	MS-63
$50	$75	$200	$350	$550	$1,250	$2,000

W-13110 · Martin 6.1-Hb.1 · 11 Strings · no dots on obverse · one dot on reverse

Style as preceding. Only one variety. Dot after HIBERNIA. *Rarity:* URS-5.

W-13120 · Martin 3-Gc and 4-Gb · 11 Strings · two dots on reverse

Style as preceding. Dots after HIBERNIA and date. In its early state reverse Gc.37a has tiny additional dot after date (Breen-160). Martin describes 127 varieties. *Rarity:* URS-16.

VG-8	F-12	VF-20	EF-40	AU-50	MS-60	MS-63
$50	$75	$200	$350	$550	$1,250	$2,000

W-13460 · Martin 4.52-Gb.8 · silver

Style as preceding, but silver. Only one variety. *Notes:* Breen-156. *Rarity:* URS-5.

Selected auction price(s): John J. Ford Jr. VII Sale (Stack's 1/2005), Choice MS PL, $40,250.

W-13470 · Martin 3-F and 5-F · 11 Strings · three dots on reverse

Style as preceding. Dots before and after HIBERNIA and date. Martin describes 19 varieties. *Rarity:* URS-13.

VG-8	F-12	VF-20	EF-40	AU-50	MS-60	MS-63
$50	$75	$200	$350	$550	$1,250	$2,000

W-13570 · Martin 4-Gd · 12 Strings · two dots on reverse

Style as preceding. Dots after HIBERNIA and date. Martin describes 15 varieties. *Rarity:* URS-12.

VG-8	F-12	VF-20	EF-40	AU-50	MS-60	MS-63
$50	$75	$200	$350	$550	$1,250	$2,000

W-13650 · Martin 4.46-Gd.3 · silver

Style as preceding, but struck in silver. Only one variety. *Notes:* Breen-156. *Rarity:* URS-4.

W-13660 · Martin 2.1-E.1 and 4.21-E.1 · 12 Strings · Star before date

Style as preceding. Martin describes two varieties and designates them as patterns. *Rarity:* URS-3.

1724

W-13690 to 13750 · Martin 4-J, 4-K, and 4-L

Designs as preceding. Die varieties. *Rarity:* URS-12.

Selected auction price(s): ANA Sale (Superior 8/2002), MS-64BD (PCGS), $6,038. Long Beach Sale (Heritage 9/2003), MS-62BN (PCGS), $1,898. John J. Ford Jr. VII Sale (Stack's 1/2005), MS BN, $1,725, $1,840; Choice MS BN, $2,760, $2,760; Choice MS BB, $3,220; Gem MS BN, $3,738; Gem MS BD, $4,025, $8,050. Long Beach Sale (Heritage 9/2005), MS-62BN (PCGS), $3,450. Dallas Sale (Heritage 12/2005), MS-65BN (NGC), $11,500. FUN Sale (Heritage 1/2007), MS-65BB (PCGS), $12,650. Henry Leon Sale (Stack's 5/2007), MS-60BN $1,725. Amherst & Waccabuc Collections (Stack's 11/2007), AU-53 (NGC), $598.

W-13690 · Martin 4-K · 11 Strings · two dots on reverse

Style as preceding. Dots after HIBERNIA and date. Martin describes six varieties. *Rarity:* URS-11 or 12.

VG-8	F-12	VF-20	EF-40	AU-50	MS-60	MS-63
$100	$160	$400	$850	$1,300	$1,500	$2,700

W-13720 · Martin 4-J · 12 Strings · two dots on reverse

Style as preceding. Dots after HIBERNIA and date. Martin describes one variety. *Rarity:* URS-5.

W-13730 · Martin 4.73-L.2 and 4.74-L.4 · 11 Strings · one dot on reverse

Style as preceding. Dot after HIBERNIA. Martin describes two varieties. *Rarity:* URS-7.

VG-8	F-12	VF-20	EF-40	AU-50	MS-60	MS-63
$100	$160	$400	$850	$1,300	$1,500	$2,700

W-13750 · 4.36-L.4 · silver

As preceding, but struck in silver. Martin describes one variety. *Notes:* Breen-167. *Rarity:* URS-5.

Selected auction price(s): John J. Ford Jr. VII Sale (Stack's 1/2005), Choice F, $37,375.

VOCE POPULI TOKENS
Ireland, 1760

History

Voce Populi coppers, mostly of halfpenny size though some were made of the smaller farthing denomination, are believed to have been struck as a speculative venture in Dublin, Ireland, by a Mr. Roche in 1760. The legend VOCE POPULI is similar to VOCE POPOLI, or "the voice of the people" found on the Georgivs Triumpho token dated 1783. As such, they have been adopted by American numismatists, although there is no evidence to suggest that Voce Populi pieces, which bear the legend HIBERNIA (Ireland) on the reverse, ever circulated on the North American continent. Sylvester S. Crosby did not include them in *The Early Coins of America*, 1875. Likewise, they were ignored in Wayte Raymond's *Standard Catalogue of United States Coins* until Walter Breen revised the section on colonial coins in 1954.

There are several different busts portrayed on various die varieties of the halfpenny issues. Robert Vlack theorizes that among those represented may be George II, George III, a pretender who claimed to be James III, or the young pretender Charles Edward, and Hely Hutchenson (provost of Dublin College). He further notes that the raised letter "P" that appears on some issues in front of the bust or below it may relate to "Princeps," as pertaining to Charles Edward, or "Provost" as relating to Hely Hutchenson.

All pieces were intended to bear the 1760 date, although due to an engraving error the numeral 6 on one halfpenny was cut as a 0, thereby given an erroneous "1700" date. This die was later altered by putting a tail on top of the zero, transforming it to the correct 6. All have plain edges. The standard reference is Jerry Zelinka's study, "The Enigmatic Voce Populi Halfpenny of 1760," in the *Colonial Newsletter*, October 1976. Farthings measure about 21 mm, halfpence 28 mm. Diameters are not consistent.

Voce Populi Farthings

W-13800 · 1760 · Large Letters

Obverse: Male portrait to the right. VOCE / POPULI at left and right borders. *Reverse:* Seated figure with harp. HIBER / NIA to left and right. Date 1760 below. *Notes:* Breen-234, Nelson-1. In the mid-20th century this issue was considered much scarcer than it seems to be today. *Rarity:* URS-7.

VG-8	F-12	VF-20	EF-40	AU-50	MS-60	MS-63
$400	$750	$2,100	$3,600	$8,000	$11,000	$15,000

W-13810 · Small Letters

Obverse: As preceding, but from a different die with smaller letters. *Reverse:* As preceding. *Notes:* Breen-236, Nelson-2. Colonial Williamsburg Foundation coin illustrated, gift of Joseph R. and Ruth P. Lasser. This is a major rarity, the extent of which has not been generally appreciated. *Rarity:* URS-3.

Voce Populi Halfpence

W-1382X · 1760

Obverse: Male portrait to the right. VOCE / POPULI at left and right borders. *Reverse:* Seated figure with harp. HIBERNIA at border. Die varieties include the word divided as HIBE RNIA and HIBER NIA. Date 1760 below. *Notes:* Breen, Nelson, and Zelinka: various dies other than those specifically listed below. The devices, particularly on the reverse, often lack detail, necessitating skill in grading such coins. Values are for a typical halfpenny (but certain other varieties are listed on the next page). *Rarity:* URS-14.

F-12	VF-20	EF-40	AU-50	MS-60	MS-63
$200	$425	$775	$1,500	$2,175	$2,850

W-13930 · VOOE

Type as preceding, but with die crack connecting top and bottom of C; a die state that has been popular and listed in various references, sometimes incorrectly called a die-cutting error. *Notes:* Breen-227, Nelson-3, Zelinka 7-E. *Rarity:* URS-11.

G-4	VG-8	F-12	VF-20	EF-40	AU-50	MS-60
$100	$175	$275	$550	$1,000	$1,950	$3,000

W-13940 · "1700"

With error date, later corrected in the die by adding a tail to the top of the first 0. *Notes:* Breen-226 and 229; Nelson-2, Zelinka 5-Da. Sometimes faked by tooling away the tail later added to the 0. Breen lists two dies with this feature, equivalent to Zelinka 4-B and 5-D. However, Zelinka states that 4-B is a regular reverse, but can appear as 1700 when a coin is well worn. *Rarity:* URS-5.

G-4	VG-8	F-12	VF-20	EF-40	AU-50
			$2,900	$5,000	

W-13950 · 1760 · P before face

General type as preceding, but with P in field in front of the face. The significance of this extra letter is not known. *Notes:* Breen-232, Nelson-12, Zelinka 15-N. Zelinka estimated 501 to 1,250 known. Scarce in high grades. Devices indistinct in areas. *Rarity:* URS-11 (based on Zelinka).

G-4	VG-8	F-12	VF-20	EF-40	AU-50
$120	$200	$375	$800	$1,800	$3,250

W-13960 · P below bust

General type as preceding, but with P below the bust. The significance of this extra letter is not known. *Notes:* Breen-233; Nelson-11, 13, and 14; Zelinka 14-L, 14-M, and 16-O. Devices indistinct in areas. *Rarity:* URS-12 (based on Zelinka).

G-4	VG-8	F-12	VF-20	EF-40	AU-50
$130	$225	$400	$850	$2,100	$4,250

1781 NORTH AMERICA TOKENS
c. 1820

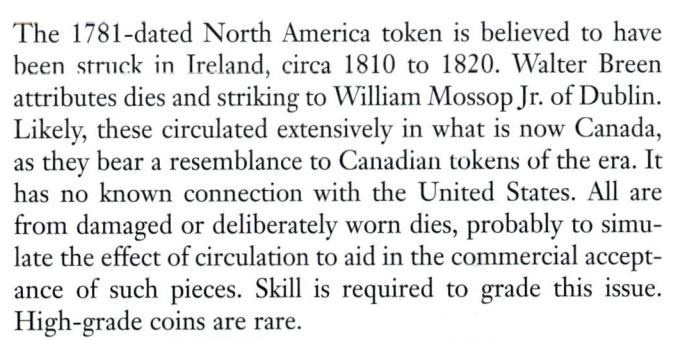

The 1781-dated North America token is believed to have been struck in Ireland, circa 1810 to 1820. Walter Breen attributes dies and striking to William Mossop Jr. of Dublin. Likely, these circulated extensively in what is now Canada, as they bear a resemblance to Canadian tokens of the era. It has no known connection with the United States. All are from damaged or deliberately worn dies, probably to simulate the effect of circulation to aid in the commercial acceptance of such pieces. Skill is required to grade this issue. High-grade coins are rare.

W-13980

Obverse: Seated goddess with left hand holding harp, evocative of Ireland. NORTH AMERICAN TOKEN around top and sides. *Reverse:* Ship sailing to the left. COMMERCE at top border. *Edge:* Plain. *Notes:* Breen-1143 (brass) and 1144 (copper), Crosby Plate IX, 21. Brass or copper. About 27.5 mm. *Rarity:* URS-11.

VG-8	F-12	VF-20	EF-40
$70	$140	$325	$825

12

19TH-CENTURY COLONIAL COPIES AND FANTASIES

COPIES OF COLONIAL COINS

Deceptive Copies of Little Value

Is it genuine or is it fake? A fake coin, counterfeit, alteration, or forgery immediately evokes thoughts of something undesirable. And, for such pieces produced after the colonial era, this is certainly true. Today, a recently made copy of a 1787 Massachusetts half cent, or a 1785 Immune Columbia copper, or a 1792 Birch cent would have no real value. The list of modern *copies* (to use an inclusive term) is a long one. Several manufacturers produce different varieties, with one New York outfit achieving large nationwide sales in the late 19th century. Modern copies, sometimes (but not always) marked with the word COPY (as required by the Hobby Protection Act, 1973), are widely available in novelty shops, including at certain National Historic Sites (such as Mount Vernon) and national parks. Reproductions of Confederate, continental, and other early paper money are widely sold as well.

Although the intention is to provide a souvenir, in many instances the pieces are separated from any information identifying them as copies and can be misleading to new owners. Any dealer with a coin shop is familiar with the dozens of such fakes brought over the counter regularly, or described on the telephone, by hopeful owners who have bought such pieces in an "estate sale," or from an antique shop, or who say it has descended in the family.

Modern forgeries are of many types and can be cast or struck. Some are made of base metal coated with copper, which if bent will snap apart and reveal a bright white interior. Somewhat more traditional are electrotype copies, made years ago to provide "fillers" for numismatists. The British Museum and the Mint Cabinet, to name just two collections, provided electrotypes as a convenience, or allowed their coins to be electrotyped. Such copies were produced by pressing each side of a genuine coin into wax, making a mold carrying an exact impression (in reverse), coating the mold with graphite or other electrically conductive substance, and then immersing it in a bath in which copper is electrodeposited. The result was a foil-like shell which was then trimmed to remove flash and filled with lead or some other material to strengthen it. The obverse and reverse halves were then joined by soldering or gluing.

Copies from new dies, some made by the spark erosion process, can be very deceptive. Many experts have been fooled by these, until closer examination and study reveals their true nature. Cast and struck copies, often made overseas, are endemic in Internet offerings and have victimized many people. John M. Kleeberg's article, "Peter Rosa's Replicas of Colonial Coins," *CNL*, April 2002, gives a long list of fakes of a sophisticated nature, made by taking impressions of genuine coins by the dental molding process, then using a Janvier-type lathe to create dies. The fakes were made by Taylor Industries of New York City. Some were marked COPY on the edge, others were not.

As to identifying copies that were made after the colonial era, from the 19th century down to the present day, but most in recent generations, no one rule fits all. Your best safeguard is to buy from a knowledgeable professional numismatist who guarantees the authenticity of his or her coins. If purchasing on the Internet, a very popular activity, you should by all means have *any* colonial coin checked carefully if it is not from a professional seller. Thousands of phony pieces are out there. In a related field, in recent decades hundreds if not thousands of Indian peace medals have turned up at gun shows, antique dealers, on the Internet, and elsewhere. More than 99 percent of these are copies or later restrikes. One contributor to this book said on the single day of March 13, 2008, there were 15 Internet auction offerings of unimportant British copper coins being falsely offered as Machin's Mills pieces.

That said, the focus turns to contemporary counterfeits, which, interestingly, can be rare, desirable, highly collectible, and very expensive in the marketplace.

Collectible Contemporary Counterfeits

When coins were struck in colonial and early America, beginning with Massachusetts silver in the 1650s, fraudsters sought to turn easy profits by producing counterfeits. In nearly all instances this was done by engraving new dies and striking coins from them. Often, the amount of silver or copper in a counterfeit was less than in an original. In most instances, particularly during the 19th century, the workmanship of counterfeit dies was less artistic and precise than dies for originals. In some instances, counterfeits were made by casting, such as the 1785 Vermont RR-5 (W-2275).

The most famous maker of contemporary counterfeits was Machin's Mills, which operated at the outlet of Orange Pond near Newburgh, New York, in the late 1790s. Chapter 7 delineates many varieties of Machin's Mills counterfeit English halfpence, and Machin's Mills imitations are listed elsewhere, such as among the Connecticut coppers. All of these are highly desirable today and meet with strong demand in the marketplace, with rare varieties often selling into the thousands of dollars. Often, a contemporary counterfeit can be far rarer than a typical original and bring a greater price. In autumn 2007 a choice Machin's Mills copper sold for over $20,000 on eBay. One of the most famous of all coins in the Connecticut series, 1787 1.4-WW, is a curious variety not minted under the contract given by that state. Just two are known, and the offering of one at auction would measurably raise the temperature of the room.

The numismatic value and demand of contemporary counterfeits varies from series to series. For a long time, counterfeits of Massachusetts silver have been integrated among regular listings, as has been done in the present text. Contemporary counterfeits of Connecticut coppers 1785 to 1788 are integrated, as are Massachusetts coppers of 1787 and 1788, although for the latter there are divided opinions as to which listing method to use. Robert A. Vlack in his set of plates of Massachusetts coins separated contemporary counterfeits, whereas the cataloger of the auction offering of the Ford Collection and Hillyer C. Ryder in his standard reference on the series integrated them without noting they were imitations. Indeed, not everyone agrees on what is an imitation and what is not.

Numismatic tradition has a lot to do with the acceptance and value of contemporary counterfeits. Should a new discovery be made of a crude counterfeit thought to have been contemporary, publication in the *C4 Newsletter* or the *Colonial Newsletter* would draw commentary, after which its significance would be accepted or rejected. Generally, a contemporary that was struck from dies is much more important than one cast in a mold. It is often difficult to differentiate an old cast from a modern one.

Early and Mid-20th Century Struck Copies

From 1900 to 1950, many struck copies were made of colonial coins. Most were identified by extra lettering or notations on the dies, or illogical combinations of motifs, or in some other way. New York City coin dealer Thomas L. Elder made copies of the 1776 Continental dollar and some "Confederatio dollars," the last having no original counterparts.

In the 1930s many different copies and medals were made in imitation of the Massachusetts Pine Tree shilling, often with new lettering relating to a particular town or anniversary observance. Horace W. Grant, a well-known dealer in Providence, Rhode Island, struck Rhode Island Ship medals from copy dies. In the 1950s Copley Coin Company (Boston) and Tatham Coin & Stamp Co. (Springfield, Massachusetts) struck and/or distributed certain copies. The intent of these copies was not to deceive, but to provide souvenirs for collectors. Today, they are readily collectible and sell for modest sums.

Collectible 19th-Century Struck Copies and Fantasies

After coin collecting became a popular hobby in the late 1850s, a strong desire arose for scarce and rare colonial American coins. In the absence of their availability in the auction room or elsewhere in the marketplace, a number of engravers and coiners produced their own versions, often identified as such. The most famous producer of struck copies was John A. Bolen, a numismatist of Springfield, Massachusetts. A competent engraver, Bolen turned out his own version of Higley, Confederatio, and other early American coins in the intended metal of copper, but also often in brass or German silver. These were sold for what they were: struck copies of interest as fillers in collections. George H. Lovett, the well-known New York City engraver, cut new dies for certain colonial coins that were marketed by Alfred S. Robinson (of Hartford, Connecticut) and others.

Thomas Wyatt, a numismatist and author, turned devious and participated in a fraud (discussed below). A. Wuesthoff, a New York dealer, turned out a fantasy Bermuda XX shilling circa 1880. Horatio N. Rust distributed copies of Fugio coppers, newly made circa 1860, complete with invented stories of how "original" dies were found. Most innovative, however, was C. Wyllys Betts. Other 19th-century makers of copies could be mentioned. Richard D. Kenney's 1952 study, *Struck Copies of Early American Coins*, is the standard reference for most such copies. Today, all are highly prized and collectible when cataloged and described as such. The John

J. Ford Jr. Collection Part XIV catalog lists and illustrates a very large selection of copies.

Several particularly rare and unusual Bolen and Betts copies have sold in the range of $5,000 to $10,000. Some examples of the relatively common 1787 Fugio fantasy Newman 104-FF have sold for over $5,000. Most copies trade for much less, the typical Bolen coin for under $1,000. For most collectors entering the field of struck copies, pieces in copper seem to be the most appealing as this metal is the same as used for the originals. Mulings with store card dies are interesting and often very rare, but not in the mainstream of interest. The Ford Collection included only a few, for example.

No account can be complete without mentioning that in their time certain especially well-made copies deceived many people. Typically, a Bolen, Betts, or other copy was sold with proper description to a collector or dealer, after which it was further traded without disclosing its true nature. Édouard Frossard, for one, was terribly embarrassed by Betts's NOVUM BELGIUM fantasy, a piece that had been recorded in an auction sale earlier, but was forgotten.

A representative selection of collectible 19th-century struck copies is given below. Selected auction prices include prices from the 2006 sale of the Ford collection (Stack's), the largest auction ever of struck copies. In the marketplace prices can vary widely, due to lack of published price information, infrequent offerings, and rarity.

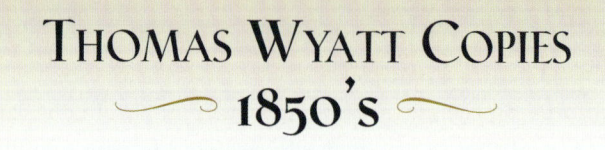

Thomas Wyatt Copies
1850's

The Chelsea Hoard

In Chelsea, Massachusetts, near Boston, a reporter for the *Boston Journal*, issue of June 16, 1856, had this experience:

> We had the pleasure of seeing today some of the Pine Tree money of Massachusetts, which was dug up some time since at Chelsea. There were a shilling, sixpence, threepence, and twopence, dated 1652, in almost as good preservation as if they had been coined one year [ago] only, every letter and figure upon them being perfectly clear and distinct; they probably have been entombed for more than one hundred and fifty years. The bottle in which they were found, and several of the coins, were purchased by a gentleman to be presented to the British Museum.

This notice caught the eye of reader "Nummus" (likely Jeremiah Colburn, leading numismatic scholar of Boston), who hastened to pen a commentary for the *Boston Transcript*, August 16, 1856, noting in part:

> It is remarkable to observe how many different means unprincipled people resort to to replenish their empty purses. Too proud to work for an honest livelihood, and too indolent to engage in some legitimate pursuit, their wits are constantly at work devising new ways to fatten themselves upon the industry of others.
>
> A few weeks since a paragraph appeared in several of our papers, stating that a large number of pine tree coins had been recently dug up in this vicinity. No sooner had this announcement been made than complete sets of this coinage poured into our city. NE shillings and sixpence, before so rare, together with some other pieces never before seen, were to be found exposed for sale in this city. . . . It has, however, turned out that all of these pieces are counterfeit, and made by a man in New York City, who represents them to be originals.

The perpetrator was one Thomas Wyatt, who lived on Mercer Street, New York City, circa 1840 to 1860. A knowledgeable numismatist, he is remembered today for his important 315-page book, *Memoirs of the Generals, Commodores, and Other Commanders, Who Distinguished Themselves in the American Army and Navy During The Wars of The Revolution, and 1812, and Who Were Presented With Medals by Congress, For Their Gallant Services. Illustrated by Eighty-Two Engravings on Steel from the Original Medals*, published by Carey & Hart, Philadelphia, in 1848. He also wrote *A Description of the National Medals of America, Presented to the Officers of the Wars of the Revolution and 1812* (New York, 1854) and once assisted Daniel E. Groux in the making of reproductions of rare U.S. medals. His interests were varied and also included natural history, religion, military history, conchology, and other fields.

Around 1856 Thomas Wyatt struck or had made to his order a dozen "sets" of Massachusetts silver coins, each containing one each of the NE shilling and sixpence; an Oak Tree shilling and twopence; a Pine Tree sixpence, threepence, and hitherto unknown one pence; and a Good Samaritan shilling. It seems that he copied the two NE designs from an earlier text with finely spaced horizontal lines on the coins to indicate depth or shading. Unaware of what original Massachusetts NE silver coins looked like, Wyatt copied the lines as well. As such, his NE sixpence and shilling are readily identifiable today. The 1652 Oak Tree twopence and 1652 Pine Tree penny are fantasies with no equivalent originals, although the denomination was presumptively illustrated in Martin Folkes's *Tables of English Gold and Silver Coins*, 1763 (which also showed the NE coins with lined fields). The Good Samaritan shilling is a copy of a famous forgery. In addition to the sets he also distributed singles, such as in the Chelsea hoard.

Wyatt's dies were acquired by Edwin Bishop, of 9 Dutch Street, New York City, who struck additional examples, including new versions in copper. W. Elliot Woodward's sale of November 1878 included this comment as part of Lot 4506, a Wyatt Good Samaritan shilling muling struck over an English gold guinea:

> Mr. Edwin Bishop, late of New York, informed me many years ago that the dies for the Wyatt counterfeits having come into his possession he struck a few sets,

regular in form; in silver and copper; that he then took an English guinea and, using the obverse dies of Wyatt's Good Samaritan and Pine Tree shillings, he struck this coin; that he made no similar one in any medal whatever, but immediately destroyed the dies.

Numismatic Aspects

NE Coinage Copies

W-14010 · sixpence · silver

Obverse: VI at one end of field, background of coin with closely spaced horizontal lines. *Reverse:* At one end of the field NE, background of coin with closely spaced horizontal lines. *Mintage:* Twelve as part of sets, plus unrecorded singles by Wyatt; unknown others by Bishop. *Rarity:* URS-5.

Selected auction price(s): John J. Ford Jr. XIV Sale (5/2006), MS, $3,737, $3,220.

W-14012 · sixpence · copper

Design as preceding, but struck in copper. *Mintage:* Small unknown quantity by Edwin Bishop. *Rarity:* URS-2 or 3(?).

W-14020 · shilling · silver

Obverse: XII at one end of field, background of coin with closely spaced horizontal lines. *Reverse:* At one end of the field NE, background of coin with closely spaced horizontal lines. *Mintage:* Twelve as part of sets, plus unrecorded singles by Wyatt; unknown others by Bishop. *Rarity:* URS-5.

Selected auction price(s): Hain Family Sale (Stack's 1/2002), MS, $3,162.50. John J. Ford Jr. XIV Sale (5/2006), VF, $2,875; MS, $2,645.

W-14022 · shilling · copper

Design as preceding, but struck in copper. *Mintage:* Small unknown quantity by Edwin Bishop. *Rarity:* URS-2 or 3.

Selected auction price(s): John J. Ford Jr. XIV Sale (5/2006), Choice MS, $2,875.

1652 Oak Tree Coinage Copies

W-14030 · twopence · silver

Obverse: Two beaded circles with MASATHVSETS within. At center, oak tree. *Reverse:* Two beaded circles with NEW ENGLAND within. At center 1652 / II. *Mintage:* Twelve as part of sets plus unrecorded singles by Wyatt; unknown others by Bishop. *Notes:* Called a Pine Tree twopence by Noe, Oak Tree twopence by Kenney. No original Oak Tree twopence was ever made, and the genuine Pine Tree twopence is dated 1662. *Rarity:* URS-4.

W-14032 · twopence · copper

Design as preceding, but struck in copper. *Mintage:* Small unknown quantity by Edwin Bishop. *Rarity:* URS-2 or 3.

W-14040 · shilling · silver

Obverse: Two beaded circles with MASATHVSETS IN within. At center, oak (?) tree. *Reverse:* Two beaded circles with NEW ENGLAND AN DOM within. At center 1652 / XII. *Mintage:* Twelve as part of sets plus unrecorded singles by Wyatt; unknown others by Bishop. *Notes:* Called a Pine Tree shilling by Noe; actually copied after Noe 1-D, an Oak Tree shilling. *Rarity:* URS-5.

Selected auction price(s): John J. Ford Jr. XIV Sale (5/2006), EF, $1,495; Choice MS, $1,150 [*sic*].

W-14042 · shilling · copper

Design as preceding, but struck in copper. *Mintage:* Small unknown quantity by Edwin Bishop. *Rarity:* URS-2 or 3.

Selected auction price(s): Hain Family Sale (Stack's 1/2002), MS, $460. John J. Ford Jr. XIV Sale (5/2006), F, $345.

1652 Pine Tree Coinage Copies

W-14050 · penny · silver

Obverse: Pine (?) tree within beaded circle with MASATHVSETS around, letters only partially visible. *Reverse:* Within beaded circle 1652 / 1. *Mintage:* Twelve as part of sets plus unrecorded singles by Wyatt; unknown others by Bishop. *Notes:* A complete fantasy, as no coins of this denomination were originally struck. *Rarity:* URS-5.

Selected auction price(s): John J. Ford Jr. XIV Sale (5/2006), AU, $575; MS, $1,840.

W-14052 · penny · copper

Design as preceding, but struck in copper. *Mintage:* Small unknown quantity by Edwin Bishop. *Rarity:* URS-2 or 3.

W-14060 · threepence · silver

Obverse: Two beaded circles with MASATHVSETS within. At center, pine tree. *Reverse:* Two beaded circles with NEW ENGLAND within. At center 1652 / III. *Mintage:* Twelve as part of sets plus unrecorded singles by Wyatt; unknown others by Bishop. *Notes:* Loosely copied from Crosby 1-A. *Rarity:* URS-5.

Selected auction price(s): John J. Ford Jr. XIV Sale (5/2006), VF, $575; MS, $575 (same price for both).

W-14070 · threepence · copper

Design as preceding, but struck in copper. *Mintage:* Small unknown quantity by Edwin Bishop. *Rarity:* URS-2 or 3.

W-14072 · sixpence · silver

Obverse: Two beaded circles with MASATHVSETS IN within. At center, pine tree. *Reverse:* Two beaded circles with NEW ENGLAND within. At center 1652 / VI. *Mintage:* Twelve as part of sets plus unrecorded singles by Wyatt; unknown others by Bishop. *Rarity:* URS-5.

Selected auction price(s): Hain Family Sale (Stack's 1/2002), MS, $460. John J. Ford Jr. XIV Sale (5/2006), EF, $960.

W-14080 · sixpence · copper

Design as preceding, but struck in copper. *Mintage:* Small unknown quantity by Edwin Bishop. *Rarity:* URS-2 or 3.

1652 Good Samaritan Coinage Copies

W-14082 · shilling · silver
Obverse: Two circles with MASATHVSETS IN within. At center, scene of the Good Samaritan per the Biblical parable. *Reverse:* NEW ENGLAND AN DOM around border. At center within beaded circle, 1652 / XII. *Mintage:* Twelve as part of sets plus unrecorded singles by Wyatt; unknown others by Bishop. *Notes:* The "original" of the Good Samaritan shilling was an alteration of a Pine Tree shilling, exposed by Eric P. Newman in *The Secret of the Good Samaritan Shilling*, 1959. *Rarity:* URS-5.

Selected auction price(s): C4 Convention (M&G 11/2001), VF-35, $1,200. John J. Ford Jr. XIV Sale (5/2006), F, $3,340; MS, $5,750; Choice MS, $6,325.

W-14090 · shilling · copper
Design as preceding, but struck in copper. *Mintage:* Small unknown quantity by Edwin Bishop. *Rarity:* URS-2 or 3.

Selected auction price(s): Hain Family Sale (Stack's 1/2002), MS, $1,610.

W-14092 · shilling · Good Samaritan / Oak Tree muling · silver
Obverse: Two circles with MASATHVSETS IN within. At center, scene of the Good Samaritan per the Biblical parable. *Reverse:* Obverse of Wyatt's Oak Tree shilling die; two beaded circles with MASATHVSETS IN within. At center, oak (?) tree. *Mintage:* One. *Notes:* Unrecorded production by Edwin Bishop. One in the Ford collection, where it is noted, "several known." *Rarity:* URS-3.

Selected auction price(s): John J. Ford Jr. XIV Sale (5/2006), $3,162.

W-14100 · shilling · gold
Design as preceding, but struck in gold. *Mintage:* One. *Notes:* Struck over an English gold guinea by Edwin Bishop. *Rarity:* URS-1.

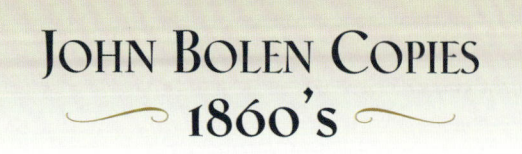

John Bolen Copies
1860's

John Adams Bolen

John Adams Bolen (1826–1907) of Springfield, Massachusetts, is one of the most interesting and, in some ways, enigmatic characters to walk across the numismatic stage. As did several others in the mid-19th century, he was at once a numismatist and a diesinker. This combination can be powerful, inasmuch as a numismatist, especially with an eye to the market, knows what will sell. As a diesinker, Bolen could create pieces that would find a ready sale, or simply to satisfy his whims. He produced many tokens and small medals, some of which very closely imitated colonial coins. The craftsmanship on his colonial copy dies was extraordinary.

Bolen was born in New York City on November 10, 1826. In the 1850s he relocated to Springfield, where he gained employment with Rumrill & Shumway, manufacturer of jewelry. By 1858 or 1859 he was working on his own account, as a sales agent for National sewing machines and as an engraver and jewelry manufacturer. The date of Bolen's first independent token production is not known, but 1861 is the date given by Bolen himself in a recollection he penned in 1904. He was listed as a "diesinker" for the first time in the 1859–1860 *Springfield Directory*, released in May 1859. Bolen's recollections were not always accurate or complete, and thus his comments must be taken with the proverbial grain of salt.

By the early 1860s, he was into diesinking full swing, and by 1870 he had created several dozen different dies and combinations. Colonial coins accounted for only a small percentage of these.

W. Elliot Woodward, the leading auctioneer of tokens and medals in the 1860s, subscribed to Bolen's productions and became one of several outlets for them. On July 2, 1862, Woodward published a circular offering for sale copies of Bolen's "U.S.A." or "Bar Cent," among other items. Woodward seems to have had mixed emotions about Bolen's products, at one time offering them for sale and at other times calling them "dangerous counterfeits."

In August 1869 the *American Journal of Numismatics* ran this commentary following Bolen's announcement of his creation of a copy of the Carolina Elephant token and a related muling:

> They are, as nearly as may be, facsimiles of the rare original. The execution of both pieces is masterly, and gives continued evidence of the remarkable talent which their artist is acknowledged to possess. We hope that he may ere long find worthy employment on some original and important work.

The comment "original" is noteworthy and reveals that Bolen's copies were so good that his talent might be best directed elsewhere, on something original of his own creation.

In the 1860s it was common practice for auction catalogers to include struck copies, electrotypes, and other non-original pieces, identified as such. There was no stigma to making or selling such pieces, so long as there was no fraudulent intent.

In the June 1868 issue of the *AJN*, Bolen noted that certain of his dies had been sold to others including A. Ramsey McCoy, Charles E. Vinton, and Francis Smith Edwards. A follow-up article by Charles Porter Nichols in the same journal, August 1868, listed additional varieties. It was evident that, in a numismatic sense, Bolen had run amok and had created all sorts of illogical mulings, off-metal pieces, and other delicacies. However, he was hardly the first to do this.

Francis Smith Edwards, M.D., of New York City, by all numismatic accounts a rascal, remains today somewhat of a shadowy figure, although in his day he was well known. No doubt his biography, if accurately delineated, would make fascinating reading today. In the 1860s he issued a copy of Gobrecht's Charles Carroll of Carrollton medal. In the same era he acquired a number of Bolen's dies and produced restrikes from them, issuing no information as to the varieties or quantities made. We know he used Bolen's Higley copper dies. It seems that he made certain Immune Columbia copies as well, with dies from another source. Other productions include Washington funeral medals and a copy of the 1796 federal half cent. George B. Mason and J.W. Kline also acquired Bolen dies and made unrecorded strikings from them.

In August 1866, the newly established *American Journal of Numismatics* published a listing, "Medal Dies Cut by J.A. Bolen, of Springfield," which had been "communicated to the Boston Numismatic Society." This was the first of many lists and commentaries that appeared in that magazine over the next several decades.

Today, Bolen copies are highly collectible and eagerly sought. Bolen's own mintage figures are unreliable, and there is no real accounting for examples made by others who bought dies from Bolen and who made special strikings, such as over silver coins. Generally, all Bolen copies are scarce today, and many are very rare. The typical size range for a Bolen copy is from the high end of 26 mm to the low end of 29 mm. As the pieces were generally struck without a collar, some are slightly out of round. Plain edge is standard. A typical collecting objective is to acquire one of each striking in copper, this being the metal of the originals. Such pieces are asterisked (*) in the following listings. The standard reference work is *The Medallic Works of John Adams Bolen, Die Sinker &c.*, Neil E. Musante, 1992.

Numismatic Aspects

Basic copy of colonial dies in copper are noted with an asterisk after the W-number.

Bar Copper Copies

W-14200* · Kenney-1 · Bolen dies 1-A · struck in copper

Obverse: USA letters entwined as a monogram. *Reverse:* Thirteen parallel bars. A copy can be distinguished from an original by whether the S passes over the A; on the original it goes under the A. *Mintage:* Sixty-five, but "most" destroyed (see below). *Notes:* Musante JAB-2. Dies made in 1862. This was the first of Bolen's colonial copies. More than any other copy, this variety is sometimes found lightly worn (deliberately, as these were popular deceptions). Sizes can vary by several tenths of a millimeter. Ford had three. After Bolen struck the copper impressions he sold the dies to W.E. Woodward, who struck 12 in silver. W.E. Woodward's sale of April 28 to May 1, 1863, included these: lot 2099, "U.S.A. or Bar Cent, from the Bolen die, in copper; the die and most of the impressions having been destroyed, these pieces are now rarer than the originals." Sold for $1. Musante considered the Woodward comment to be incorrect. Lot 2100, "Same as the last, in silver, excessively rare." Sold for $3. Lot 2101, "The same in nickel, unique." Sold for $1.25. Lot 2012, "Another in brass, the only one struck." Sold for $1.75. Lot 2013, "Same in tin, but one struck." Sold for 75¢. *Rarity:* URS-7.

AU-50	MS-60	MS-63
$400	$1,000	$2,000

W-14205 · brass

Design as preceding, but struck in brass. *Mintage:* One by W. Elliott Woodward, who bought the dies from Bolen. *Notes:* Musante JAB-2. Ford catalog: "Woodward wrote in his sale of April 28, 1863, that he instructed George H. Lovett to strike only one each in nickel, brass, and tin. These three pieces were purchased by Charles I. Bushnell.... This brass piece may or may not be the Bushnell specimen." *Rarity:* URS-1 or 2.

Selected auction price(s): John J. Ford Jr. XIV Sale (5/2006), MS, $4,025.

W-14210 · German silver

Design as preceding, but struck in German silver. *Mintage:* One by W. Elliott Woodward, who bought the dies from Bolen. *Notes:* Musante JAB-2. *Rarity:* URS-1.

W-14215 · white metal

Design as preceding, but struck in white metal. *Mintage:* One by W. Elliott Woodward, who bought the dies from Bolen. *Notes:* Musante JAB-2. *Rarity:* URS-1.

W-14220 · silver

Design as preceding, but struck in silver. *Mintage:* Twelve by W. Elliott Woodward, who bought the dies from Bolen and enlisted Lovett to do the striking. They were offered in 1863 for $4 each. *Notes:* Musante JAB-2. Ford had one. Otherwise seldom seen in the marketplace. *Rarity:* URS-4.

Selected auction price(s): John J. Ford Jr. XIV Sale (5/2006), Choice MS, $9,750.

Inimica Tyrannis / 1785 Confederatio Mulings

W-14230* · Kenney-2 · Bolen dies 2-B · Large Stars · copper

Obverse: • INIMICA TYRANNIS • / AMERICANA around border. At center, Indian standing, holding bow in left hand (to observer's right) and arrow in right hand. His right foot steps on a crown, symbolic of crushing a tyrant (Great Britain). To the right of the Indian is a large container or tree stump. Thin, widely spaced dentils around border. The die was created in the old style, with irregular lettering, and so on, in excellent imitation of the style of the 1785 original. *Reverse:* CONFEDERATIO / 1785 (large stars). Can be distinguished from an original by whether ME (AMERICANA) is joined at the top; not joined on the copy. On the genuine the lower part of the S (TYRANNIS) is nearly closed; on the copy it is open; privy mark of a dot in the Y. On the reverse of the genuine the second E points to a large ray; on the copy to a small ray. The star under the N (CONFEDERATIO) points to a small ray on the genuine; on the copy to a large ray. *Mintage:* Forty, per Bolen. *Notes:* Musante JAB-7. Dies cut in 1863. W.E. Woodward sale, March 30, 1865, Lot 197: "Confederatio, 1785; rev. Indian standing, with bow and arrow, 'Inimica Tyrannis Americana'; a new and dangerous counterfeit by Bolen. As a work of art a perfect wonder. Dies destroyed and very rare." In Woodward's sale of October 1863 two examples sold for a remarkable $8 and $10 and were purchased by ANA. Levick, *American Journal of Numismatics*, June 1868: "Dies sold to Dr. Edwards, after they had been defaced, or battered so as not to be fit to use." Edwards struck additional examples. *Rarity:* URS-7.

AU-50	MS-60	MS-63
$300	$500	$1,500

W-14235 · brass

Design as preceding, but struck in brass. *Mintage:* Not recorded. *Notes:* Musante JAB-7. One offered by W.E. Woodward in his sale of April 1866. *Rarity:* URS-1.

W-14240 · silver

Design as preceding, but struck in silver. *Mintage:* Two per Bolen. *Notes:* Musante JAB-7. Johnson (1882) stated the silver strikings were sold to W. Elliot Woodward and to James Parker (who was mentioned on the reverse of the Springfield Antiquarians Medal made by Bolen, not discussed here). Two silver impressions are in the Ford collection, one overstruck on an unidentified coin. *Rarity:* URS-2(?).

Selected auction price(s): John J. Ford Jr. XIV Sale (5/2006), MS, $8,050, $8,050.

W-14250* · Kenney-3 · Bolen dies 2-C · Small Stars · copper

Obverse: Same as preceding. *Reverse:* Small stars CONFEDERATIO reverse. • CONFEDERATIO • / 1785 around border. At center, 13 stars in a circle, with rays extending from the circle. *Mintage:* Forty, per Bolen. *Notes:* Musante JAB-8. Dies cut in 1863. Bolen said he destroyed both. Reverse sometimes seen with raised cancellation marks, perhaps from a "destroyed" die. *Rarity:* URS-7.

AU-50	MS-60	MS-63
$350	$700	$1,500

W-14255 · brass

Design as preceding, but struck in brass. *Mintage:* Not stated. *Notes:* Musante JAB-8. One reported by Richard D. Kenney. *Rarity:* URS-1(?).

W-14260 · silver

Design as preceding, but struck in silver. *Mintage:* Two, per Bolen. *Notes:* Musante JAB-8. 27.8 mm. *Rarity:* URS-2(?).

Higley Copies

W-14270* · Kenney-4 · Bolen dies 3-D · threepence · copper

Obverse: [Pointing hand] THE • VALVE • OF • THREE • PENCE. around border. At center, a standing stag faces to the viewer's left. Two lines under stag. Circle within letters is pierced by one of the stag's antlers. Plain border. Field somewhat irregular as intended. *Reverse:* [Five-pointed star made of lines] CONNECTICVT. 1737. around border. Circle within, enclosing three crowned hammers. Plain border. Field somewhat irregular as intended. Differs from original, which has a complete circle around the deer; copy has circle incomplete at bottom. Copy has privy mark, a dot in the C of PENCE. *Mintage:* Forty, per Bolen. True mintage unknown. *Notes:* Musante JAB-10. Dies cut in 1864. Bolen commented in 1904: "In 1865 I sold these dies to Dr. F.S. Edwards, of New York, but he must have had them restored as I have seen one in nickel." Five copper in the Ford collection. *Rarity:* URS-7.

AU-50	MS-60	MS-63
$350	$500	$1,800

W-14275 · brass

Design as preceding, but struck in brass. *Mintage:* True mintage unknown. Probably made by Bolen, who forgot to mention them. *Notes:* Musante JAB-10. Three in the Ford collection. *Rarity:* URS-5.

Selected auction price(s): John J. Ford Jr. XIV Sale (5/2006), AU, $230; Choice MS, $402, $920 (wide price differential).

W-14280 · German silver

Design as preceding, but struck in German silver. *Mintage:* Two per Bolen. True mintage unknown. Sometimes called "nickel." *Notes:* Musante JAB-10. "Seems pewter" piece reported in *CNL*, January 1961; not verified. Example in Stack's Americana Sale, 2001, lot 258. *Rarity:* URS-1 or 2(?).

W-14285 · silver

Design as preceding, but struck in silver. *Mintage:* Two per Bolen. True mintage unknown. In the Ford commentary, Michael J. Hodder knew of four. *Notes:* Musante JAB-10. Three in the Ford collection. *Rarity:* URS-4.

Selected auction price(s): John J. Ford Jr. XIV Sale (5/2006), MS, $1,610, $2,530, $2,990.

Elephant Token / God Preserve Carolina Mulings

W-14300* · Kenney-5 · Bolen dies 4-E · copper

Obverse: Standing elephant facing left. First variety; tusks very close to border. *Reverse:* GOD PRESERVE CAROLINA. Can be distinguished from the original by the spacing between V and E (PRESERVE); in the original V and E are widely spaced, but on the copy they are close. Also, on the original the PROPRIETORS reverse has the O cut over an earlier erroneous E; the copy lacks this feature. *Mintage:* Forty per Bolen. *Notes:* Musante JAB-33. Dies cut in 1869; said to have been canceled and gifted to the Boston Numismatic Society. *Rarity:* URS-7.

AU-50	MS-60	MS-63
$500	$1,000	$2,500

W-14305 · brass

Design as preceding, but struck in brass. *Mintage:* Five per Bolen. *Notes:* Musante JAB-33. *Rarity:* URS-2 or 3.

Selected auction price(s): John J. Ford Jr. XIV Sale (5/2006), Choice MS, $2,300.

W-14310 · lead

Design as preceding, but struck in lead. *Mintage:* One per Musante. *Notes:* Musante JAB-33. Trial piece. Details not known. *Rarity:* URS-1.

W-14320 · silver

Design as preceding, but struck in silver. *Mintage:* Two per Bolen, five per Edward Cogan comment in 1874. *Notes:* Musante JAB-33. One struck over an 1807 half dollar (Chapman brothers' sale of June 1885, lot 1441), later in the Ford collection, now in an Eastern collection (illustrated here); the half dollar was not cut down, and the Bolen dies were carefully impressed in the center, allowing significant margin of the half dollar to remain. Another Ford collection coin over an 1863 Swiss two-franc piece. *Rarity:* URS-3.

Selected auction price(s): John J. Ford Jr. XIV Sale (5/2006), Choice MS, $6,900; MS, over half dollar, $12,650.

W-14340 · Kenney unlisted "6a" · Bolen dies 4-5 · double elephants · no lettering · copper

Standing elephant facing left. First variety, combined with standing elephant facing left. Second variety (tusks slightly farther from border), early state without lettering. *Mintage:* Two. *Notes:* Musante JAB-34a. The second obverse die is similar to the first, but was not acceptable to Bolen. It was used briefly, then the next coin (see below) was created. Ford collection and Massachusetts Historical Society. *Rarity:* URS-2.

Selected auction price(s): John J. Ford Jr. XIV Sale (5/2006), AU, $3,737.

W-14360 · Kenney-6 · Bolen dies 4-6 · lettering

Standing elephant facing left. First variety, combined with standing elephant facing left. Third variety lettered ONLY TEN STRUCK, a later state of the second variety die. Bolen commented that he used this incorrect die to make two mulings with the first elephant die, after which he took the second die and added the lettering, ONLY TEN STRUCK (our obverse die 5 now changed to die 6). Ten more coins were made combining obverse 4 with 6 (see below). *Mintage:* Ten. *Notes:* Musante JAB-34. *Rarity:* URS-4.

Selected auction price(s): John J. Ford Jr. XIV Sale (5/2006), AU, $1,380; Choice MS, $3,737.

Liber Natus Libertatem Defendo / Neo Eboracus Excelsior

W-14370* · Kenney-7 · Bolen dies 7-F · copper

Obverse: [six-pointed star] LIBER NATUS LIBERTATUM DEFENDO. At center, Indian standing, quiver on his back, holding a bow in his left hand and an arrow in his right hand. Plain border. *Reverse:* NEO EBORACUS 1787 / EXCELSIOR. At center, eagle perched on upper part of globe. Dentils at border. Letters in imitation of the original copper of 1787. E (NEO) double punched. B (EBORACUS) double punched. The 7's (1787) are small. A counterfeit can be identified from the original by the following: on the original the Indian's right foot touches the ground line; on the copy it does not. The original has seven feathers in the Indian's headdress; the copy has nine. On the reverse the original has a hyphen separating NEO and EBORACUS; the copy does not. *Mintage:* Forty, per Bolen. *Notes:* Musante JAB-36. Always lightly struck at the center of both sides. Dies cut in 1869. In 1893 Bolen recalled that he destroyed both dies and then presented them to the Boston Numismatic Society. The Crosby collection sale (Cogan 1883) had 12 pieces. *Rarity:* URS-6.

AU-50	MS-60	MS-63
$600	$1,500	$2,000

W-14375 · brass

Designs as preceding, but struck in brass. *Mintage:* Five per Bolen. *Notes:* Musante JAB-36. Always lightly struck at the center. One in the Ford collection. *Rarity:* URS-2 or 3.

Selected auction price(s): John J. Ford Jr. XIV Sale (5/2006), Choice MS, $3,737.

W-14380 · silver

Designs as preceding, but struck in silver. *Mintage:* Two per Bolen. *Notes:* Musante JAB-36. Lightly struck at the center. None in the Ford collection. Somerset collection coin (1992) over an 1821 quarter. One over an 1805 quarter, maintaining its reeded edge (ex Newcomer and Cruzan collections to Eastern collection; massive rim cud at upper right of reverse, probably fatal to the die; illustrated). *Rarity:* URS-2.

George Clinton / Excelsior 1787

W-14390* · Kenney-8 · Bolen dies 8-G · copper

Obverse: Bust of Governor George Clinton facing right; facial features somewhat resembling Benjamin Franklin (?). GEORGE CLINTON at border, star after each word. *Reverse:* Arms of the State of New York, with two goddesses flanking oval, on top of which is an eagle perched on a half globe; two horizontal parallel lines below. Eagle faces to viewer's right. Below, 1787 / EXCELSIOR. Plain border. Letters in the old style in imitation of the 1787 original. Pole of goddess to right pierces two horizontal parallel lines. The 1 (1787) is missing lower right serif; first 7 small (second 7 normal). A counterfeit can be identified from the original by the following: The copy has a dot in the O (GEORGE). On the reverse of the original the first E (EXCELSIOR) is directly below the left foot; on the copy it is to the right. *Mintage:* Forty, per Bolen. *Notes:* Musante JAB-37. Breen (*Encyclopedia*) suggested they are as rare as originals. The Parker collection sale (1876) had one struck on an 1850 cent. ANS specimen with edge lettered B 40 STRUCK (from Bolen's estate; in later years he lettered the edges of certain of his copies still on hand). *Rarity:* URS-6.

AU-50	MS-60	MS-63
$750	$1,500	$2,000

W-14395 · brass

Designs as preceding, but struck in brass. *Mintage:* Five per Bolen. *Notes:* Musante JAB-37. Some with edge lettered B 5 STRUCK. Not in the Ford collection. *Rarity:* URS-3.

W-14400 · silver

Designs as preceding, but struck in silver. *Mintage:* Two per Bolen, three per Edward Cogan. Examples over 1819 (Ford; detail shown), 1822, and 1832 (ANS) quarters. *Notes:* Musante JAB-37.

Selected auction price(s): John J. Ford Jr. XIV Sale (5/2006), Choice MS, $9,775.

1785 Confederatio, Large Stars / 1785 Confederatio, Small Stars Muling

W-14440* · Kenney-9 · Bolen dies B-C · copper

Muling of two reverse dies. *Mintage:* Two per Johnson. *Notes:* Musante JAB.M-1. One in the Ford collection, another owned by the Massachusetts Historical Society, another in an Eastern collection. *Rarity:* URS-3.

Selected auction price(s): John J. Ford Jr. XIV Sale (5/2006), Choice MS, $4,025.

W-14460 · brass

Designs as preceding, but struck in brass. *Mintage:* One per Musante. *Notes:* Musante JAB.M-1. *Rarity:* URS-1.

W-14480 · silver

Designs as preceding, but struck in silver. *Mintage:* One per Bolen. *Notes:* Musante JAB.M-1. *Rarity:* URS-1.

Liber Natus Libertatem Defendo / Excelsior 1787

W-14510* · Kenney-10 · Bolen dies 7-G · copper

Obverse: Same as for W-14370. *Reverse:* Arms of the State of New York, with two goddesses flanking oval, on top of which is an eagle perched on a half globe; two horizontal parallel lines below. Eagle faces to viewer's right. Below, 1787 / EXCELSIOR. Plain border. Letters in the old style in imitation of the 1787 original. Pole of goddess to right pierces two horizontal parallel lines. In date, 1 missing lower right serif; first 7 small (second 7 normal). *Mintage:* Forty, per Bolen. *Notes:* Musante JAB.M-11. Crosby noted this was the "most easily procured" of the Bolen copies. Today, offerings are occasional at best. *Rarity:* URS-7.

AU-50	MS-60	MS-63
$600	$800	$1,500

W-14520 · brass

Designs as preceding, but struck in brass. *Mintage:* Five per Bolen. *Notes:* Musante JAB.M-11. One with edge lettered: 5 STRUCK. *Rarity:* URS-2 or 3.

W-14530 · silver

Designs as preceding, but struck in silver. *Mintage:* Two per Bolen. *Notes:* Musante JAB.M-11. One over a 1787 English shilling with original diagonally reeded edge remaining (Eastern collection ex Stack's sale of March 2000). *Rarity:* URS-1 or 2.

Other Bolen Copies

W-14550* · Kenney-11 · Bolen dies F-G · Neo Eboracus Excelsior / Excelsior 1787 muling · copper

Muling of two reverse dies. *Mintage:* Five per Bolen. *Notes:* Musante JAB.M-12, called "extremely rare and possibly unique." None in the Ford collection. Example sold in the Coin Galleries sale of November 1990. One in an Eastern collection. *Rarity:* URS-1(?).

W-14560* · Kenney-12 · Bolen dies 8-F · George Clinton / Neo Eboracus Excelsior muling · copper

Obverse: See description for W-14390. *Reverse:* NEO EBORACUS 1787 / EXCELSIOR. At center, eagle perched on upper part of globe. Dentils at border. Letters in imitation of the original copper of 1787. E (NEO) double punched. B (EBORACUS) double punched. In date, 7's small. *Mintage:* Five per Bolen. *Notes:* Musante JAB.M-13; no auction records located. Dies cut in 1869. Later canceled and presented to the Boston Numismatic Society. *Rarity:* URS-3.

Selected auction price(s): John J. Ford Jr. XIV Sale (5/2006), Choice MS, $1,495.

W-14570* · Kenney-13 · Bolen dies 7-8 · Liber Natus Libertatem Defendo / George Clinton muling · copper

Obverse: See description for W-14510. *Reverse:* Around border, GEORGE [six-pointed star] CLINTON [six-pointed star]. At center, portrait of Clinton facing right. Border with small, short, widely spaced dentils. Letters in the old style in imitation of the 1787 original. Dot inside O (GEORGE). *Mintage:* Five per Bolen. *Notes:* Musante JAB.M-14; no auction records located by him. *Rarity:* URS-1 or 2.

Selected auction price(s): John J. Ford Jr. XIV Sale (5/2006), Choice MS, $1,495.

W-14580* · Kenney-14 · Bolen dies 3-B · Higley / Confederatio With Large Stars muling · copper

Obverse: Same as preceding. *Reverse:* CONFEDERATIO / 1785 (large stars). *Mintage:* Unknown. None mentioned by Bolen. *Notes:* Musante JAB.M/E-13. In *The Numismatist*, July 1912, Edgar H. Adams commented: "HIGLEY CENT . . . joined to reverse with large stars in the sunburst. Both of these dies are by Bolen. Curiously, he does not mention this combination in his list. While he says that he sold the dies of [the Higley copy] to Dr. Edwards of New York, still he states that he destroyed the dies of the [Confederatio issues]. Nevertheless, these dies have been used in conjunction, and there are several specimens known. Copper." None in the Ford collection. Two in the American Numismatic Society. *Rarity:* URS-3.

W-14650* · Kenney-unlisted · Die 2 and Bolen store card · Inimica Tyrannis / Bolen store-card reverse muling · copper

Obverse: See description for W-14230. With marks from defacing. *Reverse:* Bolen store-card die with inscription J.A. Bolen / DIE SINKER / MEDALIST / SPRINGFIELD, MASS. *Mintage:* Not recorded. *Notes:* Musante JAB-M/E-12. Rulau-unlisted. Henry Chapman estate to Edmund A. Rice to Donald M. Miller to Eastern collection. *Rarity:* URS-2.

Selected auction price(s): John J. Ford Jr. XIV Sale (5/2006), Choice MS, $1,265.

W-14655 · brass

Designs as preceding, but struck in brass. *Mintage:* Not recorded. *Notes:* Musante JAB-M/E-12. Obverse die with marks from defacing. Rulau unlisted. Henry Chapman estate to Edmund A. Rice to Donald M. Miller to Eastern collection. *Rarity:* URS-2.

Selected auction price(s): John J. Ford Jr. XIV Sale (5/2006), Choice MS, $1,265.

W-14665 · white metal

Designs as preceding, but struck in brass. *Mintage:* Not recorded. *Notes:* Musante JAB-M/E-12. Rulau unlisted. Obverse die with marks from defacing. Described in W.E. Woodward's sale of his own collection, October 1884, lot 768: "'Inimica Tyrannis.' Reverse: Bolen's card; tin, fine, rare." *Rarity:* URS-1(?).

Selected auction price(s): John J. Ford Jr. XIV Sale (5/2006), Choice MS, $454.

W-14690* · Kenney-unlisted · Die C and Bolen store card · 1785 Confederatio With Small Stars / Bolen store-card reverse muling · copper

Obverse: As described earlier. *Reverse:* Same die as preceding. *Mintage:* Not recorded. *Notes:* Musante JAB-M/E-11. Rulau MA-Sp-20. Confederatio die with marks from defacing. Eastern collection. *Rarity:* URS-1(?).

W-14695 · brass

Obverse: As described earlier. *Reverse:* Same die as preceding. *Mintage:* Not recorded. *Notes:* Musante JAB-M/E-11. Rulau MA-Sp-20. Confederatio die with marks from defacing. *Rarity:* URS-1(?).

Selected auction price(s): New York Public Library Collection Sale (1982), an example thought unique, $352.

W-14700 · white metal

Obverse: As described earlier. *Reverse:* Same die as preceding. *Mintage:* Not recorded. *Notes:* Musante JAB-M/E-11. Rulau unlisted. Confederatio die with marks from defacing. *Rarity:* URS-1(?).

Non Dependens Status Copper 1778?

The 1778-dated Non Dependens Status copper is one of the more enduring mysteries in American numismatics. Was it hand-engraved by Paul Revere? Does it actually date from 1778? This curious coin has on the obverse the cuirassed bust of a man facing right, with NON DEPEN-DENS STATUS at the border. On the reverse a seated youth wears a headband and feathered skirt, and holds a branch in his right hand and leans on an oval shield with his left. The shield is diagonal quarters by a sword and flagstaff. In each diamond-shaped quarter is a fleur-de-lis, the symbol of France. At the border is AMER ICA, divided between R and I. The date 1778 is at the bottom border.

Early notice of this appeared 1858 in *Norton's Literary Letter No. 2*, a 46-page offering of coins, autographs, etc. The "Curiosa Americana" column included this:

> The next coin is in pure copper, and is truly a well-executed design. On the obverse is a bust facing the right, which resembles that of an Indian chief or warrior; on the shoulder, within a small circle, are to be seen a flag and sword crossed, and the *fleur de lis* of France; on the breast is a small head with wings. Legend—"NON DEPEN DENS STATUS."
>
> *Obverse:* Full length figure of an Indian seated on a globe, around the loins is an apron of feathers; in the right hand he holds a branch of tobacco, in the left a shield, with the American flag and sword crossed, and *fleur de lis* the same as on the shoulder-knot of the obverse. Around the whole is the Legend—"AMERICA, 1778." This piece is without doubt *unique*, and is supposed to be one of the many pattern pieces engraved and designed by Paul Revere.

In the same year the 1778 Non Dependens Status copper was listed in John H. Hickcox's *An Historical Account of American Coinage*, citing *Norton's* as the source. The coin attracted the notice of Montroville W. Dickeson in his *American Numismatical Manual*, 1859, who described it in detail and illustrated it on a plate.

In 1875 Crosby illustrated the coin and gave it a half-page description, concluding with, "Nothing is known of the origin or history of this piece."

Somewhere along the line, probably 1859 or so, it is thought that George H. Lovett, a New York City diesinker, made a copy version, using the illustration in *Norton's Literary Letter*, although no documentation has been located. The small word "COPY" is under the bust on the obverse, but this has been tooled away on some surviving pieces. The notation was also removed from the die, and some pieces were struck without that word. Examples are known in copper and silver. It must have been envisioned that there was a good market for copies of this well publicized unique coin.

The earliest auction record found for the original engraved coin is in W. Elliott Woodward's sale of the Finotti collection, 1862, where it sold for $70 (in the same sale a Higley copper realized $50, a 1792 silver center cent sold for $52.50, and a 1793 half cent in Extremely Fine condition brought $4).

Some have suggested that the portrait is that of Washington. However, Byron K. White, who studied the coin over many years, held the representation was of Samuel Adams, Revolutionary War patriot and firebrand, as it closely resembles a John Singleton Copley portrait of Adams (White communication to the author).

As to the Lovett-Robinson copies, Robinson stated that 100 were made in copper and just six were struck in silver. See Robinson listings below.

Numismatic Aspects

W-14800 · engraved original in copper

Design as described above, in main text. Detail differences on original: face on winged head round, somewhat similar to that on a 1787 Fugio copper. Three bands above head. S (DEPENDENS) partly on bust. On the reverse the seated figure wears six large leaves or plaits. The left of the tip under the shield touches the globe. *Notes:* In a private Eastern collection, ex Byron K. White. *Rarity:* URS-1.

ROBINSON COPIES
1860's

Alfred S. Robinson, Hartford, Connecticut banker, exchange dealer, and "great numismatist" (per the cover of an April 16, 1861, auction catalog including his material) was an early issuer of struck copies of colonial coins in addition to various tokens and medalets. Some have associated him with the Non Dependens Status copy earlier described. His most famous production is a store card featuring a copy of a Higley die on the obverse and his advertisement on the other side, introduced in the aforementioned 1861 catalog.

In 1860 at age 24 he was a clerk at the banking firm of Bissell & Company, where his father was a partner. Historian J. Doyle DeWitt believes that in this same year he began issuing tokens, the first being the Non Vi Virtute Vici copper, advertised as the "George Clinton medalet." In 1862 his father died. He became an heir, drawing a stipend of $600 from the trustees of the estate. Apparently, he was considered ill prepared to manage the family property. Robinson maintained an office in the Marble Block at 11 Central Row in Hartford. Through various unwise business decisions he drifted into deep debt. In 1872 he was elected mayor of Hartford. In September 1878 he died at age 42 of a "dropsical affection of long standing." His obituary included this: "His mental endowments were unusual. He possessed excellent literary tastes and abilities and would have been a superior man in the field of letters. But few were more thoroughly conversant with the best English authors or better acquainted with contemporary literature."

Numismatic Aspects

Basic copies of colonial and fantasy dies in copper are indicated with an asterisk after the Whitman number.

Granby (Higley) / Store Card

W-15000* · Kenney-1 · copper

Obverse: Copy of the 1737 Higley copper with VALUE ME AS YOU PLEASE and standing deer. *Reverse:* Advertisement noting Robinson as a "Banker, Numismatist, and Notary Public, Dealer in Stocks, Bonds, Notes, Land Warrants, Uncurrent Money, & All Kinds of American and Foreign Specie." *Mintage:* One hundred fifty. *Notes:* Rulau Ct-Ha-13. 27.5 mm. Rarer than the mintage suggests. Dies by George H. Lovett. Issued in early 1861. Two reverse die varieties in this series. Called the "copy of Granby" by Robinson. Mintage information from Robinson price list reproduced by Richard E. Kenney. *Rarity:* URS-7.

AU-50	MS-60	MS-63
$200	$300	$500

W-15005 · brass

Designs as preceding, but struck in brass. *Mintage:* One hundred fifty. *Notes:* Rulau Ct-Ha-14. *Rarity:* URS-8.

AU-50	MS-60	MS-63
$300	$400	$1,800

W-15010 · white metal

Designs as preceding, but struck in white metal. *Mintage:* One hundred fifty. *Notes:* Rulau Ct-Ha-15. *Rarity:* URS-7.

AU-50	MS-60	MS-63
$150	$300	$500

W-15015 · copper-nickel

Designs as preceding, but struck in copper-nickel. *Mintage:* One hundred fifty. *Rarity:* URS-7.

AU-50	MS-60	MS-63
$150	$300	$500

W-15020 · "plated"

Designs as preceding, but silver plated. *Mintage:* One hundred fifty. *Notes:* Rulau Ct-Ha-12. Listings infrequent; perhaps cataloged as white metal or copper-nickel? *Rarity:* URS-5(?).

W-15025 · silver

Designs as preceding, but struck in silver. *Mintage:* Twenty. *Notes:* Rulau Ct-Ha-11. *Rarity:* URS-4.

Selected auction price(s): John J. Ford Jr. XIV Sale (5/2006), MS, $977, $977, $977; Gem MS, $2,180.

George Clinton / Eagle Fantasy

W-15050* · Kenney-2 · copper

Obverse: Fantasy issue with portrait of George Clinton facing right, copied from the 1787 copper with NON VI VIRTUTE VICI, which originally had a different portrait. *Reverse:* Eagle perched on shield facing right. MERRIAM in tiny letters below shield. E PLURIBUS UNUM above, EXCELSIOR below. Fantasy design. *Mintage:* Fifty-four. *Notes:* Baker-13J, Fuld-WA.FA.(no date).1. 27 mm. Robinson called this the George Clinton medalet. Dies by Joseph Merriam of Boston. "Dies destroyed," per Robinson list. *Rarity:* URS-7.

AU-50	MS-60	MS-63
$150	$300	$500

W-15080 · silver

Designs as preceding, but struck in silver. *Mintage:* Six. *Notes:* Baker 13K, Fuld-WA.FA.(no date).1a.Ag. *Rarity:* URS-3.

Selected auction price(s): John J. Ford Jr. XIV Sale (5/2006), MS, $575.

1787 Brasher Doubloon Copy

W-15100* · Kenney-3 · copper

Copy of the 1787 Brasher doubloon. A counterfeit can be distinguished from the original by the absence of the signature BRASHER at the lower part of the obverse; the original has this signature, whereas the copy does not. Workmanship on the copy is modern in appearance. *Mintage:* Twenty-five. *Notes:* 29 mm. Dies by Joseph Merriam of Boston. "Dies destroyed." *Rarity:* URS-5.

Selected auction price(s): John J. Ford Jr. XIV Sale (5/2006), AU, $690; MS, $920.

W-15105 · brass

Designs as preceding, but struck in brass. *Mintage:* Twenty-five. *Rarity:* URS-5.

Selected auction price(s): John J. Ford Jr. XIV Sale (5/2006), Choice MS, $2,300.

1733 Rosa Americana Twopence Copy

W-15150* · Kenney-4 · copper

Copy of the 1733 Rosa Americana twopence. A counterfeit can be identified from the original by the following: Lettering on the obverse much larger than on the original. On the reverse the rose faces forward, while on the original it is turned slightly toward the viewer's right. *Mintage:* Forty-five. *Notes:* 33 mm. Dies by Joseph Merriam of Boston. "Dies destroyed." *Rarity:* URS-6.

AU-50	MS-60	MS-63
$250	$350	$700

W-15160 · brass

Designs as preceding, but struck in brass. *Mintage:* Forty-five. *Rarity:* URS-5.

Selected auction price(s): John J. Ford Jr. XIV Sale (5/2006), MS, $460.

W-15180 · silver

Designs as preceding, but struck in silver. *Mintage:* Ten. *Rarity:* URS-4.

Selected auction price(s): John J. Ford Jr. XIV Sale (5/2006), MS, weakly struck, $431; Choice MS, $375, $825 [wide differential].

1694 New England Elephant Token Copies

W-15200* · Kenney-5 · copper

Copy of the 1694 New England Elephant Token. A counterfeit can be identified from the original by the following: On the original the upright of E (NEW) is slightly right of the upright of L (ENGLAND); on the copy both are aligned. *Mintage:* Fifteen. *Notes:* 28 mm. Dies by Joseph Merriam of Boston. "Dies destroyed." *Rarity:* URS-5.

AU-50	MS-60	MS-63
$500	$1,300	$1,750

W-15210 · Kenney-5 · brass

Designs as preceding, but struck in brass. *Mintage:* Fifteen. *Rarity:* URS-5.

Selected auction price(s): John J. Ford Jr. XIV Sale (5/2006), MS, $1,725.

W-15210 · nickel
Mintage: Fifteen. *Rarity:* URS-5.

W-15235 · silver
Mintage: Three. *Rarity:* URS-2 or 3.
Selected auction price(s): John J. Ford Jr. XIV Sale (5/2006), Choice MS, $1,610, $1,725.

Other Robinson Copies

W-15250 · Kenney-6 · 1778 Non Dependens Status · copper
Design as described above in introduction. A counterfeit can be identified from the original as follows: on copy, face on winged head is oval and with more details; wings with more details. One band above head. S not touching bust. On the reverse the seated figure wears three rows of leaves, with 10 or more leaves in each. The left of the tip is distant from the shield. *Mintage:* One hundred. *Notes:* Dies by George H. Lovett. "COPY" on below bust on early strikings, later removed from the die. *Rarity:* URS-7.

AU-50	MS-60	MS-63
$200	$350	$600

W-15255 · silver
Dies as preceding. *Mintage:* Six. *Rarity:* URS-3 or 4.

W-15270* · Kenney-7 · 1789 Washington Large Eagle Cent · copper
Obverse: Portrait of Washington facing left as taken from the Getz Washington copper of 1792, with fantasy date 1789 below. GEORGE WASHINGTON PRESIDENT around border, obviously inspired by William Idler's copy of the Getz cent. *Reverse:* Large eagle copied from the 1791 Large Eagle cent with eagle holding ribbon inscribed UNUM E PLURIBUS. *Mintage:* Unknown. *Notes:* Baker-14, Fuld-WA.FA.1789.1, Dalton & Hamer Middlesex-242 (although this is not a Conder token). 31 mm. Struck circa 1862 or 1863. Some issued with a bronzed (dark brown) surface. Some silver-plated pieces exist. Dies by George H. Lovett of New York City. *Rarity:* URS-8.

AU-50	MS-60	MS-63
$300	$450	$900

W-15290 · silver
Mintage: Twenty-two said to have been struck. *Notes:* Fuld-WA.FA.1789.1a. *Rarity:* URS-4(?).

DICKESON COPIES
1860's

Montroville W. Dickeson

Montroville Wilson Dickeson, born on June 18, 1809, became interested in old coins in 1822, thus ranking him as a pioneer in the hobby. He went on to become a medical doctor, entrepreneur, author, and landlord. His main interest was archaeology, especially the culture of ancient Indian tribes. He excavated over 1,000 Indian burial mounds, mostly in Tennessee and Louisiana. In the 1859 his *American Numismatical Manual* was published, the first large, comprehensive book ever published on the title subject. Colonial coins were given extensive treatment.

In the 1860s he sold the Dickeson Coin & Medal Safe, manufactured by Evans and Watson in Philadephia. In February 1869 he was one of 48 numismatists illustrated on a sheet titled "Mason's Photographic Gallery of Coin Collectors of the United States, No. 1," published in *Mason's Coin and Stamp Collectors' Magazine*. At the 1876 Centennial Exhibition his coin collection was displayed in the Government Building in Fairmount Park. Likely, his 1776 Continental dollar copies were made for this occasion. Dickeson died on April 14, 1882.

Colonial Copies

Dickeson's 1859 copy of the Sommer Islands shilling, of modern fabric and hardly apt to deceive anyone with even a modest knowledge of numismatics, caused a stir, as noted by a pamphlet datelined Philadelphia, October 1859, which included this:

COIN COLLECTORS, TO THE RESCUE! THE CAROLINA ELEPHANT IN THE FIELD!!
Whereas, certain parties in the City of Brotherly Love have combined together to furnish the inhabitants of Philadelphia with counterfeit Washington cents, and 1/2 dollars, (the Lord Baltimore coinage) also the Sommer Island Shilling, or Hog Cent: We, the Coin Collectors of Philadelphia, seeing the impropriety of the above, have agreed not to purchase any of the above-mentioned pieces, or any that may be made as copies of rare coins or medals, from this date.

There have been several attempts made to re-strike rare coins within the last year or two, and it is high time that a stop should be put to it. On some of the above pieces the word COPY has been made, but in so slight a manner as to be easily erased, and then you cannot tell them from the genuine. We would especially call the attention of the curious public to the Sommer Island, or

Hog Cent, without the word COPY.... Probably VIATOR, alias George H. Hickory nuts, has something to do with the restriking of those pieces.

The commentary refers to various copies made by Robert Lovett Jr., including the Sommer Islands shilling and certain pieces for William K. Idler, both of Philadelphia.

The Sommer Islands dies were muled with irrelevant dies, a Washington token (Baker-615) and the other a store card of Evans and Watson of Philadelphia, makers of the Dickeson Coin and Medal Safe. Lovett Jr. made the dies.

The Continental Currency copy dies are said to have been made for distribution at the 1876 Centennial Exhibition. In the early 20th century the dies were owned by Thomas L. Elder, who made additional strikings and mulings from them. Later they passed to John J. Ford Jr., to Empire Coin Company, Inc., and to Robert Bashlow. John Pinches, Ltd., of England, struck certain of the later issues. Additional strikings were made in the early 1960s. Bashlow produced quantities in bronze, goldine, and silver, plus some in "various metals," the details of which were not recorded. He donated the dies to the Smithsonian Institution. Elder made various mulings in the early 20th century, combining the Continental dollar obverse with various fantasy reverses (for a listing see Hibler-Kappen, *So-Called Dollars*; 20th-century issues are beyond the scope of the present text). The Sommer Islands and Continental dollar dies still exist.

Dickeson Sommer Islands Copies

W-15400 · Kenney-1 · shilling · copper
Obverse: SOMMER ISLANDS within two beaded circles. At the center is a standing hog with XII above his back. *Reverse:* Ship sailing to the left. A counterfeit can be identified from the original by the following: On the obverse of the original, XII is close to or touches the back of the hog, X is low; on the copy the letters are properly aligned and above the hog. On the reverse of the copy a cannon is firing a broadside, with billowing smoke; feature not seen on the original. *Mintage:* Unknown for this and other Sommer Islands varieties and mulings. *Notes:* 31 mm. Misattributed by Crosby to Alfred S. Robinson. Dies made by Robert Lovett Jr. in 1859. *Rarity:* URS-5.

AU-50	MS-60	MS-63
$300	$400	$1,000

W-15410 · brass
Rarity: URS-6.

AU-50	MS-60	MS-63
$500	$900	$1,250

W-15420 · white metal
Rarity: URS-4.

W-15430 · copper-nickel
Rarity: URS-4.

W-15440 · nickel (German silver)
Rarity: URS-4.

W-15445 · Kenney-unlisted · Sommer Islands shilling obverse / Wuesthoff Sommer Islands reverse · Fantasy muling
Notes: Modern muling by Paul Franklin, 1956, combining Dickeson's obverse with the reverse of Wuesthoff's XX shilling fantasy (W-18500). *Rarity:* Unknown. Franklin kept no known records.

Selected auction price(s): John J. Ford Jr. XIV Sale (5/2006), MS, $1,150.

W-15480 · Kenney Muling-1 · Sommer Islands Ship reverse / George Washington · copper
Notes: Baker-616. *Rarity:* URS-3 or 4(?).

W-15485 · Kenney Muling-2 · white metal
Notes: Baker-616A. *Rarity:* URS-3 or 4(?).

W-15490 · Kenney Muling-3 · Sommer Islands Hog obverse / George Washington · copper
Notes: Baker-615. *Rarity:* URS-3 or 4(?).

W-15495 · Kenney Muling-4 · white metal
Notes: Baker-615A. *Rarity:* URS-3 or 4(?).

W-15510 · Kenney Muling-5 · Sommer Islands Hog obverse / Evans & Watson store card · copper
Notes: Rulau Pa-Ph-50. *Rarity:* URS-3 or 4(?).

W-15515 · Kenney Muling-6 · brass
Notes: Rulau Pa-Ph-51. *Rarity:* URS-3 or 4(?).

W-15520 · Kenney Muling-7 · white metal
Notes: Rulau Pa-Ph-52. *Rarity:* URS-3 or 4(?).

W-15525 · Kenney Muling-9 · copper-nickel
Notes: Rulau Pa-Ph-53. *Rarity:* URS-3 or 4(?).

W-15530 · Kenney Muling-10 · copper
Notes: Rulau Pa-Ph-44. *Rarity:* URS-3 or 4(?).

W-15535 · Kenney Muling-11 · brass
Notes: Rulau Pa-Ph-45. *Rarity:* URS-3 or 4(?).

W-15540 · Kenney Muling-12 · white metal
Notes: Rulau Pa-Ph-46. *Rarity:* URS-3 or 4(?).

W-15545 · Kenney Muling-13 · copper-nickel
Notes: Rulau Pa-Ph-47. *Rarity:* URS-3 or 4(?).

Dickeson Continental Dollar Copies

W-15600 · Kenney-2 · Hibler-Kappen 853 · copper
Copy of a 1776 Continental Currency dollar. A counterfeit can be identified from the original by the following: the copy has the 1776 date compact and distant from the legends to either side; on the original the date is wider and

closer to the legends. *Mintage:* Unknown. Probably dozens in the 19th century; additional pieces by Elder; 5,000 (at least) in bronze from copy dies by Robert Bashlow in the early 1960s. *Notes:* 31 mm. Dies believed to have been made in 1876. *Rarity:* URS-6 (19th century).

AU-50	MS-60	MS-63
$350	$650	$1,000

W-15610 · brass
Mintage: Unknown. Some struck in the 19th or early 20th centuries. *Rarity:* URS-5(?).

W-15625 · Kenney-2 · goldine
Mintage: At least 3,000 by Robert Bashlow in the early 1960s. Modern strikes, $15 to $25. *Rarity:* URS-12.

W-15630 · Kenney-2 · Hibler-Kappen 854 and 855 · white metal or pewter
Mintage: Unknown. Probably hundreds in the 19th century; additional pieces by Elder; 4,000 or more from copy dies distributed by Empire Coin Co. and, later, Robert Bashlow in the early 1960s. *Notes:* Modern strikes, $15 to $25. *Rarity:* URS-13.

AU-50	MS-60	MS-63
$250	$500	$800

W-15640 · Kenney-2 · Hibler-Kappen 852 · silver
Mintage: Fifty in the 1870s per John W. Haseltine; 2,000 or more in the early 1960s by Robert Bashlow from copy dies (with tiny S letter on reverse); it is not certain all were actually distributed. *Notes:* Modern strikes, $25 to $50. *Rarity:* URS-6 (19th century).

Selected auction price(s): John J. Ford Jr. XIV Sale (5/2006), 19th-century strikings, Choice MS, $920; Choice MS, $1,500.

W-15650 · Kenney-2 · Hibler-Kappen 852 · Continental Dollar · gold
Mintage: At least one modern striking over a double eagle. *Rarity:* URS-1.

Idler Copies
1860's

William K. Idler

William K. Idler (1808–1901) began his rare coin dealership in Philadelphia in 1858 in a shop at the front of his house at 109 South 11th Street. Like other pioneers in the coin trade, he also sold minerals, prints, antiques, and other collector's items. Almost immediately he established a confidential connection with one or more officers of the Philadelphia Mint, who in spring 1859 began the wholesale restriking of rarities, the making of patterns, and the production of other delicacies for the numismatic trade. Without any records being kept, many if not most of these were funneled into the marketplace through Idler. (Later, his son-in-law, John W. Haseltine, would maintain the secret connection and handle many rarities.) Idler died on June 16, 1901, by which time he had been inactive in numismatics for some time. Among his estate effects were "discovered" the first known trade dollars dated 1884 and 1885. His obituary in *The Numismatist* quoted an anonymous contributor, probably Haseltine:

> Mr. Idler was a jeweler by trade but his modest little shop on 11th Street, near Chestnut, always had in its show window a sprinkling of coins, old currency and curios, amid the regular stock, and the counter and wall cases inside were about equally divided in content between Mr. Idler's two interests in life. He, however, held to business before pleasure, and often occupied himself long with some woman or others, wanting a trinket repaired, while an impatient collector was waiting eagerly to spend 10 or 20 times the amount for coins. Mr. Idler was a portly, deliberate man, always amiable, but generally giving the impression that he had little or nothing of a special interest, with a plaintive remark or two about the difficulty of coming across anything good nowadays. Then, if no general customer was present, and you could induce him to open his safe and lay out two or three trays in a melancholy way, you would often find choice pickings and get some good bargains.
>
> All the leading Philadelphia collectors visited him at frequent intervals as well as many from other cities, and his many years of acquaintance with the numismatic world, and the regard in which he was held, caused him to be a medium of transfer of rich resources. His great age at length began to tell, members of his family became more active in the store, and he rarely came out of a little rear room. His numismatic scholars will miss him greatly.

Idler commissioned local diesinker and medalist Robert Lovett Jr. to make two copies of colonial coins, each of which was produced in several different metals and with colonial copy reverse dies as well as store card dies. Today the general types are met with easily enough, although certain metals and mulings can be scarce. Mintages are unknown except as stated, and there are likely some combinations of medals and edge styles not recorded.

Idler Copies of the Maryland Denarium

W-15660 · Kenney-2 · Maryland Denarium · copper
A counterfeit can be distinguished from the original by the legend, which on the original ends with &C; the copy ends with &CT. In addition, the copies have Idler's advertisement in tiny letters around the head: W. IDLER, DEALER IN

307

COINS, MINERALS &C PHILA, but this can be tooled away. *Notes:* This is the basic, most popular, and most relevant collectible format. *Rarity:* URS-9.

AU-50	MS-60	MS-63
$650	$800	$1,000

W-15670 · brass
Rarity: URS-8.

AU-50	MS-60	MS-63
$650	$800	$1,000

W-15675 · white metal
Rarity: URS-6.

AU-50	MS-60	MS-63
$650	$800	$1,000

W-15680 · copper-nickel
Rarity: URS-8.

AU-50	MS-60	MS-63
$650	$800	$1,000

W-15685 · nickel (German silver)
Mintage: Two. *Rarity:* URS-2(?).

W-15690 · silver
Rarity: URS-5.
Selected auction price(s): John J. Ford Jr. XIV Sale (5/2006), AU, $230; Choice MS, $1,725.

W-15700 · gold
Mintage: Two. *Rarity:* URS-1 or 2.

Maryland Denarium Mulings With Store Cards

W-15750 · Kenney unlisted · plain edge · copper
Reverse: Store card Type I: CONTINENTAL / PAPER / MONEY, / AUTOGRAPHS, / ENGRAVINGS / &C. / BOUGHT & SOLD / W. IDLER 111 N. 9TH ST. *Notes:* (Rulau) Miller Pa-223. *Rarity:* URS-5 or 6(?).

W-15751 · Kenney Muling-2 · reeded edge · copper
Notes: (Rulau) Miller Pa-224. *Rarity:* URS-5 or 6(?).

W-15755 · Kenney Muling-5 · plain edge · brass
Notes: (Rulau) Miller Pa-227. *Rarity:* URS-5 or 6(?).

W-15756 · Kenney Muling-6 · reeded edge · brass
Notes: (Rulau) Miller Pa-228. *Rarity:* URS-5 or 6(?).

W-15760 · Kenney-unlisted · plain edge · white metal
Notes: (Rulau) Miller Pa-228A. *Rarity:* URS-5 or 6(?).

W-15765 · Kenney Muling-4 · plain edge · copper-nickel
Notes: (Rulau) Miller Pa-226. *Rarity:* URS-6 or 7.

W-15766 · Kenney Muling-3 · reeded edge · copper-nickel
Notes: (Rulau) Miller Pa-225. *Rarity:* URS-6 or 7.

W-15770 · Kenney Muling-1 · reeded edge · silver
Notes: (Rulau) Miller unlisted. *Rarity:* URS-4.

W-15775 · Kenney-unlisted · plain edge · gold
Notes: Two struck. (Rulau) Miller Pa-228B. *Rarity:* URS-2.

W-15790 · Kenney-unlisted · Maryland denarium obverse / Idler's store card Type II · plain edge · copper
Reverse: Store card Type II: W. IDLER / DEALER IN / COINS, / MINERALS, / SHELLS / ANTIQUES &C. / 111 N. 9TH ST. / PHILADA. *Notes:* (Rulau) Miller Pa-228F. *Rarity:* URS-5 or 6(?).

W-15800 · Kenney-unlisted · reeded edge · brass
Notes: (Rulau) Miller Pa-228H. *Rarity:* URS-5 or 6(?).

W-15810 · Kenney-unlisted · plain edge · copper-nickel
Notes: (Rulau) Miller Pa-228G. *Rarity:* URS-7.

W-15830 · Kenney-unlisted · Maryland Denarium Reverse / Idler's Store Card Type I · plain edge · copper or bronze
Reverse: Store card Type I: CONTINENTAL / PAPER / MONEY, / AUTOGRAPHS, / ENGRAVINGS / &C. / BOUGHT & SOLD / W. IDLER 111 N. 9TH ST. *Notes:* Combination of two reverse dies. (Rulau) Miller Pa-217 and 220. *Rarity:* URS-5 or 6(?).

W-15835 · plain edge · brass
Notes: (Rulau) Miller Pa-219. *Rarity:* URS-5 or 6(?).

W-15845 · plain edge · silvered white metal
Notes: (Rulau) Miller Pa-211. *Rarity:* URS-5 or 6(?).

W-15860 · plain edge · silver
Notes: (Rulau) Miller Pa-216. *Rarity:* URS-2 or 3(?).

Idler Copies of the 1792 Washington "Half Dollar"

W-15870 · Kenney-1 · Baker-25M · copper

Copy of the 1792 Getz dies (originals struck in copper and silver and often referred to as a cent and half dollar). A counterfeit can be identified from the original by the following: On the original the period after the final A (AMERICA) is very close to a feather; on the copy it is distant. On the original the final A is opposite the eagle's talons; on the copy it is opposite the arrows. The copy has COPY lettered to the left of the tail, but on many examples this has been tooled away (these are worth considerably less). *Notes:* Baker-25, Fuld-WA.FA.1792.1. This is the basic, most popular and most relevant collectible format. *Rarity:* URS-9.

AU-50	MS-60	MS-63
$400	$900	$1,300

W-15880 · brass
Notes: Baker-25N, Fuld-WA.FA.1792.1a.Br. *Rarity:* URS-7.

AU-50	MS-60	MS-63
$750	$1,200	$1,700

W-15890 · white metal
Notes: Baker-25L, Fuld-WA.FA.1792.1b.WM. Many are silvered and achieve very attractive toning. *Rarity:* URS-6.

AU-50	MS-60	MS-63
$600	$900	$1,300

W-15910 · silver
Notes: Baker-25K, Fuld-WA.FA.1792.1c.Ag. Popular metal, as related Getz coins were struck in both copper and silver. Weights vary from about 123.5 grains to 157.5 grains. Worth less if "COPY" is removed. *Rarity:* URS-7.

AU-50	MS-60	MS-63
$600	$900	$1,850

1792 Washington "Half Dollar" Mulings With Store Cards

W-15920 · Kenney Muling-2 · copper
Notes: Baker-544A, (Rulau) Miller Pa-211. *Rarity:* URS-5 or 6(?).

W-15930 · Kenney Muling-3 · brass
Notes: Baker-544B, (Rulau) Miller Pa-212. *Rarity:* URS-5 or 6(?).

W-15940 · Kenney Muling-4 · white metal
Notes: Baker-544C, (Rulau) Miller Pa-212A. *Rarity:* URS-4 or 5(?).

W-15950 · Kenney Muling-1 · silver
Notes: Baker-544, (Rulau) Miller Pa-210. *Rarity:* URS-3 or 4(?).

W-15960 · Kenney Muling-6 · Eagle / Idler's store card · copper
Notes: Baker-544G, (Rulau) Miller Pa-214. *Rarity:* URS-5 or 6(?).

W-15965 · Kenney Muling-7 · brass
Notes: Baker-544H, (Rulau) Miller Pa-215. *Rarity:* URS-5 or 6(?).

W-15970 · Kenney Muling-8 · white metal
Notes: Baker-544I, (Rulau) Miller Pa-215A. *Rarity:* URS-4 or 5.

W-15980 · Kenney Muling-5 · silver
Notes: Baker-544F, (Rulau) Miller Pa-213. *Rarity:* URS-3 or 4(?).

THE FANTASY COINS OF C. WYLLYS BETTS 1870's

In the 1870s several dealers competed with each other in seeking public acclaim for discoveries, new interpretations of numismatic history, and the like. Casting himself as among the most erudite was Édouard Frossard, a Swiss who came to America in 1858 and by the early 1870s was active in the rare coin trade. From then until his death in 1899 he conducted over 160 auction sales. Residing in Irvington-on-Hudson, New York, he published *Numisma* from January 1877 to December 1891. This was intended to be a journal of record, with observations by the editor relating to new discoveries, research, auction sales, the activities of competitors, and more. In his catalog of the Armand Champa Library collection, modern scholar Charles Davis described *Numisma* as:

An often acid, often scholarly, always entertaining journal with important, although sometimes axe-grinding observations on the business practices of his competitors, and invaluable for reports on contemporary auctions with notices of overgrading and counterfeits liberally sprinkled in. Arrows were shot at, among others, *Doctor* Woodward (the apothecary unable to sell the false talisman to the children of Knicker), Charley Steigerwalt (the plagiarist with his big journal), *Brother* Mason (the only original Moses in the coin trade), J.W. Scott, (the Fulton St. octopod), the Chapmans (who produce quarto catalogues with margins sufficiently large for corrections), and David U. Proskey (with a level head and an India rubber conscience).

It was with pride that Frossard trumped all others in announcing in *Numisma* in November 1877 the "Discovery of a Colonial Coin Relating to New Netherlands":

On the 19th of September last, and while awaiting the opening of the Balmanno sale at Bangs & Co. in Broadway, Captain Wilson Defendorf, a well known New York collector, submitted to our inspection a copper coin of which the following description will suffice for the present:

Obverse: Earl's crown, PETER MINVIT.

Reverse: Triangular shield with slightly curving border, and beaver in field of rippling waters, NOVUM BELGIUM 1623; border serrated.

In condition this coin can be described as a somewhat weak impress, especially in certain parts of the legends, but not to any extent abraded or circulated.

Of the meaning of the words "Novum Belgium" we had previously communicated to Capt. Defendorf our opinion that they were to be translated to "New Netherlands," an assertion which we offered to prove by referring to various historical works; nothing remaining therefore but to examine the coin critically, and our impression after a thorough and minute inspection that the piece bore on its face the testimonials of age and authenticity, was shared by Mr. David Proskey, but dissented from by Mr. Ed. Cogan; these two gentlemen, Capt. Defendorf and our self, being the only ones to take part in the discussion.

Frossard went on to discuss the early history of New York, the importance of Peter Minuit, and more. A separate letter was published from Defendorf, which noted that the coin was at the moment in the possession of J.W. Scott, "but if the coin should turn out as you expect, I have no doubt but you deserve *all the credit* there may be attached in making this coin known to the people of the United States."

Frossard had not done his homework. In the same month J.W. Scott printed this in his magazine, *The Coin Collector's Journal*:

The Last Discovery

The illustration given above is one of a class of coins which have been common in all ages, and we suppose will continue to appear until the millennium; as they are usually conceived by cupidity, brought forth by lies, and adopted through ignorance. Novum Belgium is an exception to this rule only in the fact that it was made by a young man to pass away time, and sold at public auction as a fraud, so that no one could offer any excuse for being taken in by it, much less the editor of a numismatic paper, unless that the difficulty of acquiring the English language offers obstacles so insurmountable to the average foreigner as to prevent him attaining a useful knowledge of it, as he has lately shown himself incapable of even understanding such a classical (?) work as a coin sale catalogue, for we cannot suppose that any respectable person, much less one who devotes his life and talents to the education of the young, would knowingly descend to falsehood.

The coin of which we propose to give the history may be briefly described as follows:

Obverse, Beaver on shield, NOVUM BELGIVM, 1623,

Reverse, Crown, PETER MINVIT.

It is the property of Capt. Defendorf, a well-known and highly esteemed collector of this city, who became possessed of it many years ago; having purchased it along with a lot of old coins, he has kept it from that day to this without ever attaching any importance to it. On looking over a lot of his coins, he thought he would try to find out something about it. He, accordingly, carried it with him to a coin sale, and asked the opinion of a few collectors concerning it. The general opinion was that it was a fraud, which was concurred in by the writer for reasons given below, and probably would have never been again noticed had it not been for the fact that a young editor had his acutely reasoning, historical and critical faculties terribly mixed by the bewildering anticipation of being the first to have "the honor of bringing out the coin to the notice of the American collectors and numismatics." *[sic]* Whatever this curiously constructed sentence may mean, it really is amusing to think how pathetically he must have pleaded with the owner for all the credit and we certainly shall not be cruel enough to rob him of one particle of the renown which his excellent judgment and deep historic learning entitle him to receive from all well-informed numismatists.

Our reasons for not believing in the authority of the coin were:

1st. The style of engraving did not correspond with that of the period in which the coin as professed (by the date) was made.

2nd. We know of no person connected with New Amsterdam of the name of Peter Minuit, and if it was intended for Peter Minnewit we think it quite probable he knew how to spell his own name, even if his English contemporaries preferred to call him Minuit or Minuits.

3d. We thought it scarcely probable that the then (1623) Governor of New Amsterdam, Jacobson May, would have coins struck with the name of one of his successors on them. These trifles, however (although he was not ignorant of them), were not allowed to bias the judgment of our critic.

4th. Mr. Cogan, a gentleman of excellent judgment, who has grown gray in the study of numismatics, said that he knew it to be false, and gave the name of the probable maker; we never allow our opinion to stand in the way of obtaining facts, when a few hours' investigation would settle the matter.

Again, regarding the manufacture of the coin, we will show how easy it is to get up a fraud that will deceive some people. A young gentleman (we do not give his name although it is an open secret), finding time hang heavily on his hands, amused himself by engraving dies in imitation of rare coins, afterward he branched out and designed some altogether fictitious, a list of which together with his counterfeits, we subjoin. His mode of work was simply to take two large U.S. cents, and file one side perfectly smooth, and then sitting at his desk dig out the designs with his penknife, an operation requiring great labor, but not more than has been accomplished by many schoolboys in cutting out the heads on pennies. After both sides were finished, he would take another cent, and file both sides smooth, and placing this between his dies, hammer it until he obtained a pretty fair impression, which our contemporary justly described as a "somewhat weak impress, especially in certain parts of the legends, but not to any extent abraded or circulated!"

Frossard refused to give up, and in *Numisma*, January 1878, this defense was presented:

> In regard to the "Novum Belgium" coin described in our last, we reiterate our opinion, shared by several of the most prominent coin collectors in the United States, that the piece owned by Capt. Defendorf is an original coin issued in Holland sometime between the years 1625 and 1632. Of the base imitations so accurately described by our contemporary, we know nothing whatsoever, except that they undoubtedly exist. The fact, however, that counterfeit coins, postage stamp restrikes, and other abominations are on the market only gives proof of the existence of originals.
>
> At a future time we hope to present our readers additional data concerning the coin in possession of Capt. Defendorf. In the meanwhile we decline further controversy with the publishers of the C.C.J. We view the personal attacks they have made upon us with the same indifference as we do their opinions on coins, but we are ready at any time to enter into a friendly discussion of the subject with any other numismatic publication or with individuals.

In *Numisma*, March 1878, Frossard ate crow, stating that relation of the designs and inscriptions to history caused him to concentrate on that aspect of the Novum Belgium coin, rather than the characteristics of the coin itself.

The maker of the coin was C. Wyllys Betts, born in Newburgh, New York, on August 13, 1845—ironically in the city that was home to Machin's Mills decades earlier. Betts never made a secret of these and other curious productions. As J.W. Scott noted, a listing of these had been published in 1864. This was by W. Elliott Woodward in a four-page addendum to the McCoy sale, offering 45 lots under the title of *Catalogue of a Few Pieces from the Collection of C. Wyllys Betts of New Haven*. At the time Betts was a student at Yale.

Betts accommodated Frossard with a commentary for him to include in *Numisma*'s March 1878 issue (excerpted):

> It was in 1860 that I made my first attempt at die cutting, and the occasions was the receipt of a quantity of coins and medals from some New York dealers for inspection. After selecting those which my own collection lacked, I sold the rest to various collectors in New Haven, and thereupon in commemoration of this business enterprise I struck a medal with this *Obverse*: CONNECTICUT, with three pine trees in center, and the reverse with my own name, with the words, "Coins and Medals, New Haven, 1860."
>
> My next attempt at coinage was a leaden token with the inscription, "Colony of New Yorke," with the latter words being on the obverse surrounding a head. One of these tokens I sent to Mr. Mickley of Philadelphia. It was some time before I acquired sufficient skill to make impressions in any metal but lead. The dies were cut in copper or sometimes brass, and were so soft as to be often destroyed in the attempt to stamp upon copper or silver. I believe that my first successful impression upon copper was from dies having the obverse of the "Nova Eborac" and the reverse, "Immunis Columbia."
>
> The dies were cut upon coins of the halfpenny size, either worn smooth or filed away on one side. My only tools were an awl for cutting the letters and the outlines of the figures and a knife for gouging out the broader parts of the designs. When the cutting was finished each die was heated white hot and dipped into cold water. A third smooth copper of the halfpenny size was then heated and placed between the dies, and the three, being quickly rolled together in sheet lead from a tea box, to prevent them from slipping, were pounded upon an anvil with a six-pound dumb-bell. The heating process gave an air of antiquity to the pieces. . . .
>
> The earlier ones I look upon with some interest because they used to afford me a great deal of amusement, not only in the making, but in the astonishment of collectors looking over my cabinet.

In 1871 Betts completed his postgraduate studies at Yale and entered the legal profession. He left numismatics behind, consigning his collection to Edward Cogan, who sold it in a two-day auction beginning on June 1. In spring 1884 Betts's passion for the hobby was renewed with fervor. He joined the American Numismatic and Archaeological Society. Later he contributed several valuable papers on the medals of Porto Bello, counterfeit English halfpence, and other subjects. In 1886 he was the author of a 17-page study, *Counterfeit Half Pence Current in the American Colonies, and Their Issue from the Mints of Connecticut and Vermont*, adapted from a paper delivered to the Society. In 1887 he caught pneumonia, and after a week's illness died on April 27. At the time he was working on a book, published posthumously in 1894 as *American Colonial History Illustrated by Contemporary Medals*, which remains the standard text today.

The *American Journal of Numismatics* in April 1887 published Betts's obituary, including a sketch of his life, noting in part:

> His father removed to New Haven [in 1855], to give his sons the educational facilities of that city. Just before the breaking out of the Civil War, Wyllys was taken from school by reason of ill health, and coin collecting was then suggested to him as a matter of recreation and pastime; his field was in New Haven and the adjacent towns and villages. It was on one of these expeditions that he discovered what are now known as the New Haven dies of the Fugio coppers, which from the best evidence were unknown to numismatists up to that time, and had never been used. $10 was asked for them. He informed Mr. Root [sic; should be Rust] of New York of their existence, and that gentleman bought them; they are now the property of Mr. J. Colvin Randall of Philadelphia.

Thus, Betts was linked with the famous "New Haven restrikes," also discussed in this chapter.

A store card dated 1860 struck from dies cut by the youthful C. Wyllys Betts. The reverse is a fantasy die with CONNECTICUT IN around the border and vines at the center. A precocious numismatist who was confined to his home by illness much of the time, Betts amused himself by creating imaginative "colonial" coins and other fantasies.

Numismatic Aspects

Most Betts fantasies are sufficiently rare as to be effectively non-collectible. The historic Novum Belgium copper was offered in Thomas L. Elder's sale of October 28, 1916, with the poignant comment: "Is this a rare pattern for an American Colonial.... Who knows about this piece?" Later it was owned by F.C.C. Boyd. In the Ford Collection sale of June 2006 it sold for $8,625, including buyer's commission and 5 percent to an agent. Other Betts fantasies have sold for upwards of several hundred dollars. As few people know about them, demand has been low.

Betts gave certain of his fabrications to Yale, nearly 200 pieces. The largest modern offering of these was in Stack's sale of March 1993. The Ford Collection sale (May 2006) included just six coins. The listing below utilizes Woodward catalog numbers from the McCoy sale addendum, 1864, comprising 22 lots. The introduction to that offering: "Very many of the pieces here offered, are struck from excessively rare dies, recently engraved, all of which are destroyed; and every piece being the best in existence, it is the sincere wish of the owner that they meet with satisfaction." Others owned by F.C.C. Boyd (apart from those acquired by Ford) were gifted to the American Numismatic Society. It may be presumed that most are unique or nearly so.

W-17000 · Woodward-1 · (1652) Massachusetts NE sixpence
1864 catalog: N.E. sixpence (not Wyatt's), silver, unique. *Rarity:* URS-1.

W-17020 · Woodward-2 · 1653 Massachusetts Pine Tree shilling
1864 catalog: Pine Tree shilling, 1653. "Massachusetts in." "New England, Anno. 1653, XII"; silver, very fine, unique. *Notes:* 1653 is a fantasy date; originals are dated 1652. *Rarity:* URS-1.

W-17030 · Woodward-3 · 1662 Connecticut shilling
1864 catalog: Connecticut shilling. Obverse, grape vine, "Connecticut in." Reverse, "New England, An. Do. 1662, XII." Struck over an unique N.E. "shilling" (not Wyatt's); silver, very fine, excessively rare, and in respect to the N.E. shilling, unique. *Notes:* This implies that multiple pieces were made, but only one over an NE shilling. Presumably, the NE shilling was another Betts fantasy, different from Woodward-2. *Rarity:* URS-1.

W-17040 · Woodward-4 · Lord Baltimore shilling
1864 catalog: Lord Baltimore shilling; silver, very fine, unique. *Rarity:* URS-1.

W-17050 · Woodward-5 · Lord Baltimore sixpence
1864 catalog: Lord Baltimore sixpence; silver, very good, unique. *Rarity:* URS-1.

W-17060 · Woodward-6 · Lord Baltimore penny
1864 catalog: Lord Baltimore penny. Engraved, unique. *Notes:* Seemingly engraved rather than struck. *Rarity:* URS-1.

W-17070 · Woodward-7 · Colony of New Yorke · silver
1864 catalog: Obverse, Goddess of Liberty facing left. "Colony of." Reverse, bust in armor facing right. "New Yorke"; excessively rare in lead. This specimen is in silver, and unique. *Notes:* This would indicate that multiple pieces were also made in lead. 29.5 mm. *Rarity:* URS-1.

Selected auction price(s): John J. Ford Jr. XIV Sale (5/2006), MS, $538.

W-17080 · lead
Notes: One in ANS. Illustrated by John Kleeberg in "The New Yorke in America Token," 1992. *Rarity:* URS-1 or 2(?).

W-17090 · Woodward-8 · Novum Belgium · lead
1864 catalog: New York Piece. Obverse, Beaver on Shield (old coat-of-arms of New York under the Dutch government), "Novum Belgium, 1623." Reverse, Crown "Peter Masuit" (first Gov.); lead. *Notes:* Per J.W. Scott, "It will be

noticed that the Novum Belgium, bought by Mr. Nixon for 40 cents at this auction sale was lead. It will also be noticed that in the description Peter Masuit (evidently a printer's error) is described as the first governor. This mistake in regard to Minnewit being the first governor, evidently led the author to put the date of the first governor on the coin." *Rarity:* URS-1.

W-17100 · copper

Notes: 27.8 mm. This is the copper striking that caused the excitement in 1877. Ford collection, lot 557 (with two-page description). Two known, the other in ANS. *Rarity:* URS-2.

Selected auction price(s): John J. Ford Jr. XIV Sale (5/2006), MS, some mint red, $8,625.

W-17110 · Woodward-9 · 1779 Rhodia Insula / Nova Brittania 1

1864 catalog: Rhode Island Piece. Obverse, "Rhodia Orsula, 1779." [*sic*] Reverse, Nova Brittania, 1. Copper, Very fine, excessively rare. *Notes:* Seemingly, more than one was made. *Rarity:* URS-1 or 2.

W-17120 · Woodward-10 · 1783 Annapolis sixpence

1864 catalog: Annapolis sixpence, 1783; silver, very fine, unique. *Rarity:* URS-1.

W-17130 · Woodward-11 · 1785 Auctori Plebis

1864 catalog: Auctori Plebis, 1785; very fine, unique. *Notes:* Original Auctori Plebis tokens, part of the Conder series, are dated 1787. *Rarity:* URS-1.

W-17140 · Woodward-12 · 1785 Nova Constellatio / Immune Columbia

1864 catalog: Obverse, "Nova Constellatio." Reverse, "Immune Columbia, 1785." Genuine. Very fine, unique. *Rarity:* URS-1.

W-17150 · Woodward-13 · 1786 Immunis Columbia / shield

1864 catalog: Obverse, "Immunis Columbia., 1786." Reverse, shield, "E Pluribus Unum." Genuine; good, unique. *Rarity:* URS-1.

W-17160 · Woodward-14 · 1786 Non Vi Virtute Vici

1864 catalog: "Non vi virtute vici, 1786"; fine, unique. *Rarity:* URS-1.

W-17170 · 1785 Immune Columbia

Notes: 29.5 mm. Uniface obverse striking over a Nova Constellatio. Reverse is the original coin. *Rarity:* URS-1.

Selected auction price(s): John J. Ford Jr. XIV Sale (5/2006), VF, $1,092.

W-17200 · Woodward-15 · 1786 Immune Columbia / Nova Eborac

1864 catalog: "Nova Eborac." Reverse, "Immune Columbia, 1786"; very fine, excessively rare. *Notes:* 29.5 mm. At least two are known. Original Immune Columbia coppers are dated 1785. *Rarity:* URS-2.

Selected auction price(s): John J. Ford Jr. XIV Sale (5/2006), EF, $374.

W-17220 · Woodward-16 · 1785 George III / Immune Columbia

1864 catalog: "George III. Rex." Reverse, "Immune Columbia, 1785"; very fine. *Obverse:* Genuine; excessively rare. (All the dies of "Immune Columbia" are different.) *Notes:* 32.8 mm. Seemingly, more than one was made. *Rarity:* URS-1.

W-17240 · Woodward-17 · 1787 New Hampshire cent

1864 catalog: New Hampshire Cent. Obverse, Bust in armor, facing right, "Nova Hamps:" Reverse, figure of Liberty, seated facing right; "Libertas, 1787"; very fine; two struck. *Notes:* Original New Hampshire coppers are dated 1776. 30.3 mm. *Rarity:* URS-2(?).

Selected auction price(s): John J. Ford Jr. XIV Sale (5/2006), EF, $1,035.

W-17260 · Woodward-18 · 1787 Liber Natus Libertatem Defenda / Nev Eboracus Excelsior

1864 catalog: "Liber Natus Libertatem Defendo," [*sic*] Indian standing. Reverse, eagle, "Nev Eboracus, 1787, Excelsior"; very fine, unique. *Notes:* Originals have Defendo, not Defenda. *Rarity:* URS-1.

W-17280 · Woodward-19 · 1787 Liber Natus Libertatem Defenda / Excelsior

1864 catalog: Obverse, the same, Indian standing. Reverse, coat-of-arms of N.Y., "1787, Excelsior"; very fine, unique. *Rarity:* URS-1.

W-17320 · Woodward-20 · 1787 Non Vi Virtute Vici / Nev Eboracus

1864 catalog: "Non vi virtute vici." Reverse, eagle, "Nev Eboracus, 1787, Excelsior"; fine, unique. *Notes:* 31.3 mm. *Rarity:* URS-1.

Selected auction price(s): John J. Ford Jr. XIV Sale (5/2006), EF, $1,725.

W-17360 · Bar copper

Crude production with USA in irregular monogram on obverse. Reverse with light horizontal lines not well defined. Illustrated coin is struck over a 1788 RR-27 Vermont copper. Also shown is the obverse die hand-cut by Betts. *Rarity:* URS-1.

W-17390 · Woodward-21 · Washington Commander

1864 catalog: Washington medal. Obverse, bust to right. "Washington." Reverse, five-pointed star, "Commander of the Armie of Virginia"; copper, very fine; very slightly double struck; unique. *Rarity:* URS-1.

W-17300 · Woodward-22 · Washington / Kerdrig

1864 catalog: Washington medal. Obverse, two ships sailing, "George Washington." Reverse, "Payable to John Kerdrig. T.O.O.E.W.T.T.W.N." Silver, very fine, unique. Such a piece has known to have been issued in 1794, but no original is in existence. *Rarity:* URS-1.

The "New Haven Restrikes" of the Fugio Cent
1860's

When coin collecting became popular in the United States in the late 1850s, Fugio coppers were avidly sought along with other colonial and early American coins. Enduring legends arose. Perhaps the best known is the story of C. Wyllys Betts. In 1858, Betts, then 14 years old, allegedly discovered on the site of the Broome & Platt store in New Haven three sets of 1787-dated Fugio dies. These pieces differed in numerous respects from those actually used for earlier coinage, although the main features were the same. Around 1860, coins were made from these dies in copper alloy, silver, and gold, with numismatist Horatio N. Rust being involved. Rust had been honored in 1859 by dealer Augustus B. Sage, who created a medal with his portrait as part of the Numismatic Gallery series from dies cut by George H. Lovett of New York City. These became known as "New Haven restrikes." A later memorandum in Rust's hand stated:

> In 1859 I called in New Haven on my way from New York and hunted the city over all day trying to find the dies in which the Fugio Cent was struck. At evening I was at West Haven with a coin collector who directed me to a store in Chapel Street which he said descended from Broom [sic] & Platt who did the coinage. I then found the dies, bought two pairs & one odd die for $20.00.
>
> I took them to Waterbury and had 500 coins struck in copper, 50 in silver, and one in gold. I sold one pair & the odd die to a coin dealer in New York, I think it was Curtis. Later I sold the remaining pair to Randell [sic] of Penn.

Over a period of time Rust gave other versions. Modern scholarship has suggested that the dies were newly created about 1859 or 1860 by the Scovill Manufacturing Company of Waterbury, Connecticut. These copies, dated 1787 and similar in general appearance to the originals, differ in detail and, most particularly, have narrow rather than wide rings on the reverse. Neither restrikes nor from New Haven, these are usually seen in a brassy alloy, sometimes called copper. Silver impressions are rarer, and gold rarer yet.

The Fugio coppers with state names on the links, and other fantasies, may have been issued by other than Rust. Crosby listed certain of them, noting they were "supposed to be patterns."

Fugio "New Haven Restrike" Copies

Copies and fantasies from new dies made by Scovill Manufacturing Co.

W-17500 · Newman 101-AA · copper

Sun dial without date or motto; links with state names, AMERICAN CONGRESS at center. *Notes:* Obverse die unfinished. *Rarity:* URS-2.

W-17510 · Newman 101-BB · brass

Sun dial without date or motto; links with state names, eye at center. *Rarity:* URS-2.

Selected auction price(s): John J. Ford Jr. I Sale (Stack's 10/2003), MS, $4,887.50.

W-17520 · Newman 101-BB · silver

Rarity: URS-2(?).

W-17530 · Newman 101-EE · copper

Sun dial without date or motto; stars within links, WE ARE ONE at center. *Notes:* Ford's was Mint State. *Rarity:* URS-2.

Selected auction price(s): John J. Ford Jr. I Sale (Stack's 10/2003), MS, $9,775.

W-17540 · Newman 103-EE · brass

Sun with pointed chin. MIND YOUR BUSINESS with three thick dashes; stars within links, WE ARE ONE at center. *Rarity:* URS-2.

W-17550 · Newman 103-EE · silver

Rarity: URS-1.

W-17560 · Newman 104-FF · yellow bronze

Sun with pointed chin, incuse ornaments between numbers on sun dial; narrow rings on reverse. *Notes:* Mintage 500, per Horatio Rust. Most examples are struck in a yellowish bronze, sometimes called "copper," more often "brass." Color varies, probably due to striking at different times in slightly different alloys, but usually is yellowish orange. This is one of the most common of all struck copies. *Rarity:* URS-10.

AU-50	MS-60	MS-63
$700	$900	$1,200

W-17570 · Newman 104-FF · silver
Mintage: Fifty, per Horatio Rust. *Rarity:* URS-6.

AU-50	MS-60	MS-63
$3,700	$4,500	$5,500

W-17580 · Newman 104-FF · gold
Mintage: One, per Horatio Rust. *Rarity:* URS-1.

W-17590 · Newman 105-JJ · silver
Notes: Dies owned by the American Numismatic Society. James C. Spilman, *CNL*, November 1984: "Reverse JJ is almost indistinguishable from Reverse FF having been manufactured from the same master (complex) hub having all details of design and lettering resident in the hub." *Rarity:* URS-2.

OTHER MASSACHUSETTS SILVER COPIES OF IMPORTANCE

For even more copies of Massachusetts coins see Eric P. Newman, *The Secret of the Good Samaritan Shilling*, which contains several chapters on the subject.

1650 Pine Tree Shillings (Getchell Fantasy)

W-17000 · Noe-A.1 · large planchet
Obverse: Copy of a Pine Tree shilling in the old style, but with differences. MASSACHVSETS (MASSA instead of MASA) IN around border, an inscription found on no originals. At the center is a rather spindly pine tree with the innovative addition of pine cones. *Reverse:* NEW ENGLAND AN DOM around border. 1650 / XII at the center, separated by a horizontal line. *Notes:* 72.7 grains. Crosby devoted the best part of four pages (pages 63–67; see especially page 63, fig. 20) on this and the next copy. Dated 1650, these had come to light in 1854 through Ammi Brown, a Boston numismatist who was a bidder in the Dr. Lewis Roper collection sale in 1851 and was otherwise prominent in the hobby. They had been acquired from a Mr. Getchell of Boscawen (or Fisherville, contiguous settlements sometimes also listed under Concord), New Hampshire. Three went to Joseph J. Mickley for the remarkable price of $100 each. Brown considered them to be current numismatic forgeries made to sell for a profit. The maker sought not to copy originals, but to differentiate them slightly, certainly to feature them as unknown rarities, possibly as patterns. The maker of the coins remains unknown. *Rarity:* URS-1(?).

W-18001 · Noe-A.2
Obverse: Same as preceding, but die altered from MASSACHVSETS to MASSATHVSETS (C changed to T). *Reverse:* Same as preceding. *Notes:* 76.9 grains. 29 mm wide, 30.1 mm high. The Mickley coin appeared in the Ford sale, there called unique. *Rarity:* URS-1(?).

Selected auction price(s): John J. Ford Jr. XIV Sale (5/2006), MS, $5,570; to Eastern Collection (2007), $7,750.

W-18010 · Noe-B · small planchet
Obverse: MASATHVSETS IN around border. Pine tree at center, with branches gently curving upward, needles on upper part of each branch. *Reverse:* NEW ENGLAND AN DOM around border. 1650 / XII at the center. Ford sale there called unique. *Notes:* 76.9 grains. See Crosby, page 63, figure 21. *Rarity:* URS-1.

Selected auction price(s): John J. Ford Jr. XIV Sale (5/2006), $5,175.

W-18020 · Noe-C
Obverse: MASATHVSETS IN around border. Pine tree at center, with branches gently curving upward, needles on upper part of each branch. *Reverse:* NEW ENGLAND AN DOM around border. 1650 / XII at the center. *Notes:* 57.0 grains. *Rarity:* URS-1.

Selected auction price(s): John J. Ford Jr. XIV Sale (5/2006), As unique, $4,887.

1652 Good Samaritan Shillings

W-18200 · Bushnell coin

Alteration made by engraving the obverse of a 1652 Pine Tree shilling to create the biblical scene of the Good Samaritan. *Notes:* 26.1 mm. One of the most famous numismatic forgeries of all time, this piece and the next formed the subject of *The Secret of the Good Samaritan Shilling*, by Eric P. Newman, 1959. In brief, it is a naive copy of the Pembroke coin listed below. Acquired by Bushnell from a London dealer in 1859. Thomas Wyatt produced a struck copy of this fantasy (W-14100). *Rarity:* URS-1(?).

Selected auction price(s): John J. Ford Jr. XIV Sale (5/2006), VF, $46,000.

W-18205 · Pembroke coin

Counterstamped obverse of a Noe-25 Pine Tree shilling with a die illustrating the Good Samaritan proverb, with FAC SIMILE above. *Notes:* See Newman for fascinating details including the fact that FAC SIMILE may be from the Latin (Vulgate) Bible, *Vade et tu fac similiter,* or "Go thou and do likewise." From the collection of Thomas Herbert (1656–1755), eighth earl of Pembroke; illustrated in the 1746 catalog of his collection. Now in the British Museum. *Rarity:* URS-1.

OTHER MISCELLANEOUS COPIES OF IMPORTANCE

Bermuda XX Shillings (A. Wuesthoff Fantasy)

W-18500 · copper

Fantasy XX (20 shillings, or one pound) Bermuda coin copied from the 1616 Bermuda shilling. On the copy, XX above hog. *Notes:* Wuesthoff was a coin dealer at 113 Canal Street, New York City, in the 1880s. The maker of the dies is not known. The Ford catalog indicates that Paul Franklin made copper, brass, silver, and gold strikings in October 1956 (four gold copies were in the Ford sale) when the dies were on loan from F.C.C. Boyd. Ford bought and soon sold the dies, and later owners made more, including including some using Liberty Head $10 gold coins as planchets. Original gold strikings are very rare. Modern strikes in any metal are of unknown rarity; the dies may still exist. *Rarity:* URS-Unknown.

Selected auction price(s): John J. Ford Jr. XIV Sale (5/2006), strike by Paul Franklin on overly wide planchet, MS, $1,150.

W-18510 · brass

Notes: Originals made in the 1880s; restrikes 1956 to modern times.

W-18520 · silver

Notes: Originals made in the 1880s; restrikes 1956 to modern times.

Selected auction price(s): John J. Ford Jr. XIV Sale (5/2006), strike by Paul Franklin, PF, $1,380.

W-18530 · gold

Notes: Originals made in the 1880s; restrikes 1956 to modern times.

Selected auction price(s): Garrett III Sale (B&R 10/1980), EF, weakly struck, 1880s striking, $1,250. John J. Ford Jr. XIV Sale (5/2006), strikes by Paul Franklin, MS, $1,265, $1,610, $1,610, $1,725.

1785 Immune Columbia Coppers (F.S. Edwards Copy)

W-18800 · Kenney-2

Copy of the Immune Columbia cent. A counterfeit can be identified from the original by the following: On the original the hand points to the left upright of M (COLUMBIA); on the copy it points to just past the U. On the original a ray points to the lower right of the first L (CONSTELLATIO); on the copy it points to the upright. *Notes:* Kenney was unable to find an example to illustrate. Ford Lot 617: "Mr. Ford had to wait until this one appeared for sale in 1997 before he acquired an example, which should be as good a measure of its real rarity as any." Francis Smith Edwards was a notorious distributor of copies, perhaps made in England (see Eric P. Newman, *The Secret of the Good Samaritan Shilling,* p. 56), his most famous production being the 1796 federal half cent (variety with pole to cap). He is said to have sold copies Jacob Perkins's Washington funeral medal, including strikings in gold, and of the Charles Carroll of Carrollton medal. *Rarity:* URS-2 or 3(?).

Selected auction price(s): John J. Ford Jr. XIV Sale (5/2006), VF $2,300.

George Clinton / Excelsior 1787

W-18900 · copper

Unknown maker. *Notes:* Struck copy or else a struck counterfeit, work cruder than Bolen's art. Two in Ford. "Probably not a Bolen copy, but included here for its similarity." *Rarity:* URS-2(?).

Selected auction price(s): John J. Ford Jr. XIV Sale (5/2006), EF, $161; EF, $862 (wide price differential).

SELECTED BIBLIOGRAPHY

Adams, John W. *United States Numismatic Literature*. Volume 1: *Nineteenth Century Auction Catalogs*. Mission Viejo, Calif.: George Frederick Kolbe, 1982.

—— *United States Numismatic Literature*. Volume 2: *Twentieth Century Auction Catalogues*. Crestline, Calif.: George Frederick Kolbe, 1990.

—— "The Story Behind the Castorland Jeton." *The Asylum*, Vol. 25, No. 4, Fall 2007.

Adelson, Howard. *The American Numismatic Society, 1858–1958*. New York: American Numismatic Society, 1958.

American Journal of Numismatics. New York and Boston: Various issues, 1866–1912.

Anthony, Alan, Roger A. Moore, and Eric P. Newman. "Virginia Halfpence Variety Update with Revised Die Interlock Chart." *The Colonial Newsletter*, No. 127, April 2005.

Anton, William T., Jr. "A Modern Survey of the Copper Coinage of the State of New Jersey." *The Colonial Newsletter*, No. 44, July 1975.

Anton, William T., Jr., and Bruce Kesse. *The Forgotten Coins of the North American Colonies*. Author, 1990.

Asylum, The. Various issues, 1980s onward. Published by the Numismatic Bibliomania Society.

Atkins, James. *Coins and Tokens of the Possessions and Colonies of the British Empire*. London: Bernard Quaritch, 1889.

Attinelli, Emmanuel J. *Numisgraphics, or A List of Catalogues, Which Have Been Sold by Auction in the United States*. New York: author, 1876.

August, Richard. "Massachusetts Coppers Rarity Rating—A Second Opinion." *The C4 Newsletter*, Summer 1998.

August, Richard, and Edwin Sarrafian. "Machin's Mills Coins: Condition Census, Die States, Discoveries, and Estimated Rarity by Grades." *The C4 Newsletter*, Spring 1998.

Bailey, Clement F. "Dr. Samuel Higley and his Coppers." *The Numismatist*, September 1976.

Baker, W.S. *American Engravers and Their Works*. Philadelphia: Gebbie & Barrie Publishers, 1875.

—— *The Engraved Portraits of Washington*. Philadelphia: Lindsay & Baker, 1880.

—— *Medallic Portraits of Washington*. Philadelphia: Robert M. Lindsay, 1885. An annotated reprint with updated information was prepared by George J. Fuld in 1965 and issued by Krause Publications.

Barnsley, Edward R. "Miller's Connecticut Listings Updated." *The Colonial Newsletter*, No. 11, March 1964.

—— "The Problem of James F. Atlee." *The Colonial Newsletter*, No. 45, January 1975.

Bentley, Anne B. [Study of the 1776 Massachusetts copper penny, part of:] *Witness to America's Past: Two Centuries of Collecting by the Massachusetts Historical Society*. Boston: Massachusetts Historical Society, 1991.

Betts, C. Wyllys. "Counterfeit Half Pence Current in the American Colonies and Their Issue from the Mints of Connecticut and Vermont." New York: American Numismatic and Archaeological Society, 1886. Transcript of speech given to the Society.

—— *American Colonial History Illustrated by Contemporary Medals*. New York: Scott Stamp and Coin Co., Ltd., 1894.

Bonjour, Roy E. *Survey of the Rarest Vermonts*. Supplement no. 1 to the *C4 Newsletter*, April 2005.

Bowers, Q. David. *The History of United States Coinage as Illustrated by the Garrett Collection.* Published for The Johns Hopkins University, Baltimore. First printing, Los Angeles, Calif.

——— "Web of Mystery Lifts: Researcher Delves Into Unique Brasher Half Doubloon." *Coin World*, August 31, 1988.

——— *American Coin Treasures and Hoards.* Wolfeboro, NH: Bowers and Merena Galleries, 1997.

Breen, Walter H. "Survey of American Coin Hoards." *The Numismatist*, January 1952.

——— "Blundered Dies of Colonial and U.S. Coins." *Empire Topics* 2, 1958.

——— "Comment on St. Patrick's Halfpence and Farthings." *The Colonial Newsletter*, No. 22, April 1968.

——— *Walter Breen's Complete Encyclopedia of U.S. and Colonial Coins.* New York: Doubleday, 1988.

——— *Walter Breen's Encyclopedia of U.S. and Colonial Proof Coins, 1792–1977.* Albertson, N.Y.: FCI Press, 1977. Updated, Wolfeboro, N.H.: Bowers and Merena Galleries, 1989.

Bressett, Kenneth E. (ed.). *A Guide Book of United States Coins.* Atlanta, Georgia: Various modern editions. Earlier editions edited by Richard S. Yeoman.

——— "The Vermont Copper Coinage," part of *Studies on Money in Early America.* New York: American Numismatic Society, 1976.

Bryant, Norman. "The New Haven Mint." *The Colonial Newsletter*, No. 50, November 1977.

Bushnell, Charles I. *An Historical Account of the First Three Business Tokens Issued In The City of New York.* Author, 1858. Also exists with 1859 imprint.

Carlotto, Tony. *The Copper Coins of Vermont and Those Bearing the Vermont Name.* Colonial Coin Collectors Club (C4), 1998.

Carothers, Neil. *Fractional Money.* New York: Wiley, 1930.

Carlson, Carl W.A. "Tracker: An Introduction to Pedigree Research in the Field of Rare American Coins." *The American Numismatic Association Centennial Anthology*, 1991.

Chalmers, Robert. *A History of Currency in the British Colonies.* Colchester, England: John Drury, 1972. Original work published 1893.

Clark, Randy. "Connecticut Varieties of Interest or Note." Digital file of die information and characteristics.

——— "Draped to Mailed Bust Transition on a 1787 Connecticut Obverse Die." *The C4 Newsletter*, Summer 2007.

Coin Collector's Journal, The. Published by J.W. Scott & Co., New York, in the 1870s and 1880s.

Coin World. Sidney, Ohio: Amos Press, et al., 1960 to date.

Collins, Jack. *Washingtonia.* South Gate, Calif.: author, 1991.

——— *Washingtonia.* South Gate, Calif.: author, 1995.

Colonial Coin Collectors Club Newsletter; a.k.a. *C4 Newsletter.* Various issues, 1993 to date.

Colonial Newsletter, The. New York: American Numismatic Society, various issues, 1960 to date.

Crawmer, Arthur. "Standish Barry and His Threepence." Typescript furnished by the author, 2007.

Crosby, Sylvester S. *The Early Coins of America.* Boston: author, 1875.

Dalton, R., and S.H. Hamer. *English Provincial Token Coinage of the 18th Century.* London: 1910–1922.

Danforth, Brian. "St. Patrick." *The Colonial Newsletter*, No. 121, August 2002.

——— "St. Patrick Coinage Revisited." *The Colonial Newsletter*, No. 127, April 2005.

—— "Bath Metal: Composition of Rosa Americana Coins." *The C4 Newsletter*, Summer 2006.

Davis, Charles E. *American Numismatic Literature: An Annotated Survey of Auction Sales, 1980–1991.* Lincoln, Mass.: Quarterman, 1992.

DeWitt, J. Doyle. *A Century of Campaign Buttons, 1789–1959.* Hartford, Conn.: The Travelers Press, 1959.

—— *Alfred S. Robinson, Hartford Numismatist.* Hartford, Conn.: The Connecticut Historical Society, 1968.

Dickeson, Montroville W. *American Numismatical Manual.* Philadelphia: J.B. Lippincott, 1859.

Doty, Richard G. "Making Money in Early Massachusetts." *Money of Pre-Federal America.* New York: American Numismatic Society, 1992.

—— "Coinage During the Confederation: Two Near Misses for Matthew Bolton." *Coinage of the American Confederation Period.* New York: American Numismatic Society, 1996.

—— *America's Money, America's Story.* Iola, Wisc.: Krause, 1998.

—— *The Soho Mint & The Industrialization of Money.* London: Spink and The British Numismatic Society, 1998.

Douglas, Damon G. Manuscript notes on James Jarvis and Fugio coppers. Notes on New Jersey coppers. Excerpts published in the *Colonial Newsletter* and elsewhere.

—— "The Original Mint of the New Jersey Coppers." From the *Proceedings of the New Jersey Historical Society*, reprinted in the *Colonial Newsletter*, July 1968.

—— (Gary A. Trudgen, editor). *The Copper Coinage of the State of New Jersey: Annotated Manuscript of Damon G. Douglas.* New York: American Numismatic Society, 2003

Dubois, William E. *Pledges of History: A Brief Account of the Collection of Coins Belonging to the Mint of the United States, More Particularly of the Antique Specimens.* Philadelphia: C. Sherman, 1846. Second edition, New York: George P. Putnam, 1851.

Duncan, Charles V. "The Auctori Plebis Token & Related Pieces." *The Colonial Newsletter*, No. 43, April 1975.

Felt, Joseph B. *An Historical Account of Massachusetts Currency.* Boston: Printed by Perkins & Marvin, 1839.

Freidus, Daniel. "The History and Die Varieties of the Higley Coppers." *The Token: America's Other Money*, Coinage of the Americas Conference, 1994. New York: American Numismatic Society, 1995.

Fuld, George J. "Research Forum" submission concerning the 1783 Washington Unity Cent. *The Colonial Newsletter*, No. 12, June 1964.

—— "The Origin of the Washington 1783 Cents." *The Numismatist*, November 1964.

—— *Medallic Portraits of Washington.* 1965 annotated reprint of W.S. Baker's 1885 work of this title.

—— "Coinage Featuring George Washington." *Coinage of the American Confederation Period.* New York: American Numismatic Society, 1996.

Fuld, George, and Fuld, Melvin. "The Talbot, Allum & Lee Cents." *Numismatic Scrapbook Magazine*, September 1956.

Fulghum, R. Neil. "The Hunt for Carolina Elephant Tokens: Questions Regarding Genuine Specimens and Reproductions of the 1694 Token." *The Colonial Newsletter*, April 2003.

Gaspar, Graham P., and Peter P. Gaspar. "A Virginia Numismatic Discovery." *American Numismatic Society Museum Notes 27*, 1982.

Gladfelter, David D. "Mark Newby: Quaker Pioneer." *Token and Medal Society Journal*, October 1974. Reprinted in *The Colonial Newsletter*, December 1989.

—— "A Tale of Two Elephants." *The Colonial Newsletter*, No. 100, July 1995.

—— "Obverse Iconography of the Rhode Island Ship Medals." *The C4 Newsletter*, Summer 2006.

Goldstein, Erik. "Colonial Coins at Colonial Williamsburg." *The C4 Newsletter*, Summer 2004.

Guth, Ron. "The 1796 Castorland Jetons." *The MCA Advisory*, September 2007

Guttag Brothers. *Coins of the Americas.* Parts 1 and 2. New York: Guttag Brothers, 1924.

Hall, Benjamin H. *History of Eastern Vermont, From Its Earliest Settlement to the Close of the Eighteenth Century.* New York: D. Appleton & Co., 1858.

Hawkins, R.N.P. *A Dictionary of Makers of British Metallic Tickets, Checks, Medalets, Tallies and Counters 1788–1910.* London: A.H. Baldwin & Sons, 1989.

Hibler, Harold E., and Charles V. Kappen. *So-Called Dollars.* New York: The Coin and Currency Institute, 1963

Hickcox, John H. *An Historical Account of American Coinage.* Albany, N.Y.: Joel Munsell, 1858.

Historical Magazine, The. Morrisania, N.Y. Issues in Series 1, 2, and 3, 1850s and 1860s.

Hodder, Michael J. "The St. Patrick Token Coinage: A Re-evaluation of the Evidence," *The Colonial Newsletter*, No. 77, November 1987.

—— "The London, Carolina, and New England Elephant Tokens." Discussion and attribution of die varieties in the Norweb Collection 1 catalog. Bowers and Merena Galleries, 1987.

—— "Reverse J Study." *American Journal of Numismatics*, American Numismatic Society, 1989.

—— "Appleton-Massachusetts Historical Society Rhode Island Ship Token With Vlugtende." *The Colonial Newsletter*, No. 84, March 1990.

—— "The 1787 'New York' Immunis Columbia; A Mystery Re-Ravelled." *The Colonial Newsletter*, No. 87, January 1991.

—— "Ephraim Brasher's 1786 Lima Style Doubloon." *Money of Pre-Federal America.* New York: American Numismatic Society, 1992.

—— "Attitudes Toward the Coinage Right in Early Federal America: The Case of New Jersey, 1788–1794." *The Colonial Newsletter*, No. 91, July 1992.

—— "Cecil Calvert's Coinage for Maryland: A Study in History and Law." *The Colonial Newsletter*, No. 93, February 1993.

—— "The New Jersey No-Coulter Die Families." *The Colonial Newsletter*, No. 96, February 1994.

—— "More on Benjamin Dudley, Public Copper, Constellatio Novas and Fugio Cents." *The Colonial Newsletter*, No. 97, June 1994.

—— "An American Collector's Guide to the Coins of Nouvelle France." *Canada's Money.* New York: American Numismatic Society, 1994

—— "The Gloucester County, Virginia Courthouse Tokens," *The Colonial Newsletter*, No. 104, April 1997.

—— More on the Rhode Island Ship Token." *The C4 Newsletter*, Summer 2002.

Hoover, Oliver D. "A Note on the Typology of the St. Patrick Coinage in its Restoration Context." *American Journal of Numismatics*, 16–17, Second Series. New York: American Numismatic Society 2004.

Howes, Jack. "A New (and Long Overdue) Guide to the Identification of Machin's Mills Halfpence." *The C4 Newsletter*, Spring 2006.

—— "Atlee Halfpenny Vlack 5-74A: A New Discovery and Its Relevance to a Detailed Analysis of Vlack Obverse Dies 5 and 8." *The Colonial Newsletter*, No. 132, December 2006.

Hull, John. "The Diaries of John Hull, Mint-Master and Treasurer of the Colony of Massachusetts Bay." *Archæologica Americana: Transactions and Collections of the American Antiquarian Society*, vol. 3. Cambridge, Mass.: Bolles and Houghton, 1850.

Humphrey, Z. *The History of Dorset*. Rutland, Vermont: Tuttle & Company, 1924.

Jaeger, Katherine M., and Q. David Bowers. *The 100 Greatest American Medals and Tokens*. Atlanta, Georgia: Whitman, 2007.

Jordan, Louis E., and Robert H. Gore Jr. Numismatic Endowment. University of Notre Dame, Department of Special Collections. Web site compiled maintained by Louis E. Jordan.

—— "An Examination of the 'New Constellation' Coppers in Relation to the Nova Constellatio–Constellatio Nova Debate." *The Colonial Newsletter*, No. 115, December 2000.

—— *John Hull, the Mint and the Economics of Massachusetts Coinage*. The Colonial Coin Collectors Club, 2002.

—— "Somer Islands 'Hogge Money' of 1616: The Historical Context." *The Colonial Newsletter*, No. 123, August 2003.

—— "Lord Baltimore Coinage and Daily Exchange in Early Maryland." *The Colonial Newsletter*, No. 126, August–December 2004.

Kelso, William M. Jamestown: *The Buried Truth*. Charlottesville, Virginia: University of Virginia Press, 2006.

Kenney, Richard D. *Struck Copies of Early American Coins*. New York: Wayte Raymond, 1952.

—— *Early American Medalists and Die-Sinkers Prior to the Civil War*. New York: Wayte Raymond, 1954.

Kessler, Alan. *The Fugio Cents*. Newtonville, Mass.: Colony Coin Co., 1976.

Kleeberg, John M. "A Catalogue of the Exhibition of Massachusetts Silver at the American Numismatic Society." *Money of Pre-Federal America*. New York: American Numismatic Society, 1992.

—— "The New Yorke in America Token." *Money of Pre-Federal America*. New York: American Numismatic Society, 1992.

—— "The Theatre at New York." *The Token: America's Other Money*. New York: American Numismatic Society, 1995.

—— "Shipwreck of the Faithful Steward." *Coinage of the American Confederation Period*. New York: American Numismatic Society, 1996.

—— "Peter Rosa's Replicas of Colonial Coins." *The Colonial Newsletter*, No. 119, April 2002.

Lefroy, Gen. J.H. (governor of Bermuda). "The Hog Money of the Somers Islands." *American Journal of Numismatics*, July 1877.

Lipsky, Jeff. "Proposed Classification System for Sommer Islands Coinage." *The C4 Newsletter*, Winter 2001.

Lorenzo, John. "The So-Called Atlee Broken 'A' Letterpunch." *Coinage of the American Confederation Period*. New York: American Numismatic Society, 1996.

Lorenzo, John, and Roger Moore. "The 1787 Immunis Columbia: A Late Rahway / Elizabethtown Product?" *The C4 Newsletter*, Spring 1997.

Luther, C.F. "Connecticut Cents in the Yale Collection." *The Numismatist*, August 1935.

Margolis, Richard. "Matthew Boulton, Philip Parry Price Myddelton, and the Proposed Token Coinage for Kentucky." *The Colonial Newsletter*, December 1999.

Maris, Edward. *A Historical Sketch of the Coins of New Jersey*. Philadelphia: 1881.

Martin, Robert M. "George C. Perkins Collection of Connecticut Coppers: Additions & Corrections, Priced & Named." Author, 2006.

Martin, Sydney F. "US Colonial Coins in Bermuda National Collections." *The C4 Newsletter*, Fall 2004.

——— *The Hibernia Coinage of William Wood (1722–1724)*. Colonial Coin Collectors Club, 2007.

Martin, Sydney F., and Michael Ringo. "Discovery of a New U.S. Colonial Coin Type." *The Colonial Newsletter*, No. 120, August 2002

Martin, Sydney F., and Ray Williams. "Rarity Scales—Their Meaning." *The C4 Newsletter*, Fall 2006.

Mason's Monthly Illustrated Coin Collector's Magazine. Philadelphia and Boston: Ebenezer Locke Mason. Various issues, 1860s onward.

McCarthy, David. "Understanding Brasher's Doubloons." *The Brasher Bulletin*, 2006.

McCusker, John J. *Money and Exchange in Europe and America, 1600–1775: A Handbook*. Chapel Hill, N.C.: University of North Carolina Press, 1978.

Miller, Henry C., and Hillyer C. Ryder. *The State Coinages of New England*. New York: American Numismatic Society, 1920.

Moore, Roger A. "Edward Maris, M.D.—Numismatist." *The Colonial Newsletter*, No. 106, December 1997.

Moore, Roger A., Alan Anthony, and Eric P. Newman. "Virginia Halfpence Variety Update With Revised Die Interlock Chart." *The Colonial Newsletter*, No. 127, April 2005.

Mossman, Philip L. "A Weight Analysis of Abel Buell's Connecticut Coppers." *Money of Pre-Federal America*. New York: American Numismatic Society, 1992.

——— *Money of the American Colonies and Confederation: A Numismatic, Economic & Historical Correlation*. New York: American Numismatic Society, 1993.

——— "The American Confederation: The Times and Its Money." *Coinage of the American Confederation Period*. New York: American Numismatic Society, 1996.

——— "Error Coins of Pre-Federal America." *The Colonial Newsletter*, No. 125, April 2004.

Musante, Neil E. *The Medallic Works of John Adams Bolen, Die Sinker &c*. Springfield, Mass.: author, 2002.

Nelson, Philip. *The Coinage of William Wood, 1722–1733*. London: Spink & Son, Ltd., 1959. Original work published 1903.

Newman, Eric P. "The 1776 Continental Currency Coinage." *The Coin Collector's Journal*, July–August 1952.

——— "Varieties of the Fugio Cent." *The Coin Collector's Journal*, July–August 1952.

——— "A Recently Discovered Coin Solves a Vermont Numismatic Enigma." *The Centennial Publication of the American Numismatic Society*. New York: American Numismatic Society, 1958.

——— *The Secret of the Good Samaritan Shilling*. New York: American Numismatic Society, 1959.

——— "Additions to Coinage for Colonial Virginia." *Museum Notes 10*. American Numismatic Society, 1962.

——— "The James II 1/24th Real for the American Plantations." *Museum Notes 11*. American Numismatic Society, 1964.

——— "New Thoughts on the Nova Constellatio Private Copper Coinage." *Coinage of the American Confederation Period*. New York: American Numismatic Society, 1996.

——— *The United States Fugio Copper Coinage of 1787*. Jon Lusk, 2007.

Noe, Sydney P. *The Silver Coinage of Massachusetts*. Lawrence, Mass.: Quarterman, 1973.

Norton's Literary Letter. New York: 1857–1860.

Numisma. House organ published by Édouard Frossard, 1877–1891.

Numismatic News. Iola, Wisc.: Krause, 1952 to date.

Numismatist, The. American Numismatic Association. Colorado Springs, Colorado. Various issues, 1891 to date.

O'Callaghan, E.B. *The Documentary History of the State of New-York.* Four volumes. Albany, N.Y.: Weed, Parsons & Co., 1850.

Orosz, Joel J. "Robert Gilmor Jr. and the Cradle Age of American Numismatics." *Rare Coin Review* No. 58, 1985.

——— *The Eagle That Is Forgotten: Pierre Eugène Du Simitière, Founding Father of American Numismatics.* Wolfeboro, N.H.: Bowers and Merena Galleries, 1988.

Orosz, Joel J., and Carl R. Herkowitz. "George Washington and America's 'Small Beginning' in Coinage: The Fabled 1792 Half Disme." *American Journal of Numismatics,* Second Series, 18, 2003.

Packard, Michael. "Rarity Values of Massachusetts Copper Coins," *The Colonial Newsletter,* No. 77, November 1987.

——— "Auction Appearances of Massachusetts Coppers." *The Colonial Newsletter,* No. 81, August 1989.

Packard, Michael, and Tom Rinaldo. "Attributing 1787 Massachusetts Cents." *The C4 Newsletter,* Winter 1997.

Peck, C. Wilson. *English Copper, Tin and Bronze Coins in the British Museum, 1558–1958.* London: Trustees of the British Museum, 1960.

Phelps, Richard H. *Newgate of Connecticut: Its Origin and Early History.* American Publishing Co., 1876. Reprinted in 1927 by Clarence W. Seymour, Hartford, Conn.

Pietri, Angel. "The History of the Castorland Settlement." *The C4 Newsletter,* Spring 1997.

Pilcher, Edith. *Castorland: French Refugees in the Western Adirondacks, 1793–1814.* Harrison, N.Y.: Harbor Hill Books, 1985.

Pine Tree Auction Company Auction for EAC, February 15, 1975.

Prattent, Thomas, and M. Denton. *The Virtuoso's Companion and Coin Collector's Guide.* Eight volumes. London, 1795–1797.

Prime, W.C. *Coins, Medals, and Seals.* New York: Harper & Brothers, 1861.

Raymond, Wayte. *Standard Catalogue of United States Coins and Paper Money* (titles vary). Scott Stamp & Coin Co. (and others): New York, 1934 to 1957 editions.

Richardson, John M. "The Copper Coins of Vermont," published in *The Numismatist,* May 1947.

Rock, Jeff. "Corrigenda Millerensis Revisited." *The Colonial Newsletter,* No. 88, May 1991.

Rothschild, Neil. "The First Modern Connecticut Coppers Variety Collection?" *The C4 Newsletter,* Fall 2003.

Rulau, Russell. *Standard Catalogue of United States Tokens 1700–1900.* 4th edition. Iola, Wisc.: Krause, 2004.

Rulau, Russell, and George J. Fuld. *Medallic Portraits of Washington.* Second edition. Iola, Wisc.: Krause Publications, 1999.

Ryder, Hillyer. "The Colonial Coins of Vermont." Part of *State Coinages of New England.* New York: American Numismatic Society, 1920.

Schab, Henry. "The Life and Coins of John Chalmers." *The Numismatist,* November 1984.

Schilke, Oscar G., and Raphael E. Solomon. *America's Foreign Coins: An Illustrated Standard Catalogue with Valuations of Foreign Coins with Legal Tender Status in the United States 1793–1857.* New York: Coin and Currency Institute, 1964.

Scott, Kenneth. *Counterfeiting in Colonial America.* New York: Oxford University Press, 1957.

Shelby, Wayne H. "Survey of Colonial Coins Recovered in Southern New Jersey." *The C4 Newsletter,* Winter 2003.

Shurtleff, Augustine. "The Washington Coins." Published in the *Boston Evening Transcript* and reprinted as a supplement to the Bangs, Merwin & Co. listing of the Charles H. Morse Collection, October 17–18, 1860.

Siboni, Roger S. "The Not-So-Hidden Hand of Walter Mould." *The C4 Newsletter,* Winter 2004.

Siboni, Roger S, and Vicken Yegparian. "Mark Newby and His St. Patrick Halfpence." Coinage of the Americas Conference, American Numismatic Society, November 11, 2006.

Sipsey, Everett T. "New Facts and Ideas on the State Coinages: A Blend of Numismatics, History, and Genealogy." *The Colonial Newsletter,* No. 13, October 1964.

Slafter, Edmund F. "The Vermont Coinage." *Proceedings of the Vermont Historical Society,* vol. 1. Montpelier, Vermont: Vermont Historical Society, 1870.

Smith, Pete. "Vermont Coppers: Coinage of an Independent Republic." *Coinage of the American Confederation Period.* New York: American Numismatic Society, 1996.

Snelling, T. *A View of the Silver Coin and Coinage of England, From the Norman Conquest to the Present Time, Considered with Regard to Type, Legend, Sorts, Rarity, Weight, Fineness and Value, with Copper-Plates.* London: 1762. ("Printed for T. Snelling, next the Horn Tavern, in Fleet-Street. Who buys and sells all sorts of Coins and Medals.")

Snowden, James Ross. *A Description of Ancient and Modern Coins in the Cabinet of the Mint of the United States.* Philadelphia: J.B. Lippincott, 1860.

—— *The Medallic Memorials of Washington in the Mint of the United States.* Philadelphia: J.B. Lippincott & Co., 1861.

Spence, T. *The Coin Collector's Companion. Being a Descriptive Alphabetical List of the Modern Provincial, Political, and Other Copper Coins.* London: Printed for T. Spence, 1795.

Spilman, James C. "More Comments on the Fugio Cents of 1787." *The Colonial Newsletter,* No. 7, April–June 1962.

—— "Abel Buell, Our American Genius," part 2. *The Colonial Newsletter,* No. 39, February 1974.

—— "An Overview of Early American Coinage Technology." *The Colonial Newsletter,* Nos. 62–65, April and July 1982, March and July 1983.

—— "Update: CNL Fugio Weight Survey." *The Colonial Newsletter,* No. 87, January 1991.

—— "The CNLF Checklist of Early American Counterfeit Halfpence Believed Struck in America." *The Colonial Newsletter,* No. 117, August 2001.

Steimle, Frank. "A Tricentennial Review and Comments on the 'God Preserve' Elephant Tokens." *The Colonial Newsletter,* No. 99, April 1995.

Sumner, William Graham. *A History of American Currency.* New York: Henry Holt & Co., 1874.

—— *The Financier and the Finances of the American Revolution.* Vols. 1 and 2. New York: Dodd, Mead and Co., 1891.

Taxay, Don. *Counterfeit, Mis-Struck, and Unofficial U.S. Coins.* New York: Arco, 1963.

—— *U.S. Mint and Coinage.* New York: Arco, 1966.

—— *Scott's Comprehensive Catalogue of United States Coinage.* New York: Scott, 1970 (cover date 1971).

Token and Medal Society Journal. Various addresses, 1960s to date.

Trudgen, Gary A. "Machin's Mills." *The Colonial Newsletter*, No. 68, July 1984.

—— "The Mysterious Muttonhead." *Rare Coin Review* No. 63, Winter 1986–87.

—— "James Atlee's Imitation British Halfpence." *The Colonial Newsletter*, No. 75, March 1987.

—— "The Nova Eborac Coppers." *The Colonial Newsletter*, No. 99, September 1981.

—— "Matthias Ogden, New Jersey State Coiner." *The Colonial Newsletter*, No. 79, June 1988.

—— "John Bailey, New York City Coiner." *The Colonial Newsletter*, No. 85, July 1990.

—— "A Brief Look at the Life of Thomas Goadsby." *The Colonial Newsletter*, No. 90, February 1992.

—— "Samuel and James F. Atlee, Machin's Mills Partners." *The Colonial Newsletter*, No. 92, October 1992.

Vlack, Robert A. A. *Catalog of Early American Coins.* Anaheim, Calif.: Ovolon, 1963.

—— *Early American Coins.* Johnson City, N.Y.: Windsor Research, 1965.

—— "Die Varieties of St. Patrick Halfpence." *The Colonial Newsletter*, No. 21, January 1968.

—— "The Washington Coppers of '1783'," *The Colonial Newsletter*, No. 52, July 1978.

—— *An Illustrated Catalogue of the French Billon Coinage in the Americas.* Colonial Coin Collectors Club, 2004.

Weston, Byron K. "Evasion Hybrids: The Missing Link." *The Colonial Newsletter*, No. 111, August 1999.

Wierzba, Dennis P. "Revised Sheldon Rarity Ratings Estimates for NJ Coppers." *The C4 Newsletter*, Winter 1998.

Williams, Malcolm E., Peter T. Sousa, and Edward C. Harris. *Coins of Bermuda 1616–1996.* Hamilton: Bermuda Monetary Authority, 1997.

Williams, Ray. "My personal notes and observations dealing with NJ coppers." Computer database notes, October 2007.

Williamson, Raymond H. "Virginia's Early Money of Account." *The Colonial Newsletter*, No. 72, January 1986.

Woodward, W. Elliot. "Memorial Medals." *Washingtoniana*, vol. 2, by Franklin B. Hough, 1865.

Wright, Benjamin P. "The American Store or Business Cards." Published serially in *The Numismatist*, 1898–1901. Reprinted by the Token and Medal Society, 1963.

Wroth, Lawrence C. *Abel Buell of Connecticut: Silversmith, Type Founder & Engraver.* Revised and updated edition. Middletown, Conn.: Wesleyan University Press, 1958. Original work published in 1926 by the Acorn Club of Connecticut.

Zelinka, Jerry. "The Enigmatic Voce Populi Halfpenny of 1760." *The Colonial Newsletter*, No. 47, October 1976.

About the Author

Q. David Bowers became a professional numismatist as a teenager in 1953, later (1960) earning a B.A. in finance from the Pennsylvania State University, which in 1976 bestowed its Distinguished Alumnus Award on him. The author served as president of the American Numismatic Association (1983–1985) and president of the Professional Numismatists Guild (1977–1979); is a recipient of the highest honor bestowed by the ANA (the Farran Zerbe Award); was the first ANA member to be named Numismatist of the Year (1995); in 2005 was given the Lifetime Achievement Award; and has been inducted into the ANA Numismatic Hall of Fame. Bowers was given the highest honor bestowed by the Professional Numismatists Guild (the Founders' Award) and has received more "Book of the Year Award" and "Best Columnist" honors given by the Numismatic Literary Guild than has any other writer. In July 1999, in a poll published in *COINage*, "Numismatists of the Century," by Ed Reiter, Bowers was recognized in this list of just 18 names. He is the author of more than 50 books, hundreds of auction and other catalogs, and several thousand articles including columns in *Coin World* (now the longest-running by any author in numismatic history), *Paper Money*, and *The Numismatist*. His prime enjoyments in numismatics are knowing "coin people," from newcomers to old-timers, and studying the endless lore, technical aspects, and history of coins, tokens, medals, and paper money. Colonial coins have always been a favorite interest. As co-chairman of Stack's (New York City and Wolfeboro, N.H.) and numismatic director for Whitman Publishing, LLC, he is at the forefront of current events in the hobby.

The writer of the foreword, **Kenneth Bressett,** has been involved in the hobby since the 1940s. He has written many numismatic articles and is author or editor of more than a dozen related books. He is a past governor, vice president, and president of the American Numismatic Association, and a highly accomplished teacher and researcher. He has served for many years as the editor of *A Guide Book of United States Coins*—at more than 21 million copies, one of the best-selling nonfiction titles in American publishing. As a former consultant to the U.S. Mint, he was instrumental in helping to implement the 50 State Quarters® Program and in selecting many of the coins' reverse designs. Ken is a founder of the Rittenhouse Society, a past appointee to the Annual Assay Commission, a recipient of the Numismatic Literary Guild's Clemy Award, and an inductee in the Numismatic Hall of Fame (at ANA Headquarters in Colorado Springs). Colonial coins have been among his specialties for a long time.

INDEX

Act of February 21, 1857, 2
Act of May 8, 1792, 4
agricultural products, used as money, 1
Albany Church pennies, 240
Alexander, George, 189
Allan, John, 16
American Museum, 16, 17
American Numismatic Association (ANA), 24
    founding of, 18
    See also ANA Grading Service Study Committee
American Numismatic Association Certification Service (ANACS), 24
American Numismatic Society (ANS), 20, 21, 29, 95, 197
    founding of, 18
American Plantations tokens, 4, 54–57
ammunition, used as money, 1, 32, 50
ANA Grading Service Study Committee, 24
Andrews, John, 16
annealing, 7
Anton, William T. Jr., 27, 222
Articles of Confederation, 192
Ashmead, C.C., 16
assaying, 7, 192
Atlee, James F., 13, 82, 221, 222
    and Machin's Mills, 83
Atlee, Samuel, 82, 83, 221
auctions, price study of, 27–28
Auctori Plebis tokens, 248
August, Richard, 27, 222

Bailey, John, 7, 159–160, 189
Baker, W.C., 159
Baldwin, Isaac, 93
Baltimore, Lord. See Calvert, Cecil
Bank of New York, 192, 209
Bank of North America, charter of, 4
bank-note reporters, 2
Bar coppers, 241–242
    Bolen copies, 296, 297
Barnsley, Edward, 94, 95
Barnum, P.T., 16, 17
Barry, Standish, 7, 192
    coinage of, 240–241
barter system, 32, 33
Bath metal, 58
Battle of Yorktown, 5
Bayley, Simeon, 82
beaver skins, used as money, 1
Bentley, William, 16
Bermuda coinage, 278. See also Dickeson copies; Sommer Islands coinage; Wuesthoff fantasies
    twopence, Bermuda, 278
Bermuda Company, 277
Bermudez, Juan, 276
Betts, C. Wyllys, 222, 312–313, 315
    fantasy coinage of (see Betts fantasies)
    See also die-attribution numbers of Rhode Island Ship medals
Betts fantasies, 309–314
    characteristics of, 312
billon, defined, 281
Bishop, Samuel, 92, 93
bit (100 units), 73, 74
Bluestone, Barney, 65
Boelen, Jacob III, 192
Bolen copies, 21, 296–302
Bolen, John Adams, 296–297
Bonjour, Roy E., 84
Boston Numismatic Society, founding of, 18
Boyd, Frederick C.C., 20, 21, 95, 197
Bradfield, Elston G., 22
Brand, Virgil M., 20, 21, 30, 95
Brasher gold coinage
    doubloons, 17, 20, 189, 192–194
    half doubloons, 193–194
    Robinson copies of, 304
Brasher, Ephraim, 7, 10, 189, 192–193, 240–241
Brazilian currency, in the colonies, 2
Breen, Walter, 22, 75, 222, 256
    classification system of, 94
Bressett, Kenneth, 22, 84, 222
    numbering system of, 84
    See also die-attribution numbers of Vermont coppers
British Museum, 55

Brooks, David, 82, 221
Broome, Samuel, 93–94, 208
Brown, Ammi, 17
Brown, Laurence, 235
Bryant, Norman, 95
Buell, Abel, 80–81, 93, 95, 208, 209
    and Fugio coppers, 208
Buell, Benjamin, 93
Buell, William, 80–81
bullets, currency equivalents of, 32
bungtown coppers, 108, 228–229
Burger, John, 192
Bushnell, Charles I., 10, 80, 81, 93–94, 159–160, 193, 196, 243

C4. See Colonial Coin Collectors Club (C4)
    founding of, 22
Callender, Joseph, 9, 196
Calvert, Cecil, Lord Baltimore, 4, 50–52
Calvert, Philip, 50–51
Canada, use of U.S. coins, 14
Canfield, Frederick A., 21, 95
Carlotto, Tony, 84
Castine deposit, 2
Castorland, 75
Castorland medals or jetons, 13, 253–254
cattle, used as money, 32
"cent"
    first appearance on a coin made in the United States, 197
    origin of term, 197
certification of coins, 24
Chalmers coinage, 21, 71–72
Chalmers, John, 5, 7, 13, 71
Chapman brothers (S. Hudson and Henry), 18, 20
Chelsea hoard, 17
Chetwood, F.B., 160
cinquefoils, on coins, 10, 94
Clapp, Charles Edwin Sr., 21
Clarke, T. James, 21
clipping, of planchets, 35, 192
Cogan, Edward D., 18
coin auctions, 19th-century, 18
coin clubs, in America, 18
coin prices, factors affecting, 26–28

Coinage of the Americas Conference, 232
coinage, by state, 8
coins
    cut to make change, 33, 71
    distribution of in colonies, 13–14
    produced in England for use in America, 4
    scarcity of, 1, 58
Colburn, Jeremiah, 17
Coley, William, 80, 81, 82, 221
collecting, trends in, 26–28
Colonial Coin Collectors Club (C4), 29, 84, 197
    founding of, 22
colonial coins
    copies of *(see chapter 12)*
    die features of, 12
    distribution of, 13–14
    emergence of as collectible, 18
    purity of, 7
    value history of, 28
    variations in value by state, 7
colonial era, end of, 5
colonies
    coins used in, 2
    exchange rates among, 2–3
    first coins struck in, 4
commodities, 17th-century, 1
Commonwealth (England), 50–51
Company for Coining Coppers, 93, 94, 95
Conder, James, 243
Conder tokens, 15, 243–244. *See also* Liberty and Security tokens
Confederate currency, 20, 161
Confederatio coppers, 186–188
    Bolen copies of, 300–301
Connecticut
    coinage of, 10, 75, 81, 92–158
    mints in, 13, 93–94, 208
Constable, Rucker & Co., 75
Constable, William, 75
Continental Army, 69
Continental Congress, paper-money issues of, 3–4, 5, 237–238
Continental Currency
    coinage, 20, 237–240
    notes, 197, 208, 237–238

contract coinage, 13
copies
    modern, 292
    producers of, 293–294
    struck, 292, 293
copper cents, emerging popularity of, 17
copper coins
    devaluation of, 14
    overstruck, 14
    purity of, 7
    shortage of, 14
coppers panic of 1789, 14, 83, 93, 160
coulters, 161
counterfeit detectors, 2
counterfeits, 13, 14, 17, 33, 75, 83, 92, 222, 240–241
    18th-century penalty for creating, 3
    collectible, 293
    of Indian Peace medals, 293
    of Vermont coinage, 92
    Machin's Mills, 222–228
    struck vs. cast, 293
    See also chapter 12
counterstamp, 192
"country pay," 1
Cox, Albion, 82, 159
Cradock, William, 231
Craige, Ted, 95. *See also die-attribution numbers of Higley or Granby coppers, Nova Constellatio coppers, and Willow Tree, Oak Tree, and Pine Tree coinage*
Crosby, Sylvester S., 9, 11, 13, 16, 50, 80, 196, 222, 235, 236

date, on coin, 8
Davids, Richard W., 16, 17
Davis, Charles, 309–310
de la Garza, José Antonio, 242
deniers (6, 9, 12, and 30), 281–283
deniers, double, 281–282
denominations, stated on coins, 8
dentils, 10, 223
    defined, 9
Dickeson copies, 305–307
Dickeson, Montroville W., 18–19, 66, 161, 236, 266, 305–306
Diderot, Denis, 7

dies
    characteristics of, 10, 12
    creation of, 8–9
    designs of, 8–9
    lifespan of, 9
    preparation of, 8–9
    replacement of, 10
Douglas, Damon G., 159, 160, 209
drop press, 58
Du Simitière, Pierre Eugène, 15–16, 17, 160, 232
DuBois, W.E., 193
Dubois, William F., 16
Dudley, Benjamin, 73, 74

Early American Coppers Club (EAC), 22
Easy Finding Guides
    American Plantations tokens, 56–57
    Connecticut coppers, 96–100, 103–108, 111–140, 152–156
    Fugio coppers, 209–217
    Massachusetts coppers, 198–199
    New Jersey coppers, 162–176
Eckfeldt, Adam, 16, 193
Eckfeldt, Jacob, 16, 74
edge clipping, 34
edge decorations, 9–10
Edwards, Francis Smith, M.D., 297, 316
Edwards, Pierpoint, 93
evasion halfpence, 243. *See also* bungtown coppers

8-reales, in the colonies, 2
Elder, Thomas L., 228
electrodeposition, 292
electrotypes, 292
Elephant tokens, 283–285
    characteristics of, 284
    Bolen copies of, 299
    Robinson copies of, 304–305
Eliot, Rev. Andrew, 16
Elizabethtown (N.J.) mint, 159
Ellsworth, James W., 20
Empire Coin Company, 197
encapsulation, 24–25
English coins
    denominations of, 3
    halfpenny as model for colonial coins, 11
    used in colonies, 2, 3, 32
escudos, Spanish-dollar equivalent of, 2

Esten, Howard, 64
Evans, David, 241
evasion coppers, 243 (*see also* bungtown coppers)
exchange rates, among colonies, 73
   exchange-rate tables, 2, 14

fantasy coins, 293. *See also* Betts fantasies; Getchell fantasies; Novum Belgium fantasy coinage; Wuesthoff fantasies
Felt, Joseph B., 197
Fendall, Josias, 50, 51
Feversham shipwreck, 2
fish, used as money, 1, 32
five units (Nova Constellatio pattern), 73, 74
Fletcher & Gardiner, 192
fleuron, 10, 94, 96
Flint, Royal, 208
Ford, John J. Jr., 21, 74, 95, 197
foreign coins used in colonies, 2, 4, 32–33, 192
   legal-tender status of, 2, 4
fourpence (groats), Maryland, 53
Franklin, Benjamin, 208, 249
Franklin Press tokens, 249–250
Freidus, Daniel, numbering system of, 232. *See also die-attribution numbers of Higley or Granby coppers*
French colonial coinage, 281–283
Frossard, Édouard, 18, 193, 309–312
Fugio coppers, 5, 13, 29, 80, 93, 208–221
   characteristics of, 209
   minting of, 8–9
   whether struck in Vermont, 80–81
   See also New Haven restrikes
fur, used as money, 1, 32, 50
Futter, Oliver Eaton, 22

Garrett, John Work, 74
Garrett, T. Harrison, 193
Garza, Jose Antonio de la, 242
Gavit, John, 17, 18
Georgivs Triumpho token, 14, 76, 257

German currency, in the colonies, 2
German, Anthony, 230
Getchell fantasies, 315
Getz patterns, 266–267
   Idler copies, 309
Getz, Peter, 266
Gilbert, Anne, 192
Giles, James, 82, 221
Gilmor, Robert Jr., 16–17
Gladfelter, David, 3, 232
Glouccster tokens, 230–231
Goadsby, Thomas, 159
gold doubloons
   Spanish-dollar equivalent of, 2
   Brasher (*see under* Brasher gold coinage)
   of Standish Barry, 240–241
Good Samaritan coinage copies, 296
   Getchell fantasies, 315
Goodrich, John, 92, 93
grades, for colonial coins, 23–26, 84–85
grading services, 24–25
grain, used as money, 1
   currency equivalents of, 32
Granby coppers. *See* Higley or Granby coppers
Grate halfpenny tokens, 269–270
Greco, Phil, 197
Gregorian calendar, 3
Grier, James, 221
Grier, Thomas, 82
groat, equivalence of, 51
Groux, Daniel, 17
Guttag, Julius and Henry, 161–162

half doubloons. *See under* Brasher gold coinage
halfpence, counterfeit English, 223–228
Hall, Benjamin H., 80, 81
Hall, David, 24
Hall, Thomas, 94, 95
hand engraving, 8, 10
Hanover, House of, 65
Harmon, Julian, 81
Harmon, Reuben Jr., 10, 80–82, 208, 221, 222
   and Machin's Mills, 221
Harvard College, 1
Haseltine, John W., 18, 73, 161
Hays, William M., 95
Heath, Dr. George F., 18

Heaton, Augustus G., 161
Hibernia coinage, 4, 285–290
   farthings, 286–287
   halfpence, 287–290
   See also Wood, William
Hickcox, John Howard, 18, 160
Higley or Granby coppers, 8, 13, 15, 231–234
   Bolen copies of, 298
   Robinson copies of, 303–304
Higley, Dr. Samuel, 5, 231–232
Hillhouse, James, 92, 93
Hobby Protection Act, 292
Hoch, Al, 22
Hodder, Michael J., 22, 35, 52, 59, 83, 193, 197, 234, 238, 281. *See also die-attribution numbers of Maryland coinage*
hogge money, 4, 278–279
Holt, Richard, 54
Hopkins, Joseph, 92, 93
Howe, Admiral, 69
hub punch, 8
Hull, John, 13, 33–34, 39
   death of, 44

Idler copies, 307–309
Idler, William K., 307
"imaginary money," 3
Immune Columbia coinage, 16, 78–79. *See also* Wuesthoff fantasies
Immunis Columbia coppers, 14, 186–188
Indian Peace medals, counterfeit, 293
Ingersoll, Jonathan, 93
ingots, preparation of, 6
inscriptions, Latin, 8, 81, 189
Ireland, coinage of, 4

Jackson, Elias, 82, 221
Jaeger, Katherine M., 242
Janus copper, 235–236
Jarvis, James, 93, 95, 208
jolas, New Spain, 242
Jordan, Louis E., 35, 50, 75, 234–235
Julian calendar, 3

Keller, W.P., 21
Kenney, Richard, 22. *See also die-attribution numbers of Bolen copies*
Kentucky tokens, 248–249
Kesse, Bruce, 222

Kessler, Alan, 209
King David, on coinage, 280
King Farouk of Egypt, 21
Kleeberg, John, 2, 21, 69
Kosoff, Abe, 21, 24
Kraljevich, John, 223
Kreisberg, Abner, 21
Kurth, Howard, 21

landscape-type coinage, 8, 81
Large Eagle cents, 262–263
   Robinson copies of, 305
Lasser, Joseph R., 21–22
Leavenworth, Eli, 93
Leavenworth, Mark, 93
Leavenworth, William, 93
legends, Latin, 8
Letellier, John, 192
Lewis, Winslow, 17
Liberty and Security tokens, 270–271
lion daalders, 2
Liverpool halfpennies, 263–264
Lord Baltimore coinage, 50–54. *See also* Maryland coinage
Lorenzo, John, 83
Louisiana, coins relevant to, 282–283
Lovelace, Francis, 69
Lovett, Robert Jr., 161
   coinage copies of, 306, 307
Low, Lyman H., 18
lumber, used as money, 1
Lyon Mint, 282

Machin, Capt. Thomas, 13, 82, 189, 221
Machin's Mills, 6–7, 11–12, 13, 14, 75, 78, 82–83, 93, 95, 96, 196, 293
   description of, 222
   founding of, 221
   and New Jersey coppers, 160
   and New York coinage, 189
Machin's Mills coinage, 87–92, 221–229
   characteristics of, 84
   coppers, 221–229
   halfpence, 223–228
Maris, Dr. Edward, 18, 161–162. *See also die-attribution numbers of New Jersey coppers*
mark (1,000 units), 73, 75
Mark Newby coinage, 4, 161, 279–280
   characteristics of, 280

Marsh, Daniel, 159
Martin, Sydney F., 59. *See also die-attribution numbers of Hibernia coinage and Rosa Americana coinage*
Marx, Karl, 1
Maryland
   coin denominations circulated in, 51, 52 (*see also* Maryland coinage)
   early media of exchange in, 1, 50
   founding of, 50
Maryland coinage, 50–54
   Idler copies of, 307–308
   See also chapter 6
Mason, W.G., 16
Massachusetts
   denominations minted in, 35
   early commerce of, 32–33
   early media of exchange in, 1, 32
   founding of, 32
   mint at, 4, 10, 33–34, 195
   paper money of, 3
Massachusetts coinage, 4, 5, 9–10, 13, 20, 32–35, 194–208, 235–236
   characteristics of, 197
   popularity of with collectors, 45
   See also NE coinage; Pine Tree coinage; Willow Tree coinage; *and chapter 5*
medals, collecting, 18
Mehl, B. Max, 20, 22
Meigs, Henry, 93–94
Melnick, Herbert I., 74
Mickley, Joseph, 16, 161
Millbrook, Vermont, 80–81
Miller, Henry C., 94, 95
   cataloging system of, 94, 95, 96
   See also die-attribution numbers of Connecticut coppers
Mint Cabinet, 21
   formation of, 16
minting house, typical, 6
minting methods
   colonial, 6, 9–10
   of different countries, 7
minting, contracted to private individuals, 13
mints, locations of, 10
Minuit, Peter, 310, 312–313
Mitchell, Scott, 26

moneys of account, 2–3, 33, 73
Moore, Roger, 162
Morris, Gouverneur, 73–74, 75
Morris, Jacob G., 16, 17
Morris, Robert R., 73, 75
Morristown (N.J.) mint, 159
Mossman, Philip L., 94
Mould, Walter, 159
Moulton, William, 237
mousquetaires, 281, 282
Muhlenberg, Henry A., 16
Myddelton, Philip Parry Price, 250
Myddelton tokens, 24, 250–251

National Numismatic Collection, 21
NE (New England) coinage, 34, 35–54
   Wyatt counterfeits of, 295
Newby, Mark, 4, 279. *See also* Mark Newby coinage
Newgate Prison, 231
New Hampshire
   coinage of, 237
   early media of exchange in, 1
New Haven restrikes, 314–315
New Jersey coinage, 9, 10, 18, 75, 94, 159–186
   characteristics of, 160–161
   See also Mark Newby coinage
New Jersey Copper Coin Symposium, 27
New Jersey Historical Society, 21
New Jersey, mints in, 11, 13, 159
Newman, Eric P., 22, 29, 64, 65, 75, 78, 80–81, 238
   numbering system of, 65
   See also die-attribution numbers of American Plantations tokens, Continental Dollars, Fugio coppers, and Virginia coinage
New Netherlands Coin Company, 21, 22, 197
New Spain jolas, 242
New York and related coinage, 188–192, 240
New York Coin & Stamp Company, 18
New Yorke in America tokens, 69

Index

Nicholas, Robert, 64
Noe, Sydney P., 21, 34
   numbering system of, 35
   See also die-attribution numbers of Massachusetts coinage
Non Dependens Status coppers, 302–303
   Robinson copies of, 305
North America tokens, 291
North American Mint, 73–74, 75
North Wales halfpenny tokens, 272
North West Company tokens, 254
Nouvelle France, coinage for, 281–282
Nova Constellatio coppers, 7, 14, 16, 75–78, 82
Nova Constellatio patterns, 20, 73–75
Nova Eborac coppers, 189–191
Novum Belgium fantasy coinage, 310–312
numismatic auction, first in America, 17
numismatic catalogs, 18
Numismatic Gallery, 21
Numismatic Guaranty Corporation of America (NGC), 24
numismatic museums, 16–17
numismatic publications
   in 19th century, 17–18
   in 20th century, 21–22
   launching of periodicals, 17–18
numismatic societies, emergence of, 18
numismatics
   in America, 15–16
   before 1850, 15–17
   in Europe, 15
   in 20th century, 18

Oak Tree coinage, 34, 39–43
   Wyatt counterfeits of, 295
Ogden, Matthias, 159, 160
"old tenor," 4
overstrikes, 75, 94, 161

P.P.P. Myddelton tokens, 250–251
Packard, Mike, 197
Paine, George T., 69
Paine, Thomas, 251
   tokens of, 251–252
paper-money issues
   of the colonies, 2, 3
   "old tenor," 4
   18th-century, 3–4
   devaluation of, 4
Parmelee, Lorin G., 193
pattern coins, 73–75
Peale, Charles Willson, 16
pedigree, 26–27
Perkins, Jacob, 9, 196
Perpignan Mint, 281
pheons, 10, 94, 96
Philadelphia Mint, 159, 160
   and Talbot, Allum & Lee cents, 245
Philadelphia Museum, 16
Philadelphia Numismatic Society, founding of, 18
Picker, Richard, 22, 24
pieces of eight, 3
Pight, Richard, 50, 51–52
Pine Tree coinage, 4, 15, 27, 34, 43–49, 235–236
   small vs. large planchets, 43–49
   Wyatt counterfeits of, 295
   See also Getchell fantasies; Good Samaritan coinage copies
Pingo, Thomas, 65, 234
Pitt tokens, 234–235
Pitt, William, 234
planchets
   clipping of, 35, 192
   edge types of, 7
   preparation of, 6–7
Platt, Jeremiah, 93–94, 208
Poitiers Mint, 282
portrait coinage, 82
Prado, Manuel, 242
price trends, historical, 28
private gold, 20
privy marks, 35
proclamation money, 3
Professional Coin Grading Service (PCGS), founding of, 24
punch varieties, 35

quint (500 units), 73, 74–75

Rahway (N.J.) mint, 159
Randolph, Edward, papers of, 37
Raymond, Wayte, 20, 21, 22, 65, 74, 95, 197
Read, John, 231–232
reales, Spanish-dollar equivalents of, 2
Reed, Seth, 194
Reeve, John, 16
restrikes, 55
Revere, Paul, 234, 236
Rhode Island Ship medals, 69–70
Rice, Joseph, 241
Richardson, John M., 21, 83–84. *See also die-attribution numbers of Vermont coppers*
Ringo, Mike, 222
Rittenhouse Society, 22
Robinson, Alfred S., 303
Robinson copies, 303–305
rocker press, 37
Roettier, John, 54
roller marks, 25
Roper, Lewis, 16
Rosa Americana coinage, 4, 13, 15, 17, 58–64
Rucker, John, 75
Rulau, Russell, 242
Rupert (Vermont) mint, 80–81, 84
   characteristics of coinage from, 84
   landscape-type coinage of, 85–86
   merged with Machin's Mills, 82
   portrait coinage of, 86
Rust, Horatio N., 314
Ryder, Hillyer C., 20, 21, 83, 95, 197. *See also die-attribution numbers of Massachusetts and Vermont coppers*
Ryder-Richardson numbering system, 83–84

Sage, Augustus B., 16, 18
Sarrafian, Edwin, 222
Schoepf, Dr. Johann David, 71
scissel, 6–7
Scott, J.W., 310–311
screw press, 9
Sheldon Rarity Scale, 30
Sheldon, William H., 21
   grading system of, 23
Ship halfpennies, 268
Shipman, Elias, 93
Siboni, Roger S., 55
silver, sources of, 7
singletrees, 160
Slafter, Edmund F., 83
Small Eagle cents, 262–263
Smith, Adam, 1
Smith, Capt. John, 276–277
Smither, James, 234
Smithsonian Institution, 21
Snelling, Thomas, 58, 276, 284

331

Snowden, James Ross, 256
Society of Paper Money
   Collectors (SPMC), 22
sols (5 and 15), 281, 282
Somers, George, 276, 277
Sommer Islands coinage, 4,
   21, 276–279
   characteristics of, 277–278
   copies of, 305–306
sous, 281, 283
Spanish dollars, in the
   colonies, 2, 73
Spanish-American currency,
   2–3, 4, 33, 73, 192. *See
   also* American
   Plantations tokens
spark-erosion process, 292
Sparks, Jared, 73
Sparrow, Thomas, 71
Spilman, James C., 7, 22, 83,
   94, 209
sprews, 195
Standish Barry, threepence,
   241
St. Patrick's coinage, 161,
   279, 280. *See also*
   Newby, Mark
Stamp Act of March 22,
   1765, 234
Standish Barry coinage, 240–
   241
Stearns, William G., 17
Steigerwalt, Charles, 95
Stickney, Matthew A., 16
Streeter, S.S., 50
strip
   copper, 6
   preparation of, 6–7
   silver, 6
Strobridge, W.H., 18, 193
Swan, James, 194
"sweating," 192

Talbot, Allum & Lee cents,
   244–252
   characteristics of, 245
Taxay, Don, 22
Temple, Sir Thomas, 37, 39
Terranova, Anthony, 26, 209
Theatre at New York token,
   252–253
Thomas Paine tokens, 251–
   252
Thompson, Agnes, 241
Thomson, Charles, 73–74

Thomson, John, 73–74
tinpest, 55
tobacco, used as a medium of
   exchange, 1, 4, 50–51,
   277
Token and Medal Society
   (TAMS), founding of,
   22
tokens, collecting, 18
Treaty of Paris, 5
Trudgen, Gary, 222
Tuckar, Daniel, 277

U.S. Mint, 16
   equipment of, 9
   founding of, 2
Ugly Head tokens, 262
Underhill, John, 192
Unity States cents, 257–258
Universal Rarity Scale, 29,
   31

values, stated on coin, 8
Van Voorhis, Daniel, 82, 221
varieties, 26
Vermont
   history of, 79, 82
   mints in, 13, 80–81, 222
   one-shilling note of, 79
Vermont coinage, 75, 79–92,
   208
   grading, 84–85
   landscape type, 81–82, 85
   portrait type, 82, 85–92
   shield styles of, 84
Virginia
   early media of exchange
      in, 1, 64
   minting of, 10
Virginia coinage, 64–68
Virginia Company, 276, 277
Vlack, Robert A., 197, 222,
   223, 234, 281. *See also
   die-attribution numbers
   of Machin's Mills coppers,
   Washington Military
   Bust / Draped Bust
   coppers, and coins
   relevant to Louisiana*)
vlugtende, defined, 70
Voce Populi coinage, 4, 290–
   291
   farthings, 290
   halfpence, 290–291

wampum, 1, 32, 50
   currency equivalents of, 1
War of the Spanish
   Succession, 2
washing (with acid to reduce
   planchet weight), 35
Washington Cabinet of
   Medals, 256
Washington coinage, 264–
   266
Washington Double-Head
   cents, 272–274
Washington Draped Bust
   coppers, 260–262
Washington funeral medal,
   196
Washington Military Bust
   coppers, 258–260
Washington Success tokens,
   268–269
Washington, George, 255
whiffletrees, 160
White, Aaron, 4
Wilhelmina Charlotte
   Caroline, 58
William of Orange, 54
Willow Tree coinage, 9, 21,
   34, 37–49
Wilson, Rathmell, 73–74
Winthrop, John, 33
Witherle, Joshua, 195, 196
Wood, William, 4–5, 58,
   285–286. *See also*
   Hibernia coinage; Rosa
   Americana coinage
Woodbridge, Timothy, 231
Woodward, W. Elliot, 18,
   69, 240
Wormser, Charles M., 21
Wuesthoff fantasies, 316
Würtzbach, Carl, 21
Wyatt counterfeits, 293,
   294–296
Wyatt, Thomas, 17, 293
Wynn, Edmund B., 16
Wyon, Thomas, 242

Yeo, Richard, 65
Young, Matthew, 55

Zotz, James J. Jr., 242

Coin Rarities Online

Museum Quality Coinage℠

**Specializing in Rare & Historic
Early American Coins & Related Issues
(like these, for example).**

Dave Wnuck · John Agre
www.CoinRaritiesOnline.com
994 N. Colony Rd. #356, Wallingford, CT 06492
1-800-Coins-99

America's First Coinage & Paper Money

- **Finest Certified Specimens**
- **Exceptional Quality**
- **Remarkable Rarities**
- **Extraordinary Value**

Superb Opportunities with Hundreds of Items Now Available:

www.EarlyAmerican.com

Mail Bid & Internet Auctions
Direct Sales & Purchasing

Register Online
Autographs • Coins • Currency • Americana

Colonial & Continental Congress Issued Notes

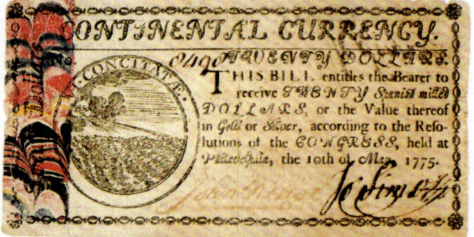

Full Descriptions & Extensive Photographs
For Every Item on Our Website:

www.EarlyAmerican.com

Participate In Our
Internet Only Sales
Held Frequently
Sign Up at Our Website Today...
Don't Miss Out On A Single Auction!

Visit Our History Store
Newly Updated Listings
of Wonderful Collector Items
Available for Immediate Purchase
First Come. First Served.
All Automated on Our Website

Specialist Market Maker For Over Three Decades in Colonial Coinage & Tokens, Washingtonia, Historic Medals, Colonial & Continental Currency, Obsolete Currency, Encased Postage Stamps, Political, Lincoln & Civil War Related, Black History, Plus Much, Much More!

Please Contact Dana Linett, President About Your Important Material

Early American • P.O. Box 3507 • Rancho Santa Fe, CA 92067
(858) 759-3290 or Fax (858) 759-1439 • Auctions@EarlyAmerican.com

WHITMAN
COIN AND COLLECTIBLES CONVENTIONS

Five shows held annually in Atlanta, Baltimore, and Philadelphia

Cobb Galleria Center, Atlanta ❉ Baltimore Convention Center, Baltimore ❉ Philadelphia Convention Center, Philadelphia

Hundreds of Dealers ❉ Thousands of Visitors ❉ Exciting Auctions

Colonial Coins • Early American Copper • Small Cents • Nickels • Silver and Gold Coins
Civil War Memorabilia • Bullion • Silver Dollars • Vintage Paper Money • Stamps and Postal Ephemera
Commemorative Coins • Territorial Gold • Rare Tokens • Fine Medals • Ancient Coins • World Coins

For more information:
404-214-4373 ❉ info@WhitmanExpo.com ❉ www.WhitmanExpo.com

Whitman COIN –AND– COLLECTIBLES CONVENTIONS

WE HAVE BEEN SELLING THE WORLD'S FINEST COLLECTIONS OF COLONIAL COINS, U.S. COINS, TOKENS, MEDALS, AND PAPER MONEY FOR OVER SEVEN DECADES

LET US BE OF SERVICE TO YOU!

Lawrence R. Stack   Christine Karstedt   Harvey G. Stack   Q. David Bowers

Call today to include your collection in one of our spectacular events.

Stack's

123 West 57th Street • New York, NY 10019 • 800-566-2580 • Fax 212-245-5018
P.O. Box 1804 • Wolfeboro, NH 03894 • 866-811-1804 • Fax 603-569-3875

Auctions • Appraisals • Retail • Since 1935
www.stacks.com • email: auction@stacks.com

VISIT US AT STACKS.COM FOR ON-LINE CATALOGUES, COLOR IMAGES AND INTERACTIVE BIDDING

"BALLPLAYERS AND INDIAN CHIEFS, SCOUNDRELS AND WAR HEROES, VIKINGS AND ELEPHANTS..."

...all of these and more await you among the *100 Greatest American Medals and Tokens!*

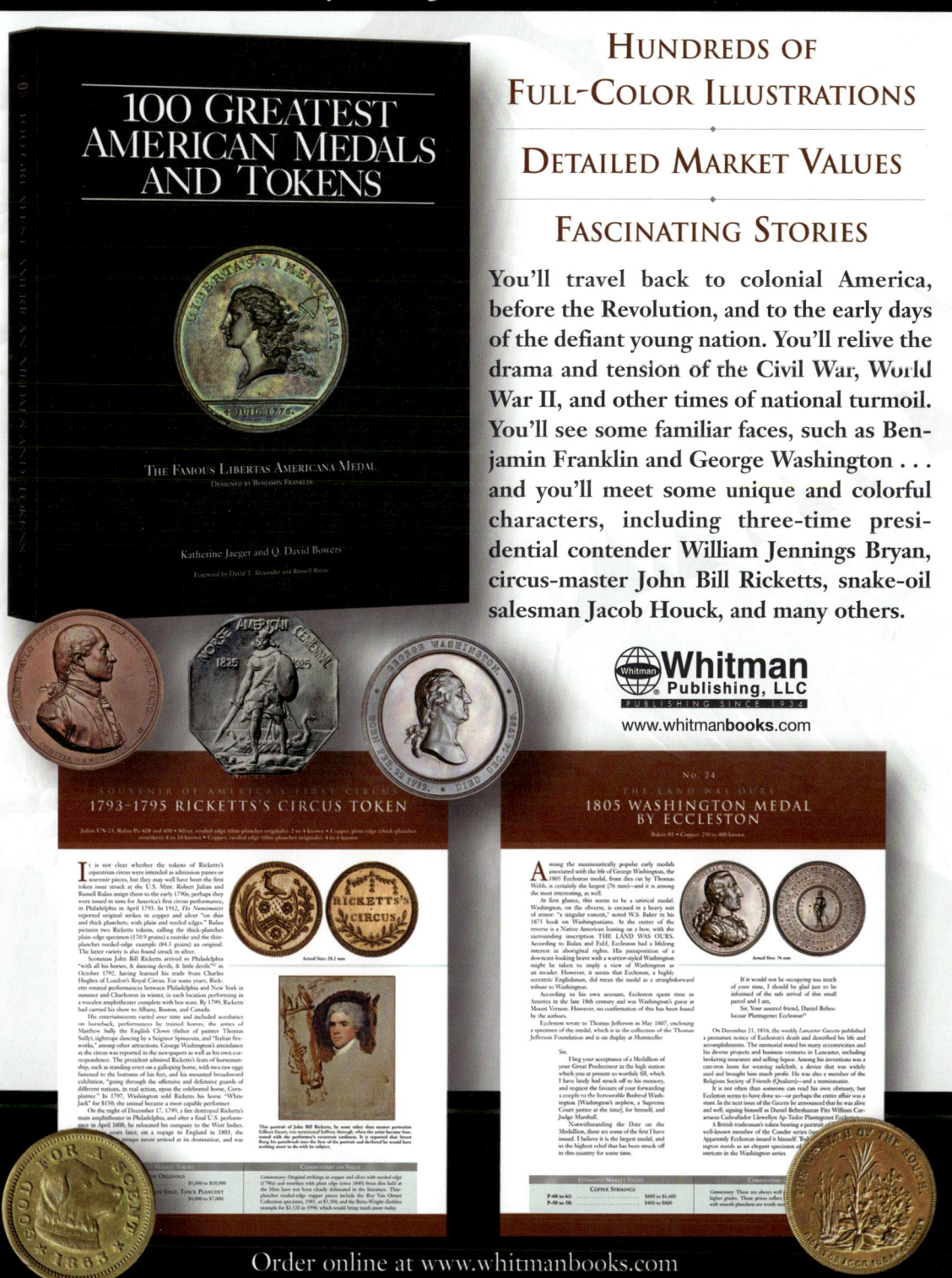

HUNDREDS OF FULL-COLOR ILLUSTRATIONS

DETAILED MARKET VALUES

FASCINATING STORIES

You'll travel back to colonial America, before the Revolution, and to the early days of the defiant young nation. You'll relive the drama and tension of the Civil War, World War II, and other times of national turmoil. You'll see some familiar faces, such as Benjamin Franklin and George Washington . . . and you'll meet some unique and colorful characters, including three-time presidential contender William Jennings Bryan, circus-master John Bill Ricketts, snake-oil salesman Jacob Houck, and many others.

Whitman Publishing, LLC
PUBLISHING SINCE 1934

www.whitmanbooks.com

Order online at www.whitmanbooks.com
Call 1-800-546-2995 • Email info@whitman**books**.com

If You Love Colonial, State, & Early American Coins, You Probably also Love Research…

And Heritage's Permanent Auction Archives Is the Best FREE Reference on the Entire Web!

1787 Brasher New York Style Doubloon.
EB Punch on Breast. XF45 NGC
Price realized: $2,990,000
HA.com/360-287001

1781 Libertas Americana Medal
MS64 PCGS
Price realized: $149,500
HA.com/444-248001

(1652) New England Shilling
AU50 PCGS
Price realized: $373,740
HA.com/454-45056

Heritage's web community has free access to our Permanent Auction Archives at HA.com, where they can view full-color enlargeable images, lot descriptions, and prices realized for more than 2 million items. Included are complete records for some 8,000 colonial issues sold. More than 25,000 early coppers sold. And thousands of eighteenth century dated issues sold by Heritage. And if you are the kind of numismatist who doesn't live by coins alone, you will be glad to know that our Archives also include complete information on more than 15,000 Colonial notes!

Heritage is the price leader because we understand that numismatics is about information, and our policy of transparency provides serious collectors and scholars with maximum information at no cost. One look is all it takes to realize that this is the greatest collector resource available on the Web. Join our free community today at HA.com.

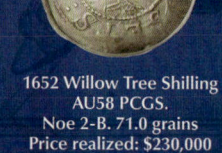

1652 Willow Tree Shilling
AU58 PCGS.
Noe 2-B. 71.0 grains
Price realized: $230,000
HA.com/422-14001

1787 Brasher New York Style Doubloon.
EB Punch on Wing. AU55 NGC
Price realized: $2,415,000
HA.com/360-287002

1776 $1 Continental Dollar CURENCY, Pewter
MS64 PCGS. Breen-1089, Newman 1-C
Price realized: $161,000
HA.com/434-178205

Receive a free copy of a catalog from any Heritage category. Register online at HA.com/book16001 or call 866-835-3243 and mention reference book16001.

The World's #1 Numismatic Auctioneer
HERITAGE HA.com
Auction Galleries

www.HA.com

Steve Ivy
Jim Halperin
Greg Rohan
Leo Frese
Warren Tucker
Todd Imhof

P·N·G

Annual Sales Exceed $700 Million • 400,000+ Online Registered Bidder-Members
3500 Maple Avenue, 17th Floor • Dallas, Texas 75219-3941 • or visit HA.com
214-528-3500 • FAX: 214-409-1425 • e-mail: Consign@HA.com
TX AUCTIONEER LICENSES: SAMUEL FOOSE 11727; ROBERT KORVER 13754; SCOTT PETERSON 13256; BOB MERRILL 13408; MIKE SADLER 16129; ANDREA VOSS 16406.
This auction subject to a 15% buyer's premium.